PRAISE FOR ADAM GOPNIK'S

Paris to the Moon

A New York Times *Notable Book of 2000*

*A New York Public Library Selection as one of the
Twenty-Five Memorable Books of 2000*

"The distinctive brilliance of Gopnik's essays lies in his ability to pick up a subject one would never have imagined it possible to think deeply about and then cover it in thoughts. . . . He is truly able to see the whole world in a grain of sand."
—*The New York Times Book Review*

"A memoir that will surely rank with the great books about Paris."
—*Montreal Gazette*

"Funny and shrewd and provocative enough to make one think hard about just why Paris remains so lovely. . . . His many essays about food are among the best I've ever read . . . simply wonderful."
—*The Boston Globe*

"Adam Gopnik's avid intelligence and nimble pen found subjects to love in Paris and in the growth of his small American family there. A conscientious, scrupulously savvy American husband and father meets contemporary France, and fireworks result, lighting up not just the Eiffel Tower."
—John Updike

"Francophiles will find this collection of essays—written during the author's stay in the City of Light at the tail end of the 20th Century—*très délicieux*."
—*People*

"Adam Gopnik has undertaken to do the French justice, much as Thomas Jefferson, Henry James and Edith Wharton did in the past. Distinguished company, to be sure, but Gopnik earns a place beside them. If anything, his take on France is more complete and various than theirs, and his wit, with its fine Manhattan edge, nicely complements the worldliness of his French hosts. The man has street smarts in spades, no matter whose streets they are."
—Raleigh-Durham *News & Record*

"Gopnik gives us an insight into French culture using the metaphors offered by everyday life." —*Los Angeles Times*

"The chronicle of an American writer's lifelong infatuation with Paris is also an extended meditation—in turns hilarious and deeply moving—on the threat of globalization, the art of parenting, and the civilizing intimacy of family life. Whether he's writing about the singularity of the Papon trial, the glory of bistro cuisine, the wacky idiosyncrasies of French kindergartens, or the vexing bureaucracy of Parisian health clubs, Gopnik's insights are infused with a formidable cultural intelligence, and his prose is as pellucid as that of any essayist. A brilliant, exhilarating book."
—Francine du Plessix Gray

"This is a delightful book, and you don't have to know anything about France to think so." —*The Arizona Republic*

"Little things that make Paris so lovable are lovingly described with verve and sparkle. Gopnik's writerly persona is smart and charming, the kind of traveling companion who can join you for dinner several nights in a row without becoming a bore. . . . This book is pretty terrific." —*Newsday*

"Adam Gopnik's *Paris to the Moon* abounds in the sensuous delights of the city—the magical carousel in the Luxembourg Gardens, the tomato dessert at Arpège, even the exquisite awfulness of the new state library. But the even greater joys of this exquisite

memoir are timeless and even placeless—the excitement of the
journey, the confusion of an outsider, and, most of all, the love of a
family."   —Jeffrey Toobin

"Gopnik is an artful reporter, dapper in his prose, sharp in his sense
of absurdity. . . . The essays are just so well put together, so airy and
trenchant and alert to their chosen topics . . . the best parts of *Paris
to the Moon* can't be beat."   —*The Seattle Times*

"Adam Gopnik is a dazzling talent—hilarious, winning, and deft—
but the surprise of *Paris to the Moon* is its quiet moral intelligence. This book begins as journalism and ends up as literature."
                                                 —Malcolm Gladwell

"Fluent and witty, delightful fodder for anyone who loves Paris or
has ever dreamed of living abroad. . . . Gopnik's essays do what the
best writing should do: they inform as they entertain."
                                                 —*Library Journal*

"An elegant stylist and master of metaphor and description." —*Book*

Paris
to the
Moon

PARIS
TO THE
MOON

Adam Gopnik

RANDOM HOUSE
TRADE PAPERBACKS
NEW YORK

2001 Random House Trade Paperback Edition
Copyright © 2000 by Adam Gopnik
Reader's guide copyright © 2001 by Random House, Inc.

RANDOM HOUSE TRADE PAPERBACKS and colophon are trademarks
of Random House, Inc.
READER'S CIRCLE and colophon are trademarks of Random House, Inc.

This work was originally published in hardcover
by Random House in 2000.

Library of Congress Cataloging-in-Publication Data
Gopnik, Adam.
Paris to the moon / Adam Gopnik.
p. cm.
ISBN 0-375-75823-2
1. Gopnik, Adam—Homes and haunts—France—Paris. 2.
Americans—France—Paris. 3.
Paris (France)—Social life and customs—20th century. I. Title.

DC718.A44 G67   2000
944'.3600413—dc21   00-037297

www.thereaderscircle.com

Printed in the United States of America

23 25 27 29 30 28 26 24

"I dare say, moreover," she pursued with an interested gravity, "that I do, that we all do here, run too much to mere eye. But how can it be helped? We're all looking at each other—and in the light of Paris one sees what things resemble. That's what the light of Paris seems always to show. It's the fault of the light of Paris—dear old light!"

"Dear Old Paris!" little Bilham echoed.

"Everything, everyone shows," Miss Barrace went on.

"But for what they really are?" Strether asked.

"Oh, I like your Boston 'reallys'! But sometimes—yes."

—*The Ambassadors*

Contents

THE WINTER CIRCUS

(An American family arrives in Paris, is greeted by bombs and strikes, and a good time is had by all.)

DISTANT ERRORS

(Emigration becomes expatriation, confusion reigns, and serenity is sought in the Luxembourg Gardens.)

LESSONS FROM THINGS

*(Food, fashion, and foibles teach their complicated lessons in
the struggle between Administration and Civilization.)*

A MACHINE TO DRAW THE WORLD

*(Serenity is found in calm and contemplation, and the deep
tragedy of history revealed. All chords are sounded and
the bells rung in the birth of a new French baby.)*

The
Winter
Circus

Paris
to the Moon

Not long after we moved to Paris, in the fall of 1995, my wife, Martha, and I saw, in the window of a shop on the rue Saint-Sulpice, a nineteenth-century engraving, done in the manner, though I'm now inclined to think not from the hand, of Daumier. It shows a train on its way from the Right Bank of Paris to the moon. The train has a steam locomotive and six cars, and it is chugging up a pretty steep track. The track is supported on two high, slender spires that seem to be anchored somewhere in the Fifth Arrondissement (you can see the Panthéon in silhouette nearby), and then the track just goes right up and touches the full moon up in the clouds. I suppose the two pillars are stronger than they look. The train is departing at twilight—presumably it's an overnight trip—and among the crowd on the ground below, only a couple of top-hatted bourgeois watch the lunar express go on its way with any interest, much less wonder. Everybody else in the crowd of thirteen or so people on the platform, mostly moms and dads and kids, are running around and making conversation and comforting children and buying tickets for the next trip and doing all the things people still do on station platforms in Paris. The device on the ticket window, like the title of the cartoon, reads: "A Railroad: From Paris to the Moon."

The cartoon is, in part, a satire on the stock market of the time and on railway share manipulations. ("Industry," the caption begins, "knows no more obstacles.") But the image cast its spell on us, at least, because it seemed to represent two notions, or romances, that had made us want to leave New York and come to Paris in the first place. One was the old nineteenth-century vision of Paris as the *naturally* modern place, the place where the future was going to happen as surely as it would happen in New York. If a train were going to run to the moon, that train would originate from the Gare du Nord, with Parisian kids getting worn out while they waited.

But the image represented another, more intense association, and that is the idea that there is, for some Americans anyway, a direct path between the sublunary city and a celestial state. Americans, Henry James wrote, "are too apt to think that Paris is the celestial city," and even if we don't quite think that, some of us do think of it as the place where tickets are sold for the train to get you there. (Ben Franklin thought this, and so did Gertrude Stein, and so did Henry Miller. It's a roomy idea.) If this notion is pretty obviously unreal, and even hair-raisingly naïve, it has at least the excuse of not being original. When they die, Wilde wrote, all good Americans go to Paris. Some of us have always tried to get there early and beat the crowds.

I've wanted to live in Paris since I was eight. I had a lot of pictures of the place in my head and even a Parisian object, what I suppose I'd have to call an icon, in my bedroom. Sometime in the mid-sixties my mother, who has a flair for the odd, ready-made present, found—I suppose in an Air France office in Philadelphia—a life-size cardboard three-dimensional cutout of a Parisian policeman. He had on a blue uniform and red kepi and blue cape, and he wore a handlebar mustache and a smile. (The smile suggests how much Art, or at any rate Air France, improves on Life, or at any rate on Paris policemen.)

My younger brother and I called the policeman Pierre, and he kept watch over our room, which also had Beatle posters and a blindingly, numbingly, excruciatingly bright red shag rug. (I had been allowed to choose the color from a choice of swatches, but I have an inability to generalize and have always made bad, over-bright guesses on curtains and carpets and, as it turned out, the shape of future events.) Although we had never gone anywhere interesting but New York, my older sister had already, on the basis of deep, illicit late-night reading of Jane Austen and *Mary Poppins*, claimed London, and I had been given Paris, partly as a consolation prize, partly because it interested me. (New York, I think, was an open city, to be divided between us, like Danzig. Our four younger brothers and sisters were given lesser principalities. We actually expected them to live in Philadelphia.)

My first images of Paris had come from the book adaptation of *The Red Balloon,* the wonderful Albert Lamorisse movie about a small boy in the Parisian neighborhood of Menilmontant who gets a magic, slightly overeager balloon, which follows him everywhere and is at last destroyed by evil boys with rocks. Curiously, it was neither a cozy nor a charming landscape. The Parisian grown-ups all treated Pascal, the boy, with a severity bordering on outright cruelty: His mother tosses the balloon right out of the Haussmannian apartment; the bus conductor shakes his head and finger and refuses to allow the balloon on the bus; the principal of the school locks him in a shed for bringing the balloon to class. The only genuine pleasure I recall that he finds in this unsmiling and rainy universe is when he leaves the balloon outside a tempting-looking bakery and goes in to buy a cake. The insouciance with which he does it—cake as a right, not a pleasure—impressed me a lot. A scowling gray universe relieved by pastry:

This was my first impression of Paris, and of them all, it was not the farthest from the truth. To this set of images were added, soon after, the overbright streets of the Madeline books, covered with vines and the little girls neat in their rows, and black and white pictures of men in suits walking through the Palais Royal, taken from a Cartier-Bresson book on the coffee table.

Pierre, though, being made of cardboard, got pretty beat up, sharing a room with two young boys, or maybe he was just both smaller and more fragile than I recall. In any case, one summer evening my parents, in a completely atypical display of hygienic decisiveness, decided that he was too beat up to keep and that it was time for him to pass away, and they put him out on the Philadelphia street for the trashman to take away.

I wept all night. He would sit out with the trash cans and would not be there in the morning. (A little later I read about Captain Dreyfus and *his* degradation, and the two uniformed and mustachioed figures got mixed up, so perhaps he had been sent to supply intimations of the other, darker side of French life. They were certainly there to be intimated.) What made me sad just then was the new knowledge that things changed, and there was nothing you could do about it. In a way, that was a Parisian emotion too.

|||

I saw the real—or anyway the physical—Paris for the first time in 1973, when I was in my early teens. I had arrived with my large, strange family, those five brothers and sisters, and a couple of hangers-on and boyfriends. There were eight of us in the back of a Citroën station wagon. I was the one with the bad adolescent mustache. My parents, college professors, were on sabbatical, at a time, just weeks before the oil crunch, when the great good wave that had lifted up college professors into the upper middle classes was still rising. At the time we all lived in Montreal, and my brothers and sisters went to a French private academy there actually run by the French government. The corridors in the school were named after Parisian streets: The Champs-Élysées led the way to the principal's office, and you took the rue Royale to the cafeteria for lunch. I was the only one in an English-speaking school and became oddly, or maybe not so oddly, the only one to fall entirely in love with France. (You can never forget, I suppose, that the Champs-Élysées once led the way to the principal's office.)

We came in through one of the *portes* of Paris, the doors that are now merely exits from the peripheral expressway but that still keep the names of the real gates of the old walled city. It was probably the porte d'Orléans. I saw a girl lean over to kiss a friend on a stopped motorbike on the cheek, twice, *here* and then *there*. The trees cast patterned light on the street. We went out for dinner and, for fifteen francs, had the best meal I had ever eaten, and most of all, nobody who lived there seemed to notice or care. The beauty and the braised trout alike were just part of life, the way we do things here.

We had spent the previous three days in London. Though the taxis were black and the buses red and Regent's Park green, the familiar street names seemed curiously to belong to another civilization, as though the city had been occupied once by another and more vivid, imperial race and had then been turned over to the pallid, gray people on the streets, who ate sandwiches that turned up at the edges. Paris, on the other hand, looked exactly as it was supposed to look. It wore its heart on its sleeve, and the strange thing was that the heart it wore so openly was in other ways so closed—mysterious, uninviting.

We settled in for a long winter. While my parents taught, I spent most of my time going to the movies with my cousin Philippe. You are supposed to be in love in Paris and Philippe and I were both in love. I was in love with Jacqueline Bisset, and he was in love with Dominique Sanda. We went to the movies all the time, looking for them both. I remember finding a fifth-run movie theater someplace in the Nineteenth Arrondissement, deep in a poor Algerian neighborhood, just in order to see Jacqueline's brief, heart-searing part in *The Life and Times of Judge Roy Bean*.

Almost incidentally, in love with Jacqueline Bisset, I fell in love with Paris. Paris—and this is the tricky thing—though it is always and indubitably itself, is also in its nature a difficult city to love for itself alone. What truly makes Paris beautiful is the intermingling of the monumental and the personal, the abstract and the footsore particular, it and you. A city of vast and impersonal set piece architecture, it is also a city of small and intricate, improvised experience. My favorite architectural detail in Paris is the little entrance up the rue de Seine, a tiny archway where, as I have since found out, you can push a *poussette* right through and get to the grand Institut de France. You aren't looking at it; and then you and the *poussette* are *in* it, right in the driveway where the academicians go. For a moment you *are* it. The Institut belongs to you. Ten steps more and you are on the pont des Arts. The passage from the big to the little is what makes Paris beautiful, and you have to be prepared to be small—to live, to trudge, to have your head down in melancholy and then lift it up, sideways—to get it.

What is true for academicians is true for adolescents with a fixation on Jacqueline Bisset. I saw Paris out of the corner of my eye, on my way to the movies, and so a love for Paris came to be one of the strongest emotions I possess. In addition, my father's friend the literary critic and pioneer deconstructionist Eugenio Donato brought me to a seminar that Roland Barthes was giving that spring. I didn't understand a word. (A few years later I met one of the French students in the class, and found out that she hadn't understood a word either.) Then we went home, back to Montreal, where my brothers and sisters returned to that French academy and I kept my French sharp by reading the sports pages every day about the Montreal Canadiens.

Two years after that first year in Paris, I used the tiny lever of my knowledge of the city to induce—I still won't say deceive—a girl, a real girl, I had fallen in love with into running away to Paris with me. Martha, who became and, twenty-five years later, remains—and I write these words with a stunned disbelief, shared only by her mother—my wife, loved Paris as much as I did, even though many of the advertised attractions (the seminar with my friend Roland Barthes, for instance) that I had promised her were suspiciously missing from our trip. If she noticed this or was bothered by it, she hasn't mentioned it yet. We spent a happy week in the Hôtel Welcome on the boulevard Saint-Germain. The hidden humanism of the classical style, the idea of the intellectual as magician and stylist, and sex in a hotel room: These were the things I took away from a childhood spent continually in a made-up Paris and an adolescence spent, fitfully, in the real one.

|||

For a long time New York intervened. Then, in the late eighties, we began to think about Paris again. We sat on the deck of a rented house on Cape Cod and, listening to old Charles Trenet records, thought . . . why not? (This was neither a hard leap nor an interesting one, since the Trenet songs we were listening to pursued the theme of Paris pretty much to the exclusion of every other human concept.) We watched *The Umbrellas of Cherbourg* over and over. We visited Paris whenever we could, as often as we could. We weren't Francophiles because we didn't know anything about France, and still don't. We were just crazy about Paris.

When our son, Luke Auden, was born, in September 1994, we knew that we would have to go to Paris soon, or we wouldn't go at all. In five years, everybody told us, he would no longer be "portable." When we were in Paris, we had hung around the parks and gardens, watching the carousels turn and the children play and thinking, This would be a nice place to be a child, or to have one. We also saw all the aspects of a New York childhood that looked less delightful. You would see the five-year-olds at a friend's house already lost in the American media, simultaneously listening to a Walkman, playing with a Game Boy, and watching a video on the VCR. Perhaps, we thought—however foolishly, however "unrealistically"—we could protect him from some of that if he spent his first five years in Paris.

"You can't run away from (a) reality, (b) American culture, (c) yourself," our friends all said, compositely. "But you can run away," we said under our breaths, and we did. We thought we might stay for good, but we knew that we would certainly stay for the last five years of the century; "We'll stay till the millennium," we could say grandly, and mean it cautiously. *The New Yorker,* where I worked, was ready to hear what I had to say about Parisian scenes and, more important, was willing to keep sending non-Parisian subjects, from Groucho Marx to the Starr Report, my way too, which let us pay Parisian rates. Martha, for her part, had become a filmmaker, and she had the great portable occupation of the late twentieth century, a screenplay to write (and rewrite and rewrite again). So we went.

The New Yorker has had lots of good writers in place in Paris, but it was James Thurber, whose blind eyes in a photograph on my desk stare at me every morning, whose writing moved me most. Thurber, though he hardly spoke a word of French, wrote once that the surface of manners in France seemed to him the most beautiful in the world, and he was right. The romance of Paris was my subject, and if it is a moony or even a loony one, it is at least the one I get, a little.

This was a hard romance to sustain in most of the last five years, when almost everybody else thought that Paris was going straight to hell. When we first started dreaming of coming to Paris, around 1989, long-termist, infrastructure-building Europe, many people said, owned the future. One only had to compare JFK and Charles de Gaulle airports, the one named after the vital young internationalist and the other after the old reactionary, to catch the irony. JFK was decrepit, dangerous, and almost unpoliced; you stumbled off your plane into, of all bizarre things, a linoleum staircase, with a sign above warning you of illegal livery drivers (whose complexions, delicately, had been made neither black nor white but swarthy, like Barbary Coast pirates). You took a taxi over roads so potholed that the infrastructure was visibly rusted out, ruined. At Charles de Gaulle Airport, on the other hand, you came to a breathtakingly modern terminal, full of odd glass corridors and long, radiating, covered walkways, and exited onto a highway so up-to-date that regular announcements of upcoming traffic were posted along with the waiting time for a reservation at the Brasserie Lipp. No one will believe this now, but that is how it seemed then. (Popular memory may be short, but it is nothing compared with the amnesia of experts.)

By 1995 all that had changed, and Paris and France seemed left out of the new all-American dispensation. London, of all places, had become the town where people went to see new art and taste new cooking. For the first time in modern history it was actually possible to live in Paris for comfort and bourgeois security and travel to London for food and sex. (My cousin Philippe had, like so many ambitious Frenchmen of his generation, actually fled Paris for London, where he had made a small fortune in banking and was about to finance his own restaurant.)

The failure of the French model and the triumph of the Anglo-American one is by now a sorry, often repeated fact. For five years hardly anyone wrote about Paris and the French except in a tone of diagnosis: how sick they were, when they got so sick, why they denied that they were sick, and if there was any chance that they would ever get better. (No.) Many journalistic *tours d' horizons* have been written in the last few years—"Whither France?" and "Whether France . . ." and "Weathering France,"

and "France: How It Withers" and "Withering France." We surf
the waves of capitalism, from crest to trough and back again, but
the funny thing is that no matter how often we ride the wave, nobody notices that it's wet. When we are on the crest, we believe
that we have climbed a mountain through our own virtuous efforts, and when we are in the trough, we believe that we have
fallen into a pit through our own vice.

Whatever else might be true, though, in the last five years of
the century, as the world became, by popular report, more "globalized" than it had ever been before, France became more *different*. "They order these matters better in France," Sterne's opening
line for *his* sentimental journey in France, had a new ring, now.
For most of two centuries, after all, what had been so different
about France was how central and cosmopolitan it was. Americans had been going to Paris for a couple of centuries to learn a
universal diplomatic language and the central artistic culture and
even the most influential manner of cooking. Yet in the time
we were there Paris seemed to pass from the place where you
learned how to do it to the place where you learned how *not* to
do it—how not to do it in the ordinary American imperial way,
the place where you learned how to do it, as the French like to
say, *autrement*, otherly. From the kind of sympathy that labor
unions get from their public to the length of time you take to eat
lunch, the way it's done in Paris now is not the way it's done in
Adelaide or Toronto or Los Angeles or Tempe or Hong Kong
or any of the studs on the broad belt of the English-speaking
imperium that now encircles the world, with New York as its
buckle. Americans still learn about differences in Paris, but now
we learn about them not because we are so much closer to the
center of things but because we are so much farther away. The
light of Paris still shows Americans things as they are (if not as
they *really* are) by showing us how things can look different in a
different light, but the light it shows them with now is more mysterious and singular, a kind of moral moonlight, a little bit harder
to see by.

There was no big story in France at the end of the century, but there were a lot of littler ones, and the littlest ones of all seemed to say the most about what makes Paris still Paris. Princesses died and prime ministers fell and intellectuals argued, gravely, about genuinely grave questions, and I wrote about all these things, but I have left most of that writing out of this book. They are important things, but the things that interested me most, in a time of plenty, were the minute variations, what a professor would call the significant absences, between living a family life in one place and living the same kind of life somewhere else. This is a story of the private life of a lucky American family living in Paris in the last five years of the century, less a tour of any horizon than just a walk around the park. To the personal essays about life in Paris, I have added some private journals I wrote every Christmas. These journals, I see in rereading them, are more pensive and even pessimistic in tone than the stories, perhaps because they are notes sent inward rather than letters sent out. (I have also included a long report on the trial of Maurice Papon because it is about the occupation and collaboration, still the great, unignorable black hole at the center of French life, still sucking in the light even of everyday pleasure.)

Family life is by its nature cocooned, and expatriate family life doubly so. We had many friends and a few intimate ones, but it is in the nature of family rhythm—up too early, asleep too soon—to place you on a margin, and to the essential joy—just the three of us!—was added the essential loneliness, *just the three of us*. What I find is left, after the politics have been removed, are mostly stories about raising a kid in foreign parts. Yet since raising a kid is the one nearly universal thing people do, and since doing it in foreign parts is the one time when you get to see most clearly all the bits of doing it that *aren't* universal—that are inflected and shaped by the local geography and mood and playground equipment—it is in its way, I hope, still a not entirely interior subject.

These stories are also, willy-nilly, about bringing up a kid in foreign parts in a funny time. What made the time funny was that there was as much peace and prosperity in the world as there has ever been and at the same time a lot of resentment directed at the United States, the country where the peace and prosperity, like the kid, came from, or which at least was taking credit for it. Paris, which in the first five years of the century seemed the capital of modern life, spent the last five years on the sidelines, brooding on what had happened. Our son's first five years, and the modern century's last five, five years to the end of the millennium and five to grade one in New York, a small subject and a large one, juxtaposed: These stories take one stretch of time and, as they used to demand in exam papers, contrast and compare.

The stories are mostly about life spent at home and include a lot—some will think too much—about the trinity of late-century bourgeois obsessions: children and cooking and spectator sports, including the spectator sport of shopping. Yet life is mostly lived by timid bodies at home, and since we see life as deeply in our pleasures as in our pains, we see the differences in lives as deeply there too. The real differences among people shine most brightly in two bedrooms and one building, with a clock ticking, five years to find out how and why. Not just how and why and in what way Paris is different from New York, but how a North American liberal, with the normal "universalist," antinationalist reflexes of the kind, might end up feeling about the idea of difference itself—about the existence of minute variations among people: which ones really matter and which ones really don't. (By the end of the decade, a new image of Paris, as a multicultural metropolis with a thriving entrepreneurial culture, was coming into place. This existed—it always had—but it seemed a little too easily pleasing to Americans, perhaps because it was so familiar, not so different after all, and looked to America for inspiration. The young soccer players on the champion French national team carefully imitated Sammy Sosa's finger-kissing when they scored their goals, and French rap, striking though it was, seemed more distinctive from its American sources than really different from them, in the same way that American impressionism in the nineteenth century was distinctive rather than different from *its* models. Anyway, while I greatly enjoyed the Sosa finger-kissing, as I enjoyed French rap, I admired even more the way that the great Zinedine Zidane, when asked about a perfect free kick he had taken, calmly said, "I am at the summit of my art.")

I looked for the large in the small, the macro in the micro, the figure in the carpet, and if some big truths passed by, I hope some significant small ones got caught. If there is a fault in reporting, after all, it is not that it is too ephemeral but that it is not ephemeral *enough,* too quickly concerned with what seems big at the time to see what is small and more likely to linger. It is, I think, the journalist's vice to believe that all history can instantly be reduced to experience: ("Pierre, an out-of-work pipe fitter in the suburb of Boulougne, is typical of the new class of *chômeurs* . . .") just as it is the scholar's vice to believe that all experience can be reduced to history ("The new world capitalist order produced a new class of *chômeurs,* of whom Pierre, a pipe fitter, was a typical case . . .").

What then, the journalist and scholar ask tetchily, what then is exactly the vice of the comic-sentimental essayist? It is of course to believe that all experience and history can be reduced to *him,* or his near relations, and the only apology I can make is that for him in this case experience and history and life were not so much reduced as all mixed up, and, scrambled together, they at least become a subject. The essayist dreams of being a prism, through which other light passes, and fears ending up merely as a mirror, showing the same old face. He has only his Self to show and only himself to blame if it doesn't show up well.

Even if experience shows no more than itself, it is still worth showing. Experience and history, I think, are actually like the two trains in that Keaton movie where Buster struggles to keep up with the big engine by pumping furiously on a handcar on the adjoining track. It looks as if the little handcar of experience and the big train of history are headed for the same place at the same speed; but in fact the big train is going where it is headed, and those of us in the handcar keep up only by working very hard, for a little while.

There are two kinds of travelers. There is the kind who goes to see what there is to see and sees it, and the kind who has an image in his head and goes out to accomplish it. The first visitor has an easier time, but I think the second visitor sees more. He is constantly comparing what he sees to what he wants, so he sees with his mind, and maybe even with his heart, or tries to. If his peripheral vision gets diminished—so that he quite literally sometimes can't see what's coming at him from the suburbs of the place he looks at—his struggle to adjust the country he looks at to the country he has inside him at least keeps him looking. It sometimes blurs, and sometimes sharpens, his eye. My head was filled with pictures of Paris, mostly black and white, and I wanted to be in them.

I am aware that my Paris, which began as a cardboard construction wearing a cape and a kepi, in many respects remains one, an invention, a Bizzaro New York, abstract where New York is specific, intricate where New York is short, though not perhaps more soulful, and that my writing about Paris is very much like my writing about New York in the first five years I lived there.

In fact it would have been a lunchtime's work for my old friend Eugenio Donato, who haunts this book as he haunts my memories of Paris, to insist that this book about Paris is *actually* about New York. A lunchtime's worth of work yet not perhaps a dinner's worth of truth. The images contain their little truth too, which I grasped even in remnant form in West Philadelphia. We all see our Paris as true, because it is. It is not an old or antiquated Paris that we love, but the persistent, modern material

Paris, carrying on in a time of postmodern immateriality, when everything seems about to dissolve into pixels. We love Paris not out of "nostalgia" but because we love the look of light on things, as opposed to the look of light *from* things, the world reduced to images radiating from screens. Paris was the site of the most beautiful commonplace civilization there has ever been: cafés, brasseries, parks, lemons on trays, dappled light on bourgeois boulevards, department stores with skylights, and windows like doors everywhere you look. If it is not so much wounded—all civilizations are that, since history wounds us all—as chastened, and overloud in its own defense, it nonetheless goes on. The persistence of this civilization in the sideshow of postmodern culture is my subject, and the life it continues to have my consolation. I don't go on a bus in Paris without still expecting my balloon to be barred and the authority figure who oversees it is still a cardboard policeman in a cape. I see the moon these days from Paris because I once saw Paris from the moon.

|||

My real life in Paris, as in New York, was spent with a few people, and, really, only with two, Martha and Luke, and when I think of Paris, I think of them: Martha and Luke in matching fur hats at the Palais Royal; waiting with Luke in the courtyard of our building for Martha to come down the stairs (in long Russian coat and Tibetan hat, cold girl, in mid-autumn); waiting with Martha in the courtyard of an odd building on the boulevard Raspail for Luke to come from his gym class, peering through the dirty windows and the cagelike grille, one child among many, and then getting a Coca-Cola, five francs from the machine. Cyril Connolly once achieved an unearned poetic effect by reciting the names of hotels on the Left Bank in wartime. I can sometimes achieve a similar one, even more unearned, though not less felt, by reciting to myself the names of restaurants where we ate lunch while Luke slept (or, occasionally, where we wished we could sleep, while Luke ate): Le Soufflé, Le Basilic, Chez André, Le Petit St. Benoît, Laduree. I believe in Le Soufflé, on a Saturday afternoon in December, in the back room, with Luke sleeping in his *poussette,* and the old couple across the neighboring banquette, who had been coming for forty years, there with their small blind dog. The waiters in white coats, the owner in a blue sports jacket, and the smell (aroma is too fancy a word) of mingled cigarettes and orange liqueurs. I am aware that this is what is called sentimental, but then we went to Paris for a sentimental reeducation—I did anyway—even though the sentiments we were instructed in were not the ones we were expecting to learn, which I believe is why they call it an education.

This book is theirs, and I ask them only to share a place at the dedication table with Henry Finder, my first and most patient reader, who had to take what it tasted like on trust.

Private Domain

A bomb went off under my bed the other morning. It was early on a gray Tuesday when I heard a flock of ambulances somewhere near my Left Bank street, making that forlorn, politely insistent two-note bleating all Paris ambulances make. I went downstairs and outside and found—nothing. The street sweeper with the green plastic broom was sweeping; the young woman who keeps the striped-pajama boutique across the street was reading her Paul Auster novel. ("You left New York for *Paris?*" she demanded incredulously when I introduced myself not long ago.) Only in the early afternoon, when *Le Monde* came out, did I realize that the Islamic terrorists who are now working in Paris had left a bomb in an underground train and that, give or take a few hundred yards, it had gone off beneath the second-floor refuge on the Left Bank that my wife and I had found this summer, after a long search. The ambulances were heading for the Gare d'Orsay, where the wounded were being taken.

"*Gardez votre sang-froid*" is the single, self-sufficient impera-
tive posted on the what-to-do-in-an-emergency placard in the
courtyard of our building, and on this occasion people had. The
bombings here, though sometimes murderous in their effects,
haven't caused any panic or even much terror. Though Parisians
believe they are superior by birth, they do not believe, as Americans do, that they are invulnerable by right. But even if our
apartment building had been officially declared the epicenter of
the bombing campaign, I don't think I'd move. Terrorism is part
of life, while a nice apartment in Paris is a miracle.

For the new French prime minister, Alain Juppé, the bombing
campaign has come as a vast, if unadmitted, relief, since he finally has a subject to talk about in public other than *l'affaire des
logements,* which has dominated the news here for four months
and once seemed likely to sink his government. For most of
those months, in fact, Juppé has probably been the only person
more preoccupied with apartments on the Left Bank than I was,
though he and I approached the matter from opposite ends. I
was trying to find one, while he was trying to explain to the
French people why he had so many and what all his relatives
were doing living in them.

Juppé has been prime minister for just under six months. He
is a long-fingered, elegant man of fifty, with the kind of enviable,
aerodynamic baldness that in America only tycoons seem able to
carry off—the Barry Diller, Larry Tisch style of baldness. Juppé
comes from a simple family down in the Landes country. He did
well in school and was eventually admitted to the École Nationale d'Administration, in Paris, the tiny institution that produces nearly the entire French political elite. He came to the
attention of an older fellow *énarque,* Jacques Chirac, and when
Chirac was mayor of Paris, in the 1980s, Juppé became his "financial adjoint"—more or less the city comptroller. Then, when
the conservative parties won the legislative elections two years
ago, Chirac, though he had prudently decided not to seek the of-

fice of prime minister, arranged for Juppé to be named the minister of foreign affairs, in which position, Bosnia aside, he was thought to have done well. So when Chirac was elected president, this May, it seemed inevitable that he would make Juppé his prime minister.

Like all ambitious French politicians, Juppé chooses to present himself as a literary man. He has actually written a book of reflections titled *La Tentation de Venise*—"The Venetian Temptation." Juppé's Venetian temptation was to retire to a house there, where he could escape from political life, admire Giorgione's *Tempestà*, drink Bellinis in the twilight, and think long, deep thoughts. *La Tentation* was regarded as a fighting campaign manifesto, since it is as necessary for an ambitious French politician to write a book explaining why he never likes to think of politics as it is for an ambitious American politician to write a book explaining why he never thinks of anything else. Juppé, ahead of the pack, had written a book asserting not only that he would rather be doing something else but that he would like to be doing it in a completely different country. The romance of retirement is still extremely powerful in France, descending, as it does, from Montaigne, who remains the model here of pensive, high-minded reclusion, even though he spent an important chunk of his life as the boss of a tough town. In Juppé's case, the descent from Montaigne, who supplies the epigraph for *La Tentation,* is easy to show: Juppé is the mayor of Bordeaux, as Montaigne was. (French politicians often hold more than one office at once, just in case.) Among French politicians, in fact, ostentatious displays of detachment are something of a competitive sport. After being succeeded as president by Chirac, François Mitterrand gave an interview to Christine Ockrent, the editor of *L'Express,* simply to announce that he was now taking long walks in Paris and looking at the sky. It was understood as his way of keeping his hand in. Not long ago the former prime minister Édouard Balladur, who had been so busy looking detached from politics that he forgot to campaign for the presidency this time around, sneaked an item into *L'Express* announcing that he too was taking walks and looking at the sky. It was the start of his comeback.

Then, at the beginning of June, the weekly comic paper *Le Canard Enchaîné* revealed that Juppé, when he was the financial adjoint to Chirac, had taken the lease on an apartment in the Sixth Arrondissement that belonged to the *domaine privé* of the City of Paris. The *domaine privé* is a peculiarly Parisian establishment, although even after four months of scandal, no one knows exactly what it is, how the City of Paris came to possess it, or how you get into it. At first many Parisians confused the *domaine privé* with the general stock of public housing that the City of Paris has built since the First World War; most of that housing is on the periphery, and a lot of it is in the less desirable neighborhoods of the Nineteenth and the Twentieth Arrondissements. It turns out, however, that the City of Paris also owns a small, semisecret group of apartments and apartment buildings that are given out at the discretion of whoever happens to be running Paris. These *domaine privé* apartments came into the hands of the Parisian government in all kinds of interesting ways. Many of them are on the beautiful old streets of the Left Bank, near the river, because of various failed city plans that left Paris with a lot of property, which the city fathers eventually started renting to one another. Until 1977 the prefects of the Paris arrondissements controlled the *domaine privé,* but then the system was reformed, which, as often happens in France, managed to make the mechanics of it even murkier. Today no one seems to know exactly how many *domaine privé* apartments there are. One estimate puts the number at about thirteen hundred; another puts it at about fifteen hundred; still another says that there are more than four thousand.

Juppé's apartment, on the lovely rue Jacob, was a lavish spread, complete with garden and terrace, that he had in effect rented to himself for a little less than three thousand dollars a month—well below the market price. When this arrangement was challenged, Juppé announced that he felt "serene" and that he couldn't see what the fuss was about, since anyone could have found out that he lived there by looking at the mailbox. There was something equally off-key about Chirac's later defense of his protégé. During a televised press conference, he declared himself "profoundly shocked" by "the exploitation of a fact that no one should contest." Here, he explained, Juppé was actually paying about three thousand dollars a month in rent, while there were tens of thousands of people in France living in subsidized apartments who did infinitely less service for the nation than Juppé.

As it happened, Martha and I arrived in Paris to look for a place just as the news of Juppé's arrangement broke, and we soon discovered what Juppé obviously knew to be the vital fact but was having a very hard time saying outright: *All* apartments in Paris that you would long to live in belong to the *domaine privé*. This is to say not that they all belong to the city government but that they can be obtained only through membership in one or another of the political or literary or fashionable *keiretsus* that dominate Paris. Though Paris is in many ways a grasping and commercial city, it is not ruled by the market in quite the way that most other Western cities are.

Martha and I, eight-month-old in tow, learned this quickly as we wandered from apartment to apartment. We discovered that apartments came in three varieties: sad apartments that no one would want; interesting apartments that would require *grands projets* to make them work; and nice apartments that had a long private history or, to put it another way, a catch and so were in a *domaine privé* of their own. This one came with a sister in America, who might or might not eventually return. Another was available only if the divorce that had led to its emptying out was concluded. (With tears in his eyes, the previous resident made it a condition that we buy the espresso machine that he and his departed love had picked out in happier days.) That one belonged to a philosopher who had changed his sexual orientation, and it was available with the proviso that if he changed it back, he would need the apartment again. The inwardness of Paris rules out the illusion created by the renting of an apartment in New York, the illusion of renewal, of starting over. An apartment in New York is a blank slate. In Paris it is an already parsed sentence, a string of imperfect verbs, hidden conditional constructions, and long, intricately wrought clauses in the past tense.

Juppé would probably have been able to survive the revelation of his living arrangements if only *Le Canard Enchaîné* hadn't published, a couple of Wednesdays later, the news that when Juppé was a city official, he had taken apartments in the *domaine privé* for his son and daughter as well and that these apartments too were right there on the rue Jacob. Then it turned out that both Juppé's ex-wife and his half brother had apartments courtesy of the City of Paris. (The former Mme. Juppé was lodged across the river, on the Right Bank, presumably out of deference to the sensibilities of the new Mme. Juppé.) At this point *l'affaire des logements* became a little more serious. *Le Canard* published a document apparently showing that Juppé had approved a rent reduction on his son's apartment from seven thousand francs per month to six thousand (a difference of about two hundred dollars). This might have contravened an all-purpose law against ethical backsliding on the part of public officials, a law whose worst penalty, sweetly enough, was that the offender would be prohibited from ever again being elected to office.

Things got so bad that Juppé had to submit to a humiliation that the French had previously considered fit only for American politicians. He had to go on television and answer questions from reporters. (De Gaulle spoke directly to the French people or else in highly choreographed press conferences; Mitterrand would tolerate a few friendly journalists but would explain to them why the questions they were asking were not of a standard that could decently be put to the president of the republic.) Juppé, by contrast, had to give one of those jumpy, undignified, I-have-nothing-to-hide performances beloved of American handlers.

Juppé did his best. He pointed out that members of the French press had been around for dinner at the now-famous apartment on the rue Jacob, and nobody had seemed upset about the apartment then. (This argument was regarded as fighting dirty. The next day *Le Monde* haughtily noted that it was not proper for guests to ask their host how much he paid in rent and who owned his apartment.) Juppé also announced that he had lowered the rent on his son's apartment only because he was afraid of contributing to a general inflation of rents in the city. It didn't help much. In July a local lawyer with Socialist party connections began filing letters of complaint against Juppé with the state district attorney in Paris, Bruno Cotte, who would therefore have to decide whether to go the Italian route and indict the prime minister of France (and, not incidentally, launch his own political career) or go the honored French route and let it all pass.

By this time I had come into possession of what I thought was the lease on an apartment and so found the later stages of *l'affaire des logements* very diverting. There is nothing like being even an honorary, part-time insider to make insiderness look cute. Then, just as we were about to leave Paris to go home and collect our furniture, I got a call from the real estate agent. "I have bad news," she announced. "Your apartment is off the market." She made it sound as though the apartment had won a prize.

Things worked out better for us than they did for the prime minister. We came back to Paris at the end of September and managed, through various routes, to find an apartment at 16 rue du Pré-aux-Clercs in the Seventh Arrondissement. The story with this one was that it belonged to a young man who had just been posted by his bank to Tokyo; the apartment was affordable because he and his wife had left it half renovated and half a wreck. On the other hand, they would want the apartment back when they returned from Japan, at some unspecified date, which makes us leap every time the doorbell rings.

Bruno Cotte has at last offered his judgment on the Juppé case. He declared that he would not indict Juppé for what he had done with the *domaine privé* apartments, provided that the prime minister of France get out of his apartment and rent one someplace else. This may have been a first in the history of jurisprudence: an eviction notice issued by a magistrate against the prime minister of a major Western power. "This was more cruel than an indictment, which at least had the savor of persecution," a veteran Parisian journalist said to me of the Cotte verdict. "An indictment might have been insupportable, but an eviction is merely ridiculous."

Naturally, American and British journalists have tried to analyze *l'affaire des logements* and, interpreting it in the light of Anglo-American politics, have concluded that Juppé has suffered because he was seen as a member of an unduly privileged elite. This is in fact almost the direct opposite of the truth. The Frenchmen who are currently the most enraged at the government—the functionaries who stopped all business in Paris several weeks ago—are not protesting against the accumulated perks of a privileged class. They are the privileged class, protesting on behalf of their accumulated perks. What made them mad about *l'affaire des logements,* and Juppé's conduct, was not that it revealed to them something they hadn't known but that it reminded them of something they knew all too well—namely, that the system of *acquis sociaux*—entitlements—runs so deep in France that to abolish it would be in some sense to abolish French life itself. Every Frenchman who is not outright destitute sits in the middle of a *domaine privé*—that is, within a domain of private benefits that he enjoys by virtue of his place in civil society. The triumph of the Fifth Republic was to have expanded that domain so that it included nearly everybody. But it may no longer be capable of any expansion at all. The people who are left outside now seem to be left outside for good. The North African immigrants, in particular, who fill the Paris *banlieue* that the police have largely abandoned are not just a minority; they are without any entrée at all. They are called, simply, the excluded. Some of them set bombs off under your bed.

Juppé's serenity is certainly gone for good. Already he is speaking plaintively of his fate. "But why have they done this to me? I am honest!" he told an interviewer recently. "Had I known, when I was foreign minister I could have moved to the quai d'Orsay, where I would have had at my disposal two hundred and eighty square meters and a chambermaid, and nobody would have reproached me at all." People agreed that he had a point, but they also noticed the way he was able to rattle off the square meters by heart.

After brooding on this affair, the French elite has decided that the cure for the kinds of hidden deals that fill French public life is transparence, which has become (along with exclusion) the word of the moment here. By *transparence* people just mean that everybody should see everything that is going on. A lot of Parisians would now settle for having a Paris that is transparent the way an ant farm is transparent: with a cutaway front so that you can see the action even if you can't affect it. But what has always given Paris its peculiar grace and favor is that things that are hidden away elsewhere (like, say, adulteries) are all out in the open here, while things that are all out in the open elsewhere are hidden away here (like, say, the way you get an apartment). A Paris you can see right through hardly seems worth having.

The
Strike

The "generalized" strike that the big French labor federations have called—making a fastidious distinction between what they're doing now and the "general" strike that they may yet get around to—has shut down Paris. The commuter and intercity trains haven't run for two weeks, not even the TGV, the famous fast train between Paris and the South. The Métro is closed down (the crickets who live beneath the rails are said to be perishing for lack of the heat they normally get from the friction of the trains running above, and their plight has become a minor cause célèbre here). There are no buses, and the post office has stopped delivering the mail. Even *le Paris touristique* has been snapped shut. The Ritz has had a dropoff in occupancy of 25 percent (at the height of the terrorist bombing campaign, a few months ago, the rate was near normal, which suggests that the rich would rather risk being blown to bits than have a hard time finding a taxi). The Louvre, like a city under siege, has been struggling to stay open and can guarantee only a narrow access corridor, leading directly from the entrance to the *Mona Lisa*. The government has even commandeered the *bateaux-mouches*—those ugly, flat-bottomed open-air tourist boats that ply the tourist sights year-round—and has turned them into ferryboats to get commuters up and down the Seine.

I think that I only really began to grasp just how serious the strike was when the chickens stopped rotating at the outdoor market in my neighborhood. Several poultry merchants there keep chickens and *coquelets* and rabbits and pheasants spitted and broiling on outdoor rotisseries all through the year, even in August and in the quiet days after Christmas. One afternoon a few days into the strike I walked over to the market to check on the progress of a turkey I had ordered from one of the *rôtisseurs*, to be sent up from the country for a belated Thanksgiving, and I noticed that he had unspitted all his birds and turned off the grill. This seemed to me one of those signs that reporters abroad are supposed to treat as portents ("It has long been said in the bazaars that when the chickens stop turning, the government will fall"), and as I approached to ask what he was doing, he gestured grimly in the direction of the boulevard Saint-Germain.

"*Ça commence*," he said grimly. It's beginning, though what, exactly, was beginning I wasn't sure.

"The turkey, it's still on its way?" I asked, with the stupid inconsequence common to people caught up in revolutions. ("*Rien*," Louis XVI noted in his diary the day the Bastille was stormed.)

He shook his head gravely, implying, I thought for a moment, that the strike might have spread to the fowl too. Then he gestured again toward the boulevard.

For about ten solid blocks, on each side of the boulevard Saint-Germain a row of tourist buses was parked; that, considering the severity with which the cops normally enforce the no-parking regulations, was in itself a near-insurrectionary sight.

The buses bore on their windshields notices indicating where their journeys had begun—Lyons, Grenoble, Bordeaux—and, in their side windows, little stickers saying "FO," for *Force Ouvrière,* or Workers' Force. (Despite the militant name, it is the more moderate of the big French labor federations.) Inside, the bus drivers looked bored and sleepy after the long trip in from the provinces. But between the two rows of buses thousands of FO members, from all across France, were marching up the boulevard, three or four abreast. Then came a rear guard of students armed with batons and occasional bricks. The noise, oddly, was confined, cozily insulated by the parked coaches, a revolution taking place in a bus depot. Farther east on the boulevard, beyond the buses, the French riot police were lined up and waiting, in helmets and shields. There wasn't any violence then, and there hasn't been too much since, but around that time it began to seem that the French were trying on, if only for a moment, long-discarded revolutionary roles, albeit in a slightly unreal setting: strikers taking buses to the revolution, students relearning the lore of the heaved cobblestone.

The strike had begun, on Friday, November 24, as a one-day job action, led by the railroad workers. The Juppé government was still in a state of self-congratulatory, mildly Gingrichian delight over the austerity measures that it had announced to reform the expensive social security system of the French state. The *cheminots,* as the railroad workers are called, hated this idea, because a lot of money is put directly into their pension fund by the government, an outright subsidy, which makes the railroad workers less employees of a profit-seeking enterprise than subsidized functionaries of a state cultural treasure, like members of the Comédie Française. (Although the train system loses money, it is one of the glories of France.) Perhaps the government doubted whether the *cheminots* could command much sympathy since their specific grievance seemed absurdly small (many of them would no longer be able to retire at fifty at full pay) and since the unions have receded as drastically in France in the past fifteen years as they have in America, maybe more so. One in every ten French workers still belongs to a union, but most of the unionized workers are ensconced for life in the public sector or in subsidized state-run enterprises. What the unions have lost in numbers, though, they have gained in freedom to maneuver and in symbolic force. They are no longer the vanguard of the revolution. Now they are the shock troops of the bourgeoisie.

Meanwhile a strike by university students, which had begun outside Paris, came to town too. The students wanted smaller classes and more money, and the government didn't foresee any possible sharing of interests between them and the *cheminots;* what's more, it didn't see how a student strike could claim center stage in a country that has suffered consistently from 10 percent unemployment. Yet the government underestimated the extraordinary hold that the word *student* has on the French imagination, a little like the hold the word *farmer* has on Americans. In fact the phrase *student movement* has in France much the same magic that the phrase *family farm* has in America, conjuring up an idealized past, even for people who never took part in a student movement or lived on a family farm. For a week the students and the *cheminots* took turns working over the Chirac-Juppé government, like a veteran tag-team wrestling pair going against a couple of beardless innocents. They did such a good job that more groups began to jump into the ring. First, the Métro workers went out, and then the postal workers, and then the employees of France Télécom. No one knows who may go next.

Though the strike has developed a quasi-revolutionary momentum, it doesn't have anything like a quasi-revolutionary ideology; the slogan of the government functionaries at the heart of the strike is, essentially, "Status quo forever." The tone is entirely middle class; it suggests a vast petit bourgeois ghost dance, trying to summon up, by its fervor and intensity, a certainty that the future will be like the *trentes glorieuses,* the glorious thirty years of French prosperity that ended in the late seventies. That is why even French people who don't belong to unions support the strike; a poll taken a week into the strike showed that just over 60 percent of them were sympathetic to it.

A few days after the demonstration, I went back to the *rôtis-seur* to see how the turkey was getting along on its way into town. "It does not look good," he said. "The strike prevents him from moving."

"Was he planning to take the TGV?" I asked.

|||

Although workers and students are striking throughout France, the strike is chiefly a Parisian event. That doesn't make it any less national, since France is a completely centralized country. To achieve in America the effect that the strikers have achieved here, it would be necessary to shut down simultaneously the New York subway, the Washington post office, and the Santa Monica Freeway. These weeks have been unusually cold, and that has made the troubles of the strike more difficult. The strike has even produced an iconography of endurance: lots of pictures of bicyclists and Rollerbladers and sailors, carrying on. But in fact the iconography is a little misleading. More typical sights are the endless *bouchons,* or traffic jams, which have made a twenty-minute trip from the Étoile to the place de Clichy last four hours. On the great boulevards and avenues there is a constant press of cars and people, marches one day and solid, immovable traffic jams the next. But if you walk only a couple of blocks away, in any direction, the city looks especially beautiful, and you can have it to yourself. Despite the strike, all the Christmas decorations are up, shiny red and gold ribbon and green garlands draped like bunting around the display windows of the boutiques. Since al-most everyone is busy not getting anywhere in a car, you can be all alone with the gleaming glass storefronts and the Christmas garlands and the sight of your own breath.

The motorcyclists have solved the traffic problem by giving up the streets and simply driving on the sidewalks. As you stroll along the boulevard, you suddenly discover a Harley-Davidson bearing down on you at high speed from among the plane trees. The motorcyclists, who would rather run over a few pedestrians than give up their Hogs, are more truly Parisian than the wan in-line skaters, since the French attitude toward any crisis is not to soldier through it but just to pretend that it isn't happening. (It was in Paris, after all, that Picasso and Sartre sat in a café for four years pretending that the Germans weren't there.)

A deeper and more dramatic version of this national habit of pretending that things haven't happened is what has shaped the strike. What the French strikers want to ignore, at least according to their critics, are the economic facts of the end of the twentieth century: "global capital," the "modern service-based economy," the "tough new competitive conditions of the twenty-first century," all of which, the critics say, can be dealt with only by a more "flexible" labor market. When are these people going to grow up and face reality? seems to be the exasperated question that others in Europe are asking. What the French feel is that for the past half century they have done pretty well by not facing reality—or, anyway, by facing it for one moment and then turning their backs on it for another, in a kind of endless inspired whirl through history. France is a uniquely lovely and supple place to live, and there is a reasonable suspicion here that the British and the Americans and the Germans are trying to hustle the French into what is called a liberal paradise, but what no one here is quite convinced is so paradisiacal. Among the nonunion-ized, petit bourgeois strike sympathizers, in particular, there is an intransigent and rather admirable level of temperamental resis-tance to the notion of "reforming" France to suit the global econ-omy. Even Bernard Thibault, the secretary-general of the *cheminots'* union, said not long ago that he was willing to negoti-ate but that his bottom line was "Citizens must never be trans-ported like merchandise."

In France, of course, not even the merchandise is transported like merchandise. When the turkey arrived at last, a week after the strike began, I got an excited call inviting me to come see it, and when I arrived, the *rôtisseur,* showing it off, pointed out to me how different it was from any bird in an American supermarket. It wasn't frozen, pumped full of cooking oil, or raised in a shed. The bird was supposed to have composed what amounted to a suicide note. "I was raised like a savage, in the forest of the Landes," the turkey's last will and testament began. "I fed on pure corn, wandered in the open air, and slept at night alone in the trees. . . ."

We talked about the strike—the *rôtisseur* seemed to have the same ambivalent sympathies as most other Frenchmen—and I sensed then that he believed that somehow the *cheminots'* strike would help him keep out the frozen turkeys, and the supermarkets they sit in, and the big chains that own the supermarkets. This belief may be as vain as the belief that a ghost dance could raise the dead and bring back the buffalo, but it is no less fervently held.

|||

The only things that have been working perfectly during the strike are what I suppose have to be called the instruments of global capitalism. The worldwide courier services are still picking up packages and sending them out overnight across the ocean, faxes buzz and communicate, and the one worker who seemed to make it nonchalantly through the streets to our house was the cable TV installer, who hooked us up so that we could watch the strike on CNN. It's that anxious-making globalized economy that the strikers are responding to, however incoherently.

Everyone here likes to compare what is going on now with what went on in '68. The real point may be that while that was, in retrospect, essentially a cultural revolution in the guise of a political one, '95 seems, so far, to be a political revolution in the form of a cultural ritual—the big student-and-worker strike—that isn't really appropriate for it. It isn't appropriate because a strike, by its nature, is unpredictably disruptive, while the emotions behind this one are deeply conservative. The strike is one more cry of the heart from people who felt blessed for a long time and now feel threatened. The turkey, not quite incidentally, was so much better than any other turkey I have ever eaten that it might have been an entirely different kind of bird.

The Winter Circus,

CHRISTMAS JOURNAL 1

It is the weather reports on CNN that will scare you most. They must come from a studio in Atlanta, like most things on the cable network, but they tell about the European weather, and only the European weather, and they treat Europe as if it were, for CNN's purposes, one solid block of air with dirt down beneath, one continuous area of high- and low-pressure systems bumping into one another over a happy common land, just like the tristate area, or "here in the Southland," or "up in the heart of the North country," or any of the other cheerful areas into which American television stations divide the country.

The job of the European weatherman (or -woman) seems to be pretty low on the CNN totem pole. They keep changing. One day it is a blow-dried midwesterner; the next a corn-fed, nicely Jane Pauleyish woman; the next a portly black guy. Each one points in turn to the big map of Europe, with the swirling satellite photo superimposed, and then, with the limitless cheeriness

of an American announcer, calls out the temperature and tomorrow's forecast for every site of the more intolerable tragedies of
the twentieth century.

"If you're headed to Warsaw tonight, you may just want to
pack that extra sweater, but if business is pulling you over on that
quick trip to St. Petersburg"—quick, impish, professional wink—
"you'd better make sure that you've got the overcoat. Looking at
snow there *all* night long.

"We're looking at sunny weather throughout Italy, from Rome
right up to Venice. Looks like another mild night in France,
though of course there'll be snow in the mountains around Savoy.
In the Basque country, some *really chilly temperatures. Nice* ski-
ing, though. More mild weather in Prague and Budapest, though
looking up at Vienna . . ." All the old capitals of Old Europe, the
sites of the ghettoes and the massacres and the opera houses,
the border with Spain where they turned the refugees away and
Walter Benjamin died in despair, all treated in the spirit, with the
same sound, that I can recall from every night in my childhood
in West Philadelphia, when "Dr." Somebody or other—a "certified meteorologist"—gave the weather for the tristate area and
threw in the highs and lows in Atlantic City "for all of you heading for the shore."

We have won as large a victory as any country has ever won—
no empire has ever stood in so much power, cultural, political,
economic, military—and all we can do is smile and say that you
might want to pack a sweater for the imperial parade.

|||

When the cable television man came to hook us up on the first
morning of the general strike, you could hear the demonstrators
out on the boulevard, singing and marching. But the bland emissary from the age of global information worked on, stringing the
wire and hooking up the decoder boxes. He finally handed us
three different remotes and then ran through the thirty-odd

channels like a priest reciting the catechism. "Here is CNN, news in America. Here is MTV. Here is French MTV," the cable man explained. "Here is Euronews, in English. Here is Euro-sport." A 49ers-Dolphins game was in progress. There it was, truly, the same familiar ribbon of information and entertainment that girdles the world now—literally (really, truly literally) encircling the atmosphere, electric rain. All you have to do is hold out a hand to catch it.

Luke, at least, has found a home, shelter from the electronic rain and global weather. He lives in the Luxembourg Gardens. We go there nearly every day, even in the chill November days among the fallen leaves. The design of the gardens is nearly perfect for a small child. There is a playground; there is a puppet theater, where he is too small to go yet, but outside the puppet theater there is a woman selling balloons, and every morning he points to his wrist and says his all-purpose word, *bu-bel,* which means balloon, ball, whatever it is meant to mean. But then, when we get to the gardens and the po-faced woman goes to tie the balloon to his wrist, he leaps back with fear and demands to have it taken off again. Approach and avoidance with older women.

He rides the carousel, the fallen leaves piled neatly all around it, and though bent-up it is a beauty. The animals are chipped, the paint is peeling, the giraffe and elephant are missing hooves and tusks, and the carousel is musicless and graceless. The older children ride the outside horses. A God-only-knows-how-old carousel motor complains and heaves and wheezes and finally picks up enough momentum to turn the platform around, while the carousel attendant hands a baton to each of the older children riding the outside horses. Then he unhooks a pear-shaped wooden egg from the roof of his little station, at the edge of the turning platform, and slips little metal rings with leather tags attached into the egg. As the children race around, the little rings drop one after another into the egg and dangle from its base, the small leather tags acting as a kind of target, a sighting mechanism, so that the children can see the rings. The older children try to catch the rings with the sticks.

It looks tricky; it looks *hard*. The kids have to hold the weather-beaten sticks up just so; there's just one angle, one way to do it. As the carousel picks up speed, it gets going whirring fast, and the hand-eye, or rather hand–eye–painted horse, coordination you need looks terrifyingly accomplished. To make things even harder, if two children are mounted one right behind the other, and the first child lances the ring, it means that the next ring, slipping down, only arrives at the base of the wooden egg as the next child arrives, making it just about impossible to aim. If the first child just knocks the ring, on the other hand, the ring starts trembling widely enough to make a good grab impossible. It is a tough game, and what makes it odder is that there is no reward for doing well at it. I have read about this game all my life: going for the Big Brass Ring! It's an American metaphor. But here there are little tin rings, and no reward for getting them except the satisfaction of having done it. You don't even get to keep the tin rings for a moment of triumph—Look, Mama!—to show the cluttered stick, rings on it like plums on the branch of a plum tree. The keeper takes back the batons before the carousel has even stopped.

It is hard for me to imagine Luke ever doing this: sitting up there, skewering his rings. For the moment, for a long moment, we sit together in the little chariots and just spin. He keeps his eyes locked on the big kids with the sticks, who come under the heading of Everything He Desires: a stick, a task, a seat on the outside horse. (For me, the sticks and rings game on the carousel looks more like a symbolic pageant. A Writer's Life: hard job, done intently, for no reason. Cioran used to walk in these gardens. I wonder if he watched this.) The reward for the Parisian children is, perhaps, the simple continuity, the reality that the spinning will never get a prize, but that it will also never stop.

After all, spinning is its own reward. There wouldn't be carousels if it weren't so.

|||

On nice days, when we don't have time to go all the way to the gardens, Luke and I go to the musical horse outside the *Oiseau de Paradis* ("Bird of Paradise"), a toy store on the boulevard Saint-Germain, and he solemnly rides up and down on it while it plays "Camptown Races." On rainy days, we go to Deyrolle on the rue du Bac. It is an extraordinary place. It is on the second floor—almost all of the second story—of one of the old *hôtels particuliers*. It is, I suppose, a taxidermists' supply house and a supplier too of educational charts. But it is also one of the great surrealist sites of Paris. Downstairs, at street level, there is the old-fashioned kind of come-hither wraparound window entrance, so that you enter a deep-set door between two vitrines, an architecture that must have been familiar once in Paris—it was the architecture of every South Street shoe store in my childhood—though it is fairly rare now. (Mostly the windows here are one sheet of plate glass, with a kind of false front showing the goods and the store behind.) But here you walk past a "seasonal" window, filled with taxidermized animals and bare minimum decor: artificial fallen leaves for autumn, cotton ball "snow" for winter, a few silk flowers for spring. Sometimes the animals inside the windows change too—an ancient, yellowing polar bear right now represents the Spirit of Christmas—but mostly it is the same bunch all year: a fox, a raccoon, a moose. (The polar bear must have been brought down on the same expedition that is celebrated in the window of a lead-soldier store on the rue des Ciseaux, which shows an otherwise unrecorded late-nineteenth-century *French* expedition to the North Pole, with the tricolor hanging over an igloo and reindeer entrecôte in a chef's *sauteuse*.)

When you open the door at Deyrolle, there is a moose on your left, and then an odd display case straight ahead, with snake embryos in little jars of formaldehyde. If you go up the stairs—and Luke will only go up the stairs clutching tightly to my chest—you will find at the top an entire bestiary waiting patiently for your arrival, not in casements or vitrines but just standing on all fours on the floor around the casements and vitrines, looking bored and social, like writers at a New York book party. They just stand there. There are several lions, genuinely terrifying in their direct address. They have been taxidermized—*reanimated* is the correct term—not to look fierce but just to look bored—these are French lions, after all—which of course makes them look more fierce.

And then a baby elephant and a jaguar and a gorilla, all just *there,* with all the other natural things—skeletons and skulls and case upon case of butterflies and beetles—all around. The walls are painted a fading blue-green; the cases are all wood and glass. The main showroom is a two-story space, with a balcony up above. They keep the ordinary farm animals, sheep and goats, up there, looking down on the stars, like the extras in *Les Enfants du Paradis.*

There are also—and this is the weirdest touch—lots of domestic animals, family pets, Siamese and Scotties and cockers, who stand there on the floor too, among the lions and jaguars, looking furtive, forlorn, a little lost. Mme. Orlovska, the owner, who has become a friend, explains that they are unclaimed taxidermized pets from the old Deyrolle regime. Apparently year after year people would come in, weeping and clutching the cold bodies of Fido and Minochette, the house pets, and beg to have them taxidermized, restored, revivified. The taxidermists would go to laborious work, and then, two or three months later, when the pet was at last stuffed into its immortality, the owner, consoled with a new living (though mortal) pet, would have forgotten all about it. No answer to calls or bills or what she calls "commands of conscience." So the unwanted permanent pets—

who were perhaps, as pets always are, mere courtesans of affection, feigning a feeling for food—got replaced, as courtesans will, and found themselves at the feet of the lions and elephants.

The big game are themselves souvenirs of a hotter time in Deyrolle's history, when hunters would have their African catches mounted and leave an extra lion or a leftover gnu to the house, as a sort of tip, like gamblers in Monte Carlo in the same period giving a chip or two to the croupier. Deyrolle makes its money now, Madame explains, mostly selling bugs and butterflies to decorators. "We can't find any large game anymore," she complains. "The laws are so absurdly tight. If a lion dies in a circus, we cannot touch it. If an elephant falls over in a zoo, we cannot reanimate it. Is it better for a thing of beauty to die and molder away than to be made a work of art?" (The government is worried, as governments will be, I suppose, that if fallen elephants are turned into merchandise, however lovely, then sooner or later elephants will not just be falling. Elephants will be nudged.)

|||

Luke is as frightened (and fascinated) by the small game as he is by the large; he clings to me tightly throughout—and then every day demands to be taken back. I think he feels about it the same way that I feel about the Baudrillard seminar I am attending at the Beaubourg. It's scary, but you learn something.

I've attended this public seminar, given by Baudrillard and friends at the Beaubourg. Jean Baudrillard is, or anyway *was*, the terror of West Broadway back in the eighties. He was the inventor of the theory of "the simulacra," among much else, and famously insisted that "reality" had disappeared and that all that was left in its place was a world of media images and simulated events. ("The Gulf War Did Not Take Place" was his famous slogan, meaning that it was a pure television production.) Before the seminar I imagined Baudrillard as tall and spectral and high-domed as Barthes had been. He turns out to be a stocky, friendly little guy in his fifties, with a leather jacket and a weather-beaten complexion.

The seminar consists of a three- or four-man panel: an economist; a sociologist; Leo Scher, the all-around thinker. Each gives a presentation, and then Baudrillard comments. The other day, for instance, the economist was giving a lecture on exponentiality. "Exponentiality is fatality," he announced grimly, and went on to point out what every first-year biology student is told, that the "exponential" proliferation of biological life—each codfish has a million codfish children; each codfish child has a million of its own children—means that the codfish, or slime mold or antelope or, for that matter, French intellectuals, would cover the world in ten or so generations, unless there were something—several somethings—there to check them.

(The girl in front of me scribbled in her book, in French, of course, "Exponentiality is Fatality.")

"Therefore," said the economist, "I propose that there must exist in the biological sphere a principle, which I will call the Regulon"—he wrote the word in capitals on the blackboard—"which prevents this from happening. I call this principle the Regulon."

No one protested, or pointed out that, as I think is the case, Darwin (among many others) had solved this problem awhile ago without recourse to the Regulon. (Predators eat most of the codfish; the rest just die. Life is hard; the Regulon is called life, or death.) Baudrillard nodded gravely at the end of the exposition. "But yours underlines the point I am making," he added, almost plaintively. He paused and then pronounced: "There is no Regulon in the Semiosphere." (And she wrote it down and underscored it: "There is no Regulon in the Semiosphere.")

There Is No Regulon in the Semiosphere. There is no way of stopping media signs from proliferating, no natural barrier to the endless flow and reproduction of electronic information, no way of keeping the CNN weatherman out of your sky. There is nothing to eat them. There Is No Regulon in the Semiosphere is an abstract way of saying that there is no "natural predator" to stop the proliferation of movies and television; they do over-whelm the world, and with it reality. It is hard to see how you save the carousel and the musical horse in a world of video games, not because the carousel and musical horse are less attractive to children than the Game Boy, but because the carousel and the musical horse are single things in one fixed place and the video games are everywhere, no Regulon to eat them up.

|||

When I lived here with my family, in the early seventies, there was nothing I liked more than walking up the boulevard Beau-marchais to the Cirque d'Hiver, the Winter Circus. It is a wooden octagon, visible from the boulevard, but set well back, on a little street of its own. A frieze, a kind of parody of the Pan-athenaic procession, runs around its roof: clowns and jugglers and acrobats in bas-relief. Inside, it has a hushed, intimate quality; the hard wooden bleachers are pitched very high. I don't recall that I ever actually went inside when I was a kid—I was too busy with movies—it just seemed like the right place to walk to. But now we've been to a winter circus at the Winter Circus. The Cirque du Soleil, from back home in Montreal, put on its slightly New Age show, and we took Luke and sat in the top rows. They brought the lights down when the circus began, as though it were a play, which struck me as an odd thing. I always think of circuses sharing the light of their spectators. (What happened to the summer circus? I used to think that the circuses must have toured all summer and then came into winter retreat on the rue Amelot. But now I suspect that there was a summer circus once too, but they closed it. The Circus. Regulon got it, I guess.)

It was a good circus, though a little long on New Age, New Vaudeville, and Zen acrobats and a little short, absent in fact, on the lions and bears I had promised Luke. (We have a standing joke about lions in Paris; as I push his *poussette*, I announce that I am terrified that there may be lions in this quarter of Paris— "and I'm so scared of lions"—and he roars, lustily.) At the end, though, the troupe took its final bow and threw those little glow-ing green bracelets up into the audience as a favor. A few came up as high as we were. The French fathers, soccer players to a man, snatched at them from the wrist as they flew up, like men slapping futilely at mosquitoes. I stood up and with years of in-competent Central Park softball under my belt, I pounded my right fist into the left and pulled one in like a pop-up. Then I handed it to Luke. The other fathers in the row looked at me with pure hate. I shrugged and have never felt so obnoxious, so proud, so imperial, so American.

|||

We have found Luke a baby-sitter, or I suppose I have to say a nanny. Her name is Nisha Shaw, she comes from Sri Lanka, has long hair in a beautiful braid and beautiful lilting English, and she is the wife of the philosopher Bernard-Henri Lévy's chauffeur. She is lovely and loving, and she sings all day to Luke in a high-pitched soprano, singing songs that seem just out of focus— "Blowin' in the Wind" and a song that begins "Softly sings the donkey/As he goes to hay/If you don't come with him/He will go away." Softly sings the donkey—the theme tune of the American liberal abroad. We have already, in a few weeks, become a strange island of Sri Lankan, Icelandic-Canadian, West Philadelphian, Franco-American civilization within a bigger culture. I imagine these are songs that she's heard over the radio and in school, songs that are part of her own little monoculture, just as we have made up ours.

Every morning as Luke and I wait for Nisha to arrive before I go to work in my office, we look out from the kitchen into the courtyard. Every morning, just at eight-fifteen, a hand emerges, holding at its end a tablecloth or a sheet or something that it shakes out. She is known as the Shaky Lady, the Aurora, or Dawn Goddess, of our home. We made up a song in her honor— Oh, Shaky Lady/Oh, Shaky Lady, be good to me"—and she seems to shake with such authority, such intensity.

The odd thing in making a big move is the knowledge that your life will be composed of hundreds of small things that you will arrive at only by trial and error, and that for all the strikes and seminars you attend, the real flavor of life will be determined, shaped, by these things. The Semiosphere comes at you in little bursts. Where will your hair be cut? What kind of coffee will you buy, and where? We have been searching for the right mocha, everywhere we go: at La Vieille France, a pastry store on the rue de Buci; at Hédiard, on the place de la Madeleine; at Whittard, an English coffee importer that has a counter in the Conran on the rue du Bac. Our old Dean & DeLuca blend is gone now, and we must find a new one. The Shaky Lady will preside over some kind of coffee, but even she cannot know quite which one, not just yet.

|||

We have been trying to furnish our place—we had minimal furniture in the New York loft, really, chairs and rugs and rattraps— and on Sundays we go up to the Marché aux Puces, the flea market, which remains a wonder, though the only fleas in it all have Platinum American Express cards. (It isn't cheap.) The Métro ride up to the porte de Clignancourt is a joy, though, just for the names of the stations in northern Paris: Château Rouge, Château d'Eau—what *was* the Red Castle? what was the *Water* Tower?—Poissonniers, Gare du Nord, with its lovely, thirties, Gabinish overtones. We come up, back home, at Odéon, under the statue of Danton, and a single limb of a chestnut tree hangs over the Métro stairs. It's dark already at five o'clock, the limb silhouetted against the moonlit sky while the crowd presses against you on the stairs. What an old place France is, the attic bursting with old caned chairs and zinc bars and peeling dressers and varnished settees. The feeling is totally different from an antiques fair in America; this is the attic of a civilization.

Today we stop at Le Biron for lunch; the restaurants up at the flea market—Le Biron, Le Voltaire—are among the few real bistros left, in the sense of simple places with some culinary pretension that maintain an air of joie de vivre. The poor madame is terribly overworked, and we feel for her, but lunch, simple chicken, takes an hour and a half. The *tarte tatin* is very good, though. After lunch, on this freezing cold day, faint light raking through the stalls, Luke and I stop at the little bar with a Django-style swing band: two gypsy guitarists with ancient electrics with f-holes, joined by a good-looking blonde with an alto sax. There's a couple smoking endless Gauloises next to us. I ordered, with a thrilling automatic feeling, a café-calva and a grenadine for Luke. They played the old American songs—"All of Me," "There Will Never Be Another You"—some Jobim too, really swinging it. Martha was off shopping at Vernaison for a plain old table. A perfect half hour.

Martha insisted on taking a cab home, declaring it too cold to get on the Métro. The cabbie, observing Luke, began a disquisition on children. Only children—we explained in French that he won't be, or we hoped he wouldn't be—are, he explained, the cause of the high modern divorce rate: The boy arrives, and the man feels jealous; there is another man in his wife's life (well, another being), and this leads to jealousy, a lover; and the whole cycle begins again. (Why a second child would cure this . . .) This is why women must have three children and stay home. "The school instructs," he explained, "but the family educates." I couldn't decide whether to give him a large or small tip.

|||

It is odd to think that for so long people came to Paris mostly for the sex. "City of the naughty spree," Auden wrote disdainfully in the twenties, "La Vie Parisienne, Les Folies-Bergère, Mademoiselle Fifi, bedroom mirrors and bidets, lingerie and adultery." These days the city's reputation for naughtiness has pretty much diminished away to nothing. Now the dirty movies get made in Amsterdam; the dirty drawings get sent in from Tokyo; and Oriental and even German towns, of all places, are the places you go for sexual experiment. (Even the bidets are gone from Paris, mostly converted into bizarre plug-in electric toilets, which roar as they chew up human waste, in a frenzy of sanitary appetite, and then send it out, chastened, down the ordinary water pipes.)

Things have become so run-down, or cleaned up, sexually here that France has even reached the point where it is running a bimbo deficit and has to import its sex objects. Just last week Sharon Stone was flown in to Paris to be made a Chevalier of Arts and Letters by the French minister of culture, M. Philippe Douste-Blazy. The award struck many Parisians as ridiculous, but it was, in its crude way, a logical part of a consistent cultural policy. Despite their reputation, the French are not really cultural chauvinists at all. They remain chauvinists about their judgment, a different thing; increasingly their judgment *is* their culture. They want to be free to continue to reinvent American culture in their own image, finding art forms where back home we saw only hackwork and actresses where we saw only bimbos. (The award to Sharon Stone was for "her services to world culture.") They don't mind if the Americans make the movies so long as they get to pass out the medals. Pinning a decoration on Sharon Stone is the perfect way of looking down your nose at U.S. cultural imperialism while simultaneously fondling its chest.

|||

The one exception to the erotic milding of Paris are the lingerie ads, which still fill the boulevards and billboards. The ads—

particularly the ones for Aubade—are sharply, unsettlingly erotic, to a male viewer, and differ from their American counterparts in not seeming particularly modern. Women are, as we would say, reduced to body parts; the Aubade ads isolate breasts or thighs or legs as relentlessly as a prep cook at KFC, each part dressed up in a somewhat rococo bit of underwear, lace and thong, in sculpted-lit black and white, very Hurrell, with a mocking "rule" underneath it—i.e., "Rule Twenty-four: Feign Indifference."

There is something stimulating but old-fashioned about these posters (which, for a week or two at a time, are everywhere, on every bus stop, on every bus). They are *coquettish,* a word I had never associated with a feeling before. For all the complaints about a new puritanism, the truth is that feminism in America has, by restoring an edge of unpredictability and danger to the way women behave and the way men react to that behavior, added to the total of tension on which desire depends. The edgy, complicated, reverse-spin coding of New York life— this skintight dress is not a come-on but its opposite, a declaration of independence meant not for you but for me—is unknown here. Here, the intellectuals wear black, and the models wear Alaïa.

The other evening, for instance, we went to a dinner party where the philosopher Bernard-Henri Lévy appeared with his wife, the amazing-looking Arielle Dombasle (who wore a bathing suit in one of those philosophical-erotic-talky French films, from the time when philosophical-erotic-talky French films were the delight of the Upper West Side). She wore a skintight lamé dress. We saw her a week or so later and she was wearing another clinging lamé dress, as though out of obligation to her own image, her own invention. *Désir* in Paris is surreptitious but not ironic; everyone has affairs, but no one has reverse-spin coding. In New York the woman in the clinging dress is probably a professor at Hunter, while the girl in all black with no makeup reading the

French papers may be Sharon Stone. You could tell by the medal, I suppose.

|||

Mostly, we shop at BHV, the department store on the rue de Rivoli, which has become our home, our Luxembourg Gardens. BHV—the Bazar de l'Hôtel de Ville, the City Hall Bazaar—is always called by its initials (bay-ash-vay), and it is an old store, one of the great nineteenth-century department stores on the Right Bank that are the children of the Galeries Lafayette. As I say, it is on the rue de Rivoli; in fact that famous Robert Doisneau photograph of the two lovers kissing is set on the rue de Rivoli just outside BHV. This is doubly ironic: first, because the narrow strip of the rue de Rivoli in front of BHV is about the last place in the world that you would want to share a passionate kiss—it would be a bit like kissing at the entrance to the BMT near Macy's—and of course, it explains why they did it anyway. They are not sundered lovers but a young couple who have managed to buy an electric oven and emerge alive. Anyone who has spent time at BHV knows that they are kissing not from an onset of passion but from gratitude at having gotten out again.

|||

BHV, in its current form, seems to have been invented by a Frenchman who visited an E. J. Korvette's in Cherry Hill, New Jersey, sometime in the early 1960s and, maddened with love, decided to reproduce it down to the least detail. There's the same smell of popcorn, the same cheery help, the same discount appliances stretching as far as the eye can see. It is the Parisian tradition that the landlord does not supply appliances. They must all be bought, and you take them with you when you leave. We had a whole run of things to buy, none of which, as lifelong Manhattan renters, we had ever had to buy before: a refrigerator, an oven, a stove. We *had*, oddly enough, once bought a wonderful French dishwasher, a Miele, silent as a Greek oracle, to add to our old loft. But we couldn't use even this, since most of the old appliances run on American 110 volts and France uses 220 volts. You either have to get the insides of the machine changed or else buy something new.

We became hypnotized, bewitched by the curious selling rhythms of BHV: a mixture of confidence, arrogance, and an American-style straightforwardness, with the odd difference that here the customer is always, entirely wrong. We bought a toaster, which promptly shorted out the first time we used it. We brought it back. "What did you toast in it?" the return man asked, haughty for all that he was wearing a regulation oversize checked vest, the uniform of BHV. "Raisin brioche," we answered honestly. He looked shocked, disgusted, appalled, though not surprised. "What do you expect if you put bread with raisins in it?" he asked. But he let us have a new one anyway.

|||

The week before Christmas I had to go out to buy Christmas tree lights at Bon Marché, the Left Bank department store. Ours didn't work, for reasons I don't understand, since a lot of the electric lamps we brought with us *do* work. Apparently some American lights shine in Paris, and some don't, don't ask why. (Henry James wrote whole novels on this theme, after all.) Instead of coming in strands that you can wrap around the tree, though, the French Christmas tree lights come in *guirlandes*—garlands—closed circles of lights without beginnings or endings. A thin cord with a plug at the end shoots out from the middle of the garland. (They cost a fortune too: twenty-five dollars for as many lights as you can get on Canal Street for five.) These garlands are packed into the box just the way strands are—light by light in little cardboard notches in a horizontal row—so it's only when you take them out of the box that you realize that what you've got is a ring, not a rope.

This means that the only way to get the Christmas lights on the Christmas tree is to lasso it. You have to get up on a ladder, hold the lights out as a loop, and then, pitching forward a bit, throw the entire garland right over the top of the tree, rodeo style. This is harder to do than it sounds and even more dangerous than it looks. I suppose you could pick up the tree and shimmy the lights on from down below, like a pair of *caleçons*, but this would require someone to pick up the tree so you could do it. I can't really see the advantages of having a garland over a string. A string is easier to use—you just start at the bottom and wrap it right around the tree, merrily ascending—and this seems to me not cultural prejudice but a practical fact. (But then all cultural prejudices seem like practical facts to the prejudiced.) Still, the garlands are all there is. Martha kept sending me back to buy more.

Even then it wasn't finished. I had had the pointed inspiration of buying blue lights for the Christmas tree this year, where in New York we always had white ones. Since we had moved, changed cultures, I couldn't think of a better marker, a clearer declaration of difference and a new beginning, than having blue lights on the tree instead of white ones. But when I brought them home and did my Roy Rogers bit again and we turned them on and then turned off the lights in the living room, no one liked the look of them. The blue lights looked, well, blue. I doggedly, painstakingly packed them back into the box, took them back to Bon Marché, and tried to exchange them for white lights.

The trouble now was that the new white lights I got were white lights that were all twinkling ones. I saw the word *clignotant* on the box, and I knew that it meant blinking, but somehow I didn't associate the word *blinking* with the concept "These lights blink off and on." It was the same thing with the garlands, come to think of it. It said *guirlande* right on the box, and I knew perfectly well what *guirlande* meant; but I am not yet able to make the transposition from what things say to what they mean. I saw the word *guirlande* on the box, but I didn't quite *believe* it. In New York I believe everything I read, even if it appears in the *New York Post*. In France I am always prepared to give words the benefit of a poetic doubt. I see the word *guirlande* and shrug and think that maybe *garland* is just the French seasonal Christmas light–specific idiom for a string. The box says, "They blink," and I think they don't.

I found this out of course only after I had already put the lights on the tree, plugged them in, and watched them blinking. I liked the effect okay, but Martha was having none of it. She thought it looked horrible—*sequiny and vulgar* were her words—so back I went to Bon Marché on the afternoon of Christmas Eve, for the third time, to buy a garland of unblinking white lights. This time the saleswoman gave me a really hard time. It was bad enough not knowing what color you want, but not even knowing if you wanted shimmer or a solid glow? I got them home at last and felt unreasonably proud of the garland of lights: a closed circle, desire and fulfillment meeting in a neat French ring, and just shining.

|||

For all the talk about globalization, the unification of the world through technology, etc., the truth is that *only* information is being globalized (and then only for people who speak English). There *is* a Regulon in the Semiosphere. It is called a plug. The necessities of life—plugs and voltages and battery types and . . . are *more* compartmentalized, more provincialized, more exhaustingly different now from country to country than what they were a century or even two centuries ago. A chamber pot, after all, was always a chamber pot in whatever country you happened to be sitting; a pen was a pen since a feather was a feather. But to plug in your computer now takes a range of plugs and adapters—three prongs and two prongs and two small prongs with a big prong and three tiny prongs in a row—that look like sexual aids for jaded courtesans in de Sade. We are unified by our machines and divided up by the outlets we use to *brancher* them.

Fish, too. Fish and plugs are the two great differences, the two things that are never quite alike from country to country. Fish are sort of alike but maddeningly not exactly alike. You have to learn the translations. A *bar* is sort of but not quite a sea bass, a *rouget* like a red snapper but actually smaller and more dapper—weirdly *snappier*. A turbot is not a flounder. Even French oysters, the most delicious in the world, have a salty, sea brine, bracing taste, not better than plump, sweet American oysters, but different—far more different than the difference, real though it is, between French lamb and American, or a French chicken and a good American one.

Globalization stops short at the baseboard and the coastline, wherever the electricity and the seafood come charging in. The reason for the differences are plain enough. You can't farm line-caught fish, and the variety of plugs is the consequence of the basic difference in the European decision to have 220-volt outlets where we have only 110. This means that the Europeans worry more about shocks. They add a third plug to ground the charge, the baseboard equivalent of a social safety net. Each country does it a little differently. The French have light, dapper, rounded three-prong plugs with two little cylindrical probes and a third, thicker one; the British have three immensely heavy prongs; and the Italians, I recall, have an odd, all-in-line arrangement. All of them feature that third grounding element to keep the shocks from passing from the surging current directly into the room and the people who live there. Only America remains ungrounded.

To make the transition from country to country, plug to plug, you also need to know more than anyone can—well, anyway, more than I do—about what things have motors and which don't. (Motors aren't adaptable, even with adapters. You have to get converters for them that turn out to be big, heavy black boxes—odd, in this day of the streamlined and transistorized—that do something or other to the current.)

I plugged in my Stylewriter Mac printer the third day here to print something out, and as it began to print, it also immediately began to smoke. Disconcerting plumes of flame shot from it, as though it were being executed in Florida. Horrible sight, particularly as *it kept on printing* even as it destructed, another symbol of the writer's life. So I had to buy a new one, whose software is all in French. I am learning French computerese: *brancher, imprimer, annuler* . . . Even the common language of the bank machine is odd. We got our bank cards from our new bank, but whereas in New York you have to punch out your code—ours was Luke's birthday—here you are assigned your code by the bank, with no appeals. You are 3431, you are 1676, that is it.

There is a separate language of appliance design in France, which we are learning as we wander, pushing the *poussette* in and out of the rows on the second floor of the BHV. Things are smaller, but they are also much quieter and more streamlined. In the kitchen, when you *branché* them, they *hum,* discreetly, impatiently. They all are slim, white, molded, with the buttons and lights neatly small, rectangular, and inset into the white plastic. The hulking, growling American appliances we had at home, with their freezers on top and their sunset brown faces, all were solid, vast and seemed to imply survivalism. You could go cruising in them. The French appliances, with their blinking lights and set-back press buttons on the front, imply sociability and connection.

It is as if all American appliances dreamed of being cars while all French appliances dreamed of being telephones. The French freezer is, in a French refrigerator, always on the bottom rather than the top and is composed of drawers and secret compartments, like an old writing desk; you are supposed to fill it with culinary billets-doux, little extras, like *petits pois,* instead of with next week's dinner, as you do in an American freezer.

Parisians love telephones, all kinds of telephones. They don't use them the way that Americans use telephones, but they just *love* them, the way that Americans love cars. (This is partly because telephones are newly arriving; when we lived here in the early seventies, a year went by, and we still didn't have a phone.) The cellular phone, which back in New York still seemed to me to be mostly in the hands of real estate agents and salespeople— those who were, in a sense, on call, biddable—is here in everyone's hands. You walk down the boulevard, and everyone is *talking,* a phone clutched to the ear. What you never see, though, is someone walking down the street with a Walkman on, as everyone does in New York. (I miss my walks with my Walkman, in fact, probably more than any other single thing about life here so far: the music, the isolation, the sense of life as a sound track, the pure release of it. Nobody here wants to shut the city out. They are talkers, not silent listeners.)

They don't have answering machines either, or at least don't rely on them to do all the work of protection and sorting and screening that New Yorkers do. If you call people, and they're home, they answer; they have the same law-abiding approach to these calls that Americans have to parking. You park where you're supposed to park, whereas people in Paris will park anywhere. It is not so much that the phone transformed France and the car transformed America as that both fitted right in, as I suppose technologies must, with what people had wanted all along. Not new desires made by new machines but new machines matching the same old needs. The phone replaced the system of pneumatic messages—the *pneus*—that used to race around Paris, and there is something *pneu* about them even now: French telephone conversations tend to be sharp, pointy, rather than expansive.

There is an odd, seemingly purposeful looking-glass quality to a lot of the things we have to buy. The Braun coffeemaker with a thermos that we had in New York is available here, but oddly only in black, whereas the one in New York was available only in white.

Luke loves BHV for the music. All day long it plays excited, taped Christmas shopping announcements, backed with appropriate tunes. Some of the tunes we recognize—it plays the *Looney Tunes* theme, for instance—and some seem vaguely familiar but are hard to name, so we give our own names to them: "The Love Theme from BHV," "BHV's Victory at Sea," and the "BHV Christmas Anthem." His ears undimmed by fifteen years of the IRT, Luke can hear them all even over the din of appliance shopping, and when he notices a favorite, he rises from his stroller, a cobra in mittens, and sways solemnly back and forth.

About five days before Christmas, BHV was decked out for the holidays—though, with the strikes shutting down transportation, there was hardly a soul in sight. Twenty years ago there was no Christmas in Paris. Oh, there was a holiday, of course, and even the gaunt, Gaullist figure of Père Noël, an ascetic and intellectualized version of Santa. But the great American department store potlatch was unknown. All that's changed beyond recognition now. That central ritual of bountiful capitalism, the department store Christmas, is in late but absurdly full bloom here, and with an American flavor so pronounced that it hardly seems American anymore, just part of an international style. The dome of Printemps, on the boulevard Haussmann, for instance, is this year decorated with stylized Stars and Stripes and life-size figures of Jimmy Dean and Marilyn and Clark and Bogie and even Babe Ruth. Now at BHV there are artificial evergreens, and tree decoration departments, and a Santa—get your picture with the old guy—and boughs of evergreen hung everywhere, and artificial snow, even though it never snows in Paris at all. On this afternoon, the "BHV Christmas Anthem" began to rise from every loudspeaker on every floor. Only now, as Luke swayed in his stroller, I could hear it clearly for the first time, loud and ringing through the almost empty store, and I understood at last why it had sounded so oddly familiar. It was the theme from *Entertainment Tonight*. Maybe there is no Regulon in the Semiosphere after all.

Distant
Errors

The Rules
of the Sport

Late last year the French government assembled a committee to choose a name for the vast new stadium that's being built in a Paris suburb. The committee included an actor, an "artiste," some functionaries, and even a few athletes. It took a long time deliberating over its choice. Names were submitted: Some people liked the idea of naming the stadium after Verlaine or Saint-Exupéry, and lots of others liked the idea of calling it Le Stade Platini, after Michel Platini, the great French soccer player. At last, in December, the committee announced that it had come to a decision, and the government decided to broadcast the verdict on television. The scene was a little like the end of the Simpson trial: the worried-looking jurors filing to their seats, the pause as the envelope was handed to the minister of youth and sports, the minister clearing his throat to read the decision to the nation. The stadium that would represent France to the world, he announced, would be called (long, dramatic pause) Le Stade de

France. The French Stadium. "Banal and beautiful at the same time," one journalist wrote. "Obvious and seductive. Timeless and unalterable."

It wasn't hard to detect, beneath the sturdy, patriotic surface of the new name, an undercurrent of ironic, derisory minimalism. The French are prepared to be formally enthusiastic about American-style stadiums and American-style sports, but they are not going to get carried away by it all. This realization first came home to me when I joined a pioneer health club on the Left Bank and spent four months unsuccessfully trying to get some exercise there.

"An American gym?" Parisians asked when I said that I was looking for someplace to work out, and at first I didn't know what to say. What would a French gym be like? Someone suggested that my wife and I join the Health Club at the Ritz; that was about as French as a gym could get. This sounded like a nice, glamorous thing to do, so we went for a trial visit. I ran out of the locker room and dived into the pool. White legs were dangling all around me—crowded to the edges, as though their owners were clinging to the sides of the pool in fear—and only after I rose to the surface did I see that the owners were all hanging from the edge of the pool, eating tea sandwiches off silver platters. Finally, after we'd done a lot of asking around, someone suggested a newly opening "New York–style" gym, which I'll call the Régiment Rouge. One afternoon Martha and I walked over to see what it was like and found it down at the end of a long, winding street. The gym was wedged into the bottom two floors of an institutional-looking Haussmann-era building. We went in and found ourselves surrounded by the virtuous sounds of Activity—sawing and hammering and other plaster dust–producing noises. The bruit seemed to be rising from a cavernlike area in the basement. At the top of a grand opera–style staircase that led to the basement were three or four fabulously chic young women in red tracksuits—the Régiment Rouge!—that still managed to be fairly form-clinging. The women all had ravishing long hair and lightly applied makeup. When we told them that we wanted to *abonner*—subscribe—one of them whisked us off to her office and gave us the full spiel on the Régiment Rouge. It was going to bring the rigorous, uncompromising spirit of the New York health club to Paris: its discipline, its toughness, its *regimental* quality. They were just in the middle of having the work done— one could hear this downstairs—and it would all be finished by the end of the month. The locker rooms, the *appareils Nautilus,* the stationary bicycles with electronic displays, the steam baths, the massage tables—everything would be not just *à l'américaine* but *très New Yorkais.* Best of all, she went on, they had organized a special "high-intensity" program in which, for the annual sum of about two thousand francs (four hundred dollars), you could make an inexorable New York–style commitment to your physique and visit the gym as often as once a week.

It was obvious that the once-a-week deal was the winner—the closer, in Mamet language—and that though she had a million arguments ready for people who thought that when it came to *forme,* once a week might be going overboard, she had nothing at all ready for people who thought once a week might not be *forme* enough. We asked her if we could possibly come more often than that, and she cautiously asked us what we meant by "often." Well, three, perhaps four times a week, we said. It was not unknown, we added quickly, apologetically, for New Yorkers to visit a gym on an impulse, almost daily. Some New Yorkers, for that matter, arranged to go to their health club every morning before work. She echoed this cautiously too: They rise from their beds and exercise vigorously before breakfast? Yes, we said weakly. That must be a wearing regimen, she commented politely.

She paused, and then she said, wonderingly, "Ah, you mean you wish to *abonner* for an infinite number of visits?" After much fooling around with numbers and hurried, hushed conferences with other members of the regiment, she arrived at a price for an infinity of *forme*. The difference between once a week and infinity, by the way, turned out to be surprisingly small, improvised prices being one of the unpredictable pleasures of Paris life. She opened dossiers for both of us; you can't do anything in France without having a dossier opened on your behalf.

A week later I dug out my old gym bag, cranked up my Walkman, and set off for the Régiment Rouge. When I arrived, the young women in the red tracksuits were still standing there. They looked more ravishing than ever. I picked out our consultant from the group and told her I was ready to get *en forme*. "Alas, the work continues," she announced. I peered down. The renovation seemed to have stopped just where it had been when I saw it before. "The *vestiaires* and the *appareils* will now be installed next month," she said. "However, we are having classes all week long, on an emergency basis, and the Régiment Rouge wishes to make you an award for your patience." Then she gave me a bag of chocolate truffles. (There is a health food store on the rue du Bac that displays in its window its own brand of chocolates and its own marque of champagne. *Tout Biologique!* a sign alongside them proclaims virtuously.) I ate one.

A week after that we got a phone call from our consultant. She proudly announced that things were ready at last, and there would be a crepe party in honor of the opening. "We will have apricot jam and *crème de marrons*," she explained. We went to the crepe party. Everyone—would-be members and the girls in the red tracksuits—walked around eating stuffed crepes and admiring the pristine, shiny, untouched Nautilus machines and exercise bikes and free weights.

A few days later I went back again to try to use the gym, but on my way into the regimen room I was stopped by another of the girls in red tracksuits. Before one could start work on the machines, she explained, it was necessary that one have a rendezvous with a *professeur*. When I arrived the next day for my rendezvous, the *professeur*—another girl in a red tracksuit—was waiting for me in the little office. She had my dossier out, and she was reviewing it seriously.

"Aren't we going to demonstrate the system of the machines?" I asked.

"Ah, that is for the future. This is the oral part of the rendezvous, where we review your body and its desires," she said. If I blushed, she certainly didn't. She made a lot of notes and then snapped my dossier shut and said that soon, she hoped, we could begin.

|||

While all this was going on, I tried to tell Parisians about it, and I could see that they couldn't see what, exactly, I thought was strange. The absence of the whole rhetoric and cult of sports and exercise is the single greatest difference between daily life in France and daily life in America. It's true that French women's magazines are as deeply preoccupied with body image and appearance as American ones. But they are confident that all problems can be solved by lotions. The number of French ointments guaranteed to eliminate fat from the female body seems limitless, and no pharmacy window is complete without a startlingly erotic ad for the Fesse-Uplift—an electrical buttock stimulator, guaranteed to eliminate fat by a steady stream of "small, not unpleasing shocks administered to the area," the ad says. *Votre Beauté,* the *Self* of France, recently had a special issue on losing weight. There were articles on electrical stimulation, on nutrition (raw carrots will help you lose weight; cooked carrots won't), on antiobesity pills, and on something called passive exercise. There was also, of course, a long article on reducing lotions. Finally, buried in the back, among the lonely-hearts ads, was a single, vaguely illicit-looking page of workout diagrams. If all else fails.

Among men, an enthusiasm for sport simply segregates you in a separate universe: You are a sportsman or you are not. The idea of sports as a lingua franca meant to pick up the slack in male conversations is completely alien here. The awkwardnesses that in America can be bridged by a hearty "See the Knicks last night?" exist here, but nobody bridges them by talking about sports. Sport is a hobby and has clinging to it any hobby's slightly disreputable air of pathos. Also, sport is an immigrant preoccupation: Whereas in America it acts as a common church, here it is still low church. There is a daily sports paper here, titled *L'Équipe*, but it is meant for enthusiasts; *Le Monde* devotes one or two pages to the subject, and *Libération* only a few pages more. Paris has one good soccer team (whereas London alone has six), but you could walk the length and breadth of Saint-Germain and not see a single bit of evidence—not a sign in a window, a pennant in a bar, or a sweater on a supporter—that it exists. France has some terrific footballers, but they play mostly in England and Italy. The nearest thing to a Magic-Michael showdown in France is the *affrontements* of the French-born players David Ginola and Eric Cantona, but those take place across the Channel, in the North of England, where Ginola plays for Newcastle and Cantona for Manchester United. Still, Ginola and Cantona are regularly dunned by *L'Équipe* to declare their love of country. "But *la France* I think of all the time! Not only when I play Manchester! She is in my head and in my heart!" Ginola declared recently. It sounded a little forced to me, but apparently *L'Équipe* was satisfied. Legend has it that among Frenchmen sex and food are supposed to take the place of sports ("Did you perhaps see the petite blonde with the immense *balcon, mon vieux?*"), but in fact they don't. What the French do to bridge the uneasy competitive silences that seem to be the price of a Y chromosome is talk about government and particularly about the incompetence of government ministers; which minister has outdone the others in self-important pomposity is viewed as a competitive event. Though the subject is different, the tone is almost exactly the same as that of American sports talk. "Did you see Léotard on the eight o'clock last night?" one Parisian man might ask another. (The news is on at eight here.) Then they both shake their heads woefully, with that half smile, half smirk that New York men reserve for Mets relief pitchers: *beyond* pathetic.

If talking about the bureaucracy takes the place of talking about sports, getting involved with the bureaucracy takes the place of exercise. Every French man and woman is engaged in a constant entanglement with one ministry or another, and I have come to realize that these entanglements are what take the place of going to a gym where people actually work out. Three or four days a week you're given something to do that is time-consuming, takes you out of yourself, is mildly painful, forces you into close proximity with strangers, and ends, usually, with a surprising rush of exhilaration: "Hey, I did it." Every French ministry is, like a Nautilus machine, thoughtfully designed to provide maximum possible resistance to your efforts, only to give way just at the moment of total mental failure. Parisians emerge from the government buildings on the Île de la Cité feeling just the way New Yorkers do after a good workout: aching and exhausted but on top of the world.

|||

A few days after my oral interview I went back to the Régiment Rouge, and this time I actually got on one of the stationary bicycles and rode it for twenty-four minutes. I was in full New York regalia (sweatpants, headband, Walkman) and did it in good New York form (Stones blasting in my headphones, crying out, "One minute!" when there was a minute left to go). By now there were other people at the gym, though the man on the bicycle next to me was going at a speed barely fast enough to sustain life, while the woman beside him, who was on a treadmill, was walking at the right speed for window-shopping on the boulevard Saint-Germain on an especially sunny day when your heart is filled with love and your pockets are filled with money; it was as though she had set the machine at "Saunter."

I got down from my bike perspiring right through my T-shirt— the first person on the Left Bank, I thought proudly, to break a sweat at a gym. I walked back to the desk. "A towel, please," I panted (in French, of course). The girl in the red tracksuit at the desk gave me a long, steady, opaque look. I thought that maybe I had got the word for towel wrong (I hadn't, though), and after I asked again and got the same look in return, I thought it wise to try to describe its function. My description sounded like a definition from Dr. Johnson's dictionary: that thing which is used in the process of removing water from the surfaces of your body in the moments after its immersion. "Ah," she said. "Of course. A towel. We have none yet." She looked off into the middle distance. "This," she said at last, "is envisaged." I looked at her dumbly, pleadingly, the reality dawning on me. Then I walked all the way home, moist as a chocolate mousse.

|||

A couple of days later I went for what I thought would be my last visit to the Préfecture de Police to get my *carte de séjour*, a process that had involved a four-ministry workout stretching over three months. The functionary seemed ready to give it to me—she was actually holding it out across the desk—but then she suddenly took one last look at the dossier the préfecture had on me and noticed something that she had somehow missed before.

"*Alors, monsieur,*" she said, "you have not yet had a physical examination to make sure that you are in sufficiently good health to remain in France."

I didn't know what to say. "I belong to a gym," I said at last, and I showed her my card from the regiment.

"Well," she said, "this will be useful for your dossier." I couldn't argue with that.

The Chill

It was a very cold winter here, and it felt even colder. "It's the dampness," every shivering Parisian explained. But really it was something else. A visitor who has walked bareheaded and oblivious through twenty arctic Canadian winters found that, out for a walk in Paris with the temperature in the high thirties, he was pulling a woolen hat over his ears and huddling in doorways and stopping in cafés to drink hot wine and then quickly heading home.

What has made it seem so cold is the French gift for social dramatization: A cold day is a cold day, and everyone conspires to give it presence. Looking cold is also a way of making it plain that you are feeling miserable, a way to dramatize the "economic horror" that has overtaken Paris. In the chill a series of smaller social pageants have been played out, including a hostage taking, a craze for a strange book on economics, a growing conviction that the way out of the crisis is for everyone to stop working, a campaign against immigrants that led to mass civil disobedience by intellectuals, and visits by two foreigners bringing messages of deliverance.

The hostage taking at the Crédit Foncier de France, a semi-public, or state-supported, mortgage lender, was the first and the most improbable of the economic dramas. The Crédit Foncier was practically bankrupt, and the government decided to fob off parts of it on anybody who wanted bits of a failing bank. Its employees then decided that the best way to persuade the government to reconsider this plan was to go to the top and kidnap the president, a M. Jérôme Meyssonier. Not only did M. Meyssonier stay on as a hostage, but he supposedly made it the only condition of his imprisonment that no photographer be allowed to take a picture of him sleeping on a cot in his office. The employees agreed, and even decided to keep the bank open for business while the boss was being held incommunicado. Then they too decided to sleep in the building, presumably as an act of solidarity with the boss they had just imprisoned.

Hostage taking of this kind has become more or less routine here, kidnapping the boss being to the French economic crisis what firing the employees was to the American one. Over the past few years a number of French bosses, including some at Moët et Chandon, have been held hostage. There's actually a nice word for telling the *patron* to go to his room and stay there: He is merely being "sequestered," which, as euphemisms go, seems a fair trade for the Anglo-Saxon *downsizing*.

The hostage takings, naturally, are almost entirely symbolic: If M. Meyssonier had really wanted to leave, he could have left. The melodrama of the "sequestration" was nonetheless mistaken by some foreign observers for the real thing. It's easy to exaggerate the scale of the French crisis; the French do it themselves. The secondary, or symbolic, point of an action is often as clear as the primary, or practical, reality, and sometimes a lot clearer. At Christmastime in 1995 many journalists were enthralled by the masses of ordinary people who were out on the streets every day in the tens of thousands, symbolically showing their solidarity with striking Métro drivers. It was easy to miss the real point, which is that what everybody was doing on the streets was walking to work.

One economic problem is especially acute here: Unemployment—or *chômage*, as it's called—has hovered around 12 percent for the last two years. Most of the other problems, the ones that create the sense of crisis, are anticipatory. They grow out of the fear that the right-wing government's tentative attempts at reform will eventually corral France into an "Anglo-Saxon" economy, where an unleashed free market will make everybody do awful jobs for no money, forever. No one is reassured by the stridently triumphal tones of American free-marketers. After a recent trip to New York one French journalist remarked that leafing through a copy of *Forbes* or *Fortune* is like reading the operating manual of a strangely sanctimonious pirate ship.

These days one popular solution to the economic crisis is for everyone to stop working. The movement to lower the universal retirement age to fifty-five is the closest thing to a mass economic uprising that the country has seen; without the support of even the labor unions, to say nothing of the bemused parties of left or right, it is sweeping the country. It started last November, when striking truck drivers blockaded highways and ports to secure their right to retire at fifty-five. The government, faced with a choice between calling out the army and giving in, gave in. There was a general feeling that social justice had been done: Truck drivers work long hours, away from their families, and letting them stop for good at fifty-five seemed fair.

Several weeks later people started to realize that after all, the truck drivers' lot wasn't that much harder than everybody else's, and the idea of universal retirement at fifty-five really took flight. In January one of the public transportation unions decided to demand universal retirement at fifty-five, and despite the opposition of the respectable left, by mid-February a poll revealed that almost 70 percent of the population was in favor of stopping work at fifty-five.

The *folie* for fifty-five can be seen as a nice populist rebound on an idea first put forward by employers. For years businesses had been able to draw on a public fund (the Fonds National pour l'Emploi) in order to encourage workers to take early retirement. At the same time, the idea of reducing the length of the work-week has been debated; many people, for instance, had pro-posed moving to a four-day week, so that a few young workers might be shoehorned in on Fridays. In the minds of many work-ing people, though, the debate about a shorter workweek got mixed up with the truck drivers' retirement coup, and the two to-gether produced a sweeping, simple, plausible-sounding solution to the *crise*: Since the unemployed would benefit if everyone worked a little bit less, wouldn't they benefit even more if every-one stopped working a lot sooner?

|||

The national craze for early retirement may be an employees' twist on an employers' gimmick, but its roots are cultural. Re-tirement isn't scary here. In America one unmentioned aspect of the Social Security debate is the feeling people have that to stop working is, in a sense, to stop living. It is the vestibule of death. In France there is no equivalent anxiety—and there are no great Florida-style gulags for the elderly. One of the striking things about Paris is that it is filled with old people who actually look old: bent, fitted out with canes, but dining and lunching and tak-ing the air and walking their small, indifferent dogs along with everybody else. The humiliations visited on old people in Amer-ica—dressed up like six-year-olds, in shorts and T-shirts and sneakers, imploding with rage—aren't common here. The ro-mance of retirement is strong. The right-wing daily *Figaro*, for in-stance, though editorially opposed to the move for very early

retirement, ran a series of pieces about the "young retired"—
people still in their forties or fifties who have managed to stop
working. The series described people who at last have time to
"reflect"; it was written in exactly the same admiring spirit that
an American daily might use for a series about old people who
are as busy as all get-out.

For Parisians the pleasure of quitting isn't far to seek. Many of
them come from the country—or, at least, feel attached to a particular village—so the idea of *returning* has a certain appeal.
They are not being sent to Florida; they are just going home. People who remain here in town find that life becomes interesting
when they stop working. Everyone who attends French public
lectures knows that the most visible, and most audible, element
in the crowd is the phalanx of the retired. Sometimes they
present a bit of a problem, since they tend to be contentious, and
when the subject comes within their purview—if it's the Third
Republic, say, or the Second World War—they feel free to speak
up and correct the lecturer.

|||

Not long ago somebody referred to the debate on Social Security
in America as being distorted by "black helicopter" thinking. In
France there is something that might be called "white helicopter" thinking. The American populist belief is that there is a
secret multinational agency ready to swoop down from the skies
and make everybody work for the government; the French populist belief is that there is a secret government agency that may
yet swoop down from the skies and give everybody a larger
pension.

L'Horreur Économique, the extreme manifesto of white helicopter thought, is the most successful book of the last several
publishing seasons. A treatise by the novelist and essayist Vi-
viane Forrester, it has sold a couple of hundred thousand copies
in six months, and in November it won the Prix Médici, which is

a little like a French Pulitzer Prize. Forrester is a minor belletrist whose earlier work included popular studies of Virginia Woolf and van Gogh. Not surprisingly, in *L'Horreur Économique* she has produced a work of political economy with all the economics, and most of the politics, left out. Unburdened by pie charts, statistics, or much else in the way of argument or evidence, the book is written in a tone of steady, murmuring apocalyptic dissent, with an occasional perky nod to a familiar neoliberal argument. The total effect is of a collaboration between Robert Reich and Rimbaud. Barely into the first chapter the author flatly announces that the logic of globalization will lead to an Auschwitz of the unemployed. "From exploitation to exclusion, from exclusion to elimination," she writes. "Is it such an unlikely scenario?"

The reader eventually comes to the realization that Forrester is not arguing against the free market, or even against globalization, but against the original sin of commerce—against buying and selling and hiring and firing and getting and spending. Her book is a pure expression of the old French romance of a radical alternative, with the ancient Catholic prejudices against usury, simony, and the rest translated into a curious kind of dinner party nihilism. Of course, the trouble with reviving the romance of the radical alternative is that the only radical alternative remaining is the extreme right-winger Jean-Marie Le Pen, who isn't romantic at all.

Laurent Joffrin, the editor of the left-wing daily *Libération,* likes to say that Forrester's book is a "symptom." "The fears are irrational, psychological, but they are real," he says. He himself is a kind of neo-Keynesian, and like many other sensible people here, he thinks that for all the hysteria, the economic *crise* is not really very deep and could be soothed by a little deficit spending. But the Keynesian medicine is forbidden by the rules of the Maastricht Treaty, which is to lead to European economic union and which, for the sake of German confidence, prohibits new deficit spending.

In any case, there's something emotionally unsatisfying about the Keynesian message. It is like going to the doctor in the certainty that you're dying of tuberculosis, only to be told that your trouble is that your shoes are too tight. In America, and even more so in England, the triumphant free market has a rhetoric, and even a kind of poetry, of its own, visible in the *Economist* and the *Spectator* and the *Telegraph*: witty, trumpet-sharp, exuberant, hardhearted. In France there is a knack of small shopkeeping and a high rhetoric of the state, but there will never be a high rhetoric of shopkeeping.

|||

By the end of February a new social movement was sweeping the papers and the streets. This one came from the left, in reaction to a new bill that attempted to appease Le Pen supporters by jumping up and down on illegal immigrants. The most obnoxious aspect of the Debré bill—named after the interior minister— was a requirement that people who had foreign guests in their homes inform the police when the foreigners left. This provision was so reminiscent of the Vichy laws, which made denouncing Jews a social obligation, that the entire French intellectual class launched a series of petitions against it. Famous artists and directors announced (theatrically, and as a dare-you-to-do-something-about-it principle, rather than as actual fact) that they were lodging illegal immigrants. The petitions flooded the newspapers and were signed by groups: directors, actors, philosophers, and even dentists. A massive demonstration was held, drawing as few as thirty thousand people (the government counting the marchers) or as many as a hundred thousand (the marchers counting themselves).

The provision was immediately withdrawn, but everyone agreed it was depressing that the government had been swayed by Le Pen's absurd notion that France's economic problems have to do with the presence of immigrants, legal or illegal. Many people, including numerous petition signers, also thought there was a depressing element of coercive self-congratulation about the marchers. The protest reached its climax when protesters, got up as deportees, arrived at the Gare de l'Est to reenact the deportations of the forties. This struck even many sympathetic watchers as being in *mauvais goût*.

|||

On a recent Saturday, at the first children's concert of the season at the beautiful new Cité de la Musique, the union of part-time artists, which had been threatening to strike over *their* pension predicament, decided instead to educate the audience. Before a Rameau pastorale began, a representative of the union harangued the five-year-olds for fifteen minutes on the role of itinerant workers in the arts, and about the modalities of their contributions to the national pension fund, and how the government was imperiling their retirement. The five-year-olds listened respectfully and then gave him a big hand.

In the midst of the economic gloom Bill Gates came to France. Not since Wilbur Wright, back in 1908, has an American arrived in France quite so imbued with the mystique of American inventiveness, industry, and technological hocus-pocus. Bill Gates came here with a masterpiece, the Leonardo Codex, and it has gone on display in the Musée du Luxembourg, but his visit seems unlikely to produce a masterpiece, as Wilbur Wright's did. Wright became the subject of one of the great portraits by the boy genius Jacques-Henri Lartigue, the Mozart of photography, which summed up the early-twentieth-century French view of American technological wizardry; grave, dignified, pure. Bill Gates doesn't have the bone structure, and anyway, the French cult of Gates is strangely indeterminate. He is described, variously, as the father of the Internet and the creator of popular computing—as anything except what he is, which is the head of a gigantic corporation. He is a symbol divorced from his invention, an aviator without an airplane.

Nonetheless he is presumed to know something. "What France needs is its own Bill Gates," the governor of the Bank of France announced. Gates's message to the French, which is essentially that buying Windows will lead to mass happiness, was symbolically linked with that of another celebrated recent visitor, the German philosopher Jürgen Habermas. Habermas is the last of Europe's "master thinkers," and he gave a series of lectures at the Collège de France. His books and lectures have been the subject of reports in *Le Monde* and *L'Express* and on the television news. It seems that Habermas has replaced his old theory of the state, which was that there is no natural basis for it outside of a bunch of human conventions, with a new theory, which is that the natural basis for the state is the human habit of arguing about whether or not it has one. The argument is somewhat opaque, but it has produced a nice catchphrase, "social communication." That, rather than the social contract, is to be the basis of the new society, and a hope now faintly glimmers that between Habermas and Gates—between the German philosopher who tells you that you need only connect and the American businessman who will sell you the software to let you do it—a new, comprehensive social theory is around the corner.

Some people just get fed up waiting. After five days in mostly happy captivity at Crédit Foncier, Jérôme Meyssonier decided that he'd had enough. "*Ça suffit*," the president announced to his employees, and that afternoon he went home. Curiously, he had become, in the interim, a kind of hero to the very people who were keeping him locked up. "Meyssonier is with us!" the employees of the Crédit Foncier cried as their boss emerged into the light. (Later in the week they added to that slogan an even better one: "The semipublic will never surrender!") On television Meyssonier was seen smiling weakly. He looked worn out and about ready to quit, but then perhaps this should not be a surprise. M. Meyssonier is fifty-five.

A Tale
of Two Cafés

I have been brooding a lot lately on what I have come to think of
as the Two-Café Problem. The form is borrowed from the old
Three-Body Problem, which perplexed mathematicians late into
the nineteenth century, and which, as I vaguely understand it, involved calculating the weird swerves and dodges that three planets worked on each other when the force of gravity was working
on them all. My problem looks simpler, because all it involves is
the interaction of a couple of places in Paris where you can eat
omelets and drink coffee. It's still pretty tricky, though, because
what fills in for gravity is the force of fashion—arbitrary, or arbi-
trary-seeming, taste—which in Paris is powerful enough to turn
planets from their orbits and make every apple fall upward.

I began to brood not long ago, on a beautiful Saturday in
October, when I arranged to meet my friend Nicole Wisniak at
the Café de Flore, on the boulevard Saint-Germain, for lunch.
Nicole is the editor, publisher, advertising account manager, and
art director of the magazine *Égoïste* and is a woman of such orig-

inal chic that in her presence I feel even more ingenuous and
American than I usually do, as though pinned to the back of my
jacket were a particularly embarrassing American license plate:
"Pennsylvania: The Keystone State" or "Explore Minnesota:
10,000 Lakes."

When we got to the Flore and looked around, upstairs and
down, we couldn't find an empty table—that kind of Saturday—
so we went outside and thought about where to go. I looked, a
little longingly, at Les Deux Magots, just down the street, on the
place Saint-Germain-des-Prés. The two cafés are separated only
by the tiny, narrow rue Saint-Benoît. I turned to Nicole. "Why
don't we just go in there?" I said.

A smile, one of slight squeamishness mixed with incapacity,
passed across Nicole's face. "I don't know," she said, at a loss for
the usual epigrammatic summary of the situation. "We used to
go there, I think . . . twenty years ago. . . ." Her voice trailed off,
and again she got a funny smile on her face. She couldn't say
why, but she knew that it was impossible.

A taboo as real as any that Malinowski studied among the Tro-
briand Islanders kept us out, though why it existed and how it
kept its spell I had no idea. Still, one of the things you learn if
you live as a curious observer (or as an observed curiosity) on the
fringes of the fashionable world in Paris is that the Flore remains
the most fashionable place in Paris, while the Deux Magots was
long ago abandoned by people who think of themselves as belonging to the world, to *ce pays-ci*—this country here, as the inhabitants of Versailles called *their* little fashionable island.
Somehow, at some point, in a past that was right around the corner but—to Nicole, at least—was irretrievable, something had
happened to make the Café de Flore the most fashionable place
in Paris and the Deux Magots the least.

|||

In Paris explanations come in a predictable sequence, no matter
what is being explained. First comes the explanation in terms of

the unique, romantic individual, then the explanation in terms of ideological absolutes, and then the explanation in terms of the futility of all explanation. So, for instance, if your clothes dryer breaks down and you want to get the people from BHV—the strange Sears, Roebuck of Paris—to come fix it, you will be told, first, that only one man knows how it works and he cannot be found (explanation in terms of the gifts of the romanticized individual); next, that it cannot be fixed for a week because of a store policy (explanation in terms of ideological necessity); and, finally, that you are perfectly right to find all this exasperating, but nothing can be done, because it is in the nature of things for a dryer to break down, dryers are like that (futility of explanation itself). "They are sensitive machines; they are ill suited to the task; no one has ever made one successfully," the store bureaucrat in charge of service says, sighing. *"C'est normal."* And what works small works big too. The same sequence that explains the broken dryer also governs the explanations of the French Revolution that have been offered by the major French historians. "Voltaire did all this!" was de La Villette's explanation (only one workman); an inevitable fight between the bourgeoisie and the aristocrats, the Marxists said (store policy); until, finally, Foucault announced that there is nothing really worth explaining in the coming of the Reign of Terror, since everything in Western culture, seen properly, is a reign of terror (all dryers are like that).

"It's a good question," a friend who has been a figure in the French media since the forties, and who eats lunch at the Flore every day, told me when I quizzed him about why, and when, exactly, and how the Flore had outstripped the Deux Magots. We were sitting, as it happened, at the Flore, eating good, wildly overpriced omelets. The downstairs room was as pleasantly red and melancholy as it always is, with its square, rather than round, tables, which give the impression that all the tables are corner tables.

In the week or so since my first inquiry I had been doing some reading. The Deux Magots and the Flore had, I knew, existed beside each other for more than a century. The Flore had long had a white marquee with green lettering, the Deux Magots a green marquee with gilt lettering. The interior of the Flore had always been decorated in red leather—what the French call moleskin— and the Deux Magots in brown. But I had only just learned that like so many timeless things in Paris, they got timeless right after the horror of the Franco-Prussian War. Although there had always been a church at Saint-Germain, the topography of the place Saint-Germain—the square itself—dates back only to the 1870s.

The Deux Magots is the modest inheritor of a silk lingerie store of that name that stood on the spot for decades, until the 1860s, when the growth of the big department stores across the river drove it out of business. The owners eventually rented out the space to a *café liquoriste,* which kept the name and started serving coffee. No one knows exactly when the two famous statues of Chinese mandarins—the Deux Magots—were installed; Anatole France, in his memoirs, written at the turn of the century, speaks of a big picture of three *magots* that used to hang in the lingerie store. The Flore, on the other hand, has no prehistory; founded in 1870, it was always a café and was called the Flore because of a statue of the goddess Flora that used to stand outside. Then, in 1880, Léonard Lipp, an Alsatian who had fled the German occupation of his province, opened a *brasserie* across the street, and the basic topography of the new square was in place.

For many years the Deux Magots was the more famous and fashionable of the two cafés. It was there that Oscar Wilde went to drink after he left England; he died about five blocks away. And it was there that Joyce went to drink Swiss white wine, with everybody except Hemingway, with whom he drank dry sherry, because Hemingway wasn't everybody. (That's how Hemingway tells it, anyway.) The presence of so much history ought to be unmanning or even just embarrassing. In Paris it isn't, not because the past is so hallowed but because it doesn't seem to be there.

The unsentimental efficiency of French commonplace civilization, of which the French café is the highest embodiment, is so
brisk that it disarms nostalgia. History keeps wiping the table off
and asking you, a little impatiently, what you'll have now.

Not until the 1940s—I had learned a lot of this in the course
of reading Olivier Todd's excellent new biography of Camus, one
of the big books here this year—did the triangle of the two cafés
and the Brasserie Lipp at Saint-Germain-des-Prés become legendary. This was when the group of *résistants* came into being,
and a culture to go with them—when Camus and Sartre and Simone de Beauvoir, as the cliché has it, brooded in one corner of
the Deux Magots while Juliette Greco sang sad songs in another.
The odd thing is that the cliché is almost entirely true. It was at
the Deux Magots, for instance, that Sartre saw his famous philosophical *garçon,* of whom he wrote, "His movement is quick and
forward, a little too precise, a little too rapid. He comes toward
the patrons with a step a little too quick. He bends forward a little too eagerly, his eyes express an interest too solicitous for the
order of the customer." (I still get waiters like that.)

Yet fifty years after the classic period, one café is more fashionable than ever and the other is not fashionable at all. You
might not see this at once. At the Flore the fashionable people
are spread out among the tables rather than concentrated in one
spot or area; they occupy the place clandestinely, following the
law of Inverse Natural Appeal. The *terrasse* of the Flore, even on
a sunny and perfect day (*especially* on a sunny and perfect day),
is off limits; the inner room, with its red moleskin banquettes, is
acceptable; but by far the most okay place to sit is upstairs (I was
sitting there now, with my friend), and the banquettes are made
of an ugly tan leatherette. (The law of Inverse Natural Appeal is
at work: The outlawed *terrasse* is, as it happens, an extraordi-
narily pleasant place to sit; the inner room is a very pleasant
place to sit; and the upstairs room is reminiscent of the cocktail
lounge of a Howard Johnson's.)

The sounds of the higher French conversation, with its lovely murmur of certainties and, rising from the banquettes, the favorite words of fashionable French people, resonated all around. *Perversité,* which means "perversity" but is used as a word of praise, suggests something—a book, a dish, a politician—that is aristocratic. *C'est normal,* which means something like "No problem" and can also refer to any political or literary situation, is different from the American phrase in that its emphasis is not on a difficulty surmounted or evaded but on the return to a familiar, homeostatic atmosphere of comfort: Something that happens may seem unusual (say, the revelation that a former defense minister might have been an East Bloc agent) but, properly understood, is not shocking at all; it's *normal,* even if a little deplorable. And from table after table, like the sound of a tolling bell, rises the connective *donc,* which just means "so" or "therefore," but which, when used in literary and worldly conversation, and rung with sufficient force, means "It must therefore follow as the night the day" and always sounds to me as conclusive as Gideon's trumpet.

"But it all has to do with the character of two men, Boubal and Cazes," my friend said. Paul Boubal was the owner of the Flore from 1939 to 1983—he died five years later—and Roger Cazes was the owner not of the Deux Magots but of the Brasserie Lipp, across the street. "That is to say, both Cazes and Boubal were from the Auvergne—they were countrymen—and though each thought the other was running a sneaky business, each respected the other and frequented the other's place. This produced, in the fifties, a natural compact, a kind of family feeling between the two places. I mean family feeling in the real sense—of dependence and suspicion and resentment. The owner of the Deux Magots was a much more timid fellow. He was left out of the compact." So the real force working was that of the Lipp; it was the third planet, perturbing the orbits of the two others.

There it was, the explanation in terms of the romantic individual in almost perfect form, along with the bonus of a touch of *terroir,* the French affection for a bit of native land. Then someone suggested that I speak to the essayist and editor Jean-Paul Enthoven, who is the author of the season's most winning collection of literary essays, *Les Enfants de Saturne.* Enthoven, I was told, would be sure to have an explanation; he could explain anything Parisian.

"Here is my hypothesis," he announced when I reached him on the phone at his office, at the publishing house of Grasset. "You must go back to the twenties and thirties, when the Flore became identified with the extreme right and the Deux Magots, by default, with the left. Charles Maurras, the founder of Action Française, used the Flore as his home base." Maurras was simultaneously one of the most important stylists in French literature—a member of the French Academy, and a crucial influence on T. S. Eliot, among other modernists—and a right-wing anti-Semite. "Before it was anyone else's place, it was Maurras's. His most famous polemic was even named after the café: 'Au Signe de Flore.' Maurras was a malevolent force, in that everything he touched was simultaneously disgraced and hallowed."

Enthoven went on to say, "This meant that by the time of the occupation, when Sartre and Simone de Beauvoir came to Saint-Germain and began their *résistance,* they had to avoid the Flore like a plague, since it had been contaminated by Maurras. But then the tourists began to crowd into the Deux Magots in order to look at Sartre and de Beauvoir. The place became overcrowded, and eventually the intellectuals noticed the emptiness of the Flore next door. By then Maurras was gone, the occupation had passed, and confronted with a choice between the pollution of Maurras and the pollution of tourism, the intellectuals chose to remake the emptiness rather than abide with the many. So they went across the street and have never returned." He stopped for a second, as if readying himself for an aphorism, and then said, "The Deux Magots was sacralized by Sartre, desacralized by the tourists, and then left vacant by history." Eighteen-seventy, 1940, I thought. Like so many lovely things in Paris, the two cafés were given shape by the first German invasion and then in one way or another were deformed by the second.

It was left to another, more dour friend to supply the futility-of-explanation explanation, over coffee at a lesser, more despairing café—neither fashionable nor unfashionable, just a place where you go to talk. "There is nothing to explain here," he said. "The explanation is a simple, Saussurean one." He was referring, I realized after a moment, to the father of modern linguistics, who was the first to point out that signs get their meanings not by being like the things they stand for but by being different from other signs: A sign for black means black because it isn't like the sign for white.

"The fashionable exists only in relation to something that is *not* that way," he went on. "The relationship between the mod-ishness of the Flore and the unmodishness of the Deux Magots isn't just possibly arbitrary. It's *necessarily* arbitrary. If you place *any* two things side by side, one will become fashionable and the other will not. It's a necessity determined by the entire idea of fashion. A world in which everything is fashionable is impossible to imagine, because it implies that there would be nothing to provide a contrast. The reason that when you place any two things side by side, one becomes chic and the other does not is that it's in the nature of desire to choose, and to choose *absolutely*. That's the mythological lesson of the great choice among the beauties: They are all beautiful—they are goddesses—and yet a man must choose. And what was the chooser's name? Paris. *C'est normal.*"

Distant Errors,

CHRISTMAS JOURNAL 2

My fax machine, which was made by the French state, always blames someone else when things go wrong. It is a Galéo 5000 model, and it is made by France Télécom and is therefore an official, or French government, product; even its name carries with it the nice implication that 4,999 other models were attempted before perfection was at last achieved by the French fax machine ministry.

You even have to go to a government telephone outlet to buy a new ribbon for it. It's a plain paper fax (you have the same expression in French, *papier ordinaire,* ordinary paper) with all the usual features. It's really very nicely designed—much better designed than its American equivalents, with that streamlined, intelligent Philippe Starck look that the French seem magically able to give to everything they make. It's reasonably efficient too—perhaps a little overtricky in loading in the sheets and unduly inclined to *bourrage de papier,* paper jams—but still . . .

It has a little glowing window on its face where it *affiches*, or posts, the events and troubles of its day, its operating life. The window flashes, for instance, a shocked, offended *Pas d'iden-tité!*—no identity!—when the fax machine at the other end doesn't "identify itself," which for some reason or another most American machines don't seem to.

But the favorite, all-purpose *affiche* of my fax machine is *er-reur distante*—distant error—which it *affiches* all the time, no matter where the error actually originates, far away or right in its own backyard. Whether the error comes from a fax machine in Lille or Los Angeles, it says that it is a distant error. When the machine itself has run out of paper, it is still a distant error. When I have forgotten to clean the ribbon heads, an error has nonetheless taken place, at a distance. Jams and overflows, missed connections, and faulty plugs: all are *erreurs distantes*. When it really *is* a distant error, it is still just another distant error. This is the French fax machine's way of getting through life. The error is distant; the problem lies someplace else; there is always somebody else to blame for your malfunctions.

French intellectuals and public people, I have on certain oc-casions come to the mordant, exasperated, and gloomy conclu-sion, share the same belief, *affiche* the same accusatory message, banding together and flashing *erreur distante,* whenever they run out of paper or ink or arguments. This morning, for instance, I saw the economist Emmanuel Todd being interviewed about his book on the economic "stagnation" of industrialized economies. He blandly announced that the U.S. economy was just as stag-nant as France's, in fact was worse because its "cultural level" (by which he meant the level of education) was so much more de-praved. Also, the United States manufactured less than it once had. Economic stagnation was the problem of all the industrial-ized economies, France was simply sharing in it, and the United States was really to blame. His debating opponent, an intelligent economist named Cohen—very poorly dressed in a brightly colored blazer and bad tortoiseshell glasses—tried to explain that this wasn't so, that the fall in manufacturing was in fact a sign of the renovation of the American economy, and that whatever its flaws in equality, the growth in America was real, that the one thing you *couldn't* call the American economy was stagnant. Todd, who looked terrific, hardly bothered to argue with him; he just made the same assertions again: The American economy is stagnant. He just *affiched,* like my fax machine *erreur distante,* and the host, terrified, nodded.

A while ago I was on a panel broadcast for France-Culture, the radio station, at the Sciences Po, the great political science school, along with Philippe Sollers and other French worthies, and we talked about the influence of American culture on France. Everyone took it for granted that the American dominance in culture was a distant error or, rather, a distant conspiracy organized by the CIA and the Disney corporation. (I was there, the sole American on the panel, to be condescended to as the representative of both Michael Eisner and William Colby, with mouse ears on my head and a listening device presumably implanted inside them.) The clichés get trotted out—that Jackson Pollock and the abstract expressionists got put over by the CIA, etc.—with a complacent certitude, and it was taken for granted that the relative decline of the prestige of French writing and painting has nothing to do with the actual decline of the quality of French writing and painting. (And yet when we got down to particulars, much of these prejudices vanished: Sollers and I actually had a reasonable debate about Roth and Updike. No American Sollers would have been able to *name* two French novelists, much less debate their value.)

What was maddening was not the anti-Americanism, which is understandable and even, in its Astérix-style resistance to American domination, admirable. What is maddening is the bland certainty, the lack of vigilant curiosity, the incapacity for critical

self-reflection, the readiness to *afficher erreur distante* and wait
for somebody else to change the paper.

|||

A wise man, an old émigré artist, when I told him, gaily, that we
were going to move to Paris, said soberly, even darkly: "Ah. So
you have at last decided not to forgo the essential Jewish experience of emigration and expatriation." I thought it was a joke, a
highly complicated, ironic joke, but still a joke, since what could
be less traumatic, in the old-fashioned émigré's sense, less Cioran and Benjamin and Celan, than moving to Paris with a baby?
But of course, what he said was true, or contained a truth. The
reality is that after a year here everything about moving to Paris
has been wonderful, and everything about emigrating to France
difficult. An immigrant is an immigrant, poor fellow: Pity him!
The errors arrive, and they tell me I brought them with me.

The loneliness of the expatriate is of an odd and complicated
kind, for it is inseparable from the feeling of being free, of having
escaped. Martha, the other day, spent the morning watching
Luke open and shut the little gates that lead into the interior gardens at the Palais Royal. He would open the gate, she explained,
walk through, watch it shut, and then walk back through again,
with the rows of violet flowers in the background. She felt, she
said, as if she had died and gone to heaven—but with the strange
feeling that dying and going to heaven mean parting, leaving, and
missing the people you left behind on earth. No wonder ghosts
at séances are so blandly encouraging; they miss you, but they
are busy watching someone else.

There is the feeling of being apart and the feeling of being a
universe apart—the immigrant's strange knowledge that the language and lore that carry on in your own living space are so
unlike the ones right outside. (This is particularly true of our
Canadian-American-Jewish–Sri Lankan–Franco-American mé-
nage, with the two-year-old at its center.) There is also the odd

knowledge, at once comforting and scary, that whatever is going on outside, you are without a predisposed opinion on it, that you have had a kind of operation, removing your instant reflexive sides-taking instinct. When French politicians debate, I think, well, everybody has a point. After a year the feeling that everything is amusing, though, bombs and strikes an act in the Winter Circus, does begin to fade, to seem less amusing in itself. When *Le Canard Enchaîné*, the satiric paper, comes out on Wednesday mornings, I buy it and generally enjoy, am even beginning to understand, most of the jokes and digs; what was largely incomprehensible to me at first is now self-evident, who is being mocked for what and why.

But I don't actually care about who is being mocked. I am simply pleased to register that what I am reading is mockery. And the slightly amused, removed feeling always breaks down as you realize that you really don't *want* to be so lofty and Olympian—or rather, that being lofty and Olympian carries within it, by tradition and precedent, the habit of wishing you could be down there in the plain, taking sides. Even the gods, actually looking down from Olympus in amusement, kept hurtling down to get laid or slug somebody.

|||

After a first winter in Paris, when the lure of the chimney and cigar smell holds you in thrall, you become accustomed to them, and then all you notice is the dark. From November to April, hardly a single day when you see the sun. The light itself is beautiful, violet and gray, but it always looks as if it were planning to snow, and then it never does.

We had the seasonal pleasure of buying a (by Canadian standards, insanely overpriced) Christmas tree. We bought it from a Greek tree-and-plant dealer on the Île de la Cité. It's a nice tree, a big fir, green and lush, but, at our insistence, without that crazy wooden cross that the French insist on nailing to the bottoms of their Christmas trees, so that you can't give them water. Ours is open, with a fresh cut, and sits in its watery pedestal, a red-and-green tripod, which we brought all the way over from Farm and Garden nursery down on Franklin Street in TriBeCa.

The logic (or fantasy) of the wooden cross on the bottoms of the trunks of the French Christmas trees, as the bemused dealer explained it to me, is that it "seals" off the tree's trunk and keeps the sap inside from drying out. The opposed American logic, our logic, of course (or is it our fantasy too?), is that an open cut will keep a dead and derooted tree "fresh" for as long as you need it, for as long as you give it water and the season lasts.

Or is the cut cross, after all, really a kind of covert, symbolic, half-hidden reminder on the part of a once entirely Catholic country of the cross-that-is-to-come, of the knowledge that even Christmas trees can't be resurrected without a miracle? Americans persuade themselves that a dead tree is still fresh if you keep pouring water on it; here there is a small guilty stirring of Catholic conscience that says, "It's dead, you know, the way everything will be. You can seal it up, but you can't keep it going. Only a miracle will bring it back to life."

|||

Naturally none of the Christmas tree garlands I bought last year works this year. Though Martha packed them away neatly when we took the tree down, they have managed to work themselves into hideous tangles, the way Christmas lights always do. If the continued existence of the Christmas tree light garlands, even though they're obviously impractical compared with strings, is proof of the strength of cultural difference, their ability to get themselves tangled is just as strong proof of cultural universality. The strands did it in New York, the garlands do it here, and there is no explaining how they do. The permanent cultural differences are language, the rituals of eating, and the habits of education; the permanent cultural universals are love of children and the capacity of Christmas lights left in a box in a closet to get themselves hopelessly tangled in knots.

|||

The American Christmas came to Paris while I was away in New York; Halloween came this year for the first time, right while we were watching, right under our noses. Linus waiting for the Great Pumpkin couldn't have been more shocked, more pleased than we were to see Halloween rising before us like a specter. The shops were suddenly filled with pumpkins and rubber masks and witches and ghost costumes and bags of candy. Apparently the American Halloween has been sneaking up bit by bit for a little while, but everyone agrees that this year the whole thing has really happened, and for the most obvious of reasons: It is a way for small shopkeepers to sell stuff before Christmas comes. *Le Monde,* sensing this brisk commercial motive, published a piece about the coming of Halloween, predictably indignant.

The essentially creepy, necrophile nature of the holiday, invisible to Americans, was harder to hide from the French. Our friends Marie and Édouard, who live with their two children, Thomas and Alexandra, across the courtyard, were dubious: The children dress up as the dead and the horrific and then demand sweets at the price of vandalism? The pleasure is located *where* exactly? Our friend Cassie says that her French mother-in-law, seeing the grandchildren dressed up as skeletons, let out a genuine shriek of distaste.

Of course, it is incumbent on Americans to reassure, gently, that it is not really a holiday of the dead at all—that like all American holidays, it is a ritual of materialism, or, to put it another way, of greed, a rite designed to teach our children that everything, even death, ends with candy. It is just *fun. Fun* is the magic American word (Our motto "Let's have fun!" is met by the French motto "Let's be amused.") Though Halloween arrived and caused parties and sales, the tradition of trick-or-treating has not really caught on here, and so Martha and several other mothers decided to have a Halloween party in Cassie's apartment. The mothers hid behind doors, so that the children could knock and get their candy. It was trick-or-treating made into an indoor sport. The French children in the party, she tells me, just didn't get it. What was the point, the French children, disconsolate as ghosts and skeletons and witches, seemed to wonder, waiting behind their doors, to be all dressed up, with nowhere to go?

|||

Luke has mounted up onto the horses on the carousel this year, although he needs to be tied on, like a parcel. To my delight, though not really to my surprise, I discovered this year that the carousel has been turning in the same manner, offering the same game, and drawing the same bemused, fascinated attention of foreigners for at least seventy-five years. I found a passage in the travel writing of Joseph Roth, the Austrian novelist, who visited the Luxembourg Gardens in 1925 and wrote about the "*manèges de chevaux de bois pour enfants.*" He describes the rings and sticks, exactly as they are today: "The owner of the merry-go-round holds in his hand, at the end of a stick, little rings lightly hung and easy to detach. All the children on the horses and in the tiny cars are armed with wands. So that when they pass before the rings, they try to unhook them, which is to say slip them onto their wand. Whoever gets the most gets a prize. They learn quick action, the value of the instant, accelerated reflexes, and the trick of adjusting one's eye." "The value of the instant . . ." Doubtless Cartier-Bresson and the rest of the "decisive moment" photographers rode on such horses, caught their rings, learned there's only one right moment in which to do it.

Roth admired the game endlessly, because it seemed so un-German, such a free and charming way to educate, without the military brutality of Teutonic schools. The funny thing is that there are now no more prizes—the same game, same carousel, but no more prizes. Nothing left to teach. You get the ring for the pleasure of having taken it. I wonder which child won the last prize and when.

|||

The differences are tiny and real. Cultures don't really encode things. They include things, and leave things out. There is, for instance, the exasperation of lunch. Lunch, as it exists in New York, doesn't exist here. Either lunch is a three-course meal—i.e., dinner, complete with two bottles of wine—or else it is to be had only at a brasserie, where the same menu—croque monsieur, omelet, salade Niçoise—is presented almost without any variation at all, as though the menu had been decreed by the state. A tuna sandwich, a bran muffin, a bowl of black bean soup—black bean soup! Yankee bean! Chicken vegetable! It is soup, beautiful soup, that I miss more than anything, not French soup, all puréed and homogenized, but American soup, with bits and things, beans and corn and even letters, in it. This can shake you up, this business of things almost but not quite being the same. A pharmacy is not quite a drugstore; a brasserie is not quite a coffee shop; a lunch is not quite a lunch. So on Sundays I have developed the habit of making soup for the week, from the good things we buy in the *marché biologique* on the boulevard Raspail. Soup and custard on Sunday nights, our salute to the land of the free.

|||

My favorite bit of evidence of the French habit of pervasive, permanent abstraction lies in the difficulties of telling people about fact checking. (I use the English word usually; there doesn't seem to be a simple French equivalent.) "Thank you so much for your help," I will say after interviewing a man of letters or politician. "I'm going to write this up, and you'll probably be hearing from what we call *une fact checker* in a couple of weeks." (I make it feminine since the fact checker usually is.)

"What do you mean, *une fact checker?*"

"Oh, it's someone to make sure that I've got all the facts right, reported them correctly."

Annoyed: "No, no, I've told you everything I know."

I, soothing: "Oh, I know you have."

Suspicious: "You mean your editor double-checks?"

"No, no, it's just a way of making sure that we haven't made a mistake in facts."

More wary and curious: "This is a way of maintaining an ideological line?"

"No, no—well, in a sense I suppose . . ." (For positivism, of which *New Yorker* fact checking is the last redoubt, *is* an ideological line; I've lived long enough in France to see that move coming. . . .)

"But really," I go on, "it's just to make sure that your dates and what we have you quoted as saying are accurate. Just to be sure."

Dubious look; there is More Here Than Meets the Eye. On occasion I even get a helpful, warning call from the subject after the fact checker has called. "You know, someone, another reporter, called me from the magazine. They were checking up on you." ("No, no, really checking on *you*," I want to say, offended, but don't—and then think he's right: They *are* checking up on me too; never thought of it that way, though.) There is a certainty in France that what assumes the guise of transparent positivism, "fact checking," is in fact a complicated plot of one kind or another, a way of enforcing ideological coherence. That there might really *be* facts worth checking is an obvious and annoying absurdity; it would be naïve to think otherwise.

I was baffled and exasperated by this until it occurred to me that you would get *exactly* the same incomprehension and suspicion if you told American intellectuals and politicians, post-interview, that a theory checker would be calling them. "It's been a pleasure speaking to you," you'd say to Al Gore or Mayor Giuliani. "And I'm going to write this up; probably in a couple of weeks a theory checker will be in touch with you."

Alarmed, suspicious: "A what?"

"You know, a theory checker. Just someone to make sure that all your premises agree with your conclusions, that there aren't any obvious errors of logic in your argument, that all your allusions flow together in a coherent stream—that kind of thing."

"What do you mean?" the American would say, alarmed. "Of course they do. I don't need to talk to a theory checker."

"Oh, no, you don't *need* to. It's for your protection, really. They just want to make sure that the theory hangs together. . . ."

The American subject would be exactly as startled and annoyed at the idea of being investigated by a theory checker as the French are by being harassed by a fact checker, since this process would claim some special status, some "privileged" place for theory. A theory checker? What an absurd waste of time, since it's apparent (to us Americans) that people don't speak in theories, that the theories they employ change, flexibly, and of necessity, from moment to moment in conversation, that the notion of limiting conversation to a rigid rule of theoretical constancy is an absurd denial of what conversation *is*.

Well, replace *fact* (and *factual*) for *theory* in that last sentence, and you have the common French view of fact checking. People don't speak in straight facts; the facts they employ to enforce their truths change, flexibly and with varying emphasis, as the conversation changes, and the notion of limiting conversation to a rigid rule of pure factual consistency is an absurd denial of what conversation ought to be. Not, of course, that the French intellectual doesn't use and respect facts, up to a useful point, any more than even the last remaining American positivist doesn't use and respect theory, up to a point. It's simply the fetishizing of one term in the game of conversation that strikes the French funny. Conversation is an organic, improvised web of fact and theory, and to pick out one bit of it for microscopic overexamination is typically American overearnest comedy.

|||

"Does this bus go across the river?" the man from Chicago demands of the Parisian bus driver, who looks blank. "I said, this bus goes across the river, or doesn't it?" I myself have been in this position, of course, more times than once, in Venice and in Tuscany, but (I choose to believe, at least) I try to make up for it with the necessary abasing looks of ignorance and sorrow and multitudes of thank-yous and head ducks, as the Japanese do here. The American in Paris just *demands*, querulously—"Now, you remember that pastry I showed you in the window? Now, I want that one"—in English, and expects the world to answer.

Sometimes the French response is muttered and comic. "Hey, does this bus go across the river?" the woman from California says, mounting onto the steps of the 63. "I wouldn't come to your country and not speak in your language," the driver says, in French. A sensitive listener would detect some frost in the manner, but the American woman doesn't: "No—I asked you, does this bus go across the river?" Or, worse, Americans ordering in English from French menus, specifying precisely, exigently, what they want in a language the waiters don't speak.

For it turns out that there is a Regulon in the Semiosphere stronger even than the plug, more agile than the fish. It's language. Language really does prevent signs or cultures from going universal. For all the endless articles in the papers and magazines about the force of globalization and international standardization, language divides and confuses people as effectively now as it ever has. It stops the fatal "exponentiality" of culture in the real world as surely as starvation stops it in the jungle. It divides absolutely, and what is really international, truly global, is, in this way, very small.

The real "crisis" in France in fact is not economic (France is in a cyclical slump; it will end) or even cultural (France is in a cyclical slump; it will end) but linguistic. French has diminished as an international language, and this will not end. When people talk about globalization, what they're really saying is that an English-speaking imperium now stretches from Adelaide to Vancouver, and that anyone who is at home in one bit of it is likely to feel at home in the other bits. You can join this global community by speaking English yourself, but that's about all. The space between the average Frenchman (or Italian or German) and the average American is just as great as it's ever been, because language remains in place, and it remains *hard*. Even after two years of speaking French all the time, I feel it. We breathe in our first language, and swim in our second.

|||

Yet there *is* a kind of authority associated with the American presence right now that is both awe-inspiring and absurd. At the Bastille Day fireworks, for instance, over on the champ-de-Mars, there is always a nice big picnic feeling, but no one pays minimal respect to the notion that people ought not to stand up in front of other people when other people are trying to watch fireworks. As happens so often in France, it is a designated bacchanal, like the playground in the Luxembourg Gardens. At the Bastille Day on the champ-de-Mars this July, in the midst of the anarchy—over on the fringes, of course, there were *flics, gendarmes,* busy arresting the vendors of those glow-in-the-dark necklaces; now, there was a *real* crime—a single American woman rose to bring order to the multitudes. She was the kind of big-boned East Coast woman you see running a progressive day camp, or working as the phys ed instructor at Dalton or Brearley, high-flown but (as she would be the first to tell you) down-to-earth. She just started ordering people around: Sit down, you down there (all this in English, of course), now make room so the little kids can see, etc. And people, at least the few hundred in earshot, actually did it. They *obeyed*, for a little while anyway.

The French believe that all errors are distant, someone else's fault. Americans believe that there is no distance, no difference, and therefore that there are no errors, that any troubles are simple misunderstandings, consequent on your not yet having spoken English loudly enough.

|||

It is, still, amazing to see how vast a screen the differences of language can be—not an opaque but a kind of translucent one. You sort of see through it, but not quite. There is a book to be written, for instance, on small errors in subtitles. In the Fred Astaire musical *Royal Wedding*, for instance, the English girl he falls for, played by Sarah Churchill (daughter of Sir Winston), is engaged to an American, whom we never see but who's called Hal—like Falstaff's prince, like a good high Englishman. That English *H*, though, was completely inaudible to the French translator who did the subtitles, and so throughout the film the absent lover is referred to in the subtitles as Al—Al like a stagehand, Al like my grandfather. If you have the habit of print addiction, so that you are listening and reading at the same time, this guy Al keeps forcing his way into the movie. "But what shall I say to Hal—that I have never loved him?" Patricia says to Fred. Down below it says, *"Et Al—qu'est-ce que je vais lui dire?"*

My other favorite subtitle was in some contemporary comedy that we went to see—we see about a movie every six months, where once I saw three a day—in which there was a reference to American talk shows. "And what do you want me to do: go on Oprah, Geraldo, or Sally Jessy?" the character asked. The translator did fine with Oprah and Geraldo but could make nothing of the last, so Sally with her glasses became a non–non sequitur question. *"Oprah, Geraldo—et sale est Jesse?"* the subtitle read— "Oprah, Geraldo—and Jesse is dirty?" This network of distant errors obviously occludes itself in front of us all the time, every day, and mostly we don't know it.

|||

There are at least three moments a month when you are ready to leap across a counter or a front seat to strangle someone: the woman at France Télécom who won't give you the fax ribbons that are there on the counter in front of her because she can't find them on the computer inventory; the chair restorer who looks at your beautiful Thonet rocker and then announces, sniffily, that it isn't worth his time; the woman who sells you a poster and then announces that she has no idea where you might go to frame it; the bus driver who won't let an exhausted pregnant woman out the front door of the bus (you're supposed to exit from the rear) from sheer bloody-mindedness. It affects Martha much less than me, leading me to suspect that it is essentially a masculine problem. My trouble is that I think like a Frenchman: I transform every encounter into a competition in status and get enraged when I lose it. As Cioran said, it's hard for me to live in a country where everyone is as irascible as I am.

At the same time, I find myself often reduced to an immigrant helplessness. We went to BHV, for instance, earlier this year to frame our "From Paris to the Moon" engraving. I have had it up in my study, an icon to write under. There's a nice do-it-yourself framing shop up there, and lacking a framer to go to, we thought we just ought to, well, do it ourselves. Back in New York we knew a framer who did our frames, and I prided myself, within limits, on having learned a thing or two about what made the right edge for the right picture. We began to sort around with simple white mats and black wooden frames. As we were doing it, a lady came up to us: a Frenchwoman in her seventies, with pearls and a strong jaw and silver hair. She had a couple of handsome flower prints that she was framing for herself. "No, no, children," she said. "You are doing that quite incorrectly. This, you see," she said, "is a nineteenth-century print. It needs a nineteenth-century mat, a nineteenth-century frame." She took the white-and-black frame away from us—put them right back—and chose a cream mat and a fake, "antiqued" gold frame. "There," she said, "*that* is the French nineteenth century," and took the frame and the print and the mat all up to the counter for us. We looked at each other sheepishly and went ahead and bought them. I used to know something about art, or thought I did, I muttered to myself, all the way home. The print actually looks pretty nice in its gold frame. When I remember the moment now, I remember my utter helplessness and how she smelled of a wonderful tea-rose perfume.

|||

The other side of French official arrogance is French improvised and elaborate courtesy. The delivery men from the department store Bon Marché called last night, to deliver the wicker kitchen organizer. "We have to be there early, because it's a small street. Six-thirty."

"It's a little too early for us," I said. "Let's make it later."

"Ah, no. It's impossible. Six-thirty or nothing."

"All right," and I hung up the phone, silently cursing French arrogance and the lack of any kind of service ethic.

Then, the next morning, at six forty-six, I was just awakened by the sound of the gentlest possible knocking on the front door—so butterfly quiet that at first I imagined that it must have been Luke Auden stirring in bed. But then there it was again, quiet but insistent. I got up, put on my robe, got to the front door, and stared out the spyglass. There were two workmen in the hallway, leaning over gently, knocking with their knuckles, as lightly as ghosts. I slipped the door open and got not a smile, but a look of acknowledgment, and they brought the kitchen organizer in with balletlike light-footedness. "Thank you," I said, "the baby is sleeping." They nodded. *We know.* I signed the invoice, and they were gone, and I went back to sleep.

|||

And then there is the chair. It started by accident one rainy Monday, after we had been to the Musée d'Orsay, and I had failed to get Luke much interested in my old favorites, Monets and Manets. I still find going to the Musée d'Orsay an infuriating, maddening experience. (Apparently, despite my superficial essays at amused blandness, I realize, reading this, that I'm a real pepperpot, a hothead, Billy Martin in France.) That vast, handsome railroad station so horribly done over in Wiener Werkstätte fashion by Gae Aulenti; the stupid, unquestioned dominance of the worst *pompier* art of the nineteenth century in the main hall as though saying, *here* are our real treasures. And the greater pain that only the *pompier* official art could look any good in such a vast and frigid space. I no longer find the taste for nineteenth-century French academic art, which can be amusing if seen small on a slide screen, the least bit likable. It is horrible, depressing beyond words, the revenge of official culture on life and youth, on reality itself. I swear to God I would take a razor to *The Romans of the Decadence* without a moment's hesitation.

And then having to take the escalator up all the way to the far upper floors—a garret, in museum terms, in order to see the great pictures, every one of which looked incomparably better in the old Jeu de Paume. It is a calculated, venom-filled insult on the part of French official culture against French civilization, revenge on the part of the academy and administration against everyone who escaped them. French official culture, having the upper hand, simply banishes French civilization to the garret, sends it to its room. What one feels, in that awful place, is violent indignation—and then an ever-increased sense of wonder that Manet and Degas and Monet, faced with the same stupidities of those same academic provocations in their own lifetimes, responded not with rage but with precision and grace and contemplative exactitude.

Paris is marked by a permanent battle between French civilization, which is the accumulated intelligence and wit of French life, and French official culture, which is the expression of the functionary system in all its pomposity and abstraction. By French civilization I mean the small shops; by French official culture I mean the big buildings. There is hardly a day when you are not wild with gratitude for something that happens in the small shops: the way that Mme. Glardon, at the pastry shop on the rue Bonaparte, carefully wraps Luke Auden's chocolate éclair in a little paper pyramid, a ribbon at its apex, knowing perfectly well, all the while, that the paper pyramid and ribbon will endure just long enough for the small boy to rip it open to get to the éclair. And hardly a day when you are not wild with dismay at something that has been begun in the big buildings, some abstraction launched on the world in smug and empty confidence.

|||

In any case, I couldn't, as it happened, get Luke much stirred by Manet or Monet (not that he was stirred by the Couture either, I'm glad to say), but searching for something that *would* stir him, I came across the handsome side chapel devoted to Daumier's portrait busts. They are caricatures of the political men of the mid-nineteenth century. Luke loved them. I held him up, and he stared at their faces behind the Plexiglas boxes and imitated each one. We guessed at the character of each one: who's mean, who's nice, who's conceited. The scary thing is that the faces are *exactly* the faces of French politicians today: Philippe Séguin, with his raccoon-circled eyes; Le Pen, with his obscene, smiling jowliness; Bruno Megret with his ratlike ordinariness. You could find the men of the left; too: Jospin's fatuous cheerfulness—they're all there.

After the success of the Daumiers, I thought of going to the park, as a release, or back to Deyrolle, for the umpteenth time, but it was raining hard, and we needed something new. "Do you want a soda?" I said, and we went over to the Courier de Lyons, the nearest thing our *haut* neighborhood has to a workingman's café. After he had a grenadine, and I a *grand crème,* and we had shared a *tarte Normande,* I noticed that there was a pinball machine—a *flipper,* as it is called in French. So I dragged a chair over, so that he could stand up on it and work the left flipper, and took control of the right flipper myself. It was an "NBA all-star" pinball machine, a true old-fashioned, pre-Atari, steel ball pinball, but with extra ramps and lights that let you shoot the ball up into hoops, get extra points, make model players jump up and down. (Luke, of course, had never seen a basketball game.) We started playing, and he loved it: the ping of the hard metal balls, the compressed springiness of the release, the fat *thwack* of the bumpers, above all the bounce of the flipper, hitting the ball back up, keeping it in play, making it go. We played three times, rushed home, and he told his momma about it. "It goes . . ." he said, and at a loss for words, he just raced his eyes, back and forth, rolled them back and forth crazily—*that's* how it goes.

Since then we go once a week to play pinball, always prefaced by a trip first to the Musée d'Orsay to look at the funny faces (while Daddy seethes at the nineteenth-century academicians and the small boy counts the minutes to the Courier de Lyons.) The funny thing is that the café changes the pinball machine every month or so, and it is always, *always,* an American machine with an American theme. Each machine has an automated bonus, something weird that happens if you get enough points, and there is something rapt and lovely, in this day of virtual everything, about the clockwork nightingale *mechanicalness* of the pinball machines, about the persistence of their metallic gears and simple slot-and-track devices. So far we have been through major-league baseball, Star Wars (Han Solo gets blasted into that carbon sheet), Jurassic Park (an egg glows and opens, and a baby dinosaur appears), Gopher Golf (a kind of parody golf, with little chipmunks that jump up, bucktoothed), and, our favorite, Monster Bash (Dracula comes out of his coffin, on a little metal track; Frankenstein, to the accompaniment of suitably stormy music—the lights on the machine actually first go off, a lovely touch—*sits up*). All the instructions on the machines are in English, of course, as are all the details. ("I love these machines, compared to video games," another aficionado at the café said to me once, sincerely, as we scored big and watched Dracula creaking out on his mechanical track. "They are, well, *so real*.")

We go once a week, always get the same grenadine-coffee-pie combo, leave a ten-franc tip; I am sure that it is illegal for a three-year-old to play pinball, and I am paying protection. After a month or so, though, I noticed something odd. When we began to play, I would always discreetly drag a café chair over from the table and put it alongside the machine for Luke to stand on. But after we had done this five or six times, over five or six weeks, I noticed that someone had quietly tucked that small café chair under the left flipper. The chair, the little bistro chair, was permanently pushed under the pinball machine, on the left, or Lukeish, side. There was no talk, no explanation; no one mentioned it, or pointed it out. No, it was a quiet, almost a grudging courtesy, offered to a short client who came regularly to take his pleasure there. Nothing has changed in our relation to that café: No one shakes our hands or offers us a false genial smile; we pay for our coffee and grenadine as we always have; we leave the tip we have always left. But that chair is always there.

Papon's
Paper Trail

Bordeaux is the town where France goes to give up. It was where the French government retreated from Paris under fire from the Prussians in 1870, and again from the kaiser's armies in 1914, and where, in June 1940, the French government fled in the face of the German advance and soon afterward met not just the fact of defeat but the utter depth of France's demoralization. A. J. Liebling wrote of those days that "there was a climate of death in Bordeaux, heavy and unhealthy like the smell of tuberoses." He recalled the wealthy men in the famous restaurants like the Chapon Fin, "heavy-jowled, waxy-faced, wearing an odd expression of relief from fear." Though the bad peace was ruled from the spa town of Vichy, Bordeaux is the place that gave the surrender its strange, bitter, bourgeois character: a nation retreating from cosmopolitan Paris back to *la France profonde*.

Bordeaux has always been a trench coat–and–train station, 1940s kind of town, and despite the mediocre, concrete modern architecture it shares with nearly all French provincial capitals, it remains one. The Chapon Fin is still in business, but it is not deathlike—merely nervous and overwrought, in the way of French provincial restaurants since the capitalists trimmed down and the only market left was German tourists.

In the spring of 1998, Bordeaux was invaded again, this time by battalions of lawyers, broadcasters, historians, and journalists, who had come to attend or participate in the trial of Maurice Papon—the former secretary-general of the Gironde, of which Bordeaux is the capital—for complicity in crimes against humanity fifty-five years ago, during the occupation. The Papon trial was the central, binding event of the past year in France, a kind of O.J. trial, without television or a glove. It was the longest, the most discouraging, the most moving, at times the most ridiculous, and certainly the most fraught trial in postwar French history.

On the last day of the trial, Wednesday, April 1, the invasion of the media became an occupation; what seemed like every European journalist resident in France, and a lot of Americans too, descended on the little square outside the Palais de Justice. The convenience of having La Concorde, a stage-set grand café right across from the Palais (doors open to the spring weather, bottles of good wine lined up on the wall), gave the end of the trial a strangely hilarious, high-hearted, yet self-subduing party spirit— a combination of Swifty Lazar's Oscar party and the Nuremberg trials.

Despite the mob, the national allegiance of every journalist was instantly recognizable. French journalists wear handsomely tailored jackets and share with English rock guitarists the secret of eternal hair: It piles up. Americans, rumpled and exhausted before the day begins, seem to be still longing for Vietnam. Even walking up and down the steps of the Palais, they looked as though they were ducking into the backwash of a helicopter rotor, weighed down by invisible dog tags. What really depressed them was the knowledge that their stories about the *procès Papon* would sneak into the paper only "between blow jobs," as one said bitterly. The British alone were exhilarated, bouncing around in bad suits. They all speak French, they all knew they would be on the front page, and secretly they knew too that their readers would not be completely unhappy with a story whose basic point was that all foreigners were like that.

The great Nazi hunter Serge Klarsfeld waited outside the courthouse too. He is in his sixties, spreading at the middle, and was dressed in a black jacket and cloth cap. "If Papon is found guilty, then the *appareil* of the state will be held responsible," he was saying to another journalist. "The French people will be saying that there is a limit, you must act on your conscience, even if you are a man motivated not by hatred but by procedures." Behind him, members of his group, the Association of Sons and Daughters of the Deported Jews of France, were reading out the names of Jewish children whom Papon was charged with having sent to their deaths.

A few moments later three British journalists rushed into La Concorde, having just heard the accused man's last speech. Like all of Papon's interventions during the trial, this one was sonorous, unremorseful, and full of literary and artistic reference. As soon as he finished, the three judges and nine jurors had gone to deliberate 764 questions of guilt or innocence, with a tray of sandwiches to see them through the night. The three Brits now sat down and ordered wine and roast chicken, and one began reading his translation of the speech as the others ate: "He said that it was a double scandal, something about Camus in here. Oh, yes, his wife's favorite writer was Camus." The reporter looked down at his notes and deciphered. "They killed his wife . . . I think." Papon's wife of sixty-six years had died, at the age of eighty-eight, the week before the trial was to end. " 'In their desperate . . . desperate search,' I think you'd put it, 'for a crime, they have killed her with . . . *petits esprits.*' What would you say? Small guns? Small steps? Little blows? Little blows. De Gaulle gave her a *Légion d'Honneur.*"

" 'With his own hands,' " one of the other journalists added, consulting his notes.

"Oh, yes. God, yes. 'With his own hands.' Then there was . . . Oh, yes. Here's when he turned to the prosecutor: 'Sir, you will go down in history—but through the servants' entrance!' " The reporter looked up, his eyes amused. "Well, that's not bad. Now something here about the absence of Germans. Oh, yes: 'Throughout the stages of this strange and surreal trial, there has been a notable absence of Germans.' A Notable Absence of Germans—sounds like a Michael Frayn play. Then something odd about Abraham sacrificing Isaac in Rembrandt, a ray of light? Staying his hand. Anyone get that?"

Everything came to a halt as a crowd of journalists who had gathered around the table tried to call to mind the light of an early Rembrandt, struggling to keep up with the tight web of cultural allusion spun by a French war criminal.

"Well, anyway," the British reporter resumed, "he called it the most beautiful light in painting. I still don't get it. He's comparing himself to the Jewish child about to be killed? Well, it's a point of view. Anyway, he stayed the hand. So that's it. Camus, his wife, no Germans, servants' entrance, bit about the light, Rembrandt, and then the sandwiches were sent in," he concluded decisively.

"Anyone see what kind of sandwiches?" an American reporter asked anxiously. The Brits laughed. But a little later the man from the *L.A. Times* said that he had seen the sandwiches go in, and he was confident that they were ham.

|||

When the French government in Bordeaux surrendered, in 1940, it was replaced by the right-wing Vichy government under the direction of Maréchal Pétain, the great French hero of the

First World War. The Vichy regime passed anti-Jewish laws that summer, before the Germans even demanded them. Two years later, at the Nazis' demand, Vichy began deporting Jews, including children, from all over the country. Although "only" 25 percent of the Jews in France were sent to death camps, this is, as the historian Robert Paxton has pointed out, a derisive figure: Jews in France were the most assimilated in Europe. If there had not been fiches and dossiers in place at the prefecture, the Germans would have had a hard time finding Jews to kill.

No one disputes that from 1942 to 1944 Maurice Papon, the secretary-general of the department of the Gironde, signed documents recording the arrest, assembly, and deportation of more than 1,500 Jews, including 220 children. The *rafles* took place between July 1942 and May 1944. The documents show that the deportees, some French, some refugees from the East, were to be sent to the transit camp of Drancy, outside Paris. Then they were to go to a *destination inconnue*. The unknown destination was Auschwitz.

Papon's history after the war is also public knowledge. By the end of 1943 Papon had begun to cooperate quietly with the resistance, and even sheltered an important Jewish *résistant*. Then, at the liberation, he delivered the prefecture to the resistance and, despite the complaints of a few locals, began a spectacular rise in the postwar French bureaucracy as an *haut fonctionnaire*. In the late fifties he became the head of the prefecture of police in Paris and, in the seventies, budget minister in the government of Giscard d'Estaing. (The division between *hauts fonctionnaires* and politicians in France is fluid; there were five *hauts fonctionnaires* in the cabinet that signed the armistice with the Germans. Today, 41 percent of the members of the National Assembly are civil servants on leave.)

Then, in 1981, Michel Slitinsky, a Bordeaux Jew who had escaped the deportations, met a historian named Michel Bergès, who had been doing work on the role of the local wine negotiants during the war. Bergès had stumbled on some interesting documents recording what the prefecture under Papon had been doing at the same time. Slitinsky eventually helped deliver the documents to the satiric newspaper *Le Canard Enchaîné*. Later, two more Bordelais, Maurice-David Matisson and René Jacob, made formal accusations against Papon. (A Frenchman can bring a charge against another Frenchman to the attention of a magistrate, who may then investigate it.) President Mitterrand did everything he could to delay the trial. French justice is under the control, or anyway the influence, of the president; Mitterrand must have felt that opening old Vichy cases was not in anyone's interest, especially his. It was only in 1995 that a formal indictment was handed down. Last October, Papon was brought from his house outside Paris to Bordeaux to stand trial.

The trial began in October and was expected to end in December, but it went on until the *poisson d'avril*—April Fools' Day. The cast of characters in the courtroom, as the trial was reported in manic detail in the Paris papers, seemed noisy and fantastic. French courtroom decorum allows far more time than would be acceptable in an American or British court for free questioning, speechifying, digressive material, and moral instruction directed by whoever is in the mood to give it toward whoever he thinks deserves to get it. This lent the event an interestingly literary air. There was the lawyer for the accused, Jean-Marc Varaut, the author of grandiloquent books on famous trials: one on Oscar Wilde, one on Jesus. There was a stream of historians: Bergès, now bizarrely on the side of the defense; the universally admired American Robert Paxton, the greatest of Vichy historians; and Henri Amouroux, "of the Institute," the most well-known historian to appear for the defense.

There was Serge Klarsfeld, whose son Arno was one of the leading civil prosecutors in the trial. (In a French courtroom, four or five separate prosecution teams—some civil, some from the government—can all argue the same case, each in its own way.) Arno drove the other prosecutors crazy. At the last minute he pleaded for a lesser penalty for Papon than *perpétuité,* the life

sentence, demanded by the *parquet,* the prosecuting government authorities. And during the trial he led a move to have the
presiding judge barred, on the ground that a relative of his had
been among the deportees. (This may have been a preemptive
strike, to keep the defense from raising the same point.) Then,
after the motion failed, he took it on himself to disassociate
Papon from other, worse war criminals, like Paul Touvier and
Klaus Barbie, whom his parents had also helped bring to justice,
announcing that, unlike them, Papon had merely signed papers.
Since the whole point of the trial was to establish that signing
papers was itself a crime, the other prosecutors understandably
developed an even more intense dislike of Arno. Arno became
the event of the trial. Out of the black robe and white kerchief
that French lawyers still wear, making them look like perpetual
Daumier drawings, he could often be seen in jeans, with his shirt
hanging out. He is handsome, but in a modelish way, with too
much hair and too open a collar. For a while before the start of
the trial, he lived with the model Carla Bruni and had been photographed in *Paris Match* with her on a romantic vacation in
Venice. Most days he arrived at the Palais on Rollerblades. Even
in America this would have been controversial. In France it was
regarded as just short of mooning the judges.

Above all, there was Papon himself, pompous and aging and
erect and unrepentant. For the first time in a French war crimes
trial, there was a figure of sufficient Mephistophelian stature to
excite a moralist. Papon may have been evil, but he was certainly
not banal. According to the rules of French trials, he was allowed
not just to speak but to pontificate, and from the courtroom
came daily dispatches recording, in the sonorous, Gaullist tones
of the high estate, his views on the trial and the witnesses
brought against him. "This testimony is moving in both its nature
and the dignity with which it was given," he said of one witness.
Or again, "I cannot help but express my emotion in the face of
this sober, painful account. It brings back heart-wrenching
memories."

The trial failed to clarify its subject, for reasons that were partly complicated and French, partly universal and human. The universal and human reason was that Papon was an old man being tried as an accomplice to murder. Complicity is hard to prove in any courtroom, and old men make bad culprits. Papon was sick—too sick, the doctors said, to be held in prison during the trial—and his wife was even sicker; after he went home for her funeral, there were those who thought that he might not come back. Whenever it seemed that the accusers had assured the necessity of his conviction, Papon stumbled, or fell sick, or a confused memory intervened, and one was reminded that here was a very old and decrepit functionary. Whenever one wanted to leave the verdict to the historians, one was reminded by some piece of heartbreaking evidence—a few words about a wife, a mother—that here in person was the instrument by which the French state casually delivered children to their murderers. We will have justice, said the ghosts. I will soon be one of you, said the guilty man. The trial went on for six months—too short a time to try Vichy, someone said, and too long a time to try Papon.

There is an idea, beloved of American editorialists, that the Vichy regime itself was on trial in Bordeaux and that France was finally "confronting its repressed past." This is a myth. The French have been obsessed with the details of Vichy for at least twenty-five years. Almost every bookstore keeps a shelf of books devoted to these four years of France's thousand-year history. Frenchmen of the left and of the right long ago accepted that Vichy was made possible by the German army but followed homegrown right-wing ideology, and was broadly popular.

What was on trial in Bordeaux was not Vichy but something more: *l'état,* the state itself, through the acts of one of its most successful representatives. The French war crimes trials of recent years, from Barbie the Gestapo man to Touvier the militiaman to Papon the *fonctionnaire,* have been moving closer to the heart of the French identity. The idea of *l'état,* the state, and its representatives, the *hauts fonctionnaires,* has a significance in

France that is incomprehensible to Americans, for whom it means, at best, the post office. *L'État* suggests far more than the mere sum of the civil service. It has the authority that the Constitution has in America, that the monarchy until recently had in Britain. (Serge July, of the newspaper *Libération,* has even referred to "the religion of the *fonction publique.*") The state is the one guarantor of permanence in a country where neither the left nor the right can quite accept the legitimacy of the other side.

In France the state intervenes between the nation, the repository of racial memory, beloved of the right, and the republic, repository of universal rights, beloved of the left. Its presence lets them coexist: The state keeps the nation from becoming too national, and the republic from becoming too republican. In France the state suggests the official, disinterested tradition of service; it means the functioning and unity of the country; it means what works. When one of the lawyers at the trial, trying to give an interview in English, was prompted with the term *civil servant* as a translation for what Papon had been, he repeated it and then visibly gagged, as though he'd swallowed a bad oyster; the idea of associating the word *servant* with the social role he was describing was just too weird.

The cult of the state makes France run. Yet every cult comes at a price. The price of constitution worship, as in America, is to make every personal question a legal question—so that every pat on every bottom, every swig on a bottle, and every pull on every cigarette seem likely to have, eventually, a law and a prosecutor of their own. The price of state worship, as in France, is that real things and events get displaced into a parallel paper universe; the state is possible only because everything has been neatly removed from life and put in a filing cabinet.

The abstraction extends into every corner of French life. The girl at the France Télécom store who is asked for a new fax ribbon finds it, places it on the counter beside her—and then spends fifteen minutes searching through her computer files, her inventory, for some evidence that such ribbons do in fact exist. The ribbon on the counter is an empirical accident; what counts is what is in the system. The reality is the list; the reality is the document. This French habit of abstraction, unlike, say, the German habit of blind obedience, is difficult to criticize, because it is linked to so many admirable things. It is linked to the French gift for generalization, for intelligent living, for the grand manner, the classical style. It not only makes the trains run on time but makes them run on time to places one would like to visit. But it was this national habit of abstraction, with its blindness to particulars, that was, in a way, on trial.

The irony was that a French courtroom attended by the French political classes was the last place to defeat, or even to test, the compulsive habit of abstraction. The language of French lawyering, like the language of the institute and the academy, is an *étatiste* language. Inside and outside a French courtroom, abstractions pile on abstractions, and by the end you are so distracted that you are unable to face plain facts: children in a cattle car being delivered to a death camp. It was not just that you could not see the trees for the forest. It was that you could not see the forest because it was covered by a map.

So the documents involving deportations that bear Papon's signature might have been official orders authorizing actions, but—crucial difference—they might have been official memorandums, recording for the benefit of the regional prefect, Maurice Sabatier, who was Papon's boss, actions already taken, a type of document that belongs in a different filing cabinet. Bergès, the historian who found the documents, was persuaded to testify that this was in fact the case. Papon was, in his own words, a mere *téléphoniste*—a receptionist, taking messages and creating memorandums. Then what to make of Sabatier's delegating to him, among other things, responsibility for Jewish affairs? Ah, but—understandable, though lamentable, confusion—this Department of Jewish Affairs was a recording bureau, not to be confused with the governmental Department of Jewish Affairs, which organized the deportations and the convoys. Papon was responsible for Jewish affairs only in a secondary sense. Anyway, he did whatever he could to protect Jews; look at the memos in which he struggles to see to it that Jewish children are sent to their parents! But those children were being sent to parents who were already dead and were therefore being sent to their own deaths. Where on paper can that be shown to have been understood? Within the paper universe of the prefecture, the unorthodox act of attaching children's files to their parents' was an act of respect for families, whatever the sad distortion in the world outside. And Papon actually insisted that the cattle cars, *wagons à bestiaux,* be replaced with passenger cars. But if he was capable of ordering the change of cars then . . . No, here again you are confusing the technical decisions of the prefecture with the policy directives of Paris—or, in this case, of Paris and Vichy. In any case, Maître Varaut, Papon's lawyer, demanded, seizing on the prosecutors' uncertainty about how hard to press their case, how could one talk about degrees of guilt in a crime against humanity? Either one was implicit in mass murder or one was not. Any other claim was illogical. One could not be 60 percent guilty, or 30 percent guilty. The paper chain proved guilt or it did not.

Only the victims seemed quite real. Marcel Stourdze, a deportee who traveled back and forth from Paris to Bordeaux every day, in order not to miss a day, testified, "When I went back to Auschwitz after the liberation, I saw that in an enormous vat they had saved all the hair. I thought that I saw the hair of my wife. Today all that hair has become white. But at the time it still bore the color of those we had loved."

|||

One of the shocks the trial offered involved the events not of 1942 but of 1961. At that time, when Papon was the head of the Paris police, the city and federal police had taken part in a massacre in which approximately two hundred Algerian demonstrators died. It was toward the end of the Algerian War, and Algerians in Paris, sympathetic to Algerian nationalism, broke a curfew and marched to the center of the city. There had been Paris policemen killed in the preceding month, and as the march pressed on, a kind of murderous free-for-all began. Many of the demonstrators, bound hand and foot, were drowned in the Seine. (The details of this atrocity, which took place in the center of Paris, remain murky and obscure.) A partial glimpse of the records of the crime appeared only last fall, in the newspaper *Libération*.

This was regarded as good news for the defense—it showed that Papon had nothing particular against Jews—but it was also seen as an attempt by the left to equate the mistakes of the Gaullist regime during the Algerian civil war with the crimes of Vichy. What came to fill the gap of real issues was, inevitably, contemporary politics. The first people to feel the sting of the Papon trial were the Gaullists, and Philippe Séguin, the leader of the remaining Gaullist party, was the first political leader to denounce the trial. De Gaulle himself, Séguin felt, had come under attack. Papon, after all, had been allowed to continue in the *fonction publique* and had been regularly promoted by Gaullist politicians.

The right discovered a response in an 850-page book called *Le Livre Noir du Communisme*, the Black Book of Communism, which appeared last November, shortly after the Papon trial had begun. It is an encyclopedia of Communist atrocities around the world, from 1917 to the present, all scrupulously recorded and presented, with a tally of a hundred million deaths. The Black Book became the subject of a polemic, focused indirectly, as everyone understood, on the *procès Papon*. Were the crimes of the Communists really comparable to the crimes of the Nazis? And if they were, didn't that make the entire apparatus of international communism, including, of course, the French Communist party and its intellectuals—slavishly Stalinist for so long—"complicit" in another way too? Were the fiches in the prefecture the only ones that mattered or could acts in that other paper universe, of poems and manifestos, be complicit in murder too?

|||

After the jury retired, the journalists waited for the verdict at La Concorde. The wine was good, a generic Merlot, and every table was taken. Nine o'clock became ten, the clouds of smoke thickened, and the gaiety rose as, one by one, filing deadlines for the next day's paper passed. Twelve o'clock and the French journalists are off the hook; three o'clock and the Brits are off! Only the Americans are going to have to file late tonight, no matter what. But then, around three-thirty, the big news comes in. The Paula Jones case has been dismissed; whatever anyone files is now set for page 2. Mildly annoying to the newspapermen, this news is disaster for the independent television crews. "I can hear them now," one cameraman says moodily, deep in his cups. " 'Ship it, ship it.' " ("Ship it" meaning "Don't even try to put it on the satellite" is the TV equivalent of "We'll call you.")

The owners of La Concorde had learned, over the months of the trial, that American journalists cannot be outdone in their pitiless pursuit of truth and blank restaurant receipts. To cries of "Fiche, fiche, fiche," the waiters slap one down with every order. A gloomy Dutch newspaperman at one table is telling stories about how often he has broken big stories, but in Dutch. "No one knows. No one cares," he says. "Cheesus could come back tomorrow, but if he comes to me, they'll know it only in Amsterdam."

The British journalists, deadlines gone, drink whiskey and begin to reminisce about other, kinder war crimes trials, where you didn't have to stay up all night for the verdict. "Take the Barbie trial," one says. "Everyone knew what the verdict would be, but the jury waited until just after midnight to announce it; that way they got an extra day's pay, six hundred francs. We all went out and got drunk with the jury and the lawyers, and then we filed and were all on the boat train home and back in London in time for dinner. Now, that was a trial for crimes against humanity that wasn't a crime against humanity."

The Klarsfelds wander in and out, waiting for the verdict like everyone else. They have been cast as wreckers, loose cannons, pursuing some odd, private agenda. Seeing them together, certainly, one finds the connection between stolid, impassive father and mercurial son hard to grasp. Daniel Schneidermann, a television journalist who has written a book about the trial, argues that the horror of their family history—Serge's father was a deportee who died in Auschwitz—has left an "emptiness" inside Arno, the emptiness of a world that, since the Holocaust, has been abandoned by God. It is probably true that Arno's aggressive gestures—the Rollerblades, the jeans, the rude interjections in court—are meant to show a certain distaste for the whole pompous system, for the parallel paper universe in all its dignity. But it is also possible that metaphysics aside, the Klarsfelds just have a shrewder take on the possibilities of the trial than their more sophisticated confreres. They understand that only an "intermediary" penalty, only some finding of guilt for Papon clearly distinguished from the great guilt of the real killers, will seem plausible to a Bordeaux jury. They are struggling to articulate, in the rhetoric of the courtroom, that there are gradations of guilt, styles of complicity, even in the Holocaust. To treat Papon as though he were equivalent to SS killers, like Barbie, is, in a sense, to draw a line again around the killings, with pure evil on one side and innocence, by implication, safely on the other.

Among the people and the talk and the stories, one bald, hard-looking man in his seventies, drinking his cognac and coffee, never leaves his table. "Who is he?" a newcomer asks.

"Nobody knows," one of the women from the wire services answers. "He's been here every day since the trial began. He hassled some of the women, but then he gave it up." She lowers her voice. "A lot of us think he may be the man from the FN." The FN, the neo-Fascist National Front, is the phantom of Vichy that everyone wishes would go to sleep.

At four-thirty in the morning it was announced that the verdict would arrive at eight. A lot of the American reporters went back to their hotel rooms, opened their windows to let in the French spring air, and turned on CNN to watch the news about the Paula Jones dismissal. It was hard, one reporter commented afterward, not to think about the extravagant good fortune of a country that had trials like that to worry about. Another, watching James Carville and Susan Carpenter-McMillan on *Larry King,* said that he found it hard, particularly after months of trying to decode French verbal combat, to remember which was which: Did the two Americans on TV actually hate each other, despite the smileyness and forced good humor? Or was the hatred the pretense, and the reality the professional prizefighter's camaraderie? He had, he said, been away from America too long to remember.

By eight everyone was back at La Concorde. Serge Klarsfeld was waiting too. Someone asked one of the Brits, who had been there all night, if anyone had any instincts about what was to happen.

"None," he said.

"No one was persuaded?"

"No one was sober," he replied.

Shortly after nine a middle-aged woman rushed into the café. She was stout and squarely built and was bent over as she ran. She had both palms held out straight in front of her, fingers spread. It was a strange, lamenting posture, like that of a Greek mourning figure.

She ran over to Klarsfeld. He nodded and wept briefly, and they held each other. Ten! The spread fingers meant that Papon had been given ten years. "And everyone against us," Klarsfeld muttered. It was a victory for him and for Arno; the jury had found Papon guilty of complicity in crimes against humanity, but not of mass murder.

Outside, the children of the deportees came to meet Klarsfeld, clasping one another and kissing cheeks. They were stout and old and plain; evil may sometimes be banal, but virtue, to its credit, always is.

In front of the courthouse the argument had already begun. "It isn't enough of a penalty!" someone cried. "You go serve ten years," Klarsfeld said, pushing him gently. The stout lady kept saying, "It was double or nothing, the *parquet*"—the government prosecutors—"wanted double or nothing." She said "double or nothing" in English. Klarsfeld said, "He was not Touvier, and he was not Barbie. The ultimate *responsables* were the Nazis. After you have looked a real Nazi in the eye, you know the difference with Papon." For the most part, the civil parties and the reporters who had been with them for six months were disappointed. "Ten years! Ten years is what you give a housebreaker," one exhausted French journalist said.

Somehow, back in Paris, the verdict seemed more tolerable. Paradoxically, the trial had concentrated so exclusively on Papon's role in Bordeaux in the forties that it had redrawn his picture, making him once again a mere prefect. In reality, he had not been one more face among the *fonctionnaires* but one of the highest, one of the great men of state, a cabinet minister. But this was a Paris reality, not a Bordeaux one, and it was only back in Paris, where the ministerial Papon could be recalled, that the scale of the achievement in Bordeaux registered. A great man of state, protected by the state, had been pursued for crimes by pitifully ordinary people—and despite that, he had at last been held responsible. It wasn't the victory over abstraction that Camus had died dreaming of. But this time nobody gave up.

In a way, the jury in the Palais de Justice had even, over sandwiches, used their imaginations to make some necessary retrospective law, and they had done it well. By saying that Papon didn't know where the trains were going, and also saying that he was guilty of crimes against humanity, they were making the right and courageous point. To deliver a child to the secret police is as large a crime against humanity as you ever need to find, no matter where you think he is going or what kind of car he is going to travel in. The men with stamps and filing cabinets now couldn't plead procedure any more than soldiers could plead orders; the *appareil* of the state would have to understand that their fiches represented people, whether they were Jews or Algerian demonstrators or refugees yet to come. The parallel paper universe now had a window.

|||

I had explained to Luke, over the course of the trial, what was going on and why I was away: A bad man had long ago done wicked things to little children, and now he would be put in jail for it. When I came home, he asked if they had put the bad man in jail, and I said, well, yes, they had. "And when the bad man got put in jail, did all the children come out?" he asked.

Of course, they hadn't even really put the bad man in jail. Papon remained free for almost another two years in various appeals—unusually so for a convicted man in France—and then, on the eve of his incarceration, fled to Switzerland. It seemed clear from the circumstances of his flight that he had some kind of internal help from the French functionary state. But he was found, quickly, within days, and brought back to France and locked up at last. In his flight he had taken the alias of La Rochefoucauld, the great French skeptic, a man of culture to the end.

Trouble at the Tower

Paris in July is pretty much left to the tourists and the people who look after them, while everyone else goes south, or west, or, in any case, away. An incident at the Eiffel Tower—which left a tourist sore, the tower closed tight for a couple of days, and an elevator operator out of a job for a while—told you everything you needed to know about what happens when you leave the tourist and his handlers alone to sort things out. What happened, if you missed it, was that a lady tourist got on the "up" elevator of the tower with a ticket for the second platform and then decided to get off at the first platform (because she felt dizzy or because she didn't, or just because she was exercising her fundamental right to get on and off an elevator whenever she felt like it). She was kept from getting off the elevator by a French elevator operator (who either gently dissuaded her or handled her a bit roughly, or else launched into a Joe Pesci–in-a-Scorsese-film attack). The woman (an American? No, a Brit! Finally the French papers settled on calling her an Anglo-Saxon) was, it turned out, a successful writer with a profound sense of indignation and a lawyer. She complained, and the company that runs the tower—it's a private business—had the elevator guy fired. But then the rest of the tower employees went out on strike in solidarity, closing down the tower and leaving a lot of indignant American and British tourists on the ground, furious at being denied their chance to be manhandled by the elevator operators.

The incident produced a certain panicky, just discernible exchange of meaningful glances for the rest of the week between the tourists and the touristed. ("So that's what they want—our lives!" "So that's what they want—our jobs!") Naturally, sympathy in France gathered quickly around the wronged operator and his striking friends, while sympathy on the Anglo-American side gathered around the roughed-up lady. This distribution of sympathy wasn't merely tribal, though. The Eiffel Tower Incident of the Summer of '97 illustrates a temperamental and even intellectual difference between the two cultures. Most Americans draw their identities from the things they buy, while the French draw theirs from the jobs they do. What we think of as "French rudeness," and what they think of as "American arrogance," arise from this difference. But she was just trying to have a good time, we think. But he was only doing his job, they think. For us, an elevator operator is only a tourist's way of getting to the top of the Eiffel Tower. For the French, a tourist is only an elevator operator's opportunity to practice his métier in a suitably impressive setting.

The metaphysics of consumerism are much studied, of course, since it seems to be the century's winning ism. (Americans have shown that whole art forms can be made through creative browsing.) Producerism, its surprisingly hardy French counterpart, is much less well diagnosed. The Eiffel Tower itself is a prime example of pure producerism, of métier mania: a thing built by an engineer as a self-sufficient work, whose only function is to stand there and be admired for having been engineered. The French ideal of a world in which everyone has a métier but no customers to trouble him is more practical than it might seem. It has been achieved, for instance, by the diplomats inside the quai d'Orsay, who create foreign policy of enormous subtlety and refinement which has absolutely no effect on anyone outside the building. It has also been achieved by IRCAM, the modern music institute, which sponsors contemporary composers who write music that so far no one has ever heard. (When the waiter at the café finally deigns to shake your hand, it does not mean that you are now a valued client. It means that you are now an honorary waiter.)

The elevator operator dreams of going to the top of the tower alone in his elevator, while the Anglo-Saxon tourist, in her heart of hearts (and he knows this; it's what terrifies him most), dreams of an automatic elevator. When the two ideals—of absolute professionalism unfettered by customers and of absolute tourism unaffected by locals—collide, trouble happens, pain is caused. Americans long for a closed society in which everything can be bought, where laborers are either hidden away or dressed up as nonhumans, so as not to be disconcerting. This place is called Disney World. The French dream of a place where everyone can practice his métier in self-enclosed perfection, with the people to be served only on sufferance, as extras, to be knocked down the moment they act up. This place, come to think of it, is called Paris in July.

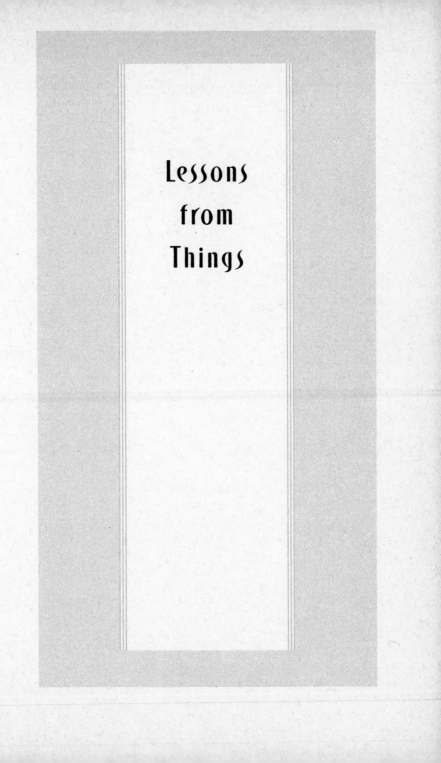

Lessons from Things

Couture
Shock

I suppose you could say that my introduction to the rites and spells of Parisian haute couture occurred early on a Sunday morning, at the Valentino show, when the ladies in the front row suddenly, and pretty much in unison, folded their programs over and began to fan themselves ferociously with the gold and brown paper. The Valentino show was being held at nine-thirty in the morning for reasons of protocol so complicated that they resembled one of those nineteenth-century diplomatic negotiations, like the Schleswig-Holstein question, comprehensible to only three people in Europe. The cream of the fashion press had turned up anyway, although Anna Wintour and Suzy Menkes and the rest had the pained, *aren't*-you-a-clever-boy-to-wake-me-up-this-early smiles otherwise seen only on parents of two-year-olds. The music had begun, Stella Tennant had come out (head angled, shoulders thrown back, hips a little forward, rolling the works) in ivory wool and silk chevron trousers with two patch

pockets, an ivory blouse with matching lace, and a beige cashmere shawl bordered in lace, looking game despite the hour and
all that lace. Then the ladies in the front row, the rich clients,
began to fan. They fanned hard, expertly—my God, it's hot in
here—just the way veteran dé-flé watchers always do. And this
was odd, because it was freezing cold inside the Salon Opéra at
the Grand Hôtel: the coldest July in Paris anyone could recall;
cassoulet and topcoat weather. But the ladies fanned as they always do, in the gasping heat of July at the collections.

I turned to a friend sitting next to me, a French television
journalist, and directed at her my version of the French shrug-
and-frown that means, Why on earth? She, in turn, made the
French O with her mouth that means, Please, my friend, discard
this elaborate pretense of naïveté. Then she shrugged too. "They
are at the collections. It is July. They fan," she said. She thought
for a moment. "It is a reflex. We watch, therefore we fan. No. I
fan, therefore I am." Then she looked around the salon and made
the encompassing shrug-and-pout-and-flex-your-hands-from-
the-wrist French gesture that in the context meant that the apparent absurdity of the act of fanning yourself in the cold is no
more absurd than the whole enterprise of traveling to Paris to
look at clothes that you will never wear, displayed on models to
whom you bear no resemblance, in order to help a designer get
people who will never attend shows like this someday to buy a
perfume or a scarf that will give them the consoling illusion that
they have a vague association with the kind of people who do attend shows like this—even though the people who attend shows
like this are the kind who fan themselves against July heat that
happens not to exist. It is these formulations—packed tight with
contradictions that spiral around, turn in on themselves, bite
their own tails, and eventually come out dressed in taffeta and
lace tulle—that give haute couture its charm, or, anyway, help it
cast its spell.

Participating in the haute couture is more like entering a

yacht in the America's Cup than it is like opening a Seventh Avenue showroom: The collections are overseen by the Chambre Syndicale de la Couture Parisienne, which demands, among other things, that its members maintain a working atelier in Paris, and put on a show each season of no fewer than fifty costumes each. Belonging is an expensive, exacting business, and every year one more house just drops out. This season there were sixteen shows—about a thousand outfits, from Stella's silky pants to the wedding dress at Saint Laurent. First an event and then a theme dominated the five days of the shows. The event was the separation of Gianfranco Ferré as head designer from the House of Dior, which was significant because it threw a major house into a "crisis," and the theme was the crisis of haute couture. Of course, haute couture is always in crisis, like Cyprus or the New York theater. But by now the crisis has become almost existential; not even a hit will help. Even very, very rich women don't buy bespoke clothes in Paris anymore, and the widely understood, though never openly articulated, justification for losing money in couture for the past twenty years or so—the loss leader justification—no longer works. By now, most fashionable people feel, the average woman who buys, say, a box of Pierre Cardin handkerchiefs is probably buying them less because of the glamorous association of Pierre Cardin haute couture than because of the glamorous association of Pierre Cardin socks and Pierre Cardin sunglasses. (As a consequence, Pierre Cardin, who seems to have figured this out, doesn't even show his haute couture line in the *défilés*.)

Fashionable people have two contradictory theories to explain the persistence of couture despite its troubles—theories usually mentioned in succession and often in the same sentence. The first—a kind of Tang and Teflon explanation, which is promoted by the Chambre—is that haute couture is the R&D wing of the fashion business, an investment in its future, since the "techniques" and "styles" that the designers wheel out today will somehow affect the kind of clothes that people wear tomorrow. (Veteran explainers offering this view can make it sound as though the *défilés* were taking place in a particle accelerator.) The other, contradictory explanation is that haute couture is the living memory of French fashion, where vanishing standards of workmanship, craftsmanship, and imagination are kept alive as a necessary act of filial piety. When you point out that both these explanations can't be true at the same time, you generally get in response a kind of Paris Zen. "Ah, you are right. Both things cannot be true at once. That is the point of haute couture," one fashion prince explained to me. Then he walked off seraphically.

|||

The haute couture remains a rite. There are the photographers, who push to get inside, and who form, on their bleachers, a little island of happy heterosexual lust amid two seas of becalmed aestheticism. They're the only free men at the collections; they whoop, whistle, and call out to the models anything they feel like calling out to the models. ("They could come out dressed in paper bags for all I care," one photographer said that morning as he looked over the Valentino program. "Well, *plastic* bags anyway.") Then there are the models themselves, who can undress and dress again so quickly that when the show is over, they climb out of the last evening dress and are on the street, wearing jeans and T-shirts and Prada knapsacks, getting a taxi before the applause has stopped. And there are the fashionable people, lining up in order not to be allowed in. (The shows never start on time, or near it, but everybody comes to the security desk and waves the invitation anyway.)

It's the clothes, of course, that differ from show to show. At Valentino the collection soon settles into a look—clothes in colors that the regular guy might describe as "sort of brown," although a fashionable person might call them chestnut, chocolate, beige, coffee, and bronze. The sequence of styles is fixed. Day wear comes first, then what are still called, touchingly, cocktail dresses, and then evening wear. Usually a wedding dress comes last, but Valentino replaced it with a long red chiffon sheath. As the models come out, almost everyone in the room begins one task of translation or another. The press has the simple job of translating the descriptions of the clothes, which are written in fashionese, into ordinary language. Valentino's program was relatively taciturn compared to most. Lacroix, for example, later in the week showed a " 'cold dawn' shot razimir spiral sheath dress with 'apricot' and 'melon' kick pleat"). Still, even Valentino's "Mordoré silk laminated ottoman pinstriped pantsuit, gold lace polo T-shirt, black cashmere shawl bordered in gold lace" became, in the margin of one journalist's program, "beige slacks." The garment industry people are looking for something—a range of colors, a shape, a new line—that they can translate from cashmere and laminated ottoman into cottons and synthetics and sell. They sketch shapes, which to the unpracticed eye all look more or less the same. A tight bodice with a big skirt represents evening wear; a short, tight jacket with big pleated flowing pants stands in for day wear. The few unattached, noncommercial, nonbuying spectators in the room are waiting for what they call a couture moment—a moment, the newcomer is assured, that is roughly equivalent to the moment in opera when the clouds of shlock lift and something crazily artificial becomes transporting.

Only the top fashion editors—at whom all the expense is in a way directed—cannot sketch or make notes, for fear of seeming rude. They leave that to their underlings and try to look interested and amused as each costume passes by. A haute couture *défilé* is an oddly heart-lifting occasion, inflected with hope. The fashion editors are hoping that one of the models' dresses will give them a point, a theme, something to write about. The fashion merchants are hoping that one of the models' dresses, suitably adapted, will make them a fortune. The aficionados are hoping that one of the models' dresses will supply a couture moment. The photographers are hoping that one of the models' dresses will fall off. The press scribbles. The photographers hoot. The ladies fan.

|||

Most of the collections are shown either in the ballroom of the Hôtel InterContinental, which is long and narrow and mock grand siècle, or, like the Valentino show, in the ballroom of the Grand Hôtel, which is high and circular and Second Empire. On Sunday afternoon, though, every fashionable person has to find a taxi or get a lift all the way out to the periphery of Paris, where John Galliano is showing his fall collection for Givenchy at the Stade Français—the old French indoor sports arena. What no one at Givenchy has considered, though, is that holding the show in a stadium means holding the waiting period before the show outside the stadium—in the open air, where few fashionable people are inclined to spend a lot of the day and, as it happens on this Sunday, in a steady Paris drizzle too.

Things get ugly fast. "It is insupportable!" one distinguished-looking dowager is crying as the rain pelts her perfectly constructed face. "I have been a Givenchy client for decades, and now I am being made to stand outside, exposed to the wind, naked to the rain!"

"In the rain! *In the rain!*" the lady next to her cries out, and she goes on, "I too have been a client for a period of time." She resists saying "decades," despite its obvious pathetic force; she is a little younger than the first lady. "The thing is insupportable."

"No! It is worse! It is a scandal!" the first lady cries, definitively. *Insupportable* is a bitter word in French, but *scandal* is a fighting one. Even the Givenchy guards at the chain-link gate, in their double-breasted jackets, are beginning to get uneasy. When the crowd gathered outside the Bastille, the trouble began after some old lady said the thing was a scandal.

At this point the fashion editor André Leon Talley comes up, pushing people aside on his way to the ritual "No, you see, *I've* been invited. What! You mean these people have too?" moment. André Leon Talley is a big guy, and for a second or two it seems likely that the guards are going to let him in. This makes the dowagers, standing behind me, plain crazy, and they charge, blind to the consequences. We are storming the Givenchy gates when the guards just give way: They open the gate and let everyone walk across the lawn toward the stadium. We file in, feeling vindicated, and take our seats. At least thirty more minutes pass before anything happens.

The Givenchy show, appropriately, takes as its subject the ever-popular fashion themes of decapitation and mass murder. Inside the stadium Galliano has constructed a Fragonard-like forest of feathery trees and dark ferns. Then, instead of sending the models one by one down a runway, he sends them out in groups, to wander around the artificial forest. The setting is meant to recall eighteenth-century French aristocratic life, and the dresses what became of it. The dress worn by Inès de la Fressange, for instance, is frankly described as an "ivory lace Empire Trench with blood pre-guillotine velvet sash." All the girls are meant to look as if they were on their way to the tumbrels, and in fact the Revolutionary-era Empire dresses, with their long, columnar lines and soft, clinging bodices, in beaded ivories and reds and champagnes and olives and emeralds, *are* quite unreal in their loveliness. They are by far the most memorable "pure" design of the week and, toned down and deblooded, the obvious tip to become this autumn's look.

|||

Haute couture, everyone says, no longer has much to do with what normal women normally wear. The besetting sin of haute couture, though, is not unreality but corniness: not that it looks like things no women would actually wear but that it looks exactly like what your aunt Ida *always* wears "for best"—that shiny black thing, say, covered with sequins and accompanied by a little shoulder-hugging jacket.

This is a thought that occurs on Monday afternoon, at the Ungaro show—a collection of pantsuits and long dresses so standard and uneventful that it gives you a lot of time to think. There is a reason, you realize, that even women who could afford to do not wear what the models in Ungaro are wearing: dresses of floor-length flowing lace. The reason is that fancy clothes look fancy, and fanciness now looks primitive. So many of the clothes, in their elaborately ostentatious materials, just seem regressive, overrich, brutally obvious. In feeling, they date back to a time when a complicated display of expensive materials was meant to be crushing evidence of wealth. Now wealth, wanting to crush, likes subtler evidence; that's why more wealthy women buy Brice Marden squares than haute couture evening clothes.

Ungaro, though, has intelligently taken his show off the runway too and put it on the floor—in principle, so that you can see the detail work on the clothes, but with the side effect that you can also see a lot of the models inside them. None of the big-name girls are here—not Linda or Naomi or Claudia—but it is the B, or no-name, models who are the most thrilling to look at. This is partly because the name models are phoning it in; Linda Evangelista, at the Givenchy show, had exactly the smug "I don't have to do this for a living anymore" look that Shecky Greene and Buddy Hackett used to have when they "dropped in" on Merv Griffin. The B list models, on the other hand, *work:* They throw out their hips, they flirt with their eyes, and when the photographers call out to them to smolder, they smolder. A great deal of time is spent—by regular guys anyway—explaining to themselves why the haute couture models are not really as desperately beautiful as you might think when they are even more beautiful than you can imagine. The trick—or, to put it another way, the consolation—is that their beauty has become so familiar that it is not so much a commodity as a commonplace. Looking at Kate Moss modeling Givenchy, you don't think, There's a heartbreakingly beautiful girl. Instead you just think, There's Kate Moss. The projected fantasy bangs up not against her inaccessibility but, paradoxically, against her familiarity. She offers not a limit-less horizon of love and elegance and great clothes but the real-ity of a known life. (You would have to avoid talking about Johnny Depp. You would have to tell her how thin she looks, or, rather—for it is the New Kate—how zaftig.)

But they are perfect! A twelve-year-old American boy who was visiting Paris that week had come equipped with his skateboard, and, to his shock, discovered in Paris not a skateboard hell but a paradise of broad, flat avenues and, at the place du Trocadéro, vast, flat concrete plazas. "How do you find Paris?" he was asked.

His eyes went round and reverent.

"*Smooth*," he said.

I find the models smooth too.

One new girl in particular is so perfectly beautiful that she seems a composite of various imaginary smoothnesses. I later learn that her name is Honor Fraser, that she is English, and that she is being tipped by the fancy as the Next Great Model; she will be Miss England in next year's Pirelli calendar. I feel like a novice horseplayer who has just picked the Kentucky Derby winner.

When the shows were over, I spoke with her about what it is like to be on the runway, instead of watching what happens there. She turned out to be a poised student of her own craft. "I love modeling couture," she said, with a passionate eagerness. "It's the only pure expression in fashion—the one part of the fashionable world where there are no commercial compromises at all. There's something terribly moving about being an element of it—being its vehicle. The purity and the exactitude that the designers devote to every tiny detail of your clothing and acces-sories, as though they were working from some image deep in their minds, which they're trying to approximate with you, the way people exhaust themselves in pursuit of an ideal—it's really very moving. It's quite extraordinary to be backstage, being made up for two hours, being transformed from who you are into this ideal of beauty that the designer keeps in the back of his mind.

"I love couture modeling too, because you have such a pure feeling of control and power when you're out there. For a tiny period of time—three or four seconds—you have the chance to hold the entire room. This may seem like a strange comparison, but I'm fascinated by comedy, and I imagine that modeling couture must feel very much like being a comedian; it's just you out there, having to win over an audience, with nothing except yourself and your attitude to do it. And then I, for one, find the clothes so lovely—those Valentino colors that aren't quite colors and yet register as though they were. I feel lucky to have been a part of it." I had never before come across someone who was articulate and knowing about her craft, was big enough to start at power forward, and looked great in a black velvet military coat with rhinestone buttons, black satin trousers, and a black silk top embroidered with black jet. (She had been wearing that, for Valentino, the first time I saw her.)

|||

Tell about the pathetic collections. A certain number of the collections seem intended to be pathetic. Olivier Lapidus's is my specimen pathetic collection. The house is full, and the B list girls do the modeling, and Olivier, who is the son of the designer Ted, looks like a very nice guy. But it is held at the Carrousel du Louvre, a place designed specially to hold collections—it is big and well lit and clean—which means, naturally, that absolutely nobody wants to show there. Olivier Lapidus comes onstage to point out that his collection is a mixture of past, present, and future and includes the first solar-paneled jacket ever made. He shows it off. You can control the solar panels, turning the heat up or down, and it also has a built-in plug that could *brancher* you right into the Internet, the first haute couture garment equipped to go on-line. The poor model has to take the plug out of the pocket and show it to the audience. Then you hear the theme from *Star Trek*. Nobody knows which way to look.

|||

Tuesday night is Christian Lacroix. The show is held in the ball-room of the Grand Hôtel, and it is by far the most intently at-tended *défilé* I have seen yet; even Mme. Chirac is here. Lacroix is of the moment. I associate his clothes with the tasteless things about the eighties, the Ivana Trump era—clothes to wear for the big settlement. Tonight, when the lights go down, Linda Evange-lista comes out in the ugliest dress I have ever seen. Even the program's words can't disguise its ugliness: "silk-crêpe dress stamped with a mauve-and-ochre-green 'reptile' design." I am settling in for a good long bath of contempt.

But then something happens. First, the music begins to take hold. In most of the collections the music is either generic "so-phisticated" soprano and synthesizer pop—the kind you associ-ate with the singer Sade—or classical chestnuts, like Albinoni and Mozart. Lacroix, though, has had someone (the program credits a Laurent Godard) with an uncanny eclectic ear arrange his music. We begin with the breathless, chimelike sounds of the Swedish group the Cardigans and switch to Joe Jackson and then, without missing a beat, land in a Bellini aria. Lacroix works through his day wear and moves into the cocktail dresses and then the evening wear. In the program he announces that he has been spending all his time lately "with Vermeer." He seems to have taken a wrong turn in the museum, for what you see is Goya: Goya's duchesses, in their mantillas and black satin dresses, but wildly remade, as though for a Balanchine ballet of the life of Goya. There are lots of satins and silks in dark colors—navy blue satin and vermilion satin and black chiffon. The layer-ing is ecclesiastical. For once, the program description actually describes the clothes: a long, lined black crepe sweater-dress tucked up over a crepe underskirt with a fuchsia faille bustle at the back, accented by a pistachio satin knot. The crepuscular colors mute the ostentation, so that it doesn't look like ostentation at all but, rather, like art, like old painting. The music turns to the Beatles' baroque period: the string part from "Eleanor Rigby" and then a long cello and harp version of "For No One." The lovely sad yet modern tunes, the twilight, and the dresses themselves create, against all odds and probabilities, something touching, and even—Honor Fraser's word is right—moving. The dresses aren't really dresses at all; they are little buildings of crepe and silk and taffeta. The girls look out from them, like Spanish ladies looking out from a second-floor window. When a model named Victoria appears in a black satin corset with Elizabethan sleeves of tulle and worn over a deep lavender-blue skirt flecked with black lace—she looks like an actress dressed up as Viola for an impossibly beautiful production of *Twelfth Night*— the audience applauds, genuinely, not politely. When Karen Mulder comes out in a silver lace dress with an iced pearl bodice, I make exclamation points in my program.

It's all too much, and that's where the loveliness—the couture moment—begins. The clothes are extravagant and unreal, but they don't seem camp. They don't seem artificial or out of this world, just symbolic of a common human hope that the world could be something other than it is—younger and more musical and less exhausting and better lit. It proposes that the little moments of seduction on which, when we look back, so much of our life depends could unfold as *formally* as they deserve to, and all dressed up. It is as if we were wishing that the rituals of sex, those moments of painful sizing up, which begin with the thought That's a nice dress, could pass by more consequentially, slowly—love walking down a runway instead of just meeting you outside the movie theater.

Couture is a romantic cartoon. It's a caricature of the romantic impulse, with a cartoon's exaggerations but a cartoon's energy and lighthearted poetry too. The thing you feel in a couture moment isn't "What a wonderful dress" or, as you do with higher kinds of art, "What a good place the world is," but, more simply,

"I'm in love." The point of haute couture may be any one of a hundred things, ninety-nine of them sordid or silly, but its subject is women wearing clothes and all the emotion that rises from women wearing clothes. Offering romance in cartoon form, couture helps preserve the habit of romance. The best moments at Lacroix or Givenchy, far from being giddy or empty, were familiar and held out the promise of the beginning of a whole familiar cycle. Soon the fantasies, translated, will become purchases—This Fall's Dresses—and these will become photographs, the kind you look at five years later (God, that dress is so mid-nineties!) to find that they have become a little piece of your time, a peg to hang a good memory on ("Remember that kind of satiny Lacroix knockoff thing you had? You looked great in that"). The sequence, one of the last romantic sequences we can count on, starts in these hotels; that they happen to be places where rich ladies cool themselves off in the cold seems a small price to pay to keep that emotion in circulation.

The emotion passes quickly, of course. In a minute Love walks back up the runway, changes into her jeans and T-shirt, and is on the phone to her agent. Still dazed by Lacroix, I stumbled across one beauty outside the hotel with her cell phone clutched in her hand. I heard her mutter, firmly, "I know I said I'd do it, but I can't. It's only Tuesday, and already I've got taffeta coming out my ass."

|||

Yves Saint Laurent, on Wednesday morning, is the last important collection, and the most "classic." Here, for once, is a really well-organized show, where everybody slips inside on time. Lacroix is the haunt of the new Gaullist French government establishment; Saint Laurent is still the favorite of the old Socialist aristocracy, and they all turn out. Jack Lang, the former culture minister, is here, looking as though he owned the place. (The Socialists loved Saint Laurent because his clothes promised the pleasures of modernity without the sacrifices of modernism; that was the Mitterrand dream.) Saint Laurent just shows Saint Laurent, beautiful clothes that he could have shown in 1980 or 1990 just as well. The music is standard opera arias. Everything gets a hand.

The big news for the photographers is that Claudia Schiffer has come to YSL, having been snubbed by Karl Lagerfeld at Chanel, and she gets the first-desk position. Claudia, though, is not what you would call a team player. While the other models only occasionally respond to the photographers' pleas for more, Claudia stands at the end of the runway for what seems like ten minutes at a time, making love to every camera in sight. The other girls, held up at the head of the runway and waiting for her to get through, give her exactly the look you see on the face of an impatient commuter at the Holland Tunnel who is stuck in the exact change lane behind a woman who has entered it on a hunch.

Then the blond, Botticelli-faced Karen Mulder comes out in the costume that every photographer has been dreaming of for years: *robe de soir courte de mousseline et satin noir*—a sheer dark silk nightgown that, for one reason or another, provides an undergarment below but not above. Karen holds one fingertip precisely in front of each breast, demurely, as she walks down the runway. The photographers go crazy. "Karen! Karen!" they moan. "*Give* us something." Karen smiles. Nothing doing. She walks right to the end of the runway—right into the heart of the photographers' lair—smiling, keeping her fingertips in place, not embarrassed but not giving anything away, either, and then she walks right back. The photographers groan, in disbelieving unison, as she disappears. You could have heard them out on the place Vendôme. "There was a fortune in it for all of us," one of them says mournfully. I notice Claudia, on her way in, giving Karen a look. You have the feeling that Claudia would have dropped her hands, pulled off the gown, and jumped off the runway to autograph the negatives.

Afterward, in the Saint Laurent dressing room, I see that, while every other outfit, on every other girl's card, includes three or four accessories, cover-ups, or undergarments, the *robe de soir,* listed on Karen Mulder's card, is, by design or mistake, all by itself—nothing to help her out at all. For the first time all week, someone had left a fashionable vacuum. She had filled it with her fingertips.

The Crisis in French Cooking

Nine o'clock on a Friday morning, and David Angelot, the *commis* at the restaurant Arpège, on the rue de Varenne, has begun to braise tomatoes for dessert. The *tomate confite farcie aux douze saveurs* is one of the few dishes in the Michelin red guide whose place on the menu has to be clarified with a parenthesis (*dessert*), indicating that though it sounds like a veggie, it eats like a sweet. It is a specialty of the kitchen of the great chef Alain Passard, which a lot of people think is the best and most poetic in Paris, and probably all France; it requires a hair-raising amount of work by the *commis,* the kitchen cabin boy; and many people who care about French cooking believe that it is a kind of hopeful portent, a sign that the creative superiority of French cooking may yet be extended indefinitely. Normally a braised tomato becomes tomato sauce. ("The limitations of this insight," one of Passard's admirers has noted gravely, "describe the limitations of Italian cuisine.") To make a tomato get sweeter without falling apart not only is technically demanding but demonstrates, with a stubborn, sublime logic, an extremely abstract botanical point. Tomatoes are not vegetables; they are fruit.

For David, who may not see M. Passard all day long, they are work. David, who is eighteen and who studied cooking at a government school just outside Lyons, cuts the tomatoes open (about fifty of them, from Morocco, in the winter), scoops them out, and makes a *farce,* a stuffing of finely chopped orange and lemon zest, sugar, ginger, mint, pistachios, star anise, cloves; then he makes a big pot of vanilla-scented caramel and braises the stuffed tomatoes in it, beating the caramel around the tomatoes vigorously for forty-five minutes without actually touching them. The tomato is a fruit and can be treated like one, but it helps to beat a lot of caramel into its body, to underline the point.

While he works, he thinks about his girlfriend (who is also a cook, and with whom he lives in an apartment in north Paris), his future, and his desire to visit Japan someday. He works in a tiny basement room in the small, two-story space of the kitchen, and he shares that room with another, more experienced assistant, Guilhem, who spends his mornings making bread. (All the bread at Arpège is made by hand.) Guilhem, while he works, thinks of going back to Washington—he calls it D.C.—where he has been before, where there is a constant demand for good French food, and where he has an offer to work in a French bakery. If David's job at Arpège embodies one of the principles of high French cooking—the gift of making things far more original than anyone can imagine—Guilhem's embodies the opposite but complementary principle: the necessity of making things much better than anybody needs. This morning he will make three kinds of bread: a sourdough raisin and nut loaf; trays of beautiful long white rolls; and a rough, round peasant bread. All the bread will be sliced and placed in baskets to be presented upstairs in the dining room, and then mostly pushed around absentmindedly on the plates of people who are looking at their menus and deciding what they really want to eat. This knowledge makes Guilhem a little bitter. He thinks about D.C.

In the main kitchen, a short flight up, Pascal Barbot, the sous-chef, is keeping things under control. The atmosphere there, with eleven serious short men in white uniforms going about intricate tasks in a cramped space, does not so much resemble the bridge of a nuclear submarine in an action movie as it does the bridge of a nuclear submarine in an action movie after it has been taken over by the Euroterrorists led by Alan Rickman: that kind of intensity, scared purposefulness, quickness, and heavy, whispered French. The kitchen is white and silver, with a few well-scrubbed copper pots hanging high up—not like the lacquered copper you see in rusticated, beam-heavy restaurant interiors but dull and scrubbed and penny-colored. The richest colors in the kitchen are those of French produce, which is always several glazes darker than American: The birds (chickens, pigeons, quail) are yellow and veined with deep violet, instead of the American white and rose. The assistant chefs start at nine o'clock and will remain at their *stages* until one o'clock the next morning. When the service begins, around twelve-thirty, they will experience an almost unendurable din, which, after a few days of work, they learn to break down into three or four distinct sounds: the *thwonk* of metal in water hitting the sides of a sink as a pot is washed by one of the Malian *plongeurs*; the higher, harsh *clank* of one clean saucepan being placed on another; the surprisingly tinny, machine-gun *rat-a-tat* of a wire whisk in a copper pot; and the crashing, the-tent-just-fell-down-on-your-head sound of hot soiled pans being thrown down onto tile to be washed again. (In a good kitchen the pans are constantly being recycled by the *plongeurs*.)

The kitchen crew includes three Americans. They have worked mostly at California and New York restaurants of the kind that one of them describes as "grill and garnish joints." They are all converts to Passardism. There is never anything entirely new in cooking, but Passard's technique is not like anybody else's. Instead of browning something over high heat in a saucepan and then roasting it in an oven, in the old French manner, or grilling it quickly over charcoal, in the new American one, Passard cooks his birds and joints *sur la plaque*: right on the stove, over extremely low heat in big braising pans, sometimes slow-cooking a baby *gigot* or a milk-fed pig in a pot for four or five hours on a bed of sweet onions and butter. "He's just *sweating* those babies," one of the Americans marvels under his breath, looking at the joints on the stoves. "Makes them cook themselves in their own fat. It's like he does everything but make them pluck their own feathers and jump into the pan. Fucking genius."

Downstairs, another of the Americans is slicing butter and teasing Guilhem about his D.C. plans. "Look at this butter," he says to himself. "That's not fucking Land o'Lakes." He turns to Guilhem. "Hey, forget about D.C.," he says. "It's cold. There are no women. Where you want to go is California. That's the promised land. Man, that's a place where you can cook *and* have a life."

Guilhem looks genuinely startled and turns to speak. "You can?" he says, softly at first, and then louder, calling out to the back of the American cook as he races up the stairs with the butter pats for the dining room. "You *can*?"

|||

Most people who love Paris love it because the first time they came they ate something better than they had ever eaten before, and kept coming back to eat it again. My first night in Paris, twenty-five years ago, I ate dinner with my enormous family in a little corner brasserie somewhere down on the unfashionable fringes of the Sixteenth Arrondissement. We were on the cut-rate American academic version of the grand tour, and we had been in London for the previous two days, where we had eaten *steamed* hamburgers and fish-and-chips in which the batter seemed to be snubbing the fish inside it as if they had never been properly introduced. On that first night in Paris we arrived late on the train, checked into a cheap hotel, and went to eat (party of eight—no, party of nine, one of my sisters having brought along a boyfriend), without much hope, at the restaurant at the corner, called something like Le Bar-B-Que. The prix-fixe menu was fifteen francs, about three dollars then. I ordered a salad Niçoise, trout baked in foil, and a cassis sorbet. It was so much better than anything I had ever eaten that I nearly wept. (My mother, I am compelled at gunpoint to add, made food like that all the time too, but a mother's cooking is a current of life, not an episode of taste.) My feelings at Le Bar-B-Que were a bit like those of Stendhal, I think it was, the first time he went to a brothel: I knew that it could be done, but I didn't know there was a place on any corner where you could walk in, pay three dollars, and get it.

That first meal in Paris was for a long time one of the few completely reliable pleasures for an American in Europe. "It was the green beans," a hardened New Yorker recalled not long ago, remembering his first meal in Paris, back in the late forties. "The green beans were like nothing I had ever known," he went on. He sat suddenly bolt upright, his eyes alight with memory.

Now, though, for the first time in several hundred years, a lot of people who live in France are worried about French cooking, and so are a lot of people who don't. The French themselves are, or claim to be, worried mostly about the high end—the end that is crowded into the Passard kitchen—and the low end. The word *crise* in connection with cooking appeared in *Le Monde* about a year ago, with the news that a restaurant near Lyons, which had earned three Michelin stars, was about to close. Meanwhile, a number of worrying polls have suggested that the old pyramid of French food, in which the base of plain dishes shared by the population pointed upward to the higher reaches of the *grande cuisine,* is collapsing. Thirty-six percent of the French people polled in one survey thought that you make mayonnaise with whole eggs (you use only yolks), 17 percent thought that you put a *travers de porc* in a pot-au-feu (you use beef), and 7 percent believed that Lucas Carton, the Paris restaurant that for a century has been one of the holiest of holies of haute cuisine, is a name for badly cooked meat. More ominously, fully 71 percent of Frenchmen named the banal *steak-frites* as their favorite *plat*; only people past sixty preferred a *blanquette de veau,* or a *gigot d'agneau,* or even a pot-au-feu, all real French cooking. (The French solution to this has been, inevitably, to create a National Council of Culinary Arts, connected to the Ministry of Culture.)

To an outsider, the real *crise* lies in the middle. That Paris first-night experience seems harder to come by. It is the unforced superiority of the cooking in the ordinary corner bistro—the *prix-fixe ordinaire*—that seems to be passing. This is partly a tribute to the international power of French cooking and to the great catching up that has been going on in the rest of the world for the past quarter century. The new visitor, trying out the trout baked in foil on his first night in Paris, will probably be comparing it with the trout baked in foil back home at, oh, Le Lac de Feu, in Cleveland—or even back home at Chez Alfie, in Leeds, or Matilda Qui Danse, in Adelaide—and the trout back home may just be better: raised wild or caught on the line. Even the cassis sorbet may not be quite as good as the kind he makes at home with his Sorbet-o-matic.

The fear—first unspoken, then whispered, then cautiously enunciated, and now loudly insisted on by certain competitors—is that the muse of cooking has migrated across the ocean to a spot in Berkeley, with occasional trips to New York and, of all places, Great Britain. People in London will even tell you, flatly, that the cooking there now is the best in the world, and they will publish this thought as though it were a statement of fact and as though the steamed hamburger and the stiff fish had been made long ago in another country. Two of the best chefs in the London cooking renaissance said to a reporter not long ago that London, along with Sydney and San Francisco, is one of the capitals of good food and that the food in Paris—"heavy, lazy, lacking in imagination"—is now among the worst in the world.

All this makes a Francophile eating in Paris feel a little like a turn-of-the-century clergyman who has just read Robert Ingersoll: You try to keep the faith, but Doubts keep creeping in. Even the most ardent Paris lover, who once blessed himself at every dinner for having escaped Schrafft's, may now find himself—as he gazes down one more unvarying menu of *boudin noir* and *saumon unilatéral* and *entrecôte bordelaise* and *poulet rôti*, eats one more bland and buttery dish—feeling a slight pang for that Cuban-Vietnamese-California grill on Amsterdam Avenue or wondering whether he might, just possibly, enjoy the New Sardinian Cooking, as featured that week on the cover of *New York*.

I would still rather eat in Paris than anywhere else in the world. The best places in Paris, like the Brasserie Balzar, on the rue des Écoles, don't just feed you well; they make you happy in a way that no other city's restaurants can. (The Balzar is the place that plays Gallant to the more famous Brasserie Lipp's Goofus.) Even in a mediocre Paris restaurant, you are part of the richest commonplace civilization that has ever been created and that extends back visibly to the previous century. In Paris restaurants can actually go into a kind of hibernation for years and awaken in a new generation: Lapérouse, the famous swanky nineteenth-century spot, has, after a long stretch of being overlooked, just come back to life, and is a good place to eat again. Reading Olivier Todd's biography of Camus, you discover that the places where Camus went to dinner in the forties (Aux Charpentiers, Le Petit St. Benoît, Aux Assassins) are places where you can go to dinner tonight. Some of Liebling's joints are still in business too: the Beaux-Arts, the Pierre à la Place Gaillon, the Closerie des Lilas.

These continuities suggest that a strong allegiance to the past acts as a drag on the present. But, after several months of pains-taking, tie-staining research, I think that the real problem lies in the French genius for laying the intellectual foundation for a rev-olution that takes place somewhere else. With movies (Méliès and the Lumière brothers invented the form and then couldn't build the industry), with airplanes, and now even with cooking, France has again and again made the first breakthrough and then got stalled. All the elements of the new cooking, as it exists today in America and in London—the openness to new techniques, the suspicion of the overelaborate, the love of surprising juxtapo-sitions—were invented in Paris long before they emigrated to London and New York and Berkeley. But in France they never coalesced into something entirely new. The Enlightenment took place here, and the Revolution worked out better somewhere else.

|||

The early seventies, when I was first in France, were, I realize now, a kind of Indian summer of French haute cuisine, the last exhalation of a tradition that had been in place for several hun-dred years. The atmosphere of French cooking was everywhere in Paris then: thick smells and posted purple mimeographed menus; the sounds of cutlery on tables and the jowly look of pro-fessional eaters emerging blinking into the light at four o'clock.

The standard, practical account of the superiority of French cooking was that it had been established in the sixteenth cen-tury, when Catherine de' Medici brought Italian cooks, then the best in the world, to Paris. It was not until after the French Rev-olution, though, when the breakup of the great aristocratic houses sent chefs out onto the street looking for someone to feed, that the style of French cooking went public. The most fa-mous and influential figure of this period—the first great chef in European history—was Antonin Carême, who worked, by turns, for Talleyrand, the future George IV, Czar Alexander I, and the

Baroness de Rothschild. He invented "presentation." His cooking looked a lot like architecture, with the dishes fitted into vast, beautiful neoclassical structures.

The unique superiority of French cooking for the next hundred years depended on the invention of the cooking associated with the name Auguste Escoffier. Escoffier's formula for food was in essence the same as Jasper Johns's formula for dada art: Take something; do something to it; then do something else to it. It was cooking that rested, above all, on the idea of the master sauce: A lump of protein was cooked in a pan, and what was left behind in the pan was "deglazed" with wine or stock, ornamented with butter or cream, and then poured back over the lump of protein. Escoffier was largely the creature of courtiers and aristocratic patrons; the great hoteliers of Europe, particularly César Ritz, sealed in place the master sauce approach that remains the unchallenged basis of haute cuisine.

It was also an article of faith, dating, perhaps, to Alexandre Dumas *père*'s famous *Grand Dictionnaire de Cuisine,* that the cooking of Carême and Escoffier had evolved from a set of provincial folk techniques. At the heart of French food lay the pot-au-feu, the bouillon pot that every peasant wife was supposed to keep on her hearth, and into which, according to legend, she threw whatever she had, to stew for the day's meal. French classic cooking was French provincial cooking gone to town.

|||

I heard another, more weirdly philosophical account of this history from a professor named Eugenio Donato, who was the most passionately intellectual eater I have ever known. Armenian-Italian, reared in Egypt and educated in France, he spoke five languages, each with a nearly opaque Akim Tamiroff accent. ("It could have been worse," he said to me once, expertly removing one mussel with the shell of another as we ate *moules marinières* somewhere on the place de la Sorbonne. "I had a friend whose parents were ardent Esperantists. He spoke five languages, each with an impenetrable Esperanto accent.") Eugenio was a literary critic whom we would now call a poststructuralist, though he called what he did philosophical criticism.

Most of the time he wandered from one American university to another—the Johnny Appleseed or Typhoid Mary of deconstruction, depending on your point of view. He had a deeply tragic personal life, though, and I think that his happiest hours were spent in Paris, eating and thinking and talking. His favorite subject was French food, and his favorite theory was that "French cooking" was foreign to France, not something that had percolated up from the old pot-au-feu but something that had been invented by fanatics at the top, as a series of powerful "metaphors"—ideas about France and Frenchness—that had then moved downward to organize the menus and, retrospectively, colonize the past. "The idea of the French chef precedes French cooking" was how he put it. Cooking for him was a form of writing—Carême and Escoffier had earned their reputations by publishing cookbooks—with literature's ability to make something up and then pretend it had been there all along.

The invention of the French restaurant, Eugenio believed, depended largely on what every assistant professor would now call an "essentialized" idea of France. One proof of this was that if the best French restaurants tended to be in Paris, the most "typical" ones tended to be in New York. Yet the more abstract and self-enclosed haute cuisine became, the more inclined its lovers were to pretend that it was a folk art, risen from the French earth unbidden. For Eugenio, the key date in this masquerade was 1855, when the wines of Médoc were classified into the famous five growths in which they remain today. "The form of metropolitan rationalization being extended to the provincial earth, *in the guise of the reflection of an order locked in the earth itself,*" he announced once, bringing his fist down on the tablecloth. He was a big man, who looked uncannily like John Madden, the football coach.

On that occasion we were eating lunch in one of the heavy, dark, smoky Lyons places that were popular in Paris then. (There is always one provincial region singled out for favor in Paris at any moment—*privileged* would have been Eugenio's word. Then it was Burgundy; now it is the southwest. This fact was grist for his thesis that the countryside was made in the city.) The restaurant was, I think, someplace over in the Seventh; it may have been Pantagruel or La Bourgogne. At lunch, in those days, Eugenio would usually begin with twelve escargots in Chablis, then go on to something like a *filet aux moelles*—a filet with bone marrow and Madeira sauce—and end, whenever he could, with a mille-feuille.

The food in those places wasn't so much "rich" as deep, dense. Each *plat* arrived looking mellow and varnished, like an old violin. Each mouthful registered like a fat organ chord in a tall church, hitting you hard and then echoing around the room: There's the bass note (the beef), there's the middle note (the marrow), and there's the treble (the Madeira in the sauce).

It couldn't last. "We have landed in the moment when the metaphors begin to devour themselves, the moment of rhetorical self-annihilation," Eugenio once said cheerfully. This meant that the food had become so rich as to be practically inedible. A recipe from the restaurant Lucas Carton that I found among a collection of menus of the time that Eugenio bequeathed to me suggests the problem. The recipe is for a *timbale des homards*. You take three lobsters, season them with salt and pepper and a little curry, sauté them in a light *mirepoix*—a mixture of chopped onions and carrots—and then simmer them with cognac, port, double cream, and fish stock for twenty minutes. Then you take out the lobsters and, keeping them warm, reduce the cooking liquid and add two egg yolks and 150 grams of sweet butter. Metaphors like that can kill you.

Something had to give, and it did. The "nouvelle cuisine" that replaced the old style has by now been reduced to a set of clichés and become a licensed subject of satire: the tiny portion on the big oval plate; the raspberry-vinegar infusion; the kiwi. This makes it difficult to remember how fundamental a revolution it worked in the way people cooked. At the same moment in the early seventies, a handful of new chefs—Michel Guérard, Paul Bocuse, Alain Senderens—began to question the do-something-to-it-then-do-something-else-to-it basis of the classic cooking. They emphasized, instead, fresh ingredients, simple treatment, an openness to Oriental techniques and spices, and a general reformist air of lightness and airiness.

The new chefs had little places all around Paris, in the outlying arrondissements, where, before, no one would have traveled for a first-rate meal. Michel Guérard was at Le Pot-au-Feu, way out in Asnières; Alain Dutournier, a little later, settled his first restaurant, Au Trou Gascon, in the extremely unfashionable Twelfth. In the sad, sedate Seventh Arrondissement, Alain Senderens opened Archestrate, first in a little space on the rue de l'Exposition, in the shadow of the Eiffel Tower, and then on the rue de Varenne.

From the beginning, the new cooking divided into two styles, into what Eugenio identified as "two rhetorics," a rhetoric of *terroir* and a rhetoric of *épices*—soil and spice. The rhetoric of the *terroir* emphasized the allegiance of new cooking to French soil; the rhetoric of the *épices* emphasized its openness to the world beyond the hexagon. The soil boys wanted to return French cooking to its roots in the regions; the spice boys wanted to take it forward to the new regions of *outre-mer*. Even as the new cooking tried to look outward, it had to reassure its audience (and itself) that it was really looking inward.

On the surface the beautiful orderly pattern continues. Alain Senderens is now in Michel Comby's place at Lucas Carton and has replaced the *timbale des homards* cooking with his own style.

Senderens's rue de Varenne Archestrate is now occupied by Alain Passard, the Senderens of his generation, while the original Archestrate is occupied by a talented young chef and his wife, just starting out, who have named the restaurant after their little girl, La Maison de Cosima.

But twenty-five years later the great leap forward seems to have stalled. A large part of the *crise* is economic: A hundred-dollar lunch is a splurge; a four-hundred-dollar lunch a moral dubiety. Worse, because of the expense, the cooking at the top places in Paris is no longer a higher extension of a commonplace civilization. It is just three-star cooking, a thing unto itself, like grand opera in the age of the microphone. Like grand opera, it is something that will soon need a subsidy to survive; the kitchen at Arpège depends on regular infusions of range-struck Americans to fill the space left by the French kids who no longer want to work eighteen-hour days for very little money while they train.

And it is like grand opera in this also: You can get too much of it, easily. It is, truth be told, often a challenge to eat—a happy challenge, and sometimes a welcome one, but a challenge nonetheless. It is just too rich, and there is just too much. The new cooking in France has become a version of the old.

At Lucas Carton you begin with, say, a plate of vegetables so young they seem dewy, beautifully done, but so bathed in butter and transformed that they are no longer particularly vegetal, and then you move on to the new lobster dish that has taken the place of the old one. Where the old lobsters were done in a cow-shedful of cream, the new lobsters are done, *épicé* style, with Madagascar vanilla bean. This is delicious, with the natural sugar of the lobster revealing the vanilla as a spice—although, for an American, the custard-colored sauce, dotted with specks of black vanilla, disconcertingly calls to mind melted lunchroom ice cream. For dessert, you might have a roasted pineapple, which is done on the same principles on which Passard's tomatoes are braised: It ends up encrusted in caramel. This is delicious too, though intensely sweet. Lunch at Lucas these days can fairly be called Napoleonic or Empire; the references to the revolutionary principles are there, but finally it's in thrall to the same old aristocratic values.

Lucas is hardly representative, but even at the lesser, less ambitious places the cooking seems stuck in a rut: a chunk of boned protein, a reduced sauce; maybe a fruit complement, to establish its "inventive" bona fides; and a puree. The style has become formulaic: a disk of meat, a disk of complement, a sauce on top. The new cooking seems to have produced less a new freedom than a revived orthodoxy—a new essentialized form of French cooking, which seems less pleasing, and certainly a lot less "modern," than the cooking that evolved at the same time from the French new cooking in other countries. The hold of the master sauté pan, and the master sauce, and the thing-in-the-middle-of-the-plate is still intact.

|||

Thinking it over, I suspect that Eugenio put his finger on the problem with the new cooking in France when it first appeared. "A revolution can sweep clean," he said, "but a reformation points forward and backward at the same time." The new cooking was, as Eugenio said, a reformation, not a revolution; it worked within the same system of Michelin stars and fifteen-man kitchens and wealthy clients that the old cooking did. It didn't make a new audience; it tried to appropriate the old one.

In America—and in England too, where the only thing you wanted to do with the national culinary tradition was lose it—the division between soil and spice wasn't a problem. You could first create the recipes and then put the ingredients in the earth yourself. The American cooks who have followed in Alice Waters's pathmaking footsteps at Chez Panisse, in Berkeley—the generation whom a lot of people think of as the children of M.F.K. Fisher—created a freewheeling, eclectic cosmopolitan cuisine: a risotto preceding a stir-fry leading to a *sabayon*. Then they went out and persuaded the local farmers to grow the things they needed.

In France the soil boys won easily. Some of what they stood for is positive and even inspiring: The *terroir* movement has a green, organic, earth-conscious element that is very good news. The *marché biologique* every Sunday morning on the boulevard Raspail has become one of the weekly Parisian wonders, full of ugly, honest fruit and rough, tasty country meat. And it is rare for any restaurant in Paris to succeed now without presenting itself as a "regional" spot—a southwest, or Provençal, or Savoyard place. (Even at the exquisite Grand Véfour, at the Palais Royal, the most beautiful restaurant in the world and a cathedral of the cosmopolitan tradition, it is thought necessary to parade around a plate of the cheeses of the chef's native Savoy.)

Yet the insistence on national, or local, tradition—on truth to *terroir*—can give even to the best new Paris restaurants a predictability that the good new places in London and New York don't share. The French, who invented the tradition of taking things over and then insisting that they were yours all along, are now shy about doing it. The cooking at a French restaurant must now, for the first time, be French. This tendency came to a head last spring, when a group of important French chefs actually issued a manifesto protesting the spread of exotic food combinations and alien spices in French cooking and calling for a return to the *terroir*.

Peter Hoffman, the owner and chef of the influential Savoy in New York, is one of those American chefs who went to France in the early eighties, were dazzled, and now find that the light has dimmed. He likes to tell about his most recent dinner at the three-star restaurant L'Ambroisie, on the place des Vosges. "We went to L'Ambroisie and had a classic French dish: hare with blood sauce. It was fabulous, everything you want rabbit with blood to be. But then I got talked into ordering one of the chef's specialties, a mille-feuille of langoustines with curry, and it was infuriating. It was a French dish with powder. It was such an insular approach, as though nobody understood that curry isn't a powder that you apply cosmetically. Nobody had read Madhur Jaffrey, or really understood that curry isn't just a spice you shake but a whole technique of cooking you have to understand."

As the writer Catharine Reynolds points out, the new cooking in America and England alike is really Mediterranean cooking, inspired by Italy, Tunisia, and Greece. It suits the fat-allergic modern palate better than the old butter and cream cooking of the north. France, which has a big window south, ought to be open to its influence yet remains resistant. The real national dish of the French right now—the cheap, available food—is couscous. But North African cooking remains segregated in couscous parlors and has not been brought into the main current. A fossilized metropolitan tradition should have been replaced by a modernized metropolitan tradition, yet what took its place was sentimental nationalism.

It was the invasion of American fast food, as much as anything, that made the French turn back to their own tradition and, for the first time, see it as something in need of self-conscious protection. Looking at America, the French don't see the children of M.F.K. Fisher; they just see the flood tides of McDonald's, which, understandably, strike fear into their hearts. The bistro became an endangered species. To make still one more *blanquette de veau* suddenly became not a habit of commonplace civilization but a form of self-defense.

|||

Waverley Root once divided all Gaul into three fats—lard, olive oil, and butter—and said that they determined the shape of French cooking. That you might be able to cook without putting any fat in the pan at all was an unthinkable notion. The charcoal grill, the brick oven, and all the other nonfat ways of cooking now seem normal everywhere except in France. People who look at cooking more practically than philosophically think that that technical lag is the heart of the problem.

"It's deglaze or die" is how Alexandra Guarnaschelli, an American cook in Paris, puts it. The master sauce approach remains the basis of French cooking, whereas elsewhere it has been overthrown by the grill. The pan and the pot have always been the basic utensils of French cooking—just what was there—in the same way that the grill was the primary element of American vernacular backyard cooking. For Americans, grilled food wasn't new but familiar, and good cooking is made up of familiar things done right. As the excellent American chefs Chris Schlesinger and John Willoughby have pointed out, grilling forced an entirely new approach to saucemaking: With no residue to deglaze, the cook had to think in terms of savory complements rather than subtle echoes. Grilling demanded chutney, fruit mustards, spice mixes. Although the French tradition included these things, they weren't part of the vernacular.

Alex has seen some of the predicament at first hand. She is twenty-seven; she arrived in France five years ago and, after training in Burgundy, became a *commis* at Guy Savoy's two-star place in the Seventeenth Arrondissement. Within a couple of years she had worked her way up to fish chef, and a little while later Savoy appointed her second-in-command at his bistro, La Butte Chaillot. (This is like a young Frenchman arriving in New York, all enthusiastic about baseball, and ending up five years later as third baseman for the Yankees.)

The other day, over coffee on the avenue Kléber, Alex, who is from New York (she went to Barnard, Mom's an editor at Scribner's, Dad's a professor), said, "I decided I wanted to chop onions, so I tried the CIA"—the Culinary Institute of America, the MIT of American cooking—"but it was like eighteen thousand a year, *tout compris,* so I decided to go to Burgundy and chop. I started learning the French way, which is half beautiful beyond belief and half 'Please shoot me.' It's by the book. Really, there's a book, and you learn it. There's a system for everything, a way to do it. You can't cut the fish that way, because *ça n'est pas bon*. You can't bone a chicken that way, because *that's* not good. 'We do it the way it's always been done in France.' When I first started at Savoy, there was one old stager who, every time I did something, would just frown and shake his head and say, 'It won't do, it won't do.' Finally, I did *exactly* what he did, and he said, 'Good, now always do it exactly the same way.' So I did. You never get a real attempt to innovate, or to use new flavors. You can change an adjective, but the sentence stays the same.

"Whenever we make a classic sauce, everybody gathers around and *argues* about it. Once we got into a two-hour argument about whether you use chervil as well as tarragon in a true béarnaise. There are certain things these days that I will not do. I will not do mayonnaise or béarnaise. Uh-uh. I don't have time for the postgame analysis.

"Of course, there's that tomato at Passard's place," she went on. "But have you seen the way the poor kid has to work to make it?"

Alex's existence helps to explain why the new cooking went deeper in America than it could in France: In America the cooking revolution was above all a middle-class revolution, even an upper-middle-class revolution. A lot of the people who made the cooking revolution in America were doing it as a second career. At the very least they were doing it after a liberal arts degree; David Angelot started slicing carrots at fifteen. The most mocked of all modern American restaurant manners—the waiter who introduces himself by name—is, on reflection, a sign of something very positive. "I'm Henry, and I'll be your waiter tonight" means, really, "You and I belong to the same social class. Tomorrow night I could be sitting there, and you could be standing here."

The French system of education, unrenovated for a long time, locks people in place. Kids emerge with an impressive respect for learning and erudition, and intimidated by it too. For an American, getting a Ph.D. is a preliminary, before you go someplace else and find your real work, like opening a restaurant. Nobody thinks of changing métiers in France because it's just too hard. In America not only the consumers of the new cooking but, more important, the producers and dealers were college-educated. I once met a pair of American academics who had gone off to live with a flock of goats and make goat cheese. They had named the goats Emily, Virginia, Jessamyn, Willa, and Ursula. It was terrific goat cheese too.

|||

Beyond these reasons—the missing grill, the resurgent nationalism, the educational trap—there may be an even deeper reason for the lull in French cooking. A new book, *L'Amateur de Cuisine,* by an unknown author, Jean-Philippe Derenne, which was published last year, offers an anatomy of French cooking—an effort to organize the materials, forms, and manners of the subject in a systematic way. "This cookbook is a book," the author writes on the first page, and then attempts to create a whole taxonomy of cooking based not on folk tradition or cosmopolitan recipes but on an analysis of plants and animals and the chemistry of what happens when you apply different kinds of heat and cold to them before you eat them. He begins his market section with the minerals (a crisp page and a half) and then passes to the plants (more than a hundred pages) and the animals, divided into those of the earth and the sky and those of fresh and salt water. (Even *"Serpents, Sauriens, Lézards, etc."* get their moment in the sun.) He gives a precise biological description of every imaginable thing there is to eat, then presents an exact analysis of every imaginable method of cooking it and shows how all the glories of cuisine rise out of the limitless intersections of these two forces. It is a vast, eleven-hundred-page volume, comprehensive and radiant; it resembles less a cookbook than a Baroque almanac, offering a timeless, secure, benevolent universe of food. Its subject isn't cooking. It's *plenty*.

Derenne is a modest and gentle scholar, not a cook or a critic or even a gourmand. He is a doctor, the head of the pulmonary department at a Paris hospital. Over lunch one afternoon at Arpège, Derenne, a small, good-natured man, with the open face and happy appetites of a Benedictine monk, said, "The same week that *L'Amateur de Cuisine* came out, I published another book, called *Acute Respiratory Failure of Chronic Obstructive Pulmonary Disease*." That was another thousand pages. This, surely, is a record for total weight by one author published in one week.

Derenne wrote the cookbook in seclusion, in the garden of his little house near Fontainebleau, only to find himself, on its publication, a new lion of the French culinary establishment: the man who wrote the book. He gets reverential, *cher maître*–type letters from Paul Bocuse. Passard himself sees him as a friend. Dr. Derenne doesn't know quite what to make of it all.

"My editor said to me, when I gave him the manuscript, 'Why, you've written the first humanist history of food.' I said, 'No, not humanist. It's a religious book, really.' I was inspired by a history of religion by Mircea Eliade, which attempted the same kind of logical organization, rising upward from the types of religious apparition into the possibilities of organized faith. I've done for cooking what that author did for belief: shown an underlying logic without attempting to make it logical."

He went on to talk about a second volume, which he's just started: "It may be called free cuisine, but really it will be about the rejected cuisine. About everything the world throws out. Shells and guts and leaves—the whole world of the rejected. This is religious too, because religion depends on being able to find the holy in the ordinary. It's putting together things banal in themselves which nonetheless become transformed into something transcendent. You know who else has this quality? Duke Ellington—he simply used what he had."

There was something surprising about Derenne's talk, an expansive, open, embracing ardor that a hundred years ago would have seemed more American than French. It seems possible that the different fates of the new cooking in France and America are a sign of a new relation between the two places.

A century ago Americans used to say that what brought them to Europe was its history. At home, there was "no sovereign, no court . . . no aristocracy . . . nor ivied ruins; no cathedrals," as Henry James's famous list has it. What really brought Americans to the Old World, though, was the allure of power: cultural power, political power, military power—imperial power, as it existed in Europe and only there. What fascinated Whistler and James in the Old World was not its age but the extreme self-consciousness that comes with power, the way that power could be seen to shimmer through manners—the way that what you wore or how you stood (or what you ate) spelled out your place in a complicated and potent social hierarchy.

Now that that power has passed into American—or, anyway, English-speaking—hands, the trappings of power that come from extreme self-consciousness are ours too. Even our cooking—especially our cooking—has become involved with power. Where you stand on, say, the spread of McDonald's is a political issue, just as where you stood on the outdoor café was in France a century ago. Even the smaller issues of the palate count. Most American women define their feminism, at least in part, in terms of their attitude toward the kitchen. A century ago the modern form of that self-consciousness was invented in Paris. The limitlessly complicated relation of what you eat and where you eat it to where you stand in the social order is the subject of, for instance, the first two chapters of Maupassant's *Bel-Ami*. But now food and cooking in France have begun to take at least a small half turn back toward their other role, as sources of nourishment, comfort, cohesion. The role of food as anxious social theater, seen at its crudest in the endless worry in Los Angeles and

New York about power tables—where you sit at Spago, what time you leave the Four Seasons—is diminishing in France. We are the worldly, corrupt ones at the table now, and the Europeans, in this regard at least, are the innocents. Even their philosophers eat for pleasure.

When the *tomate confite,* which David Angelot had been working on since nine o'clock, came out at last, Derenne tasted it. Then he said, "You see, he demonstrates for us what we knew from the first: that the tomato is a fruit. Would you call that arrogance or modesty?"

Not long after that I finally did what I had dreaded doing, though it would have been the practical thing to do all along, which was to go back to that first restaurant and see what it was like now. I walked back and found both the hotel and the restaurant, though both had changed their names—the hotel belonged now to the Best Western chain—and while in memory I had kept them on the same street, they were in fact a street apart. But the exterior of the restaurant was unmistakable; I found it by getting the Eiffel Tower in exactly the same area of my eye as it had occupied when I was fourteen. It was not far from—I am not making this up—the avenue Marcel-Proust. The restaurant is now called the Tournesol, and the less expensive prix fixe is 114 francs, or about twenty dollars. I ate à la carte. I had a little foie gras, sole meunière, and a cassis sorbet.

The food was even better than I had remembered. This proves either that (a) Proust was wrong, and you can always recapture the pleasures of your youth if you just go back to the places where you had them, or (b) there is more good cooking left in Paris than I knew, or (c) I went to the wrong place. Anyway, there's hope.

Barney in Paris

When people ask why Martha and I, not long after the birth of our first child, left New York for Paris, we can usually think of a lot of plausible-sounding reasons. They vary in tone from the high-mindedly agonized (we couldn't endure the malling of our SoHo neighborhood) to the cloyingly whimsical (we wanted to live within walking distance of the Gérard Mulot bakery, on the rue de Seine). The real reason was Barney. We had seen one after another of our friends' children—charming children of parents who parse Greek texts or write long metafictions set in the eighteenth century—sunk dumbly in front of a television set watching a man in a cheap purple dinosaur suit sing doggerel in an adenoidal voice with a chorus of overregimented eight-year-old ham actors. Just a glimpse was enough to scare a prospective parent to death: the garish Jeff Koons colors, the frantic prancing, the cynically appropriated public domain melodies. And, finally, that anthem of coercive affection—"I love you/you love me/we're a happy family"—sung, so incongruously, to the tune of "This Old Man."

The experienced reader will know of course that Barney stands here for the whole of American kiddie video culture. The experienced reader, though, is wrong. We looked forward to introducing Luke to Bugs and Bullwinkle and Bert and Ernie, and even Steve and Norm on *This Old House*. We just couldn't bear the idea of his watching Barney. The only way, we thought, to be sure that he wouldn't was to pack up everything we had and move to another country.

So, Paris. "We want him to grow up someplace where everything he sees is beautiful," we said, and though we realized that the moment our backs were turned our friends' eyes were rolling, we didn't care. We knew that our attempt to insist on a particular set of pleasures for our kid—to impose a childhood on our child—might be silly or inappropriate or even doomed. We couldn't help it, entirely. The romance of your child's childhood may be the last romance you can give up.

In our first week in our new home on the Left Bank, we were awakened early one morning by loud, oddly fugitive organ music; it sounded like a carousel yet seemed to be moving closer. We opened the long French windows, looked out—and there was an honest-to-God organ grinder coming along the street, "La Ronde" playing as he turned the crank on his hand-painted hurdy-gurdy. I found a ten-franc piece and threw it down to the street; Luke applauded; the organ grinder caught it with one hand and cheerily, nattily, tipped his cap. Things looked good.

That first year we went to a lot of circuses; in Paris there are usually six or seven in residence. We saw the Moreno-Bormann family circus, which is a true family circus: When any performer does anything slightly dangerous, the rest of the family stand around the ring calling out "Careful!" under their breaths and averting their eyes. We also saw the Mongolian National Circus, in a little tent pitched at the Arsenal. It consists of six broad-faced, smiling Mongolians, who do circus tricks appropriate to a nomadic scarcity economy—they eat a *little bit* of fire, walk on *one* broken bottle and save the shards—and finish off with an elaborate, pointless thirty-minute trick using a magician's cabinet that must have been left in Mongolia by an American illusionist sometime around 1860. (A Mongolian girl gets in the cabinet; Mongolian circus members slowly slide the swords through the slots; spend twenty minutes removing the swords from the slots; and then the girl gets out.)

We went to a lot of parks and rode a lot of carousels. In the Luxembourg Gardens is a completely unsupervised playground that's run on lines inspired by the last chapter of *Lord of the Flies*. There is a spinning red platter onto which little children are thrown by bigger ones, who whip it around, with the terrified little ones kept from flying off by sheer centripetal force. There is a weird ski lift–style conveyance that kids cling to with their fingers, dangling ten feet in the air over nothing but hard pavement. There are jungle gyms the kids climb on, to be knocked off the top bars by informal gangs of larger kids. There is not a safety belt, a padded surface, or a liability lawyer anywhere to be found. (Twenty years ago my wife and I, on our first date, saw Truffaut's *Small Change.* We loved the sequence in which a child falls out of a sixth-story window and walks away unhurt. In our early Francophile moments we saw this as charming French fantasy. In fact, it was pure cinema verité. Luke attends a weekly gym class for two-year-olds, along with heartbreakingly exquisite little girls named Amandine and Jolie and Neige. The children are routinely sent leaping from high, splintery boards onto low, uncushioned ones.)

At dusk, however, a uniformed surveillant emerges from a windowless shed at the center of the gardens and blows a whistle, and everyone goes home. The child who has his hands around your child's throat lets go, helps him up, dusts off his *tablier,* takes his mother's hand, and trudges toward the gates. The vicious big kids help the terrified small kids off the spinning red platter. The play routine at the gardens explains French history: The restrictive Old Regime, represented by the carousel, leads to the anarchy of the Revolution and the Reign of Terror, represented by the playground; then Napoleon emerges in uniform to blow his whistle and call everybody to order. (Or it could be the occupation, the Fourth Republic, and de Gaulle emerging in uniform.) Between the carousels and the circuses and a wealth of Charlie Chaplin movies, to which Luke developed a deep, sober attachment, we seemed, blessedly, to have skipped right past the *B*'s.

|||

Then, last Christmas, we went back to New York for three days. A friend brought a pile of tapes for a jet-lagged Luke to watch in the bedroom while we had dinner. I should have guessed from the ominous, atypical silence coming from the bedroom that something was off. Scooping up my exhausted little boy at the end of the evening, I noticed that he was looking unusually withdrawn. Then, right there in the backseat of a New York City taxicab, he suddenly looked up and said quietly, "Daddy, I like Barney."

"You like *what*?" I said.

"I like Barney," he said, and he turned over and went to sleep. The next morning we broke down and let him watch the video again—we were pretty jet-lagged too—and that was enough. It was like what they used to tell you about heroin: One taste, and you're hooked for good.

"I want Barney," he would announce early in the morning. He began to *whine* for Barney: "I want Barney, I want Barney." When we got back to Paris (the tapes somehow got into our bags), the need for Barney went right on. It even got worse. We'd be trying to watch one of the long, thoughtful French things that are good for your soul and your French—*Bouillon de Culture* or *Droit d'Auteurs*, or even just the dubbed version of *NYPD Blue* ("Ah, c'est un boulot difficile, ce travail de policier, Inspecteur Sipowicz")—and Luke would appear with a Barney tape. We had fled to Paris to escape our appointment with Barney, and Barney had come to meet us there.

Not wanting to be a bad or unduly coercive parent, I thought, Well, he has a right to his pleasures, but I too have a right—indeed a duty—to tell him what I think of them. We began to have a regular daily exchange.

"Daddy, I *like* Barney," he would say with elaborately feigned nonchalance, coming into my office first thing in the morning.

"Well, I don't like Barney," I would say, frankly.

"You like B.J.?" he would ask, tauntingly. B.J. is one of Barney's even more inane and adenoidal sidekicks.

"I love Ernie and Bert," I would say, trying to put a positive spin on my position. "I love the carousel. I love the circus. I love Charlie Chaplin."

"*I* like Barney," he would begin again, and it would go on.

Naturally it occurred to us that the pro-Barney campaign was a resourceful and in many ways courageous and admirable show of independence on the part of a two-and-a-half-year-old who might otherwise have been smothered by his parents' overbearing enthusiasms. We put up minimal Barney resistance. More tapes arrived from America; more tapes got popped in and played.

We tried to be tolerant, but Barney takes his toll: the braying voice, the crude direction, the inane mummery of the dancing, the witlessness of the writing. Our dreamed-of Parisian life was becoming unendurable. One afternoon around four-thirty I wandered into the bedroom, where the television is. My wife was, uncharacteristically, drinking a glass of red wine. On the little screen Barney was leading all the kids in one more rousing chorus of "I love you/you love me." We finished the bottle of Burgundy together. On the screen Barney sang, and our son moved his lips in time.

|||

What puzzled me of course was why. Loving Barney in Paris was partly a way of teasing his parents, but it was not *simply* a way of teasing his parents; it was too deep, too emotional for that. Nor had Barney yet crossed the ocean, so it wasn't any kind of peer pressure from the French kids he played with in class and in the courtyard every day. In Paris, in fact, almost all the childhood icons are those that have been in place for forty years: stuffy, bourgeois Babar; conniving, witty Astérix and Obélix; and imperturbable Lucky Luke, the Franco-American cowboy in perpetual battle with the four Dalton brothers. Although these characters from time to time appear in cartoons, they remain locked in their little worlds of satire and storytelling. There is no Barney in France, and there is no French Barney. Whatever spell was working on my son, it was entirely, residually American.

There are certain insights that can come to an American only when he is abroad, because only there does the endless ribbon of American television become segmented enough so that you can pay attention to its parts, instead of just being overwhelmed by the relentlessness of its presence. In the middle of the winter I happened to see, during some stray roundup of the year's events on CNN International, a clip of another familiar American figure, his arms around his wife and child, swaying and humming as he watched fireworks going off. Suddenly I got it. The nose; the rocking motion; above all, the squinty-eyed, aw-shucks, just-a-big-lug smile: Barney is Bill Clinton for three-year-olds. Or, rather, Bill Clinton is Barney for adults. He serves the same role for jumpy American liberals that Barney does for their children: He reassures without actually instructing. The physical resemblance alone is eerie. There's the odd combination of *hauteur* and *rondeur* (both are very tall without really being imposing), the perpetually swaying body, the unvarying smile, even the disconcerting chubby thighs—everything but the purple skin. Barney and Bill are not amiable authority figures, like the Friendly Giant and Ronald Reagan. They are, instead, representations of pure need: Wanting to be hugged, they hug.

For the first time, I also understood Clinton hating, of the violent irrational kind that, when I left America, was being prac-

ticed on the editorial page of the *Times* and in the *New Republic*
and had always seemed incomprehensible, directed, as it was, at
so anodyne a character. Suddenly I saw that the psychology of
the Clinton hater was exactly that of the Barney basher; the ob-
jections were not moral but peevishly aesthetic. Like Barney, Bill
stripped away our pet illusions by showing just how much we
could do without. We had persuaded ourselves that the modern
child needed irony, wit, humor, parody to be reached and affected; *Sesame Street* and *Bullwinkle* were our exhibits in this argument. Barney showed that this was not the case. At the same
time, we had persuaded ourselves that the modern citizen, similarly wary (he is, after all, merely the *Bullwinkle* viewer grown
old), could be recalled to liberalism only through a heightened,
self-conscious, soul-searching high-mindedness. Bill showed
that *this* was not the case. Both dinosaur and Arkansas governor
had discovered that the way to win the hearts of their countrymen was to reduce their occupation to its most primitive form.
Where Kermit the Frog, on *Sesame Street,* had sung the principle
of brotherhood to children through the poetic metaphor of his
own greenness, Barney just grabbed the kids and told them that
he loved them and that they loved him too, damn it. Where
Mario Cuomo had orated about Lincoln and the immigrants and
the metaphor of family, Bill Clinton just held out his arms and
watched people leap into them. It turns out that you don't need
to be especially witty or wise to entertain children, just as you
don't need to believe in anything much to be an extremely effective president. All you need is to know your audience's insecuri-
ties and how to keep swaying in time to them forever.

|||

We had kept Barney in quarantine, for the most part, and though
Neige and Jolie and Amandine passed through the house, it was
mostly to sing lovely French songs—"Pomme de Reinette" and
"Frère Jacques"—and play with Luke's puppet theater. Then we
decided to hold a party to celebrate the coming of spring, and I

went out to Mulot to get a four-part chocolate cake. When I came back to the apartment, half an hour later, the roomful of lively children whom I had left drawling in *haute* French was silent. They were all in the bedroom. I walked in—no cuckolded husband can ever have entered his own bedroom with more dread about what he would find there—and saw the three girls spread out on the bed, their crinolines beautifully plumped, their eyes wide, their mouths agape. Barney was in France, and the kids were loving him. The three perfect French children looked on, hardly able to understand the language, yet utterly transfixed. I held out cake. Nothing doing. Barney was swaying. B.J. was prancing. The kids on the show were mugging like crazy, and everyone was singing.

It was too late. "How do you sing that 'I loove you, you loove me'?" Amandine asked haltingly, in French, when the program ended.

"I love you, you love me," Jolie answered swiftly.

"Happy family," Luke prompted. For the next week the song resounded from the street the way "La Ronde" had, long before.

|||

A couple of weeks later, at breakfast, Luke made an announcement. "Daddy," he said, "I *don't* like Barney."

"You don't like Barney?" I asked, incredulous, delighted.

"No, I *don't* like Barney." He paused. "I like to *watch* Barney." He had stumbled, in a Barneycentric manner, on the essential formula that could be applied to almost every American spectacle: I don't like the O. J. Simpson trial, I like to *watch* the O. J. Simpson trial; I don't like Geraldo Rivera, I like to *watch* Geraldo Rivera. And most basic of all: I don't like television, I like to *watch* television. When he watches Barney now, it's with a look in his eye that I know too well and that I can only call the American look, the look of someone who, though he has seen right through it, still can't take his eyes away—one of us, despite it all.

Lessons from Things,

CHRISTMAS JOURNAL 3

A French school term that I have learned to love is *leçons de choses,* lessons from things. It refers to a whole field of study, which you learn in class, or used to, that traces civilization's progress from stuff to things. The wonderful posters in Deyrolle, which Martha and I love and have collected, were made for *leçons de choses.* They show the passage of coffee from the bean to the porcelain coffeepot, of wine from the vine and soil to the bottle, of sugar from the cane to the *clafoutis.* They always show the precise costume that the beans and grapes and stuff end up in: the château bottling, the painted coffeepot, the label on the jam jar. The Deyrolle posters simultaneously remind you that even the best things always have some stuff leaking out their edges—a bit of the barnyard, a stain of soil—and that even the worst stuff is really okay, because it can all be civilized into things. The *choses,* the things, are what matter.

Of all the *leçons de choses* I have absorbed in Paris, the most important has come from learning to cook. I cooked a bit in New

York, Thanksgiving dinner and a filet mignon or two, and summers by the grill, like every American guy. But here I cook com-
pulsively, obsessively, waking up with a *plat* in mind, balancing it
with wine and side dishes throughout the working day ("Do I dare
poach a Brussels sprout?"), shopping, anticipating six o'clock,
when I can start, waiting for the perfectly happy moment when I
begin, as one almost always does, no matter what one is cooking,
by chopping onions.

The beautiful part of cooking lies in the repetition, living the
same participles, day after day: planning, shopping, chopping,
roasting, eating, and then vowing, always, never again to start on
something so ambitious again . . . until the dawn rises, with another dream of something else. (Hunger, I find, plays a very small
role in it all.) I have learned to make fifty or sixty different dinners: roasted *poulet de Bresse, blanquette de veau à vanille; carré
d'agneau; gigot de sept heures*. I can *clafoutis* an apple, poach a
pear, peel a chestnut. Big dishes, big food. Much *too* big food,
the old cooking. (There is a little culinary bookstore on the rue
du Bac that sells menus from the turn of the century. How did
people, rich people, middle-class people, eat so much? Our
stomachs *must* have shrunk, an argument for the plasticity of appetite, or at least of tummies. Is it fashion, culture, though? Or
is it simply central heating; is it that we need fewer calories now
than then and eat like West Indians—ginger and lime and rum
marinades—because our indoor climate is now West Indian?)

I shop every day, making the rounds: the nice butcher on the
rue de Verneuil, the grumpy butcher on the rue du Bac; the expensive excellent vegetable shop on the rue de Grenelle, or the
homey mom-and-pop cheaper vegetable place on the rue de
Verneuil. The one good fish place on the rue du Bac, cheese
from Barthélemy on the rue de Grenelle (which Luke won't
enter, from dislike of the smell, and so he waits outside, picket-
ing). Maybe a bottle of wine at Le Repaire de Bacchus, where we
discuss what I'm cooking; dessert from the grumpy ladies at
Michel Chemin or the smooth, charming, expensive ladies at

Dalloyau, and then I come home, my hands torn and aching from all the plastic bags biting into them.

Shopping in Paris, even for a simple family dinner, takes a solid hour, since everything has to be picked over, made ready, sorted out. (Of course, there are supermarkets, but real supermarkets—*grands espaces,* large spaces—are not allowed into Paris proper, and, anyway, the local merchants still thrive.) The chicken must have its head cut off, its feet cut off, and then it must be gutted. There is really nothing I enjoy more than watching a good butcher gut a chicken; it is a *leçon de choses* with bloody hands. The butcher incises the gut and then reaches in and pulls out the *whole insides,* a (shocking fact this, to a supermarket-stupid American) long, squalid string of mixed-up stuff, guts and gizzard and liver and heart, and then neatly shifts the disgusting to one side and the palatable to the other. You calm down—oh, look at that, that's nice, that's nasty—although at the moment that he actually pulls out the guts, your North American nice-nasty meter has been swinging wildly from one end of the scale to the other. Guts to one side, liver and heart to the other: *That's* just stuff, but *that's* a potential thing, and what about the neck? Might possibly with a lot of work *become* a thing, but it's discardable as stuff too if you feel that way about it.

The sublime moment of cooking, though, is really the moment when nature becomes culture, stuff becomes things. It is the moment when the red onions have been chopped and the bacon has been sliced into lardons and the chestnuts have been peeled, and they are all *mijoté*ing together in the pot, and then— a specific moment—the colors begin to change, and the smells gather together just at the level of your nose. Everything begins to mottle, bend from raw to cooked. The chestnuts, if you're doing chestnuts, turn a little damp, a little weepy. That's what they do; everything *weeps*.

I suppose there must be a good evolutionary psychologist's reason for the appeal of this transformation, some smart, smutty thing about color change and female rears, but cooking isn't really like sex: appetite and satiation and appetite again. Sex is ravenous rather than reflective. The passage from stuff to things, the moment when the vegetables weep, is a meditative moment and has no point, really, except the purely ephemeral one of seeing it happen. You cook for yourself, or I do anyway. Martha picks through things, New York girl with a New York appetite, and Luke, like an astronaut, would prefer to live on a diet of milk shakes and nutrient pellets. Cooking, for middle-class, end-of-the-century people, is our only direct, not entirely debased line with the hermetic life, with Zen sitting, with just doing things without a thought. No wonder monks make good cheese.

(I tried teaching sublime and beautiful as categories to Luke the other day. He brooded. "Daddy," he said at last, "an example of the sublime: dinosaur bones. An example of the beautiful: Cressida Taylor." Cressida Taylor, I have since learned, is a four-year-old girl with a long blond braid in his class at school with whom he is, understandably, in love, and who is in fact perfectly beautiful. The other day he also came home and said, "That Cressida—she's quite a dish!" I don't know where he gets this slang. The other day I also heard him say, "Oh, brother, what a peach!" about someone or other.)

|||

The absence of stuff may be what makes writing so depressing and cooking so inviting to the writer. (To the yuppie-family-guy writer anyway. It used to be not cooking but its happy, feckless near relation drinking that writers looked forward to at twilight. Perhaps for the same reason; it gives you something to do with your hands at six o'clock other than typing.) Writing isn't the transformation of stuff into things. It is just the transformation of symbols into other symbols, as if one read recipes out loud for dinner, changing the proportions ("I'm adding fifty goddamn grams of butter!") for dramatic effect. You read out the recipe and the audience listens, and pretends to taste, the way Martha does when I force her to listen to jazz records. *Mmm, delicious.* Sometimes, if you change the proportions dramatically enough—nothing but butter! no butter at all!—the people listening gasp, as though they really *could* taste it. (This is the way Burroughs and Bukowski write.) Fortunately they never have to. Writing is a business of saying things about stuff and saying things about things and then pretending that you have cooked one into the other.

This may be why I like this year to take a fundamental *leçon de choses* by going up to Sennelier, the beautiful art supply store on the quai Voltaire, and just buying some stuff that artists use to make things. Ingres paper, or oil pastels, or just a *carnet,* a notebook. How can artists ever make anything ugly at all? you wonder; just a black mark on thick white paper is so beautiful. I feel serene surrounded by paper, having learned that things give lessons enough.

|||

We've gone traveling a lot this year, to Budapest and London many times and to Venice and to Bruges. The weather on CNN, at least, whichever hotel room you find it in (and you find it in them all) always continues cheerful. ("And, hey, would you look here? A big low-pressure area is going to drop snow *all over* the east, from Danzig right out to Ukraine. . . .") I always imagine the businessmen, selling Dunkin' Donuts franchises and Internet stocks from Bucharest to Ulan Bator, checking the weather on CNN every night. Our peculiar American toothless bite is there. (But then I recall a theory Luke and I have learned this year about the *T. rex:* that it didn't actually *bite* at all but just grabbed and tore at its prey, half the time leaving it just wounded, but with enough toxic *T. rex* slime in the wound to infect it fatally. All the *T. rex* had to do was follow the poor sick guy around and watch until he dropped. American capitalism seems to work this way too. Toothless bites, it seems, are the worst bites of all.)

We followed CNN from motel to hotel, Michelin guide to Michelin guide, as we traveled. When I was in New York, all-news radio had the stock exchange highs every day, waiting for the Dow to break a number (eight thousand? ten thousand? It breaks the next one so quickly that we can't recall), the way we waited for a ballplayer to break a record.

Traveling around France, we've been out to the Loire, down to Grenoble and the Savoy, up to Normandy. I begin to get it. France is a big, rich country. It has a lot of people; they have a lot of good things to eat; they don't see why anyone should push them around. France doesn't believe that it was once the big one, as Holland or England do, by virtue of a special mission and an exceptional national character. France believes that it is *naturally* the big one, like China or America. The big one by virtue of its size, its abundance, its obvious cultural hegemony (all cultural hegemonies are believed to be natural by the people at the core of them). It was not so terribly long ago that everybody took this status for granted, and speaking French was like speaking English now: not an accomplishment but a necessity for a cosmopolitan life. It was not so long ago that France was almost *lazily* the big one, as we are now so to be told, again and again, that not only is it not the big one but not even among the bigger ones riles the French.

|||

Luke decided this year to penetrate farther into the Luxembourg Gardens. He is the Amundsen, the Peary, though I hope not the Scott, of the Luxembourg Gardens. His whole life is devoted to penetrating its mysteries, hoping eventually to get to its core. Someday he will enter the surveillants' shed, where the policemen sit and warm their coffee and watch for park infractions, and it will be time to go home. Or else he will spend the rest of his life as a Paris policeman; he will become Pierre! On the carousel he is now up and mounted on a horse, with the leather rope tight around his waist, eyes fixed straight ahead, hands clutching the pole, still too unsure for the stick and rings, but looking at them, hard.

This year he penetrated into the inner temple of the gardens. He went to a puppet show. It was a huge move, much meditated on and discussed in advance.

"Daddy, I think I want to go to the puppet show," he said sometime this spring, and then, having chosen *Les Trois Petits Cochons*, The Three Little Pigs, as his first show, we debated for a week, before the fateful Saturday matinee arose, what it was going to be like. He would jump into bed at seven in the morning with a new theory. "I think they'll dance like this," he said worriedly one morning, putting his hands on his waist and oscillating his torso back and forth mechanically. Then he stopped and looked even more worried. What if they *did* dance like that, God help us?

"I think there will be a wolf in it," he said on another morning, "and he will look like this," and then he grimaced, horribly. (I realized that he had become a precise replica of the young Marcel getting worked up about seeing Berma for the first time. It is a French moment, though not exactly the one we had in mind, puppets as pigs rather than Sarah in Racine, still . . .)

Saturday came around at last, and we lined up at the entrance to the puppet theater, just to the left of the playground, where we have gone so many afternoons. The owner–proprietor–producer–chief puppeteer is named Francis-Claude Desarthis, and he walks up and down the gardens with a bell before each show begins, ringing hard—not ringing to be fetching but ringing to fetch. As so often in Paris, it is hard to know if the puppet theater is making a mint—it charges twenty-four francs a ticket, about five dollars, and on weekends always seem full up—or hanging on by its nails.

Desarthis's father started the theater back in the thirties. His framed picture is still in place on the facade of the theater, looking plaintively at a puppet. Many of the shows seem to have been left untouched since then. The performance of *Les Trois Petits Cochons,* for instance, uses, with slight variations, many of the devices, not to mention the music, of the Disney version of the story from the thirties. There are French touches, though. The *catastrophe,* or climax, occurs when the wolf pretends to be a minor official come to read the water meter. The pigs have to let him into the one remaining house; the French little pigs *have* to open the door to administration, even when it has an immense jaw and sixty white papier-mâché teeth. Fortunately the day is saved, first by a series of electric shocks administered by the smart pig to the wolf by way of a rigged water meter and then by a snapping crocodile that arrives wrapped in a package (who sent him isn't clear, at least not to me). Finally, before the hunter arrives, the day is really saved by a black American boxer (Joe Louis?) with gleaming white choppers and thick lips and a terrific, wolf-devastating right uppercut.

There are dances—various animal puppets leaping up and down in time—at regular intervals, even when some necessary question of the play has yet to be resolved. The line to the seventeenth-century theater—for Molière too is full of arbitrary dances—is unbroken. The puppet shows are real puppet shows. They use puppets, the kind you hold with your hand from beneath. They're big puppets, with overlarge, papier-mâché heads and long arms, but no legs.

The no-legness of the puppets puzzles and discourages Luke. Far from seeming to him an invisible artistic convention, I think that he believes it to be a notable, disturbing sign of amputation. He thinks not Well, their legs are represented by sheets of fabric but, rather, Their legs have been cut off, and they have been forced to perform in a theater! In every show the hero is always Guignol, a kind of Puck or Trickster puppet, with a long Chinese braid. It is alarming to see his face, since it is obviously modeled on that of M. Desarthis himself—or, even scarier, on that of his father, who, from his portrait on the side of the building, seems to have had more or less the same features. They have passed themselves, it seems, into Guignol, who is, interestingly, amoral. Guignol takes the splinters out of the paws of wounded tigers ("*Le pauvre,*" he soothes) but is in business for himself, and mocks and bedevils the well-meaning admirals and librarians and magistrates he always seem to encounter. (Many of these, interestingly enough, have British accents.)

So far we have seen *Les Trésors du Sultan* (first a mixup on a ship and then a second act on a desert island, including, oddly, a tiger with a thorn in its paw and that noisy, impressively snapping crocodile. Also highly Semitic caricatures of the pirates and the sultan), *Minochet* (a cat in a Paris garret), *Le Cirque en Folie* (the Mad Circus, many animals, including, again oddly enough, a tiger and a crocodile), *Le Rossignol et l'Empereur de Chine* (adapted, the sign says honorably, from the *conte* of Hans Christian Andersen, although, interestingly, a tiger and a crocodile have been added), and, of course, those pigs.

As in any vast dramatic corpus, the puppet plays are of varying styles, ranging from the classic heigh-ho heartiness of *Pigs* and *Trésors* (as they are known to scholars) to the darker, more static style of *Minochet* and *Le Vieux Château*—the problem puppet shows, as they are known. (*Le Vieux Château* begins with a long, endless sequence in a scholar's library, and *Minochet* with an act, half Céline and half Beckett, about the poor cat, Minochet, trying to have her little supper while a mad butcher searches for her to turn her into cat sausage.) All of course are in French, using voices that must have also been recorded sometime in the late thirties—you can practically see the Pathé rooster on the side of the box that the records are kept in—and since the language is idiomatic and jokey, it is often hard for me to follow. Luke, whose French, despite his going to a French school, is in and out—as Hemingway's friends said about him, you never know if he knows a lot or a little—kneels up on the seat beside me and demands translations. ("What's he saying?" "That they're going to kidnap the princess . . . no, now he's saying something else" . . . etc.)

That first performance, though, the epochal *Pigs*, was so overwhelming that he couldn't sleep, and so we tried a usually reliable soporific: walking him down to the Seine in his *poussette* to watch the boats on the river from the pont des Arts. Usually, almost always, he falls asleep on the walk back. This night, though—a wonderful May night, chestnuts in blossom, a month later than the song advertises—he couldn't sleep, and his troubled, obsessive mind kept returning to the puppet show, to the struggle 'twixt damnation and impassioned papier-mâché.

We wandered through the Sixth, taking what I still think is the most beautiful walk in the world: up the rue de Seine and then right through the little, unprepossessing-looking arch—a hole punched in a wall—that gives no promise at all that it opens right onto the esplanade of the greatest of grand siècle buildings, the Institut de France, Mazarin's great curved library topped by its perfect dome. Passing through the tiny, *poussette*-wide arch onto the curved esplanade is like walking backstage through a flat and onto a great set.

There are no guards, no guardrails—nothing between you and the great building. It's all just there, and you can push a child's *poussette* back and forth in front of the institute entrance and even lean on the door to rest, though it is the center of French civilization. It is one of those odd Parisian absences that are as strange as the pervasive presences elsewhere. (There are enough policemen in the Luxembourg Gardens to be assigned one child each, but not a single guard anywhere here.)

Luke all the while was keeping up a running, troubled commentary on *Les Trois Petits Cochons*. "Why there were two wolves?" he would spring up, sleepy, from his *poussette,* to demand. (Actually there was just one, but he would appear, with sinister effect, on either side of the proscenium.) "Why he wants to eat the pigs?" "Why that man knock him?" "Why that crocodile bite?" Why why, why . . . the question the pigs ask the wolf, that the wolf asks the hunter, that the hunter asks God—and the answer, as it comes at midnight, after all the other, patient parental answers ("Well, you see, wolves generally like to eat pigs, though that's just in the story." "Well, hunters, a long time ago, would go hunting for wolves with guns when they were a danger to people"), the final, exhausted midnight-in-the-lamplight answer, wheeling the *poussette* down the quai Voltaire, is the only answer there is, the Bible's answer to Job: because that's the way the puppet master chose to do it, because that's the way the guy who works the puppets likes to see it done.

|||

Wednesday afternoons, Luke and I take our local bus, the 63, which runs down the boulevard Saint-Germain toward his school and the Seventh Arrondissement, back up toward the Jardin des Plantes and the Fifth, to visit the dinosaur museum. Luke has been following a course in Picasso and dinosaurs in his *maternelle.* I had already taken him round the Picasso museum, which Luke liked, and the dinosaurs were an even bigger hit. He talks knowingly, familiarly, of the brachiosaurus and pterodactyl. I have told him that dinosaurs were defeated by an alliance of daddies, that *only* daddies can defeat dinosaurs. Look around, I ask, are there dinosaurs? (No.) Are there daddies? (Yes.) Well, then . . . He sees the flaw in this argument more quickly than I expected. Daddies came long after dinosaurs; daddies claimed the terrain of power only after dinosaurs had already abandoned it. That's the way the dinosaurs tell it, I say. Long discussions. Long pause. Finally: "Here's one dinosaur you can *never* defeat [dramatic pause] . . . *T. rex!*" He needs an undefeatable dinosaur, a dinosaur beyond the reach of a dad.

The entrance to the paleontology museum at the Jardin des Plantes is graced by a statue of Lamarck, with the engraving "The Father of Evolution," in giant letters, on its pedestal. Darwin, on the other hand, is nowhere in sight.

There is nothing more exasperating than French monuments to unheroic local heroes. In the Luxembourg Gardens, where I run many mornings, there are statues of the great writers of France, genuinely towering and Olympian figures—real all-stars, the greats. Baudelaire scowls at the southern end of the gardens; Delacroix is greeted by angels at the other end. I salute them both every morning, while jogging by Verlaine and Sainte-Beuve. In the midst of them all there is a statue to a man whose name I, at least, have never heard, a guy named Branly, whose pedestal proclaims him to be the father of the wireless communication, radiotelegraph, and television. I am skeptical of this claim. It is a few feet away from the small, just larger than life-size Statue of Liberty, made by Bartholdi for fund-raising back when. This Liberty looks, well, sexy, free.

At last we get to the big Hall of Evolution, and Darwin sneaks in there—sideways. He gets a plaque. The Hall is filled with stuffed animals, giraffes and elephants, from another time, all apparently done by the artisans of Deyrolle but now placed in modernized half-light, the same kind of light you see in the fish restaurants of the Seventh Arrondissement. Recessed lighting says modern in France the way that a pastel arch says postmodern in New York.

The boy, however, wants to see his dinosaurs, so we go down in the gardens to the old Hall of Paleontology, off by itself down by the entrance to the gardens. It is two floors of pure bones—all bones, wall-to-wall bones, more bones than I have ever seen. At the entrance, a few feet from the Lamarck memorial, there is a statue by Frémiet of the Eternal Struggle. It shows a great ape—a species unknown to nature, with the ears of an elephant, the face of a magazine executive, and the grin of a Santa Monica maître d'—who, clutching his (her?) infant, has just wrapped his hands around the throat of a beautiful human youth. The youth, before being killed by the ape, managed to plant his ax in the ape's side, where it has left a hideous and gaping wound, perfectly cut out in stone. It is lurid, preposterous, and loud, the most improbable memorial, and this by the guy who made the golden and boring St. Joan on the rue de Rivoli. It defeats my dusty and out-of-date attempts at iconographic analysis, despite Luke's constant questions: Why the ape, why the man . . . ? Does it represent the triumph of Lamarckian evolution? Then the man with the culture (i.e., the ax) should be triumphing over the ape. It can't represent the domination of the ape-in-man over the beauty-in-man. Is it the Triumph of the Monkey in Us? Or is it simply (simply!) a lurid showpiece? Eugenio would have pointed out that the "trope" or conceit of the ape-on-the-loose is a rich nineteenth-century Parisian one, ranging from "The Murders in the Rue Morgue" to this. Man and Ape in Evolutionary Metaphor . . . these days you could probably put it out front of the Concorde and redub it "France and America."

The dinosaurs are upstairs. They are enormous and articulated to look big. Of course, this is easy: They *are* big. But they are made to look even bigger, perhaps by contrast with the delicate beaux arts architecture. They *loom*. There is a single mold of a *T. rex* head, which turns out to be a copy taken from the New York *T. rex*. Just as the famous mechanical nightingales of Byzantium that Yeats admired so were, as you discover when you read Byzantine history, the *same damn bird,* brought out century after century to impress out-of-town visitors, until the paint was peeling off the thing, so the *T. rex* that has scared several generations of schoolchildren in the two cities is the same damn lizard, dead so many million years.

In the new New York hall, where we took Luke last Christmas, the dinosaurs look wise and cunning, balanced forward on their delicate little hands, trembling like base stealers. They have fabricated fiberglass skins too, in gleaming, subtle, elegantly understated two-tone, Armani colors. Here, in Paris, in the old museum, they are still upright and looming and stolid. There is even a brontosaurus, still called that, though I think I read that there never *were* brontosauruses, that they were a false association of two different animals.

The force—I suppose I have to say the image—of the dinosaur, as it was understood by the nineteenth century, comes through here, terrifyingly. It is like reading Conan Doyle's *The Lost World*. The giant Irish elk (a mammal and, anyway, not that amazing—just a big moose) shares pride of place here with the big lizards, as he does in Doyle's story. The reason, I suspect, is that it wasn't so much the distant, scary past that drew the nineteenth century, but the simple specter of giganticism, bigness itself. They wanted their dinosaurs to loom over them, as their tycoons did. In the "lost world" of Conan Doyle, in fact, the dinosaurs are constantly being called Gothic. They were interested in big, whereas we are interested in mean. (Was this because bigness was their problem—mass armies, mass society, massiveness—whereas meanness is ours—small wars, horrible murders?) The difference between the old Parisian and the new New York dinosaurs is the difference between an industrial dinosaur, big and dumb and looming, and the postindustrial dinosaur, swift and smart and a scavenger. We make our monsters according to the armature of our fears. They wanted what loomed over them to be huge, stolid, immovable, and a little slow, like J. P. Morgan or Mr. Frick. We want them now to be smart, fast, mean, ugly, and wearing expensive suits, like Barry Diller or Rupert Murdoch.

|||

A little while later I visited the new Bibliothèque Nationale, the big—the unbelievably vertigo-inspiringly enormous—library, out at the other end of the quai in the Thirteenth. It seems to have been designed by a committee made up of Michel Foucault, Jacques Tati, and the production designer of *The Man from U.N.C.L.E.* The whole thing is set up, way up, on a wooden platform the size of six or seven football fields, high up off the street. There is an unbelievably steep stairs, leading up to this plateau, which is like nothing so much as one of those stepped pyramids where the Aztecs plucked the hearts out of their sacrificial victims. Then there are four glass skyscrapers, each one set at one of the corners of the platform, and all very handsome, in a kind of early-sixties, post–Lever House, Skidmore, Owings & Merrill way. The vast space has been planked with teak boards, to make it "warmer," but this just makes it more slippery. They have had to put down cheap-looking runners on a sticky backing, to keep people from breaking legs. (Apparently there were quite a few victims early on.)

The vast, windswept plaza, with the four towers at its corners, is *so* vast that it creates what one would have thought would be a perfectly predictable wind tunnel effect. This not only means that you walk with your head down against the gusts, even in the middle of July, but also means that all the bushes and shrubbery that were meant to "humanize" the wooden plaza had to be put inside vertical cages of mesh, which in turn are placed between white bunkers. Left out on their own, the shrubs would just die in the wind. It looks like a bad conceptual art installation about the domination of nature by man. (This is the Foucauldian part.) A stray piece of foliage peeks out forlornly from some of the enclosures, like Hans's fingers from the witch's cage. Looking across the platform toward the tiny and impossibly steep steps, you cannot see the stairs at all; it simply looks like a platform from which one could leap, suicidally, gratefully.

Downstairs you wait at the *accueil* for your card. This is done with the usual French functionary hospitality: Who are you, what do you want, what makes you think, etc.? Finally, after an hour, you may get a card. First you visit the desk of one severely disciplinary young lady, who takes your coordinates and enters them into the single-overseeing computer system that was intended as the glory of the place. You are now sent to another young woman, who reenters and corrects all the information the first girl entered, and then asks if you are ready for your picture. (This is the Jacques Tati part.) You nod and rise, looking for the photo booth. She shakes her head gravely and tells you just to sit back. A camera, mounted to your right and above, swivels, moves down on its track, and gawks at you, musing in and out. Don't move; your hostess has just become Annie Leibovitz, she is the photographer. She clicks her mouse forward onto the next screen of her computer, and there you are: The photo system is computerized too. She waits, thoughtfully for the moment of maximum exhaustion, and snaps your picture. You can, if you crane your head a bit, see a thousand images of yourself on the screen, being entered into the system.

When you at last have your card, you begin your descent into the vast underground caverns, the *sous-sol,* where the reading rooms are. (The books are, famously, all up in the towers.) First you go to a kind of master computer terminal and enter your request for a seat. The computer lets you know that there is no room for you in *L, M,* and disdainfully awards you your number, the new you: N-51. You repeat your name to yourself.

You insert your card into a turnstile; it takes its time and then lets you pass into a tiny space with a spiked metal floor, which leads in turn toward two immense two-story-high brushed metal doors. There is no signage or any indication of where you are going—because where you are going is into *another* turnstile, *another* spiked metal floor, and *another* pair of vast metal doors. Windows and sunlight have been left far behind. Once you are through those, you get on an escalator for a *ten*-story descent into the basement; there are concrete pillars around the escalators, winsomely decorated with iron-mesh hangings, that in the context look like chintz.

When you come to the end of the escalator, there are two more turnstiles and two more windowless metal doors to pass through. Now you are into the entrance to the reading rooms, and you see that they are built around a grass court, which opens to the sky, high, high above. In the glassed-in court is a bizarre amenity, a garden—no, a small forest of immense trees, pines and evergreens mostly, all planted close together in tight rows, in the shallow green center block of grass. Their grass base is surrounded by a margin of concrete. The trees are so shallowly rooted, though—or else, according to other people, the wind sweeping down from above is so strong—that they have all had to be chained to the concrete floor. Each one has at least two guy wires leading down to stakes in the ground, crisscrossing diagonal lines of black and steel cable. The bushes above in cages, the trees below in chains.

Step up three or four shallow steps from the glass wall enclosing the trees and wires—it is absolutely forbidden, by the way, for anyone to pass through the seamless glass walls and into the garden—and you are in the main reading room: dark, gloomy, and at once terrifyingly vast without being compensatingly magnificent. It is just one huge horizontal space, broken by discreet letter indicators telling you that you have passed from N to M and onward. Searching, at last you find your seat, N-51, which is simply a single space at a vast table with several hundred such spots marked. You feel more like an ant than an archivist.

Then you search, among consoles set off near the walls, for an empty, operating computer terminal on which to make your book requests. Most of the terminals are out of order, and when you insert your identity card, they sigh and say that they are initializing. After fifteen minutes you give up and walk up and down the great hall, looking for a terminal that works. When you find one, you can penetrate the catalog fairly quickly; then you claim the page and demand the book; the computer registers that you have made the demand and tells you to go sit back down. The entire library is, in principle, served by, or subject to, the same vast, single computer system, which knows who you are, where you are, what you're doing, and what you want, can track you from visit to visit, and anticipate your interests, etc. This of course means in practice that any tiny bug in one part of the system destroys the entire operation of the library. The latest bugs are posted on photocopied sheets Scotch-taped to the terminals: Please, don't ask to "resee" your list, they say, just ask to "revise" it, etc.

Now comes the part that transcends ordinary functionary fiendishness to touch the high, misty edge of French bureaucratic-sadistic genius. The keyboard on the computer terminals is almost, *but not exactly,* an ordinary keyboard. It *looks* like an ordinary QWERTY keyboard—it doesn't just have some entirely new, Pierre Boulez–inspired keyboard, so that you're warned in advance to watch your step, or finger—but *three characters* have been moved. (I found out later that this is a standard French keyboard, but I had never used one before. Writers are married to their keyboards, as to their passports.) Q is exchanged with A, and the comma with the period, and, I think, the E with the O. This means that if you are a touch, or just a plain, mildly experienced, typist, you feel exactly as if you were having a stroke, since you have to interrupt the flow of typing each time you make a tiny error, and pretty soon you are so scared that you stop trying to maintain your normal speed and begin to hunt and peck.

On the desks there is a single red light that is supposed to illuminate when your books arrive, but these lights have never been known to work. Or, rather, they have been *occasionally* known to work. So you have to get up regularly and check your computer terminal again, to see what's up. The light may be off because the books haven't arrived yet, and it may be off because it's not working. This means that if you go to the main desk, thirty yards away, to check, and the books aren't there, everyone will be annoyed at you for taking up a place in the line. There is usually at least an hourlong wait for books and a sharp limit (eight, right now) on how many you can take out. Guess wrong, and you've wasted a day. There is no cafeteria, only an appalling, gloomy little café near the subterranean entrance, with a view of the gagged and bound trees straining toward the invisible sky. Americans working there have taken to sitting on the steps that run down toward the atrium, where there is at least some light, though of course, it is also extremely hot; given the underground location and the abundance of plate glass, you are always either freezing or baking. But clerks come to shush them. "After the shock of the first few days, you get used to it," someone says.

It is not cheap-looking, God knows, very much not. It is in the Totalitarian Luxe style, which was the Mitterrand trademark. The materials are rich: brushed steel, mesh curtains, thick carpet. The trees alone, their purchase and upkeep, must have run into the millions of dollars. The floor on the concourse is made of teak. You see the production values but worry about the production. It is the largest and most depressing of all the monuments of pompous official French culture that have been produced in France since the war, the administration's ultimate revenge on the individual. All that French wit, all that charm, all that gaiety, all that somber pessimism, even all that intelligent despair sunk deep into the earth like a missile installation, with bad sandwiches and a chained and bound garden. I ordered a book by Blondin and a picture book on Trenet, just to recall that there was something gayer in Paris, up there above, where the light was.

When I left at last and saw, on the quai, with the cars rushing by, a typically French beauty poster—this one for Lancaster sun cream: a perfect girl's bottom, bare and in full color, five times normal scale, with a gold sheen in the summer light—I was pathetically grateful for the sight of something humanly beautiful, curved and soft to the eye. French civilization is all the more a miracle, given the obstacles the French put in its way.

III

The curious thing about all of Mitterrand's *grands projets*—the Bastille Opéra, the pyramid of the Louvre, above all, this library—is that though they are big, they don't *feel* big. They don't feel big the way the dinosaur museum feels big, the way the Parisian monuments of the last century still do, even when those old monuments are actually smaller than the new ones. The new *grands projets* don't feel big so much as claustrophobic and confusing and stifling—emotionally trivial, small. The *grands projets* of the last century were either the biggest of their kind or else a kind unto themselves. The Eiffel Tower maintains its aura of height partly because it really *is* tall and big and partly because there is still nothing like it anywhere else. (The radio masts and post office towers and skyscrapers that have been built since and that in some ways resemble it really don't, since its form is uniquely feminine—not phallus into sky, but skirt into bodice into long throat.) The pyramid of the Louvre, though, looks like a shopping center, a mall, because that kind of Plexiglas and aluminum architecture has been done so much bigger elsewhere.

There is here a fundamental lesson from a thing, a *leçon d'une chose.* Architecture at its most successful passes from stuff (bricks and mortar and metal) through things (buildings) all the way to *thats,* single unforgettable objects, instantly recognizable, the thumbprints of the world. Their closed, permanent, pyramid-like *thatness* is their glory. Paris has perhaps more *thats*—the tower, the Louvre, the arch, the palace—than any city in the world, a greater concentration of distinctive monuments. Yet despite its best efforts, the *grands projets* fail to achieve the requisite *thatness.* They fail because of their comparative smallness, of course, when compared with other things in our mental library, but also because they lack something else, a kind of confidence in the things they enclose. The last thing the new Opéra makes you think of is music; the last thing the new library makes you think of is books. The paleontology museum *is* at least a semi-*that,* so filled with stuff that has been dignified into things, animal dust made hard and significant, that it becomes a *that* by virtue of the immensity of the thingness it encloses. The new library, the Bibliothèque Nationale, isn't even a thing, much less a *that.* It evokes, after you have experienced it, merely a Huh? and, like all failed monuments, in the end resolves in memory merely into a vast and barren and echoing Why?

|||

I realized this year that the appeal of jazz in France, and the reason for its holding a place so much higher in the French estimation than in America, where it remains a cult enthusiasm, is the exact equivalent of the American appreciation of impressionism (which held, and to a degree—look at the way the pictures are shown at the Musée d'Orsay!—still holds a much higher place in the American estimation than in the French one).

Jazz, like impressionism, gives dignity to comfort. Resting in an apparently artless myth of bourgeois pleasure—Gershwin and Kern melodies play the same role for the great jazzmen that the outdoor cafés in Argenteuil played for Renoir and Monet—jazz, like high impressionism, reaffirms the simple, physical basis of powerful emotion and removes it to a plane of personal expression that we recognize as art; it gives us a license to take pleasure in what really provides our pleasures. You play "All the Things You Are" and you are playing the beautiful tune, and you are playing more than the beautiful tune, in the same way that Manet is painting just the asparagus and more than the asparagus without venturing into asparagus symbols or the grand manner of the asparagus. But the tune is there, even if the more pretentious kind of jazz critic doesn't like to admit it, just as the asparagus is there, even if the more pretentious kind of art critic doesn't like to admit it. Bill Evans playing "Someday My Prince Will Come," like Manet painting a lemon, is stuff into things—into more than things, all the way into *thats*.

In every period, every century, there is one art form or another that is able to combine simple affirmation of physical pleasure with a quality of plaintive longing, and this becomes the international art form of the time. Living abroad convinces you that just as French painting was the event of the nineteenth century and Italian painting of the fifteenth—the one universal language— American popular music is the cultural event of our time. It is the one common language, the source of the deepest emotions and the most ordinary ones too. The taxi driver hums the riff from "Hotel California," and the singer Johnny Hallyday, simply by impersonating Elvis, in some decent sense inhabits Elvis (just as Childe Hassam, impersonating Monet, at some decent level inhabited him too). Every epoch has an art form into which all the energies and faiths and beliefs and creative unselfconsciousness flows. What makes them matter is their ability not to be big but *to be small meaningfully,* to be little largely, to be grandly, or intensely, diminutive.

|||

The best lesson I have learned from a thing this year, perhaps in all my time in Paris, occurred on another afternoon this spring. I was sitting on the bench under the metal and glass *porte-cochère* at the playground at the Luxembourg Gardens, watching Luke climb up the sliding board, the "toboggan," the wrong way—glancing warily over his shoulder for the surveillant to whistle him down—when I looked down at the plastic-cupped *café crème* that I had bought at the little entrance shed a few moments before. About to unwrap the sugar cube, I saw that the little paper wrapping had a picture of the poet Mallarmé on it—an odd, Benday-dot, unintentionally Lichtenstein-like portrait of him—while on the two other faces of the sugar cube there were quotes from his poems ("*Et finisse l'écho par les célestes soirs, Extase des regards scintillements des nimbes!*") and a brief, summary life ("LIBERTÉ SANS MESURE: STÉPHANE MALLARMÉ, POÈTE 1842–1898"). The fourth face just had the name of the sugar company, Begin Say. The sugarcane had not only become a sugar cube, like the one in the Deyrolle poster, but been wrapped in a picture of a poet. I saved it to keep on my desk in my writing room and for once drank my coffee unsweetened. A lesson from a thing, and thrown in for the price of the coffee too.

The
Rookie

I don't really remember how we first thought of the Rookie. I think it may have been right after I saw Luke, who had just turned three, playing with a soccer ball in the Luxembourg Gardens. It wasn't just the kicking that scared me but a kind of nonchalant bend-of-the-body European thing he did as he rose to meet the ball with his head. Next, he would be wearing those terrible shorts and bouncing the ball from foot to foot, improving his "skills." He had been born in New York, but he had no memory of it. Paris is the only home he knows. (Or, as he explained to a friend, in the third person he occasionally favors, like Bo Jackson or General de Gaulle, "He was born in New York, but then he moved to Paris and had a happy life.")

"You want to have a catch?" I said, and he looked at me blankly.

That night at bedtime I said, "Hey, I'll tell you about the Rookie." It was eight o'clock, but it was bright outside. Paris is a northern city, on a latitude with Newfoundland, as New York is a Mediterranean one, on a latitude with Naples, and so the light here in the hours between seven and nine at night is like the light in the hours between five and seven in New York. The sun is still out, but the sounds have become less purposeful—you hear smaller noises, high heels on the pavement—and though it is a pleasant time to lie in bed, it is not an easy time for a small boy to go to sleep.

I had been drawing storytelling duty for a while and had made increasingly frantic efforts to find a hit. A story about a little boy who turned into a fish in Venice hadn't gone anywhere, and a re-make of *The Hobbit* had done no box office at all. This story, though, rolled out easily. Every dad has one good bedtime story buried in him, and desperation will bring it out.

The Rookie (I said) was a small boy in Anywhere, U.S.A., in the spring of 1908. Out walking with his mom one day, he discovered that he had an uncanny gift for throwing stones at things. He picked one up and threw it so hard that it knocked a robin off its perch a mile away, and then, after his mama chided him, he threw another one, just as far but so softly that it snuggled into the nest beside the bird without breaking an egg. His parents, a little sadly but with a sense of obligation, immediately sent him off on the train to New York, to try out for the New York Giants and their great manager, John J. McGraw. All he took with him was a suitcase that his mother had packed for him, filled with things, including his bottle, that she thought might be useful in case of an emergency. (At that point the contents of the suitcase were unparticularized, but they eventually included a complete dictionary of the animal languages, a saxophone, a de-sign for the first car radio, compressed early rocket ship refueling pills, a map of Paris, a window defogger, a time machine, a Sher-lock Holmes deerstalker, a map of a secret route to the South Pole, and reindeer medicine for Santa's team.)

He got out at Grand Central, took a cab all the way uptown to the Polo Grounds—his mother had told him to take taxis in New York—and asked to see John J. McGraw. McGraw, staccato and impatient, was at first skeptical, but he finally agreed to watch while the kid threw, because he was so polite and the letter from his parents was so insistent and because, well, you never know. He called Big Six, the great Christy Mathewson, out of the dugout to watch, and Chief Meyers, the great American Indian catcher, to get behind the plate. The Chief came out, with a weary, crippled, long-suffering gait, and squatted. (I thought of the Chief as a creased veteran, though the real Chief was still in his twenties and not yet even a Giant.) The little guy walked to the mound, tugged at his cap—not a baseball cap, the cap of his knickers suit—and let fly.

Everybody was impressed, to put it mildly. "Hey, Mr. McGraw!" cried the Chief. "I ain't never seen speed like that, and ain't he got movement on it too!"

"Well," Matty said mildly, peering at the tiny, doughty figure on the mound, "when you think about it, he's more or less got to have that upward movement on his fastball, don't he?" (My ideas of credible 1908 ballplayer dialogue were heavily influenced by Ring Lardner.)

McGraw shrugged, since tryouts were one thing and baseball was another, but in the end he decided to give the kid a start that Sunday in a big benefit exhibition that the Giants were playing at the Polo Grounds against the Detroit Tigers.

I stopped. Outside we could hear the steady stop-and-start rhythmic passage of the sanitation workers. Impossibly chic, in grass green uniforms with a white stripe running down the side, the men of the *Paris Propre* come down our street every night to collect the garbage. The garbage is put out by *gardiens* in city-issued green plastic canisters, and the garbage men place the canisters on little elevators, one on each side of the rear of the truck. The containers are lifted, turned upside down, shaken out, and returned trembling to the ground. Then the truck proceeds, at a stately, serene, implacable pace; a cabdriver who gets caught behind one on a little street lets out a moan, like a man who has just been bayoneted.

At this point I decided I'd made a decent start and was getting ready to say good night. "Go on," he said, muffled but sharp, from under his covers. An order.

In the benefit exhibition that Sunday (I went on at last), the big bathtub-shaped stadium, with its strange supporting Y beams, was packed with fans, come to see the three-year-old phenom. The Rookie took the mound, throwing smoke, and it looked as though it might be a first, a perfect perfect game, twenty-seven men up, twenty-seven Ks, until, in the sixth, he had to face the Terrible Ty Cobb. (I realized that I had a problem here since Cobb should have been batting cleanup from the start; I explained that he had been late suiting up, because he insisted on extorting extra payment from the Tigers' management for playing in a charity exhibition, even though everybody else was playing for free. Cobb was just like that, I explained: terrible.) The crowd quieted as the confrontation neared. Cobb came to the plate, sneering and drawling.

"Hey, baby," he called out, taunting the Rookie. "Looks to me like you're nothin' but a *baby*." (Luke's whole body stiffened. If there was a worse insult, he hadn't heard it; Jackie Robinson, in his first year with the Brooklyn Dodgers, had never been called a name so vile.) Shaken, the Rookie lost a bit off his heater. It was still blazing, though, and Cobb just got a piece of it, dribbling it toward first; he took off, and the Rookie, who knew his assignments, dutifully scampered over to cover. Cobb came in hard, hard as he could, his spikes sharpened to razor tips, and stamped down on the Rookie's three-year-old foot. The Rookie dropped the ball. Safe! Stinking rotten way to get on base, but safe all the same. Shaking off a couple of tears, the Rookie went back to the mound. "Hey, I reckon you're a crybaby. Hey, everybody, look at the crybaby! Looks to me like you're nothin' but a *cry*baby" came the taunting Georgia drawl from first, and the Rookie pitched out of trouble. But the pain lingered, and in the top of the ninth, the Giants having pushed over one run on a hit-and-run executed by the Chief, he made a few mistakes, walked a couple of batters—hey, he was *three*—and left himself with the bases loaded and the Georgia Peach due up again. The crowd was going crazy, and now the taunting began again, worse than ever. ("Hey, baby! Hey, crybaby! Whyn't ya cry some more, crybaby?")

The Rookie knew what he had to do. In the dugout he had taken his old bottle from the suitcase his mother had packed for him when he went off to join the Giants, just in case, and stowed it under his cap. Now he dripped a couple of drops of milk onto the seams of the baseball, the Rookie's soon-to-be-notorious bottleball. It was before they brought in the rule against foreign substances on the ball, I explained. The Rookie was playing fair. ("Hey, when are you guys going to sleep?" Luke's mother's voice came from the other room. "Soon," I called back abruptly. The lights of the traffic on the boulevard Saint-Germain came in through the windows, but I didn't even draw the curtains.)

The Rookie stretched and threw, and the bottleball dipped and twisted and dipped and twisted again, curving all the way out to the third-base line and then cruising halfway toward first before finally slipping in, softly and cleanly, right across the plate, a strike at the knees. Cobb had time to take a really good cut—he had *all day*—but the pitch had him so fooled that he didn't just whiff, he twisted himself in knots while he whiffed: real knots, his whole body pulled around like a wet washrag, hands ending up back of his butt. (Luke chuckled deeply at that.) "Steer-rike-uh three," cried the umpire. The bleachers of the Polo Grounds went nuts.

The Rookie trotted off the field. "Who's the baby *now*, Mr. Cobb?" he asked, with quiet dignity, on his way back to the dugout.

My kid sat up, shot up in bed, like a mechanical doll, as

though he had a spring hinge right at his waist. Christy Mathewson (I went on) didn't say anything—that wasn't his way—but he went over as the Rookie came into the dugout, took off the Rookie's cap, and mussed up his hair. Outside, the crowd wouldn't leave. They chanted, "Rookie! Rookie!"

Now the only sound from Luke's pillow was of short, constant breathing. I had the uncanny knowledge of a kind of silent excitement, the certainty—I have witnessed it once or twice on opening night in a theater, though I had certainly never created it before myself—that what we had here was a hit. The Terrible Ty Cobb had called him a baby, and he had thrown the bottle-ball, and *then* who was the baby?

That night (I said) the Rookie was offered a contract with the Giants (doubtless a mean, exploitative contract, but I left that out), and the team got on the overnight sleeper to St. Louis, heading out to steamy Sportsman's Park. (I knew that the Browns, not the Cardinals, played there, but I liked the way it sounded.) The Chief tucked the Rookie into his berth and, before he went off to play pinochle with the guys, asked him, gruffly, "You okay, Rookie?" "I'm okay, Chief," the Rookie said, and then he listened to the sounds of the train tracks clacking and the whistle blowing and the other ballplayers in the next car, laughing and playing cards, before he fell deep asleep, somewhere outside Columbus.

"I'm okay, Chief," Luke repeated, and he did something he had never done before, or at least not in my presence: Without negotiation or hesitation, without tears or arguments or requests to come and sleep in the big bed, he rolled right over and fell asleep.

From then on we had a story about the Rookie—Luke called it the Rookie story—every night. The characters firmed up pretty quickly. The Rookie was an earnest, resourceful, somewhat high-strung little hero. The Chief was blustery and honest, wanting nothing more than to settle in with his copy of the *Police Gazette* and have a peaceful afternoon at McSorley's. The Rookie's triumph over Ty Cobb, though, had bad consequences. Cobb developed a bitter, unappeasable Tom DeLay–type enmity toward the Rookie and set himself the task of doing anything he could to destroy his career. John J. McGraw, thumbtack sharp and demanding, and Christy Mathewson, handsome and deep-voiced and friendly, though a little remote—on a couple of occasions, when the Chief left town to go on a scouting trip to Cincinnati, he was the Rookie's baby-sitter—filled out the dramatis personae.

After a couple of months I went down to the cellar of our building and got out the few baseball reference books I had brought to Paris and never unpacked. (This cellar is an honest-to-God *cave*, a stone cellar with little arches where you could keep wine. I kept meaning to bring the wine down, but I never remembered to do it, and instead the books were there, moldering away.) The 1908 National League pennant race, which I had plucked out of the air and dim memories of *The Glory of Their Times,* turned out to be even more interesting than I'd thought. It was a three-way race—Cubs, Giants, Pirates—that included Merkle's boner and the season-capping rematch it produced, and in a sense, it made baseball in America. I discovered that 1908 had been a kind of watershed year, a time when baseball had, for the last time, an air of improvisation about it, with, as someone said of those days, "stupid guys, smart guys, tough guys, mild guys, crazy guys, college men, slickers from the city, and hicks from the country." If a three-year-old with a major-league fastball *had* ever existed, 1908 would have been the right season for him to play, and he probably would have been roomed with an American Indian catcher.

I even found a wonderful photograph of the Polo Grounds in that magical year, and we hung it over Luke's bed. It shows a hundred or so fans lining up on Coogan's Bluff, overlooking the ballpark—too poor or, more likely, too cheap to buy tickets, since you can see that there are still a few seats left in center—backs turned and heads bowed as they stare down at the field. Every single one of the men (there are no women) is wearing a derby; the kids are wearing cloth caps. One kid and an elderly gent have got up on a barrel, and five men in suits and hats are standing, precarious but dignified, on a plank that slopes down from it. You can't really see a thing going on in the park—not a baseline, not a ballplayer, not a glimpse of a dugout or a bullpen, nothing except the outfield grass down below, a perfect and absolute blank. It's as good as a Magritte: the solemnly dressed businessmen, backs turned, gazing out at the bare and uneventful field. Of course Luke didn't have to be told whom they were looking at down there, and why; we both could see it plain as day. They were watching the Rookie, pitching his way out of another pinch.

Yet I began to wonder: What picture did he summon up when, night after night, he heard the words *Polo Grounds, full count, all the way to the backstop*? Not an inexact picture; no picture at all. He had never been to a baseball game, never seen a bat or a glove, never been inside a ballpark or even watched a ball game on television. He spent his days in parks where kids played soccer on dusty gravel, and you put a toe in the grass on pain of being whistled down by the surveillant, watching from his shed. No one Luke knew played baseball, no one talked about it; the words and situations were pure language, pure abstract lore. The clichés I rolled out—"He had all day," "steamy Sportsman's Park," "no foreign substances on the old pill"—what did he think, what did he see when he heard them? I knew that he wanted to hear the words as much as I needed to say them— he zipped through dessert to get to bed every night—but what did the words mean to him?

I had spent my adult life believing that storytelling depends on the credibility of its details, and now, finally, I had made up a story that someone liked, and the details had no credibility at all, no existence except as sounds. You are supposed to use a word, I had always been taught, to point at a thing and hope that the thing will somehow end up pointing at a symbol: a feeling, a state of mind. When I lived in New York, I had on occasion even brought this faith to writing students. (Not that they cared. The fetching female ones listened gravely and then came up after class to ask if I had Gary Fisketjohn's phone number.) But now I said "Polo Grounds" or "full count" and the words called up in my son a powerful reaction. What of that second range, where the words were supposed to become things, even just images in his head?

There is, I believe now, a force in stories, words in motion, that either drives them forward past things into feelings or doesn't. Sometimes the words fly right over the fence and all the way out to the feelings. Make them do it one time out of three in private, and you've got a reputation as someone who can play a little, a dad who can tell a decent bedtime story. Do it three times out of three in public, and you're Mark McGwire or Dickens.

And I needed the words too, just as words. After four years in Paris I found that though I missed American sports a lot less than I had thought I would, I missed the lore of American sports keenly. I didn't really miss sports; I missed the sports pages. I didn't miss the things—sometimes the baseball season was twenty or twenty-five games old before I knew it had started— but I missed the words that went with the things. My passion for baseball, which at one point in my life was pretty intense, is now almost gone. My team, the Montreal Expos, is on the verge of going out of business; when I visit New York, I no longer know, or can even guess, which player is wearing which cap.

I still care about the words, though. One day, shopping for dinner along the rue du Bac and waiting in one of the interminable lines that are created by the individual care of French service—a line that is briskly, infuriatingly violated by the same arrogant dyed-blond woman in a fur coat and with a great jaw— I thought, Nobody in this line but me knows what an RBI is, or who Gene Mauch was, or what Jarry Park used to look like, or what a twinight doubleheader is. And I felt yearningly, unappeasably homesick. (This was not a rational emotion, since I have lived for years with a woman who doesn't know what an RBI is either.)

The things an American who is abroad for a very long time misses—or at least the things I missed—I was discovering, weren't the things you were supposed to miss. We are supposed to come to Europe for leisure, sunshine, a more civilized pace, for slowness of various kinds. America we are supposed to miss for its speed, its friendliness, for the independence of its people and the individualism of their lives. Yet these were not the things I missed, and when I speak to Americans who have lived abroad for a long time, those are not the things they seem to miss either. I didn't miss crosstown traffic, New York taxicabs, talk radio or talk television, or the constant, appalling flow of opinion that spills out like dirty floodwater. (Paris is an argumentative but not an opinionated city; it is the ideal of every French newspaper columnist to have premises so inarguable that the opinions can more or less look after themselves while he goes to lunch.)

I didn't miss American "independence" either. If anything, I missed its opposite, American obsequiousness, that yearning, beseeching tone of a salesman trying to sell something that you never hear in statist Europe. (The French, I think somebody said, have every vice *except* obsequiousness.) Buying shoes for my son, I missed the shoe salesmen of my childhood, my own uncles among them, their glasses held together with tape, their voices keening as they got down on their knees to tie the laces and make the sale. "Now the youngster can wear this shoe as a sports shoe or a dress shoe. Yeah, you got plenty of room there at the toe, young fellow—stand up. Now show your mom these shoes. Walk around." Quieter: "I have it in burgundy, in brown, in blue . . ." A French shoe salesman, indignant at his position, laces the child's shoes in silent anger and rises to his feet pretty much shaking his fist in your face.

I found, to my surprise, that what I missed and longed for was the comforting loneliness of life in New York, a certain kind of scuffed-up soulfulness. In Paris no relationship, even one with a postman or a dry cleaner, is abstract or anonymous; human relations are carved out in a perpetual present tense. There's an intricacy of debits and credits. Things have histories. The little, quickly forgiven bumps of New York social life—the missed phone calls, the suddenly canceled lunches, the early exit from the dinner party, which are, if anything, signs of status, of "busyness"—are sources of long grievances, permanent estrangements, endless reexplanations. It isn't possible just to remove yourself from a friendship in Paris for a month or two, as you can in New York. ("What have you been doing?" "Working." "Oh.") Even the most apparently professional relationships get overloaded. The dry cleaner is recovering from cancer, and her visits to pick up the clothes are scheduled around her treatments, with enough time to talk about them; the man who puts up shelves is a jazz guitarist, and an extra hour must be budgeted in to trade licks and discuss Jim Hall. On your way down the street in the early morning to run with all the other Americans in the Luxembourg Gardens—only Americans and French riot police go running; the Americans you know by their music festival sweatshirts, the French police by their flattop cuts and thoughtful, coiled power—you hear footsteps coming after you, and you worry that you have violated some ordinance, stepped on some forbidden grass. It is the fishmonger. "The wild salmon went well?" he demands anxiously. You find a café where you feel at home—and then become reluctant to go there, since it will involve such a wearing round of handshakes and "How is Madame?"

New York is devoted to the cult of busyness, but like all cults, it has at its heart the worship of a single, unforgiving idol, the office. After the idol has been served, life can be pretty formless. The things Americans miss tend to involve that kind of formlessness, small, casual, and solitary pleasures. A psychoanalyst misses walking up Lafayette Street in her tracksuit, sipping coffee from a Styrofoam cup with the little plastic piece that pops up. My wife, having been sent the carrot cake that she missed from New York, discovered that what she really missed was standing up at the counter and eating carrot cake in the company of strangers at the Bon Vivant coffee shop. I thought I missed reading Phil Mushnick in the sports pages of the *Post*; when I read him on-line, I discovered that what I really missed was reading Phil Mushnick on the number 6 uptown train on a Monday morning around ten.

It was, in a way, the invisibility of the men up on Coogan's Bluff in 1908 that drew me to them. The consensual anonymity of men in crowds is what we are escaping when we leave, and then it is what we miss. You can be alone in Paris a lot, but it is hard to be lonely; there is always another pair of eyes, not un-friendly, appraising you. (The French husband of an American friend will not meet her in the park in his tennis shorts. He does not know who will see him, but he is sure that he will, in some way, be seen.) You are a subject, not an object, and if this is part of the narrow, centuries-old happiness of life in Paris, it is also one of the things that narrow that happiness. Walk into Central Park to watch the sea lions, and you disappear from the world for a little while. In the Luxembourg Gardens, or at the menagerie in the Jardin des Plantes, you are always conscious of the long *al-lées* leading you back the way you came; of the surveillants' shed at the center of the park, where the two uniformed men sit with their hot plate, warming up coffee and watching the world; of the lion looking back at you. We go to cities to be invisible, or to be invisible and visible by turns, and it is hard to be invisible in Paris. The light at night is too strong. Gershwin got this right at least: The car horns and the syncopations in *An American in Paris* are all French. What that American misses is the blues.

|||

After about a year of telling the Rookie story, I went to New York to give a talk, and I turned the trip into a literary mission, a sort of Rookie collecting expedition. I wanted to bring home tangible evidence of something that, as a matter of fact, had never taken place there. I bought a baseball encyclopedia and a box of books on the Cobb era and borrowed a Ken Burns video. A vintage Giants cap, child size, which I thought would be the hardest thing to find, turned out to be absurdly easy; the past is so neatly packaged now that I just walked into a memorabilia store on Lexington Avenue and found a replica cap, no problem.

When I got home, I put on the video, from the PBS *Baseball* series, which I had never seen, and we watched all those flickering, overfrantic little ghost figures racing around. One by one the faces and bodies and actions that you couldn't see in the photo above Luke's bed were being filled in. There was Ty Cobb, looking appropriately evil; there was John J. McGraw. There was pitching and batting (I realized, from Luke's comments, that he had them the wrong way around). There was baserunning.

There was Christy Mathewson, and then a picture of Matty, handsome and assured as ever, slowly dissolving into a picture of a small, serious boy with blond bangs, wearing a baseball cap and a perfectly sober expression, going into a pitching windup. I still have no idea who he actually was (it's not Christy Mathewson's kid; I've found a picture of him, and he had darker hair), but of course Luke knew, perfectly well.

"There he is," he said. "Rewind it." We watched Matty and the Rookie appear again, and then he told me to turn it off. He was uncharacteristically silent for the rest of the afternoon, but before dinner I heard him talking to his mother in the bath. "He had his hands up like this," he was saying chattily. "I don't know why."

That was enough excitement, enough reality, for one night, I thought, and it wasn't until a week later that I tried out on him a picture of the Chief—an honest-to-God picture of Chief Meyers, looking just as he ought to look.

"Hey, look, that's the Chief," I announced proudly, opening the old baseball encyclopedia at his bedside.

He paused, looked at the picture, looked back at me—peering in, for a moment—and then got a funny, guilty smile on his face that I had never seen there before.

"Oh," he said, peering intently at the picture. "I thought it was his mother."

"What do you mean?" I said, surprised.

"I mean, I knew it was—but I thought it was. I mean I knew it was a man . . . but I thought he was the mother," he concluded, stumbling a little. "I thought it was his mother."

He actually blushed, and I could sense that there was something at once so deep and so important going on in what he was trying to tell me that he feared at some other level it would seem silly. In his mind's ear, he could hear Ty Cobb calling. *Baby.*

"But remember," I said. "His mother packed the suitcase for him. He had the mama's suitcase."

"I know. I know that," he said quietly, stubbornly. "I can't—I just thought." He held his hand up to his head and tried to smile. "I thought it was a girl. I thought it was his mama."

I got it then. He knew that the words *the Chief* stood for some kind of older man—though whether he could have summoned up the kind of older man I had, a bearded grizzled forty-ish American-Indian catcher with boozy breath, I'm not sure—but the symbolic place that he occupied was so deeply maternal that it was, well, the Chief was his mother. What had been lulling him to sleep, night after night, I realized, was not the all-purpose fit. The words pointed directly to the symbol, and it was the obvious one, but it wasn't my symbol. The trouble with mental catch is that the ball you throw changes in midair into another. Staring down into the Polo Grounds, from Coogan's Bluff, what he had seen was what he needed to see, and that was the same face he saw at every window. His mother had been there at his bedside all along, and I had been too slow a reader of my own fiction to spot her lurking.

Sometime that month I began to think that it was time to

round off the Rookie story, give it a suitably grand ending, turn the legend into a myth; I would find another story. I was having a hard time thinking of new plots, and anyway, it had been two years.

It was, at last, the seventh game of the 1908 World Series. The Rookie had started three for the Giants, Matty the others. (Of course we had made the Giants, not the Cubs, grab the gonfalon on the final day.) It was the bottom of the ninth, the score tied one to one on homers by the Chief and Sam Crawford. Cobb was up. He dragged a bunt and headed for first, and this time he didn't just spike the Rookie; he actually slid into first base, razor-clad feet up. Hit hard, the Rookie held on to the ball. But the umpire ruled that the ball had rolled foul down the first-base line. The Rookie was bleeding, fed up, homesick, crowded by a ringer like Gizmo McGee, a Tiger midget pretending to be a four-year-old, and he had endured a full season (in two years) of cruel torment at the hands of this terrible man. So he did an awful thing: He loaded up and threw his best fastball right at Ty Cobb's head, threw so hard that Cobb's head came right off, popped up high, before settling back down, with a surprised look, on his shoulders.

Umpire Bill Klem checked out Cobb—he was okay; the Rookie knew what he was doing—and then looked at the Rookie. "You're outta here, Rookie," he said, giving him the longest, slowest, saddest thumbing heave-ho that the major leagues have ever seen. "There's just no throwing at people in baseball." The crowd sat silent, disbelieving. The Rookie, head bowed, walked off the field.

And (I said) he kept walking. The Chief and Matty and Mr. McGraw were waiting for him in the dugout, but he walked away from them, didn't even stop to take off his uniform in the center field clubhouse, just kept walking, right out of the Polo Grounds, day after day, week after week, until he was back in Anywhere, U.S.A., still in his uniform. His mother didn't ask any questions. She hugged him, helped him out of his uniform (she hung it in the closet), and asked him if he wanted something to eat, and the next day he went back to school. His legend grew, but he never picked up a ball again.

Luke sat up. "He did not go home to his mother," he said clearly. I felt horrible, as evil as Ty Cobb. I saw in his eyes what seemed to me not anger, exactly, but something more like doubt, religious doubt as it is described in nineteenth-century novels. What if the Rookie hadn't risen again? What if the story had been only a story? What if someone was obviously manipulating it for a moral purpose? He had the relics and the photos, but like a true believer, he knew that it was all just talk if the Rookie didn't rise again.

"He did not go home to his mother," he said again, and as quickly as I could, in a panic, I turned it around. Of course not, I said. He went home for that day, to relax. The next day a delegation from both leagues was in his front yard, insisting that he come back to the Giants. "Baseball can't survive without you, kid," said Ban Johnson, president of the American League. Even Cobb himself, bandaged and sheepish, was there. Finally the Rookie agreed to come back—"But no more dirty tricks," he said—and they played an eighth game (as they'd done once before), which he won.

"You told the story wrong," he said finally. (And the next day he said to his mother, "Daddy told the Rookie story wrong.") So the story goes on, only now it is much more under the child's control. The Rookie soon entered a Gothic phase, as the little boy began to demand scary Rookie stories ("With a real witch. Not Ty Cobb dressed up like a witch. Not the Chief dressed up like a witch. A real witch") and, more recently, a decadent phase. The current story, for instance, involves Sherlock Holmes, the genie from *Aladdin,* a *T. rex,* and the Pirate King from *Pirates of Penzance.* Having been, if only momentarily, betrayed by the story, he was doing what the literary critics would call "contesting the narrative." The story belongs to him now.

My Rookie never really played ball again, no matter how many stories I tell, any more than Sherlock Holmes really came back alive from the Reichenbach Falls, no matter how many stories Conan Doyle wrote about him afterward. I think the Rookie just went home to Anywhere, U.S.A., and back to school like all the other kids.

Luke and I tried playing a little catch this spring in the Luxembourg Gardens but gave up after about five minutes. For a present, around that time, he asked us to make him his own *carte d'identité,* marked with a *métier de journaliste*—a press pass from the government—so that he could pretend to cut through red tape. We made him an impressive-looking fake government document, with a black-and-white photo and lots of cryptic, official-looking stamps. At bedtime now before the Rookie story starts, he likes to act out a French bureaucratic drama: I play a functionary guarding an entrance to something or other who scowls at him until he haughtily flashes his *carte,* and then I let him pass with many apologetic, ah-monsieur-I-did-not-recognize grimaces and shrugs, while his mother acts out the role of irate bystander, fuming in line as the privileged functionary serenely passes by. I suppose it is about time we took him home.

I don't think about the Rookie as much as I used to, but when the bombs began to fall in Serbia I began thinking about that other Serbian conflagration, in 1914, and everything it had led to, and I realized with a start that by making the Rookie three years old in 1908, I was leaving him, unprotected, to the century's horrors. Then I did a quick calculation and realized that he would have been far too young for the First War, and just too old for the Second. The Rookie was lucky that way, I think.

A Machine to Draw the World

The World Cup,
and After

The World Cup soccer tournament got off to a strange, promising start with a pageant that closed down Paris—a seventeenth-century-style allegorical masque, with music and dance and speech, which featured four sixty-five-foot-high inflatable giants that walked across the city from four Parisian monuments (the Opéra, the Eiffel Tower, the Arc de Triomphe, and the pont Neuf) to the place de la Concorde. The giants were steel-framed latex-covered figures—dolls, really—with fork-lift trucks for feet, and hydraulic hinged arms and hips and shoulders, and even moving eyelids. They turned their heads, and shifted their gaze, and raised their arms in wonder as they slowly shuffled along the Paris streets. Each one was a different color and represented a racial type. There was Romeo, the European; Pablo, the Amerindian; Ho, the Asian; and Moussa, the African (he had purple skin). It took four hours for them to get from their starting points to the place, where they bowed to one another, and the whole spectacle was broadcast live on television, while Juliette Binoche breathed over the loudspeakers on the streets and to the audience at home. ("The giants confront each other, but do they see a stranger or themselves?" etc.) The theme of the masque seemed to be the Self and the Other; the giants, never having seen one another before—or anything else, apparently— wake in the middle of Paris, to find their Selfness in the Others. Apart from that, the commentators on French television were hard put to find something to say as the big guys inched their way along the boulevards toward this revelation and at one point were reduced to noting that the technology that had produced the hydraulic giants had military applications, leaving you with the comforting knowledge that if NATO is ever in need of a crack synchronized team of huge, slow-moving inflatable dolls, the French will be the ones to call. (One sees them cornering a particularly sluggish war criminal in a Montenegrin mountain hideaway with a very large door.)

The vague internationalist symbolism—not to speak of the snail-like pace—seemed the right allegory for the tournament. The Coupe du Monde, which includes thirty-two nations, began on Wednesday, June 10, and continues through Sunday, July 12. I set myself the task of watching it all, wanting to figure out what exactly it is that the world loves in a game that so many American sports fans will sit through only under compulsion.

I understand why people play it. When I was a teenager, I lived in London for a while, and I spent most of my time playing soccer, or at least the middle-class Kensington Gardens version of it. I even learned how to talk the game. It was the opposite of trash talking—tidy talking, I suppose you'd have to call it. If you did something good, it was brilliant; something less than brilliant was useless; if all of you were useless together, you were rubbish; and if a person did something brilliant that nonetheless became useless, everyone cried, "Oh, unlucky!" By the end of my time in London, I wasn't brilliant at the game, but I wasn't useless either. I suppose this was all faithful to the game's English-school-playing-field origins. "Thoughtful ball," a commentator on the BBC would say about a good pass. In the papers you'll read things like "The signs of decline in the still-clever but jaded Teddy Sheringham sadly became too patent to ignore." "For all his apparent world-weariness, Beckham is still young." "[Anderton] has been stubborn to the point almost of self-destruction, however, and it cannot happen again this week." This isn't sportswriting. It's end-of-term reports.

As I began watching the cup games, though, I had a hard time making a case for soccer as spectacle. I found myself torn between a cosmopolitan desire to love a game the world loves and an American suspicion that they wouldn't love it if they had a choice. The trouble wasn't the low scores, although the ribbon of late sports news often sounded like one of those condensed, hopeless, rising-and-falling monologues about marriage in Beckett: "Nil-nil. One-one. Two-one. One-one. One-nil. Nil-nil." The trouble was what the scores represent. The game has achieved a kind of tactical stasis. Things start off briskly and then fritter away into desultory shin kicking, like a *Wall Street Journal* editorial. In soccer the defense has too big an edge to keep the contest interesting, like basketball before the coming of the twenty-four-second clock or the western front before the invention of the tank.

All sports take turns being dominated by their defense or their offense, and fully evolved defensive tactics will in the end beat offensive ones, because it is always easier to break a sequence than to build one up. Eventually the defensive edge will be so enormous that to stay in business as a spectacle, a sport has to change its rules, openly or surreptitiously. The big recent change in basketball, for instance, which took place somewhere between the Julius Erving and Michael Jordan eras, was a silent modification of the rule against traveling, so that now, it seems, a player can take about as many steps as he needs—a fact that only Rabbit Angstrom has officially noted. American football changes its rules every few years to allow quarterbacks to survive and prosper. Even baseball has tinkered with the mound and the depth of the fences. Soccer players, though, have come to accept the scarcity economy—all those nil-nil draws—and just live with it, like Eskimos. The defense has such an advantage that the national sides don't need their offensive stars. In this cup two of the most inspired forwards in Europe—David Ginola, of France, Newcastle, and now Tottenham Hotspur, and Paul Gascoigne, of England and whatever pub is open—didn't even make their national teams.

Since a defensive system keeps players from getting a decent chance to score, the idea is to get an indecent one: to draw a foul so that the referee awards a penalty, which is essentially a free goal. This creates an enormous disproportion between the foul and the reward. In the first game that Italy played, against Chile, for instance, the great Roberto Baggio saved the Italians' *pancetta* by smoking the ball onto the hand of a surprised Chilean defender, who couldn't pull back in time. "Hand ball" was ruled, which, near the goal, meant an automatic penalty and a nearly automatic goal. The other, more customary method of getting a penalty is to walk into the "area" with the ball, get breathed on hard, and then immediately collapse, like a man shot by a sniper, arms and legs splayed out, while you twist in agony and beg for morphine, and your teammates smite their foreheads at the tragic waste of a young life. The referee buys this more often than you might think. Afterward the postgame did-he-fall-or-was-he-pushed argument can go on for hours.

European defenders of the game tend to put on haughty, half-amused looks when the sport is criticized and assume that the problem lies with the American doing the criticizing, who is assumed to love action for its own sake. When you point out that ice hockey, the greatest of all games, shares with soccer the basic idea of putting something into a net behind a goalkeeper and has the added bonus of actually doing it, they giggle: "Oh, dear. In ice hockey you can't see the ball, or whatever you call it. You can't follow it. Besides, they fight all the time." It does no good when you try to explain that you can always see the puck, and anyway, better to fight like heroes than to spend all your time on the sidelines bickering about who touched the ball last before it went out of bounds, the way soccer players do, even though—as a Tom Stoppard character once pointed out—there is absolutely no doubt on the part of those two players about who touched the ball last.

European soccer apologists tend to overanalyze the triumphs of their heroes. In Brazil's game against Scotland, Ronaldo, the Brazilians' star, took the ball, faked right, and then spun around to his left, leaving a defender fooled while he rushed forward into the gap. Then he let go a weak shot, and it was over. A nice move—but exactly the same move that Emmitt Smith makes three times a game with three steroid-enraged three-hundred-pound linemen draped on his back (and then Emmitt goes in to score) or that Mario Lemieux made three or four times a period after receiving radiation therapy for Hodgkin's lymphoma and having three Saskatchewan farm boys whacking at his ankles with huge clubs (and then Mario would go in to score). In the papers, though, that moment became a golden event. Rob Hughes, the estimable soccer writer for the *International Herald Tribune,* treated the three seconds of actual activity as though it were the whole of the Peloponnesian War, or a seduction by Casanova. "Receiving the ball from Cafu on the right, Ronaldo lured Colin Hendry, Scotland's biggest and most worldly defender, to him. 'Come closer, Big Colin, come to me,' the Brazilian seemed to say. And Hendry bought the invitation. Tighter and tighter he came until, suddenly, Ronaldo swiveled 180 degrees. . . ."

Soccer writers seemed as starved for entertainment as art critics; anything vaguely enjoyable gets promoted to the level of genius. In the old days, at the Kitchen, it was the rule that three recognizable notes sung in succession by Laurie Anderson heralded a new, generous lyricism. Ronaldo's magic was like a performance artist's lyricism: It existed but was apparent only against a background of numbing boredom.

In the first ten days I watched, by my count, sixteen games, including odd, hallucinatory matchups out of some fractured game of Risk: Denmark against Saudi Arabia (1–0); Croatia against Japan (1–0); Nigeria against Bulgaria (1–0). There were a few players who stood out from the general run of bowlegged men in shorts. There were Englishmen (I root for England, from residual Kensington Gardens chauvinism): the pained, gifted O. J. Simpson look-alike Paul Ince; a speedy, tiny boy with a shining morning face named Michael Owen, only eighteen and just off the Liverpool bench. The French players were dogged, unelectric, powerful, and, as many people pointed out, mostly not ethnically French, with lots of "exotic" names: Zidane, Djorkaeff, Karembeu. Though their countrymen long for the dash and élan of David Ginola and the vanished Eric Cantona, they see the functionary logic of this harder-working, intelligent side. There were the Argentines and the Germans, who never seem quite as glamorous as, say, the Brazilians and the Dutch, but who have a brutal purposefulness. Between them they have won four of the last six cups. And there were moments of wonder, when a previously unknown—and probably soon to be unknown again—ballplayer would shock himself and his team-mates with a single stunning moment. A young Cameroonian named Pierre Njanka, with no major-league experience, made his way through the entire Austrian team, his eyes wide as he ducked and swerved, stumbling forward, out of control, hardly believing what he was accomplishing, and then scored. He may spend the rest of his life defined by that run.

But such moments were mostly drowned in tedium and then by something worse. By the time the English players arrived on the scene, on Monday, June 15, everything was already ruined. Hooligans had invaded Marseilles, where England was opening against Tunisia, and not merely got drunk and beat up shop-keepers but overran a beach where Tunisian families were pic-nicking (there is a big Tunisian community in the South of France) and beat up kids and moms there. Everyone had known that they were coming. One source said that the authorities had done their best to keep out the hardboiled Category C hooligans, but some of them had managed to sneak in—a rare case of England's having a deep bench.

Though headlines about English hooligans sweep the world, they don't do justice to the terror involved. "Lager louts" and "hooligans" sound vaguely quaint, but these guys are cruel, violent, and twisted by inarticulate hatred in a way that terrifies the French and makes them wild partisans of the Scottish team. The persistence of English hooliganism—the Englishness of hooliganism—can maybe be explained by the possibility that at some half-conscious level a lot of English people are proud of their thugs and approve of their behavior. This approval consists of a toxic combination of sentimental left-wing anti-Thatcherism (a kind of *Trainspotting* pride that at least the thugs aren't businessmen) coupled with a romantic right-wing chauvinism (it's an English tradition to go to the Continent and hit foreigners). In the Marseilles attacks most of the thugs turned out not to be poor kids, or unemployed kids; they couldn't have afforded the passage over. The thugs were, apparently, mostly postal workers (what is it about mail?), and they were not going to be damaged in the eyes of their mates for having gone over to France to beat people up, or for being sent back from France for having beat people up.

|||

Despite the reports of violence from provincial fronts, Paris itself has been relatively blasé about the cup. The streets are peaceful, the mood is calm, the atmosphere pastoral. The boulevard Saint-Germain has never been so quiet. The morning after the giants' march, for instance, with Scotland and Brazil about to begin at the Stade de France, the only evidence I saw of anything unusual was the appearance of two Scotsmen in kilts waiting for a taxi on the rue du Bac. Expecting to hear a war cry ("Ay, we'll leave them samba-dancin' laddies guid and bloody"), I tentatively wished them good luck. "We'll need it!" one said feelingly, and the other chimed in, "It's simply a privilege to be playing Brazil." They turned out to be lawyers from Hong Kong—Scottish lawyers from Hong Kong, but lawyers. They talked about the Brazilian esprit, and then got in their cab and, in perfect French, ordered the driver to go to the Stade de France.

I saw Italy beat Cameroon, 3–0, from the back of a bar in Venice. Watching soccer in Italy, you have the feeling that you have wandered into a family drama more complex and intense than you can understand. Each player—Vieri, Di Biagio—was greeted with a combination of hoots, cheers, and tears so personal and heartfelt that it was almost embarrassing for an outsider to witness. With Italy into the eighth-finals (eighth-finals!), the papers, from left to right, were bursting with pride. ITALIA PADRONE! read one headline. "Italy Rules." The curious thing was that Italy played one of the dullest defensive games of all—the famous "blue chain." But this didn't seem to bother anyone. Whatever people were watching for, it wasn't for fun.

Just afterward I spoke on the phone to an English friend, a big World Cupper.

"How are you getting on with the cup?" he asked.

"It's a bit—well, don't you think it's a bit lacking in entertainment?" I said weakly.

There was a pause. "Why would you expect it to be entertaining?" he asked, reprovingly.

Perhaps that was a clue. I came back to Paris resolved not to be entertained. I watched a double-overtime confrontation between an overmatched Paraguay and an overpressed France. The Paraguayans, who looked worn out from stress, essentially surrendered the idea of scoring and kept dropping back—kicking the ball out, heading it out, willing it out, again and again. It was obvious that their desperate, gallant strategy was to force a nil-nil draw, over 120 minutes, and then "go to penalties," the shoot-out at goal where anything can happen and anyone can win. The nil-nil draw wasn't a "result" they would settle for; it was everything they dreamed of achieving. When the game finally ended, as Laurent Blanc (a traditionally French-sounding name) stumbled a ball into the Paraguayan net, what was most memorable was the subdued triumph. The French celebrated, but they did not exult; the Paraguayans cried—really cried—but they did not despair. They did not seem ruined or emptied out, as American losers do. They seemed relieved. The tears looked like tears of bitter accomplishment. We knew we were going to lose, the faces and the back pats said, but, hey, didn't we hold it off for a while? ("*Héroïque, héroïque,*" murmured the French commentator.)

The next morning I slipped in a tape I'd made of the fifth game of the NBA finals, for purposes of comparison. It was a French broadcast, and the commentators announced that the game was a test of truth—*une épreuve de vérité*—for the Utah Jazz. To my surprise, I was, after a week of starvation, used to the austerity of soccer scoring. All those basketball points seemed a little loud, a little cheap. Points coming in from left, from right, cheap points, inspired points, stupid points—goals everywhere you looked, more goals than you knew what to do with, democratic goals, all leveled and equal. It was too much, like eating whipped cream straight. And why had I never before noticed the absurd, choppy, broken rhythm of deliberate fouls and time-outs in the last two minutes of the game?

A few nights later England-Argentina—to see who would go to the quarterfinals. The match started off with two typically exasperating soccer events. After only five minutes David Seaman, the English goalkeeper, lunged for the ball, and an onrushing Argentine stumbled over him. Penalty and, inevitably, a goal. Then young Owen, who, with his brush cut, looks as if he ought to be wearing a blazer and beanie, got tripped. He acted out the death scene from *Camille* and drew a penalty himself, which was knocked in by Alan Shearer, England's captain. A few minutes later Owen raced half the length of the field—really sprinting, huffing—mesmerizing an Argentine defenseman, who kept moving back, back, defeated in his own mind, and then he sent it in: 2–1, England! With fifteen seconds left in the half, Argentina got the ball, executed a jagged, pinball-quick exchange of passes and, shockingly, the ball was bouncing in the net, and the game was tied.

At the start of the second half, David Beckham, the blond midfielder who was at the time engaged to Posh Spice, was expelled from the game, leaving England, like the Spices, a performer short. Though England scored on a corner, the goal was ruled out by the referee for a meaningless, barely visible (but undeniably real) elbow. Nothing happened in thirty minutes of overtime, and the game went into the self-parody of soccer: a series of penalty kicks. With England needing only one more to tie, David Batty, of Newcastle, stepped up and, rushing his shot, fired it right into the diving goaltender. The Argentine side rushed out into the pitch, weeping with joy and exhaustion.

The game had been marked by everything that can exasperate an American fan: the dominance of defense, the disproportion between foul and consequence, the absurd penalty shoot-out, the playacting. (In England they will be arguing did-he-fall-or-was-he-pushed about the first Argentine penalty for years.) But it had been as draining as any contest I'd ever seen.

Soccer was not meant to be enjoyed. It was meant to be experienced. The World Cup is a festival of fate: man accepting his hard circumstances, the near certainty of his failure. There is, after all, something familiar about a contest in which nobody wins and nobody pots a goal. Nil-nil is the score of life. This may be where the difficulty lies for Americans, who still look for Eden out there on the ballfield. But soccer is not meant to be an escape from life. It *is* life, in all its injustice and tedium: We seek unfair advantage, celebrate tiny moments of pleasure as though they were final victories, score goals for the wrong side. (In the first three nights of the World Cup, three of the seventeen goals were "own" goals: A player would head the ball away and watch it backspin past his own goalkeeper, his face a rapidly changing mask of decision, satisfaction, worry, disbelief, and despair.) A bad play or call in baseball—Merkle's boner or Denkinger's call—hurts, but usually there's a saving air of humor. "We're due," "It's our turn," "Wait till next year" are the cheers of American sport. We are optimists and look to sports to amplify our optimism.

In soccer tomorrow is a long way off, even in ordinary circumstances, and four years in these special ones. By then everything will be different; there are no second chances in the World Cup. It is a human contest on a nearly geologic time scale. Grievances, injustices rankle for years, decades, forever. But along with that comes, appealingly, a sense of proportion. Accepting the eventual certainty of defeat in turn liberates you to take real joy in any small victory, that one good kick. If American sports are played in paradise, soccer takes place after the fall. Even its squabbles have their echoes: Did he fall or was he pushed? It's the oldest question.

Finally, on a stray, leaking cable channel, I got to see highlights of Detroit and Washington in the Stanley Cup final. I turned it on with joy and then found, to my shock, that . . . I couldn't see the puck! It was too small, way too small—a tiny black spot on a vast white surface, with huge men in bright-colored sweaters hulking over it. When a goal was scored (and goals do get scored), I knew it only by the subsequent celebration. I squinted at the set and called in Martha, a purebred Canadian, and asked if she could follow the puck. "I could never follow the puck," she told me.

Had I been corrupted by the Old World's game or enlightened by it? Another of the old, unanswerable questions. All I knew was that I was looking forward to the next big match, between France and Italy. Anything might happen, or nothing at all.

|||

Although France didn't win the World Cup until just before midnight on Sunday, the celebrations in Paris started hours before the game began. By two o'clock in the afternoon the beeping of horns along the Seine had become a din, and the kids with their faces painted red-white-and-blue, heads poking up through the sunroofs of Peugeots racing along the quays, had become a menace. Win or lose, the *crise* was already over.

Cars are cars all over the world, of course, and horns are horns, and a victory celebration in Paris doesn't sound much different from a victory celebration in New York or, for that matter, from a traffic tieup outside the Holland Tunnel. Even the theme song of the French victory was not the "Marseillaise" but Queen's "We Are the Champions."

Anyway, the whole point of the celebration was that it wasn't a champagne occasion. It was bottled water and cheap booze and a lot of beer. What made it memorable was that, for once, the carnival atmosphere of the Latin Quarter and the Marais spilled over into official French culture, and kept right on spilling. (By Tuesday morning, it had even spilled over into the garden of the Élysée, where a visibly blanching President Chirac greeted the players to a chorus of "We Are the Champions," sung, in best Freddie Mercury English, by the crowd thronging the team.)

At one-thirty in the morning after the victory, you could take the world's most beautiful walk—beginning at the Institut de France and moving across the pont des Arts and around the cour Carrée of the Louvre and then to the Tuileries and the Champs-Élysées—and feel as if, in the presence of so many happy people, the grand siècle itself had gone a little lopsided and blissed out. Misrule ruled. A man wrapped in a tricolor was relieving himself against the front wall of the Institut de France—discreetly, with maximum esprit de corps, but, still, relieving himself. Someone was selling beer out of a cooler, violating about twelve hundred French laws in the act, and someone else had one of those pinball arcade love-o-meters set up. (Everybody's hand was hot; even an American writer saw his score shoot past "Casanova" and all the way up to *"Chaud Lapin"*—"Hot Rabbit!") Kids were singing; men were grabbing politely at girls, presumably with a memory of 1944, when the girls were said to have grabbed back. This time they didn't, but it didn't matter.

Many people had talked a lot about the ethnic mix of the French team, which was composed of players of Algerian, Basque, and Ghanaian descent, among others, but the players themselves seemed a lot less self-conscious about this than journalists did. French identity is not that hard to achieve; if you speak French, you feel French. What is hard for an immigrant or an outsider in France to achieve is French institutional acceptance, a place in the crowded, ancient French iconography. The faces you saw on the World Cup team—the faces of Zidane and Djorkaeff and Karembeu—are already part of French society. They just hadn't been integrated before into the French self-image, and now they were.

It's natural for people to hope that the victory of a multiracial team might be the beginning of the end of Le Pen and the racist National Front, but it probably won't be. The ability of sports to solve social problems is limited—the Dream Team didn't change black income levels—and anyway, Le Pen blandly claimed the victory for himself. It was a reassertion of French glory, he said, and who is more glorious about France than he? The logic of nationalism always flows downhill, toward the gutter.

The real victory on Sunday night was a victory for disorder, an unexpected blessing, bonking the head of an unprepared population. On that long, beautiful walk, there's a moment when you arrive at the gate of the Tuileries and, for the first time, see the expanse of the Champs-Élysées. On Sunday you expected to see what you always see: a line of red car lights going up the right side of the champs and a line of white lights running down the left—two perfect, side-by-side mile-long lines of red and white, framed by the Arc de Triomphe. On Sunday night, for the first time that anyone could remember, the two neat columns of light were gone. The champs, a chaos of people and cars, was a blur of indistinct movement, the lights and colors a smear of milky pink. For once Paris was all mixed up.

The Balzar
Wars

The Balzar, on the rue des Écoles, in the Fifth Arrondissement of Paris, happens to be the best restaurant in the world. It is the best restaurant in the world not because it has the best food— though the food is (or used to be) excellent—and not because it is "hot," or even particularly fashionable, but because of a hundred small things that make it a uniquely soulful and happy place.

The Balzar is a brasserie, which means that it is Alsatian in origin, serves beer, and stays open late. Over the years it has added a full dinner menu, so that it has become indistinguishable from a restaurant. For more than a hundred years the Balzar has been a family business, and each of the families has managed to keep it constant without making it stale. It's a one-story, one-room spot, small by brasserie standards—with only ninety or so covers—and has a glass front that looks out onto the street; you can see with one eye people boarding the number 63 bus in the twilight, and with the other a pretty little park dedicated to Montaigne, with plane trees and pink-flowering chestnuts.

The Balzar is a democratic place. You are greeted at the door with a handshake and a quick squint of crinkled, harried warmth, by the two maîtres d'hôtel—one always in a tuxedo, the other in a suit—and are shown to your table with a few pensive words about families, children, and the weather. There's not a trace of unctuousness or forced familiarity, no appraisal of your wallet, your last review, or your weekend gross. There are long banquettes covered with dark brown leather along the walls, and a T-shaped banquette in the middle of the room. On the tables are white linen and glasses and silver. The light—from eight round globe lamps, high above—is warm and bright, gay without being harsh. The *carte* is a long printed card, with the dishes listed on the front and the wines on the back, and it never changes. There are leeks and tomato salad and herring for starters—foie gras if you're in an expansive mood—and then the same five or so *plats:* *steak au poivre,* roast chicken, grilled sole or salmon, calf's liver, *gigot* with white and green beans. The wine list is short, and usually the best thing on it is the Réserve Balzar, a pleasant red Bordeaux. The only sauces are the *sauce au poivre* on the steak and a béarnaise for the grilled salmon. The *pommes frites* are fine, the *crème caramel* is good, the profiteroles the best in Paris.

It is the waiters—or *serveurs,* as they're called—who give the Balzar its soul. A team of the same ten men has been in place for decades: They are courteous, warmhearted, ironic (able to warn a client off a dubious *plat* with an eyebrow), and mildly lubricious. (They have been known to evaluate, sotto voce, the size and shape of a woman's rear even as they pull out the table to make way for it.) They work hard. By tradition at the Balzar, the *plats* arrive beautifully arranged on an oval platter and then are carefully transferred by the waiter to a round plate. This doubles the work but creates an effect. Whenever I am feeling blue, I like to go to the Balzar and watch a waiter gravely transfer a *steak au poivre* and its accompaniments from an oval platter to a plate, item by item. It reaffirms my faith in the sanity of superfluous civilization.

The other famous Left Bank brasserie, the Lipp, is known as a canteen for the men of power in the Fifth Republic, but when Lionel Jospin, the virtuous Socialist who is trying to transform French politics, was running for president three years ago, he made an event of being photographed, for *Paris Match,* having dinner at the Balzar. Everyone got the point.

On a Sunday night in April, Martha and I, with Luke, were sitting at a table in the back, just finishing one in a long line of good dinners and were once again refining our long-term plan to be buried at the Balzar—or, more precisely, to have the urns containing our ashes placed on the dessert counter just above the mille-feuilles and the lemon tart, and on either side of the flowers. The plaques, we decided, should read "A Faithful Client" or, better, should repeat the words of those inscriptions you see all over Paris: "Here, fallen for France . . ."

Just then Jean-Claude, the maître d' in the tuxedo, came over to our table. His gravelly *sud-ouest* voice was pitched low, and to my amazement, his eyes were glistening. "I'd like to introduce you to someone who'll be working with us," he said graciously, and he summoned a melancholy-faced, lantern-jawed man, buttoned up in a good suit, whom I had idly noticed standing by the door earlier in the evening. "This is M. Delouche," he said. I shook hands with M. Delouche and raised my eyebrows at Jean-Claude.

"The Balzar has been sold," he said. "M. Delouche is here representing the new management." He walked away quickly, and M. Delouche followed.

I grabbed our waiter as he came by the table. "The restaurant has been sold?" I said. "To whom was it sold?"

"To the Flo Group," he answered, in a strangled voice.

The Flo Group! I felt as I imagined I would feel if I had been stabbed: first surprise, then nothing, then pain. The Flo Group is the creation of an Alsatian waiter turned restaurant tycoon named Jean-Paul Bucher, and in Paris it is often referred to as the *rouleau compresseur Flo,* the Flo steamroller. It is for many people the symbol of the forces of restaurant consolidation, globalization, standardization, and even Disneyfication; Flo runs five restaurants at Disneyland Paris. Over the past thirty years Bucher has bought up some of the oldest and most famous brasseries and bistros in Paris, while also running a chain of lesser Flos, a catering business, and a chain of cheap restaurants called Hippopotamus. Some of the Flo Group restaurants—Julien, Le Boeuf sur le Toit—are actually pretty good. But even the good places have a processed, overwrought quality, and the food at one is pretty much like the food at the others. They lack all the things that the Balzar possesses so effortlessly: distinctiveness, eccentricity, and a sense of continuity.

A few moments later one of the waiters, whom I had known for a long time, and whom I'll call Thierry, came up to me and suggested, under his breath, that we meet for coffee the next day. When we met, Thierry told me the history of the Balzar, seen from below. He was in mufti, wearing jeans and a jean jacket, a standard uniform for off-duty waiters, like blue windbreakers on off-duty New York cops. The Balzar had never been a perfectly happy place, he maintained, and the *syndicat,* the union, had suffered a good deal even under the old owners. Nonetheless the *garçons* loved the work, because they liked the clients and the clients liked them. (I noticed that he referred to the waiters by the usually forbidden, old-fashioned word *garçons,* or boys, and that he also referred to their métier as *restauration,* or restaurant work. The two words together gave their profession blue-collar integrity.) He outlined their fears. The Flo people, he said, might close the Balzar "for restoration" and disperse the waiters to other Flo restaurants, all over Paris, never to be reassembled. "They express a savoir-faire that dates from 1968," he said. "Ours dates from 1894." It was said that the Flo people had arranged to have American tour groups brought to the Balzar; it was also said that they were standardizing the kitchen produce, bringing it in line with the rest of the Flo Group. More immediately, the *garçons* were appalled because the new man, M. Delouche, had been put "on the service," drawing his salary from their tips—the

15 percent service charge that is added to all French restaurant bills. (Thierry explained to me that the service charge was real and sacrosanct; before Flo took over, one of the *garçons* collected it at the end of every evening and put it in a drawer, to which each of them had a key. Now they have to wait five weeks for the same money.) It also turned out that the suit-tuxedo distinction among the greeters was a deeply significant code: A maître d' in a suit was aligned with the owner, one in a tuxedo with the staff.

Within a week or so a group of Balzar regulars, mostly editors and publishers and professors—the Balzar is around the corner from the Sorbonne—arranged to meet at the apartment of one of the staunchest clients, on the quai Anatole-France, to think about what we could do. It was a beautiful day, but ominous reports were coming in from all sides. Someone had had a doubtful sole; someone else had noticed that *oeufs crevettes,* hard-boiled eggs with shrimp, had been sneaked onto the menu. (No, no, someone else said, reassuringly, the *oeufs crevettes* were there twenty years ago; it was really a restoration.) More seriously, it was said that the waiters were being forced to rush checks to the table. It is a Balzar tradition that you can nurse even a cup of coffee and a plate of cold cuts for as long as you like. Now, it was said, after seventy minutes the waiters were forced to put the check on the table. This was—well, there was no other word for it—so American. You see this in California, someone said; he had eaten once in Santa Monica, and the young woman slapped the bill on the table after an hour and a half. (I could only imagine the waitress, on her way to her tai chi or acting class, dying on the vine while a couple of Frenchmen sat polishing off a bottle and solving the world's problems.) More horror stories were told; a keen-eyed regular claimed to have spotted a Flo Group camion parked outside the Balzar at six o'clock one morning, bringing in Flo produce.

It was obvious that something had to be done, but what? One person suggested a boycott; another person a sit-in; someone else a campaign of letter writing. We had a left, a right, and a center even before we had a party. Finally a leader emerged, a handsome, round-faced young publisher named Lorenzo Valentin. He had an excellent plan: Why not invite all the regulars we could find to reserve tables on the same night, occupy the restaurant, make a scene, and demand that Bucher meet with us? Fine, someone else said, but added that if we did it, we had to be sure not to leave the waiters, on whose behalf we were acting, "in an ambiguous position." If we sat in, occupied the restaurant, and didn't order anything, they would be the ones to suffer. Therefore we also had to order and eat dinner. Good, one woman said, but we had to be sure to hold on to the tables for the entire evening. "Eat, but eat slowly" would be our motto. Why not order foie gras on toast, she suggested; that could be spread very slowly. She mimed just how to do it, like a veteran of many a foie gras slow-down on the barricades. We all watched her studiously.

During the next two weeks, as I helped organize the occupation, I felt exhilarated, though I recognized in my exhilaration a certain hypocrisy. Like every American in France, I had spent a fair amount of time being exasperated by the French because of their inability to accept change, their refusal to accept the inevitable logic of the market, and their tendency to blame Americans for everything. As I raged against the changes at the Balzar, I began to hear people repeating to me the same tiresome and sensible logic that I had been preaching so long myself: that nothing stays the same; change must be welcomed; one must choose to live in the world as it is or live in a museum whose walls increasingly recede inward. . . . It was all true, and when it came to the Balzar, I didn't care. I would like to say that the difference was that my concern was now attached to particular people—to Thierry and Jean-Claude and the rest. But that would be giving myself too much credit for disinterestedness. The difference was not that it was happening to the Balzar. The difference was that it was happening to me. I was being asked to give up the continuity of a thousand small associations and pleasures—the night we went after we signed the lease, the night we went, still jet-lagged, after a summer away—and I didn't see why I should.

"Can't repeat the past?" says Gatsby. "Why of course you can!"
And every American schoolchild is taught that in this belief lies
Gatsby's tragedy. But why should the thought be so absurd?
Can't repeat the past? We do it every day. We build a life, or try
to, of pleasures and duties that will become routine, so that every
day will be the same day, or nearly so, "the day of our life," Randall Jarrell called it. There seemed to me nothing stranger about
my wanting to eat forever at an unchanged Balzar than about my
wanting to stay married to the same wife or be father of the same
kid. ("M. Bucher has now bought your family, and will be adding
a new child to the staff on the same terms. Change is good.
Here, try Ralphie for a while. He comes from the centralized
nursery and only speaks German, but you'll soon find that . . .")
On the day of my life, I eat dinner at the Balzar—the Balzar as it
is and was, and not some improved, Flo Group version. I realize
that one of the tricks of capitalism is to lure you into a mislead-
ingly unreciprocated love with a cash register, but what impressed me about my friends in the Balzar war was that they
weren't prepared to treat their attachment to the Balzar as somehow less real than the cash register's attachment to it.

June 25 was picked as the day for our occupation of the
Balzar. We carefully arranged to stagger our phone calls to reserve tables for that Thursday night, to avoid tipping our hand.
When my turn came, I was so nervous that I had to dial twice,
and then, in a high-pitched quaver, I reserved my table. ("*Oui,
madame,*" said an obviously bemused maître d'.) On the night I
arrived with a couple of friends. The tables filled up with regulars, gaily overacting the part of ordinary diners: Oh, how *sympa,*
you're here too, we said to each other, exchanging meaty, significant winks. We ordered apéritifs and made nervous conversation. Finally, at nine o'clock, the last regular sat down, and, with
two taps on a glass, Lorenzo Valentin rose. The revolution was
under way.

"We are here tonight," he said, "to demonstrate our sympathy with the waiters, clients, and tradition of the Balzar." Valentin stepped away from his table and addressed Bucher's man, M. Delouche, directly. Delouche clasped his hands behind his back and thrust out his chin, both obsequious and defiant. When I saw him like that, bearing the brunt of a sudden wave of disapproval—and, surely, thinking, I'm the working stiff here, these people are rich *gauchistes,* easy for them—I have to admit that a small whitecap of sympathy for him rose in my mind.

"This is not a personal assault on anyone," Lorenzo declared. "We have gathered here tonight as, shall we say, an opportunity to discuss the issue at the heart of our concerns about the recent purchase of the Balzar by the Flo Group. Our question is: Is this merely a place to eat or is it something more, and if it is something more, what is it? Our organization, Les Amis du Balzar, is here to safeguard the quality and, what's more, to defend the spirit and the staff of a place that we believe offers a respite from time itself." This was grandly said, and he got a big hand.

M. Delouche attempted to defend his position, but his voice was mostly inaudible. All you could make out was "logic," "safeguard," "continuity."

"But what about the staff?" Lorenzo demanded. "What of their continuity?"

"Les serveurs! Les serveurs!" The cry went up from around the room as we pounded the tables and hit cutlery against glasses. The waiters, their eyes fixed studiously on the floor or on the tables, continued to serve.

"Why can't this place be different from other places bought by Flo?" another protester said, rising to his feet. "We all know what Flo does. How many people here are former clients of La Coupole?"

"Anciens! Anciens!" we chanted in unison, pounding the tables some more, meaning that we used to go to La Coupole and didn't anymore.

We were building up to an impressive pitch of indignation,

but at that point the waiters began to serve the dinners that we had ordered while we were waiting to begin our protest, and this weakened the revolutionary spirit a little. There was, I sensed, a flaw in our strategy: If you take over a restaurant as an act of protest and then order dinner at the restaurant, what you have actually done is gone to the restaurant and had dinner, since a restaurant is, by definition, always occupied, by its diners. Having come to say that you just won't take it anymore, you have to add sheepishly that you *will* take it, *au point* and with béarnaise sauce. It was as if at the Boston Tea Party the patriots had boarded the ship, bought up all the boxes of tea, and then brewed them.

Nonetheless we carried on. We loudly criticized the fish; we angrily demanded a meeting with Bucher; we rose and offered memories of the Balzar, and vowed that we would fight for the Balzar yet to be.

We were hoping for a little *médiatisation,* and we got it. Pieces about the protest appeared in the magazine *Marianne* and in *Le Figaro.* Then, unfortunately, Jean-Pierre Quélin, the food critic of *Le Monde,* who is a kind of Jonathan Yardley of French restaurant writing, weighed in, announcing that the food at the Balzar had always been terrible—but that he had eaten there since the Flo Group took over, and now it was even worse, so to hell with everybody. Lorenzo thought that this might actually be a useful article for our cause: By defining the Balzar radical fringe, Quélin was allowing us to occupy the rational center.

To the surprise of my American self, Bucher sent back word that he would be delighted to meet with our association, to have breakfast with what amounted to our Directorate at the Balzar itself. At nine on a Saturday morning we assembled at the Café Sorbon, across the street and then trooped over to meet the enemy. Bucher turned out to be a simple round Alsatian, wearing an open shirt, and he spoke with the guttural accent of Alsace. We all shook hands—he had a couple of his PR people sitting behind him at a second table—and then Lorenzo Valentin, with quiet dignity, began his speech.

"We are here," he said, "as representatives of our association, to argue that your regime is not compatible with the spirit of the Balzar. This is not meant to be offensive to you—"

"Not at all," Bucher said politely.

"But without denying your right of property, we claim for ourselves a kind of right of usage." And from that premise Valentin carefully outlined our thesis that what mattered was the esprit of the Balzar and that the esprit of the Flo Group was, on the evidence, not compatible with that esprit we were defending. We asked him to keep the Balzar an autonomous brasserie, outside the Flo Group proper, and to make no changes in the staff, in the decor, or in the spirit of the place. After stating these demands, Lorenzo looked at him squarely.

I don't think any of us were prepared for what happened next. Bucher looked us over, up and down the table. "No problem," he said, a friendly, gap-toothed smile creasing his face. "No problem. Tell me, my friends, why would I want to change something that is working so well right now, something that works so effectively? I bought the Balzar because it's the crown jewel of Parisian brasseries. I bought the Balzar because I love it. What motive would I have to want it to be different? I'm here because if I weren't, McDonald's would be—and that would be too bad. I sincerely think that we are defending the same thing."

Our committee exchanged glances. Lorenzo pressed his point. "It's not just the cuisine," he said. "It's something more. A certain relaxation, the feeling of time suspended, the spirit of a place. You see, five hundred and fifty people have already joined Les Amis du Balzar."

Bucher nodded emphatically. "I know. You are to be congratulated," he said. "What an accomplishment!" After some more conversation about the cooking—he had brought out the *chef de cuisine,* who was understandably upset about the piece in *Le*

Monde—he said, "I am sixty years old. I give you a guarantee that I will keep the Balzar as it is. This wasn't a good buy for me. My accountants advised against it. My analysts advised against it. My heart and my soul told me to do it, and they're with you. A restaurant this small—it makes no sense for my chain. A hundred covers. It makes no sense for me except as the jewel in the crown of my Parisian brasseries, whose quality and values I'm going to defend."

We mumbled something and, after more handshaking, withdrew to the sidewalk. We had not anticipated the strategic advantage to Bucher of total, enthusiastic assent. We wanted to save the *steak au poivre* on the oval plate and the waiter serving it, but you couldn't argue with the man when he pointed to the steak, the plate, and the waiter and said nothing's changed. (Thierry, when he heard of our breakfast with Bucher, said, "It is the old technique of the kings of France: Treat your worst enemy like your best friend.")

I did not doubt that Bucher was being perfectly sincere, as far as it went, and that in his case as-far-as-it-went went as far it could. The Balzar would stay the same until it changed. The waiters seem encouraged by our actions. When I go to the Balzar now, Thierry, bringing a *coupe de champagne,* slips by and, under his breath, makes a toast: "À *la santé de l'association*—to the health of the association!" We repeat the toast, under our breaths. It is like being in the resistance. (But when M. Delouche comes over, we shake his hand too. Perhaps that is also like being in the resistance.)

Les Amis du Balzar has sent an eloquent new letter to Bucher, written by Lorenzo Valentin, and describing the *objet de nos préoccupations:* that no dish will come from a centralized kitchen and that there will be real autonomy for the staff, and real autonomy in the management. My Parisian self is prepared to defend the Balzar to the end, whatever it takes. My American self suspects that the Balzar will stay the same, and then it will change, and that we will love it as long as we can.

Alice
in Paris

Not long ago, in the brown dawn light of the western Paris suburbs, three Americans could be seen taking a mildly illicit walk
through the Rungis wholesale food market. The three Americans—the California chef Alice Waters, the vegetable scholar
Antoine Jacobsohn, and I—all had something on their minds,
and all were in a heightened emotional state that had its origins
in something more than the very early hour and the very chilly
weather.

Alice Waters was in a heightened emotional state because, as
many of her friends believe, she is always in a heightened emotional state, particularly when she is in the presence of fresh produce. Alice, who was wearing a wool cloche, is a small, intense,
pale, pretty, fiftyish woman, with a quiet, satisfied smile and a
shining, virtuous light in her eye, the kind of American woman
who a century ago would have been storming through saloons
with a hatchet and is now steaming fresh green beans, but with
similar motives. Her vision is rooted in the romantic Berkeley

politics that she practiced before starting her restaurant, Chez Panisse, with a ten-thousand-dollar loan twenty-seven years ago. She believes in concentric circles of social responsibility, with the reformed carrot in the backyard garden insensibly improving the family around the dinner table, the reformed family around the dinner table insensibly improving the small neighborhood merchants they shop with, the reformed neighborhood merchants improving their city, and so right on, ever upward and outward, but with the reformed carrot always there, the unmoved (though crisply cooked) mover in the center.

Earlier this year Alice was invited to open a restaurant at the Louvre, by Mme. Hélène David-Weill, the *très grande dame* who is the director of the Musée des Arts Décoratifs there. An enthusiastic article in the *Times* gave the impression that this was a fait accompli, or nearly so. In fact in September it still existed essentially only as an enthusiasm in the eye of Alice Waters, Mme. David-Weill, and Richard Overstreet, an American painter who lives in Berkeley and Paris and has been the go-between since the beginning. (Francis Ford Coppola was the first person to suggest Alice to Mme. David-Weill.) Alice had come to Paris to move the project along, and Richard had brought her together with Antoine as a possible "principal forager," on the lines of a principal dancer, for it. Rungis was the setting for their long-awaited meeting.

Antoine Jacobsohn was in a heightened emotional state because he is in a heightened emotional state whenever he visits the Rungis market. Twenty-nine years ago Rungis replaced the great Les Halles complex, which had dominated central Paris from the fifteenth century until after the Second World War and which Zola called, in a novel he devoted to it, "the belly of Paris." For Antoine, Les Halles was not just the belly of Paris but its heart, and for him the replacement of Les Halles by Rungis is the primordial sin of modern France—the destruction of Penn Station, Ebbets Field, and B. Altman's combined.

"When the market moved out of Les Halles," Antoine was saying, as he led our little party—it was illicit because, strictly speaking, you need a permit to shop at Rungis—"it effectively changed the relationship between pleasure and play and work in all of Paris. For centuries, because the market was at once a center for restaurants and for ordinary people, a whole culture grew up around it. Shopping and eating, the restaurant and the market, the stroller and the shopper, the artisan and the bourgeois—all were kept in an organic arrangement. And because many of the goods couldn't be kept overnight, it meant that what was left at the end of every day was given to the poor. But for trivial reasons—traffic and hygiene—they made the decision to move the market to Rungis, and left a hole in the heart of Paris. There was no place allotted here for the small artisan, for the small grower, or for the organic market."

He shook his head in disbelief. Antoine was raised in North Plainfield, New Jersey, by a French mother; he has a research fellowship at the Museum of Vegetable Culture, in the Paris suburb of La Courneuve, a degree in agricultural sciences from Cornell, and a perfect, crisp, contrary French mind trapped in an American body and voice box. Antoine has been known to give his friends an idealized poster of the twenty-four cultivated radishes—some lost, some extant—of the Île-de-France, and he has written beautifully, not to say longingly, of the lost monstrous spinach of Viroflay and the flat onions of Vertus.

We had been joined by Sally Clarke, of Clarke's restaurant, in London, who is one of Alice's many spiritual godchildren. The two chefs seemed torn between delight and surprise—delight in the freshness and green beauty of the vegetables, surprise at the lack of variety.

"I'm going to show you the space left for the local growers," Antoine went on. We walked through the aisles of the vast, chilly airplane hangars of vegetables: bins of *girolles,* crates of shiny eggplants. It all looked wonderful but remarkably standardized, explaining the standardization of what the average Paris green-grocer sells.

"Imagine," Antoine said. "So many radishes gone; the artichokes of Paris, almost gone; the turnips of Vaugirard, gone. There's a variety of beans that one reads about all the time in nineteenth-century texts. But gone! We've kept some seedlings of the plants in the museum, and they could be revived."

"We'll plant them in the Tuileries," Alice said softly, but with determination. One of her dreams for the restaurant is to raise a vegetable garden right outside the door.

Antoine walked along, greeting old friends and growers. "This man has excellent tomatoes," he now whispered to Alice.

"Does he grow organically?" she asked urgently. In recent years Alice has become a fanatic of organic growing.

Antoine, who had been telling Alice how the French sense of *terroir*—of the taste and traditions of a local region—was more important to authentic produce in France than the precise rules of organic growing, asked the grower. The man shrugged and then explained his situation. "He says he's giving up the business, in any case, as it happens, since it's becoming hopeless," Antoine said to Alice. (He failed to add that every French merchant, in every field, will always tell you that it's hopeless, he's going to give up the business; when French weapons salesmen go to China to sell missiles, they probably shrug when the Chinese start to bargain and say, Well, it doesn't matter, we're giving up the business anyway, it's a hopeless métier.)

Alice gave the grower a steady, encouraging look. "We just have to get the suppliers to adapt," she said. "That's what we did at Chez Panisse. You have to let them know there's the demand. You have to bring them along with you." In the early-morning light you could sense Alice Waters's eyes radiating the spiritual intensity that for so long has startled and impressed her friends and admirers and has set her apart from other chefs, making her a kind of materfamilias to a generation of chefs ranging from Sally Clarke to Michel Courtalhac, in Paris. (He keeps a photograph of

Alice in the window of his restaurant.) Aubert de Villaine, who is the codirector of the Domaine de la Romanée-Conti, the greatest wine estate in France, speaks of her in hushed tones, less as a superior hashslinger than as a kind of cross between Emily Dickinson and La Pucelle. "There's something crystalline about her, an extraordinary purity of spirit," he said not long ago. "She's one of *les vigiles en haut,* the watchman in the crow's nest, seeing far ahead. The thing I most admire about Alice is the sense that the sensual is not really sensual if it is not, *au fond,* spiritual."

Antoine nodded at another merchant across the way. "Now, this man grows excellent asparagus," he whispered. "It's interesting. Two hundred, a hundred and fifty years ago it was always green asparagus; now the demand is for white asparagus."

He went up to the grower and said, in French, "Why is it that no one any longer grows green asparagus? When was it that people went over to white asparagus?" The man gave him an incredulous look and then said, in the beautiful clear French of the Île-de-France, "You know, I would say that what you've just stated is the exact contrary of the truth." It was a perfect Parisian tone of voice—not disputatious, just suggesting a love of the shared pursuit of the truth, which, unfortunately, happens not to be in your possession right now.

Antoine made the right response. He raised his eyebrows in polite wonder while smiling only on the left side of his face, an expression that means, How greatly I respect the vigor of your opinions, however much they may call to mind the ravings of a lunatic. "What do you mean?" he demanded.

"Well, it is my experience that everyone grows green asparagus now. It's all you see for decorative *plats,* that touch of green. In the magazines, for instance, among the fashionable chefs, it's all you see, green asparagus. It has a much greater decorative effect. It's obvious."

"Ah, yes, for decorative effect," Antoine agreed calmly. Everybody won.

As they were speaking, I was poking a pile of *girolles* nearby, and wondering if I had made a mistake in not planning to serve some kind of autumnal mushroom plate for dinner the next night. I was in a heightened emotional state because I had offered to cook dinner for Alice Waters, and I had spent most of the summer worrying about what I would cook and how it would taste. I had decided to try and sneak in a little serious shopping while I was observing Alice and Antoine. I had also decided to go out later that day and buy a new set of dinner plates. I had come to both of these decisions more or less in the spirit of a man who, having in an insane moment invited Michael Jordan over to play a little one-on-one, decides that he might as well use the occasion to put down a new coat of asphalt on the driveway.

I had made up my mind to do a lamb braised for seven hours—a *gigot de sept heures,* as it's known—which would be cooked in the Provençal style, with eggplant and tomatoes. But to be in Rungis at dawn with two such devoted *terroiristes* as Alice and Antoine, for whom cooking is meaningful only if it is an expression of the place where the things are being cooked, made me feel a little guilty. I was going to have to get the tomatoes out of a can, and though the canned tomato is absolutely typical of my own *terroir,* I somehow felt that they would disapprove.

Nearby Alice had found *frisée* and watercress and was looking at them raptly—not with the greed of a hungry man seeing dinner but with the admiration of William Bennett looking at a long marriage. "There's nothing so beautiful as French watercress," she said. "I can recall walking down the rue Mouffetard in 1965, my first year in Paris. I was a girl from New Jersey who'd grown up on frozen food, and to see the baskets and baskets of greens, so many shades of green and red!

"I walked up and down the street, my eyes unbelieving," she went on. "I had never tasted an oyster. I went through Normandy, eating eighteen at a time, and drinking apple cider, and it was so wonderful that I was just carried away, and I would fall asleep by the roadside. When I got back to Berkeley, I thought of opening a creperie, and I tried to import some of the cider and found out that there was alcohol in it. That was why I kept passing out! I thought it was just the oysters and the apple juice and France." She was lost for a moment.

"You know," Antoine said, coming over, "there used to be asparagus grown in Argenteuil, just down the river from Paris—great asparagus. And they used to have figs in Argenteuil too. The white figs of Argenteuil, they were called in the nineteenth century. The trees were bent over with weights, so that the branches could be buried in the ground, to protect them all through the winter. Yet we think of figs as a southern fruit."

"Oh, we have to have them," Alice said, her eyes moist with emotion. "The white figs of Argenteuil! We'll grow them again. It can be done, you know." We had been wandering through the airplane hangars and were standing among towers of carrots and leeks, mountains of *haricots verts*. She looked upward and, Pucelle-like, seemed to be seeing before her—in a vision, as though they were already tangible, edible—the white figs of Argenteuil: an improbable Berkeley Joan, imagining her France restored to glory.

I had been thinking about various menus ever since I'd had the idea of cooking dinner for Alice, and for a while I'd thought I might do a four-hour braised leg of lamb that I had found the recipe for in the Sunday magazine of the *London Independent*. Unfortunately I had lost the issue of the magazine. I had the phone number of the editor, but I thought that it was unprofessional journalistic practice, in this day and age, to call up a fellow scandalmongering cynic and ask him if he would mind thumbing through his back issues for a recipe.

Then, this summer, I came upon a copy of a twenty-five-year-old recipe book written by the wonderful (and blind) food writer Roy Andries de Groot. The book was called *The Auberge of the Flowering Hearth*. Half cookbook, half *Lost Horizon* remake, it tells about a little inn—the Auberge of the Flowering Hearth—that the author discovered in the French Alps, while he was on an assignment to write something on how the monks down there make Chartreuse. The menu called for mussel soup, poached pears, and a *gigot de mouton de sept heures*—the same slow-cooked lamb that I had lost the recipe for but, in this case, given the whole, classic nine yards, or seven hours. Sounded great and was in the right spirit for the occasion, part of the history of the American love of French cooking.

Then I had another inspiration. As Alice Waters would have wanted, my childhood had been a series of intense family dinners, evening after evening, with their own set of "social protocols," and one of the most cherished of these family dinnertime protocols was known as Getting Someone Else to Do the Work. I decided to call Susan Herrmann Loomis, who lives in Normandy, and ask her to come to Paris to help me cook. Susan is the author of books on French and American country cooking and has a CIA-worthy gift for going into deep cover in a strange region and coming out with all its secrets. She cheerfully agreed to help, and after much discussion—she felt that the mussels would be too similar in color to the *gigot,* a feat of previsualization that increased my respect for the things a professional cook knows that an amateur doesn't—we decided that we would cook together. We scoured markets and arrived at a menu: steamed autumn vegetables with *aioli,* or garlic mayonnaise; the seven-hour lamb with eggplant and tomatoes; and an apple tart with rosemary. I went out and got the best bottle of Chartreuse I could find, to keep it honest to de Groot's memory.

While we prepared, Alice continued her tour of Paris. The idea of a restaurant turned out to have been something of an afterthought at the Musée des Arts Décoratifs, which is an annex of the Louvre, out on the rue de Rivoli. For many years, it had been a sleepy, unattended institution, filled with old clocks and settees. Mme. David-Weill's reign devoted a recent exhibition to the Tati stores, a kind of French Woolworth's, and has promised in general to be much more swinging. Still, the space that had been put aside for eating, though it looked out from the back of the museum onto the Tuileries gardens, lacked some of the amenities of modern restaurants. "It's all those kinds of basic things," Alice explained after she had seen it. "Where do the employees wash their hands? Where are the umbrellas for the rainy days? It's only ninety covers, which is even fewer than Chez Panisse." She went on, diplomatically, "It's really more of a tearoom size than anything else. I worry that the space is too small to express what we'd like to express."

In a kind of mission statement, she has described the restaurant as she imagines it: "A platform, an exhibit, a classroom, a conservatory, a laboratory, and a garden. It must be, in a phrase, an art installation in the form of a restaurant, expressing the sensuousness of food and putting people in touch with the pleasures of eating and with the connection between those pleasures and sustainable agriculture. . . . All the elements of the collaboration, from the menu to the decor, will clearly demonstrate where the food comes from and how it was grown. The emphasis is going to be on the food, the kind that makes eating a soul-nourishing experience. Amid the grandeur of the Louvre, the restaurant must feel human, reflecting the spirit of the farm, the *terroir,* and the market, and it must express the humanity of the artisans, cooks, and servers who work there."

Yet Alice seemed unperturbed by the difficulties; she has the sublime California confidence that all physical problems are susceptible to a little intense spiritual pressure. "I'm not worried," she said. "If we can solve the space problem, everything else will fall into place. I don't really want it to be an extension of Chez Panisse in Paris. There will be a vegetable garden, but more important will be establishing a relation to a whole network of suppliers. I'm going to work with Eiko Ishioka, the great Japanese designer, who will do an inspired job. And now I've found my forager, in Antoine. This restaurant could be the next step. It could be a statement about diversity on so many levels. It could be the next part of an effort to keep people from perceiving life in the unified way that the mass culture demands." (When she's asked if her daughter, Fanny, has ever gone to a McDonald's, she answers, carefully, "She may have. During a soccer match or something. But I've told her that while she's free to do it if she wants to, I would rather not get involved in that kind of activity.")

Alice is acutely aware that there are people who see something hypocritical or unreal about a woman who presides over an expensive restaurant preaching against commercial culture. This is silly, of course—if there's going to be a faith, somebody's got to live in the Vatican—but it is also false on its own terms. She has scrupulously kept Chez Panisse out of mass merchandising of any kind. There are no Chez Panisse frozen foods, no Chez Panisse canned sauces, no Chez Panisse pasta. There are only cookbooks and a line of granola. Alice Waters is in every way the anti–Wolfgang Puck. (People who know insist that the restaurant still makes remarkably little money for such a famous place.) In a speech she made recently to teachers involved with the "garden in every school" project, in California, she pointed out that "all too many kids—both rich and poor—are disconnected from civilized and humane ways of living their lives," and then added the Berkeley Basic Truth: "The sensual pleasure of eating beautiful food from the garden brings with it the moral satisfaction of doing the right thing for the planet and for yourself."

Most people feel that Alice is the figure par excellence of the great Berkeley Transformation, in which the wise children ate the revolution before it had a chance to eat them. Kermit Lynch, the wine importer, who has done more than anyone else to bring the organic revolution to French winemaking (and has been called a "hopeless romantic" for his efforts), is a product of the same history. "Alice and I both started our businesses around the same time," he recollected recently. "She started cooking for an underground newspaper in San Francisco, and I was working for the *Berkeley Barb*—and there we were. Who could have imagined that we'd end up this way? It was very political what she was doing then, and it still is." Alice herself traces the crucial moment for the creation of Chez Panisse to the defeat of Robert Scheer, now a well-known journalist in Los Angeles, whose congressional campaign she had worked for in 1966. "I was so crushed, and I thought, I'm just going to start my own world," she says.

It may be this reconciliation of utopian politics and aristocratic cooking, more than anything else, that has divided the cooking cultures of France and America. The *soixante-huitards* were as disappointed in France as they were in America, but they drove their political disappointment into more political disappointment. The culture that the French radicals were countering, after all, was already epicurean; there was no cultural space to be found in expanding it. The counterculture in America had just the opposite situation—it was Nixon who ate cottage cheese with ketchup—and anyway, the counterculture in America liked pleasure; its anthem was "Feed Your Head," not "Clear Your Head."

Over time, an obsession with sex and drugs slid imperceptibly into an obsession with children and food. This obsessiveness is what separates Alice Waters from all the other "Anglo-Saxon" restaurateurs who have arrived in Paris recently to open restaurants. (Sir Terence Conran, the London food lord, has just remade an old cabaret on the rue Mazarine, for instance, bringing the new English style to Paris.) For Alice, the idea of making the millennial restaurant in France is a way of closing a romantic circle. Like de Groot, she sees France as the cradle of organic culture in every sense: "The restaurant I imagine is a way of repaying that debt to France, of Americans taking the best of ourselves, instead of the worst of ourselves, to help recall the

French to their own best traditions, a way that my generation can repay the debt we owe to France."

|||

On the day of our dinner Kenneth Starr's report had just appeared, and all afternoon friends from New York were calling me about it. Susan Loomis and I ran back and forth from the study to the kitchen, doing a lot of "Can you believe what he's saying?" (and also a fair amount of "Can you believe what they were doing?"). I was trying to adjust the heat on the lamb when the phone rang, from Luke's school. Once again, as he often had since the term began, he had refused to take a nap, and the school wanted me to bring him home. I sighed, forgot about the report, checked the lamb, left Susan in the kitchen, and raced off to pick him up. (I thought ruefully that you could bet a million dollars that if he were in a school in New York, there would be a Nap-Averse Support Group, a special room for the dormitively challenged, and a precedent-setting lawsuit launched by the attorney father of an earlier child, guaranteeing the right of every child to refuse a nap. But this was Paris: strictly no nap, no school.) I hesitated about leaving the lamb in the oven untended, but then decided, well, seven hours. . . . Throughout the afternoon, instead of feeling, as I had hoped, like Roy de Groot luxuriating in the Alps, I felt a lot like Ray Liotta spinning in the last reel of *Goodfellas,* when he's cooking veal for his crippled brother, and the police helicopter is circling overhead, and he and the mule who's carrying the cocaine have to go and get her lucky hat.

How was the lamb? The evening went well, though all through dinner the Starr Report was being faxed to us by a friend; pages— four hundred of them—kept churning out of the machine, just a room away. You couldn't help hearing them as they arrived, and every now and then I would go in and peek at the latest revelation. There was an odd symmetry: on the one hand, at our dinner table the high priestess of the American generation that has come to believe that only through refined sensual pleasure can you re-create an ideal America; on the other, page after page of legal detail documenting the existence of those who believe that talking about ideals while pursuing sensations is just what makes this generation such a bunch of louses. It was a kind of two-course meal of radical hedonism and extreme puritanism, both as American as, well, apple pie.

But how was the lamb? Alice spoke freely about the problems that the space at the Louvre represented. Listening between the sentences, you could deduce that if she had not lost heart, she had, at least, a larger sense of how vast and difficult a project it promised to be. Susan Loomis's *aioli* was fabulous. People talked, as they do everywhere, about Clinton and Monica.

But *How was the lamb?* The wine was excellent. The *tarte aux pommes* was fine.

And the lamb? Well. The lamb had a strong resemblance to a third baseman's mitt—if I had Antoine Jacobsohn's gift for precision, I would compare it to Buddy Bell's glove, circa 1978—with interesting hints of Naugahyde, kapok, and old suede bomber jacket. There were plenty of white beans, though, and some sauce, so everyone pushed it around politely on the plate. I think I know now what went wrong: after three years of a French oven, I realized that it was easy to forget that American cookbooks were still written, so to speak, in Fahrenheit. De Groot's two hundred degrees were almost half as hot as the two hundred degrees of my Celsius oven.

I also saw that Alice Waters didn't notice. If you are playing tennis with Martina Hingis, she does not notice when your backhand is off, because she does not notice when your backhand is on. What you have is not what she would call a backhand. At least I was able to explain to the company that the lamb came from Roy de Groot's book, and I talked about what a haunting image it gave of a now-vanished French cooking culture: the iron pots on the hearth, the shy Provençale lady in the kitchen, the daily bounty from the farms and the hunters. Alice got that look in her eye. "I love that book," she said. "And I went on an expedition to the Alps just to find the auberge."

Did that perfect auberge really exist? I asked.

"Well, no, not really. Not exactly," she said, in a tone that sounded like "not at all." "I mean, yes, it didn't, not like that." She thought for a moment. "Of course, it existed for him. It still exists for us, in the minds of the people around this table. Maybe that's where the ideal restaurant always will be."

|||

Postscript: After Alice Waters left Paris, *Le Figaro* published an interview with her in which she gently reviewed her concerns about the Rungis market. THE MARKETS IN PARIS ARE SHOCKING! was the headline on the piece, whose effect, from a PR point of view, was like that of a Japanese baseball manager who, after a trip to Yankee Stadium, is quoted in a headline saying, "You call that a ballpark?" Alice Waters is learning that the real France is an inscrutable, hypersensitive place.

I have come to suspect that what is called a seven-hour lamb was really meant to be seven-hour mutton. I am aware of course that there may be other, better recipes for this dish and other, more careful cooks who have prepared it. (The four-hour lamb was great.) But it is also my suspicion that like so many vanishing things in French cooking, the seven-hour recipe was actually made for harder sheep in tougher times. In the late-modern world, where we get all the pleasure we can as soon as we can get it and on any terms we can, and none of us wants to take a nap, for fear of missing some pleasure we might otherwise have had— in a world like that, as I say, there may just be no place left for the seven-hour *gigot*.

A Machine to Draw
the World,

CHRISTMAS JOURNAL 4

In April the knock we had been fearing came on the door. The owners of our apartment were coming back from Tokyo. The Asian banking crisis had sent them back to Paris a year early, History leaping its track to knock Experience cold. It came as a shock. Three months and we would have to leave, be gone from 16 rue du Pré-aux-Clercs.

The phone call came, exasperatingly, in the French manner, the way the apartment had come: your whole life thrown upside down in an aside. "Oh, the owners are coming home and will need the apartment in July," the real estate woman said; no apology or even a "sorry for the inconvenience." We stayed up all night debating, in the way you do with big news: avoiding, digressing, suddenly feeling sick in the pit of the stomach at the thought of leaving. When we lost the apartment, we thought of going home early, and so we asked ourselves what were the things we loved in Paris, really loved, not just officially appreciated or chose to be amused at? Well, the places our child went. The Luxembourg Gardens at three in the afternoon. The Guignols, and Luke saying, "I'm so excited" before the curtain went up.

The curious thing was that with the loss of Paris threatening, we became more Parisian. The same thing, I had noted, had happened in our last few months in New York. The city, which had become increasingly difficult, suddenly seemed like a playground—people eating outside, in T-shirts and shorts and sneakers in the Italian restaurants in SoHo; the open-all-nightness of New York; the sweet funkiness—registered as it hadn't in years. When we left the loft for the last time, without trouble, with tears, the music box on Luke Auden's stroller played "Manhattan."

Now after the knock on the door, it happened to Paris. I began to cook Parisianly. I bought the chef's cookbook from Le Grand Véfour and began to make the buttery, three- and four-part dishes that I had been exasperated by before: *suprêmes de volaille,* with mint, that sort of thing. I even made soufflés again. We put Trenet back on the CD player; strangely the clarity of his French had improved enormously over three years, so that now one could understand the meaning of nearly everything he sang. Or maybe it was just a better record player.

Is this simply the unique perversity of the human heart that wants (and wants and wants) what it doesn't have—Italian food in Paris, American jazz in Saint-Germain—and, only when it is about to lose it, returns to the things that drew it to the desire in the first place? Or was there a kind of peace in it too? We would now never be Parisians or integrate; we might not even stay in town more than another eight weeks. Loss, like distance, gives permission for romance. In a better-ordered Verona, Romeo and Juliet would have grown up to be just another couple at dinner.

Finally we went for a long walk, down to see the boats, by the river, and thought, No, we're not ready to leave yet, haven't yet found a good-bye. So we moved. To a bigger, actually nicer apartment. A slight, permanent overhang of depression lifted; the new place was so bright, and it was connected to the street, the life of the city. One by one our stuff came over, three blocks from one apartment to the other.

In every move, I've noticed, there is always *something*—a roll of Christmas wrapping paper, a boxful of hangers from the dry cleaners, a metal extender whose use no one can recall—that is left over in the apartment you're leaving, which you step around in curiosity and then, on the last trip, take with you. In this case it was an antenna that belonged with something—a shortwave radio? a portable television?—which we could no longer recall, a plastic dagger, with a "Kings and Knights" sticker on it, and a hardcover of Nabokov's *Pnin,* which came from nowhere and I could never remember reading in Paris. Leaving 16 rue du Pré-aux-Clercs for the last time, I opened *Pnin* at random, to a bit about a boy's imaginary father, a king: " 'Abdication! One third of the alphabet!' coldly quipped the King, with the trace of an accent. 'The answer is no. I prefer the unknown quantity of Exile.' "

|||

Just after the move, for my birthday, Luke and Martha gave me a wonderful toy, *La Machine à Dessiner le Monde,* a machine to draw the world. Really, all it is is a camera lucida, but nicely done in plastic, with a viewing stand on top. You put a piece of vellum on it, and if the light's bright enough, and it has to be very bright, it projects the thing you're looking at right onto the paper. All you have to do is trace it.

All! For just tracing turns out to be the hardest thing of all. All the clichés and exasperating French abstractions about the insuperable difficulties of realism turn out to be plain truth when you have your machine to draw the world pointed out the window at the plane trees on the boulevard Saint-Germain, your pencil poised, and then you try to decide where to make the first mark. The world *moves* so much—shimmers and shakes like a nautch dancer, more than you can ever know when you're in it rather than looking at it. You bless any leaf that holds still long enough for you to get it. Hold still, you tell the tree, the light leaping up and down on the balustrade, as though you were talking to a small child as you try to get on its galoshes. Just *hold still*. Where you finally make the mark is mostly a question of when you finally get fed up.

Tracing becomes a deep, knotty problem, a thing to solve, and I am completely absorbed in it. I take the Machine to Draw the World to the Palais Royal or the Luxembourg Gardens and just watch the screen, pencil poised, at the translation of Paris into this single flat layer of translucent, lucid shimmer. I no longer try to circus it, or mourn it, or even learn from it, since just drawing it is enough. What you really need from the world in order to draw it is a lot of light and for everything to just stand still.

|||

Martha and I went for our Christmas lunch together at Le Grand Véfour. The Palais Royal in December: undecorated *sapins* line the arcades, and Monet smokiness hangs over the gardens. Christian David, the maître d', is suave and perfect and has been *utterly* worn out, in the five years we have lunched there twice a year, by the experience of having kids. One of his kids, Antoine, has swallowed a peanut, and he has spent six nights in a hospital; the other is having trouble at school, so David has, beneath a crackle of suave, the hollow, thousand-yard stare of the Parent.

He insisted that next time, next spring we bring Luke Auden, and I told Luke (or Luca, as he now likes to be known) about the invitation when we got home. "Is it Chinese food?" Luke asked, eyes alight with faint hope. "Or regular Paris food?" Regular Paris food, I told him. His eyes became doleful. He loves Chinese food.

One of our accomplishments of the year has been to invent Chinese takeout in Paris. There is a Chinese restaurant in the *rez-de-chaussée* of our new building, Le Coq d'Or or something, and we asked them if we could sometimes simply call them up and have them prepare the food in the kitchen and then let us come down and pick it up. They looked at us dubiously: We would call in advance and have prepared food awaiting us? Yes, we said. They could even, if it were convenient, have someone run upstairs with it; we would be glad to give this messenger a little something extra for his trouble. We now have this system worked out, and it is regarded as very piquant and original.

We were so proud that we tried to extend it to the Mexican place around the corner. This was a new place that had just opened on the little street around the corner called, of all odd things, Spicy Dinners. There is a new, depressingly Japanese–Third World–style enthusiasm in Paris for "American"-style names. Some, like Buffalo Grill, are ordinary enough. Others are alarming: Speed Rabbit Pizza, for instance, a chain that is beginning to blanket the city, with a very up-to-date image of a racing hare. I don't think that you can actually get a rabbit pizza from them, a *pizza au lapin,* but they think it looks streamlined, late century, thrillingly global. A speedy rabbit, delivering speedy food. Anyway, Spicy Dinners really did have spicy dinners, and I miss them terribly, spicy dinners. It serves Mexican food basically, though with various West Indian accents. The owner seems to be East Indian, though. We proposed that we try the same system of calling up and coming over to take out, and the owner, after a few unconvinced looks, said fine, that would be good. Around six o'clock we called in our order—burritos and chili and enchiladas—and, eyes alight with expectation (man, at last some spicy food!), went around a few minutes later. He had prepared all the dinner on normal plates—big, restauranty white china plates—and had it waiting for us. It was Parisian takeout; he trusted us with his plates. I held out my arms, and he carefully put one heavy plate after another in them, placing a second plate upside down on the first, to keep everything warm, so that I had six plates and three dinners all in my hands. I felt like a circus juggler. Luke delicately guided me home and, since I didn't have the use of my hands, had to punch out the code and push open the big courtyard door himself, while I balanced the plates and spicy food as best I could, with visions of crashing china and spilled burritos all over the boulevard. It was quite a weight. "Please bring back the plates," he had called out as we left the premises. But we ran them through the dishwasher that night, and then Nisha put them away, and we forgot all about them. A month later, when we remembered, the little spicy restaurant had gone out of business. We feel very guilty about the whole thing.

|||

Earlier in December Luke fell terribly sick—far sicker than I ever hope to see him again. We packed him off to his pediatrician, our wonderful Dr. Pierre Bitoun, who looks exactly like a kinder Groucho Marx. When we called him, he picked up the phone himself, as he always does, and said to get him over. Dr. Bitoun looked worried as hell and told us to get him to a surgeon right away. I picked Luke up in my arms, and we ran to the surgical hospital, where the gentle, grave-eyed surgeon, just emerging from an operation, examined him, said that he didn't have appendicitis but that he was very sick and that we ought to get him over to the Necker Hospital for an emergency workup. The Necker is the central children's hospital in Paris. We raced over, without an introduction, into the packed emergency ward, showed our *carnet de santé*, the pediatrician's record of inoculations and so forth. The girl at the desk barely glanced at it, and within an hour Luke had had a sonogram, an X ray, a barium enema, and various other tests and got examined by three doctors. Two and a half hours later we were back home with a diagnosis. (It turned out that Luke had salmonella poisoning.) It was only after we had left the hospital that we realized that not only had we not paid a penny but that no one had asked us to show our insurance, fill out a form, or do any of the other standard, humiliating things that happen to our American friends with sick children. Nor had any of the procedures had to be run by the profit-and-loss manager of an HMO. This is socialized medicine, of course, which the insurance companies have patriotically kept Americans from suffering under. There are times, as one reads about the uninsured and the armed and the executed, when French anti-Americanism begins to look extremely rational.

|||

The Christmas windows are weird in Paris this year. Every year, in Paris as everywhere else, the American imperium of shopping opportunities continues to rage, unbanked. Yet the windows are strange, a fin de siècle note of disquiet seeping in. Bon Marché, which usually has hordes of industrious elves and bears dancing at the end of invisible wires, this year has its windows filled with life-size human figures mechanically enacting a story of incest, bestiality, murder, and fashion narcissism. They play out an updated version of Charles Perrault's story "Peau d'Ane," in which a king in mourning for his queen threatens to force himself on his own daughter and is outwitted only by the princess's decision first to distract him with a series of overwrought holiday dresses and then by the killing of the royal donkey, whose dripping skin . . . well, it's a long story, and a strange one, and what connection it has with Christmas—or what the Parisian children, pressed toward the animated windows in their duffel coats, careful scarves bunched like packages around their throats, think of it all—is hard to imagine.

Luke and I went Christmas shopping after he recovered. He desperately believes in Santa—we have sold it hard, I don't know why—and has been trying to arrange his Christmas list to fit the dimensions of Santa's sack, which he studies in illustration. "You know what is the problem?" he says as he turns from the Bon Marché toy catalog to his Thomas Nast pictures of Santa. "I don't think that a big race set is a good idea; it won't fit." He loves the Christmas windows and a Louis Armstrong song called "Zat You, Santa Claus?"

After nearly four years in Paris he has developed a complicated, defensive sense of his own apartness, rather like his dad's.

He recognizes that his parents, his father particularly, speaks with an Accent, and this brings onto him exactly the shame that my grandfather must have felt when his Yiddish-speaking father arrived to talk to *his* teachers at a Philadelphia public school. I try to have solid, parental discussions with his teachers, but as I do, I realize, uneasily, that in his eyes I am the *alter kocker,* the comic immigrant.

"Zo, how the boy does?" he hears me saying in effect. "He is good boy, no? He is feeling out the homeworks, isn't he?" I can see his small frame shudder, just perceptibly, at his father's words. I had thought to bring him the suavity of the French gamin, and instead I have brought onto him the shame of the immigrant child.

I sense too that he is in a larger confusion: What's French, what's American, where am I? His French vocabulary is very large, but he doesn't like to use it, or show it, except in extremis. (He always seems to know the answer to the question, in even the most rapid and complicated French, "Would you like a little treat/candy/pastry?") A family is a civilization, and a language is a culture, and he is left with a sense of being doubly islanded. Watching the children at the gardens, he turns to me. "*All* children in New York speak English?" he demands. Yes, I tell him, and he imagines the unthinkable: a world of English speakers, where English is the public, not the private, language.

When we go out to eat—at the Balzar or at a nice French-American place called the Café Parisien—we play the game of Imaginary Restaurants, making up places we would like to open. (My best so far is a Franco-American inn specializing in game, called Les Fauves.) He has invented a restaurant that will be called the Toy Store Restaurant, and will serve an eclectic menu, French and American: baked chicken—fresh from the oven, hamburgers—fresh from the oven! And something everyone likes (dramatic pause): fruit salad! He has intuited his way toward a New York coffee shop.

But: "No French people," he says decisively.

"No French people!" I say, with genuine shock; increasing his French-bashing was not the reason we came here.

"No," he says. "I'm the owner, and it would be too nervous." He sees himself as the next Toots Shor, and wants to feel relaxed, ready to put an arm around his clients and pound their backs, without worrying if he remembers the word, which language he is speaking.

In other, unconscious ways he is thoroughly French and will, I fear, be lost in New York when we go back. He ate a hamburger for the first time on July 4. He took three bites, pushed it away, had some ice cream, his normal routine, but the next morning he said, "I liked the hamburger"—decisively—"but I did not like that sauce you served with it."

"What sauce?" I said, puzzled. I hadn't made a sauce.

"That *red* sauce," he said, disdainfully, with exactly the expression I have seen on the face of Jean-Pierre Quélin, the food critic of *Le Monde,* when he gets a corked glass of wine. "I did not like that *red* sauce." He means, of course, the Heinz ketchup, bought at La Grande Épicerie, in the American specialties section.

|||

When he went back to New York, his one trip, to interview at a New York nursery school, where you have to go a year and a half before you enter, he was asked what he liked to eat for breakfast, and he said, "Croissants and *confiture.*" Everybody laughed, thought it was cute, though he was being serious as hell. It is, perhaps, a truth of expatriate children that rather than grow up with two civilizations, they grow up with less than one, unable somehow to plug in the civilization at home with the big one around. They grow up, we have noticed with other kids, achingly polite and watchful and skilled, "adult," and guarded.

His one island of calm and certainty remains the Luxembourg

Gardens. He is master there, and he has his itinerary nearly perfectly arranged: first the playground, then the carousel, then the ponies, if there's time, and then a crepe from the crepe man. He rides the horses now, upright, and I feel sure that any day now he will ask for a stick.

Nothing stops the wheel, though, and now even the puppet shows have been revolutionized: Las Vegasized, Americanized, globalized. At God knows what expense, and rolling dice of a size I can only imagine, this Christmas M. Desarthis discarded the reliable run of *Cochons* and *Trésors* and launched an entirely new kind of spectacular called *La Valise Enchantée,* complete with an original recorded score, with drums and organs, and black backgrounds and animated fluorescent fish and squirrels. In terms of his little park theater this is a ratchet up of enormous dimensions—and all very well done by a staff of four new puppeteers, though with the slight tang of the lounge act.

I can only imagine that M. Desarthis, in the French manner, decided that he was slipping behind the times and thought of this as a way to modernize. It couldn't be a bigger hit with Luca, who plays the cassette we bought of the show and has committed it to memory, racing over the French word he doesn't know with suave Sid Caesar inventions: "*Quand il était très petit, sa maman s'amusait . . . hunsta whoosta weestsa. . . .*" I like the new show, but I am worried about what is going to happen to the *Cochons*.

On Christmas Eve we saw a department-store Santa at Hédiard, shopping for champagne. We stood in line behind him; Luke was not a bit shaken. When we got home, he said to his mother: "We saw Santa at Hédiard. I think he was just getting a little cheap wine for his elves."

|||

The *lycéens,* the high school students, are on strike this Christmas, and we see them march by the windows of our new apartment along the boulevard Raspail. Like the protesters in Lewis Carroll's *Sylvie and Bruno* who march with the banner "Less

Bread! More Taxes!" the *lycéens* are, officially, striking for more classes and harder teachers. But their strike has nearly universal support: The government is for it; the opposition is for it; the press is for it.

What is startling and instructive to an outsider is how earnest the French *lycéens* look as they march; they have a worn-out, exhausted, genuinely oppressed look that is miles away from the overfed, ironic complacency that American kids of the same age have. This is the consequence of the school system. The *lycéens'* normal, nonstriking day begins at eight-thirty in the morning and often runs to six o'clock in the evening and, for all the reforms that have been attempted in the last twenty years, is still conducted in an atmosphere of rote-learning, reflexive authoritarianism. (You see even ten- and eleven-year-olds emerging from school at the end of the day pale as veal, clutching for a *pain aux raisins,* starved for a little pleasure.)

|||

Outside the Galeries Lafayette are stationed official city guards in uniform and a store surveillant, telling everyone how to get up to the windows and which way to walk once you're there, directing traffic, with no appeal. Everyone meekly obeys. The authoritarian impulses shapes everything, even the traffic by the windows.

|||

The weird thing is that by taking tracing on as an ambition, I've become more in tune with the fundamental French temperament. The will toward contemplative observation is the keynote of French sensibility and tied, in ways both beautiful and horrible, to French indifference. My favorite French writers when I arrived were, dutifully, Proust and Camus and Stendhal, who generalize, brilliantly; now my favorites are Colette, Antoine Blondin, and Maupassant, who above all look, who are part of the great French Machine to Draw the World.

The greatness of Colette and Maupassant, who is the real father of modern writing, have leaked out back home (though I think Maupassant is still known as the father of the trick ending), but I think Blondin is just about completely unknown in America. He was a French newspaperman and essayist, thriving in the 1950s and 1960s, who wrote novels and reportage and essays for the French papers. He is most famous for writing a kind of all-purpose column in the French sports daily *L'Équipe*.

Blondin is a wonderful, easy writer, and what I admire most about him is the fluency, the particularizations of his language. Everything seeks a joke, but nothing misses a point. He captures tiny moments of reality: a rainy day in the stadium where someone is listening to the radio of the rugby game below, and the crackling broadcast is more real than the game it is describing, which takes you back outside the stadium, is more real than the game it describes. His most emphatic aphorism was simple: "The only duty of the writer is not to have one."

|||

Against the official French culture of the academy, the French empirical tradition has to keep itself alive in the oddest corners, like Blondin in *L'Équipe*. Manet's lemons and asparagus are its best emblems. It produces an atmosphere of *calm*. The calm of Manet's flowers, the calm of Colette's dialogue, the precious, life-enhancing calm of the Palais Royal at three in the afternoon, the last coffee on the table, the light slanting in, French calm. Has anyone ever thought how incongruous and touching the use of that word is in the Baudelaire poem, the Matisse title? "Luxe, Calme and Volupté"? Luxury, Calm and Voluptuousness. *Calm* and Voluptuousness? Not hot and voluptuous or funky and voluptuous? We have grown accustomed to it by familiarity, but really, *calm*—it is as if one put some other flat, bourgeois word in there: Luxury: nice and voluptuous? Luxury: comfy and voluptuous. And yet it works. It is the essence of the French vision. *Everybody calm down*. (Luke Auden about the excitable little boy in his class: "He was nervous, but Sonia calmed him up.") Matisse, Manet, calm us up.

|||

In France private life still turns on the closed seventeenth-century model of *ce pays ici,* this little country here. The crucial unit of social life in France is the Cohort, rather than the social Class, as in England, or the Clan, as in Italy (or the Company, as back home in America). These Parisian cohorts—loosely defined working alliances of people in politics and art and literature, who draw together in youth for one purpose or another and then remain linked, if only in mutual hatred, for life—get pulled from a lot of different social classes and clans and therefore need neutral places to inhabit. This has produced the unique Parisian commonplace civilization of parks and cafés and salons, which give the illusion of democratic entry.

It is *only* an illusion, though. What looks like a café is really a kind of club, and you can no more really enter it than you can enter White's or Boodle's in St. James's just by walking in there. The cohorts of Paris—the impressionist group is a perfect example of the kind—look open but remain essentially closed to anyone not in at their formation. Pressed beyond a polite point, they clam up as firmly as an Italian family.

John Singer Sargent's relations with the impressionists are a perfect example of how this works. Throughout the 1870s he stood right on the friendly edges of the impressionist cohort, knocking politely on the door again and again. They looked him over, but they never let him in. All that's left to the outsider is the beautiful surface. The two favorite sites of Sargent—the Luxembourg Gardens and the Winter Circus—strike a guilty chord; parks and circuses are open and seem to offer the illusion of assimilation. You end up by walking around and around the Luxembourg Gardens. French life just goes on, with its enormous insular indifference. Americans and Frenchmen always agree that they share *something,* something deeper than anything they share with any other people—the love of happiness, perhaps, or of social pleasures. Really it is this insularity that they share, as they discover sadly in the end. Americans welcome everyone with open arms and forced smiles, and in the end the immigrant-expatriates discover that that's the problem; the next man off the next boat is just as welcome too. Paris is open to anyone, but what is open isn't entirely Paris. It is another, simulacra Paris, which wraps around the real one and is there to be looked at, to be seen. About all you can do is paint it, and Sargent did that about as well as it could be done for about as long as it could be done. It was a great subject, but never Home, and Americans want home.

||||

More comfort: Food here is comfort, not theater. Last night we had our good friends B. and R. over, and we had champagne (Drappier '90) and then lemon tart from Ladurée, where Luke and I stood in line for half an hour. It's a beautiful Proustian store on the rue Royale with a pale green wooden front, old wooden tables, and absolutely no line discipline. We get *bûches* from Ladurée too. Tonight, Christmas night: a brined turkey, Brussels sprouts with *crème fraîche,* chestnut stuffing, and those *bûches de Noël.* As always in Paris, each thing has a thing associated with it, a story: The turkey was ordered, argued over (take two small ones, I don't want two small ones, etc.).

||||

I was, if anything, a slightly too complacent universalist when I arrived in Paris and have become a far too melancholic particularist as we get ready to leave, someone who believes in the spirit of places, although he always expects to be outside them, and can pay them only the compliment of eternal comparison.

Luke, once this winter, brought home the school goldfish, Swimmy, for the weekend. He got up on a chair to stare at his bowl and said hello. No answer. Then he recalled what kind of goldfish it was. "*Ça va*, Swimmy?" he said at last, "*ça va?*" speaking the goldfish's language to the goldfish.

It is better to speak to the goldfish in their own language, and better still just to jump into the bowl and become a goldfish yourself, or try to. Without that immersion you feel a constant temptation to compare them with the nongoldfish you know back home, to say what they are like, to engage in the constant stilted game of comparison. In the end it is better just to say what goldfish do than to say what they are like, goldfish, like Parisians, in the end not being "like" anything, but just busy *being,* like everything else. Yet the attempt to say what the goldfish are like—they're swimming, they're gold, oh, how they shine—is in its way the sincerest tribute to their glitter.

|||

Once again, and reliably, the Christmas lights got themselves tangled, and this time, since the ceilings in the new apartment are higher, and the tree we bought taller, I had to go out and get even more new ones. Hundreds and hundreds of dollars have now been spent by this family on French Christmas tree lights, which will have absolutely no use when we go home. I had to get on a really high ladder this year to toss them onto the tree and felt like something between Will Rogers and one of those people on the old Don Ameche circus show. Luke followed me up the ladder, "helping," and I could sense in him this year not so much admiration as sheer impatience, an almost unbeatable Oedipal urge. I can do that as well as the next guy, as well as you can.

Our Parisian friends Agnès and Richard came over this year for the tree trimming and laughed as they saw me lassoing the tree. "No, no," Agnès explained, "the idea is to hold them up in two strands and drape them on like an apron, and then they tie in the back."

"I can't believe he never thought of that," Martha said.

The real Christmas story is not about Jesus and/or Mary, or the Wise Men, but about poor Joseph, sound asleep under the stable, glad that this first time, at least, everyone is busy, and no one is counting on him to put up the lights.

|||

All I can do is trace something, flip open the red plastic lid of the machine to draw little bits of Paris. Luke's school, for instance, is on the rue Saint-Dominique. You take the 69 bus to get there, and it goes down the rue du Bac, and then along the rue de Grenelle, narrow and twisting, with the high walls and plastered fronts of schools for older children and government buildings alongside, broken now and then by a lace curtain front on a bistro where no one ever seems to go. Often, the 69 can't make the turn onto the rue de Grenelle because someone has parked on the sidewalk, half on the street. Then the bus driver just stops, blows his horn, and folds his arms. We'll wait it out, like a war. In a rush, a *high*, the bus breaks out after three minutes into the esplanade des Invalides, the huge, flat, officially forbidden lawn—though, on a Wednesday afternoon, I once did see two brave and determined Americans playing Frisbee there (you could tell they were Americans because they looked thirty and were dressed like six-year-olds). The golden covered dome of the church stands straight up behind, not looming but preening, and the Invalides itself sits below, an old military hospital with the two horses incised on its front, combining splendor with the odd barrackslike solidity, the bureaucratic confidence, of the architecture of the *grand siècle*.

The bus whizzes across, witness to this old beauty too many times, and pushes along to the real heart of the Seventh, where Grenelle warms up. The rue Cler, which breaks off it, is one of the nicest shopping and *marché* streets in Paris, and it acts as a heart for the neighborhood, warming even the chilly great avenues of Tour Maubourg and Rapp. They are lined with chestnuts and planes, and there is more art nouveau architecture there than perhaps anywhere else in Paris save the Sixteenth.

Luke's school is a block up, on the rue Saint-Dominique; Grenelle is one of those sandwiched streets, between the truly busy Saint-Dominique and the rue Cler, where there are two lingerie stores to a block (how can women *wear* so much underwear?). The school has an archway for an entrance and is set back in a deep courtyard, with geraniums and ivy tumbling over the courtyard walls. On warm days the single classroom window is open, and you see the (overregimented) kindergarten children, already in their rows. Since we still feel that eight-thirty to four-thirty is just too long a day for a four-year-old, we have arranged for me to pick up Luke every day at three.

I catch Luke's eye, and we wave. He is breaking out, free, and sometimes we have an omelet and a grenadine in the café down the street, where Luke likes to pull the lace curtains and the old lady who is always there has an old black cocker. Then, by now four o'clock, violet twilight falling, watching that sky that looks as though it were ready to snow though it never does, we get the bus back home. Going home, it goes down Saint-Dominique, gently, formally, perfectly curving across the Left Bank, rather than snaking, as Grenelle does. Saint-Dominique is lined with wonderful shops: butchers with fat-wrapped *noisettes d'agneau* and bakers with various-sized *tartes tatins*, all caramel-colored, and children's clothing stores, their windows filled with violet coats for small girls. They believe in blitz advertising in Paris; usually all the poster columns and the sides of all the buses are covered with the same image of the same single thing: Julia Roberts's teeth; or a girl, seen from shoulder to knee in black and white, perfectly lit, sculpted lit, lingerie, snapping her garters; or Johnny Hallyday's face on a new issue of *Paris Match*. Once there were a thousand images of a woman behind a gold yellow champagne glass, *Le Moment Taittinger*. That time, I remember, I looked up the rue Jean Nicot and could see lights twinkling, like fireflies, right across the Seine, filling the trees. I went to investigate another day and found out that they were just lights strung in the trees to draw tourists to the *bateaux-mouches*.

The hardest thing to convey is how lovely it all is and how that loveliness seems all you need. The ghosts that haunted you in New York or Pittsburgh will haunt you anywhere you go, because they're your ghosts and the house they haunt is you. But they become disconcerted, shaken, confused for half a minute, and in that moment on a December at four o'clock when you're walking from the bus stop to the rue Saint-Dominique and the lights are twinkling across the river—only twinkling in the *bateaux-mouches*, luring the tourists, but still . . . you feel as if you've escaped your ghosts if only because, being you, they're transfixed looking at the lights in the trees on the other bank, too, which they haven't seen before, either.

It's true that you can't run away from yourself. But we were right: You can run away.

|||

I brined the turkey for Christmas dinner in a big white pasta pot that Martha and I bought years ago on lower Broadway. I put it out on our tiny terrace overlooking the boulevard Saint-Germain, covered with foil—all night long a shiny white ceramic and silver foil American beacon on the boulevard.

|||

And a Christmas surprise! We're going to have another kid, a small French child! The big Machine to Draw the World, which traces from two objects at once and makes something of the superimposition, is drawing a new one, down in Martha's belly. Stow the elegies, pal; we *can't* leave, not quite yet.

A Handful of
Cherries

Quite a few people have asked me to tell them what happened at
the Brasserie Balzar, after its friends occupied it in order to
protest its purchase by M. Jean-Paul Bucher, the owner of a large
and (we thought) unfeeling and soulless chain of brasseries and
restaurants. I've wanted to write about it for several reasons: because it sheds some light on the French struggle with change;
because it touches on the differences between French and
American attitudes to food, which have been filling the papers a
lot lately; and because it presented me with the one moment
when for a brief moment—seconds, really—I actually felt fully
French. But I've also been reluctant to write about it because in
the end it was a sad, typical story about the struggle for small values during a fin de siècle dominated by big money.

In plain English, we fought, and we lost. Not miserably,
though, and perhaps not entirely. We saved something, if only
our amour propre, and the solidarity of our organization, so that

there is a conceivable, half-plausible sense in which, in ornamental French, we won.

The first Balzar meeting was held in June 1998, just after the purchase of the small, perfect, century-old Left Bank brasserie by Bucher. The friends of the Balzar organized a group, led by two honorable men. The first, the *délégué du personnel,* or steward of the waiters, can now emerge from behind the pathetic false mustache he was provided in my first account and appear under his real name, Claude Blanchot. The other leader was Lorenzo Valentin, a startlingly handsome and eloquent young publisher whose offices were across the street from the Balzar. We banded together a collection of regulars, the clientele—mostly writers and publishers and professors from the Sorbonne—to protect the Balzar. The first meeting was a kind of sit-down and dine strike at the Balzar itself. We infiltrated about sixty members inside to protest, and almost everyone judged it a great success.

The evening had gotten a lot of attention in the press and produced a breakfast meeting at the Balzar of our executive committee with M. Bucher himself. He freely gave any number of assurances to protect the staff, the cooking, and the distinct traditions of the place. They were, I thought at the time, both very sincerely made and utterly worthless, since he had no more obligation to keep his promises than he had to come to our apartments and cook us breakfast.

By then it was late July, though, and nothing happens in Paris in late July. (If the king could have kept things calm around the Bastille for another three weeks, France would still be a monarchy.) Right on date, August 1, everyone went away: Lorenzo to Italy and the rest of the committee to one or another French resort. (All the *garçons,* as I had learned, rather reluctantly, to call them, went home too, mostly to the small towns in the Massif Central and the South and even Alsace where they came from.) The pattern of internal emigration, as described by Balzac, youth coming to the capital, remains as powerful in France as it was a century ago. You come to Paris to make a reputation, as a writer or a waiter, intending to go home, soon, to run the local paper or to open your own brasserie on the town square, but then you don't, except in August.

We had the habit of going back to America for two or three weeks in August, to be washed over by the cold waves of American ocean and the warm spit of American opinion and to see our family. First we would go to see Martha's family in Canada (who said, Canadianly, "Oh, you live in *Paris*. How stimulating,") and then to the little shack on Cape Cod where we had first sat out and watched the sunsets and dreamed of going to Paris.

And then back home through Orly, where, bleary-eyed, air-sick, after the tightly sealed flight, we would feel our hearts lift as the taxi turned in the early-morning flat white light into the porte d'Orléans, and then up the avenue du Général Leclerc, past the place Denfert-Rochereau, where I once lived as a kid (and where I could still see the window where Melissa, the baby of the six kids in my family, had once stood and semaphored to me, across the street, not to forget the *long, round* bread.) Then past the Belfort Café (where, twenty years before, I had once sneaked down for a *pain au chocolat* and my first *café serré*) and up the boulevard Raspail, where they were already setting up the *marché biologique,* and back to our apartment. "This is home," Luke said once, and our hearts skipped, because we knew it wasn't, quite, and were glad he thought it was.

The trees would already be shedding, and the streets would be filled with brown leaves, skipping across the empty boulevards. We always missed the fall coming to Paris; coming back after Labor Day is too late. Of the great argued-out differences between New York and Paris, none is more important than the simple difference that Paris is farther north than New York is. The end of August is still mostly high summer in America, at least on the East Coast, with days in the nineties and hazy sun and hardly a hint of autumn in the air. Labor Day hits Americans like a ton of bricks; we're going back to work *so soon*? And then, of course, Americans, for all their cult of summer and fussing about summer and idealizing summer have no summer at all to speak of. The two-week paid vacation, now made for the no-collar classes almost no vacation at all by the fax machine and the computer, is a small favor taken from a restless, impatiently toe-tapping employer. In France everyone—Luke's baby-sitter, the man who sells cheeses, President Chirac, Bernard Arnault, Bernard-Henri Lévy—is guaranteed five weeks of vacation by law, and just about everyone takes it. (There would be no point even for an eager beaver, overachieving tycoon to stay on the job since there would be nobody there for him to motivate.) When people say that Paris closes down in August, they don't mean the pace slackens a little. They mean it closes, like a box.

The funny thing is that the cool weather comes to Paris right around the end of August, so that by the time everyone comes back for the *rentrée,* it feels like autumn, and everyone is ready to start life over. People, ordinary people, are actually fed up with their vacations and glad to get back to town. (I once saw one of the inconsolably grumpy women who works at Michel Chemin, the bakery near us, come in on the first day of September and actually grab the other inconsolably grumpy woman who works there and kiss her, fully, on the cheeks.)

|||

As soon as I was back in town, I got a call from Lorenzo, to tell me that things were going very badly at the Balzar. The waiters were nervous; they had felt abused and overtaken by events; their grievance hearing at the *tribunal des Prudhommes*—the labor court—had been postponed. It seemed that Bucher was about ready to fire everybody, or that at least was the rumor. Tour groups of Americans were being sent in by concierges of large hotels. Our only hope, it seemed, was to *médiatiser* some more and then to . . . well, to have another meeting. There was one called that week at Mme. de Lavigne's apartment over on the quai Anatole-France.

I was the only American there, and this unexceptional fact made me unreasonably self-satisfied—the Tom Paine of the Balzar insurrection (although it seemed to me that I recalled from some sixtyish piece of guerrilla theater that, bad omen, Tom Paine ended up in prison during the Terror and died drunk in New York). While I was away, the great afternoon paper *Le Monde* had come out with another piece outlining our struggle to save the Balzar, by the oddly dyspeptic food writer J.-P. Quélin, the Hilton Kramer of French cuisine. Why should people whose lives are devoted to the study of pleasure be so charmless, so lacking in joy, I have often wondered? The answer is simple, I now thought. They were not drawn to their subject for pleasure; it was the *absence* of pleasure they felt that made them so tense and talky. This is the Devil's Theory of what draws critics to themes, and I am sure that it is true. The people who take natural pleasure in pictures, whom you see haunting the Museum of Modern Art at lunch hour, or eating with a copy of *Le Monde* at the old Balzar, are *completed* by the pleasure, as most of us are by sex. They feel no more need to discuss it than most of us want to discuss lovemaking; the drowsy commonplaces are, for them, the appropriate speech act, the only appropriate speech act. People who don't actually enjoy eating are the ones with the attention to look around the room—where are people sitting? Who likes what?—and absorb both the abstract system of snob values and the social comedy of it. The people who actually write well about food—M.F.K. Fisher or Seymour Britchky—are oddly abstemious, austere, even, in a way, antisensual, for the same reason that Ruskin, a man who recoiled in horror at his wife's pubic hair, could write so well about the hidden message of the pointed arch. *Not really liking it much* is a precondition of art criticism of all kinds. This is why embarrassingly, thunderously obvious thoughts—beauty counts, power matters, pictures sell for money—are often presented by critics with such shocked or plaintive intensity. All critics are food fusses, not wanting to try the green stuff, even when the

Mother-MOMA tells you it's good for you, and then announce darkly that it's poison, any child can see it is. (This is why Tom Wolfe could be both absolutely right and wrong about American art. Not wanting to eat, he alone would notice the odd order of the cutlery on the table.)

|||

At the meeting there was a general feeling that we needed to placate Quélin. We had a cross section of waiters and clients there that afternoon: Claude and Guy from the staff, and a left-wing journalist who I thought was looking at me darkly, having spotted not Tom Paine but a smoothie from the CIA.

Lorenzo led off with his usual quiet authority. He was in his usual costume: a soft black turtleneck and flannel slacks, with a scarf thrown, Little Prince style, around his throat. He has a round face, with an absolutely beautiful, warm smile. He has two registers at his command: a low, troubled one that he uses when he is reviewing the agenda and another, higher, and more plaintive one that he uses when he is exhorting us publicly, for instance when we occupy the restaurant. He outlined the problems. The waiters felt abused and uncertain because the standards in the kitchen were declining and Bucher was still letting the new manager take a chunk of their service money. "How were they declining?" someone asked. The fish was no good; the sole was being parboiled before it was grilled; someone else thought a supplier was coming in from the Flo Group with ordinary beef. "Well, I had a steak there the other night," someone began . . . but we all shushed him. The food, good or bad, was not really the *point,* we all said. The point was the spirit of the Balzar. If we did not act quickly and more decisively, the brasserie, and the *garçons'* security, would be lost. The guys had decided to stage a one-day wildcat strike, and it was important for us to support them—perhaps by occupying the Balzar the same day, perhaps on the night before. In any case, the crisis of the battle was approaching, and we could not be lazy or indecisive in our actions.

Claude spoke next. He was angry and at the same time, and for the first time, a little pleading. The *garçons* were planning to walk out on Thursday, he explained, and he hoped that we, the members of the association, would come out to support them. We would have Bucher foxed coming and going.

I could sense a reluctance to do this on the part even of our elite radical circle; this would be going beyond the politesse of our arrangement with Bucher, moving toward open warfare. "*Attention!*" someone said, a real interjection in French. "This could put us in a dangerous position." I feared too that Claude's ideas about the power of the association were greater than the power of the association deserved. I noticed that he liked to say the term *the association,* and he always referred to Lorenzo as "M. le Président."

I was becoming a little dubious, especially so because Lorenzo, for some reason, I thought, kept looking at me for ideas. I said, at last, that the only threat that had any meaning to Bucher was the threat of more bad publicity; that in effect, a boycott of his other restaurants would scare him more than anything else we could do. But I was also pretty sure that Bucher would never sell, and I feared that if the *garçons* walked out, he'd just replace them. Perhaps, I hinted, I gulped—I sensed the left-wing journalist looking at me with increasing disgust—we needed to start moving toward an exit strategy (I couldn't think of the French, so I said, *scénario de sortie,* which was more or less right). Did we have an exit strategy, aside from victory? What if Bucher held fast and didn't move? Could we get the *garçons* out in decent shape and not just blow up the Balzar, so to speak?

I was rewarded with steady, opaque looks. Having arrived at the logic of war, one of us—the American—was trying to wriggle out of it at the first sign of opposition. (I remembered what an American diplomat negotiating with the Quai d'Orsay had once said to me: "It is hard enough to get them to start, and once they start, you can't get them to stop.")

Then Lorenzo and Mme. de Lavigne together raised another, stranger, and more tempting vision. What if we were to buy the Balzar? What if Bucher could be convinced that the cost to him in bad publicity and harassment was just too great, didn't make sense for his chain, and that, finally, in a moment of facesaving capitulation (but why would this be facesaving for him? I let it pass) he could sell to a group of *actionnaires*—i.e., *us*.

Lorenzo had a nice rhetorical formula for this transaction: "M. Bucher wants to join the association, but the association would like to join the Flo Group." Mme. de Lavigne had been in the restaurant business; it would not be hard to do. We could each own a little piece of the Balzar, the *garçons* too, and, run as a co-operative, a kind of writers and waiters cooperative, we could make it *rentable*.

It sounded like just about the best idea I had ever heard. Like many Americans of my generation, I am a fanatic restaurant imaginer: I think that someday I will open a restaurant called La Chanson, to serve French-American cooking: roast chicken with caramelized carrots and broccoli puree and pecan pie for dessert; then there is my favorite idea for a restaurant called Les Fauves, which would serve only game—taglietelle with wild boar, pheasant stuffed with chestnuts—or else to open—and this I was sure would make a fortune—a place to get real Montreal bagels, better than any other kind, boiled and then baked, sweet and chewy where New York bagels are bready and tasteless. . . .

So this was the hand that we would play, or try to play at least. We would have another sit-in at the Balzar, the night before the meeting, and we would threaten Bucher with still more *médiatisation*. The next day, independently, the personnel would stage their wildcat strike, and the two actions together would, somehow, sufficiently intimidate a whipsawed Bucher and he would crumble and sell us back the Balzar.

I can only say that at the time it did not seem like a completely crazy scenario. What we could not understand, I suppose, was why Bucher would want to buy the Balzar only in order to destroy it, why, after it had been clearly shown to him that he could not understand the institution, grasp its traditions, perpetuate its values, he would still want to hold on to it. For the money? It was too small for his chain; he had said as much himself. He could make more money in a single sitting at one of his Right Bank atmosphere factories—the vast art deco Boeuf sur le Toit, or the belle époque Julien—than he could in a week at Balzar. It wasn't as if we had anything against him personally; if he wanted to come and eat at the Balzar, we'd welcome him, anytime. But why own it only in order to ruin it? Where was the logic in that?

I suppose we couldn't realize, or could realize but couldn't accept, that the logic of business is not a logic in that sense. It's not only a narrow consideration of profits and losses, but a larger logic of, well, appetite. To buy something is to assert oneself, and to sell it, for whatever reason, is to collaborate in one's own diminishment. We were asking him to regurgitate in public, and even if we offered him the feather with which to tickle his own throat, he wouldn't want to do it. A man in his position couldn't afford to regurgitate, not in public, because then he would look ridiculous.

Anyway, we all clasped hands and swore to be at the Balzar on October 7 to reoccupy the place. Everybody had bought some food to the meeting—I recall that Claude had brought a particularly beautiful and fragrant Cantal, a wonderful cheese—and we soon broke for some wine. I buttonholed Guy after the meeting and asked him what we could really do, what the guys, the *garçons, really* wanted. Did they really want us to try to buy the place? He said, We want it to stay the same. To continue doing what we've always done. And to serve good food—the food isn't good enough. The food should be excellent.

This was curious, I thought. We radicals had decided that it was a red herring, so to speak, to make too much of an issue of the quality of the cooking—that wasn't the point, we insisted grandly—yet the *garçons* made much of it, made more of it than anything else. Some fundamental part of their métierhood is offended by the knowledge that the cuisine is being degraded. There is a real decent impulse on their part to put down a *plat* on the table with real enthusiasm: You'll enjoy this.

As I thought it over on my way home, it occurred to me that this is after all the deepest altruistic impulse that we have, food sharing being the most fundamental gesture of selflessness. I thought I was at last beginning to see the deeper motives, the real human basis of their indignation, beyond the few pennies here and there that they were losing. In the old regime they had been the tribal chieftains, the ones doing the sharing, and this more than compensated for their otherwise servile-seeming role. If they served good food, then they were practicing, if only by proxy, the primal role of the provider; if they served bad food, then they were just waiters in a restaurant. Beneath the "French" aspect of the Balzar wars—the mistrust of change that is not merely, or not merely foolishly and emptily, "nostalgic"—there was a deeper impulse, almost an instinctive one. Of course they wanted to protect their share of the service, and they wanted to keep their old working conditions. But they also were terrified of a loss of status, of being publicly shamed. To be a server at all is to dance on the edge of shame all the time. *"Sale métier,"* Bemelmans's waiters famously mutter to themselves as they go in and out of the kitchen, "filthy profession," and it is easy to understand why. Bucher was reducing them to food bearers, rather than food sharers, and it made them feel as if they were being eaten alive.

||||

October came, and we occupied the Balzar again. The second *réunion* had a different feeling from the first, both gayer and angrier and more hysterical. At the first meeting the near absurdity of what we were doing had given everything an edge of comedy. *Can we really be doing this? Well, yes, we are. We are!* At the second *réunion* things seemed tougher, rockier. There were far more of us, for one thing, and not everyone could find a seat. People were waiting outside, thronged outside, trying to come in. The Balzar wars had been *médiatisées* as something amusing—a *fronde parisienne,* one of the papers had called it, a Parisian civil war. Those of us on the inside knew that the real action would take place the following day, when the *garçons* walked out, and we felt both anxious not to tip their hand and eager to let them know that we were with them.

Lorenzo was sublime. At the appointed hour he rose again from his seat, "We are here tonight not to make demands, not to protest, but to inquire," he began. "We are here to inquire of M. Bucher if, though he owns the name Balzar, if anyone can purchase its spirit. Is that spirit truly for sale? Can it be bought and sold? Or can it only be protected? We are not here to criticize the cuisine or to give M. Bucher lessons in the management of his affairs. We claim no expertise in that." Lorenzo gave a just so slightly sardonic inflection to these last words, implying that this was an expertise that one would hardly want. "But we do claim to understand the spirit of this place, the thousand tiny interchanges between the *personnel* and the place that have made it something more than a place where one exchanges money for food, and from which one would go elsewhere if more food could be had for less money. We are here to inquire about the *nature* of possession, about what it means to possess something and about who truly possesses a place: the man who owns the chairs and tables or the people who sit at those tables or those who have devoted their working lives to those tables. We want to ask: To whom belongs the Balzar? Does it belong to those who own it or to those who love it? Above all, we are here to inquire if any of us can feel at home in this place if the *personnel* of the Balzar do not feel at home in it. For they are the carriers of the spirit of this place. I say to the *personnel:* We are with you, right to the end." The room exploded in applause.

People began to rise and make seconding speeches themselves. Many of them, I am bound to report, had a slight edge of anti-Americanism, although no American was involved in this struggle, one way or another. (Apart from me, I mean, and I was there strictly as an honorary Parisian, or Quisling.)

For instance, a man rose from one of the banquettes at the end and cried, "You must let Bucher know that this is not a small war!" Applause. "Not a little brushfire that can be put out." More applause. "Let them know that this will not be the Gulf War!" Wild applause. "It will be Vietnam!" Madly enthused applause.

But after the meeting I went over to talk to this Danton, and he turned out to be a French-American businessman who lives in San Francisco. He gave me his card. Finally, and one by one, the waiters came out to bow, and we rose to our feet to applaud them. They looked genuinely touched, and we swore that we would not let them be betrayed.

|||

The next day at lunch the waiters walked out. I went over to the rue des Écoles to see what was going on and found all of them on the street, in mufti, carrying placards. Their union had put out a table, and there was a petition that you could sign to show your support for the Balzaristes. The *garçons* looked happy, and Jacques, a friend of Lorenzo's, was there with a video camera, documenting the event.

Our next meeting, in late November, was the strange one. Bucher had invited a little group of us to have breakfast with him once again, and on the eve of that meeting, we decided to have a serious meeting—an *assemblée générale* of Les Amis du Balzar. We held it, now, as serious meetings should be held, not at the Balzar or in Mme. de Lavigne's apartment, but in the classroom in a film school in the Twelfth Arrondissement, at nine o'clock at night. There was a pretty good turnout, considering, but now the alacrity and lightness had been lost, and the meeting had the air of, well, of a meeting. We all sat on school chairs, uncomfortably, and Claude, looking surprisingly uncomfortable too, droned on about the position of the waiter's grievance in front of the labor court.

Then Lorenzo took over and talked about the three plans that were open to us: We could continue to *médiatiser* and agitate about the Balzar, but that did not seem like a promising strategy, since in the meantime Bucher could simply wear us (and the waiters) down. We could attempt to buy the Balzar from Bucher—but he would almost certainly not sell. (I do not know to this day why Lorenzo had become pessimistic about this possibility, though I am sure that he was right. Perhaps he had another conversation with Bucher when they arranged the breakfast meeting.) The third possibility was to raise enough money to, in effect, start our own Balzar—a Balzar *des refusés*, a real Balzar, under some other name, while Bucher's Balzar continued its impersonation. We all looked cheerful at this possibility, though it obviously demanded an infusion of capital. But a possible site had already been located farther down the rue des Écoles, and one of our members had long experience in the *restauration* . . . it might be done.

The conversation batted along, sometimes with animation, sometimes in a desultory way, for the next couple of hours. We pursued dead ends (could another, more sympathetic, buyer be found?) and digressions (what was the precise status of the *garçons* after the strike?) and kept circling around the central point. We needed to show Bucher that we were in earnest about opening another Balzar, in order to get him to, perhaps, perpetuate the current one. Like all public meetings of "causes," this one had a curious sideways, crab-walking momentum of its own. Somehow, the notion that we ought to show Bucher we were serious metamorphosed into the idea that the only way to show him that we were was to ask for a subscription of some real but small sum—say, six hundred francs, about a hundred dollars—from all the members of the association, which in turn metamorphosed into the idea that we ought to put the *idea* of the

subscription to a vote of the membership. We voted on this resolution, and it passed.

The whole thing made no sense at all, as we all knew perfectly
well the moment we left the classroom and went back out into
the cold early winter air and headed for the Métro. The sum involved was both ridiculously small—Bucher was hardly about to
be intimidated by it—and at the same time sufficiently noxious
to keep a lot of people from wanting to offer it up. (I did not look
forward to explaining to my own wife that we needed to pony up
a hundred dollars in order to open up a new brasserie.) And to
put it to a vote simply attenuated things still more. It was one of
those bizarre decisions that are arrived at in protest meetings by
a process of drift and uncertainty, in which a backwater suddenly
for a moment looks like the way to the blue ocean and then, even
when only moments later everybody knows that it's a dead end,
we still close our eyes and pretend that we are going somewhere.

I do not want to give the impression that once the drama and
steak au poivre had been removed from our movement, it lost
momentum or seriousness. The classroom was full; the debate
was intense; the purpose was firm. It was just that the strongest
part of our case was its presentation, and once we moved away
from our proscenium, there was not very much we could do. We
had moved in a single November night from ideology to politics—from what you *want* to what you do—with the usual disappointing results. "We have gone from '68 to '81 tonight," a friend
sighed in my ear as we walked home. He meant that we had gone
from utopian vision and slogans to the realities of the assumption
of power, or from Mao (the make-believe French Mao) to Mitterrand.

I walked all the way home from the Twelfth, across at the
Gare d'Austerlitz and then all the way along by the river. It was a
cold night, winter really, and the few leaves left on the trees shivered sympathetically above, like waiters carrying trays.

On November 30, that Tuesday, we met with M. Bucher early in the morning at La Coupole, the vast twenties brasserie that he owns down on the boulevard du Montparnasse. It was eight-thirty in the morning—much too early, we all agreed—but that had been M. Bucher's hour, and we did not want to change it, I suppose for fear of seeming sluggish.

Bucher was as agreeable as ever. This time, though, instead of the short sleeves and open shirt that he had worn at our first breakfast together at the Balzar, he wore a suit and tie, pressed tightly over his belly. He began by smiling and shrugging and making the significant admission that maybe M. Delouche, the new maître d', was the wrong man to be fronting the Balzar. He complained again about the *médiatisation,* meaning, I think, M. Quélin and *Le Monde,* which Lorenzo agreed had been unfortunate, but then pressed on to his hard, blunt point: The *garçons* will leave with a fat envelope, and that's it.

"They drove the old owner into the bushes like a hunted animal," he says scornfully. "Not me. All this"—he meant the war of the *garçons*—"belongs to another century." He caught himself, knowing that he mustn't seem too harsh, too "liberal." "But you know, on reflection, that's why I like it. I value it. That's why I want to be a member of your organization."

He agreed, after much tender pushing by Lorenzo, to meet himself with the *garçons*. The strike had shocked him. "Ninety-five percent of my media is about Balzar and point two percent of my business. Listen, I'll talk to them, I'll try to make them happy. But if they want to leave with a fat envelope, they can leave." He swore, forcefully, that there are no tour groups admitted to the Balzar.

Then Bucher did something, amazingly, intuitively shrewd. Before he had always spoken of the alternative to his ownership as McDonald's—"Listen, if you don't want me, maybe McDonald's will take over"—and we knew this to be pure rhetoric; McDonald's was not about to take over the Balzar, and in any case, McDonald's bashing of that kind was too generalized, too vague an ideological gesture to have any weight. It was a purely formal turn, recognizable as such. But now he turned to another potential owner.

"Listen," he said, "I hear you'd like me to sell. Okay. Maybe you want me to sell out to M. Conran? I'm sure he would love it." Terence Conran is the English restaurateur and furniture tycoon who a few weeks before had just opened his own new brasserie, L'Alcazar, over on the rue Mazarin. It was the first attempt by a major figure of the London cooking renaissance to establish a beachhead in Paris, and it had been getting a lot of press.

Bucher shrugged. "I think he has nothing to teach us about how to run a brasserie. I'm trying to defend a 'Franco-Français' tradition but . . ."

A little of the air seemed to pass right out of our movement at that moment. The anti-Americanism that lent a piquant, alarming note to the Balzar wars had been, as anti-Americanism most often is in France, not quite real, an abstract idea, a speech act with very few barbs in it. (Lorenzo, Claude, and I had once had a long debate, over dinner, about the relative merits of John Coltrane, whose pianist, McCoy Tyner, Lorenzo's brother had studied with, and Cannonball Adderley, favored by Claude.) Anti-Americanism in France at the end of the twentieth century is in fact in some ways like anti-Catholicism in England in the nineteenth century. It is a powerful, important, influential, official doctrine, but it is also not entirely real: English people imprecated against the Catholics and the pope, but that didn't stop them from loving Venice, traveling to Florence, worshiping Raphael, and filling their houses with Italian pictures. Even the much-publicized fusses about American mass-produced food and French peasants "trashing" McDonald's are almost pure media events. The French farmers knock down a McDonald's for the benefit of the French media, which publicize it in *Le Monde* in order to see what *The New York Times* will have to say about it the next day. Anti-Americanism has enormous life as an abstract ideological principle and a closed circle of media events of this kind, but outside of a tiny circle on the elite left and, surprisingly, a slightly larger one on the elite right, it has almost no life as a real emotion. But suspicion of the English is a permanent feature of the French psyche. Anti-English sentiment in France is like anti-French sentiment in nineteenth-century England: inarticulate but real. Those people just annoy the hell out of you. This contempt for the English, as opposed to the love-hate relation with Americans, is seen, for instance, in the almost open disdain that the French press has displayed in its investigation of the death of Diana Spencer, as it prefers to call her. Or at a more obscure level it can be seen in the magazine *Le Point,* which is usually pro-American in the neutral, hidden sense (it runs endless reviews of American music and movies and television). When it ran a cover story on the British invasion of the Dordogne, though, the story was full of mistrust and contempt.

So for Bucher to say that McDonald's was coming was a mere ideological gesture, instantly seen as one. But to say that he could sell out to Terence Conran was to speak to a real, and completely annoying, possibility. Afterward, when our committee gathered in a café across the street from La Coupole, with two new members of the group—whom I didn't know but whom Lorenzo had invited along after the meeting earlier that week, Lorenzo having a good left democrat's desire to keep the leadership in touch with the masses—we all felt unhappy. The two new guys were sure that there was a *complot* of some kind, a hidden history, that was being kept from them. Discussing the possibility of our new Balzar, they also seemed unable to accept the logic of capitalism in any form, including one we would own ourselves.

Above all, they were offended by the very existence, the very idea, even in a purely hypothetical form, of Terence Conran. "I wouldn't go to England and give them lessons on making tea," one of them said, bitterly. Lorenzo, I thought, looked unsettled.

|||

It was around that time that I finally went to have lunch with J.-P. Quélin, the biting food critic of *Le Monde*. I was almost, though not quite, an official emissary from the friends of the Balzar to him, hoping that he would tone it down a little. We went to Aux Fins Gourmets, the Basque bistro downstairs from our apartment, where I have been going for several years now and where, to my surprise, Quélin had never been.

Quélin turned out to be from central casting. (But then we are all from central casting: I running down, without extra forethought, from the apartment, in sneakers and sweater and beige Levi's, and at my age too.) He was wearing what I have come to think of as the Uniform, the standard gear of French journalists who still see themselves as men of letters: black and beige houndstooth jacket, white cotton shirt, black knit tie. He has a perfect hatchet face, a long jaw, a clear enunciation, and he smoked American cigarettes square in the middle of his mouth. He looked nearly exactly like Ian McKellen playing Richard III.

I came in, took my table, and noticed him, thinking, This can't be J.-P. Quélin; he looks much too characteristic for that. But of course, it was, and he smiled, sardonically, and pointed: So it is you. He had invited along his editor, who turned out to be a lovely, worried-looking, square-built blonde—a mum (French writers and their editors, Frenchmen and their mums). He was brutal with the waiters and decided at last on *haricot de mouton* and a bottle of Madiran. I had sworn to have an *omelette* and no wine at all, but took the wine as a challenge to my—well, if not to my masculinity then to my French assimilation, my right to live in Paris and call myself a writer.

We talked about cooking and restaurants. "There is an Anglo-Saxon contempt for French food and a love for it all the same," Jean-Pierre Quélin began. I tried, tactfully, to argue that while the top heights of French cuisine remain unique—Passard, Gagnaire—the everydays might be more pleasurable now in New

York or even London. He was dubious about the second proposition but agreed about the first: They are cooking, he says, at a level of originality that defies judgment, defies criticism, defies the grammar of cuisine. (This, I think, is true. When I took my brother to L'Arpège for his birthday, we got fourteen [small] courses, mostly of vegetables—*haricots verts* with peaches and raw almonds dressed with basil and fresh mint; fresh shell beans with onion ravioli and tomato coulis—that made even the best of the old cuisine look like sludge.)

We kept pouring the Madiran, and to my alarm, a second bottle followed the first. I saw the afternoon's work disappearing. In voicing my own tentative criticisms of the state of French cooking—mild and commonplace—I realized that Quélin was completely insulated from the general opinion that the new Mediterranean synthesis that reigns in New York and London is simply the thing and that the French two-tier system—three stars for the millionaires and occasions; the same old same old forever elsewhere—is defunct. He just had never heard the idea. I didn't even try to convince him otherwise, though, not that I could have.

Quélin's editor left and, the bottle still there, we began confiding—no, not confiding, engaging in that level of frank, let's-call-a-Medusa's-head-a-Medusa's-head honesty that is one of the pleasures of the end of a two-bottle lunch in Paris. We shared philosophical reflections on our sons, our lives, the impossibility of journalism. "The voluptuous cruelty of filling pages," he said, "the voluptuous cruelty of filling pages is what kills us." We talked about his time in the army in Algeria, when a Breton peasant under his command tried to rape a local girl. He stopped him, and the peasant drew his revolver: "I looked death, in all its absurdity and horror, right in the face for fifteen minutes." Then we talked about our sons. The day will come, he said, when they condescend to us, when they feel themselves to be our intellectual superiors, "and in that moment of pity we will find our pride."

It occurred to me then that the paradoxes that litter French writing are deeply felt among all French literary people. The pity and pride of paternity; the absurdity and profundity of death, the voluptuous cruelty of journalism—these antinomies are not affectations but part of a real heritage of feeling. They *mean* it. In my heart, I suppose, I don't believe that something *can* be horrible and beautiful. I am too American for that, though I suppose I believe that something can be voluptuous and cruel. A child of the occupation—his father escaped twice from prison camps, to see him as a baby—and the Algerian War, Quélin knows in his blood that it is so, that life is damnably double, whichever way it falls. It may be an affectation, but it is not a pose.

Over the third bottle—a title for a French memoir—I tried out my pet theory: that France is marked by a struggle between its pompous official culture and its matchless vernacular, commonplace civilization—and that what makes France unique is that so much of the pompous, abstract, official culture has spilled over into the popular "culture," so that every man sees himself as an aphorist, his own Montaigne in his own tower. He pointed at me again. "That," he said dramatically, "is an idea of merit. You must write it up for us in the context of cuisine." I said that I would try.

When the bill came, he handed the waiter his *carte bleue* and was told, as I knew he would be, that they don't take cards. Without looking up again at the waiter, he reached into his wallet and handed him his *Le Monde* press card. "Send it to me," he said icily, meaning the bill. The insolence was enormous. Not even an essay at a smile. Afterward, as we left, he searched out the thin, intellectual owner of the restaurant, Michel, who had been giving us the same indulgent, fixed half-smile for three years and told him that he admired his *navarin*. Michel looked at him with hungry gratitude and then at me with disbelief—*this* one brought *this* one?—and I looked back at him in quiet, sneaker-bound triumph.

That Wednesday I appeared in Quélin's column in *Le Monde,* as a *brave joyeusement américain* who had introduced him to the bistro where they still know how to master the difficult art of the *navarin,* etc. Later on that year I even made a second appearance, at Quélin's invitation, and under my own byline, explaining my theory about civilization and culture in France and even making a terrible French pun on the words *moss* and *mass.*

Quélin never again made fun of the friends of the Balzar, so I feel that this diplomatic negotiation had, at least, been well conducted. At the end of the lunch, though, I wasn't just muzzy but absolutely knocked cold by the Madiran. I went back upstairs and slept for two hours.

|||

And then it was over, all over by Christmas. One by one, the *garçons* each decided to take the "fat envelope" Bucher was offering them, and retire. They had to. There was nothing we could do. We walked into the Balzar one December evening, and everyone—Jean-Michel, Claude, Robert—was gone, gone for good. They had decided to take the fat envelope—just how fat it was I'm not sure, though it was said to be about a year's salary, in addition, of course, to their pensions—and go. Only two of the old *garçons* remained. We had lost.

Guy, who remained, spoke to me under his breath, sadly, as we shook hands, defeated. "A handful of cherries," he said softly. "They gave them a handful of cherries for a lifetime of work. What can I do? I want to work for a while longer."

I felt blue. Without the regular guys it was not the same place. They had an English menu now, and they forced it on me when they heard me speak in English to Luke. I told them to take it away and bring me the proper menu. The new *garçon* looked haughty and insulted.

I spoke to Lorenzo and Claude on the phone that week, and everyone agreed that this was the best thing for everyone: There was no sense in allowing the personnel to hang on waiting for some quixotic scheme for a new Balzar to hatch—though, they both added quickly, hatch it might, hatch it might. We rung off.

I stopped going to the Balzar. The food was fine, I was told, and I would still send visiting Americans there. But I no longer loved it, and without Jean-Pierre welcoming us, it was not the same place. Fortunately a good cookbook had appeared—by the American Daniel Young—with a couple of Balzar recipes that I liked, and I would stay home and make them for my family on Sundays: *gigot d'agneau avec flageolets* and profiteroles.

Then, one night at the beginning of May, I got a call from Claude. How was Madame and the *héritier*? Fine, fine, how was he? Oh, it was going for him. Listen, he said, the old guys had decided to come together for a night and give a dinner of their own for the people who had helped them in their fight. They would love to have us. Could we join them? Yes, of course, I said. We wouldn't miss it for the world. He gave me the date a couple of weeks off, at the end of May, and the address of a restaurant up in the Ninth, the Relais Beaujolais. The owner was a friend and was glad to be hosting the dinner.

By then Martha was already five months pregnant and very big, and it was a hot and humid night. It was a nice place, though, and we arrived at eight-thirty. There were two or three big tables set up, with familiar faces all around them. Everyone was there: Claude and Guy and Lorenzo. . . . All the *garçons* of course were in plain clothes, jeans and short-sleeve shirts mostly. There was a lot of chilled Beaujolais and a dinner of *pièce de boeuf chasseur,* roast beef in a mushroom-wine sauce.

The startling and instructive thing was that the *garçons* seemed, on the whole, happy, free, and content. They were genuinely philosophical, in the old-fashioned sense, about what had happened—meaning stoic but articulate. They could see their own situation against a broader background.

I sat across from Robert, one of the oldest of the old *garçons,* a small, mustached man in his late fifties. "A handful of cherries?" he said when I repeated, a little dolefully, Guy's comment. "Perhaps. But a handful of cherries is better than an empty hand." He was in a rust-colored short-sleeve shirt, and his mustache was turning white. "Anyway, it is only in moments of crisis that we find lucidity about ourselves—though only after the crisis is over. Still, that's enough lucidity for anyone. Anyway, it is all the lucidity that life will give you. The crucial thing is that it was *our choice*. We made it. We *chose* to leave. I'm rather old to do this. The younger fellows . . . but it's over, we made a good choice. And it was *our* choice."

We talked about more general subjects: Corsica, the Clinton affair. "We can't understand your society," he said, shaking his head, "at once so violent and so puritanical, so authoritarian and so anarchist." But of course, it turned out that he had someone, a son, in America, who was always inviting him over. He had been once and was going to go again. He liked it there.

"I love to study the problem of being," he added abruptly, and he told a long and tragic story about one of the other personnel, a maître d' who had worked at the Balzar once, whose daughter, the light of his life, had committed suicide. Her father could not stop thinking of it and talking about it, all the time, his grief so deep, while he gave orders and cleaned tables. Though I knew him, in my callowness I had never sensed the tragedy within this man.

"His problem," Robert went on gravely, "was that he could not arrive at an abstraction of himself, only at a version of *me,* a me in some other form. He could not see himself as he was, see himself from outside himself. He was trapped in himself from the failure to make himself into an abstraction."

I looked up. Lorenzo was shaking hands and, I could see, was being urged to make a speech, a toast, but he was politely declining, smiling and shaking his head. *La guerre est finie.*

"That's a formidable guy," Robert said, nodding at Lorenzo. "Once he is wound up, ah, he can go on brilliantly, passionately. And Claude too. We were lucky to have them."

I thought then that the most irritating thing about life in

France, as I had described it so sapiently to the readers of *Le Monde*—the insistence on the primacy of the unspecific, on turning things into abstractions of themselves at every turn—was really a gift. I had praised the civilization, and the culture had exasperated me, and by civilization, I had meant small shops, and by culture, big buildings. In the end, though, the small shops were special in Paris because they were always in the shadow of the big buildings. Take the small shops away (and the streets the shops sit on and the *quartiers* that the streets sit in) and you would have nothing—not René Clair or Trenet and Lartigue or the whole of this great and beautiful bourgeois civilization. But take away the big buildings, with their abstract ideas and grand manner, and the special quality of the Parisian shops—of the brasseries and cafés, of the glass houses and glass domes—their quality of being the stage sets of a modern drama, something more than just shops, would go too. The lucidity of Parisian empiricism was bought at the price of the grandiosity of Parisian abstraction, and you couldn't have one without the other, no matter how much you wanted to or how hard you tried.

We finished dinner, and I asked the owner—who had been up on a ladder most of the night, fussing with the single unworking fan that was supposed to cool off the entire *salle*—to call us a cab. My wife was large and easily tired. But just as the owner came to tell us that the cab had arrived, Claude at last rose and began to make a presentation to Lorenzo of a single immense, earthenware tray. "A gift of friendship," he said, "of simple friendship."

Lorenzo Valentin rose to his feet reluctantly, hugged Claude, and began to sit down. "No, say something, say something," everyone said. He shook his head again. People began to pound the tables, as they had done at the Balzar a year ago. Now he was on his feet again, and I could see that he was about to begin.

It seemed like a good moment for us to slip away to the taxi, and we got up and tried to duck our heads down and go back up the stairs to the front room and the street. But Claude saw us going and cried out and called for a round of applause.

I stopped and turned and bowed. I had fallen in love all over again that night with the lucidity and intelligence of Parisian civilization, and I said, in my ornate, brutally accented, abstract French that we were leaving so precipitously simply to defend the health of one more child who would—that there would be a child who would be, to be born in Paris, and who would love Paris too—who would in some way be French. It was playing to the gallery, I suppose, but it got a round of applause, and I still tell myself they meant it.

We went out into the street, found the taxi waiting in the rain, and went home. From the street, as I helped Martha into the cab, I could hear the first murmur of Lorenzo's voice, rising in interrogation, just one last time, to inquire about the complexities of ownership, the love of a *lieu,* the hold of memory, and the meaning of possession, as it is felt both by the possessor and by the possessed.

|||

I was so overtaken by the excitement of the strike and the action, and then I was so happily filled with a sense of moral indignation, and self-righteous pleasure, that I kept away from the Balzar, and for a while I didn't miss it at all. As generations of French revolutionaries have discovered, moral self-righteousness is a very good short-term substitute for pleasure, but it wears out. Now I realize that the Balzar still exists on the rue des Écoles and that I have lost it for good, and I think about the light coming in on a spring night, and the way the waiters took the food from the oval platters to the circular plates, and the simple *poulet rôti,* and how good it all was, and I miss it all the time.

Like a King

When we discovered that the child we were going to have in Paris last fall would be a girl—we already have a boy—everybody told us that we had been blessed with the *choix du roi,* the king's choice. "Why, it's the *choix du roi!*" the technician said as she looked at the sonogram, more or less in the tone of the host on *Jeopardy!* announcing the Daily Double. "It's the *choix du roi!*" said the woman in the two-hour photo place on the rue du Bac when we told her. "A little girl coming after a little boy?" said my friend Pascal, the philosopher, with evident pleasure. "Why, then, it's the *choix du roi!*"

Martha was delighted to be having a girl, however the king felt about it. She had always wanted a son and a daughter, and as she only now explained to me, one of the reasons she had been so eager to leave New York four years earlier, just after the birth of our son, was that all her friends there who had two children had two boys, and she was starting to believe that two boys were just one of the things that happened to women in New York, "like high-intensity step classes and vanilla Edensoy," as she put it. Also, she said, she was worried about having to succumb to the New York social law that compels you nowadays to name your sons exclusively after the men your grandfather used to take a *shvitz* with. In our New York circle of under-tens we already had, in addition to the requisite Maxes, a Harry, a Joe, a Sam, an Otto, and a Charlie—the whole senior staff of Benny's Market: Lowest Prices in Town. "Even if I had had another boy, at least in Paris I wouldn't have had to call him Moe," she explained.

I was pleased by the news too, of course, but a little mystified by the expression. To be brutally frank, what mystified me was why a king would choose to have any girls at all. If I were a king, I would want only boys, so that the succession would never be challenged by the sinister uncle with a mustache lurking behind my throne. Or only girls and an immortality pill. What puzzled me even more was the way the phrase, though you heard it on Parisian lips, had a slightly disconcerting air of peasants-in-the-spring ecstasy about it, the kind of thing (*"C'est le choix du roi!"*) you would expect to hear set to a Trenet tune and sung by the villagers in a Pagnol film when the baker's daughter gives birth to little Lisette.

I soon sensed, though, that while people meant it, they also didn't mean it, that it was a thing you said both as a joke and not as a joke. After four years in Paris I have come to realize that this is where the true cultural differences reside: not in those famous moments when you think that a joke was meant straight ("My goodness, the *dessert grand-mère* is not made by Grandmother!"), or you misunderstand something that was meant straight as a joke ("The *tête de veau* is actually the head of a calf!"), but in those moments when you are confronted with something that is meant both as a joke and seriously. This zone of kidding overlaid with not kidding is one that we know at home. When a New Yorker passes out cigars in the office after the birth of his child,

for instance, he is both making a joke about passing out cigars—
with unspoken but quickly grasped reference to all the episodes
of *Bewitched* and *I Love Lucy* in which Darrin or Desi or some
other fifties-ish father passed out cigars—and sincerely celebrat-
ing the birth of his child. (The proof of this doubleness is that
the cigars he passes out will actually be good to smoke, while
mockery would make do with a bad or unsmokable cigar. Nobody tried to eat Warhol's soups.)

|||

In Paris, the obstetricians all wear black. When your wife goes to
be examined, the doctor who comes out into the waiting room is
not a smart Jewish girl in a lab coat, as in New York, but a man
with a day's growth of beard, who is wearing black jeans and a
black silk shirt, like a character in a David Mamet play about
Hollywood producers.

I first became aware of this when we went to get the first of
many sonograms of the new baby. The sonogramist we had been
sent to performs in a nineteenth-century apartment in the Sixth
Arrondissement, with wainscoting and ceiling moldings and windows that open like doors. A curtain was drawn across one half
of the living room, and couples sat on two sofas in the other half,
turning the pages of *Elle* (*Elle* is a weekly in France) and waiting
to be called.

After about ten minutes the curtain parted, and the sonogram
specialist came into the room. He had on black jeans and a black
silk shirt, open at the front and plunging down toward his navel,
sleeves rolled up to the elbows. A day-old growth of beard covered his face. He smiled at us and asked us to come in. We sat
down in front of a handsome Louis XV desk—the sonogram
equipment was over in the other corner of the office—and he
asked us when the baby had been conceived. My wife gave him
the likely date.

"Was that at night or early the next day?" he asked. It took me
a moment to realize that he was kidding, and then another mo-

ment to realize that he was not, and then still another moment—
the crucial cultural gap moment—to realize that he was neither
kidding nor not kidding. That is to say, he was kidding—he knew
that it didn't matter—but he was not kidding in the sense that he
was genuinely interested, considered that it was part of his profession to view that precise moment of passion or lust with a special tenderness. The moment of conception, the sexual act, was,
in his schema, not incidental information to be handled discreetly or pushed aside altogether, as American obstetricians
do—all American "What to Expect" books begin with the test,
not the act—but the prime moment, the hallowed moment, the
first happy domino that, falling, caused all the other dominoes
that had brought the three of us together to fall, and (his eyes implied) it was our special shared knowledge that that domino had
not in fact fallen but had been nudged, deliberately, and by us.
Then he asked Martha to get undressed. There was, to my surprise, no changing room or even a curtain, so she did, like that.
(I was the only embarrassed person in the room.) The elaborate
hospital rigmarole of American hygiene and American obstet-
rics—the white coats, the dressing rooms, the lab gowns—is dispensed with. They make no sense, since a pregnant woman is
not only not sick but in a sense has doubled the sum of her
health.

We looked at the baby on the sonar screen, as though she
were a character in a Tom Clancy novel. "She's pretty," he said at
last. Then we got a package of fifteen or so pictures of our daughter in embryo, full of allure, as the receptionist said. The pictures
were stapled, in neat, ruffled rows, into a little wallet, with sans
serif lowercase type, like an e. e. cummings poem.

"In New York the obstetricians all wear white, and they all
have books out," Martha said to me one afternoon. She had
called up an obstetrician in New York that day, before her appointment with her French doctor. "She covered me with congratulations, and then she told me all these tests I ought to take.
Week ten the CVS, then in week fourteen an early amnio, and

then in weeks eighteen to twenty a targeted ultrasound to test for neural tube defects, and then I'm supposed to get genetic carrier blood tests for all these other things."

"What did the French obstetrician say when you told her that?"

"She made that 'oh' face—you know, that lips-together, 'How naïve can one be?' face—said that it was far too dangerous to do the CVS, and then she prescribed a lot of drugs for pain. I've got antispasmodics, antinausea drugs, painkillers, and some other ones too. Then she told me I could drink red wine and absolutely not to eat any raw vegetables. She keeps asking me if I've had any salad. She says 'salad' the way the doctors in New York say 'uninsured.'"

French doctors like to prescribe drugs as much as New York doctors like to publish books. I suppose that it fulfills a similar need for self-expression with a pen, without having to go to the trouble of having your photograph taken with a professional yet humane grin. You cannot go into a French doctor's office for a cinder in your eye and emerge without a six-part prescription, made up of pills of different sizes to be taken at irregular intervals.

I wanted to meet Martha's doctor, who would be delivering the baby while I "coached"—I am of the Phil Jackson school as a coach; you might not actually see me doing much, but I contribute a lot to the winning atmosphere—and so I accompanied her to the next appointment. We sat in the waiting room and read *Elle* some more. By now Martha was nervous. An American friend who lives in Normandy had gone into labor a few days before, only to find that all the anesthesiologists had gone out on strike that morning. She had delivered the baby, her second, without any epidural.

"I want to go to a place where the anesthesiologists are scabs," Martha said. "Or nuns or something. I don't want to go to a place where the man with the epidural is on a picket line."

While we were in the waiting room, a man in black jeans and a black silk shirt with the sleeves rolled up, and with a Pat Riley hairstyle, peeked in and mischievously summoned one of the women in the waiting room.

"Who's that?" I asked.

"The other obstetrician," Martha said.

"Does he always dress like that?" I demanded.

"Oh, yes. He's very nice. He examined me last time."

Martha's doctor was wearing black stretch slacks, a black tank top, and a handsome gold necklace. She was very exacting about appearances. "You have gained too much weight," she said to Martha, who had in fact gained less than with her first pregnancy. "Start swimming, stop eating." (Martha says that a friend who went for an appointment two months after the birth of her second baby was told by the same doctor, "You look terrible. And do something about your hair.") We did another sonogram. "Look at her, she's pretty," the doctor said as we looked at the sonogram. "There's her *fille*," she said, pointing to the sex. Then she again counseled Martha to swim more and gave her a prescription for sleeping pills. We talked a bit about the approach of those hard, exhausting first weeks with a newborn. "Get a night nurse," she advised. "Go out with your husband. Be happy again."

In New York, in other words, pregnancy is a medical condition that, after proper care by people in white coats and a brief hospital stay, can have a "positive outcome." In Paris it is something that has happened because of sex, which, with help and counsel, can end with your being set free to go out and have more sex. In New York pregnancy is a ward in the house of medicine; in Paris it is a chapter in a sentimental education, a strange consequence of the pleasures of the body.

In America, we have managed to sexualize everything—cars, refrigerators, computers, Congress—except the natural consequences of sex. Though it is de rigueur for every pregnant supermodel to have her picture taken when she is full-bellied, it is always the same picture. She covers her breasts, she is swaddled below in some way, and she looks off into the middle distance, not dreamily, as she might when wearing lingerie, but slightly anxiously, as though she could not remember if she had left her husband's electric guitar turned on. The subject, the hidden subject, is not the apotheosis of sexuality but its transcendence into maternal instinct: babe into mother by way of baby.

In France, though, a pregnant woman is alive, since she has demonstrated both her availability and her fecundity: We Have a Winner. Though Lamaze method childbirth began here, it remains cultish and sectarian. Most women nurse for three months, no more. (It shrinks your breasts and gives you an uncomfortable accessory.) And when the anesthesiologists are not striking, they are, as our baby-sitter says, fully busy. (Two French friends of ours talk about natural childbirth: "What is the English for *accouchement sans douleur*?" one asks. "A lie," the other answers.)

The prohibition on uncooked vegetables, by the way, turns out to have a solid scientific basis. Toxoplasmosis—a mild parasitic infection that is devastating to unborn children—though it's rare in America (it's that thing you can get from cat litter), is common in France. Red wine is recommended, in turn, because it is high in iron and acts as an effective antispasmodic.

|||

By law a French woman who is going to have a baby is guaranteed—not merely allowed but pretty much compelled—to stay four or five nights in a clinic or a hospital. In New York, when our son, Luke, was born—in the Klingenstein Pavilion of Mount Sinai Hospital—we had two days to have the baby, bond, and get out. French law is specific and protective about the rights of pregnant women. If you are a salaried employee, you get six weeks of prenatal leave and ten weeks of paid leave after the baby is born. For a third child, you get eight weeks off and eighteen more, and if you have three at once, you get, in all, forty-six weeks of paid leave. (The leave is paid, through a complicated formula, by your employer and the state.) The law is as finely tuned as a viola d'amore. There is even a beautiful added *remarque,* right there on the government document: *"Les artistes du spectacle, les mannequins des maisons de couture,"* and others who do work that is plainly incompatible with the state of pregnancy (i.e., a bigger belly) are assured of paid leave after the twenty-first week. In France, Cindy and Paulina and the rest would not just be having their pictures taken. They would already be on the dole.

The system, Martha's doctor observed once during a visit, is "royal for the users, good for the doctors, and expensive for the society." There are many rational arguments to be made about whether or not the outcomes justify the expenditures, and in any case, the level of care that the French have insisted on may be unsustainable. But the people who are being treated "royally" are ordinary people—everybody. For many, perhaps most, French people, life at the end of the century in the American imperium may look a bit like a typical transatlantic flight, with the airless, roomless, comfortless coach packed as tightly as possible, so that the maximum dollars can be squeezed out of every seat, with a few rich people up front. I am American enough to understand that this is, so to speak, one of the prices of mass travel—that there is no such thing as a free lunch, or clinic—and yet have become French enough to feel, stubbornly, that legroom and a little air should not be luxuries for the rich and that in a prosperous society all pregnant women should have three sonograms and four nights in a hospital, if they want to. It doesn't seem particularly royal to have four nights in a clinic when you have a baby or aristocratically spoiled to think that a woman should keep her job and have some paid leave afterward, even sixteen weeks, if she happens to be a mannequin in an haute couture house. All human desires short of simple survival are luxurious, and a mother's desire to have a slightly queenly experience of childbirth—a lying in rather than a pushing out and a going home—

seems as well worth paying for as a tobacco subsidy or another tank.

|||

In preparation for our own four-night stay we had first to search for the right clinic. Friends recommended two: the Clinique Sainte-Isabelle, in the leafy suburb of Neuilly, and the Clinique Belvedere, in Boulogne-Billancourt. We went to tour them. Both clinics had a pastoral, flower-bed, medical but not quite hospital feel, like the sanitarium to which they pack off Nicole in *Tender Is the Night*. I liked the Belvedere best. The rooms there had a nice faded white and pale blue look, like the room in *Madeline* where she goes to have her appendix taken out and sees the crack in the ceiling that has a habit of sometimes looking like a rabbit. The cracks in the ceiling at the Belvedere were expressive too, and for a premium you could have a room with French doors leading out onto the garden. (The ordinary rooms were less grand, though they mostly had garden views too.) But what I really liked about the place were the clippings in the formal salon—the waiting room—downstairs, which was filled with dusty silk roses and blue and gold Louis XVI furniture. The clippings chronicled the birth of minor nobility in the halls of the Belvedere. A Bonapartist pretender had been born there, I remember, and also I think a prince of Yugoslavia. I liked the kingly company, particularly since it was such cheesy kingly company.

Martha, though, as we toured the clinics, kept asking gentle, pointed questions about labor relations with the anesthesiologists. Now, the anesthesiologists here—were they unionized? Did they have enough vacation time? Would the clinic manager say that they were happy with their working conditions? How long had it been since they signed a contract? Were there any, well, radicals among them, the kind of ex-Trotskyite *soixante-huitards* who might suddenly call for mass action by the workers? Eventually, we settled on the Clinique Sainte-Isabelle, which seemed to be the sensible, primly bourgeois choice of all our friends and which had a couple of full-time anesthesiologists on call, neither of whom looked like a sansculotte.

Everything was going along fine, in fact, until our meeting with the *sage-femme,* the wise woman, or, in American, the midwife. She was in yet another of the suburban clinics, an odd Jacques Tati modern place. This meeting was brisk, and it concentrated on two essential points: breathing and lying. The breathing bit we had heard about before—you are supposed to breathe from the diaphragm—but she emphasized that it was just as important, for a happy birth, to remember never to tell a taxi driver that you are in labor. Whatever you do, she said, don't say that you're in labor, or might be in labor, because no taxi driver in Paris will take a pregnant woman to her clinic, for fear of her having the baby in his car. (You can't call an ambulance because an ambulance won't go over the city line, and our clinic was out in Neuilly.)

Then how were we going to get to the clinic? Martha asked. (We don't have a car.) It's no problem, I interrupted, we'll simply walk over to the taxi stand. (You can't call a taxi, because there is a stand right across the street from our apartment.)

"I won't be able to stroll across the street and stand in line if I'm in labor," she objected. "I'll wait in the courtyard. Just get him to do the *demi-tour.*"

At these words my heart was stricken. *Demi-tour* means literally a U-turn, but in Paris it is also a half-metaphysical possibility that exists on the boulevard Saint-Germain just across the street from our apartment building. The boulevard itself runs one-way, from east to west. There is, however, a narrow lane carved out on it, for buses and taxis, that runs the other way, toward the place de la Concorde and the quai d'Orsay and, eventually, if you turn right over a bridge, toward Neuilly and the clinic too. Leading off this lane, at a single light about a hundred feet from our building, there is a small, discreet curved arrow marked on the asphalt. This arrow means that a taxicab—and only a taxicab—can make a U-turn there and go the other way, with the rest of the traffic. In principle, I could get a cab going against the traffic, have him do the *demi-tour*, pick up my pregnant wife, and then go back against the traffic. The trouble is that, though I have sometimes succeeded in persuading taxi drivers, when we arrive from the airport, to make the *demi-tour*, I have just as often failed. "It's impossible," the cabbie will tell you, when you ask him to do it.

"No, there is an arrow printed on the pavement that advertises the possibility of this maneuver," I will say. (When I'm under stress, my French becomes very abstract.)

"I've been driving a taxi for twenty years, and it doesn't exist," the cabbie will say. Then you either give up or get hot under the collar, and neither approach helps.

If I asked a Paris cabdriver to attempt the *demi-tour* at, say, five in the morning, to pick up a very pregnant-looking woman, he would know that the only reason was that she was in labor, and to the insult of being instructed would come the injury of being asked to ruin his cab.

For the next few weeks I became obsessed by the logic and strategies of the *demi-tour*. What if I couldn't pull it off? The only thing to do was to rehearse, just as we had done in New York in the Lamaze class. So I began walking over to the taxi station at all hours of the day and night, getting in a cab, asking the driver to make the *demi-tour*, and then going, well, someplace or other. Then I walked home. Sometimes the driver made the *demi-tour*, and sometimes he didn't. I was determined to keep practicing, until it felt as natural as breathing.

We still hadn't got to the bottom of the whole *choix du roi* thing. Martha had decided to give in to the obstetrician's insistence that she start swimming, and one day, with Luke, we got into a cab to go to the pool. The taxi driver was wearing a short-sleeved shirt, and had gray hair and a lot of metal teeth. Suddenly he chuckled and said, of Luke, "Why, he speaks so well. Tell me, is it a little sister or a brother?" A sister, we said, and I grimaced and tightened inside as I prepared myself for the response, which, of course, came on cue. "Ah," he said, slapping the steering wheel. *"C'est le choix du roi!"*

I was so fed up that I said, "Please explain it to me." It was an ironic, rhetorical question. But he didn't miss a beat.

"I will be happy to explain it," he said, and he actually pulled over to the curb, near the Hôtel de Crillon, so that he could speak in peace. "In Latin countries we have what we call Salic law, which means that only your son can inherit the throne. You Anglo-Saxons, you don't follow Salic law." I let the Anglo-Saxon thing go by. "For your Anglo-Saxon royal families, it doesn't matter if the king has a *nana* or a *mec*." A *nana* is a doll, and a *mec* is a guy. "But you see, a French king, under Salic law, had to consolidate his hold on the throne by having a boy. And he had to have a girl, so that she could be offered in marriage to another king, and in this way the royal possessions would be expanded, since the daughter's son would be a king too. He," he said, gesturing toward Luke in the backseat, "is your strong piece, to be kept in reserve, while she"—he gestured toward Martha's belly—"is your pawn to build your empire. That's why it's the king's choice: first a boy to hold the throne, then a girl to get another. *Tendresse* has nothing to do with it. That is why it is the *choix du roi.*

"It is very odd," he went on expansively, "because in the Hundred Years' War the king of England, as duc de Guyenne, a title he had inherited from his grandfather, was subject to Salic law too. The story of how this worked itself out in the making of the two monarchies is a passionately interesting piece of history. I recommend the series *Les Rois Maudits* [the damned or cursed kings], which is a fascinating study of this history, particularly of the acts of John the Good and what he did as an act of policy to accommodate the Salic principle. The books are by Maurice

Druon, of the Académie Française, and I heartily recommend them. Passionately interesting."

We sat in stunned silence.

"Ask him does he do *demi-tours,*" said Martha.

|||

"You're wearing stripes?" she asked. I had put on a striped shirt a few minutes before, in the excitement, but I quickly changed it. I put on a suit and tie, in fact—a nice maroon cotton number— thinking that though my New York child had been born with me watching in jeans and a collarless shirt, my French kid ought to see a dad who had a touch more finish.

The drama had begun a few hours earlier, in the middle of the night, and now it was five o'clock and we were on our way to the clinic. At five-thirty, with a baby-sitter for Luke and a suitcase in hand, we were out on the boulevard. I walked to the curb, held my breath, saw that there were cabs at the taxi stand, and, head down, told Martha to wait where she was while I started across the street, preparing to ask a taxi driver to make the *demi-tour,* my moment come at last.

Far down the boulevard, a single cab with a firelight light appeared. Martha stepped out into the street, just as though it were five-thirty in the evening on Sixth Avenue, got her right hand up in that weird New York Nazi taxi salute, and cried, "Taxi!" The guy came skidding to a stop. She got in, and I followed.

"Twenty-four boulevard du Château in Neuilly," I commanded, my voice pitched a little too high (as it also tends to get in French). "Just cross the street and make the *demi-tour,*" I added fairly casually, and docilely, at five-thirty in the morning, he swung the cab over to the taxi lane, on other side of the street, and did a full U-turn. He flew along the boulevard. I took the hand of my queen.

"You've got him going the wrong way," she whispered.

He was too. I waited a few blocks and then told him that I had made a mistake, could he turn around and go the other way? He shrugged and did.

When we got to the clinic, it was shut tight, no lights on at all. The advantages of a big hospital up on Madison Avenue became a little clearer. No one was answering the door, a thing I doubt happens much at Mount Sinai. We banged and cried out, "*Allô!* Is anybody there?" Finally, an incredibly weary-looking *sage-femme*—not our own—wearing sweater and slippers, sighed, let us in, hooked Martha up to an IV, and asked to see our papers. She shuffled through them.

"Where is your blood test for the dossier?" she asked at last.

"The doctor has it," I said. "She'll be here soon."

"That the doctor has it is of no consequence," the nurse said. "If your wife wishes to have an epidural, she must have that paper."

"It's all the way back home," I protested, but of course, nothing doing. It looked as though Martha's epidural, having escaped French syndicalism, was about to be done in by French bureaucracy. Having lived in France long enough to know there was no choice, I found another taxi, rushed all the way home, ran upstairs, tore open the filing cabinet, found the paper, and then took a taxi back, setting some kind of land speed record for trips from central Paris to Neuilly. The *sage-femme* slipped the paper into the dossier, yawned, put the dossier down on a radiator, and nobody ever looked at it or referred to it again.

The labor got complicated, for various reasons—basically the baby at the last moment decided to turn sideways—and Martha's doctor, acting with the quiet sureness that is the other side of Parisian insouciance, did an emergency cesarean. It turned out that behind a small, quaint-looking white door down in the basement there was a bloc—a warren of blindingly white-lit, state-of-the-art operating and recovery rooms. They hadn't shown it to us when we toured the clinic, of course. It seemed very French, the nuclear power plant hidden in the *bocage*.

The baby came out mad, yelling at the top of her lungs. In New York the nurses had snatched the baby and taken him off to be washed behind a big glass nursery window and then had dressed him in prison garb, the same white nightshirt and cap that the hundred other babies in the nursery had on. (The next day there was also an elaborate maximum security procedure of reading off the bracelet numbers of mother and child whenever either one wanted to nurse.) Here, after the *sage-femme* and I had given her a bath, and the *sage-femme* had taped her umbilical remnant, the *sage-femme* turned to me.

"Where are her clothes?" she asked. I said I didn't know, upstairs in the suitcase, I guessed, and she said, "You'd better get them," so I ran up, and came back down to the bloc with the white onesie and a lovely white-and-pink-trimmed baby-style cat suit, which her mother had bought at Bonpoint a few days before. All by myself I carefully dressed the five-minute-old squalling newborn and took her back to her mother, in the recovery room. A day later I would walk the six blocks to the *mairie,* the city hall, of Neuilly-sur-Seine and register her birth. The New York birth certificate had been a fill-in-the-blanks, choose-one-box business, which we had filled in on our way out of the hospital. The French birth certificate was like the first paragraph of a nineteenth-century novel, with the baby's parents' names, their occupations, the years of their births and of their emigration, their residence, and her number, baby number 2365 born in Neuilly in 1999. (It's got a big hospital too.) After that, of course, would come the weeks of exhaustion and 3:00 A.M. feedings, which are remarkably alike from place to place.

But just then, looking at the sleeping mom and the tiny newborn in her arms, I had a genuine moment of what I can only call revelation, religious vision. When people talk about what it is to have a baby, they usually talk about starting over, a clean slate, endless possibility, a new beginning, but I saw that that is not it at all. A birth is not a rebirth. It's a weighty event. A baby is an absolute object of nature *and* an absolute subject of civilization, screaming in her new Bonpoint jumper. Life is nothing but an unchanging sea of nature, the same endless and undifferentiating human wave of lust and pain, and is still subject to a set of tiny cultural articulations and antinomies and dualities and distinctions and hair-splittings so fine that they produce, in the end, this single American baby lying in a French nursery in her own fine new clothes, sipping her sugar bottle. In a telescopic universe, we choose to see microscopically, and the blessing is that what we see is not an illusion but what is really there: a singularity in the cosmos, another baby born in a Paris suburb. The universe is kidding, and the universe is not kidding. The world is a meaningless place, and we are weird, replicating mammals on its surface, yet the whole purpose of the universe since it began was, in a way, to produce this baby, who is the tiny end point of a funnel that goes back to the beginning of time, a singularity that history was pointing toward from the start. That history didn't know it was pointing toward Olivia—and, of course, toward Salome over in the other corner of the nursery and little François just arrived, not to mention Max and Otto and possibly even Moe, just now checking in at Mount Sinai—doesn't change the fact that it was. We didn't know we were pointing to her either, until she got here. The universe doesn't need a purpose if life goes on. You sink back and hear the nurse cooing in French to the mother and child ("*Ah, calme-toi, ma biche, ma biche,*" she says. "Be calm, my doe, my doe," but which one is she talking to?) and feel as completely useless as any other male animal after a birth and, at the same time, somehow serenely powerful, beyond care or criticism, since you have taken part in the only really majestic choice we get to make in life, which is to continue it.

Angels
Dining at the Ritz

When Martha was still pregnant, we decided to join the pool at the Ritz hotel on the place Vendôme for eight weeks. We had, as I've said, thought about it once before, during our adventures at the Régiment Rouge, but had gotten scared off by the expense and by all those tea sandwiches on silver platters. For four years we had been swimming at the public pool of the Sixth Arrondissement near the old Saint-Germain market, a nice place, with families splashing in one part and solitary fierce-looking swimmers doing laps in the other—though, like every French public institution, terribly overcharged with functionaries, in this case officious, functionary lifeguards. But then the same friend who had invited us there that first time invited us to the Ritz pool again, to spend a Sunday away from the August heat. With Martha pregnant and more or less immobile, we weren't able to go away anyway, even though everyone in Paris goes away in August. (The five-week mandatory vacation is part of the inheritance of the old Popular Front of the thirties, one of the laws put over by the saintly Socialist leader Léon Blum.) Anyway, we couldn't go anywhere, not with Martha that big, and we were cool and comfortable at the pool. Paris is hot in August—really, suddenly hot—and not many places are air-conditioned. Even the ones that claim to be *climatisés* are not really air-conditioned as public places are in New York. Instead a trickle of chilly air floats someplace around the baseboards.

The pool at the Ritz hotel in Paris—they actually call the place the Ritz Health Club, in English, although I think this is designed less as a concession to Americans than as a lingering sign of old-fashioned Parisian Anglomania, like calling the Jockey Club in Paris the Jockey Club—is intended to look "Pompeian" in a way that I suppose makes a strong case for Mount Vesuvius and molten lava. There is a high domed skylight, held up by painted Ionic columns with rosettes along their pillars and bordered by a bas-relief frieze of classical figures standing around in a line, as though waiting to check out of the hotel. There is a trompe l'oeil ceiling painting of old Roman bathers looking down at contemporary French swimmers, with more colored architectural drawings of Roman temple fronts decorating the locker rooms and the showers, and, on either side of the pool, two enormous murals of Romans in togas standing around on terraces, all painted in a style someplace between Victorian-Academic and New York Pizzeria.

My favorite detail at the Ritz pool is a pair of mosaics on the bottom of the pool, right where the shallow end starts to incline and deepen a little, of two comely and topless mermaids, with long blond hair—tresses, really—floating off to one side. With one hand they reach down modestly; with the other each holds up one half of the great seal of the Ritz. (Where most mermaids have fishtails that begin at their waists, these mermaids have fishtails that begin only at their shins.) These are real mosaics, by the way, assembled shiny shard by shiny shard, and they probably would be a treasure if they had actually been made by a Roman artisan and dug up by an archaeologist. The line between art and kitsch is largely measured in ruin.

Martha felt cool there, and cool matters a lot to a nine-month pregnant woman. We sat by the edge of the pool in white terry-cloth robes, surrounded by thin rich women with very high hair, who were listlessly turning the pages of magazines and occasionally going into the pool to swim. They swam like nervous poodles, with their heads held high, high, *high*—up out of the water on their long necks, protecting their perfect helmets of hair from the least drop of moisture.

We ate lunch up on the curved terrace overlooking the pool and thought, only with a little guilt, Well, this *is* nice. So we inquired and found that we could get an eight-week nonpeak hours, never-on-Sunday family membership for a lot less than it cost us to rent a cottage on Cape Cod every summer for two weeks—and on Cape Cod, we *work* all day and night, sweeping the sand out of the house and bringing up the laundry and stoking up the grill and then cleaning up the kitchen. So with a slightly nervous sense of extravagance, we decided to subscribe to the Ritz pool for the minimum off-hours "family" membership, a little joke, we assured ourselves, laid at the altar of the old Hemingway-Flanner Paris. I felt a little guilty about it, I guess—I felt a lot guilty about it, really—but I also thought that Léon Blum, all things considered, wouldn't get too mad at me. I gave it a vaguely Socialist feeling; it was our five weeks.

Since our experience at the Régiment Rouge I had been improvising exercise. For a while we had gone running with the rest of the Americans, and the French riot police, around the Luxembourg Gardens. The gardens are filled with busts and statues of writers, which make it easy to mark your progress as a runner. A half lap of the gardens, for instance, takes you right to a bust of Sainte-Beuve, the good literary critic whom Proust attacked; the two-thirds point is marked by another bust, this one of

Baudelaire; and then finally, completing the circuit, you go past the Delacroix monument, with angels looking up admiringly at his haughty, mustachioed head. At the start I could do a Baudelaire and then, after a couple of months' practice, two full Delacroix's, not bad. The trouble was that the great men seemed to look out disdainfully from their pedestals at the absurdity of Americans running today in order to run more tomorrow. Get drunk instead, Baudelaire seemed to counsel, intelligently, with his scowl. Eventually we bought a stationary bike, and I tried to do twenty-four minutes a day on it, re-creating the conditions of the New York Health and Racquet Club on Thirteenth Street, more or less in the dubious, perverse spirit of a British lieutenant wearing flannel and drinking tea at five o'clock in the Sahara. I had even bought a pair of dumbbells.

After a couple of weeks, though, Martha was too big to do much of anything, and then Olivia Esmé Claire, our beautiful little girl, was born. But we still had six weeks to work out on the membership, so Luke Auden and I kept going. I was nervous and interested. I associated the Ritz with a kind of high life that makes me uneasy, and this is not because I do not like expensive and "exclusive" pleasures, but because I do, and always feel unskilled in their enjoyment. I knew that the Ritz in Paris had once been dashing and elegant but also knew that now there was, as with so many old places of luxury, a note of unhappy rootlessness to the place. It was the capital of the non-Paris Paris. It had what we would have called at my high school bad karma. While we were living in Paris, it had been the place where Pamela Harriman had passed out—"I go badly," she had said, and went—and where Princess Diana too had left on that last car trip. English politicians in particular seemed to come to grief there; one prominent MP, I had vaguely heard, had spent a night, had it paid for by the wrong person, and lost his reputation. There was about it now, for all that it was still frequented by high-living Parisians, a note less of old Parisian high life than of new, late-century overclass big money, with big money's unhappiness about it, that high-strung video surveillance watchfulness of the very, very rich. I liked arriving at the Ritz and having a little *commis* in uniform spin the revolving door for me, but I was always worried about the way I looked when he did. I am hedonistic but not at all heedless, a bad combination. I watch the meter in the limousine, the revolving door as it spins.

Luke of course took it for granted, as children take all things. He learned to swim there, first backstroke, then "frontstroke." I felt a vague feeling of paternal pride about it, though I hadn't really taught him. Just dropped him in, really.

Then something really nice, genuinely terrific happened. Earlier that year, at the school he went to at the American Church, he had fallen in love. The little girl was named Cressida Taylor. She was the dish, the girl he had said was "quite a dish." (I had finally tracked the expression down to a three-hour compilation of Warner Brothers' *Looney Tunes* from the forties that we had bought for him. Bugs Bunny says it about, well, about a dish.) I met her at the school, and she *was* quite a dish, the most beautiful five-year-old girl I have ever seen. She had fair skin, and high blue eyes, and two long golden braids of hair, mermaid tresses, really, and an Audrey Hepburn voice, that elegant, piping accent of children who have been raised in both French and English. (Her mother was a sensible Englishwoman, and her father, I think, some kind of French banker.)

Unquestionably a dish, she was also a peach. It had been Cressida who had finally gotten Luke past the nap crisis at school, generously holding his hand when the teachers would insist that the children "take a rest" and he would go into a panic. She had come over to play a few times. (No one used the expression *play date* in Paris. Kids just came over, played, and then their mothers picked them up and took them home.) They played intensely, and there was, I thought, fondly, a kind of Gilberte and Marcel quality to their playing. They just *played,* you see, and all the other things that pass between boys and girls just passed, without comment or too much oversight from their parents. Martha was relieved at least. In love with her son, she was already worried about the woman who would take him away, and I think that she would have betrothed them on the spot, like seventeenth-century royalty, if she could have. But Cressida had left his school, and now we saw her, wistfully, only every now and again.

On that memorable Wednesday afternoon Luke and I went to the pool. Though he liked to swim, he went, to my puzzlement, mostly to take home the little shower caps that were placed all around the locker rooms. They were just shower caps, but they came in blue cardboard boxes, with the Ritz coat of arms printed in gold on them, and he would sneak home ten or eleven at a time, tucking them under his arms, hiding them in the pockets of his white terry-cloth peignoir, and then sticking them in his jacket—why and to what end, I was never sure.

We were strangers at the Ritz. I was nervous, self-conscious about seeming too loud or too American. "Let's kiss the mermaids," Luke would insist, every time we went swimming, and though they were scarcely five feet down, within easy dive-and-kiss distance, I never could. I was too self-conscious about splashing a lot on my way down, my flattish feet waving, and about what the ladies with the tall hair would think about it. Luke couldn't do it either, since five feet was still far too deep for him to go, but he tried, manfully, and didn't care if he splashed or not.

On this Wednesday, though, after the furtive theft of a few shower caps, and the endless irritating "Please stand *still!*" of a father changing a kid into his swim trunks, we got to the pool. Normally he couldn't wait to jump in, but now he stood utterly still at the edge of the water. I saw his small, skinny body in the madras trunks stiffen, and then he got a shy, embarrassed smile on his face and backed away.

"Daddy, look," he whispered.

"What?" I said.

"Daddy, look," he repeated urgently, still under his breath. "It's Cressida."

It was too. *And* the most beautiful thing I had ever seen, right there in the middle of the Paris Ritz pool. She was floating as elegantly as an angel, just above the mermaids, a little on her side, her long blond braids trailing in the water behind her. I think my heart stopped a little bit at that moment too.

Luke's certainly had stopped and then restarted. He leaped right in, before I could stop him, and head up—like a puppy, like a millionaire's wife—he swam out to his love in the water.

Cressida, it turned out, after a few minutes of splashing, happy greeting, was there with her best friend and constant companion Ada. (The year before, Luke had complained to me about how inseparable they were: "It's like they're twins or something.") Ada turned out to be a startling, ideal, central casting best friend, with a throaty, husky Glynis Johns–Demi Moore voice, the perfect sultry sidekick to perfect radiant beauty. They both were there with Cressida's nanny, a jolly Australian girl named Shari, who played the trombone, and whom I can describe only by saying that she looked like a jolly Australian girl who played the trombone.

The two little girls were excellent swimmers, veterans of the Ritz pool, I supposed. They splashed back and forth easily, and Luke manfully struggled after them, head up, losing it, swallowing water and coming up exhausted and clinging to the side and spitting out, his face scrunched up in misery, but then shaking his head violently ("I'm fine! I'm fine!") when I came up and, a little too paternal, a little too obvious, pounded him on the back and asked him if he was okay. Then he shot back out to the girls in the middle of the pool. Pretty quickly he worked out a good method of getting around; first clinging to the side of the pool, then shooting out in backstroke, and then going into a quick three-stroke combined breaststroke–doggy paddle over to the girls—a wonderful simulacrum of a guy who is just an easy, varied swimmer. (He swam, I realized, exactly the way that after five years I spoke French, which also involved a lot of clinging to the side of the pool and sudden bravura dashes out to the deep end to impress the girls, or listeners.)

I hovered around him, worried—I was snob enough to be tickled that he had learned to swim at the Ritz pool in Paris but insecure enough to worry about what his mother would say if I *lost* him at the Ritz pool; after all, it was, at its deep end, effectively as deep as the ocean, three times over the head of a small boy—only to have him shake me off, again and again.

I didn't mind, really. I have never seen a human being before in a state of pure liquid unadulterated joy. The little girls, to my surprise, for I had had more bitter experiences at his age, seemed to accept him absolutely as an equal and fellow diver and Ritz habitué, a *bec-fin* of this damp *beau monde*, albeit one with a bit of water in his lungs from time to time. And if his lungs *were* filling up with water, swallow by swallow, he didn't care. He just followed the red bathing suit and the blond braid, wherever they led him.

The Australian au pair and I huddled around the edges of the pool and made conversation. She had been in Paris for only a couple of weeks, she explained, had flown right over from Sydney. She seemed unperturbed, not even much interested in her surroundings, Australians being like that, I suppose: From the Sydney beach to the Ritz pool, all just water, isn't it?

After about half an hour Ada paddled over. "I want a *chocolat chaud*," she said, imperiously. She looked at me just the way that Lorelei Lee must have looked at *her* sugar daddy at the Paris Ritz, so I gathered up the children—Luke could barely speak, he was so filled with water—and we went up to the café on the terrace overlooking the pool. I strode up as boldly as I could manage to the white-shirted attendant behind the counter and ordered three hot chocolates and three cakes for the children and then a *café crème* for me and a Badoit for the Australian girl. I shuddered inside, imagining what it was all going to cost. As I say, I am hedonistic but not heedless, and like Luke, only with less fortitude, I knew that I was out of my depth and swallowing water.

After a mysterious fifteen-minute wait the attendant reemerged with the chocolate in silver pitchers and the cake—simple pound cake with lemon glaze—on silver plates and served them to the children. Ada looked bored and indifferent and demanded some more *lait chaud* for her chocolate, after she had tasted it. She soon had a chocolate mustache, but it didn't make her look like a child. She looked more like Aramis, the youngest and most imperious of the musketeers.

Luke, never a big eater, watched Cressida. I saw what there was to watch: She sipped her chocolate daintily but not as one making a big deal about daintiness. She was just a naturally elegant sipper. I drank my coffee, gulped it, really, and thought, gracelessly enough, about the bill running up. The two girls chatted in the way children do, effortlessly and seamlessly and in this case in two languages but without actually seeming to exchange information. ("You know what? You're a *Looney Tunes*." Laughter. "No, *Oscar* is a *Looney Tunes*." More laughter, in which Luke joined.)

After the first hot chocolate had been dispensed with, Ada summoned over the waiter with a wave of her hand and said, *"Encore un chocolat chaud"*—that is, "Another hot chocolate." "Say please," I said instantly. She gave me a steady, opaque, not-only-are-you-not-my-father-but-you-couldn't-begin-to-*afford*-to-be-my-father look. But then she said please. We all went for a second round, hot chocolate and cake and bottled water, and I felt like Charlie Chaplin in *The Immigrant*—it had been Luke's favorite movie, back when he would stay home all day and watch Chaplin videos while I worked—when Edna Purviance starts ordering beans and he reaches into his pocket to count his change and finds the quarter he had picked up on the sidewalk isn't there anymore. A third round of cake followed the second round of hot chocolate—Luke left his untouched, leaving three cakes on the plate in all, which I eventually ate—and then I told Luke it was time to go.

"No," he said definitely. And the children ran back down the stairs to the pool and played some more, dodging in and out among the chaise longues. I went over to the attendant, asked for the check, and signed it, trying to feign the nonchalance of Papa ordering another bottle of Dom Pérignon for Sister Dietrich, of Dodi Fayed before his last journey.

I got him home at last, around six o'clock. Martha was mildly irascible, nursing the baby on a chaise longue near the window, all by herself all afternoon, but she melted a little when I told her the story. "You won't believe who we met at the pool today," I began. Luke seemed quietly happy, nonchalant. The improbability of the encounter simply hadn't struck him. That Cressida Taylor would be swimming in a red one-piece at the Ritz pool on the same Wednesday afternoon that we were there . . . He had no sense of the size of the world or even of Paris. His haunts were the world's haunts; his world was the world. This is an emotion shared, I suppose, only by children and aristocrats; everyone goes where we go. Where else would you expect to meet people? (I have none of it and in my heart always expect to be alone, the one man sitting awkwardly at a table in the wrong restaurant after everyone else has left it. When I see my wife and children coming down the boulevard to meet me, I am dazzled. The baby, Olivia, was, I could see, a little like me, constantly pulling away from her mother's breast to give me the same anxious, reassuring smile: *You of all people! Here of all places!*)

For the next four weeks we went every Wednesday to the pool at the Ritz, to meet Ada and Cressida and their nanny and to swim and treat to hot chocolate and cake. Although Ada was a constant presence ("I don't think I shall swim today," she would say. "She's a bit moody," Cressida would explain, unemotionally), I could sense that a bond, a romance had begun between Luke and Cressida, in the simple sense that the unstated had emerged from the informal. I recognized the signs: It lay not in their having fun together but in their not *needing* to have fun together, in a quiet, you-here-me-there, however-deep-you-can-go-in-the-deep-end-I'll-go-deeper understanding. I remembered the words that Gilberte had said to Marcel, somewhere in Proust, I think in that beautiful section titled "Place-Names: The Name," where the two children—if they are children; I can never really figure out in Proust if they are eight or eighteen—meet at the Champs-Élysées. "Now we can begin," Gilberte says. "You are on *my* side." The two of them were on the same side too.

You are on my side. Martha and I had once always been on the same side too, and without thinking about it at all. Now, here in the city that a notion of romance, a need for one last romantic adventure, had led us to, we found that we didn't care for each other less, yet loved each other differently. Our moving to Paris, which was intended, almost too self-consciously, I suppose, to extend that feeling—to keep each other on each other's side without the fretfulness and noise of New York life, without dinner parties and gallery openings and Burmese takeout and the number 6 uptown for life—had had the unexpected effect of plopping us down in the same pool with the same hot chocolate to sip day after day after day, and this at a time when we both were already, so to speak, practiced swimmers. We began to take almost too much pleasure, I suppose, almost too much delight, in the passage of our son's first romance because it recalled to us the landscape of limitations that surround all romance, the way that romance is a thing always best allied to difficulty: the water pouring into your lungs; the trombone-playing Australian looking over your shoulder and calling you into a towel; the encumbering presence of a moody hot chocolate–addicted best friend. Martha and I had always been so close; but now we were so *near*, and that is different.

We had run away to Paris that first time, twenty years earlier, back when we had known each other for six months, and even though it would be possible to say that that first time we were merely playing at running away, since we had families and houses waiting safely for us back in Montreal, the truth is that the existence of the families and houses was what made it, weirdly, not play at all. There really was someone back there waiting for you with a towel and calling you out of the pool, and we had decided not to listen. This time running away *was* a kind of play, since there was no one to run away from save ourselves, and your self always catches up.

Perhaps in the end this is why Paris is "romantic." It marries both the voluptuous and restricted. It is not the yeses but the noes of Paris, not the licenses it offers love but the prohibitions it puts in its way, that makes it powerful. All the noes of French life, the way that each gate to each park is bounded by that endless ten-thousand-word fine-print announcement from the government dictating all the things you are absolutely *not* allowed to do in the park, contribute in some odd way to the romance of Paris. Strictness, rules, disciplines, boundaries dam the libido, as Freud knew, even when you are five, and make it overflow backward. It is the knowledge of how awkward your splashing feet will look to the rich women on the chaises that prevents you, tantalizingly, from kissing the mermaid's invisible nipple.

Sometimes now, watching Martha—watching her nurse the new baby, or just lying beside her at night and watching her sleep, practically gobbling up sleep, her brow furrowed, in her new mother exhaustion—I thought that though I knew her better than I had ever known anyone, I didn't know her now nearly as well as I had when our days were broken with the thousand small distractions of life in New York. She had been my Cressida, unique in a pool, and in Paris had had to evolve from a fantasy figure into a reality principle for a chaotic husband and a small boy and then a baby. In New York we would meet at dinner and spill out the day's discontents, and they were always discontents with other people. Our discontents now crystallized not so much around each other—we hadn't come to that quite yet—as around tiny things that we held each other responsible for and that each of us pursued with silent, independent fury. Instead of rebelling together against our common prohibitions, we nursed our little exasperations.

I, for instance, had become absolutely furious about the long hallway in our apartment, which ran all the way from the kitchen, where I cooked, way in the back, to the dining room up in front, a constant jostling corridor of plates, forgotten Évian water, and spilled spices, like a trade route in the Byzantine Empire. Back and forth we went, again and again, breakfast, lunch, and dinner. (Kitchens in Parisian apartments are always off at the back, at the end of a long corridor, since there were originally no kitchens, or else because they were for servants, who were expected to be Out There in Back.) I didn't exactly blame Martha for the length of time it took to get dinner to the table, cold, but I didn't exactly *forgive* her for it either.

Martha's exasperation, for which she didn't exactly blame me, but which she thought I might have done something about if I were a more efficient person than I am, was the absence of a decent copy shop. She looked after the bills and the dry cleaning and the rent—all the small logistics of life—and she couldn't find places where you could just go in, hand in a document, and have them copy and collate it, one, two, three, just like that. They had instead machines where you had to feed in two-franc pieces, page by page. (The government discourages video rental stores in Paris, in order to protect the little repertory cinemas whose business, it's quite true, would otherwise be destroyed. I don't know who's being protected by the discouragement of Kinko's-style copy shops; the remaining scriveners and clerks and copyists, I suppose.) The absence of napkins drove her crazy, too. She loved order and cleanliness, and the refusal of a French take-out shop to give more than one napkin per sandwich made her wild. "They *hoard* napkins," she would complain. "It's as though it's still wartime." New York, America, where paper napkins shower down like confetti on New Year's Eve, had become, in her memory, napkin heaven, napkin world.

One day, when I was working in my little office on the latest subject that the office at home had sent in, Martha came storming into my office.

"What's this?" she said, angry as I had ever seen her, waving a sheaf of envelopes and white paper with a blue and gold crest on it.

"What's what?" I asked, though I knew, or thought I knew.

"These bills," she cried. "What is this all *for*?"

"Hot chocolate," I said weakly.

"Hot chocolate," she repeated scornfully.

"And cake," I added.

"Do you know how much this costs?" she said.

"Of course I know. But what can I do? It's Cressida."

"Say no." She looked at me darkly. "That's a lot of hot chocolate," she added suspiciously.

"It's Ada too," I explained. "She has a habit."

She walked away. I wondered if she really thought I might be having an affair at the Ritz and if, in some secret way, she wished I were.

|||

Three weeks, and then four went by, and I depended on the children's happiness to support, to float my own. Luke and I, in the *vestiaire*, would always have the same two conversations or variations on them. First we would have a sharp, pointed exchange about the nature of buoyancy. What makes people float in water? Well, people are lighter than water, I explained. If you were made of water yourself or well, metal, or something, you would sink. He thought this sounded weird, and I thought so too, actually. People certainly don't *seem* lighter than water. They seem just the opposite. People seem heavy as can be compared with water. People are *obviously* heavier than water; just touch them and then touch water. I knew it was the right answer, but it seemed as unconvincing to me as it did to him. Then we would discuss the conventions of nudity. Why was it okay to be nude in the *vestiaire* but not in the pool or around the pool? It was a matter of custom and convention, I explained, or tried to. The metaphysics of modesty was even harder to explain than the physics of floating.

I joked with him about the little girls. The sublime Ada and the glorious Cressida, I called them, and those became their names. "What means *sublime*?" he demanded, and I gave some more examples of things, besides Ada, that were scary but irresistible (though I will say right here that I have never met anyone quite as sublime as Ada).

(What *does* make things float, by the way? That they are lighter than the thing they float in sounds fine when you say it— I know it is the right answer—but it is not a convincing answer, because things, however much lighter they may be than the thing they float in, are still so heavy, too heavy to stay up.)

Finally, after about four weeks of joy, Luke had to miss a Wednesday session, I forget precisely why: His class was going on a trip to a goat farm to see how chèvre is made or off to an apple farm to help press cider. They were always doing things like that. Anyway, I went to the Ritz myself, as always, feeling the eyes of al Fayed on me, in the person of the sunglassed security men who hid discreetly at the entrance. I got into my swimming suit, my body tensed for the contest to get Luke's suit on and get him pointed in the right direction, down toward the pool, and I was a little disconcerted when I found I didn't have to do it.

The girls were already in the water.

"Where's Luca?" Cressida cried when she saw me. "Where's Luca?" She always called him Luca, in the Italian manner, and said it with that funny trans-European intonation, the accent oddly placed on the first syllable: "Where's *Loo*-ka?," just like Audrey Hepburn saying, "Take the *pic*-ture," in *Funny Face*.

He couldn't come, I explained; his school was doing something that day.

"I'm so sad," she said, and made a face. "I'm so very sad. I wanted to swim with Luca." And she swam away, inconsolable. I swam a little myself, and then I slipped away before I could buy hot chocolate for the rich little girls, half expecting to be expelled from the Ritz, a child masher, buying hot chocolate only to serve his son's romance.

I enjoyed having the Ritz to myself, for once, though, before we had to leave it. I went down to the *hammam*—that's what the French call a steam bath—and read the instructions. There were nearly as many prohibitions as those posted on the gates to the public park, although these were more varied. Translated, they read:

1. *The shower is obligatory before using the installations.*
2. *It is forbidden to shave in the sauna.*
3. *Reading of newspapers is strongly discouraged in the hammam and sauna.*
4. *Children of less than twelve years are not authorized to use the installations.*

"Obligatory," "forbidden," "strongly discouraged," and "not authorized": four ways of saying "not allowed," each slightly different, each implying slightly different penalties. Such elegant variations on the theme of No! And these intended for the rich too. *You can't do that here,* the French taste for order reaching even into the rich man's locker room. Who would *want* to read a newspaper in the steam bath? The ink would get all over your hand. It was like the warnings on the park gates. Who aside from a French functionary would think so encyclopedically about all the things you can't do in a park? But then only if you can't, do you want to. If you can, you don't.

When I got home, I sought Luke out right away.

"Hey, you've made quite a score with Cressida," I said. "She was just broken up because you weren't there today."

"What did she say?" he asked.

"She said, 'Where's Luca? I miss Luca, I wish Luca were here to swim.' Like that. *Nothing* would cheer her up." He seemed to take it only half in.

The next Wednesday came, and I stopped work early and went to collect the bathing trunks and towels.

"Hey, come on, let's hustle up," I said to Luke when he came home after a half day of school. "We have to go to the pool today to meet Ada and Cressida."

He shrugged. "Daddy, I don't really feel like going."

I was dumbfounded, really struck dumb.

"You don't?" I said at last. "Why not?"

"I just don't feel like it," he said, and went into his room to play.

Fifteen minutes later I tried again. "C'mon," I said, "the sublime Ada and the divine Cressida are expecting us."

"I just don't feel like going," he repeated. Then he looked up at me, a strange half-smile that I had never seen before on his face. "Daddy," he said, "what will Cressida say if I'm not there?"

"She'll say she's sad," I said, not sure where we were going.

"No, but what will she say *exactly*? What *exactly* will she say?"

Then I got it. "I don't know. I guess, 'Where's Luca? I wish Luca were here? I miss Luca so much.'"

"What else?"

"I don't know. Just like that."

"No, say exactly what she would say. Tell me *exactly* what she would say." His face was shining.

"You know." I groped. " 'I miss Luca. I wish he would come swimming with me.' " I felt vaguely as if I were reciting pornography.

"I'm not going," he repeated.

The eternal, painful truth of love had struck. Proust wasn't exaggerating, I realized. Five *was* fifteen, five slipped into fifteen—or thirty-five, or fifty for that matter, I suppose—seamlessly. He was struggling with the oldest romantic-erotic question. Was there more pleasure to be found in sharing Cressida's company or in feeling the power that he held by making her suffer from his absence? More pleasure to be found in sharing joy or in denying joy, in knowing that he now possessed the power to make her miserable, change her entire emotional state, simply by not being there?

I was already at the door, and was already turning the handle to leave, when he popped out of his room at last.

"Okay," he said, "I'll go." I was glad, of course. We went to the pool, and they had a good time, though I noticed that now Cressida, ever so slightly, swam toward him. I bought a lot of hot chocolate, and everybody drank it.

I told Martha the story that night, and she seemed somehow stirred. She wanted to know what Cressida had said, too.

"Well, what exactly *did* she say?" she said. "What exactly did she say when she saw him?" His absence was alive in her too.

Was it an accident or not that we shared a bottle of champagne, our own *chocolat chaud,* that night for the first time since she had become big with Olivia, right in the living room, with Tony Bennett singing the English lyrics of our favorite old Michel Legrand song, one of the songs that had gotten us here onto the boulevard Saint-Germain, "You Must Believe in Spring"? Could it have been that her son's first thrill of sadism with a woman had reawakened her own sense of the fragility of desire, of the urge to renewal that runs through the eternal possibility that Wednesday will come and someone will *not* be at the pool, no matter how many wet Wednesdays there have been before? I don't know. There was at least for a moment present again between us the central elements of love: buoyancy, seminudity, and uncertainty, that mixture of imperfect faith and intoxicating drink that is desire.

|||

Our *abonnement* was running out that next week. From now on, I knew, we would have to cadge invitations to swim on Wednesday from Cressida and Ada and couldn't just show up as equals. But I didn't have the heart, the courage to explain to Luke that we were rubes, just visiting, trespassers of a kind. I just told Luke that we wouldn't be swimming there anymore. It didn't seem to bother him any more than our going there together had impressed him. In childhood, I suppose, you are always a little lighter than your circumstances and just keep floating. He worried more about getting his pleasures than about keeping them. He would make me promise him things, in precise order: "First we'll go to the pool, then we'll have hot chocolate, then we'll have dinner, then we'll play a game, then we'll have the Rookie story. . . ." He knew that if he didn't get a contract written down in advance, you could lose any part of it, and that worried him. On the other hand, he didn't worry that the pleasures would ever run out. Life was full of good stuff. The budget of pleasures is tighter in childhood, but the economy of pleasure at least is always in surplus.

We had one last thing to do, of course. We had tried to kiss the mermaid so many times, and we had always failed, because he was too short and I was too scared.

"Let's just *touch* the mermaid," he said wisely, this time, and we held our breaths together, and then we did.

When we were getting ready to leave Paris, I found several hundred shower caps, pristine in their gold and blue boxes, hidden in his bottom drawer.

One Last
Ride

Paris won the century, against all odds. At least we won the party, which is the next best thing to dominating the period. In London they had built a giant wheel and a giant dome and a great big rhetoric of newness to greet the next thousand years. In New York, unduly jumpy despite all the money and power, our friends' major millennial ambition seemed to be to keep out of midtown. One couple we knew had decided to drive down from the country, where they were hunkering down in Y2K alert, park on Ninety-sixth Street, go to a midtown party, and then get back in the car and get home, before the lightning struck, keeping Times Square at a safe and wary distance.

But that was New York, where everything was happening anyway, one millennial party more or less hardly mattered, everybody there was probably on to the next millennium anyway. London was more annoying. We would arrive at Waterloo Station on the Eurostar—transplanted Americans, of course, but still pa-

triotic Parisians—and feel vaguely ashamed, cheesed off, even
sort of country cousinish. Where did London come by this feeling of confidence, this sense of entitlement, all this girder and
vinyl construction? My cousin Philippe, who had once wandered
with me through the outer arrondissements of Paris in search of
von Stroheim festivals and Dominique Sanda memorabilia, had
moved to London now too and was dropping me e-mails about
the progress of his fish restaurant, disparaging the provincial
cooking in the country he had left behind.

Yet on the night, Paris shone, scored a clear and beautiful triumph. It had, to be sure, been a weird run-up through Christmas
week. A siege of flu had struck Europe. It hit our family right in
the kisser. Everyone was sick. I had been banished to the sofa, in
fear that my flu would spread to the baby. (It did anyway.) I shook
with the chills on the sofa all night, only to find a fevered Luke
sympathetically jumping in every night alongside me. (Sympathetic? Or just so satisfied by the idea that Daddy had at last
been banished from the marriage bed that he wanted to make
sure that he didn't stray back?) Anyway, there is nothing so
strangely comforting in sickness as the feeling of an all-elbows-
and-knees five-year-old with a 103-degree fever, shaking alongside you on a narrow velvet sofa.

It was Christmas Eve by the time we had all recovered, and
Martha and I had to crowd all our shopping into that single day,
rushing from Au Nain Bleu for a two-wheeler with training
wheels for Luke up to Bonpoint for a sea green tulle first dress
for Olivia, and then quickly into line at Ladurée for our *bûche de
Noël*. (We actually got summoned out of line, as people who had
wisely ordered in advance, and got our *bûche* from an efficient
but unprepossessing-looking Ladurée bakery truck, parked at
the curb on the rue Royale.) Parisians are efficient Christmas
shoppers, I suppose, or maybe everybody else was home sick
with the flu. Anyway, the rue Royale was pretty much empty by
five o'clock, and Martha and I, walking out into the pure violet
and gray light of the place de la Concorde at twilight in Decem-

ber, had it to ourselves. The Concorde at Christmas at five o'clock has as many subtly distinguished shades of gray as a pair of flannel pants painted by Manet.

Christmas was nice. Luke liked his two-wheeler enough to want to try it out right away (with training wheels) in the little park down the rue du Bac, and after a single fall, he went right around the bust of Chateaubriand on it. The flower store on the commercial part of the street was, to our surprise, open, although there was no one minding the store. We searched a little and found the entire flower family having Christmas lunch in the little shed behind the flowers. The madame wiped her mouth and sold us some tulips and threw in some of the painted white twigs as a gift. Everyone came out to admire Luke's red and chrome two-wheeler.

On Christmas night the wind, following the viruses, socked it to Paris all over again. We woke up at five in the morning, thinking that someone was trying to push open our front door. Nobody there. It was just the wind, blowing away inside the building— blowing so strongly even in the corridors that it pressed against every door. Then we went to look out the windows and saw it blowing so hard that you felt, at least, as if you could see it, as streaking lines of force, like the pen streaks behind Superman's cape. A hundred-plus-miles-an-hour wind blew for an hour. It lifted up the awning on the café across the way, tore wooden shutters off old buildings, and even made the outer walls of our building shake—really shake, *stone* shaking, a scary sound. The winds lifted all the Christmas trees that lined the street right up and sent them blowing like tumbleweeds down the boulevard Saint-Germain. One of them still had its lights on, plugged in on a long cord, writhing and blinking.

There was a lot of damage outside Paris—the park at Versailles may be a century returning to what it was—and even in Paris most of the parks, including the little one where Luke had taken his first bike ride, were closed for a few days. But the city was more or less patched up by New Year's Eve, or Saint Silvestre, as the French more often call it. We went out for a walk at six and went back to the Concorde with the children, the baby sleeping in her *poussette*. There were wheels, small Ferris wheels, set up all along the Champs-Élysées, and then one big Ferris wheel, covered with white lights, at the Concorde—a big wheel, sure, but the same wheel they put up there every Christmas, no big London-type deal.

It was a winter evening like every other winter evening in Paris: the temperature somewhere in the forties, with a little damp mist and a white-gray sky. The whole place had a nice, easy, almost small-town flavor. People strolled. A guy climbed up the face of the obelisk in the center of the place and then climbed back down. The police grabbed him, and the crowd booed. We went home, bedtime for the kids, thinking, only a little ruefully, that with two children, the night of the millennium in Paris wouldn't be a lot different from Arbor Day in Kalamazoo: Bedtimes (and bedtime stories and bedtime stalls and bedtime nursing) rule all, even a fete that came once a thousand years. Millennial time is public time, history time; children's bedtimes are experience time, the real clock that ticks in life.

Then, at midnight, we opened our living-room windows and stepped out onto the tiny balcony outside. We had the TV on, CNN bringing the millennium from around the world. The London party, for all its buildup, seemed, we thought from watching it—and even heard from a few English friends who had called— actually a bit of a dud, with long lines and damp squibs and a nonworking Ferris wheel (our wheels were smaller, but they spun like crazy). We felt meanly, smugly glad.

Then we heard bangs from away down left down the boulevard, over by the Invalides, and a muffled roar. We looked at the television screen and saw the Eiffel Tower, all lit up. They had set up fireworks so that they began at the base of the tower, exploding in gold and violet around its piers, and then dramatically in gold bursts and haloes, working their way up to the top. As the fireworks reached the top, the entire tower turned on; twenty thousand or so small flashbulbs that had been wired to the tower went off at once, blinking hyperfast. The tiny constant explosions of the little bulbs made the tower look as though it had been carbonated, injected with seltzer bubbles. It was a beautiful sight. I thought of going out to see it firsthand, like a responsible reporter, but it was late—hey, come to think of it, it was *after midnight*—and anyway, the children were asleep. So we watched the whole thing on TV, and were proud anyway, one last virtual CNN experience, but with a living room window open, and the cold air coming in, and one ear at least hearing the muffled bangs of the real thing taking place a few blocks away.

I was still kicking myself for missing the show when about a week later Luke and I went to the big Ferris wheel for an afterschool ride and stopped to buy a crepe *crème de marrons*—still his favorite Paris treat—and then decided (I decided; Luke accepted) to walk home across the Concorde bridge. We stopped to admire the searchlight that had also been placed on the top of the tower, sweeping around Paris, when suddenly the whole damn thing exploded all over again, the thousands of little flashing lights sparkling and shooting off and raising hell, just the way they had on New Year's Eve. I looked at my watch; it was five forty-seven on an ordinary Wednesday. Either an *haut fonctionnaire* in the mayor's office, following an inscrutable but precise schedule, had set the whole thing off again on the minute, maybe in honor of some visiting dignitary, or some elevator operator or janitor working in the base of the tower had thrown the switch again, just for the hell of it. Either some official in a big building had set it off, or else it was just some little guy with a taste for mischief—culture or civilization, one or the other, and you would never know which just by looking.

The tower with all its dancing lights, seen real, looked a thousand times more beautiful than it had on television, though it also looked a little as if it had been hung with a giant garland of those vulgar, blinking Christmas lights that Martha had nixed for our tree that first Christmas, when Luke was still a baby. "It looks like champagne," Luke said, and we laughed, he with pleasure at scoring a simile, and I with pleasure that the simile he had scored was, well, so French. We stood on the Concorde bridge and watched the towering, immense spire sizzle for five minutes, and then ten.

I thought: Here we were, at the end of the century and *that's* what we have to get excited about, same old belle époque, fin de siècle stuff, champagne, and the Eiffel Tower? That exhausted stuff, that dead stuff. Only it isn't dead, or even really sick or, in a certain sense, even old. It's here right now, we're looking at it right now, Luke is young in Paris right now, and in that sense, the sparkling tower is the same age he is. He's going to take it with him through life, not as part of the lost glory of the French past but as part of what happened to him when he was a kid. "It looks like champagne," he said again, meaning to please me. I recalled a night not long before when I had been trying to read one of those knotty, dense books about evolution and consciousness that are popular now and had come across an argument about whether, as a human invention, you should value more Newton's *Principia* or the Eiffel Tower. The argument, surprisingly, came down in favor of Eiffel, on the grounds that the principles of physics have a permanent general existence outside ourselves and, had Newton never existed, would eventually have been discovered by Schnewton, while the tower, in all its particulars, could have been built only in Paris at Eiffel's moment by Eiffel, even though it was, after all, only a "minor piece of romantic engineering."

|||

We went to New York first in December and then in January, to find a place to live. The forces drawing us home were pretty strong and even pretty attractive: We wanted Luke to go to a New York school, for one thing. "We have a beautiful existence in Paris, but not a full life," Martha said, summing it up, "and in New York we have a full life and an unbeautiful existence."

Luke had come to associate French, for us the language of romance and the exotic, with authority and order, with school. It was his German. Sometimes, at home, he would pretend to be Zeus and call out to his French teachers from the top of Mount Olympus. "*Oui, oui, oui?*" he would then say, mimicking their high, humorless accents as they turned their heads to look up at the god on the mountain. Then, zap, right between the eyes with a thunderbolt. He would produce what I believe is called a mirthless laugh, even with French administration at last.

Martha had at least been allowed to glimpse a proper copy shop in Paris. It was down near the rue Vavin, just outside the Luxembourg Gardens. We came across it one day, on one of our last strolls, walking home from the playground. A vast glass front, pristine, humming, superfast color Xerox machines, ten or twenty of them, right in front, eager attendants in white T-shirts, ready to collate a manuscript or laser-copy a photograph: It was her Xanadu, right there where you needed it and just as we were leaving.

When we got back, still cold February weather, we went up to the Luxembourg Gardens again, and Luke, slightly to my surprise, said that he wanted to go on the carousel. Martha sat on the little bench with Olivia, nursing discreetly. ("You can't really nurse in Paris openly," she said the other day, "the way I could in New York. I'm always putting on a scarf, and I feel people staring at me. It's not puritanical, really, more sort of the opposite. It's that baring your breast here is really meaningful and loaded.")

Luke got up on one of the beat-up and beautiful old horses. There were a couple of other kids up there too in the cold weather—Paris winter, neither bitter nor chilly nor sunny, life under the perpetual gray skies. Luke asked for a stick when the guy offered them around and held it tight, and I recalled the near baby who had come to Paris five years before.

The carousel started up, and Luke, back absolutely straight, brow slightly creased, watched the man holding the rings. His stick dipped to pick up the ring, and angled to let the ring with its little leather tag drop to its end. *One*. Once around again the second time, back straight, stick out, ring on—perfect. The carousel picked up speed, and since it has no music, the only sound you could hear was the sound of the ancient wheezing fan belt going faster and faster as it drove the horses and carriages around. Bang, bang—two more rings, picking them like cherries: back straight, stick out, unsmiling, taking one ring after another and slipping it down his wood baton.

I was unreasonably pleased and then felt a little guilty about my own pleasure. It seemed so American, so competitive; the French fathers on the bench just sat there, watching with sober pleasure, not seeing even a carousel as a competitive sport. But as Luke whirled around, now really going fast, and grabbed still another ring—I only knew it now by the slight clang of wood on metal and the ring missing—I couldn't help myself.

"Hey, sir"—I call him sir a lot, Johnsonianly—"you're unconscious."

Luke, a blur of gray coat on the brown horse.

"What means *unconscious*?" I heard him ask, his voice clear and then fading away as the carousel whipped him around.

"It means you're doing great without even thinking about it," I called out.

The carousel was beginning to slow down now—the normal five-minute ride at an end. I saw the man's hand on the lever, bringing the ride to its close.

"Daddy," Luke said, and I thought I heard a little concern in his voice, a small edge of worry, "Daddy, I *am* thinking about it," he said, and he didn't even try for the one last ring that the man held out, before the carousel stopped for good and the man took back the stick and shook off the rings, so dearly won, to give to the next child who would get up on the carousel in the Luxembourg Gardens and give it a try.

Paris to the Moon

Adam Gopnik

A Reader's Guide

Questions for Discussion

1. Throughout *Paris to the Moon,* Adam Gopnik seems to be writing about small things—Christmas lights, fax machines, children's stories—but he tries to find in them larger truths about French and American life. Can the shape of big things be found by studying small ones? Is it really possible to "see the world in a grain of sand"? What overlooked small things in our American life seem to resonate with larger meanings?

2. Although composed of separate essays, the book follows a thread toward a larger meaning: that the "commonplace civilization" of Paris is beautiful but its official culture is often oppressive. What kinds of evidence, small and large, does Gopnik collect to illustrate this idea? In "Papon's Paper Trail," how does this lighthearted observation turn serious? In the chapters about the Balzar wars, how are the author's feelings finally resolved?

3. Can we find a similar distinction between "civilization" and "official culture" in America? Do you agree with the notion Gopnik alludes to in "Barney in Paris" that media culture is our official culture? Do you think his urge to "protect" his child from the "weather on CNN" in favor of the "civilization of the carousel" is admirable or foolish?

To print out copies of this or other Random House Reader's Guides, visit us at www.atrandom.com/rgg.

4. Although *Paris to the Moon* is not a novel, it has a novelistic shape, with characters we come to know. Are there "secret stories" in the book? Does Gopnik want us to sense something about the development of his feelings about his child? About his wife? Has the narrator changed or matured by the end? In what way are "all chords sounded" by the birth of a new child?

5. "The Rookie" is one of the most popular stories in the book. Why do you think this is so? The author seems to be saying that American life gives the "gift of loneliness"; do you agree? If you were away from home for a long time, what elements of American culture do you think you would miss?

6. Throughout the book, Gopnik compares France and America. What are the most frequent points of comparison? Where do you think he favors America, and where France? Which do you favor?

7. At the end of *Paris to the Moon,* when the family decides to return to America, Martha says, "In Paris we have a beautiful existence but not a full life, and in New York we have a full life but an unbeautiful existence." The author has said that this distinction is central to his experience of being an expatriate. Do you think it's a valid distinction? Given the choice, which would you prefer?

Further Reading

Books about Paris and France stretch out to the end of the horizon, and fill libraries. But the subcategory of books about Americans in Paris is smaller, and still choice. Of twentieth-century books, A. J. Liebling's *Between Meals: An Appetite For Paris* is pure gold, as is his *The Road Back to Paris*. Janet Flanner's *Paris Journals* are collections of her letters from Paris for *The New Yorker*, and are full of condensed, stylized French history. Henry James's *A Little Tour in France* is the classic literary guidebook, and James Thurber's wonderful stories of his mishaps in France are included in *My World and Welcome to It* and in *The Thurber Carnival*, particularly the stories "A Ride with Olympy" and "Memoirs of a Drudge." Ernest Hemingway's *A Moveable Feast* is probably the most famous twentieth-century Paris memoir, though it is more about Americans than about Paris.

Novels about Americans in Paris make up an even longer and richer list. They include Henry James's *The American* and *The Ambassadors*. Hemingway's *The Sun Also Rises* is the classic story of American expatriates in Paris in the 1920s, and in Irwin Shaw's *Collected Stories* there is many a glimpse of American expatriates in the 1950s. F. Scott Fitzgerald's "Babylon Revisited" is probably the saddest and most beautiful story about an American in Paris after the crash—and the fall.

Finally, George Gershwin's great tone poem "An American in Paris," which is heard often in the background of *Paris to the Moon*, has been recorded many times. The best version is Leonard Bernstein's 1959 recording, made with the Columbia Symphony Orchestra; it is available on CD. Gershwin's piece was the basis for a not-bad Gene Kelly movie directed by Vincente Minnelli, widely available on video.

ADAM GOPNIK has been writing for *The New Yorker* since 1986, and his work for the magazine has twice won the National Magazine Award for Essay and Criticism as well as the George Polk Award for Magazine Reporting. He broadcasts regularly for the Canadian Broadcasting Corporation, and is the author of the article on the culture of the United States in the last two editions of the *Encyclopedia Britannica*. From 1995 to 2000 Gopnik lived in Paris, where the newspaper *Le Monde* profiled him as a "witty and Voltairean commentator on French life," and the weekly magazine *Le Point* wrote, "It is impossible to resist delighting in the nuances of his articles, for the details concerning French culture that one discovers even when one is French oneself." He now lives in New York with his wife, Martha Parker, and their two children, Luke Auden and Olivia Esmé Claire.

ABOUT THE TYPE

This book was set in Fairfield, the first typeface from the hand of the distinguished American artist and engraver Rudolph Ruzicka (1883–1978). In its structure Fairfield displays the sober and sane qualities of the master craftsman whose talent has long been dedicated to clarity. It is this trait that accounts for the trim grace and vigor, the spirited design and sensitive balance, of this original typeface.

Recent titles in the series

A BRIEF GUIDE TO THE

SUPERNATURAL

LEO RUICKBIE

ROBINSON

Constable & Robinson Ltd
55–56 Russell Square
London WC1B 4HP
www.constablerobinson.com

First published in the UK by Robinson,
an imprint of Constable & Robinson Ltd, 2012

A copy of the British Library Cataloguing in
Publication data is available from the British Library

ISBN: 978-1-84901-675-9

Printed and bound in the UK

1 3 5 7 9 10 8 6 4 2

First published in the United States in 2011 by Running Press Book Publishers,
A Member of the Perseus Books Group

‘‘ble at special discounts for bulk purchases
other organizations. For more
ent at the Perseus Books Group,
03, or call (800) 810-4145,
eusbooks.com.

‘-0
r: 2011933253

1

this printing

NNING PRESS
PHILADELPHIA · LONDON

To Antje and Morgana

CAUTION TO THE READER

Before reading the contents of this book,—

PLEASE NOTE

1. —That the narratives printed in these pages had better not be read by any one of tender years, of morbid excitability, or of excessively nervous temperament.
2. —That the latest students of the subject concur in the solemn warning addressed in the Sacred Writings to those who have dealings with familiar spirits, or who expose themselves to the horrible consequences of possession.
3. —That as the latent possibilities of our complex personality are so imperfectly understood, all experimenting in hypnotism, spiritualism, etc., excepting in the most careful and reverent spirit, by the most level-headed persons, had much better be avoided.

This Caution is printed here at the suggestion of *Catholics*, *Theosophists*, and *Spiritualists*, who declare themselves to be profoundly convinced of its *necessity*.

An actual notice first printed in W. T. Stead, 'Real Ghost Stories: A Record of Authentic Apparitions', *Review of Reviews*, London, December 1891; here reproduced from the 1897 revised edition, p. xiii.

Contents

Foreword

A little while ago I was interviewed on a radio station and the presenter decided to get right back to basics with his first question: 'What does paranormal mean – what *is* the paranormal?' he asked me.

Since I was then the editor of a magazine called *Paranormal* the interviewer had every reason to expect me to answer that question quickly and concisely but . . . in truth, I had to think about it. When it comes to the paranormal the 'simple' questions can be the hardest to answer.

The word paranormal simply means 'beyond the normal', in the same way the word supernatural means 'beyond the natural'. But how far beyond? That's the nub of it.

For many who say they 'believe in the paranormal' the word presumes the acceptance of a spirit world, a world beyond our own with laws different from our scientific laws. For them the paranormal is merely a foyer that leads to the great halls of religion. This is not true of everyone who accepts the reality of paranormal phenomena, however.

Personally, I believe that a great deal of that which is currently 'beyond the natural' will in time be understood as natural. That is to say, it will one day be brought into the realm of science (provided the scientific establishment ever gets round to taking an interest).

Are poltergeists mischievous spirits or the effects of some energy source not currently known to science? Are ghosts the returning dead or images created by our brains in response to some external stimulus we don't understand? If it is found that extraterrestrials really are visiting us, isn't it likely we will also find they are employing principles of some alien science in order to do so?

I think it likely most of the phenomena discussed by Dr Leo Ruickbie in this fascinating book will one day be understood by science.

The few sound-bites laymen like me pick up of quantum physics research implies that the gap between the supernatural and the natural is narrowing. We hear of particles that can arrive at a destination before leaving their point of origin and of particles which, once connected, remain mysteriously linked to each other even when they are light years apart. Such phenomena sound paranormal to me and yet, if true, they are effects manifesting in the natural world at the most fundamental level.

It should also be borne in mind that even the existence of spirits needn't fall forever outside the precincts of science. The idea of a multi-dimensional universe is an old one: who is to say that 'the spirit world' and any number of 'heavens' might not each represent one of these dimensions and that the barrier between them and our world can be – and is being – routinely broached? Maybe some future science will one day be able to understand and quantify what today we currently think of as firmly beyond, indeed antagonistic, to science.

Nevertheless, I doubt very much that one explanation – such as multiple dimensions or, more prosaically, hallucinations – will ever be found to cover the whole gamut of the 'paranormal'.

Taking all the above into consideration, it's no wonder I found it so hard to answer that radio presenter's deceptively simple question during a live broadcast. I was pleased, however, to have been forced to reconsider that central concept of 'what is paranormal?' once again.

In this book Leo Ruickbie takes on the same challenge – to dissect, examine and ratify the paranormal in a *Brief Guide*. It's no easy task but one he is certainly well equipped to accomplish.

He achieves his goal with insight, scholarship and admirable good humour and readability.

Of course, Dr Ruickbie makes no claim to fully explain the phenomena he examines. What he does do is illuminate tantalizing glimpses as he descends into the paranormal's 'bottomless pit' (as he describes it in his introduction). The real fascination of the paranormal for me is that for now it does remain dark and unknown. Paranormal events challenge our perceptions of the world around us and beg important questions about the universe and our place within it.

It's not just the truth that's out there – to quote an iconic TV series – the paranormal is, too. It really is. In your town. In your street. Maybe in your own home. The weird and inexplicable happens to ordinary people somewhere in the world every single day. Before you go in search of it, though, you will need a guide. How lucky for you that you have this excellent one in your hands.

Richard Holland, Editor, UncannyUK.com
and former editor of *Paranormal* magazine

Introduction

Neither Normal Nor Natural

At the edge of what we know, a dark continent of legend and belief stretches to a distant vanishing point. It is a realm inhabited by strange entities – ghosts, poltergeists, the undead, angels, demons, extraterrestrials – and it is a realm explained by strange ideas from the occult to modern parapsychology involving ancient gods, magical powers, alternative universes and multi-dimensional space. From novels *The Exorcist* to *Twilight*, from films *Poltergeist* to *Underworld*, from television programmes *The X-Files* to *Buffy the Vampire Slayer*, from video games *Doom* to *Resident Evil*, our thoughts and fears are drawn to this dark world of the supernatural. It has never been more popular than now.

Human history is also the history of the non-human and the unreal. Throughout our recorded history – from rock carving to the internet – the human race has made reference to another, radically different order of beings and alternatives to physical reality. In referring to this, the term 'paranormal' has come to replace 'supernatural' in scientific discourse on the subject, but they are, essentially, the same. The 'supernatural' is a dissident subject. It deals with things that mainstream science cannot allow, but in which many believe, yet rarely has the same privileges as religion. However, it is also an essential subject. From our earliest myths to our latest fears, the supernatural has always been with us. To paraphrase William James, to study the supernatural is the best way of understanding the natural; certainly it is bound to be more interesting.

The field of the supernatural is often divided sharply between believers and sceptics. At the extremes there are those who will believe anything and those who will deny everything. To avoid such divisiveness, let us think of the supernatural in a different way. If literature is the willing suspension of disbelief, then science is the willing suspension of belief. But let us go further and suspend both belief and disbelief. Let us look at the evidence, that quirky will-o'-the-wisp that promises proof while leading us into the bog of oblivion. And to help us avoid divisiveness and think about this subject in a new way, let us take a new name for it. We need something fashionable, something popular and obscure at the same time: we need quantum physics. I want us to think of the supernatural as 'quantum normality' – a world where things can suddenly appear and disappear, and be in two places at once, a world where there is still room for the astonishing and unlikely. Let us adopt a 'quantum' position ourselves: what follows might be true or it might not be, and it is both of these things until we peek into the box containing Schrödinger's cat and collapse the probability wave function. Not least as history, the supernatural is an undeniable social fact, whether it is real or not.

The supernatural is a vast subject whose boundaries are unfathomable. It is everything beyond the natural. But what is natural? Is it the paranormal – everything beyond the normal? But again, what is normal? In fact, reports of paranormal occurrences are so frequent that we might be better thinking of them as normal. It is often the case, as American writer Elbert Hubbard once put it, that 'the supernatural is the natural not yet understood'.[1] Science is constantly pushing our understanding of what constitutes the natural order of things.

As history it is impossible to define a beginning. Enigmatic cave drawings may hint at supernatural ideas and beliefs, but it is not certain that they do, and if they do, what do they mean? That is why this book is organized thematically. A rough timeline

---

[1] Hubbard, 'The Open Road: Afoot with the Fra', *The Fra*, 1.2, May 1908, p. 22.

can occasionally be drawn through the chapters, particularly the later ones, but they are written primarily as stand-alone guides to key concepts and fields of study within the broad envelope of 'supernatural'.

As a guide to what should be in a book about the supernatural I have, of course, considered the demands and desires of popular culture, but more particularly I have looked to specialist publications such as *Paranormal* magazine and *Fortean Times*, dedicated encyclopaedias on the subject and the scientific literature, such as that produced by the members of the Society for Psychical Research over the last 130 or so years. Today, the supernatural/paranormal encompasses everything from building your own UFO to reanimating corpses with voodoo.

To reflect and, hopefully, organize that expansive range, the book is divided into two parts. The first deals with what I have called supernatural entities. This mostly covers what are considered to be spirits: spirits of the dead (ghosts and possibly poltergeists), spirits of the dead believed to have reanimated their physical forms ('the undead'), good spirits (angels), and evil spirits (demons). I have also included extraterrestrials and UFOs since they are described by witnesses and believers in ways reminiscent of some of the older categories of spirits, such as angels and demons. The second part deals with ways in which humankind has tried to communicate with and control these supernatural entities and tap into the whole range of powers that are thought to be paranormal in origin and function. I have called these 'approaches to the supernatural', since they cover a broad range of activity from magic to science.

Finally, it must be borne in mind that this book is a guide and a *brief* guide at that. Each subject I cover has volumes, sometimes whole libraries, devoted to it. Thus more might have been included – religious visions of gods, God and saints, the fairies and monsters of folklore and the cryptids of current cryptozoology – but as with every project there has to be a point where one draws the line and this book was never intended to be an encyclopaedia of the subject. Sanity is learning what to overlook. Whilst I have endeavoured to delve deeply into the subjects I do cover, due to the constraints of space and the purpose of this book it has not been possible to touch the bottom of what is, essentially, a bottomless pit – or even several bottomless pits. It is not intended to be an academic textbook, but it is written in a way that it can be relied upon. To allow the reader to follow up the sources consulted I have included full references in the notes and as is usual in historical research I have used primary sources wherever possible supplemented by the latest research where necessary. For those new to these subjects I have tried to provide a solid starting-point; for those already familiar with them, hopefully, an enjoyable overview with a few surprises along the way. For everyone, these are simply some of the most astonishing stories that have ever been told.

The Experiments

For most people, most of the time, they find out things from other people. A tells B a ghost story, B writes it down and C reads it, and so on, although especially important is the part where C tells D who then gets B's book out of the library and tracks down A, interviews all those involved, reads all the source material, weighs the evidence and writes a book like this one. Here I want to give you the opportunity to find out something for yourself by actually doing it. The reason is that I want to involve you in some of the issues surrounding the investigation of the supernatural. I have devised three simple experiments that you can try right now.

Experiment 1: Mind-Reading

You will need a pen or pencil and a blank sheet of paper. When you have these rounded up, in your mind's eye, I want you to see a simple geometrical shape. Got it? Make it larger, draw it on the paper, then, inside this space I want you to try and get another geometrical shape, and draw that, too. Now you should have two shapes, one inside the other. At the end of the book I will tell you what you have drawn.

Experiment 2: Thought-Transference

From my secret location in central Europe I am now going to mentally project a number between 1 and 50. To make things easier, both digits are odd numbers, but not the same number, so that it could be 15 but not 11, for example. Open up your mind. Write down the number you receive.

Experiment 3: Psychokinesis

Uri Geller once performed a live paranormal event on television where he told viewers that his psychic powers would reactivate their old, broken clocks and watches. Many people were amazed to find out that it worked. We are going to do the same thing right now. Find an old wind-up watch that no longer works, hold it in your hands for some minutes, concentrating on making it work, as I broadcast my psychic powers to operate on the machinery. You should hold it for at least ten minutes, repeating 'work, mend, work'. It might help if you hold a copy of this book in your other hand.

Part I: Supernatural Entities

Millions of spiritual creatures walk the earth
Unseen, both when we wake and when we sleep.
– John Milton, Paradise Lost, 1667

Sir, to leave things out of a book, merely because people
tell you they will not be believed, is meanness.
– Samuel Johnson, 21 March 1772
(James Boswell's The Life of Samuel Johnson)

1. Ghosts

'Tales of Headless Coachmen and a Lonely Nun': it was early summer, 1929, when news reached the *Daily Mirror* from a forgotten hamlet in a remote corner of Essex. Unusual events were disrupting the lives of the local rector and his household. The rector had written requesting the name of a reputable society involved in psychical research that could help him put an end to the disturbances. The paper dispatched one of its most experienced reporters, V. C. Wall, to investigate. The name of the village was Borley.[2]

Even when it was full of life, the rectory had an air of foreboding. A charmless red brick mansion built in the early 1860s by the Revd Henry Bull to accommodate his vast family of fourteen children, it stood, it was said, on the site of a medieval monastery. In 1928, the rectory, after being turned down by twelve other clergymen, had become the home of Revd Guy Eric Smith and his wife Mabel, despite the warnings. 'It had a sinister reputation,' said Sidney Glanville, one of the later investigators, 'and the huge, melancholy house could not have been very inviting.' Wall told his readers that the strange events the Smiths related to him had all the makings of 'a first-class ghost story'.[3]

---

[2] Sidney Glanville, 'The Strange Happenings at Borley Rectory', *Fate*, October 1951, p. 95.

[3] V. C. Wall, 'Ghost Visits to a Rectory', *Daily Mirror,* 10 June 1929; Glanville, p. 91; Eric J. Dingwall, et al., 'The Haunting of Borley Rectory', *Proceedings of the Society for Psychical Research*, 51.186, January 1956, p. 28. The journalist V. C. Wall did not put his byline to the stories, but he is named by Harry Price,

When the Smiths arrived from India, they found that the rectory had fallen into severe disrepair. There was no mains water, the cisterns were filthy, and fresh water had to be pumped from a well in the courtyard – when it worked. The roof leaked. There was no gas or electricity. It was cold and difficult to heat, and only part of the twenty-three-room mansion was habitable. Unmanaged trees had grown up tall and nigh encircling, almost hiding the house from the sun. The Smiths were about to embark on what they would later describe as 'the darkest years of their life'.[4]

For the Smiths, it began with the sound of footsteps: slow, dragging footsteps echoing from an unoccupied room. The reverend stayed up one night, hockey stick at the ready, waiting for the footsteps to cross the room's floor. They did not disappoint. Although he saw nothing, the sound of feet wearing what he took for slippers began to drag themselves over the bare floorboards. The reverend swung his hockey stick, whistling through the air, at the spot where he thought the footsteps were. But the invisible feet kept their pace across the room.[5]

On another occasion, Mrs Smith was in the library, apparently investigating the nooks and crannies of the house. A large Victorian bookcase stretched the length of one wall with the top half glass fronted and the bottom given over to cupboards. Inside one of the cupboards Mrs Smith found a football-sized parcel. There was no label or indication as to what was inside and so, like Pandora in the Greek myth, she started to unwrap the layers of paper. Inside was a human skull. Revd Smith interred it in the nearby graveyard after a short service, but soon after, mysterious taps started to sound from the mirror on Mrs Smith's dressing table whenever she approached it. According to a certain Mr Hardy, a workman at Borley, the strange phenomena became so intense after the burial that it was decided to restore the skull to its previous place.[6]

The End of Borley Rectory, Harrap & Co., 1946, p. 178.

[4] Glanville, pp. 90, 94; Dingwall, et al., 1956, pp. 28–9.

[5] Wall, 'Ghost Visits to a Rectory'.

[6] Glanville, p. 95. Glanville interviewed the Smiths on 6 October 1937 and

Mystery lights were seen in unoccupied parts of the building. In the library, the heavy wooden shutters to the French windows would slam shut. Doors would be locked and unlocked. Keys would mysteriously vanish. Bells would ring for the servants from empty rooms. The reverend heard whispering voices in the passage outside his bedroom. At one point, someone or something shouted 'Don't, Carlos'.[7]

A servant girl brought all the way from London gave her notice after only two days. She had, she said, seen the ghost of a nun walking in the woods at the back of the house and at another time leaning over a gate near the house. Another servant girl claimed to have seen an 'old-fashioned coach' on the lawn. The previous rector, already dead, had himself told the story of how, when walking along the road outside the rectory one night, he had seen a coach drive by, driven by two headless coachmen. Wall related that 'the villagers dread the neighbourhood of the rectory after dark, and will not pass it'.[8]

Wall's explanation was that, according to local legend, a groom at the monastery and a nun from a nearby convent had fallen in love 'several hundred years ago'. They would meet illicitly in the woods, pledging their love for one another and planning their elopement. When the day came for them to escape, another groom brought a coach round to the woods. But the lovers quarrelled and in a fit of rage, the groom strangled the nun. He was caught and both grooms were beheaded. According to another version, the monks caught all three red-handed, beheaded the grooms and walled up the nun alive within the monastery. In subsequent versions it was a monk and nun who had fallen in love, with the same grisly ending.[9]

heard this story first-hand. Price gives the same details, p. 20, with the addition of Hardy's testimony.

[7] Glanville, pp. 94–6.

[8] Wall, 'Ghost Visits to a Rectory'.

[9] Wall, 'Ghost Visits to a Rectory'; V. C. Wall, 'Mystery Light in Haunted Wood', *Daily Mirror*, 11 June 1929; Peter Underwood, *The A–Z of British Ghosts*, Chancellor Press, 1992, p. 31.

The Smiths' experiences were not the first time that ghosts had been reported at Borley. The stories in the *Daily Mirror* prompted a Mrs E. Myford of Newport to write in about her own encounter with the ghost. She had grown up in the area where 'it was common talk that the rectory was haunted'. 'Many people,' she said, 'declared that they had seen figures walking at the bottom of the garden.' Despite that she became an under-nursemaid there in 1886. Installed in what was, according to the other servants, the 'haunted bedroom', she had to wait two weeks before the ghost made itself known. In the dead of night she was woken by the sound of someone walking down the corridor towards her room. It was a slightly muffled, scuffling sound, as if the approaching person were wearing slippers. She expected that it was the head nurse come to wake her as she did at six every morning, but when no one came into the room her thoughts turned to 'the ghost'. Next morning the other maids all denied having walked down to her room. The young Mrs Myford became so nervous that she handed in her notice and never again ventured down by the house after sunset.[10]

Colchester Grammar School's former headmaster, P. Shaw Jeffrey, MA, told veteran ghost hunter Peter Underwood that he had seen the ghostly nun several times when he had visited the rectory in 1885 or 1886. Ethel Bull, one of the last surviving children of Revd Bull, told how she and two of her sisters had seen the nun gliding along the so-called 'Nun's Walk' in the late afternoon of 28 July 1900 – 28 July being the traditional date of the nun's appearance. Another sister was called from the house and promptly decided that there was nothing strange at all about the nun and approached to enquire whether she wanted anything. That was when the nun vanished. One of their brothers, Harry Bull, went on to become a parson and took over the parish after his father: he, too, claimed to have seen the nun, as well as being awakened, along with the rest of the household, by

---

[10] V. C. Wall, 'Haunted Room in a Rectory', *Daily Mirror*, 12 June 1929.

the loud and unaccountable ringing of bells. He also frequently met the dwarfish figure of an old man on the lawn.[11]

Wall and a photographer decided to spend the night in the woods to try and see the ghosts themselves. Gamely, Revd Smith joined them, professing not to believe in ghosts. After some time, they noticed a mysterious light appear in a disused wing of the building. Neither Wall nor his photographer seemed anxious to investigate, so the reverend volunteered. They saw the reverend light a lamp next to the mysterious light, but when they approached, the mystery light winked out. The intrepid reporters were then badly scared by a maid coming out to ask if they would like coffee. Undeterred, they examined some tree stumps that looked a bit like nuns, before finally calling it a night. That was when they decided to call in Harry Price, Honorary Director of the National Laboratory of Psychic Research.[12]

With Price on site, Wall's till then rather tongue-in-cheek account took on a new note of seriousness. This time he claimed to have actually seen the 'nun' moving in the deep shadows at the edge of the woods. By this time the ghost or ghosts seemed to have learnt a few new tricks. After he had investigated the shadowy figure, a pane of glass from the porch 'hurtled to the ground'. As he went inside, a vase flew past the reporter's head and smashed against the iron stove in the hallway. Waiting on the stairs in darkness to see if anything else would happen, a mothball struck Wall on the head. Then from about 1 a.m. to 4 a.m., Wall, the rector and his wife, as well as Price and his secretary Lucy Kaye, communicated with the spirit as it made a series of raps on the back of a mirror. The spirit told them that he was the late Revd Harry Bull.[13]

The press attention brought sightseers in their 'hundreds' to gawp at the house and 'at night the headlights of their cars may

[11] Underwood, p. 31; Glanville, p. 92.

[12] Wall, 'Mystery Light in Haunted Wood'; Wall, 'Haunted Room in a Rectory'.

[13] V. C. Wall, 'Weird Night in Haunted House', *Daily Mirror*, 14 June 1929; V. C. Wall, 'Shy Ghost of Borley Rectory', *Daily Mirror*, 17 June 1929.

be seen for miles around'. One enterprising company was even
running a bus service to the rectory with the slogan 'come and
see the Borley ghost'. Instances of 'rowdyism' were disrupting
the neighbourhood and the reverend appealed to people to be 'a
little more considerate when they come here'. People were trampling the flower beds and peering through the windows. The
police were called. By 17 June 1929, just a week after Wall's first
story, this ugly old building had become 'the now famous
rectory'. And this was only the beginning.[14]

These experiences, the public interest, the subsequent investigations and reports of further phenomena would award Borley
Rectory the name of 'the most haunted house in England'.
There are, arguably, more haunted places. The Theatre Royal
on Drury Lane, London, claims over 500 ghosts, for example.[15]
However, no other case has become so talked about nor been as
controversial. Borley Rectory is either the best authenticated
case of a haunted house, or one of the most heinous frauds ever
perpetrated.

Defining Ghosts

Nuns, white ladies, green ladies, blue ladies, headless horsemen,
as well as coachmen, drummer-boys, underground pipers,
marching soldiers, fighting armies, phantom coaches, ghost
trains, spectral pets – all these and more are the sorts of spirits
that people believe have come back from the dead or the past to
haunt us. It was once calculated that Warwickshire had a ghost
for every square mile, which, if it were a representative figure,
would mean that the United Kingdom alone must be troubled
by some 94,000 spirits of the dead.[16]

---

[14] Wall, 'Shy Ghost of Borley Rectory'; Glanville, p. 96.
[15] John Spencer and Anne Spencer, *The Ghost Handbook*, Boxtree, 1998, pp.
8, 110, according to tourguide Nina Smirnoff.
[16] William Purcell Witcutt, 'Notes on Warwickshire Folklore', *Folklore* 55,
2 (1944), p. 72; I have widened the estimate made by Owen Davies in *The
Haunted: A Social History of Ghosts*, Palgrave Macmillan, 2009, p. 1, for England to include the whole of the UK.

In every culture, in every age, we find people who have seen ghosts. Many more believe in them. A 2001 Gallup poll found that 38 per cent of Americans believed in ghosts with an unaccountably larger 42 per cent believing in haunted houses. At around the same time in Britain, the Consumer Analysis Group found that 57 per cent believed in ghosts. In 1882 the then newly formed Society for Psychical Research (SPR) surveyed 17,000 people and found that nearly 10 per cent had had a ghostly experience. [17]

The terminology that has grown up around hauntings is almost as varied as the hauntings themselves: ghost, phantom, phantasm, shade, shadow, spectre, spook, apparition, wraith, poltergeist (which we will examine separately). We also find a number of more obscure words, such as *lemures, larvae, umbrae mortuorum, spectra* and so on. Then there are new terms, such as orbs, EVP, shadow people.

No definitive typology has emerged, but many authors have sought to order this jumble of terminology. For Ludwig Lavater writing in the sixteenth century, *lemures* and *larvae* were generic terms for the ghosts of the dead, somewhat like *umbrae mortuorum* – shades of the dead – whilst *spectra* referred to 'a substance without a body' that yet could be heard or seen. *Lemures* were also 'evil and hurtful shapes which appear in the night'. *Visum* (also *Visio, Visiones*) he equated with the Greek *phantasia*, a realistic fantasy occurring in sleep or near sleep, to be differentiated (it is not clear how) from a *phasma*. For King James VI and I, writing in his *Daemonologie* at the end of the sixteenth century, the peculiarly Scottish wraiths were the spirits of the newly dead, or soon to die, and, undoubtedly influenced by Lavater, *lemures* and *spectra* haunted houses in various terrifying appearances and with much noise.[18]

---

[17] Brad Steiger and Sherry Steiger, *Gale Encyclopedia of the Unusual and Unexplained*, Gale, 2003, vol. 3, p. 2; George Stuart, 'What is a Ghost?', *Paranormal*, June 2010, p. 59.

[18] Ludwig (also Lewes) Lavater, *Das Gespensterbuch*, 1569, English trans. published as *Of Ghostes and Spirites Walking by Nyght*, 1572, pp. 1–3; James VI and

It is clear that many of these concepts were taken from Latin sources. The Romans had a name for a class of spirits who protected and guided human beings: *genii*. Lavater noted that we have two: one that encourages good deeds and another that encourages the opposite. The term *genius* was a personification of the creative powers, depicted in Etruscan and Roman art as naked winged males. Under Greek influence this became fused with the concept of *daimon*, but the Romans continued their particular belief in a *genius loci*, spirit of place. Lavater also plumbed the depths of Greek and Roman folklore concerning evil spirits, referring to Mormo and Gilo, as well as the Gorgones, Empusae, Lamiae and others (see the chapter on demons). Among the Romans it was believed that evil spirits of the dead wandered the night. Called *lemures* (*larvae*) these ghost-demons could be appeased at the feast of the Lemuria (9 November and 13 May) with black beans scattered at midnight.[19]

In the earliest literature of the Ancient Near East we find many of the same concerns as today, especially with what happens after death. Confronted with a corpse they wondered, as do we all, where the life force that so recently had energized and characterized that body had gone. And in that mysterious place, what did the dead do? The bizarre complexities of Egyptian funerary customs, from the technical wonders of mummification and the gigantic pyramids, to the range of spells in *The Book of the Dead* to prevent such horrors as having to eat dung in the afterlife, attest to this deepest of concerns. The deceased continued as a multiplicity of spiritual forms called *ka*, *ba* and *ah*. In Coptic the *ah* becomes a demonic aspect, but otherwise the dead are not necessarily considered to be ill-disposed towards the living. The dead could be called upon for help and likewise the living could help the dead. Provisions, tools, money, jewels, weapons, warriors and slaves have all been

---

I, *Daemonologie*, 1597, p. 57; see also Davies, pp. 2–3. Spellings modernized.
[19] Manfred Lurker, *Routledge Dictionary of Gods and Goddesses, Devils and Demons*, Routledge, 2004, pp. 68, 111; Lavater, pp. 3, 5.

buried with the dead at one time or another to assist in the deceased's afterlife existence.[20]

We are familiar with the differential fates of the righteous and the ignominious dead: Valhalla for the valiant Northern warrior, the gloomy halls of Hel for the rest; the Elysian Fields for the Heroic Greek, the Meadows of Asphodel for the indifferent and Tartarus for the wicked; Heaven for the good Christian, Hell for everyone else, with Limbo added later as a compromise. In contrast to the idyllic Field of Offerings (or Reeds) that awaited the Egyptian, the Mesopotamians believed that the dead lived in perpetual darkness eating mud and filth and drinking foul water in 'the land of no return'. Given such an unenviable future, the unwelcome attentions of angry ghosts were greatly feared. Reflecting funerary taboos, it was believed by the Babylonians that the spirit of an uninterred corpse remained on the earth as a potentially harmful ghost.[21]

Similar ideas continued to be influential right up until our own times. The Revd J. C. Atkinson (1814–1900) reported the belief current in his Yorkshire parish that if a body on its way to be buried was not carried up the 'church road', then its ghost would return. An inverted form of this idea can be read in the story of the restless Borley skull.[22]

We see from this it was commonly believed that ghosts behaved in a purposeful manner. As well as protesting against the improper implementation of funerary customs, they also returned to right other wrongs. Ghosts interceded in legal cases, as when the spirit of Sir Walter Long's (c. 1591–1672) first wife allegedly scared the wits out of a clerk who was preparing the legal papers enabling Long's second wife to disinherit her stepson. In 1660 the spirit of Robert Parkin supposedly appeared to

---

[20] K. van der Toorn, Bob Becking and Pieter Willem van der Horst (eds), *Dictionary of Deities and Demons in the Bible* [*DDD*], 2nd ed., Brill/Eerdmans, 1999, pp. 223–5.

[21] *DDD*, pp. 223–31, 309–12.

[22] *Routledge Dict. Gods*, p. 60; John Christopher Atkinson, *Forty Years in a Moorland Parish*, Macmillan, 1891, pp. 219–20.

Robert Hope of Appleby in the parish church, crying out 'I am murdered' over and over, which instigated the local Justice of the Peace to begin a murder enquiry. Borley's ghostly nun was likewise believed to have returned because of her cruel murder. The vengeful ghost had its counterpart in the repentant ghost. Remorseful murderers were also believed to occasionally return to reveal their crimes. Other ghosts appeared to mark the date of their death, especially in the case of suicides, whilst others simply continued to do what they had always done and followed their everyday routine. In very rare, but most interesting cases, spirits of the dead return to warn the living, make prophecies, or even to give evidence of the afterlife.[23]

Fictional ghosts are always purposeful. One need only think of the ghost of Hamlet's father who returns to reveal his murder to his son and incite him to exact revenge in Shakespeare's *Hamlet* (c. 1599–1601), or the ghost of the murdered Banquo returning to haunt his killer in *Macbeth* (c. 1603–7). The spirits in Charles Dickens' *A Christmas Carol* (1843) play a central role in transforming the character of Ebenezer Scrooge with grim and prophetic messages. With such precedents it is no wonder that the purposeful ghost continues to be a theme in popular culture. The Oscar-winning film *Ghost* (1990) had Patrick Swayze trying to warn his fiancée, played by Demi Moore, and bring his killers to justice. In *The Sixth Sense* (1999) spirits of the dead use a young boy who can see and communicate with them to resolve their untimely deaths, which ultimately allows Bruce Willis's character to come to terms with his own death and express his true feelings for his wife. In the 2008 film *Ghost Town* with Ricky Gervais, the spirits of the dead were trapped on the earth because of unfinished business with the living. Of course, this is as much a technical requirement as it is a reflection of popular belief: a ghost without a purpose is not a good plot device.

The main problem for earlier writers was a theological one:

---

[23] Davies, pp. 4–6.

how could a spirit return before the resurrection? For James VI and I, it was entirely possible for the Devil and witches to root up bodies, like swine, to borrow his comparison, and use them for their own ends, especially in the case of unfaithful persons.[24] The crucial point for us is that we see a differentiation between visions or fantasies and the spirits themselves. Earlier writers were well aware that some people saw things that were not there, but did not use this to explain (or explain away) all such incorporeal manifestations.

Writers such as James VI and I remained certain that, if they were not the malicious manipulations of witches and devils, ghosts were spirits of the dead. The problem is that, given the range of apparent phenomena reported, which includes 'ghosts' of the living, 'ghosts' of the future, even 'ghosts' of inanimate objects, and, under certain experimental conditions, artificially created 'ghosts', they cannot all be spirits of the dead.

Ghostology

When the Swedish scientist Carolus Linnaeus proposed his classification of the Earth's life forms in the eighteenth century he looked to the organisms' reproductive systems to differentiate them. If ghosts are the mirror and inverse of the living then we should develop a classification based on their *destructive* systems, that is, the nature of their functional interaction, not with each other, but with the living. However, in some cases ghosts appear to have no functional interaction with the living, leaving us with a classification based largely on appearance. We should also expect that a process of *unnatural* selection has matched the pace of evolution to produce the currently reported range of phenomena.

Even before the ghosts of modern machinery were reported people wondered why ghosts of the dead appeared wearing clothes. One of the earliest to pose the question was the philosopher Thomas Hobbes in 1651 within the wider debate of the

[24] James VI and I, p. 36.

problem of the spirit or soul itself. Hobbes surely knows the answer now, as it is said that his ghost can be heard muttering and singing to itself at Hardwick Hall in Derbyshire where he died. Popular culture solutions, like that given in the film *Ghost Town* (2008), is that ghosts wear the clothes (or lack of them) they died in. This seems logical for all those cavaliers, nuns, monks, and so on, but there are cases of ghosts reportedly appearing in different clothes at different times, or wearing apparently new clothes. In 1852, one writer mockingly posed the solution that the clothes were ghosts too, the spirits of 'all the socks that never came home from the wash' and so on. In fact, ghost socks may not be entirely out of the question. In the late 1960s a flock of supernatural headgear – top hats, bonnets, caps – flew through a house in Killakee, Ireland, during a poltergeist outbreak.[25]

What would be the ghost story without the phantom coach replete with ghostly horseteam? The idea of ghostly coaches and carriages is a well-known staple of the ghost story. We have already seen how one featured so prominently in the early period of the Borley Rectory haunting. Others career about the highways and byways of Britain: a headless coachman drives his team of four black horses through Brockley Combe in Somerset; in the 1970s a car driver was alarmed to see an old coach and horses bearing down on him outside Bungay in Suffolk; the ghost of Boudicca, Queen of the Celtic Iceni tribe and thorn in the Romans' side in the first century CE, has been seen driving her chariot along the old Roman road Ermine Street as it passes near Cammeringham in Lincolnshire.[26] But with the development of technology we have also seen an evolution of apparitions to include trains, cars, lorries, ships and aeroplanes.

---

[25] Thomas Hobbes, *Leviathan*, 1651, p. 374; *Saturday Review*, 19 July 1852, p. 268; Anna Claybourne, *Ghosts and Hauntings*, Usborne, 2000, p. 2; Richard Freeman, 'Just Too Weird!', *Paranormal*, 50, August 2010, p. 44. On the question of different/new clothes see the cases given in Elizabeth Nowotny-Keane, *Amazing Encounters: Direct Communication from the Afterlife*, David Lovell, 2009, pp. 21, 92.

[26] Spencer, pp. 185–8.

On 28 December 1879 the evening train on the Edinburgh to Aberdeen line was battling stormy weather to reach Dundee station on time. As North British Locomotive 224 and six carriages pulled out onto the Tay Bridge, severe gales estimated to be Force 10 or 11 on the Beaufort scale lashed what was then, at nearly two miles, the longest rail bridge in the world. As the train steamed onto the highest middle section the structure gave way, sending engine, carriages, passengers and all plummeting 88 feet into the dark waves below. 'And the Demon of the air seem'd to say,' as the poet William McGonagall put it, '"I'll blow down the Bridge of Tay".' All of the estimated sixty to seventy-five passengers were lost. The stumps of the old foundations can still be seen running alongside the new bridge, and on 28 December every year at approximately 7.15 p.m. the ghost of the train can be seen charging headlong into the darkness and its doom, or so it is said. Dundee-based group Paranormal Discovery attempted to investigate the haunting in 2007. As well as noting that ghost stories were still doing the rounds in the local pub, several team members witnessed unexplained lights.[27]

Across Britain the Age of Rail has left its mark. The Southend to Sheffield line has a ghostly ticket inspector who was killed in 1913 whilst saving a child who had fallen onto the tracks. A sleeping car said to have been used as a brothel by the Germans during WWII, which is now in the National Railway Museum, is thought to be haunted; as well as the museum itself. In the 1950s the dilapidated parcels depot, Mayfield Station, was reputedly haunted by the ghost of a workman who had fallen to his death down a deep shaft there. Stockholm's metro is said to be haunted by the *Silverpilen* ('Silver Arrow'), an unpainted aluminium train from the mid 1960s. With more than 250 route miles and over 270 stations, the London Underground also has

[27] Tom Martin, taybridgedisaster.co.uk, accessed 4 September 2010; Paranormal Discovery, http://www.paranormaldiscovery.co.uk/taybridge.htm, accessed 4 September 2010; William McGonagall, 'The Tay Bridge Disaster', 1880, in Chris Hunt (ed.), *William McGonagall: Collected Poems*, Birlinn, 2006.

its share of ghosts: an ancient Egyptian in the disused British Museum station; a man in black at Marble Arch; and the sounds of screaming still heard more than half a century after the wartime Bethnal Green station disaster.[28]

If not actually haunted, the car in which Archduke Franz Ferdinand and his wife were assassinated in Sarajevo on 28 June 1914 certainly had the reputation of being cursed. Successive owners met accident and death until the car was destroyed during an Allied bombing raid on Vienna in WWII. One of the earliest ghost cars is the chauffeur-driven 1920 Daimler Landaulette seen by a driver in 1967 in Devonshire on the Modbury to Garabridge road. The Revd David Warner of Wombwell, Yorkshire, was surprised one day when his car switched itself on and drove off. 'If it acts possessed again,' he said, 'I shall have to exorcise it.' Other incidents involve car lights being seen approaching then mysteriously vanishing, such as those seen outside Moretonhampstead in 1969 and at Penhill Beacon in the late 1990s.[29]

The first 'phantom lorry' appeared in 1930 during the inquest into the death of motorcyclist Charles Ridgway on the A75 between Hyde and Mottram-in-Longdale. According to Ridgway's cousin, Albert Collinson, who had been riding pillion and was seriously injured in the accident, a lorry had backed out of a narrow opening in front of them, causing Ridgway to swerve and lose control of his motorbike. The police found no such opening and no lorry tracks. But the investigation did reveal that the area was a mysterious accident black spot, despite being a straight stretch of well-maintained road. More accidents were to follow. One even involved a pedestrian who was apparently run over by the phantom lorry. One of London's trademark red double-decker buses haunted the junction of St Mark's

---

[28] Spencer, pp. 196–8; Bengt af Klintberg, *Råttan i pizzan*, Nordstedts Förlag, 1992; David Brandon, 'Spooks on the Tube', *Paranormal*, 55, January 2011, pp. 14–19.

[29] Nigel Blundell and Roger Boar, *The World's Greatest Ghosts*, Octopus, 1983, pp. 117–18, 129; Spencer, pp. 191–3.

Road and Cambridge Gardens in Kensington, causing several accidents before the dangerous bend was remodelled.[30]

Even a stretch of modern road, the A616 bypass around Stocksbridge in South Yorkshire, has acquired a reputation for being haunted. Car accidents are attributed to the phantom monk, seen on several occasions by private security guards, police officers, and many others. The well-known UFO researcher and lecturer in journalism Dr David Clarke covered the stories as a reporter for the *Sheffield Star*, coming up with the memorable headline 'Ghostly Stories of Police 'n' Spectre'.[31]

The seven seas play host to many hauntings, none more famous than the legendary *Flying Dutchman*. One of the most dramatic sightings came from a sixteen-year-old midshipman aboard HMS *Inconstant* as it steamed off the coast of Australia on 11 July 1881: 'At 4 a.m. *The Flying Dutchman* crossed our bows. She emitted a strange phosphorescent light as of a phantom ship all aglow'. The young sailor was Prince George, later King George V of Great Britain. A total of thirteen other men witnessed the apparition that morning and it has been sighted many times since. The schooner *Lady Lovibond* sank with all hands on 13 February 1748 and has reputedly appeared every fifty years to the day off the coast of southern England. A WWII landing craft flying the Cross of Lorraine, the flag of the Free French forces, was sighted in difficult weather off the coast of Devon in 1959, fourteen years after the end of the war.[32]

Ghosts also appear onboard ship. A phantom appeared to Captain Rogers of the *Society* as it made for Virginia, New England, in 1664, whose timely warning saved the vessel from shipwreck. The WWI German submarine UB65 was reputedly haunted by the ghost of its second officer, despite being

---

[30] Spencer, pp. 188–9, 190.

[31] Steve Mera and Kirst D'Raven, 'Taking Stock of Stocksbridge', *Paranormal*, 55, January 2011, pp. 58–63 – the authors were sceptical about the stories and reported that a man calling himself 'Dave from Wakefield' had confessed to staging the 'haunting' himself.

[32] Blundell and Boar, pp. 92–3.

exorcised by a Lutheran pastor, until destroyed by a mysterious explosion in 1918. John Smith, ship's engineer aboard the *Queen Mary* said he heard sounds like rushing water. In 1988 Tony Cornell and William Roll used a sound-activated recorder to capture bangs, rushing water and human cries. During WWII the *Queen Mary* had collided with a British frigate: some 300 men had been lost that day. These were not the only ghosts still onboard. Davy Jones's Locker will no doubt continue to give a momentary lease of freedom upon the surface to all those poor souls lost at sea.[33]

After the Wright Brothers' historic flight in 1903, it could only be a matter of time before the skies were filled with their share of ghosts, too. Bircham Newton aerodrome in Norfolk saw service through both world wars and, if accounts are to be believed, is still doing so despite being disused. A film crew there to shoot a management training video instead caught sounds of aircraft engines, human voices and machinery; in fact, all the noise and bustle of a busy hangar in active use. Other members of the film crew also saw ghostly figures in RAF uniform and enquiries revealed a history of hauntings. A lone Spitfire can sometimes still be heard as it returns from a sortie to the famous Battle of Britain airfield at Biggin Hill in Kent. Some witnesses even claim to have seen it perform a victory roll over the runway. The villagers of Hawkinge near Folkestone have heard the unforgettable drone of a Nazi V1 'flying bomb' flying overhead decades after the event.[34]

Of course phantom objects are not restricted to forms of transport. H. Porten claimed to see the face of his dead father in a worn area of wall in his living room in the 1950s. A haunted concrete floor at Street Real 5, Bélmez de la Moraleda, Spain, has produced mysterious images of faces since 1971. Known as

---

[33] Dennis Bardens, *Ghosts and Hauntings*, Zeus, 1965, p. 220; Blundell and Boar, pp. 92–3, 97–9; William Roll, Review of Tony Cornell, *Investigating the Paranormal*, Parapsychology Foundation, 2002, *Journal of Parapsychology*, 67, 2003, p. 191.

[34] Blundell and Boar, pp. 121–3.

La Casa de las Caras ('The House of the Faces') the property has drawn thousands to witness the allegedly paranormal phenomena. The German parapsychologist Hans Bender sealed some of the faces under transparent plastic and, when they continued to develop, was convinced that they must be paranormal in origin. The theory was that the phenomena were unconscious 'thoughtography' produced by the house's owner, María Gómez Cámara. However, it has also been suggested that several constituents of paint found in a chemical analysis of the floor, oxidizing substances, or even chemical stain removers were used to artificially manufacture the faces.[35]

Clocks often become paranormal foci, perhaps because of their connection to time and hence mortality. The winged hourglass, symbolizing *tempus fugit*, is a frequent *memento mori* and funerary motif. A haunted grandfather clock terrified Elliott O'Donnell (1872–1965) at a friend's house one Christmas with erratic ticking, violent rocking motions and even, at one point, speaking prior to the death of its owner. It was not the only such oddity O'Donnell had come across. He told of other spirit-infested grandfather clocks: one that whined whenever catastrophe loomed for its owners; one that made a thumping noise to portend death; and one where a hooded face would sometimes peer out instead of the clock face. Keeping up with the times, a letter writer to *Paranormal* magazine claimed to have a haunted clock-radio that patriotically turned itself on for the national anthem on Radio 4 and then off again.[36]

Furniture itself can also acquire a supernatural reputation. An old oak chest, blood-stained and coffin-shaped, reputedly caused paranormal disturbances at Stanbury Manor in West

[35] H. Porten, *The Miracle of the Walls: A Revelation of Life After Death*, self-published, 1954; César Tort, 'Bélmez Faces Turned Out to Be Suspiciously Picture-like Images', *Skeptical Inquirer* 19 (2), March/April 1995, p. 4; Luis Ruiz Noguez, 'Are the Faces of Bélmez Permanent Paranormal Objects?', *Journal of the Society for Psychical Research*, 59, 1993, pp. 161–71.

[36] Elliott O'Donnell, *Byways of Ghost-Land*, William Rider and Son, 1911, pp. 34–7; Rachel [no surname], 'Somewhat Alarmed', *Paranormal*, 50, August 2010, p. 77.

Yorkshire, leading then owner Mr T. A. Ley to nickname the entity 'Old George'. Mrs Barbara L. Barnes of Waterside, Barton-on-Humber, got more than she bargained for when she bought an antique chair. She and one of her children reported seeing the apparition of a kindly old man sitting in it on more than one occasion. A haunted wheelchair trundled about on its own in a house on Starnes Avenue, Asheville, North Carolina. Rocking chairs that rock by themselves are, of course, another mainstay of the ghost story, but there are attested cases, such as the rocking chair that belonged to Stella Metchling in Charlotte, North Carolina.[37]

I remember an odd occurrence that happened to me in the summer of 2008. It was the opening day of my first exhibition on witchcraft. The town in France where I lived at the time had graciously lent one of its historic buildings, a restored pigeonier called Le Colombier. The exhibits had all been installed the night before, the doors stood open and we stood waiting as the clock ticked down to our official opening. As we waited, a chair made of bent tubular metal collapsed slowly as if a heavy weight had sat down upon it. There were five of us in the room and all of us watched the chair crumple. I was rather pleased – it was a suitable beginning to an exhibition on witchcraft, after all – but the two town employees who worked there looked at each other nervously. No one had been sitting on the chair prior to its collapse. As far as I know it was relatively new: there were no obvious signs of wear and tear. But the logical explanation is that it must have been metal fatigue. Judging by the scared looks, not everyone else was so sure.[38]

Strange indeed, but not quite as terrifying as Elliott O'Donnell's story of the 'Boggle Chair'. Staying in another grand country house for Christmas, as was his wont, O'Donnell, because of his special interests, was conducted to the haunted

---

[37] Bardens, pp. 226, 228–31.
[38] 'La Sorcellerie en France', 15–29 June 2008, Bureau du Tourisme, Le Colombier, Place du Colombier, Mouzon, Ardennes.

room to there spend the night. The room was coffin-shaped, darkly panelled, swathed in ominous shadows and 'charged to the very utmost with superphysical impressions'. Filled with vintage wine and good food, O'Donnell bravely managed to fall asleep almost at once. He was soon woken by creaking sounds coming from a black ebony chair. O'Donnell reasonably dismissed the sound as the usual creaking of old wood, but as he listened he became aware of the sound of 'stealthy respiration'. As he looked in the direction of the chair he could see 'two, long, pale, and wholly evil eyes' that held him transfixed. The spell was only broken by the arrival of noisy carollers outside the house. O'Donnell sat up on two subsequent nights to observe the phenomenon. He was not disappointed. On the third night, lying paralysed in bed, he was strangled into unconsciousness by the malevolent entity, or so he said. The chair had been bought in Bruges and it had either been the one in which a wicked monk called Gaboni had died or had stood in the studio of a painter of the grotesque, where, it was suggested, it had absorbed his bizarre thoughtforms.[39]

Reports emerged from Ghana in 2009 of another 'haunted chair'. Apparently, the then Ghanaian Parliament's Minority Leader, Alban Bagbin, was 'very uncomfortable' on his new seat after a 'piece of traditional concoction' was discovered affixed to its underside. This was later described as 'a piece of lead probably laced with juju'. As the new parliament convened on its first day, he 'nearly fell off' the chair, sparking rumours of supernatural involvement. A three-man committee was formed to investigate the matter.[40]

---

[39] O'Donnell, pp. 230–43.

[40] 'Parliament Investigates "Haunted" Chair Saga', ModernGhana.com, 28 January 2009, http://www.modernghana.com/news2/200463/1/parliament-investigates-haunted-chair-saga.html, 3 September 2010; 'Parliament Investigates "Haunted" Chair Saga', ThinkGhana.com, 28 January 2009, http://www.thinkghana.com/tools/printnews/news.php?contentid=26229, accessed 3 September 2010; 'MPs Hunt Juju', ModernGhana.com, 29 January 2010, http://www.modernghana.com/news/200591/1/mps-hunt-juju.html, 3 September 2010.

Certain pictures themselves by their verisimilitude seem closer to magic than art and haunted by the figures depicted in them. In 1965 Dennis Bardens (1911–2004), journalist and creator of BBC TV's *Panorama* programme, recalled having inadvertently given a haunted picture as a present. A friend of the occult artist Austin Osman Spare (1886–1956), Bardens once gave one of the artist's pictures to an unidentified female friend. It was one of Spare's 'Magical Stelle', a mysterious coded invocation to Spare's inner demons. Bardens' friend was soon desperate to return the work, blaming a run of bad luck on it. 'The thing,' said Bardens, 'seemed to have a baleful influence'.[41]

In 2000 Bill Stoneham's 1972 painting *The Hands Resist Him* was put up for auction on eBay. It shows a five-year-old boy standing next to a life-size female doll in front of a glass door. Behind them hands are pressed up against the glass. In the sale's description it was claimed that the figures could come to life: 'One morning our four-and-a-half-year-old daughter claimed that the children in the picture were fighting and coming into the room during the night.' There was even a photograph showing the doll threatening the boy with a gun. Quickly becoming known as 'the haunted eBay painting', thousands of curious visitors were accessing the page, some reporting that it made them violently ill, faint, or feel as though an 'unseen entity' had gripped them, whilst children reportedly screamed on seeing it. Bidding went from an initial $199 to end at $1,050. A lengthy disclaimer sought to absolve the sellers from any legal liability resulting from these claims.[42]

Sports equipment has also been known to exhibit supernatural phenomena. In 2005 a woman in St George, Ontario, Canada, bought a set of antique lawn bowls from a junk shop. That night she was woken by a loud thunk and the sound of one of the balls rolling across the floor. There is even the story of a haunted trampoline in the US. Three children all aged around

---

[41] Bardens, p. 233.
[42] Gavin Bevis, 'The eBay Haunted Painting', BBC.co.uk, July 2002.

nine years old were lying on a trampoline when they saw a face appear underneath it: an orange face with black hair and black-and-blue eyes. The trampoline then started shaking violently and the face let out a terrifying scream. The children ran inside and watched as a gang of spirits appeared to take over their playground, bouncing on the trampoline, swinging on the swings and bobbing up and down on the see-saw. However, the most unlikely ghost has to be the bag of soot that lurks in a lane in Crowborough, East Sussex, waiting to pounce on unsuspecting passers-by.[43]

The most notable absence in the list of ghostly inanimate objects is buildings. Whilst the 'haunted house' is the basis of so many cases, there is no apparitional house in itself. Why this should be so is not clear. The range of locations is diverse in the extreme, from castles and stately homes to council houses and lampposts. The grander sorts of building probably feature more often in the ghost hunter's guidebooks simply because they have been around the longest, although there is an argument that the types of construction materials themselves could be contributory if not actually causal. The single exception I have uncovered so far is Sir Victor Goddard's sighting of an airfield, complete with hangars, aircraft and personnel, about five years before it was built, and here we must note that this is much more in the nature of a premonition than a classic haunting.[44]

G. W. Lambert categorized a number of cases involving buildings and features of the landscape as 'phantom scenery'. The most famous cases were the vanishing buildings/features of Boscastle, Bradfield St George, Hailsham, Man Sands and Versailles. Members of the Society for Psychical Research managed to track down these alleged phantoms and establish

---

[43] Richard Freeman, 'Just Too Weird!', *Paranormal*, 50, August 2010, pp. 42, 44; 'Strawberry Girl', 'Haunted Bowling Balls', About.com, January 2008, http://paranormal.about.com/library/blstory_january08_05.htm, accessed 2 September 2010; Maddie, 'Haunted Trampoline', About.com, June 2008, http://paranormal.about.com/library/blstory_june08_21.htm, accessed 2 September 2010.
[44] Blundell and Boar, p. 116.

that they were real. The explanation then was simply one of what Lambert called 'mislocation': the percipients looked in the wrong places when searching for the original feature. Only the Georgian house in Hadleigh that apparently appeared and disappeared one day in 1946 remained undiscovered by diligent researchers, at least until the late 1990s. Melvin Harris found the house on maps of a local authority neighbouring those that had already been checked.[45]

Orbs

Who could forget the scene in the film *The Omen* when successive photographs of the priest show a dark, spear-like shape moving towards him? Invisible to the naked eye, it seemed as though the camera that never lies could also capture the supernatural. For many ghost hunters it also seems as if their cameras have recorded an invisible paranormal reality lurking beyond the grasp of our human senses. The internet buzzes with talk of spirit orbs, ghost orbs, even unicorn orbs, as well as plasmoids, 'ectoplasm', vortices and rods. 'In the hundreds of Orb pictures we have examined we have seen the spirits of those who have passed away', argue Diana Cooper and Kathy Crosswell in their 2009 book *Enlightenment Through Orbs*. The International Ghost Hunters Society stated 'we discovered that an orb represented the soul of a departed person'. However, according to Maurice Townsend, writing for the Association for the Scientific Study of Anomalous Phenomena (ASSAP) website, 'there is overwhelming evidence that orbs are out of focus bits of dust and raindrops'.[46]

---

[45] G. W. Lambert, 'Phantom Scenery', *Journal of the Society of Psychical Research*, 42, 1963, pp. 1–6; M. H. Coleman, 'Phantom Scenery', *Journal of the Society of Psychical Research*, 63, 1998–99, pp. 47–8.

[46] Diana Cooper and Kathy Crosswell, *Enlightenment Through Orbs*, Findhorn Press, 2009, p. 55. International Ghost Hunters Society (IGHS) quoted in John Potts, 'Ghost Hunting in the Twenty-First Century', in James Houran

Giant shadows of unseen people across the tunnel wall, running, intent on killing – it is one of the most abiding images of the film *28 Days Later*, but for some it has also become a hideous reality. The earlier shades and shadows – the Greek *skia* (σκιά) and Latin *umbra* of the Classical world – have found a new lease of life, if one can use that term, as 'shadow people'. Often seen as a new phenomenon, the concept is not a new one, but it has become extremely popular. The range of interpretation is drifting, too, from ghosts to extraterrestrials to the undead to demons to angels, although they rarely seem to be benign.

In the early years of the twentieth century, Elliott O'Donnell recounted a time when he met what he described as 'a tall, black figure, its polished ebony skin shining in the moonbeams'. It moved without sound and had no face, only two sinister slit-like eyes. Then there was the haunted oak chest from Limerick, bought by a Mrs McNeill, that acted like a magnet to shadowy entities: 'She actually saw them gliding towards the house, in shoals . . . Shadows of all sorts . . .'[47]

One of the earliest encounters with the new shadow people was reported by the editor of *Paranormal* magazine, Richard Holland. In 1976 during a second phase of poltergeist activity in Holland's childhood, he started to see 'swiftly moving shadows' out of the corner of his eye. Ranging from six to ten inches in length they would 'slither across the floor like slicks of oil'. Maurice Towns recalled how, as a child in 1979, he saw 'a huge dark muscular male shadow materialize in front of me' on Exposition Boulevard, Los Angeles. One dark morning in 2007 he saw what he thought was the same shadow figure again. In 1983 a woman called Dottie was disturbed by her cat's growling one night after going to bed. In the

---

(ed.), *From Shaman to Scientist*, Scarecrow Press, 2004, p. 221. The IGHS claims to have coined the word 'orbs' in 1996. Maurice Townsend, 'Orbs – Are They Paranormal?', Association for the Scientific Study of Anomalous Phenomena, 2007, http://www.assap.org/newsite/articles/Paranormal%20orbs. html, accessed 17 December 2010.

[47] Brad Steiger, 'Who are the Shadow People?', *Paranormal*, 44, February 2010, pp. 54–9; O'Donnell, pp. 36, 41.

dim light she could make out a 'black shadow of a man with a hat on'. He was standing flat against the wall and the percipient thought he was trying to hide from the cat. When she switched on her bedside light the figure disappeared, but the cat went over to investigate the spot and 'sniffed and sniffed'. Dottie concluded, 'I'll never forget it and I know they are real'. Another early experience was recorded in 1999 by someone known only as Tracy G.: 'Often at night, but only when I am driving, I can see these dark shadows dashing across the road as I drive. They first started out to be cats, and on the highways I see people.' In 2000 another shadow cat joined the supernatural menagerie of an invisible bird and a 'black lizard' said to be haunting an American house. A shapeless black form lurks about the 'Devil's Elbow' on the B6105 in Longendale, UK. Possibly the earliest experience reported comes from author Jason Offut, who interviewed a man who said he had seen shadow people as a child in the late 1940s.[48]

As well as visible effects, there are ghostly phenomena of sound, smell and touch, but thankfully not taste. Footsteps and voices are common. The smell of lavender seems a favourite of the otherworld. I frequently get unaccountable wafts of a flowery odour as I sit in my study, seemingly from the corner of the room where I keep a picture of my late grandmother, although I would not go so far as to connect the two. At other times, things brush past people, or even, disturbingly, seem to apply direct physical force such as shoves, kicks, pokes and strangulation. And of

---

[48] Richard Holland, 'The Editor's Experience', *Paranormal*, 44, February 2010, p. 58; Maurice Towns, 'Muscular Shadow Man Stalker', About. com, September 2010, http://paranormal.about.com/od/shadowpeople/a/tales_10_09_19t.htm, accessed 2 September 2010; Dottie, 'Shadow Man with Hat', About.com, September 2010, http://paranormal.about.com/od/shadowpeople/a/tales_10_09_07t.htm, accessed 2 September 2010; Tracy G., 'Dark Shadows', About.com, December 1999, http://paranormal.about.com/library/blstory_december99.htm, accessed 2 September 2010; Kamala, 'Shadow Animals', About.com, January 2000, http://paranormal.about.com/library/blstory_january00.htm, accessed 2 September 2010; Paul Devereux, *Paranormal Review*, 15, 2000, p. 28. The 'shadow people' had, at this stage, not yet made it into popular collections, such as Guiley, *Enc. of Ghosts*. Jason Offutt, *Darkness Walks: The Shadow People Among Us*, Anomalist Books, 2009.

course, we also get reports of a 'sixth sense': awareness of presence, of being watched, or of feeling 'spooked'.

Electronic Voice Phenomena (EVP)

In the summer of 1959 the Swedish artist and film-maker Friedrich Jurgenson (1903–87) was recording bird song. When he played the tapes back he was surprised to hear faint voices. Intrigued, he conducted further experiments into what he called 'voices from space'. When he heard the voice of his deceased mother calling him by her pet name for him, he was convinced that he had established 'a radio-link with the dead'. The Latvian scientist Dr Konstantin Raudive (1906–74), then lecturing at the University of Uppsala, heard about Jurgenson's work and after making over 100,000 recordings of his own published his findings as *Breakthrough: An Amazing Experiment in Electronic Communication with the Dead* (1971). This led to the phenomena being called Raudive Voices for a time. Generally, the recordings sound like a word, or a short group of words of few syllables, what Dr Carlo Tajna called the 'psychophonic style'. Other researchers, such as David Ellis and Professor James Alcock, have suggested that such 'voices' could be misinterpreted terrestrial radio signals, static interference effects, or auditory apophenia (also pareidolia) – where the brain finds meaningful patterns in random stimuli. Professor Hans Bender in Germany thought that the effect might be a demonstration of psychokinesis, rather than a spiritual phenomenon. After the early audio experiments, German pensioner Klaus Schreiber became famous for receiving images of his dead relatives on a television set in the 1980s. Using a variation of Schreiber's technique, Martin Wenzel even claimed to have received a picture of Jurgenson. The range of phenomena reported has grown to include telephone, video, television and computers – leading to the new term 'instrumental transcommunication' (ITC).[49]

---

[49] See David Ellis, 'Listening to the "Raudive Voices"', *Journal of the Society of*

Ghost Hunters

Haunted House. – Responsible persons of leisure and intelligence, intrepid, critical, and unbiased, are invited to join rota
of observers in a year's night and day investigation of alleged
haunted house in Home Counties. Printed instructions
supplied. Scientific training or ability to operate simple instruments an advantage. House situated in lonely hamlet, so own
car is essential.

When Harry Price's advert for ghost hunters appeared in *The
Times* on 25 May 1937, 200 people applied. After careful screening, he chose forty-eight to help him investigate the infamous
Borley Rectory. Each of his ghost hunters, or 'Official Observers'
as they were called, was required to sign the '"Haunted House" –
Declaration Form', Price's unofficial secrets act, which prevented
any of his observers from acting independently. Price published
two books on the rectory and was writing another when he died in
1948, and it was this work, perhaps more than his other interests,
that has kept his name alive. Dr Paul Tabori called his 1950 biography *Harry Price – The Biography of a Ghost Hunter*.

Price was not, however, the first ghost hunter. An early case
of a 'ghost-detector' was recounted in the first issue of *The
Spiritual Magazine* in January 1860. Events took place twenty
years earlier in 1840 at 'the far-famed house' of Willington
Mill, near Newcastle. A certain Joseph Proctor, described as 'a
plain unimaginative Quaker', complaining of being troubled
by an apparition, attracted the aid of Edward Drury of
Sunderland, 'a valiant and self-confident man' and 'ghost-
detector'. Determined to solve the mystery, Drury and an
accomplice searched the house from cellar to garret to rule out

---

Psychical Research, 48, 1975, pp. 31–42; Arthur S. Berger, Gerd H. Hovelmann
and Walter von Lucadou, 'Spirit Extras on Video Tape?', *Journal of the Society of Psychical Research*, 58, 1992, pp. 153ff; James Alcock, 'Electronic Voice
Phenomena: Voices of the Dead?', *Skeptical Inquirer*, 21 December 2004.

any 'contrivances being played off upon them'. Drury then stationed himself in the haunted room, armed with pistols, whilst his confederate watched the stairs outside the door. At around midnight, as the candles had burnt low, 'the well-known female figure issued from the closet near Drury, walked or glided slowly past him, and approached his friend on the landing'. The writer notes that this was the moment to seize the phantom or discharge a pistol at it. Some say that he did try and grab the ghost, others that Drury's valiant character failed him. By all accounts, he screamed and collapsed on the floor. Briefly coming round, 'he went out of one fit into another till three o'clock in the morning'. His constant refrain was 'there she is. Keep her off. For God's sake, keep her off'. Proctor and his friend feared he had lost his mind, but he recovered after many weeks' recuperation. Drury's career as a 'ghost-detector' was singularly short and unsuccessful.[50]

William Hope Hodgson entertained the reading public in 1913 with his stories of a paranormal investigator in *Carnacki the Ghost Finder*. However, the first person to use the term 'ghost hunter' of himself was Elliott O'Donnell in the title of his 1916 book *Twenty Years' Experience as a Ghost Hunter*. In 1928 he published *Confessions of a Ghost Hunter*. Price caught on to the term and published his own *Confessions of a Ghost Hunter* in 1936 with chapters on the 'Talking Mongoose' and 'How to Test a Medium'.[51]

In 1937 Harry Price supplied instructions to his observers in the form of an eight-page booklet called 'The Alleged Haunting at B—— Rectory – Instructions for Observers', the colour of its cover lending it the more informal title of the 'Blue Book'. This covered such things as how to write up reports and what to do when dealing with unexplained phenomena. The Society for Psychical Research also sets out some guidelines on its website for today's investigators:[52]

---

[50] 'Modern Sadducism', *Spiritual Magazine*, 1.1, 1860, pp. 15–16; W. T. Stead, *Real Ghost Stories*, Grant Richards, 1897, pp. 261, 264–5.

[51] Davies, p. 95.

[52] Adapted from 'Notes for Investigators', spr.ac.uk, 2009, http://www.spr.ac.uk/main/page/notes-investigators-paranormal, accessed 16 December 2010.

1. Do not go by yourself.
2. Keep your relations with the experients/witnesses as relaxed and friendly as possible.
3. Keep an open mind.
4. Be tactful, or even reticent, in expressing your views.
5. Do not play the amateur psychiatrist.
6. Respect the confidentiality of the case.
7. Take particular care where children are involved.
8. Avoid publicity.
9. Learn from one's mistakes.

Price was involved with the first live broadcast from a haunted house. On 10 March 1936 the BBC rigged up four microphones to record the 'muffled footsteps and tappings, a cellar door which opens suddenly, and cold, uncanny winds' that writer G. B. Harrison said were reputed to haunt Dean Manor near Rochester in Kent. Price revealed his ghost-hunting methodology to listeners. Wax and powdered starch were sprinkled on the floor to detect footprints. Powdered graphite was used to dust for fingerprints. Thermometers were set up to record temperature drops – long associated with ghostly manifestations. The thermometer 'fluctuated inexplicably', said Harrison, but all he and the other listeners heard was 'the usual crackling in their loud-speakers'.[53]

Popular US TV shows *Ghost Hunters* and *Ghost Hunters International* feature the use of high-end equipment ranging from the K2 Deluxe EMF Meter, the Zoom H4N Handy Recorder for portable digital audio recording, to the Phonic Personal Audio Assistant for professional real-time digital audio analysis. Other investigators construct their own custom apparatus. Tony Cornell and Howard Wilkinson built what they called the SPIDER (Spontaneous Psychophysical Incident Data Electronic

---

[53] George Bagshawe Harrison, *The Day Before Yesterday: Being a Journal of the Year 1936*, Cobden-Sanderson, 1938, p. 65; Davies, p. 95. Also reported in the *Revue Métaphysique*, 1936, p. 157.

Popular Ghost-Hunting Equipment

Air Ion Counter	detects natural and artificial ion levels, either scaled to show negative ions (Negative Ion Detector, or NID) or both negative and positive ions
EMF Meter	measures a varying electromagnetic field (EMF) caused by AC or DC fields, usually calibrated to the frequency of mains electricity 50 Hz (US) and 60 Hz (European)
Gauss Meter	measures the polarity and strength of a static magnetic field in milli-Gauss (mG) or nanoTesla (nT) used to measure the earth's geomagnetic field, also described as a magnetometer
Beam Barrier Alarm	uses a transmitter and receiver unit to create an invisible infra-red beam barrier, triggering an alarm when broken
Motion Detector	uses a passive infra-red field to detect movement within a given area, typically 60 to 110° arc, triggering an alarm or other function
Hygro-Thermometer	measures maximum and minimum ranges of humidity, typically 20–99% relative humidity (RH); some models combine temperature measurement
IR Thermometer	non-contact thermometer using infra-red to measure ranges from -33 to +250°C in some models

Recorder), a complex array of sensors and cameras.[54] While this sort of kit would set the ghost hunter back several thousand pounds, for about a hundred pounds the beginner can assemble the basics of today's gadget-led investigation.

The typical starter kit includes a Gauss meter, beam barrier alarm, IR thermometer and a torch.[55] With these the ghost hunter can measure electromagnetic fields and temperature, set up an infra-red beam alarm to detect intruders (who may or may not be supernatural) and, most importantly, see in the dark. The range of devices available to measure everything from humidity to air ionization and ELF to LUX can be quite bewildering. Aimed at diverse professionals – sound engineers, electricians, health and environmental inspectors, etc. – such equipment requires technical expertise to operate and interpret correctly.

Without the benefit of any of this modern gadgetry, investigators at Borley were still able to come to some conclusions about the haunting. In 1947 the legendary ghost hunter Peter Underwood visited Borley for the first time. The burnt out ruins had already been demolished in 1944, but the paranormal anomalies associated with the site persisted. Underwood spent a night there with a colleague and both of them heard unaccountable footsteps in the dark. Rather than any specific instrumentation readings, he cited the number of years over which paranormal phenomena have been reported, the many witnesses to such phenomena and the diversity of the phenomena themselves as convincing proof of the claims associated with the site. After sixty years researching the haunting, he concluded that 'I do think Borley Rectory justified the term "the most haunted house in England"'. Ubiquitous bungalows now blight the spot, but for many it has become something of a paranormal pilgrimage site.[56]

---

[54] See Tony Cornell, *Investigating the Paranormal*, Helix Press, 2002; and the review in *Journal of Parapsychology*, 67, 2003, p. 190.
[55] Starter kit as advertised in *Paranormal*, March 2010, back cover, priced at £104.99.
[56] John Stoker, 'Memoirs of a Ghost-Hunting Man', *Paranormal*, March 2010, p. 55.

Poltergeists

'Marianne get help' read the writing scrawled on the wall: sharp, angular letters amidst illegible scribbles. Bravely, Marianne replied, writing underneath 'I cannot understand, tell me more'. Some days later more messages appeared: 'lights – Mass and prayers'; and on the opposite wall, 'Marianne please get help'. Marianne Foyster, her husband, Revd Lionel Algernon Foyster, MA, and their adopted daughter Adelaide, then two-and-a-half years old, had moved into Borley Rectory on 16 October 1930, only months after the haunting had driven out the beleaguered Smiths.[57]

'It can be said without fear of contradiction,' wrote Harry Price, 'that the Foyster occupation coincided with the noisiest, most violent, and most dangerous period in the whole recorded history of the Borley manifestations.' What began as a classic haunting, with nuns and headless coachmen, was turning into a much more serious poltergeist infestation. Price recalled a case in Amherst, Nova Scotia, during 1878–9, called 'The Great Amherst Mystery', that centred around a young girl called Esther Cox. She was threatened several times in mysterious written messages, including one on the bedroom wall that read 'Esther Cox you are mine to kill'. Did the Borley poltergeist ask Marianne for help, or was it warning her that she needed it?[58]

The idea that poltergeists were spirits of the dead is a relatively recent one. Up until the nineteenth century poltergeists were generally seen as the result of witchcraft or demonic interference, rather than spirits of the dead. The case now called the Epworth Poltergeist was not known as such by the Wesley family at its centre. Samuel Wesley referred to it as a 'deaf and dumb devil', whilst his daughter Emily called it 'Old Jeffrey' and attributed it to the spells of a witch or

---

[57] Glanville, pp. 97, 99.
[58] Price, pp. 64, 195.

cunningman. Writing in German, the theologian Martin Luther (1483–1546) was the first person to use the word 'poltergeist', meaning 'noisy spirit', in print. For Luther the answer was simple: poltergeists were the work of the Devil and one need only quote something of the Bible for them to go away, although he admitted that in some instances one just had to let the poltergeist get on with it. It would be another 300 years before it entered the English language via Catherine Crowe's book *The Night-Side of Nature* (1848). But it took Harry Price to popularize the term.[59]

[59] Davies, pp. 31–2, 74; Martin Luther, 'Ein Sermon auff das Evangelion von dem reychen man und armen Lazaro', first published 1523, in Ernst Ludwig Enders (ed.), *Dr Martin Luther's sämmtliche Werke: Kirchenpostille*, vol. 4, Hender & Zimmer, 1869, p. 17. See also 'Von Poltergeistern' and 'Historia, wie ein Poltergeist einen Pfarrherrn geplagt habe ...' in Martin Luther, *D. Martin Luther's sämmtliche Schriften, vol. 22: D. Martin Luther's Tischreden oder Colloquia*, vol. 3, Sebauer'sche Buchhandlung, 1846, pp. 34–6.

2. The Undead

The undead – vampires, mummies, zombies, and the rest – represent our collective fears of death (and sometimes life as well). As well they might – one need only think of the cold earth and the burrowing worm to cast a cloud over even the brightest day. Darkness and decay await us all, and heaven is but a compost heap of mouldering bones.

In their traditional aspects vampires embody the fear of the dead's return for revenge; mummies – within their original Egyptian cosmology – are an attempt to transcend death and live in the afterlife; and the Haitian zombies, the slave's fear of servitude after death. But all of them have been transformed in modern culture. Vampires have become a dream of triumph over death and power without conscience. Mummies now represent the revenge of the dead. The zombies we see from George A. Romero onwards are in actuality a fear of modern life, that we are dead to life without realizing it in our modern faceless, consumerist culture, controlled by the black magicians of advertising and government. With the modern zombie, it is ordinary people – our friends and neighbours – who become the enemy, an auto-immune disorder of society. With the modern vampire, it is extraordinary people – strangers and foreigners – who become the object of desire. In their many representations the undead tell us more about ourselves – the living – than they do about the dead. Perhaps that is because they themselves are not dead either. Before Boris Karloff played the mummy and Bela Lugosi Count Dracula, people really did believe that the dead could return from the grave and, what is more, they very often had what they thought was the evidence to prove it.

Vampires

In 1725 Frombald, the Imperial Provisor of the Gradisker District of the Holy Roman Empire, received a deputation of villagers from 'Kisolova', thought to be modern Kisiljevo in what is now the Republic of Serbia. The villagers were in a state of great alarm. One of their neighbours, a man by the name of Peter Plogojoviz, had died ten weeks ago and buried according to local custom. However, Peter had come back.[60]

His wife said that he had knocked on the door and demanded his *opanki*, the traditional peasant footwear of the region. After she fled the village, other people started saying that they had seen Peter, too. But not just seen him. They said Peter visited them in the night and lay upon them with such force that they felt the life being squeezed out of them. In 24 hours they were dead. Within the space of eight days, nine people had died from Peter's nightly visits. The villagers knew exactly what he was: one of the 'Vampyri', as Frombald carefully noted. To make sure, they wanted to exhume the body and look for the tell-tale signs – the body undecomposed, and the hair, beard and nails still growing – and they wanted the Imperial Provisor and a priest to be present. Frombald told them they would have to wait whilst he sent a request to his superiors in Belgrade. The villagers refused to wait, threatening to leave the village *en masse* before the vampire could kill everyone, as had happened, they

---

[60] Frombald, 'Copia eines Schreibens aus dem Gradisker District', *Wienerisches Diarium*, 58, 21 July 1725, Kayserliche Hof-Buchdruckerey, pp. 11–12. 'Kisolova' is the word used in the original text, but many later accounts use 'Kisilova'. 'Plogojowitz' is often given, as well as 'Plogojovic', but 'Plogojoviz' is the form as first published in 1725. See also Jutta Nowosadtko, 'Der "Vampyrus Serviensis" und sein Habitat: Impressionen von der österreichischen Militärgrenze', *Militär und Gesellschaft in der Frühen Neuzeit*, 8, 2004, 2, pp. 151–67.

said, sometime before. Frombald explained to them the necessity of waiting. Frombald ordered them to wait. Frombald no doubt shouted at them. But the Kisolovans were adamant. Frombald must have mulled the situation over carefully. Serbia had recently been snatched out of the jaws of the Ottoman Turks and the region remained politically tense. A deserted village could have repercussions, not least with his superiors. So it was, that he found himself taking the road to Kisolova with the priest and an escort of villagers.

As they entered the village, they found, no doubt to their surprise, that the body had already been dug up. Frombald lost no time in inspecting it:

> First, from the body and its grave there was not the slightest smell of death. The body, except the nose, which was fallen in, was very fresh. The hair and beard, also the nails, the old ones having fallen away, had grown on him. The old skin, which was somewhat whitish, had peeled off and a fresh new one had come out under it. The face, hands and also feet, and the whole body, were so recreated that they, in his lifetime, could not have been more complete. In his mouth, not without surprise, did I see fresh blood, which, after the general opinion, he had sucked from those killed by him. In sum, all the indications were presented which these people (as already noted above) should themselves have.[61]

As Frombald and the priest observed the scene – the fresh earth around the grave, the extraordinary condition of the body – the villagers were already busy sharpening a stake. Forthwith, they drove it through the heart of the corpse. Frombald was aghast as fresh blood spurted from the corpse's ears and mouth, and the priest must have blushed at the 'other wild signs' that Frombald declined to describe in his report 'out of high respect'. The body was then burnt to ashes. Frombald was careful to

---

[61] Frombald, my translation.

point out that if any mistake had been made in this matter – the desecration of a grave and the summary execution of someone who may not have been quite dead, come to mind – then all blame should rest squarely on the fear-crazed peasants.

On 26 January 1732 a report was submitted by Johann Flückinger, regimental surgeon to Baron Fürstenbusch's Infantry Regiment, to Army Headquarters Belgrade. Earlier in the month, he and several other officers had investigated a series of suspicious deaths in the village of 'Medwedia' in Serbia. The accused was a local 'Heyduck' named Arnod Paole or Arnond Parle (often written 'Arnold Paule' in modern accounts). The problem for the investigators was that five years earlier Paole had broken his neck in a fall from a haycart before allegedly committing the crimes. Locals told Flückinger that Paole had been plagued by a vampire some years previously near 'Cassova' in Turkish Serbia, but claimed to have cured himself by eating earth from the vampire's grave and smearing himself with its blood. However, twenty or thirty days after his death people started complaining that Paole had returned from the grave to torment them. Four people subsequently died. The local head-man, who had experience of these matters, ordered them to dig up Paole. His body had not decomposed and fresh blood was seen to come out of eyes, nose and ears; his nails and skin had fallen off to be replaced by new growth. According to local custom, they pierced his heart with a stake whereupon he uttered a loud cry. They burnt the remains to ashes and similarly disposed of the bodies of his victims.[62]

---

[62] W.S.G.E., *Acten-mäßige und Umständliche Relation von denen Vampiren oder Menschen-Saugern, Welche sich in diesem und vorigen Jahren, im Königreich Servien herfürgethan,* Augusto Martini, 1732, pp. 9–15; Johann Christoph Harenberg, *Vernünftige und Christliche Gedancken über die Vampirs,* Meißner, 1733, pp. 27–35. A number of variations between the two are to be noted. The date of the inquiry is given as 7 January in W.S.G.E., and both 7 and 17 January in Harenberg. Due to the inconsistent spelling of the period, the regimental surgeon is Flückinger in W.S.G.E., Flickinger in Harenberg; we find Arnod Paole in W.S.G.E., Arnond Parle in Harenberg; and the village is Medwedia in W.S.G.E., Meduegia in Harenberg. See also Klaus Hamberger

However, according to the locals, some of them had eaten the meat of livestock attacked by Paole. Within three months seventeen people died, some without any apparent disease, in the short space of only two or three days. The officers marched down to the cemetery and ordered the graves of the victims to be opened. Flückinger spread out his instruments and conducted a series of thirteen autopsies, which he carefully documented. A sixty-year-old woman called Miliza was found to be fat and healthy looking, more so, said those who had known her, than she had been in life. She had eaten the meat of sheep killed by vampires and was suspected of spreading the contagion further. The twenty-year-old Stanvicka (or Stanioicka), daughter-in-law of the Heyduck Joviza, was still florid and healthy looking with fresh blood coming from her nose. A bruise was found under her ear, one finger long. It was said that, whilst still alive, she had awoken one night with screams and in great anguish, saying that Joviza's dead son Millove (or Milloe) had returned from the grave and tried to strangle her. Within days she was dead. Other bodies were found to be in a state of normal decomposition despite, Flückinger noted, being buried in close proximity to those in the vampiric condition. Local gypsies were given the task of decapitating the bodies, which were then burnt and the ashes scattered in the Morava river. The decomposed bodies were reburied.

Then there was the case of Stephen Hubner. Some time in the year 1567 Hubner returned to the town of Trutnov in what is today the Czech Republic. The problem was that Hubner had died five months previously. Various deaths amongst the townspeople and their livestock were attributed to him. The magistrate ordered his body to be exhumed. Being found in the vampiric condition the body was decapitated and burnt, and the bodies of those buried next to him were burnt as well to prevent any spread of vampirism.[63]

(ed.), *Mortuus non mordet: Kommentierte Dokumentation zum Vampirismus 1689–1791*, Turia und Kant, 1992, pp. 49–54.

[63] Dudley Wright, *Vampires and Vampirism*, W. Rider, 1914, p. 168; Montague Summers, *The Vampire in Europe, His Kith and Kin*, Kegan Paul, Trench,

These incidents sparked off a public debate and a flurry of publications across the Holy Roman Empire and beyond. There had been an earlier discussion in the late seventeenth century, but now there were apparently well-authenticated cases to consider. In Leipzig, Michael Ranft published on the 'chewing dead' in 1728. In Jena, John Christian Stock wrote of the 'bloody cadavers' in 1732. In the same year, *A Curious and Very Wonderful Relation* about the Serbian 'blood-suckers' was published and further discussed by the medical practitioner Gottlob Vogt in his *Vampiren*. The following year, the theologian and Director of the Essen Gymnasium, Joannis Henr. Zopfius, presided over Christianus Fridericus van Dalen's public defence of the argument that 'Vampyres, which come out of the graves in the night-time, rush upon people sleeping in their beds, suck out all their blood, and destroy them'. The Archbishop of Trani, Italy, Giuseppe Davanzati, penned his own dissertation, winning the praise of Pope Benedict XIV for his efforts. The biblical scholar Dom Augustin Calmet noted in 1746 that:[64]

In this present age and for about sixty years past, we have been the hearers and witnesses of a new series of extraordinary incidents and occurrences. Hungary, Moravia, Silesia, Poland, are the principal theatre of these happenings. For here we are told that dead men, men who have been dead for several months, I say, return from the tomb.

Trubner and Co., 1928, p. 159. Wright gives the German name of Trautenau for the village; Summers, p. 159, 'Treautenau'.

[64] Michael Ranft, *De Masticatione Mortuorum in Tumulis*, Augustus Martinus, 1728; Johann Christian Stock, *Dissertatio de Cadaveribus Sanguisugis*, Littertis Hornianis, 1732; W.S.G.E., *Curieuse und sehr wunderbare Relation, von denen sich neuer Dingen in Servien erzeigenden Blut-Saugern oder Vampyrs*, n.p., 1732; Gottlob Heinrich Vogt, *Kurtzes Bedencken Von denen Acten-maeßigen Relationen Wegen derer Vampiren, Oder Menschen- Und Vieh-Aussaugern*, Augustus Martinus, 1732; Joannis Henricus Zopfius, *Dissertatio de Vamypris Serviensibus*, J. Sas, 1733; Giuseppe Davanzati, *Dissertazione sopra I Vampiri*, Fratelli Raimondi, 1744; Augustin Calmet, *Traité sur les Apparitions des Esprits et sur les Vampires*, Debure l'aine, 1751, trans. in Summers, p. 27. See also Hamberger. My thanks to librarian Hanke Immega, Aurich, for clarifying the question of the authorship of Zopfius, *Dissertatio*.

In 'The Travels of Three English Gentlemen', published in 1745, the word vampire first entered the English language. Staying in a town they called Laubach (Laibach, now Ljubljana) in what was then the Duchy of Carniola and now Slovenia, their unnamed landlord told them that:

Vampyres are supposed to be the Bodies of deceased Persons, animated by evil Spirits, which come out of the Graves, in the Night-time, suck the Blood of many of the Living, and thereby destroy them.[65]

Of course, the vampire did not first stir in the eighteenth century. We might trace the theme of blood-sucking back to the demonesses Lamia and Lilith, and the Empusae, Lamiae and Lilitum (see the chapter on demons). The idea of the dead returning from the grave is likewise ancient. We might think of the Nordic *draugr* who haunted burial howes and barrows, abusing those who ventured too close with harsh words and stone-throwing, or even sallying forth, sometimes with other undead companions, to ravage the land and slay the people. Then there are flesh-eating, blood-drinking fairies known in the folklore of Ireland and Scotland: *glaistigs, leanan sidhe* and *baobhan sith* – entities that used an attractive female countenance to seduce and destroy unwary males; as well as the night-walking corpses, the *marbh bheo*; and the blood-sucking *dearg-dul*. The folklore of Greece is haunted by the *strigla*, akin to the Italian *strega* and Roman *strix*, a witch who can assume the shape of a bird and so visit her victims and suck their blood. The genuine vampire in this region is the *vourkolakas* or *vrykolakas*, a term that further north shades into the werewolf as the Polish *vilkolak*.[66]

---

[65] Published in *The Harleian Miscellany*, 4, 1745, p. 358. Summers, p. 26, following the *OED*, stated that this was written in 1734.

[66] For the *draugr* see the story of Hrapp in the Icelandic *Laxdoela Saga* (c. 13th century) and that of Thorolf Halt-foot in the *Eyrbyggia Saga* (14th century). William Scrope told of a vampire encounter in the Scottish Highlands in his *The Art of Deer-Stalking*, A. Spottiswoode, 1838, p. 241. The living belief in the

In 2009 archaeologists excavating a mass grave on the Venetian island of Lazzaretto Nuovo discovered the skeleton of a woman with a brick rammed into her mouth. News quickly spread that they had unearthed a vampire. Matteo Borrini of the University of Florence explained that the brick had been placed there to prevent the corpse from chewing its shroud. He claimed that these remains, buried in 1576 following a plague outbreak, constituted the first vampire to have been forensically examined, although Peer Moore-Jansen of Wichita State University said similar skeletons had previously been found in Poland. Post-mortem practices to prevent the return of the dead have a long history.[67]

Noises, especially grunting 'like the sound of porkers', according to Philipp Rohr in 1679, were frequently heard emanating from graveyards, particularly, it was said, during plague epidemics. When the bodies were inspected many of them were found with torn shrouds and bitten or even partially eaten limbs, leading to the theory that the dead had done it to themselves. These 'chewing dead' were widely blamed for spreading the plague.[68]

Even after all the stakings and burnings, the vampire did not find eternal peace in the eighteenth century. Vampires prowled the area in and around Danzig, according to reports from 1820 and 1855. The occultist Dr Franz Hartmann (1838–1912) claimed to know of a number of vampire cases. A certain couple

---

Baobhan Sith was recorded as late as 1908 on the Island of Bernera, Lewis, in 'Fairy Tales', *The Celtic Review*, 5.18, October 1908, pp. 155–71. Bob Curran, *Vampires: A Field Guide to Creatures that Stalk the Night*, Career Press, 2005, pp. 55–79; Rennell Rodd, *The Customs and Lore of Modern Greece*, David Stott, 1892, p. 187; John Cuthbert Lawson, *Modern Greek Folklore and Ancient Greek Religion*, Cambridge University Press, 1910, pp. 364f.

[67] '"Vampire" Discovered in Mass Grave', *New Scientist*, 2698, 7 March 2009; Owen Davies, *The Haunted: A Social History of Ghosts*, Palgrave Macmillan, 2009, p. 71.

[68] Henerici Kornmanni, *De Miraculis Mortuorum*, I. Wolffii, 1610; Philippus Rohr, *Dissertatio Historico-Philosophica de Masticatione Mortuorum*, Michaelis Vogtii, 1679.

in Vienna in the 1880s had the misfortune to have a vampire for an uncle, who not only metaphorically bled them dry, but also consumed the life energy of the lawyer they had engaged to contest the uncle's sharp practice. Shortly before 1895, a young woman living near Vienna was troubled by the vampiric spirit of a spurned suitor who had committed suicide. Another incident from 1909 described as 'An Authenticated Case of Vampirism' reads like *Dracula* fan fiction. In 1900 Augustus J. C. Hare published his autobiography in which we find the story of Captain Fisher's encounter with the fearful vampire of Croglin Grange in Cumberland.[69]

Before they had faced the ghosts of Borley, Harry Price's National Laboratory of Psychical Research (NLPR) had encountered the vampire. In 1926 the Countess Wassilko-Serecki brought a thirteen-year-old Romanian peasant girl to London. The girl, Eleonore Zügun, was being tormented by an entity she called Dracu, the Devil. Captain Neil Gow of the NLPR began the investigation, noting on Monday, 4 October 1926 at 3.20 p.m., that 'Eleonore cried out. Showed marks on back of left hand like teeth marks'. Drinking tea less than an hour later, she 'suddenly gave a cry [. . .] there was a mark on her right hand similar to that caused by a bite'. The captain recorded that 'Both rows of teeth were indicated'. There are other instances of poltergeist activity causing bite marks, such as the bat-like 'puncture marks' noted in the Indianapolis 'Biting Poltergeist' case.[70]

In 1892 F. S. Krauss said that the Serbians still daubed tar crosses on their doors to ward off vampires. By the 1970s

---

[69] Hartmann, 'A Modern Case of Vampirism', *Lucifer*, 4, May 1889, pp. 241f; Hartmann, *Borderland*, III, 1895, cited in Summers, pp. 163–4 – also Hartmann, 'A Miller of D---', *The Occult Review*, November 1924, pp. 258–9; Augustus Hare, *The Story of My Life*, vol. 4, George Allen, 1900, pp. 203–8; Hartmann, 'An Authenticated Vampire Story', *The Occult Review*, September 1909; Summers, pp. 160–1.

[70] *Proceedings of the National Laboratory of Psychical Research*, 1, 1927, quoted in Summers, pp. 5–6; William George Roll, *The Poltergeist*, Cosimo, 2004, pp. 56ff.

Andrew Mackenzie, former Vice-President of the Society for Psychical Research and a frequent traveller to Eastern Europe in search of the paranormal, was unable to find anyone in Transylvania who believed in vampires. The vampires had moved. Like Bram Stoker's Count Dracula, they had left the romantic castles and forested wildernesses to descend upon the modern urban environment.[71]

When Rosemary Guiley interviewed three dozen or so self-proclaimed vampires for her book *Vampires Among Us* it was a disappointment to find that none of them claimed to have come back from the dead, surely the essential requirement of being a vampire, or to be centuries old. Guiley observed that those who called themselves vampires tended to be introverted and claimed an abusive childhood background. As a reviewer remarked: 'vampirism tended to be confined to wearing black, staying up late, and drinking a little blood every now and again'. [72]

'I tried different things,' said the twenty-something woman calling herself Hirudo. 'I was always thirsty, so I would drink gallons and gallons of water. But the craving didn't go away.' She was somewhat tall, red hair pulled back, swathed in a military greatcoat and talking to a journalist in a pub in Burnt Oak, London. 'It just clicked,' she continued. 'I knew I had this specific craving for blood.' For some that craving would become almost impossible to bear. The journalist in this case lived to tell the tale, but not everyone would be so lucky.[73]

Susan Walsh was an attractive blue-eyed blonde, making a living as a stripper in New York and trying to break into journalism with a story on vampirism. There were wild rumours of

---

[71] Friedrich Salomo Krauss, 'Vampyre im südslavischen Volksglauben', *Globus*, lxi, 1892, p. 326; Eric Farge, 'Obituary: Andrew Mackenzie, 1911–2001', *Journal of the Society of Psychical Research*, 66.2, 2002, p. 128; see Andrew Mackenzie, *Dracula Country: Travels and Folk Beliefs in Romania*, Arthur Baker, 1977.

[72] Rosemary Ellen Guiley, *Vampires Among Us*, Pocket Books, 1992; reviewed by Tom Ruffles in *Paranormal Review*, 1993, p. 49.

[73] Nick Compton, 'In Search of the Urban Vampires', *This is London*, 5 April 2002.

Mafia involvement and a government-vampire conspiracy to rule the world. She had allegedly told friends that she was frightened for her life and her boyfriend at the time said that she had been receiving anything up to fifteen threatening calls a day. One of Walsh's contacts in the vampire scene had warned that 'If you begin to hunt for vampires, the vampires will begin to hunt for you.' Walsh disappeared in 1996.[74]

When police were called to the flat of Aaron Homer and his girlfriend Amanda Williamson in 2010, they found a trail of blood leading up to the front door. Homer said that Williamson had been attacked, but the police found stab victim Robert Maley nearby. They were into 'vampire stuff and paganism' Maley told police, alleging that Homer had stabbed him after he refused to let the couple drink his blood. The homeless Maley had been staying with the couple and had apparently let them drink his blood in the past. He was lucky to escape with his life.[75]

For some it was pure blood lust, for others it was the supernatural attraction of blood as the life-force that drove them to murder. From the infamous Countess Bathory in the early 1600s, to the mysterious Atlas Vampire in the 1930s, to Richard Trenton Chase, the 'Vampire of Sacramento', in the 1970s, the 'Vampire Rapist' John Brennan Crutchley convicted in 1986, to 1990s murderer Roderick Ferrell who claimed to be a 500-year-old vampire called Vesago, there have always been individuals willing to cross the line.

'Pitch-black vampire seeks princess of darkness who hates everything and everyone.' When Manuela read those words in an advert in a heavy metal magazine in 2000 she knew she had

---

[74] Katherine Ramsland, *Piercing the Darkness: Undercover With the Vampires in America Today*, HarperPrism, 1998, pp. 1–4; T. A. Kevlin, *Headless Man in Topless Bar: Studies of 725 Cases of Strip Club Related Criminal Homicides*, Dog Ear Publishing, 2007, pp. 55–6.

[75] Michael Sheridan, 'Blood-Sucking "Vampires" Arrested for Attacking Homeless Man with Knife in Arizona, Police Say', *New York Daily News*, 10 October 2010.

found her soul mate. Daniel Ruda was a car-parts salesman in Bochum, Germany, who shared her love of the dark side. When she first met Daniel, Manuela had already been initiated into the underground vampire scene in London. 'We went out at night, to cemeteries, in ruins and in the woods,' she said. 'We drank blood together from willing donors.' She had even had special fangs fitted. With Daniel she would eventually turn to unwilling donors. Manuela would later deny it was murder, saying that Satan had ordered them to kill thirty-three-year-old Frank Haagen on 6 July 2001. Daniel smashed him on the head with a hammer before Manuela 'heard the command to stab him in the heart'. They then carved a pentagram into his flesh and drank his blood. The couple remained defiant in court as the judge handed down sentences of fifteen years for Daniel and thirteen years for Manuela.[76]

In Australia the high-profile trial of Evangelos Goussis for the shooting of crime boss Lewis Moran took the headlines in 2008, but an informant also implicated him in the murder of a self-confessed vampire. In 2003 the twenty-eight-year-old victim, a male prostitute called Shane Chartres-Abbott, was on trial for the brutal rape of a client. Before the violent assault Chartres-Abbott allegedly told his victim, a thirty-year-old Thai woman, that he was a 200-year-old vampire who drank blood to stay young. The woman was later found unconscious and covered in blood. There were teeth marks on her thigh and part of her tongue had been bitten off. Chartres-Abbott was later shot dead as he made his way to the County Court to give evidence. In 2009 a reward of Aus$ 1 million was offered for information to solve the case of the so-called 'gigolo vampire'.[77]

---

[76] 'Satanists Killed Man "on Devil's Orders"', BBC News, 18 January 2002; Rebecca Jones, 'Judgement Day for German Satanists', BBC News, 30 January 2002; Tony Helm, 'Last Kiss as Satanist Killers are Locked Up', *Daily Telegraph*, 1 February 2002. The *Daily Telegraph* gave the victim's name as Hackerts.

[77] Elissa Hunt, et al., 'Evangelos Goussis Named in Vampire Murder', *Herald Sun*, 30 May 2008; Keith Moor, 'Six Murder Charges Loom in "Vampire" Case', *Herald Sun*, 26 October, 2009 Keith Moor, 'Behind the Vampire Gigolo

Lead bullets are not the traditional way of dealing with supernatural blood-suckers. With instances of the true vampire diminishing, new strains of the monster have appeared. In 1896 Dr Hatmann detailed the 'psychic sponge', mental vampires who 'unconsciously vampirize every sensitive person with whom they come in contact'. He related the case of an old woman who hired young maids expressly for the purpose of absorbing them in this manner. In 1924 Dr Eugene Osty, director of the Institut Métapsychique Internationale, described the baneful animal magnetism of 'heart-vampires who burn and devour all affection approaching them'. But it would be Dion Fortune in 1930 who would establish the idea of what she called 'psychic parasitism' and what would later be known as psychic vampirism.[78]

'We thirst for life,' explained self-described psychic vampire Michelle Belanger, 'and we feed upon it.' Of course, Fortune offered advice on protecting oneself from psychic vampires. It would take a little longer for would-be psychic vampires to get their own manual. Belanger has written widely on the topic, as well as appearing on television programmes, such as History Channel's *Vampire Secrets* (2006), which also covered the disappearance of Susan Walsh. According to Belanger, 'a psychic vampire is a person who needs to take human energy from others in order to maintain their health and well-being'.[79]

Want to 'live beyond the usual human lifespan' and 'get your way with people'? The Temple of the Vampire, a legal entity in the USA since 1989, teaches that the vampire is a living god and offers you the chance to join their ranks for a membership fee

Shane Chartres-Abbott Murder', *Herald Sun*, 26 October 2009.

[78] Hartmann cited in Summers, pp. 134–5, as *Borderland*, III.3, July 1896, pp. 353–8; Eugene Osty, *Supernormal Faculties in Man: An Experimental Study*, trans. Stanley de Brath, Methuen & Co., 1923, p. 150; Dion Fortune, *Psychic Self-Defence*, Rider, 1930.

[79] Michelle Belanger, *The Vampire Codex*, self-published, c. 2000; re-released as *The Psychic Vampire Codex*, Weiser, 2004. Eleanor Goodman, 'Go Suck Yourself: Psychic Vampires', *Bizarre*, Hallowe'en 2008, p. 88; http://www.vampiretemple. com/, accessed 16 September 2010.

of $75. The Temple of the Vampire is only one of many organizations that have appeared, like blood stains on Count Dracula's shirt front, to celebrate the vampire lifestyle and network its followers. Others include Belanger's House Kheperu, Sanguinarius.org and the Vampyre Connexion.

Vampires are currently enjoying a vogue not seen since the eighteenth century. From Anne Rice's seminal *Interview With the Vampire* to Stephenie Meyer's *Twilight* saga a vein of popular interest has been tapped and shows no sign of running dry. Despite this, the latest research shows that very few people actually believe in vampires today: only 3 per cent in the UK.[80]

Some have looked to rare medical conditions to account for the origination of vampire beliefs. The disease of porphyria whose symptoms are photosensitivity and anaemia is a particular favourite. Blood drinking as a medical treatment in the case of porphyria is ineffective, however. Whilst a condition like porphyria might resemble folk ideas of vampirism it cannot explain them since these folk beliefs are specifically concerned with the problem of the returning dead, not with human illness.[81]

The condition of Plogojoviz's body seemed abnormal – paranormal – to the villagers, even to the Imperial Provisor and the regimental surgeon, but modern medicine has discovered that many of the traditional signs of vampirism are in fact part of the natural process of decomposition. When Frombald and Flückinger saw that the 'old' skin of the vampires had fallen away and had been replaced by a 'new' one, they were not entirely wrong. They had only incorrectly interpreted what we today know is 'skin slippage', the process by which the epidermis comes away from the dermis. The 'new' nails observed were probably simply the nailbeds themselves. The full and

---

[80] Populus, 'Morals, Ethics and Religion Survey', 8–9 April 2005, http://www.populus.co.uk/the-sun-moral-attitudes-090405.html, accessed 17 September 2010.

[81] Paul Barber, 'Staking Claims: The Vampires of Folklore and Legend', in Kendrick Frazier (ed.), *Encounters with the Paranormal*, Prometheus Books, 1998, pp. 374ff, first published in *Skeptical Inquirer*, 20.2, March–April 1996.

'healthy' appearance was caused by gases released during decomposition which bloat the body, hence the old woman who looked better fed than when alive. The florid or ruddy appearance can result from livor mortis (lividity) as the tissues become saturated with blood. The presence of 'fresh', i.e. liquid, blood is also possible: although blood normally coagulates at death, decomposition can cause it to liquefy again. The presence of blood in and around the mouth, taken as a sign of the vampire having sucked blood from the living, is caused by gas putting pressure on the lungs, so forcing blood from the lungs up into the mouth and nose.[82]

However, for all our medical advances we are still left with some untidy, indeed disturbing anomalies. What of the alleged sightings of the dead? What of the people who supposedly died after being visited by Plogojoviz, Paole and the rest? What of the marks on Stanvicka's neck?

Mummies

They could only work in winter. Even in November the sun was bright and warming. The shadows hid in the folds and wrinkles of the bare hills. It was a broken landscape. Lunar. A parched wadi at the edge of the vast desert, the 'hunting-ground of the tomb robber': the Valley of the Kings. And it was Howard Carter's last chance.[83]

The American lawyer and Egyptologist Theodore M. Davis had already pronounced the Valley to be 'exhausted' in 1912 after uncovering some thirty tombs. Carter knew the odds were against him. For five years, from 1917 to 1922, Carter had been working amongst 'open or half-filled mummy pits, heaps of rubbish, great mounds of rock debris, with, here and there, fragments of coffins and shreds of linen mummy-wrappings protruding from the sand'. The necropolis of Thebes was one

---

[82] Barber, pp. 374ff.
[83] George Edward Carnarvon and Howard Carter, *Five Years' Explorations at Thebes*, Oxford University Press, 1912, p. 1.

huge desecrated grave. Now, his patron, George Edward, 5th Earl of Carnarvon, had finally run out of patience.[84]

The valley echoed to the clatter of tools and voices in Arabic, as it had done on innumerable days past. They were digging near the tomb of Ramses VI, underneath the ancient remains of workmen's huts, when a stone step was discovered. It was the first of sixteen leading downwards into the sand. At the bottom of the steps they found a sealed doorway. There were hieroglyphs: Anubis over nine foes. The seal of the Royal Necropolis. Carter knew he had found the tomb of someone important; a tomb that was much older than that of Ramses VI above it. 'It was,' he said, 'a thrilling moment.' It had taken days to get this far, but now darkness was again descending and the full moon was already high. Carter had the hole refilled as a safeguard and returned home to cable Lord Carnarvon:[85]

At last have made wonderful discovery in Valley. A magnificent tomb with seals intact. Recovered same for your arrival. Congratulations.

When Carnarvon arrived, he had the sunken staircase cleared. This time they uncovered the whole of the sealed doorway and discovered seals bearing the cartouche of a royal name. It read: 'Living Image of Amun, Ruler of Upper Heliopolis'. They had found the tomb of Tutankhamun.

Breaking through the first wall they entered a tunnel heaped with debris. Laboriously clearing it all away they came to another sealed door again bearing the seals of the Royal Necropolis and Tutankhamun. Carter carefully broke a hole wide enough for them to see the astonishing sights within; the

[84] Theodore M. Davis, *The Tombs of Harmhabi and Touatânkhamanou*, Constable & Co., 1912; Carnarvon and Carter, p. 1.

[85] Howard Carter, *Tutankhamun: Anatomy of an Excavation. Howard Carter's Diaries*, pt 1, Griffith Institute, 2004, http://www.griffith.ox.ac.uk/gri/4sea1not. html, accessed 18 September 2010. John Venn and John Archibald Venn, *Alumni Cantabrigienses*, Cambridge University Press, 10 vols, 1922–58, pp. 337–8.

lamplight illuminated an Aladdin's cave of treasure guarded by the gilded and monstrous statuary of the funeral chamber.

Now would begin the slow and painstaking excavation of the tomb. It would be 16 February 1923 by the time they were ready to enter the burial chamber itself. But already strange incidents had been reported. A *New York Times* correspondent wired his paper with tales of what the native staff had supposedly said was 'a warning from the spirit of the departed King against further intrusion on the privacy of his tomb'. According to the journalist, Carter had installed a canary 'to relieve his loneliness'. Sitting down to dinner on 'the day the tomb was opened', the party was alarmed by a disturbance on the veranda and rushing out to investigate they 'found that a serpent of similar type to that in the crowns had grabbed the canary. They killed the serpent, but the canary died'.[86]

According to the former Chief Inspector of Antiquities for Upper Egypt, Arthur Weigall, this was a royal cobra: 'rare in Egypt, and seldom seen in winter [. . .] each Pharaoh wore this symbol upon his forehead'. He added:

> Those who believed in omens, therefore, interpreted this incident as meaning that the spirit of the newly-found Pharaoh, in its correct form of royal cobra, had killed the excavator's happiness symbolized by the song-bird.[87]

As he was about to enter the tomb, Carnarvon joked to the others that with all the chairs down there they could give a concert. Standing at the retaining wall of the tomb, Weigall, now a correspondent for the *Daily Mail*, turned to his neighbour: 'If he goes down in that spirit, I give him six weeks to live.' Carnarvon's half-brother, Colonel Aubrey Herbert, had also

[86] 'Times Man Views Splendors of Tomb of Tutankhamen', *The New York Times*, 22 December 1922.

[87] Quoted in Boris de Zirkoff, 'The Mystery of Egyptian Mummies', *The Theosophical Path*, 38.2, February 1930, p. 136.

entered the tomb. He is reported to have said, 'Something dreadful is going to happen to our family.'[88]

The theosophist Boris de Zirkoff, writing in 1930, said that above the unbroken seals to the tomb was an inscription:

> As for any man who shall enter into this tomb, as his mortu-
> ary possession, I will seize him like a wild fowl; he shall be
> judged for it by the Great God. The hand which dares to spoil
> my form will be annihilated; crushed will be the bones of
> those who desecrate my body, my images and the effigies of
> my *ka*.[89]

Shortly afterwards Carnarvon was bitten by an insect and developed blood poisoning. Carter rushed from the excavations to visit his sick bed at the Continental-Savoy Hotel, Cairo. 'Found Ld. C. very ill', he wrote in his diary for 21 March. Carnarvon's weakened constitution then fell prey to pneumonia. He died at 2 a.m. on 5 April 1923. He was fifty-six. The rumours quickly started.

The day after Carnarvon died *The New York Times* reported that 'Occultists advance stories of angered gods'. Back at the family seat of Highclere Castle, his three-legged dog Susie apparently howled at the moment of her master's death before collapsing lifeless herself. It was said that a number of people cancelled their bookings when they discovered that they would be sailing on the same ship as Lady Carnarvon and her husband's remains. In 1928 Mr E. Fothergill came to the conclusion, in his lecture entitled 'The Curse of Tut-Ankh-Amen', that Carnarvon's death had indeed been the result of supernatural assassination.[90]

---

[88] Weigall quoted in Julie Hankey, *A Passion for Egypt: Arthur Weigall, Tutankhamun and the 'Curse of the Pharaohs'*, I. B. Tauris, p. 4.; Herbert quoted in de Zirkoff, p. 137.

[89] De Zirkoff, p. 136.

[90] 'Carnarvon's Death Spreads Theories About Vengeance', *The New York Times*, 6 April 1923 – the story itself is dated 5 April; 'Carnarvon is Dead of

'Almost simultaneously with Lord Carnarvon's death,' wrote de Zirkoff, 'Howard Carter [. . .] was stricken down. Physicians could not diagnose his case. Death seemed imminent.' He lived, but by September 1923 Colonel Aubrey was dead. Carnarvon's friend George Jay Gould, another visitor to the tomb, died soon after. Other visitors met similar fates. Woolf Joel, heir to the 'Diamond King' Solly Joel, died of 'a strange malady'. In 1924 Sir Archibald Douglas Reid, engaged to X-ray the mummy, retired to bed feeling unwell and died some days later. That same year Professor Laffleur of McGill University died 'in a most mysterious way'. In September of that year H. G. Evelyn-White died by his own hand, saying in his suicide note, 'I knew there was a curse on me'. Professor Paul Casanova of the Collège de France died while at work in the tomb 'of the same mysterious illness'. Prince Ali Fahmy Bey was shot dead by his wife, whilst his secretary Hallah Ben passed away 'and the cause of his death was never ascertained'. In March 1926 Professor George Bénédite, Director of Egyptian Antiquities at the Louvre, 'died suddenly'. Countess Evelyn Waddington-Greeley committed suicide in Chicago. In 1930 the Hon. Richard Bethell 'was found dead at the Bath Club, Mayfair': he had jumped to his death. When the hearse carrying his body accidentally killed a boy, this, too, was attributed to the curse, as was the death of Weigall himself in 1934.[91]

The Director of the Egyptian Section of the Metropolitan

an Insect's Bite at Pharaoh's Tomb', *The New York Times*, 5 April 1923; 'Notes on Periodicals', *Journal of the Society of Psychical Research*, 24, 1928, p. 375; de Zirkoff, p. 137; Robert Hardman, '£12m Curse of King Tut', *Daily Mail*, 6 August 2009.

[91] De Zirkoff, p. 137 – J. C. Madrus had tabulated the curse-stricken victims for *The New York Times*, 28 March 1928; 'Aged Peer Dies in Seven Story Leap in London, Reviving Talk of Tut-ankh-Amen "Curse"', *The New York Times*, 22 February 1930; 'Hearse with Lord Westbury's Body Kills Boy; Museum Death also Laid to "Pharaoh's Curse"', *The New York Times*, 26 February 1930; 'A King's So-Called "Curse"', *The New York Times*, 9 March 1930; 'Death of Mr A. Weigall, Tut-ank-Amen Curse Recalled', *Daily Mail*, 3 January 1934; 'Curse of the Pharaohs Denied by Winlock', *The New York Times*, 26 January 1934; Hankey, p. 3.

Museum of Modern Art, New York, Herbert Winlock, refuted the idea of the curse. Speaking to reporters from *The New York Times* in 1934 he stated that only six of the original twenty-four people present at the opening of the tomb had died. Still, 25 per cent seems like a high mortality rate. Other accounts, such as that given by de Zirkoff, had already found thirteen victims with additional reports bringing the total to as many as fifteen, and more could no doubt be found.

Carter marvelled at how the body of Tutankhamun had escaped the depredations of robbers and miscreants through its millennia of repose and half-wonderingly added 'we may believe, as those ancient Thebans might readily claim, that Tut·ankh·Amen's long security is due to Amen·Re's protection'.[92] Protection for the pharaoh; a curse to everyone else – except in the Middle Ages.

Our word 'mummy' entered the language in the Middle Ages from medieval Latin *mumia* (and Old French *mumie*) as a medicinal ingredient. In a circa 1400 translation of Lanfranc's *Chirurgia Magnia* (1296) we read a recipe: 'take [. . .] mirre, sarcocol, mummie (*v.r.* mumie) [. . .] & leie it on þe nucha'. In 1615 we read its first use in the modern sense in George Sandys' travelogue *A Relation of a Journey*: 'The Mummes (lying in a place where many generations have had their sepultures) not far above Memphis'. The word comes ultimately from Arabic *mūmiyā*, 'embalmed body', derived from the embalming wax *mūm.*[93]

Ground to a powder, mummy was good for everything from abscesses to fractures and as an antidote to poison. It was a stock ingredient on apothecaries' shelves from the twelfth to seventeenth centuries and did not fall out of use until well into the eighteenth century. Indeed, one German pharmaceutical company was still listing 'genuine Egyptian mummy' in its catalogue in 1908. The great sixteenth-century mystico-physician

---

[92] Howard Carter, *The Tomb of Tut-Ankh-Amen*, Cambridge University Press, 2010, p. 38.
[93] Guido Lanfranc of Milan, *Chirurgia Magnia*, 1296; George Sandys, *A Relation of a Journey*, W. Barrett, 1615.

Paracelsus mixed his own 'balsam of mummy' and the even less appetizing 'treacle of mummy'. This popularity derived from the mistaken idea that mummies were preserved using bitumen – resin is used – and the belief among the ancients of bitumen's great therapeutic value. The Roman writer Pliny the Elder (23–79 CE) described all sorts of medicinal uses for bitumen, from eye infections to leprosy. The Greek writer and physician Pedanius Dioscorides (c. 40–90 CE) further cemented belief in its efficacy in his influential *De Materia Medica*.[94]

Over time the idea transferred itself from the supposed bitumen content to the actual cadaver. As well as mummy remedies, Paracelsus prescribed the use of human blood, fat, marrow and even excrement on the homeopathic principle that like cures like, showing how the body itself could be seen as a drug. The high demand for medicinal bodies led Oswald Croll (c.1560–1608), a professor at the University of Marburg in Germany, to posthumously publish a recipe for making one's own mummy, ideally from the 'Carcase of a red Man' who had been executed at the age of twenty-four – the youth and vigour of the living body was thought to be retained by the corpse. Mummy was included in the Royal College of Physicians' *Pharmacopoeia Londinensis* of 1618, which was officially sanctioned by King James VI and I, and in later editions. In 1752, Dr Johnson's friend Dr Robert James described mummy as 'a resinous, hardened, black shining Surface, of a somewhat acrid and bitterish Taste, and of a fragrant Smell'. He noted that there were three different types then available: the best was the 'Arabian', embalmed with 'Aloes, Myrrh and Balsam' and 'obtained in Sepulchres'; next was the 'Egyptian', 'a Liquament of Carcases seasoned with

---

[94] Warren R. Dawson, 'Mummy as a Drug', *Proceedings of the Royal Society of Medicine*, 21, 1927, pp. 34–9; Mark Greener, 'Corpses and Robbers', *Paranormal*, 52, October 2010, p. 27; Pliny, *Natural History*, v, 15; Louise Noble, '"And Make Two Pasties of Your Shameful Heads": Medicinal Cannibalism and Healing the Body Politic in Titus Andronicus', *English Literary History*, 70, 2003, p. 686.

Pissasphaltus'; and least was 'a Carcase torrified under the Sand, by the Heat of the Sun'.[95]

Whilst this horrifying medical cannibalism had turned many a poor patient into a ghoul, it is perhaps in Louis Penicher's *Traité des Embaumemens* of 1699 that we get the first horror story concerning the mummy. According to Penicher, a Polish traveller acquired two mummies in Alexandria, undoubtedly for medicinal uses, and had them shipped out. On board he was apparently tormented by strange dreams of two ghostly figures. Fearing the worst as the seas grew stormy, he ordered the bodies to be thrown over the side, and calm was restored.[96]

The nineteenth century would see such snippets of travellers' tales become fully fledged mummy stories. Perhaps the first mummy to be brought back to life is found in Jane C. Loudon's *The Mummy!* of 1827, which owes much to Mary Shelley's *Frankenstein*. Another hops out of the pages of Theophile Gautier's rather ludicrous romance *The Mummy's Foot* of 1840. Edgar Allen Poe had a group of scientists electrically revive a mummy in his 1845 social satire *Some Words With a Mummy*. We read of 'The dark, parchment-like skin, wrinkled and rough' in the anonymous *The Mummy's Soul* of 1862. Louisa May Alcott, famous for *Little Women*, has been identified as the anonymous author of *Lost in a Pyramid; or the Mummy's Curse* published in 1869. The popularity of the mummy was such that even Sir Arthur Conan Doyle turned his hand to the subject, first in 1890 with *The Ring of Thoth*, then in 1892 with the short story *Lot No. 249*. Here he presented the mummy in what is now a familiar role as the Golem-like automaton controlled by a diabolical, vengeful master. Bram Stoker, the creator of *Dracula*,

---

[95] Oswald Croll, *Basilica chymica*, n.p., 1609, trans. John Hartman as *Bazilica Chymica & Praxis Chymiatricae. Or Royal and Practical Chymistry*, John Starkey and Thomas Passinger, 1670, p. 156; Royal College of Physicians, *Pharmacopoeia Londinensis*, John Marriot, 1618; Robert James, *Pharmacopœia Universalis, or a New Universal Dispensatory*, 2nd ed., J. Hodges, 1752, p. 340; Noble, pp. 677–708.

[96] Louis Penicher, *Traité des Embaumemens selon les Anciens et les Modernes*, Barthelemy Girin, 1699, pp. 70–4.

published *The Jewel of Seven Stars* in 1903, but forsook the animated corpse for a ghost. The theme was now firmly cemented, embalmed as it were, in the horror genre.[97]

After Carnarvon's death, the media turned to the great writers of the day for their explanations. H. Rider Haggard – whose *She* echoed some of the mummy themes – wisely refused to comment on the curse. Conan Doyle, however, already searching for his dead son in the darkened séance rooms of Spiritualism, was drawn out to remark upon the possibility of 'elementals' within the tomb.[98]

The Curse of Tutankhamun is not the only mummy curse. There is the British Museum's 'unlucky mummy', for example, which was said, incorrectly, to have sunk the *Titanic*. However, it is the Curse of Tutankhamun that has remained the most enduring in the popular imagination. Anything untoward that happens to Lord Carnarvon's descendants is routinely reported as an effect, or possible effect, of the curse.[99] Indeed, anything untoward that happens to anyone remotely connected with the tomb of Tutankhamun is attributed to the curse. When she came into possession of samples taken from the tomb in the 1920s for bacteriological analysis, author Lesley-Ann Jones implicated the curse in a run of bad luck that took her to the brink of death with meningitis, skin cancer and violent robbery.[100]

But what of Howard Carter himself? He had been the one to find the tomb and break its aeons of grimly hallowed taboo. Surely he must have been blasted by the curse? Carter made no

---

[97] Lisa Hopkins, 'Jane C. Loudon's *The Mummy!*', *Cardiff Corvey: Reading the Romantic Text*, 10, June 2003; Jasmine Day, *The Mummy's Curse: Mummymania in the English-Speaking World*, Routledge, 2006, p. 56; Carter Lupton, '"Mummymania" for the Masses', in Sally MacDonald and Michael Rice (eds), *Consuming Ancient Egypt*, Left Coast Press, 2009, pp. 26–30.

[98] Lupton, p. 32.

[99] Richard Kay, 'Tut! Tut! That's One Earl of a Mistake', *Daily Mail*, 17 April 2009.

[100] Lesley-Ann Jones, 'Am I Cursed by King Tut?', *Daily Mail*, 17 October 2007. Despite denying that she believed in the curse, Jones laid out a long list of disasters that she clearly attributed to it.

note of any curse inscription above the entrance to the tomb. Under the headline 'Carter Ignores Curse Idea', *The New York Times* reported that he had 'Never thought of it'.[101] Carter made no note of the alleged death of his canary in his diary. He either thought it of little significance, or it never happened at all. Carter was not 'stricken down' by a mysterious ailment after Carnarvon's death, but, as his diary reveals, carried on working. Carter died at home in Kensington, London, in 1939 at the age of sixty-four, seventeen years after first setting foot inside the tomb of Tutankhamun.

Archaeology as a profession is often a dangerous one. In delving into the earth and digging amongst the dead, archaeologists are exposed to a range of diseases from tetanus to anthrax, as well as accidental injury. Consequently, it has been suggested that the deaths of those who entered the tomb of Tutankhamun were caused by infectious agents, possibly developing histoplasmosis, for example, from exposure to bats. However, research by Mark Nelson at the Department of Epidemiology and Preventive Medicine, Monash University, Australia, found that most of the Westerners likely to have been exposed to the curse at the time of the tomb's opening lived for another twenty years before dying at the average age of seventy. He concluded that 'there was no significant association between exposure to the mummy's curse and survival and thus no evidence to support the existence of a mummy's curse'. Speaking about the curse in 2009, the current Lord Carnarvon, great-grandson of the Egyptologist, said 'Well, I've been into Tutankhamun's tomb and I'm still breathing.'[102]

---

[101] 'Carter Ignores Curse Idea', *The New York Times*, 14 April 1923.

[102] G. Dean, 'The Curse of the Pharaohs', *World Medicine*, 10, 1975, pp. 17–21; H. A. Waldron, 'Occupational Health and the Archaeologist', *British Journal of Industrial Medicine*, 42.12, December 1985, pp. 793–4; Mark R. Nelson, 'The Mummy's Curse: Historical Cohort Study', *British Medical Journal*, 21 December 2002, 325(7378), pp. 1482–4; Carnarvon quoted in Robert Hardman, '£12m Curse of King Tut', *Daily Mail*, 6 August 2009.

Zombies

> I am teeming with corpses
> Teeming with death rattles
> I am a tide of wounds
> Of cries of pus of blood clots
> I graze on the pastures
> Of millions of my dead
> I am shepherd of terror.[103]

It was spring 1918. The terrible slaughter in Europe had yet to come to an end. Across the ocean, untouched by heavy artillery and poison gas, yet still a pawn in the Great Game, the Caribbean islands roasted in the sun, steeped in cruelty and indolence, simmering rebellion, and voodoo. To American President Theodore Roosevelt, 'beautiful, venomous, tropical [. . .] a land of savage negroes'.[104] And that spring it was a bumper sugar cane harvest.

The Haitian-American Sugar Company (Hasco) had a modern processing plant outside Port-au-Prince in the cane fields of the Plaine du Cul-de-Sac. They paid low wages, but gave regular work, and this season they were hiring everybody and anybody. They came in droves, whole families, even whole villages, from the plains and the mountains beyond. Amongst them was Ti Joseph from Colombier with his wife Croyance and a nine-strong work gang. There was something strange in the way Joseph's workers shuffled along, clothed in rags and giving no answer when spoken to. Joseph said they were simple people from the isolated mountain country around Morne-au-Diable, the Devil's Peak, on the Dominican border, frightened by the huge factory and its marshalling yards.

Joseph's team kept themselves to themselves. People wondered

---

[103] René Depestre, *Un Arc-en-ciel pour l'occident chrétien*, 1967, quoted in Joan Dayan, *Haiti, History and the Gods*, University of California Press, 1998, p. 38.
[104] Roosevelt in 1906, quoted in Markmann Ellis, *The History of Gothic Fiction*, Edinburgh University Press, 2000, p. 218.

why Croyance kept two pots on the fire and why she and her husband ate from one, whilst the workers ate from the other. From the neighbouring camps they might have seen her add a pinch of salt to the one and not the other. But they worked hard and every Saturday Joseph collected their wages. When the Fête Dieu came round even Hasco granted the workers a long week-end and Joseph set off to Port-au-Prince with the money clinking in his pockets, leaving Croyance to look after the workers. But Croyance got bored looking after the workers at their isolated camp and convincing herself that she might do some-thing to cheer up the dull, expressionless crew, she led them into Croix de Bouquet to see the religious procession. The workers were unmoved by the pageant, so she bought them *tablettes pistaches*, pistachio nut and cane sugar biscuits. Little did she know, the pistachios had been salted. When the workers bit into the biscuits it was as if their consciousness flooded back and with it a terrible realization. Croyance could do nothing as they abandoned her and made their way back to their village, desper-ate and determined.

As they approached the village, friends and relatives recog-nized them. Some thought it must be a miracle, but the others knew the truth. Joseph's former work gang stumbled through the collection of huts and out again, taking the path to the grave-yard. They were zombies, reanimated by the black magic of Joseph, restored to their senses by the taste of salt. They clawed their way back into their graves, finding peace again at last.

The villagers turned to black magic themselves, hiring a *bokor* to curse Ti Joseph. Impatient to wait for the magic to work, some of them also laid an ambush. Going down to the plain they waited for him to pass and hacked him to pieces with their machetes.

William Buehler Seabrook had heard the story first-hand, or so he said, sitting on a farmer's porch and trading stories of the supernatural – of firehags, demons and vampires – as the full moon rose over the cotton fields. But even here, on what he would later call 'the magic island', Seabrook did not believe the storyteller. So the farmer promised to show him a zombie, several, in fact: 'If you ride with me tomorrow, I will show you dead men working in the cane fields'.[105]

Seabrook had joined Field Section No. 8 of the Franco-American Ambulance Corps and saw action at Verdun in 1916. He came home with a medal and joined the *Augusta Chronicle* in Georgia, but a strange inner drive would take him to the ends of the earth, metaphorically as well as literally. In 1920 he sat up all night drinking a gallon of moonshine corn spirit with the infamous magician Aleister Crowley as they experimented in communicating without human language. He would go on to travel Arabia, publishing his account in 1927, and found himself in Haiti in the late 1920s. In 1929 he would publish his experiences as *The Magic Island* – 'a most interesting and level-headed book', according to a contemporary reviewer for the *Journal of the Society for Psychical Research*. Afterwards he would travel Africa, living with the Gueré cannibals and tasting human flesh. 'It was,' he said, 'like good, fully developed veal.'[106]

In the 1920s Haiti still had most of its original forest cover before its spiralling population cut down all but 2 per cent of it for fuel. Sugar was still its most important cash crop. It was also then occupied by the USA. A rebellion had been crushed by force of arms. The Marine Corps had been installed to run the provinces and the country was under martial law. One marine, Sergeant Faustin Wirkus, would be proclaimed King Faustin II by his loyal subjects of the Haitian island Île de la Gonâve, to the great embarrassment of the republic's president. Seabrook was there to see it.[107]

---

[105] William Seabrook, *The Magic Island*, George C. Harrap & Co., 1929, excerpted in Bill Pronzini (ed.), *Tales of the Dead*, Crown/Bonanza, 1986, pp. 77–88.

[106] William Seabrook, *No Hiding Place: An Autobiography*, J. B. Lippincott Company, 1942, pp. 149, 164, 166; H.D.S., *Diary of Section VIII*, privately published, 1917; *The Rotarian*, 10.1, January 1917, p. 68; William Seabrook, *Witchcraft: Its Power in the World Today*, Harcourt, Brace and Company, 1940, pp. 223–4; *Journal of the Society of Psychical Research*, 25, 1929, p. 96; 'Books: Black & White', *Time*, 6 April 1931.

[107] Richard A. Haggerty, *Haiti: A Country Study*, GPO for the Library of Con-

Seabrook was then living in the high country of La Gonâve in a peasant *lakou*, a communal compound of half a dozen thatched huts typical of the region. He lived like 'an adopted son' to the 'old black priestess' Maman Célie and would sink his soul into the 'living, vital, violent, bloody, flaming Religion' of voodoo. And the farmer, Constant Polynice, would be true to his word.[108]

They rode out together across the Plaine Mapou, through deserted cane fields until, near Picmy, Polynice spotted a group of four workers a hundred yards up on the terraced slope. He recognized the woman as Lamercie and they approached. The three other workers continued hacking at the rough, stony ground with their machetes 'like automatons'. Seabrook thought there was 'something about them unnatural and strange'. Polynice touched one of them and signalled him to rise from his toil. What Seabrook then saw 'came as a rather sickening shock':[109]

> The eyes were the worst. It was not my imagination. They were in truth like the eyes of a dead man, not blind, but staring, unfocused, unseeing. The whole face, for that matter, was bad enough. It was vacant, as if there was nothing behind it.[110]

Zombie Origins

Seabrook was probably the first person to describe the full horror of the Haitian reanimated corpse, although earlier references to the word can be found. The French were early aware of the word and its meaning. Pierre-Corneille Blesseboise (1646– c. 1700) wrote a novel on the theme in 1697 called *Le Zombi du Grand-Pérou* – the zombi being, as his later editor the poet

---

gress, 1989. Seabrook wrote about Wirkus in *The Magic Island* as well as contributing the introduction to Faustin Wirkus and Taney Dudley, *The White King of La Gonave*, Doubleday, Doran & Co., 1931.

[108] Seabrook, *No Hiding Place*, pp. 278, 280.

[109] Pronzini, p. 86.

[110] Pronzini, p. 86.

Guillaume Apollinaire pointed out, a spirit, phantom, or sorcerer, and muttered darkly of midnight orgies. It was some years later in 1819 that the poet Robert Southey noted that 'zombi' was used as the title of the chief of the Palmares negroes in Brazil, and thereby introduced the word into the English language. His explanation was that it came from the Angolan word for 'deity', although Southey noted that the Brazilian historian Sebastiao da Rocha Pitta had said that the word meant 'devil'. Southey rejected this meaning, but Maximilian Schele de Vere would later note in 1872 how the word 'zombi' was used for 'a phantom or ghost' and 'not infrequently heard in the Southern States in nurseries and among servants'. This was the understanding the French writer Moreau de Saint-Méry had in 1797 when he said 'zombi' was a Creole word meaning 'spirit, revenant'. Schele de Vere suggested that it was a Creole corruption of the Spanish *sombra*, 'shadow, shade', which could also mean a ghost. However, Southey's was the more accurate etymology. In Angola and other parts of West Africa they speak, amongst many others, the Kongo language and following the deportation of human slave labour from this region the language formed the basis for Creole spoken in the Caribbean. In Kongo we find *nzambi*, 'god, spirit', and *zumbi*, 'fetish', clearly indicating supernatural meanings.[111]

The travel writer and literary critic Lafcadio Hearn (1850–1904) was commissioned by *Harper's Magazine* in 1887 to investigate the folklore and culture of the West Indies. He took a cruise to French Guiana and later spent two years on Martinique where he learnt of the zombie. He described costumed, dancing natives taking part in the carnival in St Pierre in 1887: *ti nègue*

---

[111] Pierre-Corneille Blesseboise, *L'ouvre de Pierre-Corneille Blessebois*, ed. Guillaume Apollinaire, Bibliothéque des curieux, 1921, pp. 219–82; Médéric Louis Élie Moreau de Saint-Méry, *Description Topographique, Physique, Civile, Politique et Historique de la Partie Française de L'Isle Saint-Dominique*, self-published, 1797, pp. 47f; Southey, *History of Brazil*, vol. 3, Longman, Hurst, Rees, Orme and Brown, 1819, p. 24; Sebastiao da Rocha Pitta, *Historia da America Portugueza*, F. A. da Silva, 1880 [1730], p. 536; Maximilian Schele de Vere, *Americanisms: The English of the New World*, C. Scribner & Co., 1872, p. 138.

gouos-sirop, Creole for 'little molasses negro', covered in molasses and soot; the *guiablesse* ('she-devil') dressed in black; the *Bon-Dié* ('Good God'); and the Devil with his *zombis*, a crowd of hundreds of chanting boys. Da Rocha Pitta was not wrong and Hearn's first-hand testimony would concur with Schele de Vere. There was something more here than Southey had realized, or even Seabrook had discovered.[112]

Hearn had heard the word *zombi* in common phrases – *I ni pè zombi mênm gran-jou*, 'he is afraid of ghosts even in broad daylight' – but a doubt remained that they were not exactly like ghosts. He quizzed Adou, the daughter of the woman who rented him his lodgings. 'It is something which "makes disorder at night",' she told him, just like our 'things that go bump in the night'. She was afraid of passing the cemetery at night because the dead folk, *moun-mò*, would keep her there, but the *zombi* was not one of the dead: 'the *moun-mò* are not zombis. The zombis go everywhere: the dead folk remain in the graveyard.' Hearn probed for more: 'It is the zombis who make all those noises at night one cannot understand . . . Or, again, if I were to see a dog that high,' she held her hand five feet above the ground, 'coming into our house at night, I would scream: "*Mi Zombi!*"' The mother stopped her cooking to join in the debate. 'You pass along the high-road at night, and you see a great fire, and the more you walk to get to it the more it moves away: it is the zombi makes that,' she explained. 'Or a horse *with only three legs* passes you: that is a zombi.'[113]

From Ezekiel's vision of the Valley of the Dry Bones (Ezekiel 37) and the resurrection of the dead supposed to occur at the Final Judgement of the Judaeo-Christian imagination to the *draugr*, Wild Hunt and walking dead of Europe, the dead who come back is certainly not an unknown concept in the West. Hearn's fairy-like shape-shifting bogeyman would find himself

---

[112] Lafcadio Hearn, 'La Verette and the Carnival in St. Pierre, Martinique', *Harper's Magazine*, October 1888, pp. 737–48; and Lafcadio Hearn, *Two Years in the French West Indies*, Harper & Brothers, 1890, pp. 181f.
[113] Hearn, *Two Years*, pp. 161–3.

at home in Scotland or Ireland. But Seabrook's Haitian zombie is unique. One finds distant echoes of the homunculus or golem – the artificial magical monsters of the Renaissance – but the slave dead are peculiar to the country and culture that created them.

Zombie Culture

It would not stay that way. Director Victor Halperin's *White Zombie* (1932) stuck to the folklore, portraying zombies as undead slaves. The modern zombie did not start out as a zombie. Richard Matheson's 1954 novel *I Am Legend* described an apocalyptic future in which most of the earth's population have succumbed to a mysterious disease that turns both living and dead into vampires, perhaps drawing on a similar pandemic theme in H. G. Wells' *The Shape of Things to Come* (1933). Vincent Price and Charlton Heston starred in film adaptations – *The Last Man on Earth* (1964) and *The Omega Man* (1971), respectively – that brought Matheson's story to even wider audiences. Often seen as the creator of the modern zombie, George A. Romero's inspiration for his 1968 film *Night of the Living Dead* was Matheson's novel and the 1964 film. Crucially, however, during the film the zombies are referred to as ghouls. This is the key.

The ghoul, from Arabic *ghūl*, 'demon', is a creature of the burial ground and wasteland whose characteristic trait is an appetite for human flesh. Like Seabrook, the ghoul has a taste for 'good, fully developed veal'. First mentioned in English in the 1786 translation of William Beckford's novel *Vathek*, it is this creature that Romero has emerge from the graveyard and assault his beleaguered characters. It is this creature that is subsequently and erroneously called a zombie. Romero's subsequent films detailing the 'zombie apocalypse' have cemented the idea of the flesh-eating zombie loosed from its origins in West African and Caribbean culture.

Some people have interpreted all of this as an obsession with race – Matheson's diseased hordes as blacks, Stoker's Dracula as the Jew[114] – but this reflects current concerns, more particularly, current academic concerns. The parasitic, aristocratic Dracula was more obviously a class critique, if anything; and Matheson's hordes were the reverse, the great unwashed, although, it has to be said, there were incidental and understated signs that this was a demonologist's version of *The Planet of the Apes*. Instead, today we find people identifying with the zombie as a form of social protest and aspiring to be vampires/vampirized as an expression of teenage sexual awakening.

Some philosophers and cognitive scientists have involved themselves in arguments over the 'philosophical zombie', a postulated functional human being that is otherwise devoid of conscious experience. Some have suggested that we are already 'zombies'. Professor Daniel Dennett, co-director of the Center for Cognitive Studies, Tufts University, USA, argued that the self is 'no more than a fiction which serves as a reference point for the narratives which the brain constructs'. Take that with a pinch of salt.[115]

What differentiates Seabrook's Haitian zombie from its near undead relatives, the vampire and the mummy, is the role of the sorcerer in creating it. Some instances of the mummy in literature are governed by this theme, most notably Conan Doyle's *Lot No. 249*. But where the vampire and the mummy are most typically aspects of the vengeful or unplacated dead, the zombie is here the sorcerer's slave in a colonialism of the spirit. Hearn's Martiniquan zombi was something much more like one of the fairies in Celtic folklore: a terrifying supernatural entity that could assume a variety of forms. It is only in later fictional interpretations that the zombie takes on the mantle of the restless dead and

---

[114] Mikhail Lyubansky, 'Are the Fangs Real? Vampires as Racial Metaphor in the Anita Blake and Twilight Novels', *Psychology Today*, 10 April 2010, http://www.psychologytoday.com/blog/between-the-lines/201004/are-the-fangs-real-vampires-racial-metaphor-in-the-anita-blake-and-twi, accessed 24 September 2010.

[115] Daniel C. Dennett, *Consciousness Explained*, Penguin, 1991. This whole subject is a minefield and this not the place to venture into it.

appropriates the function of the ghoul to become the flesh-eating monster of the 'zombie apocalypse'.

Zombie Explanations

As he stared into those lifeless eyes, Seabrook felt all his certainties slipping away. Here he was face to face with the supernatural. But then he remembered something similar he had once seen: a lobotomized dog in a laboratory – alive but devoid of the higher mental processes. More for his own sanity than anything else, Seabrook concluded that the zombies were 'poor ordinary demented human beings, idiots'. Polynice was less convinced. 'How could it be,' he asked, 'that over and over again, people who have stood by and seen their own relatives buried have, sometimes soon, sometimes months or years afterward, found those relatives working as zombies?'[116]

Seabrook got his answer some time later, sitting with a certain Dr Antoine Villiers in his book-lined study. According to Seabrook, after he raised the subject of zombies, Villiers took down an edition of the *Code pénal* from the shelves and read out Article 249: 'Also shall be qualified as attempted murder the employment which may be made against any person of substances which, without causing actual death, produce a lethargic coma more or less prolonged. If, after administering of such substances, the person has been buried, the act shall be considered murder no matter what result follows.' This has been quoted repeatedly ever since. What Article 249 of the *Code pénal* actually stated was that 'homicide committed wilfully is termed murder', nothing more. In the second edition of the *Code* published in 1938 this became 'Murder shall carry the death penalty, when preceded, accompanied or followed by another crime or misdemeanour'. The death penalty has since been amended to penal servitude for life. There was no mention of 'substances' or burial and of Dr Antoine Villiers there is no trace.[117]

---

[116] Seabrook in Pronzini, p. 87.

[117] Seabrook in Pronzini, p. 87; *Code pénal d'Haiti*, L'Imprimerie du

However, Seabrook's substance-induced zombification found support in the work of Zora Neale Hurston (1891–1960) and Wade Davis (1953–). In her 1938 book *Tell My Horse*, Hurston claimed 'I know that there are Zombis in Haiti' after she supposedly met one. With the Maroons in the St Catharine Mountains of Jamaica she had already been party to 'The Nine Night', a riotous funerary rite whose purpose was to prevent the 'duppy', walking dead, from returning. Later in Haiti, she took part in another funerary ritual where the corpse suddenly 'sat up with its staring eyes, bowed its head and fell back again', or so she said. So when she was introduced to a zombie, she was primed to believe that 'people have been called back from the dead' and snapped a photograph of the creature as proof.[118]

Dr Rulx Leon, director-general of the Service d'Hygiene, had told her of Felicia Felix-Mentor, currently lodged in a government hospital. Hurston rushed over to see her, later recalling 'That blank face with the dead eyes. The eyelids were white all around the eyes as if they had been burnt with acid'.[119]

The case was examined by Dr Louis Mars, Professor of Psychiatry at the School of Medicine and of Social Psychology at the Institute of Ethnology, Port-au-Prince, and a public health officer for the government. Mars recounted the alleged zombie's history. On the morning of 24 October 1936, an elderly woman dressed in rags caused 'tumultuous and frenzied consternation' when she was discovered wandering in a confused state in the village of Ennery in the foothills of the Puylboreau mountain

---

Gouvernement, 1826, p. 61; Auguste Albert Héraux, *Code pénal avec les dernières modifications, annoté*, 2nd ed., Aug. A. Héraux, 1938, p. 66. Amended 4 July 1988: *Le Code pénal haitien*, http://www.oas.org/juridico/mla/fr/hti/fr_hti_penal.html and http://www.crijhaiti.com/fr/?page=article_code_penal accessed 27 September 2010. There was an author called Antoine Villiers, apparently a chemist, writing in French at the beginning of the twentieth century, but there is no compelling reason to connect the two, other than name alone.

[118] Paul Witcover, *Zora Neale Hurston*, Holloway House Publishing, 1994, pp. 148–9.

[119] Quoted in Robert E. Hemenway, *Zora Neale Hurston: A Literary Biography*, University of Illinois Press, p. 250.

range. She appeared to be suffering from dementia, as well as some sort of eye disease. Her eyelashes had fallen out and to protect herself from the harsh and painful glare of the sun she had covered her face with some tattered dark-coloured material, adding to her uncanny appearance. The owner of a farm near the village claimed to recognize her, believing the woman to be his sister, Felicia Felix-Mentor, who had died in 1907. Felicia, like his sister, had a limp. Felicia herself was not able to confirm or deny any of this: 'all her answers were unintelligible and irrelevant'. Mars thought her schizophrenic. He had her legs X-rayed and discovered that, unlike the real Felicia who had limped in life after sustaining a fracture, this woman had no such injuries and her limp got better with hospital care. 'I have never met anyone in Haiti,' he said, 'who was able to testify to me that he had seen a Zombi.'[120]

Hurston testified: 'I saw the broken remnant, relic, or refuse of Felicia Felix-Mentor in a hospital yard.' But she did not, or would not, look beyond the explanations of her informants. She considered that zombies could be created either by the sorcerer sucking out the soul of the victim, calling upon one of the violent *Petro loas* (spirits), or secretly administering a special poison. She was convinced that 'if science ever gets to the bottom of Voodoo in Haiti and Africa, it will be found that some important medical secrets, still unknown to medical science, give it its power'.[121]

Wade Davis would claim to have discovered those secrets. In the spring of 1980 a middle-aged man introduced himself to a woman in the village of l'Estère, central Haiti, using the private childhood nickname of her brother. Her brother had died in 1962. He said he was Clairvius Narcisse, zombified by his brother after a dispute over land and forced to work as a slave on a sugar plantation. His family and about 200 other people recognized him. Dr Lamarque Douyon, director of the Centre

---

[120] Hemenway, p. 250; Louis P. Mars, 'The Story of the Zombi in Haiti', *Man: A Record of Anthropological Science*, XLV, 22, March–April 1945, pp. 38–40.
[121] Hemenway, p. 250; Zora Neale Hurston, *Dust Tracks on a Road*, 2nd ed., University of Illinois Press, 1984, p. 205.

de Psychiatrie et Neurologie, Port-au-Prince, examined the case. He discovered that Narcisse had indeed been declared dead in 1962 and concluded that poison must have been used to lower his vital functions to the point where he could be mistaken for dead.[122]

Investigating this lead, Davis travelled to Haiti to collect samples of the so-called *coup poudre*, 'blow' or 'strike powder', a magical preparation said to cause illness or death. All of the samples contained hallucinogenic plants and animals such as tarantulas, snakes and millipedes. Also thrown into the mix was a species of toad, *Bufo marinus*, and two genera of puffer fish, *Diodon hystrix* and *Sphoerides testudineus*, all of which are deadly poisonous in the extreme. The puffer fish contains tetrodotoxin, a nerve toxin so lethal that an amount the size of a pinhead is sufficient to cause death. Because of this the puffer fish has become a macho delicacy in Japan where specially licensed chefs prepare the dish so that it is not lethal, at least most of the time. The symptoms of tetrodotoxin poisoning – paralysis, reduced heartbeat and respiration – can lead to the victim being certified clinically dead when still alive, as sometimes happens in the case of unlucky Japanese diners and, so Davis thought, victims of zombification. At lower doses the victim usually recovers. Terence Hines, a professor of psychology and neurology, pointed out that a paralysed individual who appears to be dead does not a 'zombie' make. Davis argued that a paste containing the poisonous hallucinogenic plants *Datura stramonium* or *Datura metel* is then fed to the 'zombie' to produce what he calls 'an induced state of psychotic delirium'. His critics, however, have cried 'fraud' and 'bad science', claiming that Davis's samples were either devoid of tetrodotoxin or did not contain enough to produce the supposed effects.[123]

---

[122] Wade Davis, *The Serpent and the Rainbow*, Simon & Schuster, 1985, and *Passage of Darkness: The Ethnobiology of the Haitian Zombie*, University of North Carolina Press, 1988; Catherine Caufield, 'The Chemistry of the Living Dead', *New Scientist*, 15 December 1983, p. 796.

[123] Nick Saunders, 'Law and Order in the Land of the Living Dead', *New*

Whatever the zombies are, they are still out there. A German traveller to Jamaica in the late 1980s told friends that he had encountered a zombie in the jungle. Like Seabrook he described the eyes as being the worst. Other recent encounters have been closer to home. It was revealed in 2010 that the police in Wales had received sixteen reports of zombies since 2005. Another zombie sighting hit the headlines in February 2008. A sewage treatment plant at Prince William Parade in Eastbourne, East Sussex, is reputedly the stalking ground of what workers have called a 'zombie'. A Southern Water employee told reporters 'I dread doing the night shift. It's not funny going to work and worrying that a zombie might be around the corner.' Although no one has been torn to pieces and consumed by the undead prowler, à la George A. Romero, workers have reported hearing voices and seeing a shadowy figure.[124]

Scientist, 7 August 1986, p. 47; Davis quoted in Caufield, p. 796; Terence Hines, 'Zombies and Tetrodotoxin', *Skeptical Inquirer*, May–June 2008, pp. 60–2; W. Booth, 'Voodoo Science', *Science*, 240.4850, 15 April 1988, pp. 274–7.
[124] The German traveller's tale was reported to me personally, 10 October 2010; 'Welsh in Fear of Witches and Demons', *Paranormal*, 53, November 2010, p. 10; Alan Murdie, 'Ghostwatch', *Fortean Times*, 267, October 2010, p. 17.

3. Angels

The summer sun that Sunday morning was darkly shrouded in cloud and mist. The church bell was yet quiet and the townspeople slept on. Beyond their dreams and wooden doors, a fine drizzle slowly soaked the men in khaki. Crouching behind makeshift barricades and in hastily dug scrape trenches, they rubbed sleep from their eyes and loaded their rifles. Distant shots and cries had already punctuated the grey dawn and for the soldiers the atmosphere was heavy with expectation. As the old clock tower chimed 9 a.m. the artillery of General Alexander von Kluck's First Army opened fire on the British Expeditionary Force (BEF). It was 23 August 1914. The first battle of World War I between the British and Germans had begun: the Battle of Mons.[125]

The BEF, so famously maligned as 'that contemptible little army', had crossed the English Channel and made its way with great haste to join the French Fifth Army. Only the British now found themselves outnumbered almost three to one and the army they had been sent to support was in full retreat. They had to hold the Germans, or France would fall.

---

[125] David Clarke, *The Angel of Mons: Phantom Soldiers and Ghostly Guardians*, John Wiley & Sons, 2005, p. 43; Herbert Arthur Stewart, *From Mons to Loos*, W. Blackwood, 1916, p. 19; W. Douglas Newton, *The Undying Story*, E. P. Dutton & Co., 1915, p. 12; Sir James E. Edmonds, *Military Operations, France and Belgium, 1914*, Macmillan & Co., 1937, p. 76. Lord Ernest Hamilton gives an incorrect account of the weather in *The First Seven Divisions*, E. P. Dutton & Co., 1916, p. 20.

Consisting of four infantry divisions and one cavalry division, less than 100,000 men in total, the BEF was divided into two main groupings: I Corps and II Corps. The II Corps were stretched along a twenty-mile line north of the Belgian town of Mons with the Eighth and Ninth Infantry Brigades holding an exposed section along the bend in the canal between Nimy and Obourg. It was here that two battalions from the Middlesex and Royal Fusiliers regiments bore the brunt of the bombardment: 'the sky precipitated to steel, and shivered fragments into the British'; and 'as the heat of the day increased, so did the fury of that terrific cannonade.'[126]

Fast on the heels of the shells came advancing infantry columns of the German IX Corps. Here, the shattered line faced an enemy perhaps ten times as strong. As the casualties mounted, the Second Royal Irish were moved up to support. Corporal John Lucy was among them and later recalled his amazement as the rapid rifle fire of the British knocked the Germans down in waves.[127]

Undeterred, the Germans began pushing to the west and east, trying to encircle the exposed salient. Faced with the likelihood of being cut off and wiped out, the British began to pull back. They were between the hammer and the anvil. The future of the war, of Europe, hung in the balance. Only a miracle could save them.

'There is the story of the "Angels of Mons" going strong through the II Corps,' wrote John Charteris in a letter dated 5 September 1914. Later to become Chief Intelligence Officer, the Glaswegian was at the time aide-de-camp to Lieutenant-General Sir Douglas Haig, commander of the I Corps. His letter continued: 'of how the angel of the Lord on the traditional white horse, and clad all in white with flaming sword, faced the advancing Germans at Mons and forbade their further progress'.[128]

---

[126] Quotations from Newton, p. 15; Arthur Machen, 'The Bowmen', *Evening News*, 29 September 1914, in Clarke, p. 247.

[127] John Frederick Lucy, *There's a Devil in the Drum*, Faber & Faber, 1938.

[128] John Charteris, *At GHQ*, Cassell and Co., 1931, pp. 25–6.

Of Sarah Marrable, a clergyman's daughter, it was reported in the press that 'she told me she knew the officers, both of whom had themselves seen the angels who saved the left wing from the Germans when they came right upon them during our retreat from Mons'. Phyllis Campbell, a nineteen-year-old volunteer nurse serving with the French Red Cross, later said that she had spoken to one of the wounded from Mons who told her that 'he saw at a critical moment an angel with outstretched wings – like a luminous cloud between the advancing Germans and themselves. The Germans could not advance to destroy them'.[129]

It seemed like that miracle had happened. The outnumbered and outmanoeuvred BEF had escaped certain destruction. The number of German dead has never been disclosed, but is estimated in the range of 5,000 to 10,000. Against this the British lost 1,600 men. However, over the course of what was called the Great Retirement as the BEF retreated more than 200 miles in 13 days, British losses would rise to 15,000.[130]

The rumour of angelic reinforcements spread quickly, gaining greater conviction and variety in every retelling. Charteris' letter notwithstanding, the writer Arthur Machen argued that he had started it all with his short story 'The Bowmen' published in the *Evening News* on 29 September 1914, but few people wanted to believe him and much apparent evidence to the contrary was quickly forthcoming. Today, the official battlefield guidebook published by the City of Mons Tourist Board states that 'angels descended from heaven dressed as archers stopping the Germans in their tracks' with similar text appearing on the city's official website. It has been described as 'the single most influential paranormal event in British history'. It was certainly the most important angelic encounter in British history. In the

---

[129] For Marrable see *Hereford Times*, 3 April 1915; for Campbell see Alexander Boddy interviewed by the *Sunderland Echo*, 16 August 1915, quoted in Clarke, p. 134.
[130] Alan John Percivale Taylor, *English History, 1914–1945*, Oxford University Press, 1965, p. 9.

slaughter of industrialized warfare, angels had entered the modern world.[131]

The Origin of Angels

The Angels of Mons were not the cute little figures from the top of the Christmas Tree, but warrior spirits straight out of the Old Testament. Marrable herself said she was reminded of the story of the siege of Dothan.[132] Claimed to have been written sometime in the sixth century BCE, the second book of Kings relates a legend concerning the Hebrew prophet Elisha that reputedly took place several hundred years earlier in the ninth century BCE. The Assyrian armies had surrounded the city of Dothan, intent on capturing Elisha. His servant despaired, but Elisha told him 'they that be with us are more than they that be with them' and suddenly the servant saw that 'the mountain was full of horses and chariots of fire round about Elisha' that protected them (2 Kings 6:16–17).

It is appropriate that Marrable should have been reminded of the Old Testament. Our word 'angel' comes from the Greek *aggelos* (ἄγγελος), a masculine noun used by Jewish scribes in Alexandria in the third to second centuries BCE to translate more than 200 occurrences of the Hebrew word *mal'āk*, meaning messenger, found in the *Tanakh* or Hebrew scriptures, which, for Christians, have become the Old Testament. The Hebrew was originally employed to mean a messenger in general, either spiritual or human. Prophets (Haggai 1:13), priests (Malachi 2:7) and kings (1 Samuel 29:9) could all be messengers of God. In the earlier books of the Old Testament human agents are usually meant with a transition to supernatural beings occurring in the later books, increasing from the third century BCE onwards. This

---

[131] Yves Bourdon, *Mons: August 1914: Notes on the Mons Battlefield*, City of Mons Tourist Board, 1987, quoted in Clarke, p. 45; www.mons.be accessed 15 July 2010; Kevin McClure, 'Visions of Comfort and Catastrophe' in Hilary Evans (ed.), *Frontiers of Reality*, Aquarian Press, 1991, p. 170. For a pro position see Ralph Shirley, *The Angel Warriors at Mons*, Newspaper Publicity Co., 1915.

[132] Clarke, p. 123.

development was shaped by the appearance of Jewish apocalyptic literature, the take up of popular belief and by the influence of other pagan religions. It appears likely that the supernatural angel developed as a means of maintaining Jewish monotheism by denying the messenger full godhead, especially as we find such roles paralleled by gods in all of ancient Near Eastern mythology. In other Mesopotamian belief systems the concept of supernatural messengers is well attested. There is even a Mesopotamian (Akkadian) messenger god called Malak.[133]

The earliest appearance of angels in the Old Testament is not with Elisha, but with the mythological character Abraham in Genesis. Traditionally ascribed to the authorship of Moses, the book of Genesis is thought to have been composed by a variety of authors in the sixth century BCE at the earliest.[134] Here we read 'And the Lord appeared unto him [. . .] And he lift up his eyes and looked, and lo, three men stood by him' (Genesis 18:1–2). The three are described as human with no mention of wings or white robes. They are not even sufficiently distinguished from 'the Lord', so that later Christians could interpret the group as a

---

[133] K. van der Toorn, Bob Becking and Pieter Willem van der Horst (eds), *Dictionary of Deities and Demons in the Bible* [*DDD*], 2nd ed., Brill/Eerdmans, 1999, pp. 45–9, 51. Clarke, pp. 17–18 and David Albert Jones, *Angels: A History*, Oxford University Press, 2010, p. 12, argue for a Zoroastrian influence, but the evidence for this is weak and contradictory.

[134] Dating the Bible is both controversial and problematic, if not to say confusing. The oldest surviving biblical manuscripts, the so-called Dead Sea Scrolls, all date from the second century BCE to the first century CE. However, the oldest supposed translation, the Greek Septuagint or LXX, dates from the third to second centuries BCE, although the oldest surviving manuscripts only date from the second century BCE (see Natalio Fernandez Marcos, *Scribes and Translators*, Brill, 1994, p. 7). Origination in this period is generally confirmed by textual analysis of later versions of the Bible that find a Hellenistic historical background to many of these texts. Traditional views ascribing extremely ancient authorship to these texts are not supported by the evidence. Thomas L. Thompson, a biblical scholar academically ostracized by conservative theologians for his views, put it forcefully when he said 'Not only has archaeology not proven a single event of the patriarchal traditions to be historical, it has not shown any of the traditions to be likely' (*The Historicity of the Patriarchal Narratives*, Walter de Gruyter, 1974, p. 328).

symbol of the Trinity, as is often found in Byzantine and medieval Russian art, such as the famous icon known as *The Hospitality of Abraham* or *The Holy Trinity* by Andrei Rublev.[135]

Often appearing singly, especially as the 'angel of Yahweh', they were also grouped as a 'camp' (Genesis 32:2–3) and envisioned travelling between heaven and earth by means of a ladder (Psalms 91:11–12). When not employed in the specific messenger role, they offered blessings and praise to Yahweh (Psalms 103:20, 148:2) and increasingly served in a protective capacity for believers (Daniel 3:28, 6:23; Baruch 6:6 [Epistle Jeremiah 6]) such as Elisha.

Only two angels are mentioned by name in the canonical books of the Old Testament: Michael (Daniel 10:13, 21, 12:1; Revelation 12:7) and Gabriel (Daniel 8:16, 9:21). The infamous 'fallen angel', Satan, only appeared as the legalistic role of 'the accuser' and not as the name of a divine being at this stage. Significantly, both the names Michael and Gabriel end with *-el*, as would later angelic names, and therein lies a tale.

Between the world wars in spring 1928, a peasant was ploughing his strip of rented land south of Minet-el-Beida in Syria when he struck something hard just under the surface. He had occasionally unearthed antiquities before, so it was with a keen interest that he knelt to the ground and swept away the earth with his hand. This time, however, he discovered more than an old broken vase. It was a chambered tomb full of pottery. As he and his friends began systematically looting the site and selling the pieces to local dealers, it accidentally came to the notice of the local governor. He called in the archaeologists (with armed guards) and slowly the ancient Canaanite city of Ugarit (modern Ras Shamra) emerged from the dust. Amongst the ruins they discovered thousands of clay tablets, some complete but most in fragments, dating from 1600–1200 BCE, that have overturned our understanding of the Bible.[136]

---

[135] Jones, p. 2.
[136] Edinburgh Ras Shamra Project, http://www2.div.ed.ac.uk/other/ugarit// home.htm, accessed 19 July 2010; Victor Harold Matthews, *Judges and Ruth*, Oxford University Press, 2004, p. 79.

The noun *'el* occurs more than 200 times in the Old Testament; in Ugarit over 500 references were discovered to a supreme god called El. The *-el* ending of both Michael and Gabriel comes from this Canaanite god El whom the Jews first worshipped as a separate entity before merging with the god Yahweh, so we read of 'El, the god of Israel' (Genesis 33:20) and 'El, the god of your father' (Genesis 46:3). The 'lord' that appears to Abraham with his two angels, the 'lord' that Abraham worships, is El Elyon ('El the Highest One') and 'creator of heaven and earth' (Genesis 14:18–24). Michael means 'like El', or more commonly 'who is like God', whilst the name Gabriel is usually taken to mean 'man of El', but is perhaps more accurately understood as 'El is my hero/warrior'. These two angelic names thus record the very roots of Judaism. Michael himself may also have once been a god in his own right and is tentatively connected with the Canaanite deity Mikal and in Islam this is still the name for him.[137]

Both Michael and Gabriel make their appearances in the book of Daniel. Daniel, 'my judge is El', was already a legendary figure in the time of Ezekiel and ultimately derives from the mythical Canaanite king *Dn'il*, whose ancient (but different) story was discovered amongst the ruins of Urgarit. Traditionally attributed to Daniel in the time of the Babylonian kings Nebuchadnezzar II (reigned 605–562 BCE) and Belshazzar (incorrectly identified as his son), the book is the work of several authors at different periods of history. Michael and Gabriel appear within a distinct group of chapters (7–12) confidently dated to between 168–164 BCE.[138]

The book of Daniel begins with Nebuchadnezzar's siege of Jerusalem in 598 BCE. His army of infantry, chariot and cavalry surrounded the city, deploying the tried siege methodologies of

---

[137] Mark W. Chavalas, *Mesopotamia and the Bible*, Continuum, 2003, p. 258; *DDD*, pp. 338, 912. Manfred Lurker, *Routledge Dictionary of Gods and Goddesses, Devils and Demons*, Routledge, 2004, p. 125. For Michael a derivation from the Persian deity Vohumanô has also been suggested, *DDD*, p. 569.

[138] *DDD*, pp. 219–29; Paul J. Achtemeier and Roger S. Boraas (eds), *HarperCollins Bible Dictionary*, HarperCollins, 1996, pp. 223–4, 743–4.

battering ram, escalade, sapping and starvation. The Jews might have been expecting divine intervention. An earlier siege by the Assyrians in the eighth century BCE had been broken, according to the legend, by the miraculous appearance of the 'angel of Yahweh' who single-handedly slew the 185,000 strong besieging force (2 Kings 18–19).

However, when Nebuchadnezzar himself arrived outside the walls in 597 the Judean king Jehoiachin surrendered the city. The victorious forces took Daniel and several others – 'certain of the children of Israel, and of the king's seed, and of the princes' (Daniel 1:3) – back with them to Babylon. This was the beginning of the Jewish captivity or exile and a large proportion of the Jewish population was taken prisoner, perhaps as many as 10,000 people. Yet Daniel and his companions fared especially well. They were raised in the Babylonian court, taught 'the learning and tongue of the Chaldeans' (Daniel 1:4) and 'God gave them knowledge and skill in all learning and wisdom' (Daniel 1:17). Now known as Belteshazzar among the Babylonians, Daniel in particular 'had understanding in all visions and dreams' (Daniel 1:17) and Nebuchadnezzar thought him 'ten times better than all the magicians and astrologers that were in all his realm' (Daniel 1:20), calling him 'master magician' (Daniel 4:9).[139]

After a successful career interpreting Nebuchadnezzar's dreams as his chief wizard and surviving being thrown into the lion's den after the old king died, Daniel began to have his own prophetic dreams. When he is unable to interpret the second of these concerning a fight between a ram and a billy goat, he 'heard a man's voice [. . .] which called, and said, Gabriel, make this man to understand the vision' (Daniel 8:15). An angel then appeared to him – 'behold, there stood before me as the appearance of a man' (Daniel 8:15) – and, as 'Daniel' explains, 'I was afraid, and fell upon my face' (Daniel 8:16), however, he was still dreaming as he continued 'I was in a deep sleep' (Daniel 8:18).

---

[139] Paul Bently Kern, *Ancient Siege Warfare*, Indiana University Press, 1999, pp. 44–5.

Some time later, after the historically suspect 'Darius the Median' had conquered Babylonia, Daniel became somewhat hysterical over Jeremiah's prophecy that the 'desolation of Jerusalem' (Daniel 9:2) would last seventy years. He donned sackcloth and ashes, fasted and offered a long, emotional prayer to his god asking for forgiveness. In the midst of all this teeth-gnashing 'the man Gabriel, whom I had seen in the vision at the beginning, being caused to fly swiftly, touched me about the time of the evening oblation. And he informed me, and talked with me' (Daniel 9:21–2). The angel explains the prophecy in terms of 'seventy weeks' (Daniel 9:24), usually taken to mean 'seventy weeks of years', i.e., 70 times seven, or 490 years.

The angel Gabriel appeared to Daniel in human shape. There was otherwise nothing remarkable about him. He appeared in dreams or in altered states induced by fasting. His precise function was to interpret dreams and prophecies. Michael, on the other hand, was more dramatically introduced. Daniel was again fasting: 'I ate no pleasant bread, neither came flesh nor wine in my mouth' (Daniel 10:3). After three weeks of this he experienced a vision:

> Then I lifted up mine eyes, and looked, and behold a certain man clothed in linen, whose loins were girded with fine gold of Uphaz. His body also as like beryl, and his face as the appearance of lightning, and his eyes as lamps of fire, and his arms and feet like in colour to polished brass, and the voice of his words like the voice of a multitude. (Daniel 10:5–6)

Daniel passed out – 'then was I in a deep sleep on my face' (Daniel 10:9) – but the vision seemed to pick him up and spoke:

> Fear not, Daniel: for from the first day that thou didst set thine heart to understand, and to chasten thyself before thy God, thy words were heard, and I am come for thy words. But the prince of the kingdom of Persia withstood me one and twenty days: but, lo, Michael, one of the chief princes,

came to help me; and remained there with the kings of Persia.
(Daniel 10:13–14)

This, then, was not Michael, for the being referred to Michael as
having helped him. Neither was it Gabriel, who always appeared as
a man and not so obviously supernatural in origin. Mysteriously,
he is not named at all. He is described as 'the servant of this my
lord' (Daniel 10:17), so is clearly an intermediate divine being; an
angel. Michael is 'one of the chief princes'; for Daniel he is 'Michael
your prince' (Daniel 10:21). Later he is identified as 'the great
prince which standeth for the children of thy people' (Daniel 12:1),
i.e., he is the specific angel of the Jews. Together, the unnamed
angel and Michael defeat the 'prince' of Persia, evidently another
angelic being, showing that it was thought that each kingdom or
people had its own protective spirit and that, like the kingdoms and
people on earth, they came into conflict with one another.

The unnamed angel delivered a thinly disguised version of
Hellenistic history, ending with the persecution of the Jews by
Antiochus Epiphanes. He prophesies the death of Epiphanes,
that Michael will be victorious and that the dead will rise from
the grave to be either rewarded with eternal life or everlasting
damnation. Daniel is told to 'shut up the words, and seal the
book' until the End Times (Daniel 12:4).

Additional orders of supernatural beings from the Old
Testament – the cherubim and seraphim – would come to be
classed as angels. In the book of Ezekiel, the legendary prophet
Ezekiel – traditionally another Babylonian captive – has a series
of visions. In the first, Ezekiel is by the river Chebar, a tributary
canal of the Euphrates river, to the south-east of Babylon:

> And I looked, and, behold, a whirlwind came out of the north,
> a great cloud, and a fire infolding itself, and a brightness was
> about it, and out of the midst thereof as the colour of amber,
> out of the midst of the fire. Also out of the midst thereof came
> the likeness of four living creatures. And this was their appear-
> ance; they had the likeness of a man. (Ezekiel 1:4–5)

However, these were strange-looking men. They had four faces – a man's, a lion's, an ox's and an eagle's – four wings, the soles of their feet were like the soles of calves' feet, and they shone with the colour of burnished brass (Ezekiel 1:6–7, 10). They appeared 'like burning coals of fire' and 'out of the fire went forth lightning' (Ezekiel 1:13). These cherubim then resolved into a psychedelic four-wheeled chariot with strange rings (wheel-rims) full of eyes and above it Ezekiel saw a throne bearing Yahweh (Ezekiel 16–28). Yahweh delivers a series of speeches about Israel and the wicked dying and so on, which we can safely skip over.

In all, the term 'cherubim' occurs ninety-one times in the Hebrew Bible, referring to a variety of supernatural or monstrous beings having the presence of wings in common. The cherubim are, in particular, directly associated with the Hebrew deity as his steed (Psalms 17), his chariot (1 Chronicles 18), or his throne (2 Kings 19:15). In Genesis (3:24), Yahweh sets the cherubim to guard the entrance to the Garden of Eden after expelling Adam and Eve. According to various Bible legends, images of cherubim were used extensively in the ornamentation and furnishings of the Jerusalem temple. Gold figures of cherubim were said to adorn the top of the Ark of the Covenant (Exodus 25:18–21). Cherubim were said to be embroidered on the Veil of the Tabernacle (Exodus 26:31). The exterior and interior panelling of the temple was said to be engraved with cherubim (1 Kings 6, 7). Solomon supposedly had two enormous gold-plated olivewood statues of cherubim made to stand either side of the Ark (1 Kings 6:23; 2 Chronicles 3:11). Cherubim were clearly an important and meaningful motif, quite distinct from the messenger angel.

The origin of the word is disputed, but the most likely theory is that it comes from the Akkadian *k ribu* or *kuribu*, terms denoting genii in Mesopotamian mythology and art. Cherubim are functionally and iconographically prefigured by the Egyptian sphinx, the human-headed winged lion. The sphinx functioned as a throne guardian, becoming artistically integral to the throne itself in a later Syrian development, and a simpler lion-paw throne is known from the city of Ugarit as the throne of El. Additionally, the cherub is almost certainly connected with the Mesopotamian winged half-human, half-animal protective spirits called *lamassu* and *shedu*. We find sphinx-like human-headed winged lions, although the human-headed winged bull is the more well-known representation. These then were the cherubim: fierce sacred beings that would be undoubtedly perturbed by their current representation as overweight children (*putti*), so famously evoked by Raphael in his *Sistine Madonna* (c. 1513–14) and now reproduced on everything from biscuit tins to Christmas cards.[140]

But the cherubim were not alone. In the book of Isaiah, the prophet Isaiah has a vision of strange beings attending God. These are the seraphim (Isaiah 6:1–7) who surround God's throne, singing 'Holy, holy, holy is the Lord of hosts. All the earth is filled with his glory' – the so-called *trishagion*. Seraphim is the plural of *seraph* (*sarap*), 'the burning one'. In Isaiah they are described as having six wings: two to cover their faces, two to cover their 'feet' and two with which to fly. Elsewhere (Numbers 21:6–8; Deuteronomy 8:15) they appear as 'fiery serpents'. In searching for the origin of these beings some have suggested a connection with the seven thunders of Baal; however, iconographic evidence points to the Egyptian uraeus serpent. The uraeus was a cobra – its poison being the 'burning' – sometimes represented with two or four wings and was a motif well known from scarabs and seals in Palestine. In Isaiah (6) they stand above Yahweh just as the uraeus stands on the forehead of Egyptian gods and kings. It is unlikely that an early Israelite would have seen these beings as angels, *mal'akh* (messengers), and it is only in later interpretation that they have become organized into a strict hierarchy of angelic beings.[141]

---

[140] *Harp. Coll. BD*, pp. 175–6; *DDD*, pp. 189–92; *Jewish Encyclopedia*, 12 vols, 1901–06, pp. 13–16.

[141] *DDD*, pp.742–3; Othmar Keel, *Jahwe-Visionen und Siegelkunst*, Verlag Katholisches Bibelwerk, 1977, pp. 70–124.

Apocryphal Angels and Archangels

> And behold! He cometh with ten thousands of holy ones
> To execute judgement upon all,
> And to destroy the ungodly[142]

The archangels enter with Enoch. Enoch, the mythical seventh patriarch from the time of the creation – more ancient than Moses – who lived 365 years, walked with God and was mysteriously 'taken' by him (Genesis 5:18–24). He seems to have been partly modelled on the seventh king of Sippar in Mesopotamia, the hero-magician Emmeduranki, and partly on a contemporary of Emmeduranki called Utuabzu, the seventh sage who was taken up to heaven. According to tradition, Enoch also composed a book or books: the so-called Ethiopic Apocalypse of Enoch (1 Enoch),[143] the Slavonic Apocalypse of Enoch also known as The Secret Book of Enoch (2 Enoch),[144] and the later Hebrew Book

---

[142] 1 Enoch, 1:9. All quotations are from the English translation by R. H. Charles, *The Book of Enoch*, Society for Promoting Christian Knowledge, 1917.

[143] There were 29 manuscripts of 1 Enoch written in the cryptic Ge'ez or Ethiopic language scattered across Europe and America from various eras, none of them earlier than the sixteenth century. It was only in 1886–7 that a partial Greek version, apparently a translation of a Hebrew or Aramaic text, was discovered during excavations at Akhmîm on the banks of the Nile by the Mission Archéologique Française. This Greek version was dated about the sixth century CE and had been the basis for the later Ethiopic texts. It would take until 1947 and the famous discovery of the Dead Sea Scrolls at Qumran (Cave 4) to produce evidence of the original. The oldest of these discoveries – The Astronomical Book and The Book of the Watchers – were dated to between the end of the third century and the first half of the second century BCE. See J. T. Milik, *The Books of Enoch: Aramaic Fragments from Qumran Cave 4*, Clarendon, 1976, p. 7; John Joseph Collins, *The Apocalyptic Imagination: An Introduction to Jewish Apocalyptic Literature*, Eerdmans, 1998, p. 44.

[144] 2 Enoch was not known outside of Eastern Europe for over 1,000 years. It only came to Western attention when the German *Jahrbücher für Protestantische Theologie* made mention of it in 1892. It is believed to have been written around the first century CE by a Hellenistic Jew or Jews in Egypt, probably Alexandria, and to have had a direct influence on the New Testament. It appears to be a Slavic translation of a now lost Greek text and is only preserved in medieval

of Enoch (3 Enoch).[145] These texts, another biblical mystery in themselves, are classed as apocryphal, which means that they are not an accepted part of the Christian canon. However, their influence on Christianity and later Jewish mysticism is undoubted. Without Enoch there would be no archangels.[146]

From the Greek *arch-* (ἀρχ-), 'to rule', and *aggelos*, as we saw above, the archangels are the officer class of the heavenly host. We have already seen how Michael and Gabriel held an exalted status as specifically named angels, with Michael the 'great prince' (Daniel 12:1),[147] and in Joshua we find a captain of the heavenly army (Joshua 5:13–15), hinting at a hierarchy of Yahweh's supernatural subordinates, but this idea is not fully developed until 1 Enoch. The archangels are at first only four, Michael, Uriel (Greek) or Suryal (Ethiopic), Raphael and Gabriel (1 Enoch 9), being later expanded with the addition of Raguel, Saraqâêl, and Remiel (1 Enoch 20). They are particularly known as 'the holy angels who watch' (1 Enoch 20:1), hence the appellation 'the watchers'. This already gives them a guardian aspect, but their remit is broad and impersonal. Uriel is described as 'over the world and over Tartarus' (1 Enoch 20:2). Raphael is 'over the spirits of men' (1 Enoch 20:3). Raguel 'takes vengeance on the world of the luminaries' (1 Enoch 20:4). Michael 'is set over the best part of mankind [and] over chaos' (1 Enoch 20:5). Saraqâêl is 'over the spirits, who sin in spirit' (1 Enoch 20:6). Gabriel is

---

and later manuscripts, the oldest being fourteenth century. See Robert Henry Charles and William Richard Morfill, *The Book of the Secrets of Enoch*, Clarendon, 1896, pp. xi–xxvi.

[145] 3 Enoch is also known as The Book of the Palaces, The Book of Rabbi Ishmael the High Priest and The Revelation of the Metatron. 3 Enoch gives its source as the High Priest Rabbi Ishmael (90–135 CE); however, it is generally dated to the first half of the ninth century CE. See Hugo Odeberg, *The Hebrew Book of Enoch*, Cambridge University Press, 1928, p. 27.

[146] *Harp. Coll. BD*, p. 293, 895; *DDD*, p. 80; Gershom G. Scholem, *Major Trends in Jewish Mysticism*, Schocken, 1961, p. 67; Collins, *Apocalyptic*, pp. 45–6.

[147] It has been argued that given the early date of 1 Enoch, the book of Daniel already demonstrates a second phase in the development of Michael, see *DDD*, p. 569.

'over Paradise and the serpents and the Cherubim' (1 Enoch 20:7). Finally, Remiel is 'set over those who rise', i.e., at the Last Judgement (1 Enoch 20:8).

Archangels

1 Enoch	3 Enoch	2 Esdras (4 Ezra)	Testament of Solomon	Gregory the Great*	Pseudo-Dionysius**	Raziel***	Blessed Angels****
Uriel	Mikael	Michael	Mikael	Michael	Michael	Gabriel	Raphael
Raphael	Gabriel	Gabriel	Gabriel	Gabriel	Gabriel	Famuel	Gabriel
Raguel	Shatqiel	Uriel	Uriel	Raphael	Raphael	Michael	Chamuel
Michael	Baradiel	Raphael	Sabrael	Uriel	Uriel	Uriel	Michael
Saraqâêl	Shachaqiel	Gabuthelon	Arael	Simiel	Chamuel	Raphael	Adabiel
Gabriel	Baraqiel	Beburos	Iaoth	Orifiel	Jophiel	Israel	Haniel
Remiel	Sidriel	Zebuleon	Adonael	Zachariel	Zadkiel	Uzziel	Zaphiel
		Aker					
		Arphugitonos					

*Gregory the Great (540–604 CE), *Moralia in Job*, in M. Adriaen (ed.), *Corpus Christianorum Series Latina*, Turnhout, 1979, iv.xxviii.i.9.

**Pseudo-Dionysius the Areopagite, *De Coelesti Hierarchia* (Celestial Hierarchy), chap. vi-ix.

***The so-called 'throne angels', from 'The Book of the Angel Raziel', thirteenth century. See Steve Savedow (trans.), *Sepher Rezial [sic]: The Book of the Angel Rezial*, Red Wheel/Weiser, 2000.

****Thomas Heywood, *The Hierarchy of the Blessed Angels*, Adam Islip, 1635,

Archangels

Raphael 'was sent to heal' (Tobit 3:17) and describes himself as 'one of the seven holy angels' (Tobit 12:15). He is 'set over all disease and every wound of the children of the people' (1 Enoch 40:9). Raguel is the 'friend of God', although compare Ra'uel, 'the terrifier'. Remiel is doubtless the angel Jeremiel ('El is merciful') found in 2 Esdras ([4 Ezra] 4:36), as we also have a Syriac version that reads Ramael. The names come from the Hebrew root *rûm*, 'to be high, exalted' plus the usual '-el' ending, thus we get Ramiel, Rumiel and Eremiel. In 2 Baruch (55:3) he 'presides over true visions', but confusingly in 1 Enoch (6:7) he is also one of the fallen angels. The name Uriel is known in the Old Testament as a personal name, derived from either 'light' (Hebrew) or 'fire' (Aramaic). As an archangel he is connected with astrology (1 Enoch 72–82), later becoming a revealing angel (2 Esdras [4 Ezra] where his name is sometimes given as Phanuel). Uriel is also sometimes written as Sariel, Suriel and Suryal (Suriyel), linking him with Saraqâêl, who is also sometimes named Sariel, and even Remiel. More variations of these names exist, confusing their roles and identities as separable beings.[148]

As well as the archangels, Enoch describes 'the sleepless ones who guard the throne of his glory' (1 Enoch 71:7). These are the seraphim, cherubim and ophanim. The new group here, the ophanim, takes its name from the Hebrew for 'wheel', leading some to identify these beings with the strange wheels mentioned in Ezekiel (1:15–21) and the 'wheels as burning fire' on the throne of the 'Ancient of Days' in Daniel (7–9). They are later termed 'thrones', although in 1 Enoch they are clearly distinct from the throne of God.

The rank and file angels, the 'host of the heavens' (1 Enoch 61:10), the 'troops of hosts', 'children of heaven' and 'the heavenly household' are designated as 'ministering angels' (*malᵃ'ke ha-ššārēp*) and are organized in 'camps', 'companies' or 'parties'

---

[148] *DDD*, pp. 81, 466–7, 688, 885–6; *Jewish Enc.*; Gustav Davidson, *A Dictionary of Angels*, The Free Press, 1971, pp. 238–9, 258.

(3 Enoch 5:2). In all, 1 Enoch designates seven classes of supernatural beings:

> And He will summon all the host of the heavens, and all the
> holy ones above, and the host of God, the Cherubic, Seraphin
> [*sic*] and Ophannin [*sic*], and all the angels of power, and all
> the angels of principalities, and the Elect One, and the other
> powers on the earth (and) over the water. (1 Enoch 61:10)

In 2 Enoch, the prophet is taken up to heaven by two angels,
Samuil and Ragnil (33:6), rising through seven heavens to
witness:

> A very great light and all the fiery hosts of great archangels,
> and incorporeal powers and lordships, and principalities, and
> powers; cherubim and seraphim, thrones and the watchful-
> ness of many eyes. There were ten troops, a station of
> brightness, and I was afraid and trembled with a great terror.
> (2 Enoch 10:1)

Unlike 1 Enoch, there are now supposed to be ten orders of
spirits here who stand upon ten steps, which only works if we
take the 'very great light' to also be some sort of being.[149] Finally,
in 3 Enoch, the prophet ascends to heaven in a storm chariot
and, after being transformed into fire and lightning, becomes
the angel Metatron.

Angels in the Christian Era

Angels take on a wider range of functions in the New Testament.
When Jesus supposedly tells the story of a poor man who dies
and is 'carried by the angels to Abraham's bosom' (Luke 16:22)
we see that angels now assume the role of psychopompos, guiding or leading the spirit (soul) after death. Mark (12:25) records

---

[149] Rutherford H. Platt solved the problem by simply amending the text to read
'nine regiments' in his *The Lost Books of the Bible*, Alpha House, 1926.

Jesus as having said that the risen will live like angels in heaven. Angels appear on earth (Gabriel in Luke 1–2), in dreams (Matthew 1:20, 2:13, 19), bring messages from God and offer assistance (e.g. Acts 5:19). Raphael helps Tobias (Tobit 5:4–12:22) drive out the demon who killed an earlier husband of his bride Sarah (8:2–3). The most detailed account is given in the Book of Revelation where more than a third of all angel references in the New Testament occur.[150]

The Book of Revelation is traditionally attributed to John the Apostle and appears to have been composed some time in the first or second centuries CE. It only became a canonical book of the New Testament in 397 CE at the Council of Carthage and when Martin Luther came to translate the Bible into German in the sixteenth century he placed it on his list of suspect texts, the Antilegomena. Its position has always been an uncertain one. Like Ezekiel, John sees four 'living creatures' before the throne of God (4:4–11). He witnesses the Lamb of God break the Seven Seals, unleashing the Horsemen of the Apocalypse, natural catastrophe and the Final Judgement. Judgement begins with seven angels sounding seven trumpets to bring further destruction, release Abaddon's army from the bottomless pit and set loose four angels to kill a third of humanity. There is a great battle in heaven between Michael and 'the dragon', also known as 'the Devil, and Satan' (12:7, 9). Both lead armies of angels, but Michael is triumphant and the Devil 'was cast out into the earth, and his angels were cast out with him' (12:9).

Further attempts to establish an intelligible hierarchy of angels continued to be made. The fifth-century writer known as Pseudo-Dionysius the Areopagite no doubt saw the problem with Enoch's arithmetic and described what has become the classic threefold hierarchy of three spheres of three choirs. In the first sphere we find seraphim, cherubim and thrones, in the second, dominions, virtues, powers, and in the third, principalities, archangels and

---

[150] *DDD*, pp. 50–2.

angels.[151] Showing its influence, we find it repeated in the thirteenth century by Thomas Aquinas in his influential *Summa Theologica*. The Christian writers generally agreed on what should come at the top and bottom of the hierarchy, but repeatedly re-ordered and sometimes enlarged the middle ranks.

Keeping Enoch's number ten, the medieval Jewish scholar Moses Maimonides presented an influential schema in the twelfth century of Chajjoth, Ophannim, Arellim, Chashmallim, Seraphim, Mal'achim, Elohim, Bene Elohim, Kerubim, Ishim. The thirteenth-century cabbalist Abraham ben Isaac of Granada had a different list in his *Berit Menuhah* of Arellim, Ishim, Bene Elohim, Mal'achim, Chashmallim, Tarshishim, Shina'nim, Kerubim, Ophannim, Seraphim. Ten had important connotations for the cabbalists as it related to the ten sephiroth (emanations) of the Tree of Life and hence reflected the universal order.[152]

---

[151] Pseudo-Dionysius the Areopagite, *De Coelesti Hierarchia* (Celestial Hierarchy), chap. vi–ix.

[152] Maimonides, *Mishne Thora* S. I.; Jesode Thora C. 2, quoted in Charles and Morfill, p. 25.

Christian Angelic Hierarchies[153]

4th Century St Ambrose	*Apostolic Constitutions*	5th Century Pseudo-Dionysius	6th Century Gregory the Great	7th - 8th Centuries Isidore of Seville	St John Damascene	12th Century Hildegard of Bingen
Seraphim	Seraphim	Seraphim	Seraphim	Seraphim	Seraphim	Seraphim
Cherubim	Cherubim	Cherubim	Cherubim	Cherubim	Cherubim	Cherubim
Dominations	Aeons	Thrones	Thrones	Powers	Thrones	Thrones
Thrones	Hosts	Dominions	Dominations	Principalities	Dominions	Dominations
Principalities	Powers	Virtues	Principalities	Virtues	Powers	Principalities
Potentates (Powers)	Authorities	Powers	Powers	Dominations	Authorities (Virtues)	Powers
Virtues	Principalities	Principalities	Virtues	Thrones	Rulers (Principalities)	Virtues
Archangels	Thrones	Archangels	Archangels	Archangels	Archangels	Archangels
Angels	Archangels	Angels	Angels	Angels	Angels	Angels
	Angels					
	Dominions					

[153] St Ambrose, *Apologia Prophetae David*, 5, fourth century; Clement of Rome (attributed to), *Apostolic Constitutions*, fourth century (purporting to be first century); Gregory the Great, also St Gregory (c. 540–604), *Homiliarum in Ezechielem Prophetam*, sixth century; Isidore of Seville (c. 560–636), *Etymologiae*, Bk 7, seventh century; St John Damascene (c. 676–c. 754–87), *De Fide Orthodoxa*; Hildegard of Bingen, *The Letters of Hildegard of Bingen*, trans. Joseph L. Baird and Radd K. Ehrman, Oxford University Press, 1998, p. 65; and Hildegard of Bingen, *Scivias*, trans. Columba Hart and Jane Bishop, Paulist Press, 1990, Bk 1, 6, composed 1141–51.

As one of the so-called 'religions of the book', Islam shares much of its mythological framework with Judaism and Christianity. According to the Qur'an, when Allah created Adam he ordered the angels to prostrate themselves before him. One of them refused: Azazel. 'Me thou hast created of smoke-less fire, and shall I reverence a creature made of dust?' Allah banished him from heaven to be known henceforth as Iblis (or Eblis), deriving either from the Arabic for 'despair' or a corruption of the Greek *diabolos*, and he became the enemy of humankind – *al-shaytan*, 'the satan'. The other angels remained at their place beside the throne of Allah, arranged in four orders: throne bearers, cherubim, archangels, and the lesser angels. There are four archangels: Jibril (Gabriel), the revealer; Mikal (Michael), the provider; Isra'il (Azrael), the angel of death; and Israfil (Raphael), who puts souls into bodies and is ordered to sound the trumpet announcing *Qiyamah*, the Last Judgement. The angels record the deeds of humans, both good and bad, occasionally interceding with God on their behalf. They reward the good and punish the wicked, and escort the soul at death.[154]

In 610 CE, according to tradition, Allah sent an angel to reveal the Qur'an to Muhammad. After receiving a thorough beating from the angel, Muhammad thought that he might be possessed by evil spirits, djinn, and decided to throw himself from a mountain-top. A voice spoke out as he was about to do so, saying: 'O Muhammad, thou art God's apostle and I am Gabriel.' Reassured, Muhammad was able to go on and continue receiving the Qur'an. There is an interesting range of paranormal phenomena described here: visionary dreams, poltergeist-like activity, possession (or fear of it), and auditory hallucinations, with apparent angelic intervention proving crucial to the story.[155]

---

[154] Oliver Leaman (ed.), *The Qur'an: An Encyclopedia*, Routledge, 2006, pp. 105, 179–81.

[155] Quotation from the Hadith *Sahih al-Bukhari* 1.3; Muhammad ibn Jarir Al-Tabari, *Tarikh al-Rasul Wa al-Muluk (History of the Prophets and Kings)*, Brill, 1879–1901, I, p. 1151; David A. Leeming, Kathryn Madden and Stanton Marlan (eds), *Encyclopedia of Psychology and Religion*, Springer, 2010, p. 37;

Although the term 'angel' develops out of a Judaeo-Christian context, the idea of divine messengers or intermediary spirits between humans and the gods is also found in other cultures. In Chinese and Japanese religion there are a number of beings with roles similar to the angels of the West. Hinduism has its messengers known as angiris. In Buddhism a Bodhisattva functions in a comparable manner. In pagan Europe, Hermes and Iris of the Greeks take the role of divine heralds, in the North, Odin's son Hermod took this part, and swans often appear in Celtic mythology as messengers from the Otherworld.[156]

Guardian Angels

He shall give His angels charge over thee, to keep thee in all thy ways. (Psalms 91:11)

It happened some years ago when I was still a student. It was an ordinary day and I was walking down an ordinary London street. My head was in the clouds and I was paying little attention to the world around me. A sidestreet broke the pavement and as I lifted my foot from the kerb, a voice in my head, so it seemed, shouted 'Car!' I stopped dead as a car shot out from the sidestreet at speed, missing me by inches. As I was to later find out, the experience is not uncommon, with many people attributing such phenomena to the intervention of guardian angels.

Almost every other person thinks they have a guardian angel watching over them. According to a 1993 survey of US adults, 46 per cent believed that they had a guardian angel. As reported in 2010, this figure had risen to 53 per cent. It is a popular idea – that we have a special supernatural bodyguard looking out for us – but where does it come from and did one really save me that fateful day in London?[157]

Leaman, p. 509.

[156] *Enc. Psych. Rel.*, p. 36.

[157] 'Angels Among Us', *Time*, 27 December 1993, p. 56; Christopher Bader, F. Carson Mencken and Joseph Baker, *Paranormal America*, New York University

Again the trail takes us back to Mesopotamia for the origin of current ideas about guardian angels. In the later Assyrian period we find winged creatures guarding temple and palace gates – such as the two colossal statues that once guarded the entrance to Sargon II's throne room in the eighth century BCE, for example. These creatures derive from the female *lama* (Sumerian), or *lamassu* (Akkadian) and the male *shedu*, winged half-human, half-animal hybrids. They also functioned as personal guardians, protecting against evil spirits, and carrying the individual's homage to the gods and bringing back divine blessing. It was a saying that 'he who has no god when he walks in the street wears a headache like a garment' because illnesses, such as headaches, were believed to be caused by demonic forces. Spells were used to invoke their protection, such as this one originally written in cuneiform:[158]

> *ilušîdu damiḳtu ilu[lamassu damiḳtu]* [. . .] *-kiš itti-yà* ('may the favourable [shedu] and favourable lamassu [. . .] [be] with me!')[159]

In both the Old and New Testaments this type of magic is rejected and angels, particularly guardian angels, are only available to the faithful. In the Old Testament, 'the angel of the Lord encampeth round about them that fear him, and delivereth them' (Psalms 34:7) – fearing the Lord is meant in a positive sense in this context. In the New Testament, angels are 'ministering spirits, sent forth to minister for them who shall be heirs of salvation' (Hebrews 1:14). Later Christian writers were less exacting. In the second century CE St Justin the Martyr said 'every man is attended with a guardian angel'. St Jerome (c.

Press, 2010, p. 184, using Baylor Religion Survey data, 2005 and 2007.
[158] *Routledge Dict. Gods*, 2004, pp. 109, 169; Felix Guirand (ed.), *New Larousse Encyclopedia of Mythology*, trans. Richard Aldington and Delano Ames, Crescent Books, 1987, p. 74.
[159] Leonard W. King, *Babylonian Magic and Sorcery*, Weiser, 2000 [1896], pp. 82, 84.

347–420) implied as much when he said 'Great is the dignity of souls, who have from their birth a delegate angel, commissioned from heaven, for their custody'. Thomas Aquinas (1225–74) did not disagree.[160]

In the mythology of Northern Europe we know of Heimdall (Heimdallr), the 'guardian of the gods' who may also have functioned as a boundary figure, or perhaps derived from a household spirit – the lack of surviving sources makes this speculative. The gradual feminization of the Judaic male angels brings them into greater sympathy with the Northern valkyries. Known amongst the Germans in general as *idisi*, amongst the Anglo-Saxons as *waelcryie*, and amongst the Norse as *valkyrja*, the name means 'she who chooses warriors destined to die in battle'. They were the shield-maidens of Odin who chose the most heroic of the battle slain to join the gods in Valhalla and granted victory to the chieftain who won their favour. They either travelled through the air on winged horses, or they could fly through the air unaided as swan-maidens clothed in white feathers. But the conception of being looked after by a supernatural entity is better expressed in the form of the *fylgia* (or *fylgja*), who performed the role of personal and tribal protector, and who could also appear as an omen of death. In the *Lay of Helgi Hjörvarðsson*, Hedin encounters his brother Helgi's *fylgia* in the form of a woman riding a wolf with reins of serpents, which Helgi interprets, correctly as it turns out, as a sign of his impending death.[161]

There are many accounts of the actions of guardian angels. In 1847 John Mason Neale, better known for his Christmas carols such as 'Good King Wenceslas', told two stories of being saved by angels. In the first, a Derbyshire child falls into a stream

---

[160] Quoted in G. W. Hart, 'Guardian Angels', in L.P. (ed.), *A Book of Angels*, 1906, p. 243. Thomas Aquinas, *Summa*, Pt 1, quest. 113, §4.

[161] John Lindow, *Norse Mythology*, Oxford University Press, 2001, pp. 95–6, 167, 171; *New Larousse*, pp. 254, 283; Benjamin Thorpe, *Northern Mythology*, vol. 1, E. Lumley, 1851, pp. 113–14, referring to Helgakviða Hjörvarðssonar, Poetic Edda, various editions.

and is about to drown when she is pulled out by 'a beautiful lady, clad in white'. Nobody of that description could be found, so the thankful parents concluded that she must have been an angel. In the second, a widower and his two children visit the rambling old house of a friend. The children set off to explore and are about to stumble into a deep and uncovered well in the cellar when the figure of their deceased mother appears and prevents them. Neale was not sure whether to declare this spirit that of the mother, or of an angel in her shape.[162]

A story told by the Revd G. W. Hart in 1906 concerns a girl in America who was run over by a tram and thought to have been killed. She was taken home and though apparently unhurt, lay in some sort of comatose condition for a long time. Surprisingly, she regained consciousness and explained that a being in white had lifted the tram wheels one after the other as they passed over her, preventing them from crushing her. Two red lines were discernible on her body, apparently the course of the wheels.[163]

A similar story from the 1960s recounts how a young girl called Lucy was rushed into casualty at St Mary's Hospital, Paddington, after having been run over by a lorry. A policeman had seen both the front and rear wheels roll over her. The lorry driver had felt the bumps. Examining her, medical staff found only one small bruise on her shoulder. As they were about to send her off to be X-rayed, she opened her eyes and asked 'Where is that man in white?' Thinking she meant him, the doctor approached her bed. 'No, no,' said Lucy, 'the man in the long shiny dress.' She explained that this man had picked up the wheels as the lorry went over her. 'The wheels did not touch me,' she said. Lucy was discharged the next day.[164]

Another of Hart's stories begins with a deathbed confession.

---

[162] John Mason Neale, *The Unseen World: Communications with It, Real or Imaginary,* James Burns, 1847, p. 190.

[163] Hart, pp. 246–8.

[164] Told by Judith Shrimpton, GP, in Emma Heathcote-James, *Seeing Angels,* John Blake Publishing, 2001, pp. 74–5.

A Cornish collier, taken grievously ill, confesses in the presence of a priest to having planned to rob a well-to-do farmer on his return from market. The farmer was known to make the journey home by night, alone and with his purse bulging from the day's profits. As the miner and a confederate lay in ambush, the horse-drawn trap approaching, one of them cried out, 'Good God! There are two of them.' They fled. When asked about it later, the farmer stated that he was alone as always, but that he had on that night, as on many another, felt the presence of angels.[165]

According to research, about 18 per cent of reported angelic experiences involve some sort of guardian aspect, a life-saving act or the prevention of an accident. As with my own experience, many other people report hearing voices that impart information their conscious mind was unaware of at the time. For example, a woman is woken by a voice telling her that the water boiler is overheating and she is able to get help in time to prevent it exploding.[166]

Other accounts are more coincidental, often involving the apparent disappearance of, or inability to trace a human who renders (often unintentional) aid and is subsequently interpreted as an angel. A woman walking alone at night finds herself in a dangerous part of the city when another woman appears 'almost out of nowhere' and leads her through the danger only to vanish afterwards. A woman on crutches is harassed at a bus-stop by an aggressive drunk; she prays to God and a black sports car of 'unique design' pulls up from which a blond-haired driver warns the tramp off. Whatever the quality of these reports, they do demonstrate the continuing belief in personal guardian angels able to directly interfere in the mundane world.[167]

The darker side to this is that sometimes these heart-lifting stories of miraculous help in the hour of our greatest need are

---

[165] Hart, pp. 246–8.

[166] Heathcote-James, pp. 241–2; Judith White (1970) in Heathcote-James, pp. 115–17.

[167] Caroline Plant (undated), Vanessa Lillingston-Price (1986) in Heathcote-James, pp. 63–4, 66.

deliberately manufactured to propagate political or religious positions. Machen was one of the few honest enough to immediately disclaim that his story of the bowmen was based on anything other than his own imagination, but even then it was written to bolster public opinion that God was on the side of British in the war against 'the Hun'. An uplifting story widely circulated on the internet – and one that found its way into Heathcote-James' academic study – is that of 'A Dad's Story' (also known as 'The Birdies'). In this story a three-year-old boy called Brian is trapped under a garage door, but is saved from death by what he called 'the birdies', apparently angelic beings who prevent the automatic door from crushing him and bring his mother to the rescue. The story, originally entitled 'Free the Birdies' was apparently written in 1994 by a Mormon using the name Lloyd Glenn to promote temple attendance and observances amongst other members of the Church of Latter Day Saints. Attempts to contact Lloyd Glenn to verify his story have all failed, but the story continues to make the rounds.[168]

Experiencing Angels

Men's nerves and imagination play weird pranks in these strenuous times.

– Brigadier-General John Charteris[169]

From small beginnings the story of the Angels of Mons became an almost undeniable historical fact and unpatriotic to question. An apparently miraculous escape demanded a miraculous explanation. Machen was taken to task for his claims to have

---

[168] Heathcote-James (pp. 75–8) failed to find him, but reproduced the story as true anyway, against her own stated methodology (pp. 28–9). It was also reported that the producer for the US television programme 'Beyond Chance' had also tried with the same result (http://www.near-death.com/forum/fake/000/02.html, accessed 29 July 2010). See the analysis at http://www.snopes.com/glurge/birdies.asp.

[169] Charteris, pp. 25–6.

made the whole thing up. Soldiers and nurses swore blind that they knew someone who had seen the angels. As the years wore on, more 'evidence' was forthcoming despite the growing distance from the event itself. Even as the last of the surviving veterans passed away, stories were still coming out. Just after his 101st birthday in 1980, John Ewings, who had served in the Royal Inniskilling Fusiliers at Mons, told a BBC interviewer how 'I just looked up and the clouds parted [. . .] and this man came out with a flaming sword [. . .] what I thought I saw was an angel'. As late as 2000, Joyce Trott told of her father's experiences at the battle: '[there] was an eerie sound and there was a white light across the hill and they saw these crowds on horses riding across the top of the hill'.[170]

For the various writers and compilers of the Bible and other religious texts it was self-evident that angels were real and enacted God's will, either as messengers or in more hands-on roles, slaying unbelievers, saving prophets and preparing to decimate humanity at the Last Judgement. Like the Angels of Mons, these angels became undeniably factual and for the believer to question them was irreverent. However, when Charteris was looking into the Angels of Mons legend he was more ready to ascribe the phenomenon to psychological factors, but admitted that he could not find out how the story arose. The writer Arthur Machen claimed that the legend was created when he published *The Bowmen*, leading to a situation not unlike that of the Russian cosmonauts' supposed angel sighting onboard Salyut 7 in 1985. Originally reported – we should say *invented* – in the US tabloid *Weekly World News*, the story went on to become widely cited as a factual event.[171] The problem for Machen's version is that Charteris' comments are dated just

---

[170] John Ewings, BBC Northern Ireland, 22 May 1980, quoted in Clarke, pp. 52–3; Joyce Trott, BBC Everyman 'Angels', first broadcast on BBC1, 12 December 2000, quoted in Heathcote-James, pp. 70–1.
[171] 'Huge Angels Seen in Space', *Weekly World News*, 22 October 1985; for an analysis see Leo Ruickbie, 'Angels in Space', *Paranormal*, 56, February 2011, pp. 54–7.

days after the Battle of Mons and three weeks before the publication of 'The Bowmen'. Not only that, but the accounts that started coming back from the frontlines told of winged angels, supernatural cavalry, divine lights, mysterious clouds and not so much of ghostly archers from Agincourt as in Machen's tale. So what really did happen?

Other than broader surveys conducted by organizations like Gallup, the only serious in-depth study of angel experiences was carried out in the late 1990s by Emma Heathcote-James, then a PhD theology student at Birmingham University. After numerous calls for information on national television and in the press, including the BBC and *The Times*, she received 350 written replies from people claiming to have had some sort of angel experience.

Respondents' definitions of what constituted an 'angel' ranged from the traditional being in white with wings to any helpful incident with some sort of mysterious element, including strange smells and lights. Looking closely at her figures, we see that she found only 168 people who claimed to have seen an angel. Of these 109 reported seeing what we would traditionally think of as an angel. A typical experience ran along the following lines: '[He] looked like an angel with long flowing robes and wings'; or 'she looks rather like a Pre-Raphaelite goddess in a Burn[e]-Jones painting'. For a New Age angel-therapist like Doreen Virtue, 'Angels are glowing beings, filled with the inner radiance of God's love. Angels have soft, feathery wings'.[172]

Most people who claimed to have had an angel experience were aged thirty-one to fifty at the time and lived in the south-east of England – factors influenced by Heathcote-James's methodology and geography, as she acknowledged. More women than men reported such experiences and were generally more likely to see a traditional-style angel. This again is in line with demographic expectations. Virtue reported that about 80 to

[172] Heathcote-James, pp. 23–4, 32–3, 69, 248: describes 48 per cent as having seen a 'traditional' (31.1 per cent) or humanoid being (16.9 per cent); Doreen Virtue, http://www.angeltherapy.com/faq.php, accessed 23 July 2010.

85 per cent of her audience was female, seeing the male section split between a larger number of homosexual men and fewer of what she calls 'drag-alongs' – heterosexual men who reluctantly accompany wives or girlfriends. It would seem most probable that more women than men report angel experiences nowadays because more women are currently interested in angels. It is not surprising given their heritage that most people who see angels are Christians. The men unloading their bolt-action Lee-Enfield rifles with the speed of machine guns into the ranks of advancing Germans at Mons were Christians.[173]

The timing of the angels' fateful intervention at Mons is uncertain. Legend has fixed it at the height of the engagement, but a series of running battles was fought as the BEF tried to remove itself from the path of the German juggernaut. As well as various rearguard actions there was the retreat itself: a herculean marathon under blazing summer skies with an eighty-pound kit, little or no food and sometimes barely four hours of sleep. The first stage of the retreat from Mons to the regrouping point at Bavay involved a thirty-six-hour forced march with no sleep at all. The men of the Middlesex Regiment were described as 'stumbling along more like ghosts than living soldiers'. The Northumberland Fusiliers were 'a column of automatons that dragged along through the darkness of the night'. Private Frank Richards, 2 Royal Welsh Fusiliers, told how 'we retired all night with fixed bayonets, many sleeping as they marched'.[174]

In such conditions men reported seeing strange bright lights,

---

[173] Heathcote-James, pp. 233–4, 236, 240. Virtue quoted in 'Angel's Wings and Human Prayer', *New Age Retailer*, 20 July 2005, reproduced on http://www. angeltherapy.com/view_article.php?article_id=33, accessed 23 July 2010. According to Heathcote-James (p. 237), they were 53.1 per cent Christian, comprising: 39.1 per cent Protestant, 6.3 per cent Catholic, 3.4 per cent 'Christian Convert' and 4.3 per cent lapsed Christian of unspecified denomination. Buddhists, Jews, Muslims, New Agers, even agnostics and atheists, also reported angel type experiences.

[174] Regimental History, Middlesex Regiment, 24 August 1914; Regimental History, 5th Regiment, Northumberland Fusiliers, 24 August 1914; Frank Richards, *Old Soldiers Never Die*, Faber, 1964, p. 19; Clarke, pp. 48–50.

sheets of water along the roadside, bodies of soldiers on foot and horseback, trees turned into villages, castles appeared out of nothing, and one soldier kept ducking his head to avoid imaginary arches across the road. As Richards wrote, 'very nearly everyone were [*sic*] seeing things, we were all so dead beat'.[175]

It is a known fact that sleep deprivation causes hallucinations. Michael Golder, a professor of psychiatry at George Washington University, put it this way: 'a person who has been sleep-deprived for 72 hours is as susceptible to hallucinations as someone taking LSD'. Abnormally high body temperature, hunger and thirst have also been linked with hallucinations. Men marching without sleep, with little food in hot summer weather under stress of battle present ideal subjects for spontaneous hallucinations.[176]

Hallucinations are not as rare as we might think. When 500 people assessed as mentally 'normal' were questioned on the subject in the 1960s, 125 reported having had at least one hallucination. Included amongst these was 'seeing an angel in church during service'.[177] In his 1958 book, *Flying Saucers: A Modern Myth of Things Seen in the Skies*, Carl Gustav Jung specifically used the 'evidence' of the Angels of Mons to argue that the soldiers had experienced a 'non-pathological' vision, or what he would term a 'visionary rumour', simply, a rumour experienced in a visual as opposed to aural form. According to Jung, the extreme psychological stresses on these soldiers created a collective vision based on a shared symbolism reflecting unconscious wishes.

Psychologist Dr Susan Blackmore argued that angel experiences were produced by endorphins released during pain or shock. However, only a relatively few of Heathcote-James'

---

[175] Regimental History, 5th Regiment, Northumberland Fusiliers, 24 August 1914; A. Johnstone, letter to the *Evening News*, 11 August 1915; Richards, p. 19.
[176] Golder quoted in Rachel Horn, 'What Happens When We Hallucinate?', *Popular Science*, October 2006, p. 104; Peter D. Slade and Richard P. Bentall, *Sensory Deception: A Scientific Analysis of Hallucination*, Taylor & Francis, 1988, p. 33.
[177] Slade and Bentall, p. 70.

respondents reported an angel experience at the greatest moment of pain or shock, that is, during or after an accident.[178] According to Heathcote-James' research, the largest number of angelic experiences occurred in the bedroom rather than on the battlefield or at the scene of an accident. Although this is not specific enough to confirm that the people involved were actually asleep or on the point of sleep, this peak in the evidence does suggest typical hypnogogic (falling asleep) or hypopompic (waking up) states, that is, vivid sensory experiences associated with either falling asleep or waking up – a phenomenon medically described as early as 1848. People today seem to encounter angels in the same way that Daniel first encountered Gabriel: in their dreams, or dream-like states.[179]

Angels today are seen in an almost entirely positive aspect, but one of the abiding problems has always been deciding whose side they are on. They were clearly not on the side of the Assyrian armies when the 'chariots of fire' came to Elisha's assistance at the siege of Dothan. The Angels of Mons were no angels to the Germans, but when the first German soldiers were taken prisoner in the early days of WWI, guards were surprised to read *Gott mit uns* ('God is with us') on their belt buckles. As it says in the New Testament, 'Even Satan disguises himself as an angel of light' (2 Corinthians 11:14), and as we might add ourselves, even hell has its angels.

---

[178] Blackmore quoted in 'The Extraordinary Rise and Rise of Angels', *Cosmopolitan*, December 1997, p. 40, and Heathcote-James, p. 253; approx. 1.5 per cent reported an angel experience during or after an accident, although Heathcote-James does not give the exact figures.

[179] Slade and Bentall, p. 19; Heathcote-James, pp. 191, 239–40, 254 – 30 per cent of experiences occurred in the bedroom with another 9.5 per cent taking place in hospital rooms. Many more of the examples she quotes in her book involve relaxed states of mind, although she gives no analysis of this other than by location.

4. Demons

The priest approached the bed, a forced smile on his face. His words were kindly as he addressed the girl bound to the bed frame, trying to ignore the scratches and bruises mottling her puffy, beaten face.

'Hello, Regan. I'm a friend of your mother. I'd like to help you.'

The girl looked at him. 'You might loosen the straps then?'

'I'm afraid you might hurt yourself, Regan.'

'I'm not Regan.'

'I see. Well then, let's introduce ourselves. I'm Damien Karras.'

'And I'm the Devil. Now kindly undo these straps!'

It is an unforgettable encounter in a film that would be regarded as the scariest of all time.[180] As one of the taglines to *The Exorcist* put it 'Somewhere between science and superstition, there is another world. The world of darkness.' And millions of us have gone there – at least director William Friedkin's version of it.

This world of darkness is one in which swarming hordes of demons, ranked in innumerable legions under the command of mighty warlords of hell, press at the defences of our everyday lives. The fires burn below, white-hot in readiness for the damned, as fallen angels, wings singed and perfumed with brimstone, oil the machinery of destruction in preparation for the End Times. This is the theological reality. Sophisticated modern clerics may

---

[180] AMC/Harris Interactive poll, 2006.

play down the notion of the Devil, but the Church is founded upon the rock of resistance to the forces of (perceived) evil. Demonologists down the ages have analysed and classified them, sometimes fought them, and constantly warned us of their unceasing efforts to conquer our souls. If they are right, the thought alone is enough to drive us mad. The problem is that the subject of demons is far from straightforward.

What is a Demon?

Demons are divine. Literally. The word comes from the Greek *daimon* (δαίμων, Latin *daemon*), meaning 'divinity' from the age of Homer onward. It could refer to a specific god or goddess, or denote deity in general. Even in Ancient Greece they argued about its etymology. In the fifth century BCE the philosopher Plato said that the word originally meant 'knowing'. Some modern scholars prefer an origination from a root meaning 'to divide (destinies)', in the sense of distributing 'fate' or 'destiny', or the spirit controlling one's fate.[181]

Daimones, like other Classical supernatural entities, were morally ambivalent. *Daimones* caused *eudaimonia* (εὐδαιμονία), 'good fortune', as well as *kakodaimonia* (κακοδαιμονία), 'bad luck', or 'evil fate' – or even possession by an evil spirit. The poet Hesiod, who lived around 700 BCE, explained that these *daimones* were the souls of those who had lived during the Golden Age and who now watched over humankind as 'guardians of mortal men'. Plato later added that *daimones* were 'between gods and mortals' and, like angels, mediated between the two. Socrates' famous *daimon* seems to have been predisposed towards the good and was said to offer him advice. Also in the fifth century BCE, the philosopher Empedocles taught that the *daimon* was an 'occult self', or soul, that endured through successive incarnations.[182]

---

[181] Henry George Liddell and Robert Scott, *A Greek–English Lexicon*, Clarendon Press, 1940; K. van der Toorn, Bob Becking and Pieter Willem van der Horst (eds), *Dictionary of Deities and Demons in the Bible* [*DDD*], 2nd ed., Brill/Eerdmans, 1999, p. 235.

[182] Plato, *Cratylus* 398b, *Symposium* 202e; Hesiod, *Works and Days* 109–93;

Generally, *daimones* were seen as a class of spirit below the gods of Olympus, such as Zeus and Hera. Although in principle they could be either good or bad, this is not to say that the Greeks were lacking any conception of evil spirits. There was also a large number of entirely unpleasant *daimones*, euphemistically referred to as the 'other daimon', lurking in the shadows of the Greek worldview. Illness itself was a *daimon*, but also bore specific names such as Hepiales (also Epiales), the personification of fever, Enodius who caused diarrhoea and the fluttering, fairy-like Keres who loved to cause madness, blindness and even blisters, as well as stir up hate and discord. Like the Keres, other evil spirits were seen as responsible for social unrest, such as Eris ('strife'), 'insatiable in her fury', whilst others like Lamia ('gluttonous' or 'lecherous'), the blood-sucking child-killer and shark-like mother of the dog-headed sea monster Scylla, reigned over specific realms of human misery. Lamia, descended from the Akkadian demoness Lamashtu, was often counted amongst the Empusae ('forcers-in') who were said to frighten travellers on lonely roads and sexually assault men. Later a whole class of vampirizing she-devils came to be known as the lamiae, forerunners of the later succubi.[183]

Damaging or dangerous natural phenomena were also seen as spiritual entities. The three Gorgons – Stheino ('mighty'), Euryale ('wide wandering') and Medusa ('cunning') – represented the destroying power of the thunderstorm, their basilisk stare the lightning flash, whilst at the same time being the ultimate incarnation of the evil eye. The storm winds were also personified as the Harpies ('snatchers'). They were said to live in the entrance to the underworld called the Strophades, or in a

Liddell and Scott; E. R. Dodds, *The Greeks and the Irrational*, University of California Press, 1963, p. 153; *DDD*, p. 235.

[183] Walter Burkert, *Greek Religion*, Harvard University Press, 2000, pp. 180–1; Dodds, pp. 6–8; Cesidio R. Simboli, *Disease-Spirits and Divine Cures Among the Greeks and Romans*, Doctoral Thesis, Columbia University, 1921; Robert Graves, *The Greek Myths*, Penguin, 1992, pp. 189–90; *DDD*, p. 521.

cave on Crete, and were sent by the gods to carry people off to their doom or, paradoxically, bring life.[184]

One group of beings was so feared that they were known euphemistically as the Eumenides, the 'gracious' or 'kind ones'. Whilst everyone knew they were the Erinyes, 'the angry ones', they preferred not to name them out loud. The Romans would come to call them the Furies (*Furiae*). According to Hesiod, they were born of the blood of the primordial sky-god Uranus, murdered by his son Kronos. Aeschylus called them 'the children of Eternal Night'. Their eyes dripped blood, their skin was the colour of coal, sometimes with dog's faces, or Gorgon eyes, bat-winged to show the swiftness of their vengeance, serpents entwining their brows. They carried blazing torches and brass-studded whips. Despite their fearsome reputation their purpose was in itself not evil. They avenged perjury and murder, and upheld the moral order, embodying the judgement or curse pronounced upon a criminal.[185]

Vast ranks of the Nameless Ones of the underworld, tempting sirens, oracular and tomb-haunting sphinxes, sea-monsters, Ladon the dragon, the snake-woman Echidne, the 'goat-shanked *daimon*' Pan, and the corpse-eating Euronymous: many more such entities can be named, for the Ancient Greeks had a fully developed pantheon of horrors – gods, monsters and *daimones* – to account for all of the various destructive natural forces and human maladies that one could imagine. We should be careful in calling them personifications, since, in reality, this is how the Ancient Greeks actually understood these things: as *daimones*. They could be placated by ritual and even the Erinyes were known to have shown mercy at least once. The Greeks

---

[184] Homer, *Iliad*, 16.150; Hesiod, *Theogonia* 265; Aeschylus, *Eumenides*, 50, *Prometheus* 819; Ovid, *Metamorphoses*, 4.742; Virgil, *Aeneid*, 3, and *Georgia* 3.274. Felix Guirand (ed.), *New Larousse Encyclopedia of Mythology*, trans. Richard Aldington and Delano Ames, Crescent Books, 1987, p. 198; John Davidson Beazley, *The Development of Attic Black Figure*, University of California Press, 1986, p. 13; Graves, p. 244; Jane Ellen Harrison, *Prolegomena to the Study of Greek Religion*, Cambridge University Press, 1908, pp. 179–80, 187–8, 196.

[185] Also written Erinnyes. *New Larousse*, pp. 186–7; Graves, p. 122.

interacted with the *daimones*, seeing their inescapability and their functional necessity as supernatural agents (and, indeed, relatives) of the higher gods. Things would not stay that way.[186]

Demonization

Just as angels in the Judaeo-Christian tradition were both good and evil, so were *daimones* in the Greek. It was only in the politically charged culture-clash of the Hellenistic period that the Greek *daimones* became demonized and fixed in their entirely evil aspect. Alexander the Great had brought the ancient Near East under Greek control in the fourth century BCE. After his death, power was divided amongst his generals with Seleucus gaining control of Babylonia, instituting a monarchy and the succession of the line of the Seleucids. The defining moment was the suppression of Judaism under Antiochus Epiphanes, the Seleucid King of Judea, and the subsequent revolt led by Judas Maccabeus in 167 BCE. Antiochus had rededicated the temple of Jerusalem to Zeus; and Maccabeus destroyed the altar in 165. Greek culture was despised and hence the Greek *daimon* could only be evil. The Jews threw down Mount Olympus, home of the Greek gods, and made of it a hell, so that we read in the *Testament of Solomon* (first to fifth centuries CE) of seven female demons who spend part of their time on Olympus (8:4).[187]

---

[186] Aeschylus, *Eumenides*; Pausanius, *Description of Greece*, 10.28.1–10.29.1; Burkert, p. 421.

[187] David Albert Jones, *Angels: A History*, Oxford University Press, 2010, pp. 111–12; *DDD*, pp. 646, 938. The Old Testament contains no reference to Olympus. The Bible is a complex piece of literature that cannot be taken at face value. The earliest known biblical texts exist in fragments of the Greek Septuagint (Rahlfs 801, 819, 957) and Hebrew/Aramaic Dead Sea Scrolls (the Isaiah scroll: 1QIsaᵃ) dating from the second century BCE. The earliest and most complete Christian Bible (Old and New Testaments) only dates from the fourth century CE, known in two forms as the Codex Sinaiticus and the Codex Vaticanus (LXXᴮ), and is written in Greek. The earliest and most complete version of the Hebrew Bible in Hebrew is the so-called Masoretic Text and dates from the ninth and tenth centuries CE. The Hebrew Bible itself transmits the tradition that the Torah was written/assembled under divine inspiration by 'Ezra', in the fifth century BCE. The best evidence based on archaeology

The Greek translation of the Hebrew scriptures, the Septuagint, used the word 'demon' in a general masking of nuances into a homogenous evil. Where the Hebrew text talked of the national deities of non-Jews, tutelary spirits (*sedim*) and other pagan gods, the Greek talked only of demons. But even in the Old Testament the older sense of an intermediary performing the dictates of the divine will remained. Yahweh sends an evil spirit to torment Saul (1 Samuel 16:14), a lying spirit of false prophecy to lead Ahab astray (Exodus 12:23), a 'destroyer' (1 Corinthians 10:10), and a 'son of God' called Satan is sent to test Job.

Absorbing their religious ideas from regionally dominant cultures, the Hebrews inevitably acquired the rich demonology of Mesopotamia. Like the Greeks, the Mesopotamians saw natural forces and catastrophes – fire, hail, famine, pestilence – as spiritual entities sent by the gods, or themselves the offspring of the gods. The baby-snatching Pashittu, for example, was supposedly sent by the gods to control human population size. The plague god Resheph, represented in Ugarit as an archer, appears in Psalms (91:5–6) as 'the arrow flying by day' and the 'poisonous Qeteb' in Deuteronomy (32:24).[188]

Other spirits embody the inherent dangers of the desert and lonely places. In dark alleyways, Rabişu ('the croucher'), lay in ambush and we find him indirectly referred to in Genesis (4:7): sin crouching at Cain's door like a demon. Medical divination texts from the Old Babylonian period use phrases such as 'a *rabişu* has seized him' and 'he has walked in the path of a *rabişu*'. A typology of such demons developed, so we read of 'the *rabişu* of the road', 'the *rabişu* of the roof' and 'the *rabişu* of the lavatory'. Interestingly, *rabişu* was also the title of a high official in Mesopotamia as well as being applied as a title to some of the gods in a positive sense.[189]

---

would indicate that the oldest portions of the Bible, the Torah, were composed in the Hellenistic period and not in the second millennium BCE when they purport to have been written.

[188] *DDD*, pp. 572, 673.

[189] *DDD*, pp. 236, 682, 853. See W. G. Lambert and A. R. Millard, *Atra-hasis:*

Lilith makes her entry into the Old Testament as the 'screech owl' in Isaiah (34:14) and the 'terror of the night' in Psalms (91:5). The Hebrew *lîlît* is popularly believed to come from *laylâ*, 'night', although it actually derives from Akkadian *lilītu*, which itself comes from Sumerian *lil*. Evidence of belief in her is older than Yahweh, dating from the third millennium BCE. In the Epic of Gilgamesh we read of the demon *ki-sikil-lil-lá* who makes her lair in the trunk of a tree planted by the goddess Inanna (Ishtar). In Akkadian writings three related storm demons are often mentioned as *lilû*, *lilītu* and *(w)ardat lilî*. *Lilû* is the storm wind from the south-west. *Lilītu* is imagined flying like a bird and can escape from a house through the window. Lilith assimilated the similar Lamashtu during the Middle Babylonian period, leading to her migration to the Syrian region.[190]

In later Jewish traditions, Lilith is described as a demon with long hair and wings, and men are warned not to sleep alone in case she visits them. She is said to be Adam's first wife, or later mistress, with whom she conceived a vast brood of demons. She is even said to have been the Queen of Sheba (also called Zemargad): a beautiful woman from her head to her navel, flaming fire below. The lover of the demons Samael and Asmedai, she would also be called the Devil's grandmother and the progenitrix of witches and witchcraft. She was said to fly over the rooftops at night, sniffing for mothers' milk. She could take any form she desired in order to enter the house; mention is made of a black cat, a broom, or even a strand of black hair. Once inside she would either try and strangle the child or steal the afterbirth as food for her own children. In other stories she would steal newborn children and eat them. She appears as Obyzouth in the *Testament of Solomon*, 'a woman whose body and limbs were veiled by her long hair'.[191]

The Babylonian Story of the Flood, Clarendon Press, 1969, III, vii 3–4. For the medical texts see René Labat, *Traité akkadien de diagnostics et pronostics medicaux*, Brill, 1951, 34:23, 158:12, 182:40, 188:13 and 214:11.
[190] *DDD*, pp. 520–1, 851–2.
[191] Chester Charlton McCown, *The Testament of Solomon*, J. C. Hinrichs, 1922,

A thousand superstitions sprang up around this dangerous demoness. Special amulets could protect against her. In the *Testament of Solomon* she is counteracted by the angel Apharoph and if the new mother should write Obyzouth on a piece of paper and hang it up, then Lilith will avoid her. The blood of circumcision is said to be preserved by God as a ward against the injurious attentions of Lilith. If a child smiles on the night of the Sabbath, then Lilith is playing with it and it should be smacked three times on the nose. An old German baptism ritual went *Vivat Eva, foras Lilith* ('Long live Eve, out with Lilith'), apparently drawing on a Jewish exorcism formula. Today the tide has turned and brave or reckless magicians meet in smoky temples to invoke her:[192]

> Dark is she, but brilliant! Black are her wings, black on black! Her lips are red as rose, kissing all of the Universe! She is Lilith, who leadeth forth the hordes of the Abyss, and leadeth man to liberation![193]

Another demon who was always a demon curiously does not appear in the officially sanctioned version of the Bible. Asmodeus in the Apocryphal Book of Tobit (3:8–17) is a corruption of two words from the East Iranian language Avestan: *aēšma-*, 'wrath' and *daēuua*, 'threat, menace', which form the compound *xēšm-dēw* in Middle Persian (Pahlavi), meaning 'demon of wrath'

---

p. 13; *Shishim Sippurei Am* in Howard Schwartz, *Tree of Souls: The Mythology of Judaism*, Oxford University Press, 2007, p. 224.

[192] *DDD*, p. 521. For Talmudic references see Erubin 100b, Niddah 24b, and Shabbath 151b. Other traditions: *The Alphabet of Ben Sira*, c. eighth to tenth centuries CE; Herman Leberecht Strack, *The Jew and Human Sacrifice*, Bloch, 1909, p. 129, referring to the 'Zohar' to Leviticus 14 and 19; G. Lammert, *Volksmedizin und medizinischer Aberglaube*, F. A. Julien, 1869, p. 170; Schwartz, p. 221.

[193] Joseph Max and 'Lilith Darkchilde', 'Invocation of Lilith', 1994, revised 2002, http://home.comcast.net/~max555/rites/lilith_1.htm, accessed 12 August 2010, now widely disseminated on the internet. Max describes himself as an initiate of the Autonomatrix Guild of Chaos Magicians and 'Imperator General' of the Open Source Order of the Golden Dawn.

– usually transcribed as Aeshma Daeva. Aeshma first appears in the second millennium BCE in the collection of sacred Zoroastrian hymns called Gathas as the demon who brings illness and evil to mankind. In later texts he is described as wielding a 'bloody club' and additionally presides over drunkenness. In Tobit, Asmodeus kills seven successive husbands of Sara out of jealousy, leading to a reputation for conjugal discord that reappears in the *Testament of Solomon* (2:3). In other Jewish writings he acquires the title 'king of demons' and usurps the throne of Solomon. He finds his way into the books of magic (grimoires) as Asmoday. He plays a major role in the Solomonic grimoires (see the chapter on Magic). In the medieval *Key of Solomon* he leads the Golab, 'genii of wrath and sedition', as 'Samuel the Black'. He is the thirty-second spirit of the seventeenth century *Lesser Key of Solomon*, described as a 'great king', invoked for skill in mathematics and invisibility. However, lechery would become Asmodeus' special theological function by the sixteenth century. As a crowning achievement, the nineteenth-century French occultist Jacques Auguste Simon Collin de Plancy has Asmodeus seducing Eve.[194]

To this adopted demonology the Hebrews added a degradation and demonization of the gods of neighbouring peoples, so that the beliefs of their enemies became a swamp of stinking devils. Such was the fate of Beelzebub, in particular.

When the King of Israel, Ochozias (also Ahaziah), fell out of a window in Samaria and did himself an injury, he sent messengers to Ekron (Accaron) to find out from Beelzebub whether he would recover. Yahweh was understandably upset to be slighted

---

[194] Michael Arnoud Cor de Vaan, *The Avestan Vowels*, Rodopi, 2003, p. 351; *DDD*, pp. 106–8, 581–2; Kenneth McLeish, *Myth and Legends of the World Explored*, Bloomsbury, 1996, p. 87; Geoffrey W. Dennis, *The Encyclopedia of Jewish Myth, Magic and Mysticism*, Llewellyn, 2007, p. 22; Joseph H. Peterson (ed.), *The Lesser Key of Solomon*, Weiser, 2001, p. 21; S. Liddell MacGregor Mathers, *The Key of Solomon*, George Redway, 1888, p. 122; J. A. S. Collin de Plancy, *Dictionnaire infernal*, Société Nationale, 1845, p. 46. For the Zoroastrian references see the Gathas (Yasna 29:2 and 30:6), as well as Yasna 10:8, 97, 57:10–25.

like this and sent 'an angel of the Lord' to tell Elias to intercept the messengers and inform them that because of his actions Ochozias would not recover. As the Bible tells it he did not, of course, recover.

Worshipped at Ekron, one of the five major cities of the Philistines, Baal Zebub was clearly seen as an important oracular deity. The name is interpreted as Lord (Baal) of the Flies (Zebub) and the Greek Septuagint rendered the name as 'Baal the fly' (Βααλ μυῖα). However, the Greek translation by Symmachus in the second century CE, as well as references in the New Testament, give the name as Beezeboul and Beelzeboul (Βεελζεβουλ), suggesting an entirely different meaning. Beelzeboul finds accord with the titles *zbl* ('prince'), *zbl b'l* ('prince Baal') and *zbl b'l 'ars* ('prince, lord of the underworld') used in texts discovered at Ugarit. In the Old Testament *zebul* is used to mean 'residence' or 'high house'. In Ugaritic incantations Baal is called upon to dispel the demon of disease. What this shows is that 'Beelzebub' is in fact a derogatory pun on the god's real name of Baal Zebul ('Baal the Prince', or perhaps understood by the Jews as 'Lord of the High Place').[195]

There were plenty of other Baals around at the time. Meaning 'lord', *ba'al* was frequently attached to a number of other names, as well as being the particular name of a Canaanite god. The Old Testament uses the word about ninety times, but it is much older than that, dating back to the third millennium inscription from the ancient Mesopotamian city at Abu Ṣalabikh in what is now Iraq. From texts dated to around 1350 BCE, Baal is known to have been a god of the Ugaritic pantheon, being termed a son of El.[196] His known period of worship extends from the second millennium

---

[195] OT: 2 Kings 1:2–6. NT: Matthew 10:25, 12:24, 27; Mark 3:22; Luke 11:15, 18–19. M. Dietrich and O. Loretz, 'Die Ba'al-Titel *b'l ars* und *aliy qrdm*', *Ugarit-Forschungen*, 12, 1980, pp. 391–3; *DDD* pp. 154–5. For the Ugaritic incantations see Ras-Ibn-Hani tablets, field numbers I.16, 1–3.

[196] See R. D. Biggs, *Inscriptions from Tell Abu Salabikh*, The University of Chicago Press, 1974; Dietrich and Loretz, pp. 391–3. Generally speaking, all the Ugarit gods were children of El.

BCE to about 200 BC. Baal found his way into the temples of Egypt and Phoenician colonization spread his cult throughout the Mediterranean. It is unsurprising that Baal was worshipped by the ancient Israelites in the early Iron Age, as we see in numerous Old Testament references to things like 'an altar of Baal in the house of Baal' (1 Kings 16:32) and 'the priest of Baal' (2 Kings 11:18) until suppressed by the adherents of the Yahweh cult – a fact that colours these various references to Baal.[197]

Baal and Baalim (plural) were worshipped in high places, including rooftops, as well as in temples. The shrine would comprise an image of the deity or a cone-shaped sacred stone, the *baetylion*, representing the abode of the god, or otherwise a sacred pole or pillar. Incense was burnt, libations poured, animals sacrificed. The priests led wild dances around the altar, working themselves into a frenzy so that they could cut themselves with knives until they ran with blood. The congregation would kiss the representations of Baal and indulge in immoral practices. At least that is the view presented in the Old Testament.[198]

As well as Baal Zebul, two other *ba'al* form names became demonized by the Yahweh cultists: Beelphegor and Baal-Berith. Beelphegor (Septuagint) or Baalpeor was the *ba'al* of Phogor/ Peor, a mountain in the land of the Moabites, lying in the highlands to the east of the Dead Sea. The Israelites also worshipped this god, again before suppression by the Yahwehists, with rites depicted as involving the familiar immoral practices. The tradition developed in the Rabbinical literature that these especially involved indecent exposure and a novel application of the act of defecation. He is generally known as Belphegor in the demonological and magical literature, so we find him in the *Key of Solomon* as chief of the disputers (*Tagaririm*).[199]

---

[197] *DDD*, pp. 132ff; Michael Jordan, *Dictionary of Gods and Goddesses*, Facts on File, 2004, p. 41.

[198] The OT references are numerous, but see especially 1 Kings 14, 16, 18, and 2 Kings 10–1, 17, 21, 23.

[199] Numbers 23:28, 25; Deuteronomy 3:29; Talmud: Sanhedrin 64a, 106a; Abodah Zarah, 44a; and Rashi's commentary on Numbers 25:3 (Sifrei Balak

Baal-Berith, 'Lord of the Covenant', was a Canaanite fertility god also worshipped by the Israelites (Judges 9:33). This covenant god provides the model for the later idea amongst the Jews that they had entered into a divine covenant with Yahweh. Stripped of the title 'Baal', Berith ended up as one of the seventy-two demons of the Solomon legend.[200]

Moloch (Molech), Milton's 'horrid King besmear'd with blood' is, like *ba'al*, an epithet, meaning in this case 'ruler, king' from the Semitic root *mlk*. A god *Mlk* was known in Ugarit with variations such as Malik at Ebla and the underworld god Muluk is also attested. In addition, entities called *maliku* received funerary offerings at Mari, either as spirits of the dead or chthonic (underworld) gods. All this points to an ancient underworld deity connected to a cult of the ancestral dead. Another god formerly worshipped by the Israelites, the Hebrew scriptures describe the Yahwehists' suppression of a cult of forbidden sexual relations with non-Jews (Leviticus 20:5) and/or a cult of child sacrifice (Leviticus 18:21): to 'make his son or his daughter to pass through the fire to Molech' (2 Kings 23:10). The Jewish centre of this cult was just outside Jerusalem at Tophet ('place of abomination') in the valley of Geennom; a temple erected by Solomon (1 Kings 11:7). He was denounced as an 'abomination' (1 Kings 11:7) and his followers were stoned to death (Leviticus 20:2). In the *Key of Solomon* he becomes with Satan one of the two chiefs of the Thamiel, or Double-Headed Ones, 'demons of revolt and anarchy', who are locked in battle against the Chaioth Ha-Qadesh, the Intelligences of the Divine Tetragram.[201]

---

1); 'Ancient Fragment of the Key of Solomon', in Mathers, p. 122.

[200] *DDD*, pp. 141–3. On the covenant question Mulder in the *DDD* argues contrary, but his position is unconvincing and somewhat overstated; see in support Yehezkel Kaufmann, *The Religion of Israel*, University of Chicago Press, 1960, pp. 138–9. At the very least, Baal-Berith demonstrates that the covenant was not a unique idea amongst the Jews.

[201] *DDD*, pp. 539–41, 581–5; John Milton, *Paradise Lost*, S. Simmons, 1674 [1667], Bk I, l. 392; Mathers, p. 121. Eissfeldt suggested that the name derived from the technical Punic term *molk/mulk* used in reference to a cult of child

Another Moloch, the sun god Adramelech (Semitic *'addir-melek)* of the city of Sepharvaim on the Euphrates, worshipped with the burnt offerings of children (2 Kings 17:31), becomes a demon in the Seventh Book of Moses. In Friedrich Gottlieb Klopstock's religious epic *The Messiah* (1748–73) he is described as 'the enemy of God, greater in malice, guile, ambition, and mischief than Satan, a fiend more curst'. In the nineteenth century Collin de Plancy assigned him the role of Grand-Chancellor of Hell, gentleman-in-waiting to the King of the Demons, and President of the High Council of Devils. He takes the form of a mule plumed with peacock's feathers.[202]

The ancient Hebrews angered Yahweh yet again, according to the Bible (Judges 2:13, 10:6; 1 Samuel 7:3–4, 12:10), by worshipping Ashtaroth. Solomon imported Ashtoreth 'the goddess of the Zidonians' to keep his 700 wives happy (1 Kings 11:5, 33; 2). Ranked alongside Baal and the Baalim, Ashtaroth (Ashtoreth) was in fact the great goddess Astarte (Ishtar in Akkadian) whom the Phoenicians ('Zidonians') equated with the Greek love goddess Aphrodite. She is generally thought to be a personification of the planet Venus (the Latin name for Aphrodite). Her name is found on texts recovered from Ugarit and ancient Egypt, and she is incorporated into the Greek pantheon as a wife of Kronos. She was the 'Queen of Heaven' with jurisdiction over procreation and to some extent healing. By the time Josiah came to destroy her shrine she was relegated to the status of 'abomination' (2 Kings 23:13). Strangely, the magical tradition took Ashtaroth over as male, whilst also preserving the female Astarte. Thus, according to Collin de Plancy, Ashtaroth (Astaroth) is a powerful grand-duke of hell, and Astarte retains her Venusian sex-goddess appeal. In the *Key of Solomon*, as 'the impure Venus of the Syrians', she leads the Gamchicoth, 'Disturbers of Souls'.[203]

---

sacrifice, but this is still controversial. See Otto Eissfeldt, *Molk als Opferbegriff im Punischen und Hebräischen und das Ende des Gottes Moloch*, Niemeyer, 1935.
[202] Klopstock quoted in Gustav Davidson, *A Dictionary of Angels*, The Free Press, 1971, p. 8; de Plancy, p. 6, pictured in the 1863 ed.
[203] *DDD*, pp. 109–14; de Plancy, pp. 47–8; Mathers, p. 122. Ashtaroth is also

To these lists of imported demons and demonized gods, the Hebrews had something to add that was uniquely their own. 'Wickedness' comes with the name of Belial (*bĕliyya'al*): 'a Spirit more lewd' said Milton, 'fell not from Heaven'. Biblical scholars argue over the origin and function of the word, but it seems most likely to be composed of *bĕlî* 'not', and **ya'al*, 'to be worthy, to be of value'. Belial is 'not worthy'. He is 'the spirit of darkness'. He is impurity and lying. His wickedness is inducing people to worship other gods (Deuteronomy 13:14), perjury (e.g., 1 Kings 21:10), inhospitableness (e.g., Judges 19:22), getting women drunk in Yahweh's sanctuary (1 Samuel 1:13–17), priestly lechery (1 Samuel 2:12–22), and so on. He was the false messiah to the Samaritans. As Antichrist he came down from heaven to torment the world under the name of the Emperor Nero. From him come the seven spirits of seduction that enter humans at birth. He is so diabolical that he is sometimes called 'the Devil' himself, or else Belial is seen as the Devil's proper name. To the writer of the Book of Jubilees, all non-Jews are 'sons of Belial'. For later Christian writers, Belial stands in direct contrast to Christ.[204]

In the Qumran texts, *maśțēmâ* ('hostility') is the destructive purpose of Belial as well as being the title 'Angel of Hostility' given to him. But in the Book of Jubilees *maśțēmâ* develops as an independent entity. Here he is Mastemah, the prince of demons who leads his forces to destroy the sons of Noah. After Noah complains to his God, Mastemah's army is reduced to a tenth of its former size and the sons of Noah are taught medicine by the angels so that they might resist the remaining evil spirits. It is Mastemah who prompts the Hebrew God to test

---

the name of a city (Joshua 9:10, 12:4, 13:12, 31; 1 Chronicles 6:71). She was also worshipped as Atargatis, a compound of Astarte and Anat, *DDD*, p. 114.
[204] Milton, Bk I; *DDD*, pp. 169–71. Also called Beliar and Belior in the pseudographical *Testament of Levi* (18:4, 19:1). Rabbinical and Apocryphal references in order of mention: Levi 19; Joseph 7, 10; Reuben 4, 5; Simeon 5; Issachar 6–7; Daniel 5; Asher i, 3; Sibyllines 3:63, 4:2; Reuben 2; Levi 3; Jubilees 15:32. Belial is synonymous with the Devil in the Vulgate translation. 2 Corinthians 6:15.

Abraham through the sacrifice of his son Isaac. It is Mastemah who aids the Egyptians in trying to eliminate Moses. But he is still seen in the service of the Hebrew God as the spirit who kills the firstborn in Egypt. In Exodus (12:12) it is 'the Lord' himself who does this. The chosen people are saved because of the magical use of lambs' blood that turns Mastemah from their doors.[205]

Demonization was also the inevitable attitude of Christianity. In a book that set out to prove the superiority of Christianity over paganism, Eusebius of Caesarea (c. 263–339 CE) argued that the Greek *daimon* came from a word meaning 'to fear'. Although only a religio-political etymology at best, Eusebius nonetheless reflected the Christian view.[206] The New Testament is full of demons. They are the unclean spirits (Mark 5) who cruelly torment people (Matthew 15:22).

There were also some new additions. From being a place name in the Old Testament, Abaddon is recreated as demon in the New. From the common Semitic root meaning 'to destroy' found in Ugaritic and Aramaic as *'bd* and Akkadian as *abātu*, *'baddôn* is used in the Old Testament to mean 'place of destruction' and in the Babylonian Talmud is used as one of the names of Gehenna (hell). 1 Enoch (20:2) tells of a specific angel of *baddôn*, which in Revelation (9:11) becomes a proper name in itself. When the fifth angel blows his trumpet, 'a star' falls from heaven and is given the key of 'the bottomless pit' (Revelation 9:1). He unlocks hell, venting huge clouds of smoke and armoured locusts with lions' teeth and scorpions' tails (Revelation 9:2–10). The locusts 'had a king over them, which is the angel of the bottomless pit, whose name in the Hebrew tongue is Abaddon, but in the Greek tongue hath his name Apollyon' (Revelation 9:11). The Greek name alludes to Apollo who was worshipped from the eighth century BCE up to the

---

[205] *DDD*, pp. 553–4; Qumran 1QM 13:4, 1QM 13:11, 4Q 286 10 2:2; Jubilees, 10:1–13, 17:16, 48, 49, equated with Satan in Jub 10:11.
[206] Eusebius, *Praeparatio Evangelica*, 4.5.142.

sixth century CE as both a god of pestilence and destruction, and as a god of healing. Here we most likely see a fusing of Hebrew and Greek concepts, as opposed to outright demonization of an existing deity.[207]

Mammon, one of the most well-known of the demons, is also a later creation. The word is Aramaic meaning 'that in which one puts trust' with the sense of 'money, riches' with the negative connotation developing subsequently. It becomes the name of a demon only in the New Testament with the familiar line 'You cannot serve God and Mammon' attributed to Jesus (Luke 16:13, Matthew 6:24). His character is more fully realized in the late sixteenth century in Spenser's *The Faerie Queene* and Milton's *Paradise Lost* of 1667 as 'Mammon, the least erected Spirit that fell'. Spenser described him as 'an uncouth, savage, and uncivil wight', sooty-bearded, smoke-blackened and miserly hoarding his gold. According to Milton, he taught men to mine 'the bowels of their mother Earth for treasures better hid'. Collin de Plancy added a touch of satirical humour in 1845 when he described Mammon as Hell's ambassador to England.[208]

My Name is Legion

A complex demonology developed, attributing demons to a growing range of human activities and ailments, with various attempts to order and enumerate these swarming hordes of hell. The eleventh-century Byzantine writer, Michael Psellus, described six demonic species using the four-fold schema of the elements and augmenting them with underground and light-hating varieties. They are: Igneous, Aerial, Earthly, Aqueous, Subterranean and Lucifugus. In the sixteenth century Peter Binsfeld, suffragan bishop of Trier in Germany, witch-hunter

---

[207] *DDD*, pp. 1, 74–7. There are some foreshadowings of personification in Proverbs 27:20 and Job 26:5–6.
[208] *DDD*, pp. 542–3. Robert C. Fox, 'The Character of Mammon in *Paradise Lost*', *The Review of English Studies*, 1962, XIII.49, pp. 30–9; Edmund Spenser, *The Faerie Queen*, Bk II.7.3; Milton, Bk I, ll 679, 687–8; de Plancy, p. 145 – the ambassador ascription occurs only in this, the sixth edition.

and author of *De confessionibus maleficorum et sagarum* ('The Confessions of Evil-doers and Witches', 1589), matched the seven deadly sins to the seven deadliest demons: Pride is Lucifer, Avarice is Mammon, Lechery is Asmodeus, Anger is Satan, Gluttony is Beelzebub, Envy is Leviathan and Sloth is Belphegor. He was following something of a trend. There was a particular devil for everything imaginable, including wearing the then fashionable baggy trousers, according to a German sermon of the sixteenth century.[209]

Where the Old Testament knew only Satan and a colourful handful of demons and demonized gods, the New Testament would introduce the idea of a vast, numberless horde of demonic entities. According to Mark (5:1–9), Jesus encountered a possessed man 'dwelling among the tombs' in the 'country of the Gadarenes'. He demanded that the 'unclean spirit' reveal its name to him, but the answer was instead, 'My name is Legion: for we are many.' Around this time, a Roman legion would have numbered about 6,000 men. The apocryphal Gospel of Nicodemus added 'several legions of devils'. According to the usual interpretation of Revelation (12:4), a third of all the angels fell with Satan: 'And his tail drew the third part of the stars of heaven, and did cast them to the earth'. The Cistercian abbot Richalmus in the thirteenth century thought that the demons were as plentiful and incalculable as grains of sand. But with more ingenuity Johannes Wierus (c. 1515–88) came up with a precise reckoning. Each legion numbered 6,666 – a far more diabolical figure than the Romans could muster – and with 1,111 legions under the Satanic banner, the ranks of demons totalled 7,405,926. Professor Martinus Barrhaus, a theologian at Basel in the sixteenth century, went further still, counting 2,665,866,746,664 demons.[210]

---

[209] Michael Psellus, *Psellus' Dialogue on the Operation of Demons*, trans. Marcus Collisson, James Tegg, 1843; Andreas Musculus, *Vom Hosen Teuffel*, Johann Eichhorn, 1555.

[210] Maximilian Rudwin, *The Devil in Legend and Literature*, Open Court, 1931, pp. 17–25; Keith L. Roos, *The Devil in 16th Century German Literature*, Herbert Lang, 1972, p. 52.

Demonic Hierarchies: Kings of Demon[211]

1584 Scot, *Discoverie of Witchcraft*	17th c. *Lesser Key of Solomon*	1667 Milton, *Paradise Lost*	1690–1720 *Sacred Magic of Abramelin*	Dr Rudd, *Angel Magic*	1801 Barrett, *The Magus*
Amaymon	Amaymon	Satan	Lucifer	Beelzebub	Beelzebub
Gorson	Corson	Beelzebub	Leviathan	Python	Pytho
Zimimar	Zimimay (Ziminiar)	Mammon	Satan	Belial	Belial
Goap	Göap	Moloch	Belial	Asmodeus	Asmodeus
Baëll	Bael	Chemos (Peor)	Astarot (Ashtaroth)	Sathan	Satan
Purson (Curson)	Paimon	Baalim, Ashtaroth	Magot	Merizim	Meririm
Bileth	Beleth	Astoreth (Astarte)	Asmodee (Asmodeus)	Apollyon (Abaddon)	Apollyon (Abaddon)
Paimon	Purson	Thammuz	Belzebud (Beelzebub)	Astaroth	Astaroth
Beliall	Asmoday	Dagon	Oriens	Mammon	Mammon
Sidonay (Asmoday)	Viné	Rimmon	Paimon		
Vine	Balam	Ahaz	Ariton		
Zagan	Zagan	Osiris, Isis, [H]Orus	Amaimon		
Balam	Belial	Belial			

Prince of Demons: The Devil

The Demon and demons. The Devil and devils. It was the Fourth Lateran Council in 1215 that made the official distinction between 'the Devil and the other demons'. But the tendency had already been observed in the fourth century CE Latin version of the Bible known as the Vulgate. For a particular reason, as we shall see, *diabolus* was used of the chief of the evil forces, whilst *daemon* was used of his subordinates, although Christian tradition affirms that there is no difference of nature between them.[212]

The Devil, we should not forget, is a relative newcomer, a supernatural immigrant. Unlike the *daimones* he does not appear amongst the personnel of the Ancient Greek Underworld. The pagan peoples of Europe had their own bogies and beasties to

---

[211] Aleister Crowley (ed.), *The Goetia: The Lesser Key of Solomon the King*, trans. S. Liddel MacGregor Mathers, Weiser, 1997 [1904]. The seventy-two spirits of the Goetia are ruled over by 'the Four Great Kings', which are listed here together with spirits designated as kings amongst the seventy-two. The book claims to be compiled and edited from numerous manuscripts in diverse languages, four of which are listed, pp. 23–5, but undated and unreferenced. The editor of this volume, Hymenaeus Beta, mentions British Library Sloane 2731, p. 90, which is dated 1687; 'a manuscript codex by Dr Rudd' is also mentioned, p. 69. Some of the goetic manuscripts in the British Museum date back to the fourteenth century, but most survive from the seventeenth. Reginald Scot, *The Discoverie of Witchcraft*, 1584, Dover, 1972, pp. 217–25; p. 226 gives the four 'principall divels' that head this list. Scot's was the first English translation of a similar list appearing in Wierus' *De praestigiis daemonum*, 1583, as the *Pseudomonarchia daemonum* also identified as T.R., *Secretum secretorum*, 1570, by Scot. S. Liddel MacGregor Mathers, *The Book of the Sacred Magic of Abramelin the Mage*, J. M. Watkins, 1900, pp. 104, 110–11, dated 1458, but Mathers identifies the handwriting as being late seventeenth or early eighteenth century. Harley 6482, British Museum, published as Adam McLean (ed.), *A Treatise on Angel Magic*, Weiser, 2006, dated by McLean to 1699–1714, but argued to be the copy of an earlier manuscript. The spirits here mentioned are listed on pp. 69–70. Francis Barrett, *The Magus*, Lackington, Alley and Co., 1801, Bk II, pp. 46–7.

[212] 'Diabolus enim et alii daemones', Fourth Lateran Council, 1215, see Leonard E. Boyle, 'The Fourth Lateran Council and Manuals of Popular Theology', in Thomas J. Heffernan (ed.), *The Popular Literature of Medieval England*, University of Tennessee Press, 1985, pp. 30–43.

worry about, from Loki leading the *jötnar* and hordes of Hel into the last battle against the Norse gods, to the Morrigan and Caoránach, so-called mother of demons, and the whole race of Faery who bedevilled the Celts, and, as we saw, the *kakodaimones* who made life a misery for the Greeks. The Devil is one particular representation of the combat myth between good and evil found in many religious traditions.

The word *devil* only entered the English language in the eighth century coming via Latin from the Greek *diabolos* (διάβολος). From the verb *diaballo*, meaning 'to throw across' or 'to cross over', the word had the connotations of 'slanderous' and 'defamatory' as an adjective, and 'enmity' and 'quarrel' as a noun. In the sense of 'slanderer', the Greek was used in the third to first century BCE translations of the Hebrew Bible for *satan*.[213]

The Devil as we know him today began his career as Satan – the Accuser or Adversary – with the Hebrew deity Yahweh. We first find Satan in the Book of Job (1:6): 'when the sons of God came to present themselves before the Lord, and Satan came also among them'. Yahweh boasted that in Job he had an exemplary believer, but Satan suggested that God's protection was what kept Job in the fold. 'Does Job fear God in vain?' he asked. Here the classic role of tempter is first played out, tempting not man, but God.

Yahweh succumbed and granted Satan his commission: 'Behold, all that he hath is in thy power; only upon himself put not forth thine hand' (Job 1:12). Satan got to work. Job's oxen were stolen and his servants murdered, 'the fire of God' destroyed his sheep and some more servants, his camels were stolen and yet more servants were slaughtered, and a violent wind blew down the house where his brother and children were feasting, crushing them all to death.

Job was understandably distraught, but kept his faith. Satan was not one to give up easily and persuaded Yahweh to

---

[213] *DDD*, p. 244.

grant him further permission to abuse Job. A plague of boils followed and Job threw himself on a dunghill, wishing for death. His wife and friends all tried to turn him against Yahweh, but Job refused to blame him. Yahweh finally relented and decided Job should be rewarded for his loyalty. The spots cleared up, he had more children, amassed an even greater fortune and lived to 140.

Satan appears again in the Book of Zechariah (3:1–2), a text supposedly written by one of the so-called minor prophets Zechariah about the year 520 BCE. In a vision Zechariah saw 'Joshua the high priest standing before the angel of the Lord, and Satan standing at his right hand to resist him'. But Yahweh took a shine to the raggedly attired Joshua and said to Satan 'The Lord rebuke thee, O Satan!' Here Satan was clearly acting in his role of accuser and Joshua, like Job before him, is cleared of all charges.

In other supposedly sixth century BCE biblical texts we read of Satan standing up against Israel and inciting David to make a census (1 Chronicles 21) and Satan is equated with the 'Angel of Yahweh' who gave Balaam such a hard time about his ass (Numbers 22). Confusing matters, 'satan' in the more general sense of adversity or accusation also crops up in several other books of the Old Testament.

One of the more popular stories about the origin of the Devil as a fallen angel is told of the 'sons of God', whom we should understand as angels or 'the watchers' (1 Enoch 6:2), who, lusting after mortal women, descended from heaven and seduced them. A race of 'giants' (γίγαντες) was born – often thought to be the *nephilim*, 'the fallen ones', described in Genesis (6:3) and Numbers (13:33) – and then drowned in the Flood. Their spirits became the demons (1 Enoch 15:8–16:1), led by Azazel. Azazel – whose name might be derived from *'zz*, 'to be strong', and *'l*, 'god', or *'ez*, 'goat', and *'ozel*, 'to go away', as in 'scapegoat' – was a desert demon (Leviticus 16:8–10), who was both a messenger for Satan (1 Enoch 54:6), and the Devil himself (Jubilees 10:1–11). Then there is the tale of the angel who refused to revere Adam and was thrown out of heaven with his supporters.[214]

As similar sounding or acting beings the Devil enjoys further adventures in the non-canonical Apocrypha. He is the author of evil (Wisdom 2:24), he is Satanail who was thrown from heaven with his rebel angels (2 Enoch 19) and the seducer of Eve in the Garden of Eden (2 Enoch 31). He is equated with Mastemah in the Book of Jubilees. He is the licentious Asmodeus in the Book of Tobit. He is Sammael in the Martyrdom of Isaiah, bringing 'apostasy, sin, magic and the persecution of the righteous' (2:4–11). He becomes Samael, the angel of death and 'chief of satans' in the Jewish Talmud.

However, it was in Christianity that the Devil was to play his greatest role. In the New Testament the temptation in the wilderness is one of the keystones of Jesus' career, recounted in three of the four Gospels (Matthew 4, Mark 1, Luke 4). Jesus was specifically 'led up of the spirit into the wilderness to be tempted of the Devil' (Matthew 4:1). Dating from the first century CE these writings all tell the story of how the Devil appeared to Jesus during his forty days and nights of fasting in the desert. The brief details in Mark are fleshed out in Matthew and Luke with the addition of dialogue.

'The tempter' approached Jesus, saying 'If thou be the Son of God, command that these stones be made bread'. Jesus retorted with 'Man shall not live by bread alone'. The Devil then took him to the top of the Temple in Jerusalem and said 'If thou be the Son of God, cast thyself down: for it is written, He shall give his angels charge concerning thee: and in their hands they shall bear thee up'. Jesus replied 'Thou shalt not tempt the Lord thy God'. The Devil tried again, taking him to the summit of a high mountain, showing him the world stretched out below, saying

---

[214] *DDD*, pp. 128–31, 246, 344–5, 618–20. For the giant references see 1 Enoch 6–16, Genesis 6:1–4, Jude 6, 2 Peter 2:4. For the Adam story see The Life of Adam and Eve 13–15 in Hedley Frederick Davis Sparks, *The Apocryphal Old Testament*, Oxford University Press, 1984, p. 150, Tertullian, *De Patientia*, 5, and Qur'an 15:26–35.

'All these things will I give thee, if thou wilt fall down and worship me'. Jesus replied 'Get thee hence, Satan: for it is written, Thou shalt worship the Lord thy God, and only him shalt thou serve' (Matthew 4:3–11). Satan's role here is little different from that played out in the Old Testament, but it would not stay that way.

According to the Gospel of Luke (10:18), Jesus told his followers: 'I beheld Satan as lightning fall from heaven'. In the Book of Revelation, which only found its way into the Bible in 367 CE, we read: 'And the great dragon was cast out, that old serpent, called the Devil, and Satan, which deceiveth the whole world: he was cast out into the earth, and his angels were cast out with him' (12:9). Here the differing concepts and terminology of 'devil' and 'satan' are specifically equated. Both texts bring to the fore the ejection of evil from heaven, recalling the tradition of the Nephilim as 'the fallen ones'.

Later Church writers, such as Tertullian and Origen in the second and third centuries CE, identified Satan with a character called Lucifer (Isaiah 14:12): 'How thou art fallen from heaven, O Lucifer, son of the morning!' Isaiah was actually comparing the King of Babylon to the 'morning star' – *helel* in Hebrew, *lucifer* ('light-bearer') in Latin – which is the planet we call Venus. From this misinterpretation, and much influenced by the dramatic war in heaven depicted in The Secret Book of Enoch (2 Enoch), the Church Fathers developed the idea of Satan as Lucifer the Fallen Angel, as well as the original serpentine tempter in the Garden of Eden.[215]

After such a useful career with Yahweh why did Satan fall? We already had lust as a motivation in Enoch, but Eusebius of Caesarea said it was the worst of the Seven Deadly Sins: pride. For we read in John (1, 3:8) that 'the Devil sinneth from the beginning' and in Ecclesiasticus (10:15) that 'Pride is the beginning of all sin'. Misinterpreting another Old Testament passage

---

[215] Jeffrey Burton Russell, *The Devil: Perceptions of Evil from Antiquity to Primitive Christianity*, Cornell University Press, 1987, pp. 195, 229. Henry Angsar Kelly, *Satan: A Biography*, Cambridge University Press, 2006, pp. 178–9, 194ff.

concerning the King of Tyre, the Church Fathers thought they had found further reference to Satan when they read 'Thou hast been in Eden [. . .] Thou art the anointed cherub [. . .] Thou wast perfect [. . .] till iniquity was found in thee [. . .] I will cast thee to the ground' (Ezekiel 28:1–19). It read like a description of an angel cast out of heaven and we get further evidence of pride, or more precisely vanity: 'Thine heart was lifted up because of thy beauty'.[216]

But this beauty would not survive the fall from heaven. At the Council of Toledo in 447 CE we get the first official description of the Devil:

> A large black monstrous apparition with horns on his head, cloven hooves – or one cloven hoof – ass's ears, hair, claws, fiery eyes, terrible teeth, an immense phallus, and a sulphurous smell.[217]

It proved to be an enduring look. The medieval mystery plays scared their audiences with such monstrous and well-endowed devils. The Devil's large appendage and what he did with it would be a constant concern of the witch trials in the early modern period. The French demonologist Nicholas Remy noted that, at her trial in 1568, Alexée Drigie described it as being as 'long as some kitchen utensils' when only half erect. This demonic sexuality was heightened still further by the popular representation of naked witches and Freud would suggest characteristically that 'their great broomstick was probably the great lord Penis'. During the reign of James VI and I, the Devil still took an indecent form on the stage, appearing suchwise in Middleton and Rowley's play *A Courtly Masque* of 1620, for example. Black-faced phallic demons cavorted in the public streets during carnival in Germany. The

[216] Kelly, p. 193.
[217] Pennethorne Hughes, *Witchcraft*, Penguin, 1965, p. 104; and without the 'one cloven hoof' in Jeffrey Burton Russell, *Lucifer: The Devil in the Middle Ages*, Cornell University Press, 1986, p. 69.

influential French occultist Eliphas Lévi's depiction of the
Bouc de Sabbat ('Sabbatic Goat') carried forward the idea of
the Devil as a symbol of the generative powers into the nineteenth century, representing him with a fulsome bosom and a
large rod entwined with serpents (caduceus) emerging from
some cloth draped over the creature's loins, not to mention the
horns and cloven hooves.[218]

When the authors of the infamous witch-hunters' manual,
the *Malleus Maleficarum*, explicitly made the connection in the
fifteenth century between the ancient fertility spirits, the 'Satyrs',
'Fauns' and 'Pans', and demonic 'Incubi', they were drawing on
the authority of early Christian writers, such as Augustine of
Hippo (354–430). There was clearly a continuing, centuries-
long process of identifying the Christian demonic with elements
of classical mythology. But the process did not end there.[219]

As Christianity spread through Europe its missionaries identified every god and goddess they came across as so many
disguises of the Devil sent to lead people from the Gospel. For
example, the Council of Leptinnes (744) added a new clause to
the rite of baptism to 'renounce all the works of the demon, and
all his words, and Thor, and Odin, and Saxnot, and all evil
beings that are like them'. Egbert, first Archbishop of York in the
eighth century, prohibited what were called 'offerings to devils'.
The Canon Episcopi (dated to 906) described how 'some

---

[218] Nicholas Remy, *Demonolatry*, trans. E. A. Aswin, John Rodker, 1930[1595],
Bk I, Ch. VI, p. 14; Thomas Middleton and William Rowley, *A Courtly Masque:
The Device Called, The World Tost at Tennis*, Edward Wright, 1620; Maximilian
Rudwin, *The Origin of the German Carnival Comedy*, Stechert & Co., 1920,
pp. 35–6, 43–4; Eliphas Lévi, *Transcendental Magic: Its Doctrine and Ritual*,
trans. A. E. Waite. William Rider & Son, 1923, description p. xxii, depiction
p. 180 – first published as *Dogme et rituel de la haute magie*, G. Baillière, 1861;
Montague Summers, *The History of Witchcraft and Demonology*, pp. 277–8 and
see also 98–100; Robert Muchembled, *A History of the Devil: From the Middle
Ages to the Present*, Polity Press, 2003, pp. 17, 46–51, 66, Freud quoted on p.
209; Leo Ruickbie, 'Witchcraft: The Naked Truth', paper presented to Miller's
Academy, 21 April 2009.
[219] Heinrich Institoris and Jakob Sprenger, *Malleus Maleficarum*, trans. Montague Summers, Dover, 1928 [1487], Pt 1, Q. 3, p. 24.

wicked women, perverted by the Devil [. . .] ride upon certain beasts with Diana, the goddess of pagans'. Thus the Church assembled its own theological Frankenstein's monster and sparked it into life with the raw current of fear.[220]

The Devil's image, too, began to change. In a strange turn towards decency he would take to wearing human clothes. Innumerable witch trial records would describe someone attired in the fashions of the day. The descriptions from the late sixteenth century into the seventeenth century largely agree that he most often appeared as a large black man dressed in black. He had other colours to his wardrobe, but black was his favourite; 'as proof,' said the demonologist Henri Boguet, 'that his study is only to do evil; for evil [. . .] is symbolised by black'. He was sometimes young, sometimes old, sometimes female, usually male, sometimes crippled and frequently unable to conceal his cloven hooves. He could take animal form, even appear as a priest, the Virgin Mary, or Jesus himself, but his most alarming manifestation is undoubtedly in cases of possession.[221]

Possession

'I believe this was a genuine case of possession,' Father Walter Halloran told *The Kansas City Star* newspaper in 1995 when they asked about an exorcism that had taken place at the Alexian Brothers Hospital, St Louis, Maryland, USA, in 1949. It was the case that had inspired twenty-year-old English Literature student William Peter Blatty to write *The Exorcist* years later. Possession, the belief that the human personality has been taken over by another entity, is a universal social experience recorded throughout history. It manifests in diverse ways with multiple symptoms, often of a terrifying and violent nature, but the fundamental aspect is the loss of conscious control of one's mind and body. Within Western culture it is

---

[220] Leo Ruickbie, *Witchcraft Out of the Shadows*, Robert Hale, 2004, pp. 61, 65.
[221] Henri Boguet, *Discours Exécrable des Sorciers*, Romain de Beauvais, 1603.

most usual to see this experience in terms of Christianity and talk of 'demonic possession' and being 'possessed by the Devil'. In the fifteenth century the *Malleus Maleficarum* stated that 'devils can enter the heads and other parts of the body of men, and can move the inner mental images from place to place'. Possession is still defined by the Catholic Church as 'the domination by the demon over man's bodily organs and his lower spiritual faculties'. According to research, 41 per cent of Americans today believe that this can actually happen and the Church has reported a huge rise in requests for exorcism.[222]

The Church identifies three signs of possession that particularly distinguish it from psychological disorders: the ability to speak in a language unknown to the possessed individual, or to understand it when it is spoken; to be able to see into the future, or discover 'hidden events'; and having any other powers that are 'beyond the subject's age and natural condition'. However, others have counted many more, such as nineteenth-century French writer P. L. Jacob:[223]

1. Believing that one is possessed
2. Leading a bad life
3. Living beyond society
4. Being ill for a long time with unusual symptoms

---

[222] Mark Opsasnick, 'The Haunted Boy of Cottage City: The Cold Hard Facts Behind the Story that Inspired *The Exorcist*', *Strange Magazine*, 20, December 1998; Halloran quoted in '*The Exorcist* Fairly Close to the Mark', *National Catholic Reporter*, 1 September 2000; William Peter Blatty, *The Exorcist*, Harper & Row, 1971; *Malleus Maleficarum*, Pt 2, Ch. X; *De Exorcismis et Supplicationibus Quibusdam*, Libreria Editrice Vaticana, 2003; Frank Newport and Maura Strausberg, 'Americans' Belief in Psychic and Paranormal Phenomena is Up Over Last Decade', Gallup, 8 June 2001, http://www.gallup.com/poll/4483/americans-belief-psychic-paranormal-phenomena-over-last-decade.aspx, accessed 18 January 2011 – a further 16 per cent were unsure; 'Huge Rise in Calls to Cast Out Demons', *Paranormal*, 56, February 2011, p. 8.

[223] *The Roman Ritual: Complete Edition*, trans. Philip T. Weller, Bruce Publishing Co., 1964.

5. Blaspheming the name of God and speaking often of the Devil
6. Making a pact with the Devil
7. Having dealings with spirits
8. Having a terrible and horrible facial expression
9. Being tired of life and despairing
10. Being furious and doing violence
11. Screaming and crying like a beast[224]

Some of the most dramatic manifestations of possession occurred in several French convents during the seventeenth century. In Aix-en-Provence in 1611 two possessions cost Father Louis Gaufridi his life. At Louviers in 1647 more than fourteen possessions led to the imprisonment of Sister Madeleine Bavent and the execution of Father Thomas Boullé. The Mother Superior, Barbara Buvée, was lucky enough to be acquitted at Auxonne in 1650 following her trial for the possession of eight people. The most infamous case, however, was the mass possession of Ursuline nuns at Loudun in 1634 which saw Father Urbain Grandier being burnt to death, along with the pacts and magical writings he was alleged to have made. An eye-witness to the possessions, Monsieur des Niau, Counsellor at la Flèche, described the scene:[225]

When the Exorcist gave some order to the Devil, the nuns suddenly passed from a state of quiet into the most terrible convulsions [. . .] They struck their chests and backs with their heads, as if they had had their neck broken, and with inconceivable rapidity [. . .] their faces became so frightful one could not bear to look at them [. . .] they threw themselves back till their heads touched their feet and walked in this position [. . .] They uttered cries so horrible and so loud

---

[224] P. L. Jacob, *Curiosités Infernales*, Garnier, 1886, my translation.
[225] Leo Ruickbie, *La Sorcellerie en France: Catalogue de l'Exposition*, Witchology, 2009, n.p.

that nothing like it was ever heard before; they made use of expressions so indecent as to shame the most debauched men, while their acts, both in exposing themselves and inviting lewd behaviour from those present, would have astonished the inmates of the lowest brothel in the country.[226]

Whilst religious and popular explanations continue to draw on the spirit world, modern psychiatry explains possession as a dissociative state with the alarming physical displays categorized as psychogenic seizures or pseudoseizures, that is, non-epileptic, stress-related fits. However, psychiatrists themselves do not always make that diagnosis. With many years' experience in psychiatry, the late Dr Arthur Guirdham came to the conclusion that 'people who insist that possession cannot exist have never seen a case or, if they have, have been so blinkered by prejudice that they have temporarily lost the capacity to assess symptoms'.[227]

Demons Today

The Church today has moved away from such crude personifications as 'demons' and 'the Devil'. Neither he nor his imps should be thought of as the horned and cloven-hooved fiends we are so familiar with, but instead as an abstract force for evil. Likewise, God himself should not be thought of as a white-bearded old man, but as a nebulous supreme good. In a confidential poll of Catholic priests conducted in 1960, 80 per cent said they did not believe in the Devil.[228]

It is an example of what an episcopal conference in Italy organized by the Theological Institute of Assisi would warn against: the 'extreme rationalism that denies the existence of the Devil'.[229] This development caused the Vatican's chief exorcist,

---

[226] Edmund Goldsmith (ed.), *The History of the Devils of Loudun*, 3 vols, privately published, 1887, vol. 2, pp. 35–44.

[227] Arthur Guirdham, *The Psyche in Medicine*, Spearman, 1978, p. 55.

[228] Morgan Scott Peck, *Glimpses of the Devil*, Free Press, 2005, p. 2.

[229] ZENIT, 11 May 2000.

Father Gabriel Amorth, to express his deep concern. After claiming to have performed an incredible 70,000 exorcisms, Amorth is convinced that the Devil exists. He even went so far as to state recently that 'the Devil is at work inside the Vatican'.[230] 'We have a clergy and an Episcopate who no longer believe in the Devil,' he said in another interview, adding, 'meanwhile, the Satanic sects prosper'.[231]

So what of the supposed 'Satanic sects'? Surely they believe in the Devil and his demons? It came as a shock to find myself included in that last category when the Jesus-is-Savior.com website 'reviewed' my first book on witchcraft, *Witchcraft Out of the Shadows*. Under the heading of 'Wicca = Satan' , Wicca – a modern witchcraft-inspired religion – was denounced as the 'false religion of the Devil'. It is a common enough charge made by Christian fundamentalists, but it is not the way the Wiccans themselves see it.

Most books on Wicca by Wiccans or sympathizers categorically state that Wiccans neither worship nor believe in the Devil. According to Gerald Gardner, the founder of Wicca, 'The Devil' was the medieval honorific for the leader of a coven of witches, now obsolete, or a term of disparagement for the same used by the Church – he argued both ends. The first was an idea he got from Margaret Murray's *The Witch-Cult in Western Europe* – a book that sought to prove that witchcraft was an organized pagan religion antecedent to Christianity. Gardner went to great lengths to stress that as a supernatural entity 'The Devil is, or rather was, an invention of the Church'. Of course, the press immediately denounced him as a 'whitewasher of witchcraft'.[232]

It would have surprised Gardner to find himself in agreement with a real Satanist. When Anton Szandor LaVey founded the

---

[230] *The Times*, 11 March 2010.
[231] *30 Days*, June 2000.
[232] Gerald B. Gardner, *Witchcraft Today*, Rider and Co., 1954, pp. 43–4; Margaret Murray, *The Witch-Cult in Western Europe*, Clarendon Press, 1921; *Sunday Pictorial*, 12 June 1955.

Church of Satan in 1966 and proclaimed himself the Black Pope he had no intention of actually worshipping Satan. Like Gardner, he turned things on their head. In one of his Nine Satanic Statements he asserted that 'Satan has been the best friend the [Christian] church has ever had, as he has kept it in business all these years!'[233]

For LaVey, Satan was symbolic of his rejection of Christianity and 1960s counter-culture values, and representative of his own philosophy of life rather than an actual entity. In *The Satanic Bible* he made it clear that 'most Satanists do not accept Satan as an anthropomorphic being with cloven hooves, a barbed tail, and horns'. Forty years on, the current High Priest of the Church of Satan, Peter H. Gilmore, continues this interpretation: 'Satanists do not believe in the supernatural, in neither God nor the Devil . . . Satan is not a conscious entity to be worshipped'. Instead, Gilmore says that 'Satan is a symbol of Man living as his prideful, carnal nature dictates'.[234]

With the Church, witches and even Satanists withdrawing from the idea of a supreme personality of evil, just who does believe in the Devil? Research has shown that around two in three ordinary Americans believe in the Devil and that more than one in three believe that they have been tempted by him. About one in five people – again in America – believe that 'most evil in the world is caused by the Devil' and a little fewer than one in two believe that he has an army of demons to help him.[235]

[233] Anton Szandor LaVey, *The Satanic Bible*, Avon Books, 1969, p. 25.

[234] Peter H. Gilmore, 'Satanism: The Feared Religion', churchofsatan.com, no date, stated to have been first published in *A New Age: Essays on Current Religious Beliefs and Practices*, Merrimac Books, 1992.

[235] Jennifer Robinson, 'The Devil and the Demographic Details', Gallup, 25 February 2003, http://www.gallup.com/poll/7858/devil-demographic-details.aspx, accessed 30 March 2010; Frank Newport, 'Americans More Likely to Believe in God Than Devil, Heaven More Than Hell', Gallup, 13 June 2007, http://www.gallup.com/poll/27877/americans-more-likely-believe-god-than-devil-heaven-more-than-hell.aspx, accessed 30 March 2010; Princeton Survey Research Associates for *Newsweek*, published as Kenneth L. Woodward, 'Do We Need Satan?', *Newsweek*, 13 November, 1995; Christopher Bader, F. Carson Mencken and Joseph Baker, *Paranormal*

Many health professionals also believe. Dealing directly with alleged cases of possession, psychiatrists M. Scott Peck and Richard E. Gallagher both came to the conclusion that the condition was real with the inevitable implication that there must be a Devil and/or demons. 'I would never again doubt the existence of Satan,' wrote Peck. 'Even those who doubt such a phenomenon exists,' said Gallagher, 'may find the following example rather persuasive'. They documented a range of extraordinary events, including levitation, psychokinesis and clairvoyance.[236]

After years of working with violent criminals, Rex Beaber, professor of medicine at the University of California, began to wonder if there really was 'an extra force, a dark force, that works through humans and perpetrates terror'.[237] Certainly this is something some violent criminals themselves believe. 'I believe in Satan,' said serial killer Richard Ramirez in a 1994 interview. 'I believe evil is a force that is beyond us and that we just have to invite him in.' Ramirez was a petty burglar with a drug addiction who terrified Los Angeles in 1984–5 as the sadistic 'Night Stalker'. During one of his attacks, he forced the victim to repeat 'I love Satan' as he raped her. At his preliminary court hearings, Richard Ramirez flashed a reversed pentagram on the palm of his hand to reporters and shouted 'Hail Satan!' Ramirez was eventually convicted on thirteen counts of murder in 1989.[238]

Other murderers have believed that they were actually trying to kill the Devil himself. When police found mixed martial arts fighter Jarrod Wyatt on 21 March 2010, covered in blood and standing over the body of his friend Taylor Powell, he told them

America, New York University Press, 2010, pp. 161–3, quoting from the Baylor Religion Survey, Wave 2, 2007.

[236] Peck, p. 238; Richard E. Gallagher, 'A Case of Demonic Possession', *New Oxford Review*, March 2008.

[237] Rex Julian Beaber, 'The Pathology of Evil', *Los Angeles Times*, 6 January 1985.

[238] 'Interview with Richard Ramirez', *Feast of Hate and Fear*, 6, 1996, http://feastofhateandfear.com/archives/night_stalker.html, accessed 15 December 2010; Michael Newton, *Raising Hell*, Warner, 1994, pp. 305–9; Peter Vronsky, *Serial Killers: The Method and Madness of Monsters*, Penguin, 2004.

'Satan was in that dude'. Wyatt had allegedly ripped out Powell's still beating heart and cooked it, as well as tearing off his tongue and a large part of his face, because he believed that his friend was the Devil. It was thought that they had been experimenting with hallucinogenic mushrooms. Speaking in his defence, lawyer James Fallman said 'My client was trying to silence the Devil.' Three psychiatrists have declared him sane.[239]

A demon was originally the morally neutral *daimon*, but underlying the Greek word there was always a universal conception of destroying forces, often invisible – disease, famine, natural catastrophe – whose restless, indiscriminate actions seemed like the work of evil supernatural powers. Demons became a way to explain these events and a means by which they could be magically controlled.

Whilst a rich demonology inherited from Babylonia continued to be developed and expounded with the incorporation of imagery from Classical mythology and European paganism, the Christian Church tended towards centralizing the powers of darkness in the single figure of the Devil. Jesus is tempted by the Devil. Martin Luther sees the Devil. They did not toy with mere demons. Even in modern culture, the character of Regan in *The Exorcist* is possessed by the Devil.

Towards the end of the film *The Exorcist* the priest-hero Karras asks the older Father Merrin, 'Why her? Why this girl?' Merrin replies, 'I think the point is to make us despair. To see ourselves as [. . .] animal and ugly. To make us reject the possibility that God could love us.' It was Satan and Job all over again. Only this time there would be no happy ending. Merrin dies of a heart attack and Karras, suddenly possessed himself, throws himself out of a window, tumbling down those infamous long narrow steps to his death.

As Joseph Conrad once wrote, 'The belief in a supernatural source of evil is not necessary; men alone are quite capable of

---

[239] John Driscoll, 'Klamath Suspect Wyatt Will Answer to Murder Charges', *The Times-Standard*, 27 May 2010; Anthony Skeens, 'DA Wants Death Penalty Option', *The Daily Triplicate*, 9 May 2011.

every wickedness'. Where stories like *The Exorcist* reinforce the Christian worldview, history shows us that the Devil and his demons will always be things we create ourselves, whether as an explanation for the misfortunes of life, a projection of our guilt for causing some of those misfortunes, or simply the face our mind gives to our innermost fears. The apparent evidence of possession cases and the efficacy of exorcism is suggestive, tempting, but ultimately not conclusive. As we understand more about the human mind we claim more of the territory that was once held by the diabolical, but the question and hence the possibility will long remain. As the French Decadent poet Charles Baudelaire once wrote, 'the greatest trick of the Devil is to persuade you that he does not exist'. And surely 200 million Americans cannot be wrong?[240]

[240] Charles Baudelaire, 'Le Joueur généreux', Le Spleen de Paris, *le Figaro*, 7–14 February 1864; Joseph Conrad, *Under Western Eyes*, 1911, Part Second, IV.

5. Extraterrestrials

It was a clear summer's afternoon on Tuesday, 24 June 1947, as Kenneth Arnold (1915–84) flew over the jagged Cascade mountain range, Washington State, USA. He was making a routine business flight from Chehalis to Yakima, but there was a $10,000 reward being offered to find a missing C-46 US Marine Corps transport. He veered his three-seater, single-engined Callair off course and headed towards Mount Rainier, the 4,392-metre-high stratovolcano that dominated the skyline. After an hour he turned back on course. 'The air was so smooth that day that it was a real pleasure flying,' he recalled. He sat back in his seat and enjoyed the view. A bright flash caught his attention. Off to his left he spotted nine objects flying at high speed. He described them as 'shaped like a pie plate', or 'flat like a pie pan and somewhat bat shaped', and 'saucer-like'. They moved 'like fish flipping in the sun'. They were so highly reflective that it was 'as if someone had started an arc light in front of my eyes'. He estimated that they were travelling at something like 1,200 miles an hour at an altitude of 10,000 feet.[241]

---

[241] Bill Bequette, 'Boise Flyer Maintains He Saw 'Em', *East Oregonian*, 26 June 1947; *Chicago Daily Tribune*, 26 June 1947; Frank M. Brown, Confidential Memorandum, Incident 4AF 1208 I, 16 July 1947; Ted Bloecher, *The UFO Wave of 1947*, NICAP, 1967, http://nicap.org/waves/Wave47Rpt/ReportUFOWave1947_Cover.htm, accessed 30 September 2010. The original newspaper articles and other documents for 1947 have been archived by Jan L. Aldrich, 'Project 1947', http://www.project1947.com.

Arnold was a successful businessman. He ran his own company, Great Western Fire Control Supply, selling and installing a range of fire-fighting equipment. His aeroplane had just cost him $5,000. He was also a thirty-two-year-old family man – married with two children – and had recently bought a new house on the outskirts of Boise. He was an Eagle Scout, a college football star and a Red Cross Life Saving Examiner, liked and respected in the community. He had three years' flying experience, regularly clocking up to a 100 hours a month. He could land his 'crate' in a cow pasture and the worst mishap had been a flat tyre. Arnold was what constituted a reliable witness and an experienced flyer. And now, flying across the mountains, he was about to be plunged into a celebrity he had never sought and change the face of history.[242]

Arnold ran through the likely explanations for the mysterious objects. Perhaps they were snow geese? 'But geese don't fly that high – and, anyway, what would geese be doing going south for this time of year?' Perhaps they were jet-engined planes? But 'their motion was wrong for jet jobs'. Perhaps the window was causing the reflections? He rolled down his window, but could still see the objects.[243]

They were also too fast. The Americans' new Lockheed P-80 Shooting Star jet fighter had only clocked 623 mph at Muroc Army Air Field, California, and Chuck Yeager was yet to make his historic flight in the experimental Bell X-1. Although two German pilots during WWII – Hans Guido Mutke in a Messerschmitt Me 262 and Heini Dittmar in a Messerschmitt Me 163 – had reportedly broken the sound barrier with speeds in excess of 1,062km/h (670m/h), this had only been achieved in a steep dive. Whatever Arnold had seen, supposing his calculations were correct, defied what was then technologically possible for a piloted aircraft.[244]

---

[242] Brown, Memorandum.

[243] Bequette, *East Oregonian*, 26 June 1947.

[244] Michael David Hall and Wendy Ann Connors, *Alfred Loedding and the Great Flying Saucer Wave of 1947*, Rose Press, 1998, p. 25. Muroc was later renamed

The local press quickly picked up the story. As news spread, apparently confirmatory reports started coming in. A Mr Savage from Oklahoma City saw something streak overhead: 'The machine, or whatever it was, was a shiny silvery color – very big – and was moving at a terrific rate of speed.' W. I. Davenport, a carpenter in the Midwest, said he saw nine fast moving objects from the roof of a house he was working on. E. H. Sprinkle of Eugene claimed to have photographed seven strange objects. George Clover of Bellingham saw three fast moving, shiny objects 'like kites'. Some time later prospector Fred Johnson reported to both the Air Force and the FBI that he had observed flying objects near Mt Adams on the 24th, estimated at an altitude of 300m (1,000 feet) and of 9m (30 feet) diameter. As they passed overhead, his compass needle swung wildly from side to side.[245]

In all, at least twenty sightings were reported for 24 June 1947. As excitement mounted, Arnold found himself at the centre of increasing interest, most of it unwanted. A preacher telephoned to tell him that his sighting was a forewarning of the end of the world. A woman rushed out of a café after seeing Arnold inside, shrieking, 'There's the man who saw the men from Mars.' One of the newspapers said Arnold 'would like to get on one of his 1200-mile-an-hour "flying saucers" and escape from the furor.' The flying saucer had been born.[246]

Arnold's encounter is often seen as the beginning of the modern UFO phenomenon.[247] In some ways it was, although

---

Edwards Air Force Base. Ferdinand C. W. Käsmann, *Die schnellsten Jets der Welt*, Aviatic-Verlag, 1999, pp. 17, 122. At 20°C, sea level, the speed of sound is 1,236 km/h (768m/h), but as temperature and molecular mass decrease at higher altitudes the speed of sound also decreases.

[245] Savage and Davenport quoted in 'Flying Disk Mystery Grows', *Oregon Journal*, 26 June 1947; Sprinkle and Clover quoted in 'Flying Saucer Story Grows', *The Oregonian*, 28 June 1947; Johnson in Bruce Maccabee, 'Strong Magnetic Field Detected Following a Sighting of an Unidentified Flying Object', *Journal of Scientific Exploration*, 8, 1994, p. 359.

[246] Bloecher, §I–3; 'Harassed Saucer-Sighter Would Like to Escape Fuss', *Statesman Journal*, 28 June 1947.

[247] See Gordon Stein (ed.), *The Encyclopedia of the Paranormal*, Prometheus Books, 1996, p. 767; or Stuart Gordon, *The Paranormal:An Illustrated Encyclopedia*, Head-

there were earlier sightings noted without having to reinterpret religious experiences or meteorological phenomena. Between the years 1890 and 1945 there were two peaks in the UFO-type events reported for which date, time, latitude and longitude were known: 1896–7 saw a wave of 'airship' sightings; in 1909 there was a 'phantom aircraft' wave.[248] June to July 1947 also exhibited a surge of sightings, with the highest number of eighty-two separate reports logged for 7 July alone. American ufologist Ted Bloecher (1929–) would document more than 850 cases for these two months.[249]

The sightings go on. Three soldiers at Tern Hill barracks, Shropshire, reported strange lights 'like rotating cubes with multiple colours' in June 2008, only hours before a police helicopter gave chase to an unidentified craft near Cardiff some eighty miles away.[250] Four UFOs were supposedly photographed over London in March 2009.[251] A 'comet-like fireball' or 'twinkling spotlight' closed Xiaoshan airport in Hangzhou, China, when it showed up on radar on 7 July 2010.[252] A 'hyperdimensional UFO' was reported as firing 'a ray of light or directed energy beam' in the vicinity of the White House, Washington, D.C., on 20 July 2010.[253] The number of UFO reports is over-

line, 1992, p. 672, for example. According to Hall and Connors, p. 144, the USAF also dates the UFO phenomenon from this time.

[248] Peter A. Sturrock, 'Time-Series Analysis of a Catalog of UFO Events: Evidence of a Local-Sidereal-Time Modulation', *Journal of Scientific Exploration*, 18, 2004, p. 401.

[249] Larry Hatch, *U*UFO Database, http://web.archive.org/web/20060701162649/ www.larryhatch.net/YDAY47.html, accessed 29 September 2010; Bloecher, abstract.

[250] 'Soldier Spots 13 UFOs Above Barracks', *Daily Telegraph*, 25 June 2008; 'Invasion of the Bobby Snatchers: Police Helicopter has Close Encounter with a UFO', *Daily Mail*, 20 June 2008.

[251] Sarah Knapton, 'UFOs Photographed Over London', *Daily Telegraph*, 18 March 2009.

[252] Wang Xiang, 'Experts Probe Hangzhou UFO Sighting', ShanghaiDaily. com, 14 July 2010; 'Chinese Airport Closed After Fiery UFO is Spotted Flying Over City', *Daily Mail*, 16 July 2010.

[253] Mark Fraser, 'Sightings', *Paranormal*, 52, October 2010, p. 13.

whelming. By June 2006 Larry Hatch had documented 18,552 UFO-type events, even filtering out known hoaxes and misidentified meteorological phenomena. Are extraterrestrials really out there?[254] Even Arnold had difficulty accepting what he saw, but as he said, 'I must believe my eyes.'[255]

Closer Encounters

Worried that the saucers posed a threat to national security, Arnold immediately reported his sightings to the military. Ignoring almost all of what Arnold had said, the newspapers had already found their explanations. A Lieutenant Colonel Harold E. Turner, Army Air Force, was on record as saying that the discs were the circular exhaust pipes of jets. The science editor for Associated Press, Howard W. Blakeslee, said that what Arnold saw was simply sunlight reflecting from ordinary aircraft.[256]

With everyone trying to explain it all away, Arnold stuck to his story, only complaining that neither the FBI nor the military seemed to be taking his report seriously. 'If I was running the country,' he told reporters, 'and someone reported something unusual, I'd certainly want to know more about it.'[257]

However, some quarters of the military had taken Arnold's report seriously. Two intelligence officers from Hamilton Field, California – Captain William Davidson and Lieutenant Frank Brown – were assigned to investigate the case. After questioning Arnold in a hotel room for six hours, their official report read:

---

[254] http://web.archive.org/web/20060701162858/www.larryhatch.net/AL-LABOUT.html, accessed 29 September 2010.

[255] 'Bug-Eyed Salesman Reports Fast-Flying Mystery Planes', *The Norman Transcript*, 26 June 1947.

[256] Bill Bequette, 'Experts Reach Deep Into Bag to Explain "Flying Discs"', *East Oregonian*, 28 June 1947.

[257] '"Flying Saucer" Observer Says No One Can Change His Mind', *Idaho Statesman*, 28 June 1947.

It is the personal opinion of the interviewer that Mr Arnold actually saw what he stated he saw. It is difficult to believe that a man of [his] character and apparent integrity would state that he saw objects and write up a report to the extent that he did if he did not see them.[258]

Forced to accept that Arnold was a reliable witness, military intelligence were left with a troubling conclusion: he *had* seen flying discs. But events were about to move to another level. Fifteen days after Arnold's sighting, on Tuesday, 8 July 1947, the *Roswell Daily Record* ran a front-page story under the headline 'RAAF Captures Flying Saucer on Ranch in Roswell Region':

> The intelligence office of the 509th Bombardment group at Roswell Army Field announced at noon today, that the field has come into possession of a flying saucer. According to information released by the department, over authority of Maj. J. A. Marcel, intelligence officer, the disk was recovered on a ranch in the Roswell vicinity, after an unidentified rancher had notified Sheriff Geo. Wilcox, here, that he had found the instrument on his premises. Major Marcel and a detail from his department went to the ranch and recovered the disk, it was stated. After the intelligence officer here had inspected the instrument it was flown to higher headquarters. The intelligence office stated that no details of the saucer's construction or its appearance had been revealed.[259]

The 509th had flown the Boeing B-29 Superfortresses that dropped the atomic bomb on Hiroshima and Nagasaki. It was then the world's only operational atomic bomber squadron, so at the very least, the area around their base was highly sensitive

---

[258] Quoted in Bloecher, 1–2.
[259] Transcription of the article at http://ufologie.net/rw/p/rdr8jul1947.htm, accessed 13 October 2010.

and the possibility that their airspace had been penetrated by unidentified craft must have been extremely worrying.

The newspaper went on to suggest that events unfolded on the night of Wednesday, 2 July 1947, when Mr and Mrs Dan Wilmot saw 'a large glowing object' speed across the sky at around 10 o'clock. Mr Wilmot estimated that it was travelling at about 400 to 500 miles an hour at an altitude of 1,500 feet. It was oval shaped and about 15 to 20 feet in diameter. Others said that they had seen a strange blue light at about 3 a.m. The evening edition of the *Los Angeles Herald-Express* for 8 July 1947 was already printing the official explanation that the object was a 'radar weather target'. The *Seattle Daily Times* quoted Brigadier General Roger Ramey as saying the object was of 'flimsy construction; almost like a box kite' and covered with something like tinfoil. The next day the news-papers were printing reports that the object had been discovered three weeks earlier and even that unnamed Army Air Force sources had ruled out the possibility that it was some sort of weather kite.[260]

The unidentified rancher had meanwhile been identified as William Ware Brazel and now gave his account of the story. He told the *Roswell Daily Record* that, on 14 June, he and his eight-year-old son Vernon were about seven or eight miles out from the J. B. Foster Ranch when they discovered 'a large area of bright wreckage made up of rubber strips, tinfoil, a rather tough paper and sticks'. It was only on 4 July that he went back to the spot to recover the debris. When he heard about the flying discs he wondered whether he had acciden-tally found one. In town some days later he mentioned his find to Sheriff George Wilcox. Wilcox contacted the Roswell Army Air Field (RAAF) and Major Marcel, accompanied by

---

[260] 'Army Finds "Flying Saucer", General believes it is radar weather target', *Los Angeles Herald-Express*, 8 July 1947; 'Disk lands on ranch in N.M. – is held by Army', *Seattle Daily Times*, 8 July 1947; 'Only Meager Details of Flying Disc Given – Kite-Like Device Found in N.M. Studied by Army', *The Wyoming Eagle*, 9 July 1947.

a man in plain clothes, went back with Brazel to examine and remove the evidence.[261]

Brazel had found weather balloons on his ranch before. 'I am sure,' he told the newspaper, 'that what I found was not any weather observation balloon.' But on the same day the *Roswell Daily Record* also published Brigadier General Ramey's conclusion that the mysterious object was, after all, just a high-altitude weather balloon. A reward of $3,000 was offered for evidence of alien activity. Soon people were handing in 'a spinning gadget of aluminium' and 'a piece of metal' that allegedly 'took 6300 degrees of heat to melt'. By 10 July 1947 the French newspaper *L'Aurore* was already suggesting a cover-up. So what had been found?[262]

Foo-Files

On 23 September 1947 the commanding officer of Air Materiel [*sic*] Command (AMC), General Nathan F. Twining, wrote to the commanding officer of the US Air Force (USAF), Brigadier General George Schulgen.[263] The word SECRET was stamped in large letters on all three pages of the memo. As Twining indicated, he had already conducted a preliminary investigation of the 'so-called "Flying Disks"', involving Intelligence T-2 and Aircraft Laboratory Engineering Division T-3, and was now submitting his findings. He detailed the discs' commonly reported characteristics:[264]

---

[261] 'Harassed Rancher Who Located "Saucer" Sorry He Told About It', *Roswell Daily Record*, 9 July 1947.

[262] 'Gen. Ramey Empties Roswell Saucer', *Roswell Daily Record*, 9 July 1947; 'AAF "Flying Saucer" Merely Weather Box-Kite', *The Washington Post*, 9 July 1947; '"Disk" Near Bomb Test Site is Just a Weather Balloon', *The New York Times*, 9 July 1947; 'Les "Soucoupes Volantes" Gardent Leur Mystère', *L'Aurore*, 10 July 1947.

[263] The US Army Air Forces (USAAF) had been redesignated the US Air Force (USAF) from 18 September 1947, becoming a separate military service under the terms of the National Security Act, 1947.

[264] Edward J. Ruppelt, *The Report on Unidentified Flying Objects*, Doubleday & Company, 1956, pp. 15–16, gives Air Technical Intelligence Center; Curtis

1. Metallic or light reflecting surface.
2. Absence of trail, except in a few instances when the object apparently was operating under high performance conditions.
3. Circular or elliptical in shape, flat on bottom and domed on top.
4. Several reports of well kept formation flights varying from three to nine objects.
5. Normally no associated sound, except in three instances a substantial rumbling roar was noted.
6. Level flight speeds normally above 300 knots are estimated.[265]

'The phenomenon reported,' Twining concluded, 'is something real and not visionary or fictitious.' He recommended that Army Air Force Headquarters instigate a 'detailed study'. This became Air Materiel Command's Project XS-304, codename 'Project Sign'. The Allied military had been receiving reports of mysterious craft – dubbed 'foo fighters' by US pilots – towards the end of WWII and 'ghost rockets' had haunted Scandinavian skies in the summer of 1946, but only now would a systematic study be undertaken. Although there has been some controversy over the existence of an earlier investigation into UFOs called Majestic 12 (also Majic-12 and MJ-12), Project Sign was the first documented (and uncontested) official investigation by the USAF.[266]

Initiated on 22 January 1948 and conducted at Wright-Patterson Air Force Base, Dayton, Ohio, by the Technical

---

Peebles, *Watch the Skies*, Smithsonian Institution Press, 1994, p. 250; Stanton T. Friedman, *Flying Saucers and Science*, Career Press, 2008, p. 115. So-called Twining Memo, 'AMC Opinion Concerning "Flying Discs"', TSDIN/HMM/ig/6-4100, 23 September 1947.

[265] Twining Memo.

[266] Hall and Conors gave the project number as HT-304, but Project Sign's own Technical Report, February 1949, gives XS-304; 'Science: Foo-Fighter', *Time*, 15 January 1945; on 'ghost rockets' see USAFE Item 14, TT 1524, (Top Secret), 4 November 1948, declassified 1997, National Archives, Washington, D.C. Reports of so-called 'ghost rockets' became widespread across Europe during the course of 1946.

Intelligence Division, Project Sign was classified 'restricted' and given priority 2A – 1A being the highest rating. The Air Force were serious about this one. Most of that concern was around the possibility that the UFOs could be some new Soviet aircraft or guided rocketry, especially utilizing captured Nazi technology. But as they examined the cases, it seemed less and less likely that the Soviets could be behind them – they were simply too extraordinary.[267]

Among the many cases investigated, several stood out. Captain Thomas F. Mantell, Jr, flying an Air National Guard F-51, intercepted a UFO over Kentucky on 7 January 1948. As Mantell took the pursuit above the safety limit of 15,000 feet for flying without oxygen, radio contact with the pilot was lost. His crashed F-51 was recovered from the William J. Phillips farm near Franklin, Kentucky. First Venus, then a US Navy Skyhook research balloon were blamed for the incident. First Lieutenant Robert W. Meyers was leading a flight of P-47s of the 67th Fighter Group, Central Philippines, when he encountered something like a silver 'half-moon' with a 'turtle back' flying beneath him. He too lost radio contact as he attempted pursuit, but the UFO easily outmanoeuvred him and escaped at high speed. It sounded like an experimental 'flying wing', but nothing fitting that description was known to be operating in the region. On 24 July 1948, Eastern Airlines DC-3 Flight 576 narrowly avoided a mid-air collision as a UFO travelling at 800 mph closed to within 700 feet of the aeroplane as it flew over Alabama. Captain Clarence S. Chiles and First Officer John B. Whitted clearly observed a wingless cylindrical object with two rows of windows, trailing 50 feet of flame behind it. Passenger Clarence L. McKelvie also reported seeing a 'strange, eerie

---

[267] Ruppelt, pp. 16, 30. Hall and Connors, p. 117. Hall and Connors give a start date of 11 February 1948, whilst the Technical Report and Project 'Saucer' Press Release both give 22 January 1948. According to the Project Blue Book, 'History of the Project', 1 February 1966, NARA Blue Book, Roll 87, T1206-87, the Technical Intelligence Division, AMC, issued Technical Instruction No. 2185 on 11 February 1948 relating to the creation of Sign.

streak of light'. Sign investigators told the pilots that they had seen a fireball, but Chiles and Whitted insisted that it had been a craft of some sort.[268]

By early 1949, Project Sign was ready to report. Technical Report No. F-TR-2274-IA was prepared by missile specialist Lawrence H. Treuttnet and reserve Army Air Force colonel Albert B. Deyarmond and released in February 1949. It was based on analysis of 243 US and 30 non-US cases, of which only 20 per cent had been positively identified as 'conventional aerial objects'. Treuttnet and Deyarmond concluded that 'No definite evidence is yet available to confirm or disprove the actual existence of unidentified flying objects as new and unknown types of aircraft', although they noted that because the study was still ongoing, no definitive conclusion could yet be reached.[269]

On 27 April 1949 the National Military Establishment Office of Public Information in Washington, D.C., issued a press release entitled 'Project "Saucer"', detailing the work and findings of then still classified Project Sign. Claiming to have identified about 30 per cent of cases investigated as weather balloons, aircraft, birds, flares, astronomical phenomena, optical illusions and mass hallucinations, the press release still conceded that the final answer had not been reached. But this apparent honesty belied the real purpose of the release, which was to assuage public fears: 'The "saucers" are not a joke. Neither are they cause for alarm to the population.' It was the equivalent of *The Hitchhiker's Guide to the Galaxy*'s 'Don't Panic'.[270]

But the USAF had panicked, although for different reasons. With Project Sign leaning closer to an extraterrestrial explanation, essentially as the only explanation left, the top brass deemed it necessary to shake things up. A Top Secret 'Estimate

---

[268] Hall and Connors, pp. 133–40; Ruppelt, pp. 31–40.

[269] http://www.bluebookarchive.org/page.aspx?PageCode=MAXW-PBB1-8, accessed 21 October 2010.

[270] 'Project "Saucer"', Memorandum to the Press No. M 26 – 49, National Military Establishment Office of Public Information, Washington, D.C., 27 April 1949.

of the Situation' had been made, apparently concluding that UFOs were real, but as Captain Edward J. Ruppelt, later director of UFO research, explained, 'it was kicked back'. No copies of this Estimate have so far been unearthed by ufologists. On 11 February 1949, Sign was redesignated Project Grudge and new personnel were assigned to conduct the research. In his *Report on Unidentified Flying Objects*, Ruppelt called this period 'the Dark Ages'. The name Grudge was evidently more than just a random moniker.[271]

In August 1949 Grudge released the 600-page-long 'Unidentified Flying Objects – Project Grudge', Technical Report No. 102-AC-49/15-100 – the 'Grudge Report'. After analysing 244 cases it concluded that UFOs were one of four things:[272]

a) misinterpretation of conventional objects,
b) mass hysteria or 'War Nerves',
c) hoaxes and/or
d) psychopathological persons.[273]

Writer John A. Keel, famous for *The Mothman Prophecies*, described Grudge as 'hundreds of pages of irrelevant nonsense'.[274] Based on Grudge's findings the AMC recommended that research be reduced in scope. Grudge quickly stagnated. It was finally announced on 27 December 1949 in a USAF press conference that the project had been terminated. Work continued on the possibly paranormal 'green fireballs', codenamed Project Twinkle, and even Grudge was still lingering in the background. According to Ruppelt, when the USAF's Director of Intelligence, Major General (later Lieutenant General) Charles P. Cabell got the full measure of the sorry

---

[271] Ruppelt, p. 59; 'History of the Project', n.p., gives 16 December 1948 as the date of redesignation.

[272] Ruppelt, pp. 65–8; 'History of the Project', n.p.

[273] 'History of the Project', n.p.

[274] John A. Keel, 'The Man Who Invented Flying Saucers', *Fortean Times*, 41, 1983, pp. 52–7.

state Grudge was in he demanded that a new project be set up. In September 1951, Ruppelt took over Grudge and a new series of monthly reports started appearing from November 1951. In March 1952, Grudge was redesignated Project Blue Book.[275]

An area of about 13m³ (42 cubic feet) in the US National Archives is occupied by the text records of Project Blue Book. This is estimated to contain about 84,000 pages, all of which can be read on 94 rolls of 35mm microfilm. Luckily, the Public Affairs Division of the Wright-Patterson Air Force Base produced a fact sheet in 1985 that summarized the findings. In the period from 1947 to 1969 a total of 12,618 sightings had been reported: 701 remained unidentified.[276]

Despite the initial impetus from General Cabell, the official line from the Pentagon continued to be less than constructive. Ruppelt applied for a transfer. In 1956 he published his landmark book *The Report on Unidentified Flying Objects* documenting the many incredible contacts he had investigated, yet Ruppelt remained agnostic. He was not a believer, he said, but also added:

> Every time I begin to get skeptical I think of the other reports, the many reports made by experienced pilots and radar operators, scientists, and other people who know what they're looking at. These reports were thoroughly investigated and they are still unknowns.[277]

Strictly speaking, then, he had to admit that there were unidentified flying objects and only tentatively raised the possibility that 'Maybe the earth is being visited by interplanetary spaceships'. Even with such an even-handed approach he seems to

---

[275] Ruppelt, p. 65; Status Report No. 1, Project Grudge, 30 November 1951, http://www.bluebookarchive.org/page.aspx?PageCode=MAXW-PBB1-498, accessed 21 October 2010; 'History of the Project', n.p.

[276] US National Archives, http://www.archives.gov/foia/ufos.html, accessed 13 October 2010. The Blue Book Archive website at http://www.bluebookarchive.org/ has about 10 per cent of this material online.

[277] Ruppelt, p. 242.

have ruffled a few feathers. The Commander, ATIC, wrote to the Secretary of the Air Force in 1958 concerning the book. Undermining Ruppelt's credibility as an expert, he dismissed his conclusions as 'questionable'. He had proved Ruppelt's oft made point: the Air Force only wanted *identified* flying objects and certainly did not want to hear about extraterrestrials.[278]

UFO sightings and radar contacts continued and were just as remarkable as before, and Blue Book was just as far away from solving the problem. Not long after Ruppelt left, Blue Book Special Report No. 14 had to concede that 'It can never be absolutely proven that "flying saucers" do not exist'. Completed on 17 March 1954, it was declassified and released to the public on 5 May 1955. The USAF on its own could not get rid of the unidentifieds, but they were adamant that it was 'highly improbable' that they were the product of 'technological developments outside the range of present-day scientific knowledge'. By 1966 the USAF were receiving more than 2,000 letters a year from people demanding to know more about the UFO investigations.[279]

As part of Blue Book, the USAF had contracted the University of Colorado to conduct an independent Scientific Study of Unidentified Objects, the 'Colorado Project' or 'Condon Committee', under the direction of Edward U. Condon.[280] With admirable restraint, Karl Pflock characterized this study as 'not so independent and not so scientific'.[281] Evidence was later

---

[278] Ruppelt, p. 243; Cmdr, ATIC, to Sec[retar]y of Air Force, OIS, 23 May 1958, Document T1206-87, NARA Blue Book Roll No. 87, Page ID: NARA-PBB87-335-339, http://www.bluebookarchive.org/page.aspx?PageCode=NARA-PBB87-336, accessed 27 October 2010.

[279] 'History of the Report', n.p.; 'Extract from Special Report #14', Document T1206-86, NARA Blue Book Roll No. 86, Page ID: NARA-PBB86-881, http://www.bluebookarchive.org/page.aspx?PageCode=NARA-PBB86-881, accessed 27 October 2010.

[280] Reproduced online at http://www.project1947.com/shg/condon/index.html and http://files.ncas.org/condon/ with the permission of the Regents of the University of Colorado.

[281] Karl T. Pflock, Review of Richard H. Hall, *Alien Invasion or Human Fantasy?*, Mount Rainier, 2004, *Journal of Scientific Exploration*, 18, 2004, p. 710.

forthcoming that Condon and others had held secret meetings with the CIA and that the CIA contributed to the project, neither facts being mentioned in the Condon Report itself. The project's much touted scientific methodology also met with serious criticism.[282] But the USAF had what it wanted: a way out of the UFO maze. Shored up by Condon they could now confidently state:

> The conclusions of Project BLUE BOOK are: (1) no UFO reported, investigated, and evaluated by the Air Force has ever given any indication of threat to our national security; (2) there has been no evidence submitted to or discovered by the Air Force that sightings categorized as "unidentified" represent technological developments or principles beyond the range of present-day scientific knowledge; and (3) there has been no evidence indicating that sightings categorized as "unidentified" are extraterrestrial vehicles.[283]

On 17 December 1969, the Secretary of the Air Force terminated Project Blue Book. There would be no further plans to investigate UFOs again. But the Americans were not the only ones to investigate the UFO phenomenon. With news of the Argentinian Air Force forming a commission to investigate UFOs and the New Zealand Defence Force declassifying its UFO files, the search is far from over.[284]

---

[282] Peter A. Sturrock, 'An Analysis of the Condon Report on the Colorado UFO Project', *Journal of Scientific Exploration*, 1.1, 1987, pp. 75ff.

[283] 'U.S. Air Force Fact Sheet Concerning UFOs and Project BLUE BOOK', January 1985, US National Archives, http://www.archives.gov/foia/ufos.html, accessed 13 October 2010.

[284] 'USAF Fact Sheet'; 'Argentina to Record UFO Sightings', *AFP*, 29 December 2010; 'New Zealand Releases UFO Files', *Daily Telegraph*, 23 December 2010.

Official UFO Investigations

Name	Country	Organization	Period Active
Majestic 12 (contested)	USA	Inter-governmental	1946–54?
Project Sign	USA	US Air Force (USAF)	1948
Project Grudge	USA	US Air Force (USAF)	1949–1
Project Magnet	Canada	Dept of Transport	1950–4
Flying Saucer Working Party	UK	Ministry of Defence (MoD)	1950–51
Robertson Panel	USA	Central Intelligence Agency (CIA)	1952, 1953
Project Blue Book	USA	US Air Force (USAF)	1952–69
Condon Committee (Condon Report)	USA	University of Colorado	1966–8
GEPAN/SEPRA/GEIPAN	France	Centre National d'Études Spatiales (CNES)	1977–
Project Condign	UK	Defence Intelligence Staff (DIS)	1997–2000

In 1999 the French public woke up to an astounding report published by weekly news and entertainment magazine *VSD*. In 'Les OVNI et la Defense: A quoi doit-on se préparer?' ('UFOS and Defence: What Must We Be Prepared For?') about 200,000 people read of hundreds of UFO cases with the conclusion that aliens were probably out there and 'critical vigilance' was required. Specifically, the report argued that the UFO phenomenon was worthy of continued serious investigation because it could not be ruled out that some sort of non-human technology was involved and that this necessarily had ramifications for national security. The implication was also there that the US government was being less than open with its information, particularly as regards Roswell. The report was produced by a group calling itself COMETA – the 'Committee for In-Depth Studies' – comprised of twelve private individuals formerly involved with the prestigious Institut des Hautes Études de Défense Nationale (IHEDN), including generals, an admiral and a police superintendent, amongst others, under retired air force general Denis Letty. It was endorsed by heavyweight figures such as General Bernard Norlain of the French Air Force and a former director of IHEDN, as well as André Lebeau, former president of Centre National d'Études Spatiales (CNES). Originally only sent to top officials, including then President Jacques Chirac and Prime Minister Lionel Jospin, the report garnered the reputation of being an official document. However, as a private initiative it did not carry the weight that many had hoped for it.[285]

On 22 March 2007 the French space agency CNES released via its website the equivalent of 100,000 A4 pages of eye-witness

---

[285] Bruce Maccabee, 'DVD Review: *Out of the Blue: The Definitive Investigation of the UFO Phenomenon*', 2004, *Journal of Scientific Exploration*, 22, 2008, p. 453; Mark Rodeghier, 'The 1999 French Report on UFOs and Defense', *International UFO Reporter*, Summer 2000, pp. 20–3; Claude Maugé 'A Commentary on COMETA', trans. Jacques Vallée, *Journal of Scientific Exploration*, 15, 2001, pp. 139–42; Gildas Bourdais, 'The French Report on UFOs and Defense: A Summary', CUFOS, http://www.cufos.org/cometa.html, accessed 21 December 2010.

reports, photographs, film footage and audio recordings of some 1,650 sightings documented since 1954. Printed out and piled high this amount would stand as tall as a three-storey building. Within three hours demand crashed the CNES servers.

Jacques Patenet, head of the Group d'Études et d'Information sur les Phénomènes Aérospatiaux Non Identifiés (GEIPAN), the CNES UFO team, was equivocal: 'The data that we are releasing doesn't demonstrate the presence of extraterrestrial beings, but it doesn't demonstrate the impossibility of such presence either'. Of the 1,650 cases he said, 'a few dozen are very intriguing and can be called UFOs', or about 28 per cent according to their figures. CNES still receives about a hundred new reports every year.[286]

When the UK's Ministry of Defence (MoD) declassified files in 2006 it was discovered that they had collected more than 10,000 eye-witness accounts. In 2007 Dr David Clarke, Dr Joe McGonagle and Gary Anthony campaigned to have the MoD release all of its UFO files to the public. In 2008 the British Government released its most comprehensive files on UFO sightings. Compiled by the Ministry of Defence between 1978 and 2002 the files were made available under the Freedom of Information Act (FOIA) with further releases planned for following years. The Flying Saucer Working Party (FSWP) had already reported on the problem as long ago as 1951. It came to entirely negative conclusions as to whether UFOs were of extraterrestrial origin. But then the FSWP had relied on the USAF's entirely negative Project Grudge. However, the MoD continued to operate a UFO 'desk' until 2009 before a round of budgetry cuts deemed its

---

[286] Molly Moore, 'French Get a Look at Nation's UFO Files', *Washington Post*, 23 March 2007. 'The Plain Truth of the Matter', CNES, March 2007, http://www.cnes.fr/web/CNES-en/5871-the-plain-truth-of-the-matter.php, accessed 24 March 2010. 'GEIPAN UAP Investigation Unit Opens its Files', CNES, 26 March 2007, http://www.cnes.fr/web/CNES-en/5866-geipan-uap-investigation-unit-opens-its-files.php, accessed 24 March 2010. See www.cnes-geipan.fr.

cost of £50,000 a year an expendable luxury. The MoD, whilst stating that it has no opinion on extraterrestrials, said that 'in over fifty years, no UFO report has revealed any evidence of a potential threat to the United Kingdom'. The last recorded entry, dated 30 November 2009, took place at 19:40 in Wilnecote, Staffordshire: 'Strange orange light coming from the North, clear night, no port and starboard indicators, translucent halo, lasted 1 min 20 secs, constant speed, straight line.'[287]

Roswell today is no longer the sleepy rural town that it was. It is now a major tourist attraction with an annual UFO festival, the Roswell International UFO Museum and Research Center and at least three competing crash sites. The museum was founded by Lieutenant Walter Haut, who had issued the fateful press release on 8 July 1947, and Glenn Dennis. Registered as a non-profit educational organization in 1991, it opened to visitors in autumn 1992. The museum claims to attract upwards of 150,000 people a year.[288]

As well as the tourism, additional evidence or interpretations continue to surface, keeping the Roswell controversy alive and kicking. Bible code hunters even found the word

---

[287] David Clarke and Andy Roberts, *Out of the Shadows: UFOs, the Establishment and Official Cover Up*, Piatkus Books, 2002; Finlo Rohrer, 'Saucers in the Sky', BBC News Magazine, 4 July 2007; Graham Tibbetts, 'British Government Releases UFO Files', *Daily Telegraph*, 13 May 2008; Andrew Hough, 'MoD Department that Investigated UFO Sightings "Closed"', *Daily Telegraph*, 4 December 2009; HQ Air Command, 'Closure of UFO Hotline', MoD, 31 December 2008/1 March 2010, http://www.mod.uk/DefenceInternet/FreedomOfInformation/PublicationScheme/SearchPublicationScheme/ClosureOfUfoHelpdesk.htm, accessed 23 October 2010; Air Command, 'UFO Reports 2009', MoD, p. 39, http://www.mod.uk/NR/rdonlyres/41A2F229-95B9-47E5-99C6-CB242838A03C/0/ufo_report_2009.pdf, accessed 23 October 2010.

[288] Dennis Stacey, Review of Karl T. Pflock, *Roswell: Inconvenient Facts and the Will to Believe*, Prometheus, 2001, *Journal of Scientific Exploration*, 15, 2001, p. 429; http://www.roswellufomuseum.com/about.htm, accessed 23 October 2010.

Top 10 UFO Encounters

Case	Date	Location	Alleged Occurrence
Kenneth Arnold	1947	Washington State, USA	nine 'flying discs' sighted
Roswell	1947	New Mexico, USA	UFO crash
Mantell	1948	Kentucky, USA	UFO pursuit
Chiles-Whitted	1948	Alabama, USA	UFO near-collision
Washington D.C.	1952	District of Columbia, USA	sightings and radar contacts
1966-7 UFO Wave	1966-7	USA and Canada	mass sightings documented
Shag Harbour	1967	Nova Scotia, Canada	UFO crash
Tehran	1976	Tehran, Iran	jets scrambled to intercept UFO
Rendlesham Forest	1980	Suffolk, UK	RAF base close encounter
Belgian UFO Wave	1989-90	Wallonia, Belgium	mass black triangle sightings

'Roswell' hidden in Genesis 31:28, adding to the aura.[289] But the significant new findings came from an alleged crash eye-witness, new analysis of a 1947 photograph, and archaeological digs in the supposed crash area.

In 1996 the deathbed confession of Jim Ragsdale was published along with a sworn affidavit attesting to its authenticity. He claimed not only to have seen the alleged flying disc crash, but also to have investigated the wreckage. He described seeing an instrument panel, chairs and four dead alien bodies through a hole in the fuselage. It looked like the truth was finally out. However, using the forensic psychology procedures of Statement Validity Analysis and Fact Pattern Analysis, James Houran and Stephen Porter found that Ragdale's statement did not resemble true memory recall and was factually inconsistent.[290]

A photograph taken of Brigadier General Ramey and Colonel Thomas J. DuBose examining the remains of a balloon was released to quiet the public. But even this has become evidence of proof, at least for some. Ramey is shown holding a piece of paper, which some people have said makes clear reference to a crashed UFO of alien origins. The piece of paper is barely, if at all, legible and experiments by James Houran and Kevin Randle have shown that interpretations of its contents are entirely due to the reader's expectations.[291]

---

[289] Matt Lamy, *100 Strangest Mysteries*, Barnes & Nobles 2007, p. 100. Using equidistant letter sequencing you can find almost anything in the Bible, or any long text such as *Moby Dick*, *War and Peace*, etc.

[290] Jim Ragsdale, *The Jim Ragsdale Story: A Closer Look at the Roswell Incident*, Jim Ragsdale Productions, 1996; James Houran and Stephen Porter, 'Statement Validity Analysis of "The Jim Ragsdale Story": Implication for the Roswell Incident', *Journal of Scientific Exploration*, 12.1, 1998, pp. 57–71.

[291] James Houran and Kevin Randle, '"A Message in a Bottle:" Confounds in Deciphering the Ramey Memo from the Roswell UFO Case', *Journal of Scientific Exploration*, 16.1, 2002, pp. 45–66. The photograph is held by the Fort Worth-Star Telegram Photograph Collection, The University of Texas at Arlington Libraries. As a reader of *Journal of Scientific Exploration* (16, 2002, pp. 662–3), James Westwood, pointed out, if this letter was in any way an official military communication then it should have been recorded and filed. Randle had indeed searched for the document, but to no avail.

In 2002 the SCI FI Channel sponsored archaeologists from the University of New Mexico to excavate at the alleged crash site. Working under project leader Dr William Doleman, they reputedly discovered 'historical materials of uncertain origin' and suggestive furrows. Some members of the team were certain that they were under government surveillance and feared that there might be a sabotage attempt. In the end, the nine-day excavation went ahead unmolested. Aerial photographs of the region from 1946 may indicate that at least one of the features discovered was already present before the supposed crash event took place.[292]

Area 51

Area 51 is a US Air Force base in Nevada, about 800 miles away from Roswell, New Mexico. It is primarily a testing site for secret aircraft and weapons projects. For example, the U-2 spy plane of the 1950s was tested and developed here. It is a restricted area with the 'use of deadly force' authorized to protect it. Largely because of this secrecy, Area 51 is rumoured to house wreckage from the alleged Roswell UFO crash and other crashes, as well as the bodies of extraterrestrials.

About 20,000 people signed the Roswell Declaration demanding that the US government release all its files on the Roswell Incident. It was sent to the US Congress in 1997. Kent Jeffrey was one of those instrumental in organizing the campaign, but after studying all of the evidence that has since become available he has reversed his earlier position on Roswell. Twining also noted that there was a 'lack of physical evidence in the shape of crash-recovered exhibits'. This was a secret memo from one high-ranking officer to another; if any evidence of a crashed UFO had been recovered at Roswell, he would surely

---

[292] William H. Doleman, Thomas J. Carey and Donald R. Schmitt, *The Roswell Dig Diaries*, Pocket Books, 2004; reviewed by Kevin Randle in *Journal of Scientific Exploration*, 18, 2004, pp. 706–10.

have mentioned it. Many have challenged such conflicting evidence as signs of deception. Karl Pflock, for one, argued that there was a cover-up, but that what was being covered up was not an extraterrestrial crash but the government's own top-secret balloon experiment to detect Soviet nuclear testing called Project Mogul. This was certainly one of the explanations being forwarded by the USAF itself.[293]

Project Blue Book wrote off Kenneth Arnold's sighting as a mirage. The USAF fact sheet ended on tetchy note, pointing to the ongoing public interest in the question: 'There are not now nor ever have been, any extraterrestrial visitors or equipment on Wright-Patterson Air Force Base'. Of course, this could lead some to deduce that any extraterrestrial visitors or equipment that the USAF did have must have been taken somewhere else.[294]

Closest Encounters

Do you remember hearing or seeing the word TRONDANT and knowing that it has a secret meaning for you?

'I saw a glimmer of silver reflecting from the metal frame between the door and the windscreen and then to the left over my head was this massive craft.' Bridget Grant, described by the *Sun* as a 'UFO magnet', claims to have had seventeen close

---

[293] Twining Memo. Others remain convinced that a UFO had crashed and was examined at Roswell, e.g., Philip Corso and William Birnes, *The Day After Roswell*, Pocket Books/Simon & Schuster, 1997.

[294] 'USAF Fact Sheet'. See Kent Jeffrey, 'Roswell – Anatomy of a Myth', *Journal of Scientific Exploration*, 12.1, 1998, pp. 79–101, for an argument against a UFO crash at Roswell and the replies from Michael Swords and Robert M. Wood in that same issue. For the final official position see USAF, *The Roswell Report: Fact Versus Fiction in the New Mexico Desert*, US Government Printing Office, 1995, and USAF, *The Roswell Report: Case Closed*, Barnes & Noble, 1997. As a further guide, the bibliography for Randle's *Roswell Encyclopedia*, although omitted from the book, has been published in *Journal of Scientific Exploration*, 15, 2001, pp. 425ff.

Hynek's UFO Classification System

I – Long Range (more than 500 feet)

Nocturnal Lights	N	Light seen at night
Daylight Discs	D	Light seen during the day
Radar-Visual	R	Sighting with radar contact

II – Close Range (less than 500 feet)

Close Encounter of the First Kind	CE1	Close range sighting of a UFO
Close Encounter of the Second Kind	CE2	Physical evidence after a UFO sighting
Close Encounter of the Third Kind	CE3	Contact with the occupant of a UFO

Dr J. Allen Hynek (1910–86) was a prominent astronomer and the director of the Lindheimer Astronomical Research Center at Northwestern University, USA. After serving as scientific adviser to the US Air Force UFO projects Sign, Grudge and Blue Book, he founded the Center for UFO Studies (CUFOS). He presented his classification in *The UFO Experience: A Scientific Enquiry*, Corgi Books, 1972, and *The Hynek UFO Report*, Sphere Books, 1977.

encounters with aliens in the last forty years. She is not alone. It is said that *The X-Files* creator Chris Carter got the idea for the series after reading the 1991 Roper Survey claiming that 3.7 million people in the USA believe that they have been abducted by aliens. If he had waited a year Carter could have read the more astonishing estimate that as many as 15 million Americans may believe that they have been abducted by aliens.[295]

The classic abduction case is that of American couple Betty and Barney Hill who claimed to have been kidnapped by aliens in 1961. Abductees differ from contactees – people who claim to have made contact with extraterrestrials. The abductee is usually forcibly captured and may be subjected to invasive techniques that would be illegal under almost all earthling legal systems. The contactee, in contrast, usually makes contact with benign entities who have some message for humanity, typically involving world peace. Whilst abduction always involves the report of a physical process, 'contact' can be broadly defined from 'telepathic' communication to actual physical meeting. Several contactees, such as George King and Claude Vorilhon, have gone on to found religious movements based on their experiences.

A large number of supposed alien abduction claims are based on memories said to have been recalled under hypnosis. The problem is that most clinical researchers are coming to the conclusion that memories are not recalled under hypnosis but created; that is, they are false but have the full weight of apparent past experience to convince the subject. Investigating abductees, Susan Clancy, then a postdoctoral fellow at Harvard, found that her sample group of eleven exhibited a tendency to develop false memories (using the Deese/Reodiger-McDermott paradigm) and had a higher than average score on a test for schizotopy. She concluded that abductees were virtually schizophrenic with a marked tendency towards 'magical thinking' and 'perceptual aberration'. It was later said, rather cruelly, of Betty Hill that she was 'unable to distinguish between a landed UFO and a streetlight'. 'As far as science knows,' Clancy concluded, 'no one is being abducted by aliens.'[296]

---

[295] David M. Jacobs, *Secret Life: Firsthand Accounts of UFO Abductions*, Simon & Schuster, 1992; Tim Spanton, 'Brit Housewife is UFO Magnet', the *Sun*, 11 November 2010; 'X Appeal: The X-Files Builds a Cult Following by Following the Occult', *Entertainment Weekly*, 214, 18 March 1994.

[296] Susan Clancy, *Abducted: How People Come to Believe They were Kidnapped*

By the way, if you did remember hearing or seeing the word TRONDANT then your return for the 1991 Roper Survey would have been discarded on the grounds of 'positive response bias', meaning that you will agree to anything. That immediately disqualified 1 per cent of the sample. The problem is that the survey's dramatic claims were based on answers from only 2 per cent of the remaining sample. In 1981 the psychologists Sheryl C. Wilson and Theodore X. Barber identified the fantasy-prone personality – the type of person who has intense fantasies often to the point where they cannot tell them apart from reality. Their research showed that 4 per cent of the general population fell into this category.[297]

The classic experiment on abduction was conducted in 1977 by Professor Alvin 'Corky' Lawson (1929–2010) of California State University. Recruiting a group of sixteen volunteers with little or no knowledge of abductions, he hypnotized them and asked them a set of eight questions. Almost all of his subjects 'gave us interesting narratives with many specific incidents about getting onboard, seeing alien creatures, having an examination, interacting with the aliens, and being returned'. Comparing these artificially created abduction accounts with those purporting to be real he discovered that there was very little significant difference between them. If correct, Lawson's research suggests that, although only 4 per cent of people are fantasy prone, almost

by Aliens, Harvard University Press, 2005, p. 129; David M. Jacobs, review of Clancy's *Abducted, Journal of Scientific Exploration*, 20, 2006, pp. 307, 309: Beth Potier, 'Starship Memories', *Harvard University Gazette*, 31 October 2002; Bruce Grierson, 'A Bad Trip Down Memory Lane', *The New York Times*, 27 July 2003; Leonard S. Newman and Roy F. Baumeister, 'Toward an Explanation of the UFO Abduction Phenomenon: Hypnotic Elaboration, Extraterrestrial Sado-masochism, and Spurious Memories', *Psychological Inquiry*, 7, 1996, pp. 99–126. Betty Hill comment in Robert Sheaffer, 'Over the Hill on UFO Abductions', *Skeptical Inquirer*, 31.6, November/December 2007.

[297] Sheryl C. Wilson and Theodore X. Barber, 'The Fantasy-Prone Personal-ity: Implications for Understanding Imagery, Hypnosis, and Parapsychological Phenomena', in Anees A. Sheikh (ed.), *Imagery: Current Theory, Research and Application*, John Wiley and Sons, 1983, pp. 340–90.

everyone will develop a relevant fantasy narrative under the right circumstances.[298]

However, before we dismiss alien abduction on these grounds, long-standing researcher Associate Professor David M. Jacobs of Temple University, Philadelphia, noted that abductees were reporting a range of obscure procedures (which they themselves did not understand) that had not been reported by the press and which found agreement with other abduction accounts of which they were unaware. When people are allegedly abducted their absence is often noted by others: the police might be called out, search parties organized, etc. When they return they often have unaccounted for marks on their bodies, broken bones, stains on their clothing – clothing which may even be on inside out, back to front or be someone else's entirely. Sometimes there are even eye-witnesses. In-depth psychological testing by Budd Hopkins in 1983 has also demonstrated an absence of mental illness among abductees. Some researchers, such as Clancy and psychologist Dr Susan Blackmore, have explained many more of these claims as the product of sleep paralysis hallucinations. That was not what Jacobs discovered. Out of approximately 700 cases, Jacobs found that only 40 per cent took place in bed at night, and that not all of these people were asleep. Jenny Randles conducted a similar experiment to Lawson's in 1987 and with twenty subjects using creative visualization produced none of the classic abduction motifs. Even Clancy had to admit, 'you can't disprove alien abductions'.[299]

---

[298] Peter Brookesmith, 'Necrolog: Alvin Lawson', *Fortean Times*, 270, January 2010, pp. 28–9.

[299] Jacobs, review of Clancy's *Abducted*, pp. 305–6, 311; William J. Cromie, 'Alien Abduction Claims Explained', *Harvard University Gazette*, 22 September 2005; Brookesmith, p. 29. See also Kevin D. Randle, et al., *The Abduction Enigma*, Forge, 1999, who argue that there is no scientific evidence for alien abductions. James Houran, Review of Kevin D. Randle, *The Abduction Enigma, Journal of Scientific Exploration*, 14, 2000, pp. 476–7. In reviewing Clancy's *Abducted*, the reviewer argued that all debunkers make one or more mistakes in not knowing the evidence, ignoring it, or distorting it, see *Journal of Scientific Exploration*, 20, 2006, p. 303. Susan Blackmore and Marcus Cox, 'Alien Abductions, Sleep Paralysis and the Temporal Lobe', *European Journal of UFO and Abduction Studies*, 1, 2000, pp. 113–18.

Notable Abductees

Name	Date	Location(s)	Further Reading
Elizabeth Klarer	1954–63	Kwa-Zulu Natal, South Africa	—, *Beyond the Light Barrier* (1980)
Antonio Villas Boas	1957	Minas Gerais, Brazil	
Betty and Barney Hill	1961	New Hampshire, USA	—, *The Interrupted Journey* (1966)
Herbert Schirmer	1967	Nebraska, USA	
Charles Hickson and Calvin Parker	1973	Mississippi, USA	William Mendez, *UFO Contact at Pascagoula* (1983)
Travis Walton	1975	Arizona, USA	—, *The Walton Experience* (1978)
Jack and Jim Weiner, Chuck Rak, and Charlie Foltz	1976	Maine, USA	Raymond E. Fowler, *The Allagash Abductions* (1993)
Robert Taylor	1979	Scotland, UK	
Bridget Grant	1970s?–93	Various, UK and USA	— and Nick Pope, *The Alien Within* (forthcoming)
Louis Whitley Strieber	1985	New York State, USA	—, *Communion: A True Story* (1987)
Kirsan Ilyumzhinov	1997	Kalmykia, Russian Federation	—, *The President's Crown of Thorns* (1998)

The evidence is unexplained. The interpretations are conflicting. There is clearly still a mystery here, even if it turns out to be
more psychological than extraterrestrial. As James Houran
noted, 'even if humankind is not being abducted by aliens [. . .]
the abduction phenomenon has value outside the immediate
context of ufology'.[300]

For those concerned about the problem, or simply wishing to
hedge their bets, alien abduction insurance is provided by the
UFO Abduction Insurance Company, also known as the St
Lawrence Agency, based in Florida. Their $10 million policy is
available for $19.95, although any successful claimants are only
entitled to receive $1 a year for the next ten million years.
Goodfellow Rebecca Ingrams Pearson Ltd of London apparently sold suicide cult Heaven's Gate just such a policy in 1996.
For $1,000 a year the insured would receive a $1 million payout
in the event of abduction, impregnation or death caused by
aliens. The thirty-nine members of Heaven's Gate committed
mass suicide, believing that a UFO travelling alongside the
Hale-Bopp comet was sent to collect them. Under the terms of
the policy, suicide rendered the contract null and void. Managing
director Simon Burgess is reported as saying 'There has never
been a genuine claim for alien abduction'. According to
Investment News, the company has sold some 4,000 alien protection policies.[301]

---

[300] Houran, p. 477. See also the important contribution by A. Pritchard, et. al.
(eds), *Alien Discussions: Proceedings of the Abduction Study Conference*, North
Cambridge Press, 1994.

[301] Vicki Haddock, 'Don't Sweat Alien Threat', *San Francisco Chronicle*, 18
October 1998; Louise Jury, 'Cult Insured Against Aliens', the *Independent*, 31
March 1997; Gary S. Mogel, 'Antidote to Alien Impregnation? Insurance',
Investment News, 21 May 2007. Kimberly Lankford, 'Weird Insurance', *CBS
MoneyWatch*, October 1998, stated that 20,000 such policies had been sold.
The UFO Abduction Insurance Co., offers what are essentially novelty documents payable to Comp-Pay Services, Inc., see www.ufo2001.com, accessed
26 October 2010. There are other websites, such as www.abductioninsurance.
net, offering similar products. Goodfellow Rebecca Ingrams Pearson Ltd, is
now registered as British Insurance Limited based in Maidstone, Kent, according to Companies House records accessed 26 October 2010.

Notable Contactees[302]

Name	Contact	Founder of	Author of
Daniel Fry	1949	Understanding, Inc.	*The White Sands Incident* (1954)
George Van Tassel	1951	The Giant Rock Spacecraft Convention	*I Rode a Flying Saucer* (1952)
George Adamski	1952	Adamski Foundation	*Flying Saucers Have Landed*, with Desmond Leslie (1953)
Truman Bethurum	c. 1953	Sanctuary of Thought	*The Voice of the Planet Clarion* (1957)
Gloria Lee	1953	Cosmon Research Foundation	*Why We Are Here!* (1959)
George King	1954	Aetherius Society	*You Are Responsible!* (1961)
Allen Noonan, aka Allen Michael	1954	Universal Industrial Church of the New World Comforter	*The Everlasting Gospel* (1973)
Gabriel Green	c. 1957	Amalgamated Flying Saucer Clubs of America, Inc., Universal Flying Saucer Party	*Let's Face Facts About Flying Saucers* (1967)
Claude Vorilhon, aka Raël	1973	The Raël Movement (Raëlism)	*Le Livre qui dit la vérité* ('The Book Which Tells the Truth') (1974)
Eduard 'Billy' Meier	1975	*Freie Interessengemeinschaft für Grenz- und Geisteswissenschaften und Ufologiestudien* ('Free Community of Interests for the Fringe and Spiritual Sciences and Ufological Studies')	*Talmud Jmmanuel* (2005)
Ivo A. Benda	1997	Universe People, Cosmic People of Light Powers	*Rozhovory s poučením od mých přátel z vesmíru* ('Interviews with Instructions from my Friends from the Universe') (1997)

[302] These are dates of alleged contact provided by or for the individuals listed.

Final Frontiers

Chrononauts from the future. Hypoterrestrials from inner space. Ultraterrestrials from other dimensions or the collective unconscious. Unidentified Flying Angels or demonic fallen angels from Hell. It might even be suggested that UFO should stand for Unidentified Flying Organism. That UFOs are alien spacecraft is only the least exotic explanation that has been proposed for the phenomenon.[303]

In the March 1945 issue of the sci-fi magazine *Amazing Stories*, editor Raymond Palmer published a rewritten account by a psychologically troubled welder called Richard Sharpe Shaver (1907–c. 1975) of his encounters with a race of underground beings, the 'Abandondero' or simply Dero for short, in 'I Remember Lemuria'. A supposedly abandoned remnant of a race of giants who left earth thousands of years ago, the Dero delight in dangerously depraved sexual orgies and the harassment of top-dwellers. The story was a massive success, boosting *Amazing Stories'* circulation from 25,000 to 250,000 a month by the end of the year. Palmer bought up everything Shaver had on the Dero – reams and reams of it, apparently – and commissioned more, sitting up into the wee small hours rewriting it all as what would become known as 'The Shaver Mystery'. Soon people were writing in with their own horrifying experiences. One reader – later identified as self-described 'disruption agent' Fred Lee Crisman – pleaded 'For heaven's sake, drop the whole thing! You are playing with dynamite'. Crisman claimed that in the final months of World War II he had narrowly escaped with his life from a cave in the northern foothills of the Karakoram after a deadly firefight with unidentified subterranean assailants.[304]

---

[303] Nick Redfern, 'What is a UFO?', *Paranormal*, 50, August 2010, pp. 58–63; Brad Steiger, 'Are UFOs Alive?', *UFO Digest*, 19 August 2008, http://www. ufodigest.com/news/0808/areufosalive.html, accessed 6 November 2010; Nick Redfern, 'From the Heavens or from Hell?' *Paranormal*, 54, December 2010, pp. 58–63; Leo Ruickbie, 'Angels in Space', *Paranormal*, 56, February 2011, pp. 54–7.

[304] John A. Keel, 'The Man Who Invented Flying Saucers', *Fortean Times*, 41, 1983, pp. 52–7. See also Michael Barkun, *A Culture of Conspiracy: Apocalyptic*

Robert Ernst Dickhoff, founder of the American Buddhist Society and Fellowship, described in his 1951 book *Agharta: The Subterranean World*, how Martians had established colonies on earth, creating a vast network of underground tunnels. Milinko S. Stevic, an engineer from what was then Yugoslavia, toured the USA in the 1970s telling all who would listen that a world of cities and tunnels existed below the surface, and that Adolf Hitler had even used them to escape war-torn Germany and take up residence in New Jersey. This innerverse was the Atlantean Empire of a race so advanced that they cruised our wildest dreams (particularly Stevic's) in their UFOs.[305] So when E. A. Guest later claimed that whilst working for the US military his father had seen a classified briefing on Roswell as the crash site of a craft from inner, not outer, space, the scene had already been set. The late Mac Tonnies took the theme further, arguing that what we had previously thought of as fairies, ghosts, demons, or even extraterrestrials, were so many manifestations of the subterraneans' psychological warfare and advanced technology. Abductions are their harvesting of human DNA in an attempt to treat a debilitating genetic syndrome. Roswell he explained as the crash of one of their surveillance devices. Eoin Colfer's *Artemis Fowl* fantasy world of techno-fairies never sounded more plausible.[306]

In the 1970s the shadow of the Devil fell across ufology. John Godwin, author of *Occult America* (1972), had already seen the connection between the Dero and the traditional religious idea of demons. In 1975 John Keel also argued that there was a more than suggestive parallel between the experiences of UFO

Visions in Contemporary America, University of California Press, 2003.
[305] John Godwin, 'The Lost Worlds of Mysticism', the *Oakland Tribune*, 12 August 1972, excerpted from John Godwin, *Occult America*, Doubleday & Company, 1972.
[306] E. A. Guest, 'The Other Paradigm', *Fate*, April 2005, republished in *The Best of Roswell: From the Files of Fate Magazine*, Galde Press, 2007; Redfern, 'What is a UFO?'p. 60; Nigel Watson, 'They Came from Planet Earth', *Paranormal*, 49, July 2010, pp. 25–9; Mac Tonnies, *The Cryptoterrestrials*, Anomalist Books, 2010.

eye-witnesses and possession cases. Like Tonnies he also saw a broader picture. Of UFO eye-witnesses he said:

> Many, I found, suffered certain medical symptoms such as temporary amnesia, severe headaches, muscular spasms, excessive thirst and other effects, all of which have been observed throughout history in religious miracles, demonology, occult phenomena, and contact with fairies. All of these manifestations clearly share a common source or cause.[307]

Others were convinced that the common source or cause was the Devil. By the end of the 1970s, George Knewstub and Roger Stanway, leading figures in the British UFO Research Organization (BUFORA), had reached this conclusion. Stanway himself based this on personal experience. After a sudden and unwanted desire to throw himself in front of a train deep within the bowels of the earth in London's Underground, overcome by reciting a prayer from St John's Gospel, he became convinced that the forces of evil were at work.[308]

The rumoured Collins Elite – a secret conclave of top US government, military and intelligence staff – would agree. When ufologist Nick Redfern tracked down Anglican priest Ray Boeche in 2006 he uncovered an astonishing twist in the UFO conspiracy theory. Boeche was not just any Anglican priest, he had founded the Fortean Research Center and was a former regional director for the Mutual UFO Network (MUFON). Perhaps this was why two Department of Defense (DoD) physicists arranged a clandestine meeting with him. According to Boeche's story they gave him information that not only confirmed the presence of what they called 'non-human entities', but also that many within the DoD believe that they are in actuality demonic beings. Kennedy Space

---

[307] Quoted in Redfern, 'What is a UFO?', p. 63.

[308] Redfern, 'What is a UFO?', p. 63. See also Nick Redfern, *Final Events and the Secret Government Group on Demonic UFOs and the Afterlife*, Anomalist Books, 2010.

Center researcher Joe Jordan is on record as saying 'we're dealing with fallen angels'.[309]

The 'aliens', whatever their provenance, come in all manner of guises. Over the years people have reported seeing blond-haired 'Space-Brothers', hairy dwarves, flying jellyfish, huge bananas, scaly-skinned reptilians, giant humanoids, as well as the familiar 'little green men' and 'greys'.[310]

With so much apparent evidence of *something*, at least, and so many strange and conflicting theories, what is the answer? Veteran UFO expert Professor Michael D. Swords characterized UFO research as an 'intellectual vortex which can easily addict you, draw you in, and still tell you very little about the fundamentals which lie below'.[311] Despite the problems, he was still willing to come to at least one very definite conclusion about the phenomenon.

'They're here,' said Swords in 2006, adding 'They've been here in some force at least since World War Two.'[312] But that is not something you will hear from the authorities. Most official governmental investigations into UFOs have now been terminated after reaching the conclusion that there are no UFOs. This is a conclusion that many people are unwilling to accept. There are millions in the USA alone, where almost one in four people believe that UFOs are alien spacecraft and nearly one in five claim to have seen one. Even the official investigations had to admit that they could not explain everything. Then there are the many sightings from reliable witnesses, experienced enough

---

[309] Redfern, 'From the Heavens or from Hell?', pp. 59–60, 63.

[310] Nick Redfern, 'Know Your Aliens', *Paranormal*, 53, November 2010, pp. 40–5. On jellyfish see, for example, the 13 October sighting reported by Lisa Karpova, 'New Yorkers Wave "Hi" to Jellyfish UFOs', *Pravda*, 21 October 2010 – children later claimed that the UFOs were balloons that had escaped from a surprise party for their unfortunately named teacher Andrea Craparo: 'UFO? NYC Kids Say No [. . .]', *New York Daily News*, 14 October 2010.

[311] Michael D. Swords, 'A Guide to UFO Research', *Journal of Scientific Exploration*, 7, 1993, p. 68.

[312] Michael D. Swords, 'Ufology', *Journal of Scientific Exploration*, 20, 2006, p. 572.

SETI

In 1961 the astronomer Frank Drake formulated the so-called Drake Equation that appeared to show that, logically, there must be many extraterrestrial civilizations in the universe. But it did not answer the obvious question. In 1950 the physicist Enrico Fermi had made an off-the-cuff remark that 'if there are extraterrestrials, then where are they?' – the so-called Fermi Paradox. To tackle the problem, Drake was instrumental in organizing a meeting to discuss the ways and means of finding the missing extraterrestrials and the Search for Extraterrestrial Intelligence (SETI) was born. Today it is the name for a number of different projects with the common aim of finding evidence that we are not alone in the universe. For example, one project called SETI@home is a computer programme that uses idle processing power to analyse radio signals. A SETI Institute was founded in 1984 to further advance the search. Currently, it has a staff of over 150 scientists and others. In October 2010 it was reported that a signal discovered two years earlier by scientists at the University of Western Sydney had originated from the solar system of red dwarf star Gliese 581 in the constellation of Libra, which may contain the habitable planet Gliese 581g.

with aerial phenomena to know when they are seeing something out of the ordinary. Decades after Roswell, 80 per cent of Americans believe that their government is hiding evidence of extraterrestrial life.[313]

On 27 September 2010, seasoned UFO investigator Robert Hastings held a conference at the National Press Club in Washington, D.C., on UFO interference with nuclear weapons facilities. He had talked to 120 US military personnel about the

---

[313] Christopher Bader, F. Carson Mencken and Joseph Baker, *Paranormal America*, New York University Press, 2010, p. 73; 'Poll: U.S. Hiding Knowledge of Aliens', CNN, 15 June 1997.

problem and seven of them were now willing to go public with their experiences. One of them, former ICBM (Inter-Continental Ballistic Missile) launch officer Captain Robert Salas, described how ten nuclear Minuteman missiles under his command became unlaunchable after a perimeter guard reported a UFO hovering over the Malmstrom Air Force Base, Montana, in 1967. Colonel Charles Halt recalled his UFO encounter at RAF Bentwaters near Ipswich in 1980. 'I believe – these gentlemen believe,' Hastings told reporters, 'that this planet is being visited by beings from another world.'[314]

After scoffing at Hastings' press conference, *The Washington Post*'s columnist John Kelly drew an entirely warranted flurry of abusive emails. Among them was one from 'Art' in Olney. His father had been a US Navy fighter pilot in World War II and one of the first recruits to the fledgling National Security Agency (NSA). He recalled sitting down to dinner with his family as a boy. At the time the media was full of news about UFO sightings. 'You see all those UFO reports in the news?' asked his father. 'Believe it.' Art added that he never spoke of it again.[315]

---

[314] 'Robert Hastings Presents Major UFO Press Conference in Washington, DC, September 27th 2010', Press Release, 15 September 2010; 'UFOs Eyed Nukes, Ex-Air Force Personnel Say', http://news.blogs.cnn.com/2010/09/27/ufos-showed-interest-in-nukes-ex-air-force-personnel-say/, 27 September 2010; Tony Harnden, 'Aliens "Tried to Warn US and Russia They Were Playing With Fire During Cold War"', *Daily Telegraph*, 28 September 2010.
[315] John Kelly, 'UFO Visits to Nuclear Facilities? Hmmmm', *Washington Post*, 27 September 2010; John Kelly 'Close Encounters with UFOs (Unexpectedly Furious Observers)', *Washington Post*, 5 October 2010.

Part II: Approaches to the Supernatural

Do you believe then that the sciences would have arisen and grown up if the sorcerers, alchemists, astrologers and witches had not been their forerunners; those who, with their promisings and foreshadowings had first to create a thirst, a hunger, and a taste for *hidden and forbidden* powers?
– Nietzsche, *Die fröhliche Wissenschaft*, 1882

The most beautiful thing we can experience is the mysterious. It is the source of all true art and science.
– Albert Einstein, 'What I Believe', 1930

If the doors of perception were cleansed, every thing would appear to man as it is, infinite.
– William Blake, *The Marriage of Heaven and Hell*, c. 1793

6. Magic

He made with a wand a Circle in the dust, and within that
many more Circles and Characters: [. . .] then began Doctor
Faustus to call for Mephostophiles [*sic*] the Spirit, and to
charge him in the name of Beelzebub to appear.[316]

So begins the legend of Doctor Faustus, the infamous sixteenth-
century magician, with his descent into diabolism to take an
everlasting place in literature. According to the 'History of Dr
Johann Faust, the far-bestriding Magician and Black Artist' –
the almost contemporary book that claimed to be biographical,
even autobiographical in parts – there is a cry 'as if hell had
been opened' and Mephistopheles (to use the usual spelling)
falls to earth like a bolt of lightning. Although the book is a
Protestant morality tale – perhaps even a retrospective witchcraft trial – in which Faustus is punished with a gratuitously
violent death and eternal damnation for his unchristian curiosity, it comes from an age in which most people believed in the
actual existence of demons, devils and a supreme evil being.
The real Dr Faustus' contemporary, the German theologian
Martin Luther, famously threw his inkpot at the Devil, such was
his belief in the Archfiend's actual and tangible existence. Here,

---

[316] 'P.F.', *The Historie of the Damnable Life, and the Deserved Death of Doctor Iohn
Faustus*, Thomas Orwin, 1592, p. 2, English translation of the anonymous *His-
toria von D. Johann Fausten, dem weitbeschreyten Zauberer und Schwarzkünstler*,
Johann Spies, 1587.

however, evil spirits are not enough – Faustus must invoke them using magic, a strange interplay of wand, circles, characters, and words. Magic is the bizarre science of the supernatural.[317]

Magic in Theory

There are many definitions and theories of what magic is. Aleister Crowley, the British occultist almost as legendary as Faustus, most famously said that 'Magick' – the 'k' was important, but that is another story – was 'The Science and Art of causing Change to occur in conformity with Will'. Certainly, the successful invocation of Mephistopheles was in conformity with Faustus' supposed will, but it is still a long way off from explaining how it is all meant to work. Crowley spent another 500 pages in *Magick in Theory and Practice* talking about it and telling us how to do it, but he still did not *explain* it.[318]

It was instead one of Crowley's contemporaries, a Scotsman called James George Frazer (later 'Sir'), who came up with quite possibly the most influential explanation of how magic is believed to work. Born in Glasgow in 1854, Frazer left for Cambridge to study the classics and, inspired by Sir Edward Tylor's *Primitive Culture*, social anthropology. His researches led to the publication of *The Golden Bough: A Study in Comparative Religion* in several editions and eventually twelve volumes from 1890 to 1915. He admitted himself that the book was 'one of the hothouse plants of the Victorian age [. . .] it grew and grew and grew'.[319]

The Golden Bough was a hit, particularly after the twelve massive volumes were edited into one with the slightly snappier subtitle *A Study in Magic and Religion*. It influenced such eminent people as

---

[317] See Leo Ruickbie, *Faustus: The Life and Times of a Renaissance Magician*, The History Press, 2009.

[318] Aleister Crowley, *Magick*, privately published, 1929.

[319] Sir J. G. Frazer, *The Golden Bough: A Study in Comparative Religion*, 2 vols, Macmillan & Co., 1890, and other editions. Due to the number of editions, I shall refer to the 1922 abridged edition by chapter and section number. Frazer on *The Golden Bough* quoted in George W. Stocking, 'Introduction', in Sir J. G. Frazer, *The Golden Bough*, Penguin, 1998. Sir Edward Tylor, *Primitive Culture: Researches into the Development of Mythology, Philosophy, Religion, Art, and Custom*, 2 vols, J. Murray, 1871.

the writers A. E. Housman, D. H. Lawrence and T. S. Eliot. Crowley, another Cambridge man, quoted a large chunk in support of his theories in *Magick*. H. P. Lovecraft mentioned it in 'The Call of Cthulhu'. And director Francis Ford Coppola slipped a copy of the book into his 1979 masterpiece *Apocalypse Now*.[320]

Frazer's general theory was that civilization progresses from magic to religion to science. It was a typical nineteenth-century viewpoint, much out of fashion nowadays, especially as quantum physics almost seems to have taken us back to magic. However, what inspired people about Frazer's work was his romantic theory of the Sacred King. The Sacred King represents the solar god as the principal of vegetation who must be seasonally sacrificed to ensure the continuing fertility of the land. This was the idea behind the 1973 cult film *The Wicker Man*. It was this that Coppola was referring to in the showdown between Martin Sheen's character and Marlon Brando as the crazed jungle warlord he is sent to assassinate.

In order to get to this idea, Frazer first had to deal with magic. Frazer ranged across the known universe of the imagination revealed in classical literature, ethnographies and travellers' accounts of strange peoples in distant lands, in forgotten times, in search of the answer. He wondered why among certain North American tribes, a figure drawn in sand, ashes or clay and then stabbed was believed to affect the physical body of the victim. He discovered that the Peruvian Indians had a spell called 'burning the soul' that involved making images out of fat and grain to resemble the intended victim which were then burnt on the road he or she was expected to take. He read of a Malay charm instructing the magician to take something of the victim: nail-pairings, hair and eyebrow clippings, spittle – enough to represent every part of him – to mix these with wax taken from an abandoned beehive and shape it to a human likeness. The magician should then roast the wax figure over a flame for seven nights, saying:[321]

---

[320] H. P. Lovecraft, 'The Call of Cthulhu', *Weird Tales*, February 1928.
[321] Frazer, Ch. 3, §. 2.

It is not the wax that I am scorching,
It is the liver, heart, and spleen of so-and-so that I scorch.[322]

Frazer wondered why, in darkest Sussex, only fifty years before, a maid had remonstrated with her mistress against throwing away the baby-teeth of the children. The maid had believed that they would be gnawed by wild beasts and that the harm done to the teeth would strike their former owners. As proof, she pointed to the example of poor old Master Simmons, who, it was said, had grown a pig's tooth in his upper jaw because his mother had thrown one of his baby-teeth into the pigs' trough.[323]

The answer to all this, Frazer decided, was sympathy. Not the sort of sympathy you got from your mother when, as a child, you fell over and grazed your knee. More, as Frazer put it, 'that things act on each other at a distance through a secret sympathy', hence his general term 'sympathetic magic'. Sympathetic magic, he said, operated according to either (or both) of two principles: the Law of Similarity and the Law of Contagion. According to the Law of Similarity, the magician believes he can produce an effect by imitating it, hence stabbing figures in the sand. He also called this homoeopathic magic, that like affects like. According to the Law of Contagion, the magician, or Sussex maid, believes that things that have once been in contact with each other remain in contact even when separated.[324]

In his *Confessions*, Crowley neatly summed up Frazer's theory: 'magic he defines as science which does not work'. Frazer's theory was not so very different from that of his hero Edward Tylor. Tylor had earlier argued that magic was an error in thinking of the 'lowest known stages of civilization' where an imagined connection between things was mistaken as a real one. This has been the general interpretation ever since, although Crowley preferred to look at science as magic that worked.[325]

---

[322] Frazer, Ch. 3, §. 2.
[323] Frazer, Ch. 3, §. 3.
[324] Frazer, Ch. 3, §. 1.
[325] Aleister Crowley, *The Confessions of Aleister Crowley: An Autohagiography*,

Frazer was far from sympathetic himself when he said that these principles were readily familiar 'to the crude intelligence not only of the savage, but of ignorant and dull-witted people everywhere'. Frazer was surely wrong to attribute the idea of sympathetic magic solely to 'the savage' and simple-minded. Sigmund Freud – 'that creature Freud', as Frazer called him – labelled it 'magical thinking' and his observations led him to believe that it was a universal developmental stage exhibited by children and retained by certain types of neurotics. He did not believe that it worked either.[326]

Of course, if you start out with the preconception that magic does not work, then your theory is going to reflect that and you naturally have to account for it in terms of human failing or under-development. Even in 1900 the great pioneering psychologist William James was surprised that Frazer had not considered, indeed knew nothing about, psychical research. When Crowley – according to the well-known story told by Dennis Wheatley – made a wax figure of the Master of John's (not Frazer) and stabbed it in the leg, he did not think that he was either ignorant or stupid when the same tutor later fell down some steps and broke his ankle. He thought magic worked; at least he did with regard to his better-documented experiments. And he is not alone.[327]

When a group of psychologists from Harvard and Princeton got together to try some fiendish experiments on unwitting students – presumably neither savage nor stupid – they made some surprising discoveries. They got the voodoo dolls out, made the subjects watch basketball (twice), and American football. In all four studies they found that the students believed that their magical actions or thoughts had influenced the target. When participants stuck pins in a doll representing a confederate of the researchers who then complained of spontaneous symptoms,

Routledge & Kegan Paul, 1979 [1929], pp. 127, 517. Tylor, vol. 1, pp. 112, 116.
[326] Frazer, Ch. 3, §. 1; Stocking, 'Introduction' and *Delimiting Anthropology: Occasional Essays and Reflections*, University of Wisconsin Press, 2001, p. 159; Sigmund Freud, *Totem und Tabu*, Hugo Heller & Cie, 1913.
[327] Dennis Wheatley, *The Devil And All His Works*, Hutchinson, 1971, p. 273.

they believed that they had caused them; and when the participants were told to imagine positive outcomes for both staged and
real-life sports scenarios, they again believed that they had caused
them when they occurred. Even when a positive outcome was not
forthcoming, the participants felt responsible for that, too. The
students thought they had paranormal powers, but not the
psychologists of course.[328]

Like Tylor and Frazer more than a hundred years before them,
the psychologists also talked about 'common cognitive errors',
'apparent mental causation' and even cited *The Golden Bough*. But
again their premise was that magic does not work and their experimental design reflected this. It could be argued that what they had
done was prove you can trick people into thinking magically. Even
Frazer conceded that 'imagination acts upon man as really as does
gravitation, and may kill him as certainly as a dose of prussic acid'.
Was he admitting that magic could, in effect, work?

Magic in Writing

The aspiring magician today is well-served by a vast publishing
industry supplying everything from the most obscure and rare
titles to common-or-garden DIY manuals on the magic arts, but
it was not always so. The magician Faustus lived during the
beginning of the great print revolution, but even then the materials of greatest interest to him were not yet part of that revolution.
The books of magic, or grimoires, that he sought were handwrit-
ten and circulated in secret to avoid the hostile attentions of the
Church. For these reasons and because of the nature of the
material within, such grimoires acquired the reputation, not just
as books on magic, but as magical books in themselves.

In cataloguing what he called 'the forbidden arts', the
Bavarian physician, writer and diplomat, Johannes Hartlieb (c.
1400–68), was concerned that his own book, in the wrong
hands, could be used as a grimoire. Hartlieb was detailed

---

[328] Emily Pronin, et al., 'Everyday Magical Powers', *Journal of Personality and Social Psychology*, 2006, 91.2, pp. 218–31.

enough in his descriptions, but stopped short of giving practical instructions. Even if it fell into the wrong hands, little harm could come of it. Hartlieb only served to whet the appetite.[329]

Despite this coyness, Hartlieb had himself given some pointers when he named the various texts being used in black magic: *Sigillum Salomonis, Clavicula Salomonis, Hierarchia* and *Schemhamphoras.* The *Sigillum* (Seal) and *Clavicula* (Key) were of a genre fancifully ascribed to King Solomon, generally thought to have reigned from around 970 to 928 BCE. Out of the legendary wisdom of Solomon, spiced with his dabbling in exotic cults, grew a tradition of Solomon the magician, perhaps as early as the second century BCE, but no earlier.[330] It was rather the Jewish historian Flavius Josephus who first alluded to a Solomonic magic text in the first century CE, describing the alleged powers of the legendary king:[331]

> God also enabled him to learn that skill which expels demons, which is a science useful and sanative to men. He composed such incantations also by which distempers are alleviated. And he left behind him the manner of using exorcisms, by which they drive away demons, so that they never return; and this method of cure is of great force unto this day.[332]

This was the Solomon who used a magic ring to compel legions of demons to build the Temple in Jerusalem, as we read in the pseudepigraphical *Testament of Solomon.* It is the earliest magical book attributed to Solomon despite being composed some time during the first to fifth centuries CE by authors unknown. It is a description of the various demons, their particular sphere of

---

[329] Hartlieb, p. 125.

[330] Owen Davies, *Grimoires: A History of Magic Books*, Oxford University Press, 2009, p. 12.

[331] Flavius Josephus, *Antiquities of the Jews*, trans. William Whiston, Applegate, 1855, p. 216. Reginald Scot, *The Discoverie of Witchcraft*, William Brome, 1584, Dover reprint, 1972, p. 264; S. Liddel MacGregor Mathers (ed. and trans.), *The Key of Solomon*, George Redway, 1888, pp. v, viii.

[332] Josephus, Ch. 2, §. 5.

mischief, and the correct angel to invoke against them. For example, Asmodeus causes strife between newly weds, but may be defeated by invoking Raphael and smoking the liver and gall of a fish over hot ashes. According to the Book of Tobit (6:7), Raphael himself teaches Tobias a similar exorcism ritual: 'Touching the heart and the liver [of a fish], if a devil or an evil spirit trouble any, we must make a smoke thereof before the man or the woman, and the party shall be no more vexed'. From the beginning, Solomonic magic was essentially about controlling spiritual entities. Far from being an ineffectual science it was theologically logical.[333]

We find Solomon and the power of his seal in the medieval *Picatrix* (see below) and whispers of his mysterious book (or books) are to be found in the writings of the Byzantine scholars Michael Psellus, Nicetas Choniates and Michael Glycas in the eleventh to twelfth centuries CE, as well as Roger Bacon in the thirteenth century, for example. Still in the thirteenth century, William of Auvergne, the Bishop of Paris, roundly condemned Solomonic magic, showing its pervasive influence, and singled out the *Liber sacer* as 'a cursed and execrable book'. Johannes Trithemius, occult scholar and sometime abbot of Sponheim in Germany, later catalogued a *Clavicula Solomonis* in 1508 amongst other magical texts. Another German scholar, Johannes Reuchlin, in his great work on the cabbala of 1517, mentioned a book 'inscribed "to Solomon" under Raziel's name'. Several manuscripts dated 1564 in the British Library also make this connection between Solomon and Raziel. But there are few surviving early examples. Of the manuscripts in the British Library catalogued under the name of Solomon (Salomon) the earliest *Key* texts are from the second half of the sixteenth century. Elements of Solomonic magic – the 'Almadel' and the ring of Solomon – survive in fifteenth-century manuscripts found in Florence and Paris, and there is also an 'Ars notoria Salomonis' dating from the thirteenth century in the British Library.[334]

---

[333] Chester Charlton McCown, *The Testament of Solomon*, J. C. Hinrichs, 1922.
[334] Lynn Thorndike, *A History of Magic and Experimental Science*, 8 vols,

A text like the late-sixteenth-century *Kay* [*sic*] *of Knowledge* attributed to Solomon described a complete system of magic.[335] The full procedure is made explicit. Instructions on when and how to conjure the spirits are illustrated with diagrams of the magical circles and signs pertinent to each operation and descriptions of the tools needed. One reads of the right way to extract the blood of a bat and consecrate virgin parchment. A Solomonic grimoire was a working manual of magic.

The *Schemhamphoras* is also part of this Solomonic genre. This 'Schemhamphoras' (also 'Shemhamphorash') is *Shem ham-M'forash*, the great cabbalistic name of God. Out of this name are derived seventy-two spirits – the spirits said to have been commanded by Solomon. These are the spirits we find in Johannes Wierus's *Pseudomonarchia Daemonum* ('The False Monarchy of Demons') of 1577 and Reginald Scot's *Discoverie of Witchcraft* of 1584, although neither Wierus nor Scot listed all seventy-two. Wierus said he had taken his list from an older text called the *Book of the Offices of Spirits, or the Book of Sayings of Emperor Solomon Concerning the Princes and Kings of the Demons.*[336] In 1508 Trithemius had also mentioned a *De officio spirituum* attributed to Solomon and it is possible that the two are, if not the same, then certainly similar. Hartlieb's *Hierarchia* is an otherwise unknown text, but by its name would seem to indicate some sort of table of spirits, perhaps similar to the *Schemhamphoras* and *De officio*.

Columbia University Press, 1923–58, vol. 1, pp. 279ff; Johannes Trithemius, *Antipalus maleficiorum*, c.1500, in Johannes Busaeus, ed., *Paralipomena opusculum Petri Blesensis et Joannis Trithemii aliorumque*, Ioannem Wulffrath, 1605, pp. 291–311; Johannes Reuchlin, *On the Art of the Kabbalah*, trans. Martin and Sarah Goodman, Bison Books, 1993, p. 95 – cf. London, British Library, Sloane 3826, fol. 1ʳ-57ʳ; 'Salomon. King of Israel. Sepher Raziel: A Magical Treatise 1564', London, British Library, Sloane MSS 3826, 3846, 3847; 'Ars Notoria', British Library, Sloane 1712.

[335] London, British Library, Additional MS 36674.

[336] Wierus of course knew it by its Latin title *Liber officiorum spirituum, seu Liber dictus Empto. Salomonis, de principibus & regibus dæmoniorum.* See Johannes Wierus, *De praestigiis daemonum*, Joannem Oporinum, 1577.

Famous Grimoires

Title	Quotation	Example Spell	Dating
Testament of Solomon	Testament of Solomon, son of David, who was king in Jerusalem, and mastered and controlled all spirits of the air, on the earth, and under the earth.	The liver of the fish and its gall I hung on the spike of a reed, and burned it over Asmodeus	1st–5th centuries CE
Picatrix ('The Goal of the Wise')	I set forth such miraculous and confusing matters from all the sciences for this reason only, that you may be purified for the earnest study of these marvellous arts and may achieve what the ancient sages achieved.	Of examples of figures, and the forms of imagery that call down the help of the planets	11th century
The Sworn Book of Honorius (Liber Juratus, or Liber Sacer/Sacratus)	One whose name was Honorius, the son of Euclid, master of the Thebians, [. . .] through the council of a certain angel whose name was Hocroel, did write seven volumes of art magic.	How a man should obtain his will by every angel	13th/14th century
The Key of Solomon (Clavicula Salomonis)	The secret of secrets [. . .] I have written them in this Key, so that like as a key openeth a treasure-house, so this alone may open the knowledge and understanding of magical arts and sciences.	Experiment of invisibility	14th–16th centuries
Arbatel de Magia Veterum ('Arbatel of the Magic of the Ancients')	The greatest precept of Magic is, to know what every man ought to receive for his use from the assisting Spirit, and what to refuse.	n/a	1575

Title	Description	Purpose	Date
The Lesser Key of Solomon (*Lemegeton Clavicula Salomonis*, also *The Goetia*)	This Book contains all the names, orders, and offices of all the spirits Salomon ever conversed with. The seals and characters belonging to each spirit, and the manner of calling them forth to visible appearance.	Zepar . . . his office is to cause women to love men and to bring them together in love	17th century
The Sacred Magic of Abramelin the Mage	The sacred mystery by which I entered into the knowledge of the holy angels, enjoying their sight and their sacred conversation, from whom at length I received afterwards the foundation of the Veritable Magic, and how to command and dominate the evil spirits.	To find and take possession of all kinds of treasures, provided that they be not at all (magically) guarded	17th/18th century
The Sixth and Seventh Books of Moses	Revealed by God the Almighty to his faithful servant Moses, on Mount Sinai, *intervalle lucis*, and in this manner they also came into the hands of Aaron, Caleb, Joshua, and finally to David and his son Solomon and their high priest Zadoc.	The Eleventh Table gives luck and fortune; its spirits give the treasures of the sea	18th century
Le Petit Albert ('The Little Albert')	It may well be called a universal treasure, because in its small size it contains marvellous capabilities of rewarding all mankind.	To remove rotten teeth without pain	1782
Grimorium Verum ('The True Grimoire')	The most approved Keys of Solomon the Hebrew Rabbin, wherein the most hidden secrets, both natural and supernatural, are immediately exhibited.	To make a girl dance in the nude	19th century
Le Grand Grimoire	This great book is most rare, most sought after in our lands, which for its rarity is called after the Rabbis, the true Great Work.	To win anytime one plays the lottery	19th century

Picatrix

When the late-fourteenth-century Arab historian Ibn Khaldun spoke out against magic he had one book to hand, a book whose author the satirist Rabelais later called 'the reverend father in the Devil [. . .] rector of the Diabolical faculty'. It was called in Arabic *Ghâyat al-Hakîm fi'l-sihr* ('The Goal of the Wise') or, as it was known in Europe, *Picatrix*. As Ibn Khaldun wrote:[337]

> These are sciences showing how human souls may become prepared to exercise an influence upon the world of the elements, either without or with the aid of celestial matters. The first kind is sorcery, the second kind is talismans. These sciences are forbidden by the various religious laws, because they are harmful and require [their practitioners] to direct themselves to [beings] other than God, such as stars and other things.[338]

It was written in Arabic sometime between 1047 and 1051, somewhere in Spain. King Alfonso X of Castile later commanded a translation into Spanish in 1256, possibly by the King's personal physician Rabbi Yehuda ben Moshe, and from this came the Latin translation, the most influential of which was thought to have been produced by Aegidius de Thebaldis, translator of Ptolemy's *Tetrabiblos*. The manuscript was copied and re-copied, but only published in the twentieth century. Today some seventeen copies have survived the ravages of time and the fires of the Inquisition. The important Renaissance humanist Giovanni Pico della Mirandola was known to possess a copy. His son Gian Francesco Pico may also have seen it, although he called it 'a most vain book, full of superstitions'. Trithemius denounced it as being full of 'many things that are frivolous, superstitious, and diabolical' – and he would not be the last. Its

---

[337] Eugenio Garin, *Astrology in the Renaissance: The Zodiac of Life*, Arkana, 1983, pp. 46–7.
[338] Quoted in Garin, p. 42.

influence can be seen in the work of the influential occultist Agrippa von Nettesheim, a contemporary of Faustus.[339]

But what is it about the *Picatrix* that gave it such a subterranean reputation? It is a confused, disordered mass, divided haphazardly into four books. It begins dramatically enough by revealing the reasons for writing the book: to illuminate a closely kept secret of the ancient philosophers, the secret of magic. The reader is admonished to preserve the secret from the uneducated. The text interweaves astrology, astronomy and magic, moving from Greek stellar theory to practical advice on how to influence the cosmos. Religion makes its appearance, but seen through a magician's lens. We are immersed in the legendary prehistory of Egypt and the astro-magical aphorisms of a mysterious Babylonian called 'Utârid, as well as the philosophy of Plato, Aristotle and Hippocrates, and the divinatory uses of the Qur'an.

The *Picatrix* attempts to divide its subject into talismanic magic, celestial worship and incantatory practices, but the barriers between them are porous and the forms intermingle. Instructions are given on the correct constellations to be used in making talismans with examples of incantations to make them effective. The signs of the zodiac are considered in great depth with a reverent personification of the planets that raises them to the level of gods to be worshipped and, as the book is written by a magician, invoked. There is talk of djinn, demons and angels, of love magic and the correct method of attracting the planetary energies. Details are given of how the planets should be worshipped according to the ways of the Sabians, including child sacrifice. There are Nabatean prayers to Saturn and the Sun, descriptions of the ceremonies for each planet with examples of amulets and talismans. There are formulae and

---

[339] Helmut Ritter and Martin Plessner, trans., *'Picatrix.' Das Ziel der Weisen von Pseudo-Magriti*, Warburg Institute, 1962; Elizabeth M. Butler, *Ritual Magic*, Cambridge University Press, 1949, p. 48; Garin, pp. 48, 50; Trithemius, *Antipaulus Maleficiorum* quoted in Noel L. Brann, *Trithemius and Magical Theology*, State University of New York Press, 1999, p. 67; Daniel Pickering Walker, *Spiritual and Demonic Magic*, Sutton, 2000, pp. 147, 182, n. 5.

ceremonies for incense to honour the planets said to have been devised by Buddha, perfumes given by God to Moses and 'Indian' enchantments. There are extracts from the *Book of Poisons* and an ancient temple book said to have been discovered in the days of Cleopatra.

The Moorish influence is unmistakable and the Spanish origin would seem vouchsafed. Celestial mysticism and the violent rites of the Sabians are clearly heretical to the Church, but it is undoubtedly the practical instructions given on the manufacture and correct use of talismans that gives this book the sulphurous reputation that so quickly accrued to it. With a manual such as this the magician could do a brisk trade in talismans.

Whilst the text may at times be confused and disjointed a clear picture emerges of a magical astrology designed not only to interpret the stars, but to harness their power. 'The roots of magic,' says *Picatrix*, 'are the movements of the planets'. Drawing on the ninth of the *Karpos* from the Ptolemaic *Centiloquium*, the *Picatrix* states 'All things in this world obey the celestial forms'.[340] With such a manual the whole world would be at the magician's feet, or so he – and his clients – might think.

The *Picatrix* goes beyond even the promise of ultimate power. It offers an all-embracing conception of reality. It is a conception that sharply differs from that of orthodox Christianity. It is a challenge to and refutation of Christianity, and it offers an alternative. No wonder, then, that the *Picatrix* was so feared and its reputation tarred with the accusation of black magic.

Owning the Grimoires

A few years before Hartlieb came to serve Albrecht III, Duke of Bavaria, in Munich, a court case heard in Briançon in 1437 threw some light on the sort of people who owned grimoires. The trial concerned one Jubertus of Bavaria, a sixty-year-old man from Regensburg in the east of that province, arraigned before the judge on charges of flying to nocturnal assemblies,

---

[340] Quotations from Garin, p. 49.

murdering children and black magic. In his confession Jubertus spoke of a man called Johannes Cunalis, a priest and plebian of Munich. Jubertus had served Cunalis for ten years and witnessed how he kept a book of necromancy, which when opened by him brought forth three demons. Cunalis was a Satanist of the first rank. He worshipped the Devil as his god with sacrilegious rites, showing his buttocks to the east before making a cross on the floor that he spat on, stamped on, urinated and finally defecated on. Cunalis had also made a pact with his demons, leaving them his body and soul after death. The use of torture in extracting this confession is not mentioned, but as it was commonplace it cannot be ruled out. Cunalis was also just the kind of man to have written or compiled a grimoire.[341]

Jubertus had also been in Vienna about the year 1435 where he had been causing a commotion. He had cursed someone called Johannes Fabri of Vienna and had been boasting about it just before his arrest. He had also set Cunalis' three demons on three drunken cooks who had refused to let him drink in a tavern. The demons seized them as they staggered out into the night after their revelry, throwing one down a well, another into the privy of the Dominicans and the other into the privy of the Franciscans. The one they pitched down the well died, but the other two were discovered by the friars at matins – one can imagine the looks on their faces – and rescued.

Here Cunalis' book had already reached such magical proportions that the simple act of opening it unleashed three demons that had been seemingly bound within. Other grimoires, such as the *Enchiridion of Pope Leo* conferred magical powers in other ways. According to legend, Pope Leo III gave Charlemagne a collection of prayers – the *Enchiridion* – as he was leaving Rome in 800 CE with the instructions to always carry it with him and recite it daily. It would confer divine

---

[341] Joseph Hansen (ed.), *Quellen und Untersuchungen zur Geschichte des Hexenwahns und der grossen Hexenverfolgung im Mittelalter*, Georgi, 1901, pp. 539–44; Richard Kieckhefer, *Forbidden Rites: A Necromancer's Manual of the Fifteenth Century*, Sutton, 1997, pp. 30–2.

protection so that Charlemagne might pass through all dangers unharmed and triumph over his enemies.

Picatrix and the other grimoires belong to that genre that would have fed every Christian book-burning for a thousand years. The number of survivals is low, but given the extent of that book-burning it is likely that at one time a great number of such texts was in circulation. Indeed, one scholar investigating the matter of German *Loosbücher* (lot or divination books) in the late nineteenth century thought that, from the number of examples surviving in the libraries of his day, the fifteenth century must have been 'rich in such books'. Certainly, when the Visitation of the Saxon Church peered into the activities of village pastors and churchwardens in Germany during 1527–8 it uncovered an embarrassing hoard of magical books.[342]

In the twentieth century, the German Lutheran minister and anti-magical campaigner Kurt Koch was still warning that grimoires 'circulate among people like poisonous gases, poisoning their very minds and souls' and complained about the 'flood of magical conjuration which washes the Alps'. Such concerns led to Planet-Verlag, the German publisher of the *Sixth and Seventh Books of Moses*, being taken to court in 1956. Found guilty of being 'a danger to the general public', they were fined and ordered to destroy their remaining stock. Reactions were no less strong to J. K. Rowling's *Harry Potter* books. However, the demand is so high that such determined persecution has failed to prevent the continued dissemination of magical literature.[343]

---

[342] Johann Sotzmann, 'Die Loosbücher des Mittelalters', *Serapeum*, 20, 1851, pp. 307–8; R. Po-chia Hsia, *The Myth of Ritual Murder: Jews and Magic in Reformation Germany*, Yale University Press, 1988, p. 135.

[343] A. E. Waite, *The Book of Ceremonial Magic*, pp. 40–2; Kurt Koch, *Between Christ and Satan*, Kregel, 1962, p. 131; Davies, pp. 256–60; Leo Ruickbie, '"Either Must Die at the Hand of the Other": Religious Reactions to Harry Potter', in Jennifer P. Sims (ed.), *The Sociology of Harry Potter*, Zossima, forthcoming.

Magic with Spirits

The spirit or soul, the animating, personalizing 'thing' that drives and defines the human being always seemed like a thing apart, a 'ghost in the machine'. When we sleep, where does it go? When we die, where does it go? In folklore, custom and magic there is a long tradition of what Frazer called 'the external soul'. Traditionally, the shaman had the power to send forth his soul at will and to conjure the souls of others out of their bodies. The Siberian Yakuts, for example, say that every shaman puts his soul (or one of his souls) in an animal and hides it away. The weakest must take dogs, the strongest may choose the stallion, elk, black bear, wild boar, or eagle. Here, and in similar accounts from the Americas, Africa and Australia, we have the origin of the witch's familiar. Such spirits did not only belong to individuals. Recalling shamanistic notions of tribal spirits, the Lachlan clan of Rum in the Western Isles had a taboo on deer-stalking as it was believed that family and animal shared the same fate.[344]

The shaman, the witch and the werewolf have long been thought to be able to venture out of the physical human body and travel this world or others as spirit. It is a shamanic idea that we find in tales of witches and sorcerers turning into cats and wolves, that the spirit can take an animal form, which when harmed causes reciprocal damage to the physical body. Among the Koryak people of north-eastern Siberia it was said that in days of old 'there was no sharp distinction between men, animals, and other objects' and everyone could transform themselves into animals – a practice since reserved for shamans. It is still a superstition not to suddenly awake a dreaming sleeper for fear that their soul, thought to be beyond the body and participating in the dreamworld, may not return in time. The Yakut shaman Tyusypyut boasted that 'nobody can find my *ie-kyla* [external soul], it lies hidden far away in

[344] Frazer, Ch. 67, §. 1; James M. MacKinlay, *Folklore of Scottish Lochs and Springs*, William Hodge & Co., 1893, ch. XIV.

the stony mountains of Edzhigansk'. Many folktales preserve this idea.[345]

From Norway 'the giant who had no heart in his body' devises a complicated concealment to ensure his invulnerability. 'Far, far away in a lake,' explains the giant, 'lies an island, on that island stands a church, in that church is a well, in that well swims a duck, in that duck there is an egg, and in that egg there lies my heart.' The hero, of course, manages to get the egg and, crushing it, destroys the giant. In Scotland we find the story of another giant who kept his soul out of harm's way in an egg, and of the Uille Bheist, the monstrous sea-maiden, who did likewise. From Russia comes the story of Koshchei the Deathless whose 'death' is again hidden in an egg.[346]

There are many more examples from across Europe. A soul is kept 'in a stone, in the head of a bird, in the head of a leveret, in the middle head of a seven-headed hydra' in Rome; 'in a pigeon, in a hare, in the silver tusk of a wild boar' in Albania; 'in a board, in the heart of a fox, in a mountain' in Serbia; 'in an egg, which is within a duck, which is within a stag, which is under a tree' in old Bohemia; 'in a light, in an egg, in a duck, in a pond, in a mountain' in Transylvania. The Indian folktale of the evil magician Punchkin proceeds along similar lines. Needless to say, the hero in these tales manages to overcome the obstacles and lay his hands on the magician's or monster's soul and, with the typical bloodthirstiness of the old fairy-tales, proceeds to rip it apart or crush it in front of the villain.[347]

---

[345] A. E. Crawley, *The Idea of the Soul*, Adam and Charles Black, 1909, p. 148; M. A. Czaplicka, *Aboriginal Siberia: A Study in Social Anthropology*, Clarendon Press, 1914, Pt III, Ch. 13, §. 2.

[346] Sir George Webbe Dasent, *Popular Tales from the Norse*, 2nd ed., David Douglas, 1912 [1859], p. 66; J. F. Campbell, *Popular Tales of the West Highlands*, 2 vols, Edmonston and Douglas, 1860, vol. 1, p. 11; Campbell, vol. 1, p. 82; William Ralston Shedden Ralston, *Russian Fairy Tales: A Choice Collection of Muscovite Folk-Lore*, Hurst & Co., 1873, p. 114.

[347] Mary Frere, *Old Deccan Days; or Hindoo Fairy Legends, Current in Southern India. Collected from Oral Tradition*, John Murray, 1868, pp. 1–12; Joseph Jacobs, *Indian Fairy Tales*, David Nutt, 1912, n.p., 'Story Notes, IV. Punchkin';

The shaman could also extract the soul for beneficial ends. When a family moves into a new house, an event of spiritual peril on the island of Sulawesi, the witchdoctor collects their souls in a bag to safeguard them, returning them when they are safely installed. Among the Dyaks of south-eastern Borneo, the witchdoctor preserves the soul of a newborn infant in half a coconut which he covers with a cloth and places on a small platform suspended from the rafters. The souls of the newly born are also temporarily kept in coconuts on the Kei Islands. In Alaska, the Eskimo medicine-man takes the soul of a sick child and places it in an amulet – a 'soul-box' – which he then further protects by stowing in his medicine-bag. The North American Haida shaman tempts the soul of an invalid into a hollow bone and keeps it safe until the body is well again. In 1995 the ethnologist Elizabeth McAlister reported that this form of magic was still practised in Haiti. Country people might put the *nanm*, 'soul', of their children in a bottle before sending them to school in Port-au-Prince to magically protect them. Birth, moving, illness – and, indeed, going to school – these were critical moments requiring additional magical security.[348]

The soul could also be united with another living thing, to thrive as it thrives, or wither as it withers. Only part externalized, the soul is shared between human and plant, or human and animal. Uniting with a plant usually served as an external indicator of health. In many parts of the world – from Europe to Papua New Guinea to West Africa – a tree is planted at the birth of a child and serves to act as a barometer of its fate. The Edgewell Tree near Dalhousie Castle in Scotland was a portent

Ralston, p. 120. See also E. Clodd, 'The Philosophy of Punchkin', *Folk-Lore Journal,* vol. 2, and George W. Cox, *Mythology of the Aryan Nations,* vol. 1, Longmans, Green & Co., 1870, pp. 135–42.

[348] Frazer, Ch. 67, §. 1; Frederick Starr, 'Dress and Adornment: IV. Religious Dress', *Popular Science,* December 1891, p. 196; Elizabeth McAlister, 'A Sorcerer's Bottle: The Visual Art of Magic in Haiti', in Donald J. Cosentino, (ed.), *Sacred Arts of Haitian Vodou,* UCLA Fowler Museum of Cultural History, 1995, p. 317.

for the welfare of a whole family line and, as Sir Walter Scott's visit in 1829 showed, something of a tourist attraction.[349]

Various forms of black magic could also be used to attack the soul or spirit by forcing or luring it out of the body. The *Tjilaiyu* ceremony of the Kakadu tribe aims at capturing a victim's *yalmuru*, 'spirit', and causing him to thus come into harm's way. The charm involves securing some of the victim's excrement to lure the *yalmuru* into a fire pit. A Malay charm to steal someone's soul involves taking sand or earth from the person's footprint. In the third century BCE, Clearchus, a pupil of Aristotle's, reported an incident in which a magician tapped a boy with his 'soul-drawing wand' (*psychoulkos rhabdos*) and drew out his soul for a time, leaving the body insensible to pain as if dead. However, as any good shaman will tell you, it is not just the souls of the living that can be captured.[350]

Necromagia

When Avie Woodbury had had enough of the two ghosts that were haunting her home in Christchurch, New Zealand, she called in an exorcist. This 'exorcist' from her local Spiritualist church identified one of the spirits as that of Les Graham, who had died in the house in the 1920s. Les was mischievous, but weak. The other spirit was that of a little girl and was much stronger, able to move objects and activate appliances, according to Woodbury. The exorcist was apparently able to trap the two spirits in bottles of what was said to be holy water. 'The holy water dulls the spirits' energy,' explained Woodbury, 'sort of puts them to sleep.' She added that 'We have had no activity since they were bottled on July 15th 2009. So I believe they are in the bottles.'

---

[349] Frazer, Ch. 67, §. 2; Sir Walter Scott, entry for 13 May 1829, *The Journal of Sir Walter Scott from the Original Manuscript at Abbotsford*, vol. 2, Burt Franklin, 1890.

[350] Sir Baldwin Spencer, *Native Tribes of the Northern Territory of Australia*, Macmillan, 1914; [Sir] R. O. Winstedt, *Shaman, Saiva and Sufi*, Constable & Company, 1925; Daniel Ogden, *Magic, Witchcraft and Ghosts in the Greek and Roman Worlds: A Sourcebook*, Oxford University Press, 2002, p. 171.

Sleeping or not, she still felt scared by their presence and put the two little bottles, half-filled with blue liquid, up for sale on the New Zealand auction site TradeMe. Worldwide press coverage helped draw almost 215,000 page views and boost the winning bid to NZ$5,000 (£2,339 approx.). John Deese of Florida used to sell his bottled ghosts for a more affordable US$20 (£13) and such items occasionally surface on eBay.[351]

In October 2010, in a small village in Malaysia, hundreds of people gathered outside the home of Siti Balqis Mohd Nor when they heard that her possessing spirits were about to be exorcised. The twenty-two-year-old had for the past two months been allegedly vanishing and re-appearing in unusual locations, once inside a cement mixer. Her parents had spent thousands of *ringgit*, employing around a hundred native shamans, or *bomoh*, to try and cure their daughter. After a newspaper highlighted her story, two *bomoh* came forward, waiving their fee. With onlookers jostling to take photographs and video outside, the *bomoh* emerged to say that they had cast out nine djinns and imprisoned them in special containers – large, ordinary-looking jars with a layer of mixed material in the bottom. As one *bomoh* chanted inside, the other waited by the door, catching the spirits as they tried to flee. It is not reported whether anyone in the crowd managed to capture this on film, but the jars were lined up on the bonnet of a car afterwards to the delight of snappers. The *bomoh* said that they would finally dispose of the djinns by throwing the containers into the sea. Siti Balqis told reporters that 'I am relieved to be able to live without fear of suddenly finding myself alone in strange places'. Clearly, it was believed that the djinns, like Woodbury's ghosts, could be extracted and relocated by

---

[351] 'For Sale: "Two Captured Ghosts, Trapped Inside Bottles of Holy Water to Make Them Sleepy"', *Daily Mail*, 8 March 2010; 'TradeMe: Ghost Auction Involved Bogus Bidders', *3 News*, 9 March 2010; 'Fla. Man Selling Ghosts', http://www.clickorlando.com/news/16388581/detail.html, 25 May 2008, accessed 3 January 2011; 'Purported Exorcised Poltergeist Ghost in a Bottle/ Wicca' being sold on eBay.co.uk, accessed 13 May 2011.

magical means, prompting us to wonder what the essential difference between the two might be.[352]

TheHouseofVoodoo.com offers a nice line in Zombie Spirit Bottles. According to their website, Bianca, 'the powerful New Orleans Voodoo Queen', uses a 'voodoo hoodoo ritual spell' known only to her to capture the spirits and force them into the bottles. Without making any guarantees, Bianca 'does acknowledge that strange things have been known to happen when one is in possession of one of these unique fetishes'. As we saw in the chapter on 'The Undead', the word 'zombie' comes from *nzambi*, 'god, spirit', or *zumbi*, 'fetish', in the Kongo language. To make such a bottle, according to the website, one ties a colourful glass receptacle to a tree, cobalt blue being traditional. As sunlight sparkles and shines through the glass, evil spirits are attracted to it and, entering, find themselves so seduced by the dazzling refractions that they remain within. Highly decorative works of art in themselves, Bianca's Zombie Spirit Bottles are currently retailing at US$350.[353]

Quite accidentally it seems, Elizabeth McAlister found herself being given a spirit bottle as a gift by a *bokor*, or 'sorcerer', in Haiti in the 1990s. She thought at first that she had inadvertently commissioned a piece of art that would make a pretty ornament for her coffee table until she found out it held two zombies. She explains that a zombie is 'a part of the soul that is stolen and made to work'. These are not the shuffling, or lately, sprinting, cannibal corpses beloved of George A. Romero and others, but '*zonbi* [*sic*] *astral*, a dead person's spirit that is magically captured and contained', usually also involving the magically induced premature death of the said person. The victim enters a limbic state – killed 'by the hands of man' but not yet 'by the hand of God' – and in this condition can be made to serve the *bokor*.[354]

---

[352] Mohammad Ishak, '2 Bomoh Capture 9 Djinns', *New Straits Times*, 10 October 2010. *Bomoh* was used in both the singular and plural in the article.

[353] http://www.thehouseofvoodoo.com/item_oddities/zombies/x25/, accessed 2 October 2010.

[354] McAlister, pp. 305–21.

McAlister watched as the *bokor* placed two human skulls on the floor, doused them with rum and set light to them. Blue flame danced over the grinning death's heads. It flickered and died, leaving a spicy perfume in the air. The sorcerer bent over the skulls and shaved a strip of bone from each. He then burnt a US one-dollar bill on the blade of a knife and mixed the ashes with the skull shavings. He tipped these into an empty rum bottle, adding liquor, leaves, perfume and a strange pink powder. The bottle was wrapped in the colours of the Petwo nation spirits – red, white and black – and decorated with pins, magnets, open scissors, four round mirrors, and a woman's earring. McAlister's bottle was a *wanga*, a magical working. As her research took her deeper into voodoo, she would also discover that it was 'a living grave'.[355]

The Haitian *bokor*'s zombie bottle is a descendant of the *nkisi* (*minkisi*, pl.) known amongst the people of the Congo Basin. Usually translated as 'charm' or 'fetish', it is more specifically a spirit container, manufactured and manipulated by a human operator, the *nganga-nkisi*. White clay, to symbolize the land of the dead, or earth from the grave itself, is used to hold the zombie within its new tomb. A variation of the zombie bottle is the *nganga* of the Palo Monte Mayombe religion in Cuba. Originally meaning 'medicine-man', *nganga* is here used for the 'spirit pot', often made of iron and looking not unlike a witch's cauldron. Like supernatural Tamagotchis these bottles and pots also need care and attention, and regular feeding – just remember not to give them salt.[356]

Such dealings with the dead were classified by medieval and later writers as necromancy, from the Greek *nekrós*, 'dead', and *manteia*, 'divination'. It was dangerous magic. The Bohemian poet, Johannes von Tepl (c. 1350–c. 1415) described it in grisly terms: 'with the sacrificial fingers of the dead and sigils (talismans) the formidable spirit is conjured'. It is no surprise that

---

[355] McAlister, pp. 306–7, 312, 314.
[356] McAlister, p. 310–11; Judith Bettelheim, 'Palo Monte Mayombe and its Influence on Cuban Contemporary Art', *African Arts*, 34.2, 2001, pp. 36–49, 94–6.

Hartlieb catalogued it as one of 'the forbidden arts'. The theologians of this period denied that the spirits of the dead were actually raised through necromancy, asserting that their places were instead taken by dissembling demons. This meant that necromancy was in effect to consort with demons and accordingly defined as black magic, or nigromancy from the Latin *niger*, 'black'. Although Hartlieb did not make such a sophisticated argument, he was clear about the Devil's involvement: 'He who wants to practice this art must make various offerings to the Devil [. . .] vow to him and be in league with him'. In the sixteenth century, Agrippa also described this dark art in similar terms:[357]

> *Necromancy* hath its name, because it worketh on the bodies of the dead, and giveth answers by the ghosts and apparitions of the dead, and subterrany spirits, alluring them into the carcasses of the dead, by certain hellish charms, and infernal invocations, and by deadly sacrifices, and wicked oblations.[358]

However, he was more specific than Hartlieb on the mechanisms behind this art. He furnished his description with a plethora of classical and biblical references to Odysseus and Circe, and Saul and the Witch of Endor, amongst others. The dramatic story of Saul, King of Israel, turning to the Witch of Endor to call up the spirit of the Prophet Samuel was an especially popular one amongst occultists and demonologists as both a proof of necromancy and an example of its prohibition. But behind the obvious learning was the primitive theory that 'souls after death do as yet love their body which they left'. From this it followed that those who have not been given a proper burial or who have died a

---

[357] Von Tepl, *Der Ackermann und der Tod*, 1401, trans. Felix Genzmer, Philipp Reclam, 1984; Johannes Hartlieb, *Das Buch der Verbotenen Künste*, trans. Falk Eisermann and Eckhard Graf, Eugen Diedrichs Verlag, 1998 [1456], p. 69, my translation; Richard Kieckhefer, *Magic in the Middle Ages*, Canto, 1989:152–3; Ruickbie, *Faustus*, pp. 40–1.

[358] Heinrich Cornelius Agrippa von Nettesheim, *De occulta philosophia libri tres*, n.p., 1533, trans. John French as *Three Books of Occult Philosophy*, Gregory Moule, 1651, pp. 489–90.

violent death still linger about their corpse or place of death. Such spirits can be 'allured' by the use of things that in life they found dear, but more importantly 'the souls of the dead cannot be called up without blood and a carcasse'. The best places for necromancy were duly considered to be 'burial places and places of execution, and where public slaughters have lately been made, or where the carcasses of the slain, not as yet expiated, nor rightly buried'. The same idea is expressed in the *Secretum Secretorum* document reproduced by Reginald Scot in 1584 with an even more graphic account of 'the maister standing at the head of the grave'. Unlike Hartlieb and the theological view, Agrippa took a classical stance and would seem to have believed that the dead could be made to answer the magician's interrogations. He even extended this necromantic theory to make the argument that the Christian saints listen most attentively to appeals made in the presence of their relics.[359]

Angel Magic

She ignored the voice in her head telling her that her car was going to be stolen. She had been hearing voices all her life and had learnt not to listen to them. It was a summer afternoon in 1995, the woman was in her late thirties pulling into a car park in her open-top convertible. Two men approached her; one was holding a knife, the other a gun. They made a grab for her car keys and her purse when 'one of my angels just said, "Scream"'. That stopped them in their tracks, but they were still armed and dangerous: 'then, God had placed in the parking lot a woman who leaned on the horn of her car'. The noise drew the attention of a crowd leaving a nearby church and her attackers ran off. 'I almost died,' she later said, 'by not listening to my angels.' She claims the experience changed her life and now travels the world telling people about angels.[360]

---

[359] Agrippa, p. 489; Scot, p. 232.
[360] Ray Hemachandra, 'Angel's Wings and Human Prayer', *New Age Retailer*, 20 July 2005, quoted on http://www.angeltherapy.com/view_article.php?article_id=28, accessed 22 July 2010.

Described on her website as 'a spiritual doctor of psychology and a fourth-generation metaphysician', Doreen Virtue (which she insists is her real name) claims to hold a number of degrees in 'counselling psychology'[361] and has written over twenty books on subjects as diverse as the chakras, health, diet, 'Crystal Children', 'Indigo Children', unicorns, and, of course, angels. Her titles include *Angel Words* (2011), *The Angel Therapy Handbook* (2011), *How to Hear Your Angels* (2007), *Angel Medicine* (2004), *Healing with the Angels* (1999) – there are too many to list them all. She even teaches 'Angel Therapy' courses for would-be practitioners. Over the course of four days Virtue and her staff perform 'short theatrical productions with audience participation' for those paying $1,555 per person. Sales of over 700,000 copies of Virtue's *Messages from Your Angels* card deck were reported in its first year.[362]

According to Virtue, 'angels are real' and everyone has at least two guardian angels in addition to a spirit guide who are ready to 'assist with our careers, health issues, love lives, families and homes'. Some of her angel magic includes asking that guardian angels be stationed at all of your doors and windows to protect you as you sleep, or visualize the archangel Raphael giving you 'a blanket of green healing energy' that you then pull over you. If you do not feel like doing any of this yourself, never fear: 'at night, before I fall asleep', says Virtue, 'I surround the planet with white light' – not forgetting to 'put light into all my products that are in [retailers'] stores'.[363]

---

[361] She claims to hold BA, MA and PhD degrees. Her PhD in counselling psychology is from the California Coast University (CCU), an unaccredited institution at the time of her enrolment and reported to be a 'diploma mill' in the *Dallas Observer*. The CCU was only accredited in 2005 by the US Distance Education and Training Council. Additionally, the psychiatric hospitals at which she claims to have held high positions are both now closed, and a journalist investigating her story was unable to verify these claims. See Jesse Hyde, 'Little Boy Blue', *Dallas Observer*, 9 March 2006.

[362] http://www.angeltherapy.com/about.php, accessed 22 July 2010; www.doreenvirtuellc.com, accessed 22 July 2010; Deirdre Donahue, 'Kits Help Booksellers Reach Nirvana', *USA Today*, 21 July 2003.

[363] Hemachandra; L. A. Justice, 'Heal your spirit with an angel's help', *Sun*, 7 March 2005, quoted on http://www.angeltherapy.com/view_article.

'In June 1994 Margaret Neylon was unemployed, depressed and broke,' according to the biography on her website. 'Then her angel told her "Give a course called 'Talking With Angels'."' 'You don't have to be mad to have an angel,' she says. Aiming squarely at a very particular market segment, her book *Angel Magic* is decorated with sworly text and a cute little 'cherub'.[364]

Cassandra Eason has also written a book called *Angel Magic*. A prolific writer of New Age books for many years – she has over eighty titles to her credit – Eason is perhaps most widely known as the dream analyst on *Big Brother* (series three). She also runs a course on angels. Called 'Touched by Angels' it covers working with guardian angels, archangels, angelology, healing and so on for £75. One can have an angel spell cast by Eason for £30, or an astrological-crystal-angel reading for £50. Also presenting herself as a psychic, she was asked by a UK newspaper in 2006 to predict the winning lottery numbers. As the balls rolled for a record roll-over EuroMillions draw of €126 million, her number did not come up.[365]

The roots of angel magic go deeper, of course. The *Testament of Solomon* is essentially a grimoire of angelic invocation. The surviving Greco-Roman magical papyri from Egypt of the second century BCE to the fifth century CE contain such spells of supplication as that which implores the 'excellent ruling angels' to intercede against the sufferer's fever and another that names Michael, Gabriel, Raphael, and others, as well as charms to drive out possessing demons. Some books on angel magic claimed to have been given by angels themselves, such as the third- or fourth-century CE *Sefer Ha-Razim* supposedly given by the angel Raziel to Noah and the medieval *Sefer Raziel Ha-Malach* supposedly given by Raziel to Adam. The Coptic manuscript known as 'The

---

php?article_id=28, accessed 22 July 2010.

[364] Margaret Neylon, *Angel Magic: All About Angels and How to Bring their Magic into your Life*, Thorsons, 2001; http://www.margaretneylon.com/about.html, accessed 28 July 2010.

[365] Cassandra Eason, *Angel Magic*, Little, Brown, 2010; Amit Roy, '3 in Europe get lottery lucky', the *Telegraph* [India], 5 February 2006.

Magical Book of Mary and the Angels', dating from the ninth to tenth centuries CE contains such invocatory lines as 'let the angels and the archangels appear to me today'. The Elizabethan polymath and magician John Dee famously developed his Enochian system of magic during communications with supposed angels in the late sixteenth century. A certain Dr Rudd produced *A Treatise on Angel Magic* in the seventeenth century with instructions on how to conjure angels to 'visible appearance'. Even Crowley's *Magick* is a work on angel magic, amongst other things, leading to the highest goal of invoking one's 'Holy Guardian Angel'.[366]

Magic Today

Despite Faustus' example at the beginning of this chapter, invoking the Devil is much out of fashion these days. Most witches and pagans I interviewed for my doctoral research used magic for healing (36.9 per cent), or for either personal (20 per cent) or social (18.5 per cent) development. For comparison, a survey running on the internet for over a year has found that out of 968 replies the largest number (35.8 per cent) wanted to use magic to change their relationships. Health came next (21.1 per cent) with job third (16.3 per cent). Sex (12.6 per cent) came bottom of the list after family (14.2 per cent).[367]

---

[366] Spells catalogued as PGM LXXXVIII. 1–19, PGM XC. 1–13 and PGM IV. 86–7 in Hans Dieter Betz (ed.), *The Greek Magical Papyri in Translation*, vol. I, University of Chicago Press, 1996, pp. 38, 302; Michael A. Morgan, *Sepher Ha-Razim: The Book of Mysteries*, Society of Biblical Literature, 1983; see also the scholarly edition by Bill Rebiger and Peter Schäfer (eds), *Sefer ha-Razim I und II – Das Buch der Geheimnisse I und II*, Mohr Siebeck, 2009; P. Heid Inv. Kopt. 685, Institut für Papyrologie, Ruprecht-Karls-Universität, Heidelberg, published by Marvin Meyer (ed.), *The Magical Book of Mary and the Angels*, Universitäts-verlag C. Winter, 1996; quotation p. 13; Rudd, *A Treatise on Angel Magic*, British Library MS. Harley 6482; John Dee, 'Claves Angelicæ', British Library, Sloane 3191, and 'The Book of Enoch', British Library, Sloane 3189 and 2599.

[367] Leo Ruickbie, 'The Re-Enchanters: Theorising Re-Enchantment and Testing for its Presence in Modern Witchcraft', unpublished PhD thesis, King's College, London, 2005; see Leo Ruickbie, *Witchcraft Out of the Shadows*, Robert Hale, 2004, p. 205; 'If you could magickally improve one area of your life, what would it be?' 14 February 2009 to 2 August 2010, http://naturalwicca.

Historically, magic was generally seen as the work of spirits. The complicated repertoire that emerged in the grimoires of circles and talismans was seen as a means of influencing, even commanding, spiritual entities. It was also seen as working with the spirit. The spirit could, according to our examples, be either extracted for personal protection or trapped for nefarious purposes. In folklore it is usually the villain of the piece who hides his soul; in magic it is the practitioner who can both send forth his or her own soul and extract the souls of others. Given the belief in an afterlife, it was thought that the dead could also be manipulated in this way. The principal technique to use someone else's soul relies upon sympathetic magic, according to Frazer. Something of the person, such as a bone shaving, or something having been in contact with the person, such as earth from a footprint, can be used to capture and control the soul whether the person is living or dead. Spirits of the dead could also be simply attracted by the potent symbols of life: blood and flesh. 'Higher' spirits, such as angels, can be both supplicated and commanded, although 'spells' like Virtue's green blanket are rather more imaginative exercises.

In contrast to these historical views, I found that magical practitioners in post-industrial Britain mainly described magic as a form of transformative energy or mental technique, but as we have seen there are practitioners around the world – from Haiti to Malaysia – who are still interpreting and using magic from the perspective of spirits. However they might define this mysterious technique, there are also those still using the old grimoires – especially the *Key of Solomon* – just as the real Faustus might have done in his day, 500 years ago.

com/index.php/component/poll/1-life, accessed 8 August 2010. Note that 968 is the number of returns received and may not be an accurate reflection of the number of people who took part. The online survey also used fixed categories that will have influenced the returns made.

7. Spiritualism

Snow was still on the ground and storm clouds threatened more. Dark came early to the door and drafts whistled coldly through the cracks. But that was not the reason the Fox family had taken to sleeping in one room. As night fell, pitch black and silent as the grave, upon their humble house in a lonely hamlet, it started again. Invisible hands hammered wild blows upon the walls and doors as they lay shivering in their beds.

The place was known as the 'Burned Over District', a region that got its name from the wild-fires of religious revival that frequently swept through the lives of its inhabitants. Here, in an isolated settlement called Hydesville in the far north of New York State, in 1848, lived two sisters – Catherine (Kate, Katie or Cathie), aged twelve, and Margaretta (Maggie), aged fifteen – with their parents, John and Margaret, in a 'simple wooden homestead'. From these humble beginnings, the Fox sisters would become an international sensation – and the world would come to believe that the spirits of the dead could communicate with the living.[368]

---

[368] Ann Leah Underhill, *The Missing Link in Modern Spiritualism*, T. R. Knox, 1885, p. 7 – Underhill was one of the married names of Leah Fox and as she explained (note, p. 40) Catherine was called Cathie by her parents, but later Katie by the public; Frank Podmore, *Modern Spiritualism: A History and a Criticism*, Methuen, 1902, pp. 179–80; Thomas Olman Todd, *Hydesville: The Story of the Rochester Knockings*, Keystone Press, 1905, p. 18; Amy Lehman, *Victorian Women and the Theatre of Trance*, McFarland, 2009, p. 79. Also of interest is Emma Hardinge Britten, *Modern American Spiritualism*, self-published, 1870.

In 1848 revolution was in the air. The barricades were up in Paris and a Second Republic was declared. The March Revolution had thrown Germany into turmoil. The Italian states were up in arms against Austria. In Tipperary the Irish rebelled against British rule. In London the Chartists marched on Parliament. Karl Marx and Friedrich Engels published their *Communist Manifesto*. But in this out of the way corner of rural North America, these two young girls were about to start their own revolution.

The Foxes moved into the house in Hydesville in December 1847. Faint nocturnal knocking sounds started to be heard in January of the new year, growing stronger into February and March. Additional phenomena began to be reported: chairs were moved, bedclothes would be whisked off sleepers, Katie said she felt a cold hand upon her face. Eventually, noises could be heard all over the house. As Mr and Mrs Fox stood either side of a door, they could hear knocking on the door between them. 'We heard footsteps in the pantry and walking downstairs,' said Mrs Fox. She thought 'the house must be haunted by some unhappy, restless spirit.' Events reached a crescendo on the night of Friday, 31 March.[369]

As the family huddled in a single bedroom together, the knocks echoed in the darkness. The father, John Fox, tried the doors and windows, looking for the source of the noise, but he knew it was fruitless – he had tried many times before. Then Katie called out, 'Here, Mr Splitfoot, do as I do'. She clapped her hands together a number of times. The mysterious knockings responded with the same number of sounds. Maggie tried next. 'Now do as I do,' she said, 'count one, two, three, four,' clapping whilst she did so. The raps answered in kind, four times. Maggie was too frightened to try the experiment a second time. Katie, however, in what her mother described as 'her childish simplicity', had an explanation: 'O mother, I

---

[369] Signed testimony of Margaret Fox dated 11 April 1848, in Underhill, pp. 5–10.

know what it is; tomorrow is April-fool day, and it's somebody trying to fool us'.[370]

Mrs Fox decided to try and test it with a question 'that no one in the place could answer'. She asked it how old her children were. Mrs Fox had had seven children, of which only six were still living. The knocking rapped out the correct ages for six children, paused then gave three more knocks. The seventh child had died at the age of three. Then she asked 'Is this a human being that answers my questions so correctly?' No answer. 'Is it a spirit?' 'Yes' came the knocks in reply.[371]

According to all accounts, Mrs Fox's questioning revealed that the knocks were being made by a thirty-one-year-old pedlar who had been murdered for his money, leaving a widow, now also dead, and five children. His body was buried in the cellar. By now the children were 'clinging to each other and trembling with terror'. The Foxes called in their neighbours, the Redfields, as witnesses. They then called others. Soon the Deuslers, the Hydes and the Jewells were crowding into the bedroom. The questioning continued with William Deusler leading the inter-rogation. The sum of money involved had been $500. The crime had been perpetrated about five years ago in the east bedroom on a Tuesday at midnight. His throat had been cut with a butcher's knife. Mrs Fox took the children and left the house. Deusler said he left at about midnight. Mr Fox and others stayed the night trying to find out more about the case. On Saturday night the questioning continued.[372]

News spread fast. The next evening Deusler reckoned that there were as many as 300 people in and around the Foxes' house. Deusler noted amongst them Hiram Soverhill, Esq., one

---

[370] Underhill, p. 7; Todd, pp. 27–33; Lehman, p. 80. Todd says that Katie made only movements with her hands, Podmore, p. 180, and Lehman says finger snapping, but Mrs Fox's testimony reprinted in Underhill states 'clapping'.

[371] Underhill, p. 7. Todd, p. 35, gave a different account of the questioning procedure.

[372] Underhill, pp. 7–9; Todd, pp. 35, 37–40. On pp. 37–42 Todd reproduces the signed testimony of Deusler dated 12 April 1848.

of the Republican 'Young Men', sometime school-teacher, constable and 'overseer of the poor', and Volney Brown, a former officer of the 39th Infantry, both evidently citizens of some standing. They, too, asked questions and had their answers sounded out in knocks.[373]

Committees of friends and neighbours were formed and stationed round the house, alert to any attempt at deception. The noises grew quieter as the witching hour approached and some of the crowd began to dissipate. The Foxes' son, David, and some others started digging in the cellar until they hit water at a depth of 3 feet (1m) and had to give up.[374]

By Sunday 500 people had gathered. The small cottage was jam-packed with the curious. They were milling through the rooms. They were peering in through the windows. They were everywhere. When he arrived in the afternoon, Deusler had the house cleared.[375]

With one of the Foxes' sons-in-law, Stephen Smith, and several others, Deusler went into the cellar and asked the spirit if a body had been buried there. For the first time the noises would now be reported as being heard during the hours of daylight. 'The moment I asked the question,' wrote Deusler, 'there was a sound like the falling of a stick [. . .] on the floor in the bedroom over our heads.' He sent Smith up to investigate, but he came promptly back and said the room was empty. It is not clear where the Fox family were at this point. Deusler tried to recreate the sound by dropping objects on the floor, but was unable to do so. He reported that there was only one floor between the bedroom and the cellar, allowing no hiding place for anything that might have been used to make the noise. He

---

[373] Underhill, p. 9; Todd, p. 40; 'Young Men of Arcadia', *The Western Argus*, 10 September 1834; George W. Cowles (ed.), *Landmarks of Wayne County, New York*, D. Mason & Co., 1895, pp. 358, 364; L. H. Clark, *Military History of Wayne County, N.Y.; The County in the Civil War*, Clark, Hulett & Gaylord, 1883, pp. 178, 184.

[374] Testimony of David S. Fox, dated 11 April 1848, in Underhill, pp. 18–19.

[375] Dr Campell's account reproduced in Britten, p. 34; Todd, pp. 40, 43.

repeated the questions on Monday night and got the same response. He finished his account by saying that he had never believed in haunted houses before, but that this was 'a mystery to me which I am unable to solve'.[376]

On Monday, David Fox led others in digging up the cellar again, bailing out the water as it rushed in. Again they had to abandon work. He came back on Tuesday with a pump, but not even pumping and hand-bailing the water could lower the level. There was little more they could do until the year brought hot weather and a dry season.[377]

On 11 April, both John and Margaret Fox made signed statements of all that had transpired. Margaret was clearly much put out by events. 'I am very sorry,' she wrote, 'that there has been so much excitement about it. It has been a great deal of trouble to us.' John expressed similar feelings: 'It has caused a great deal of trouble and anxiety. Hundreds have visited the house, so that it is impossible for us to attend to our daily occupations.' Margaret remained agnostic, at a loss to account for the noises. She was not, as she wrote, 'a believer in haunted houses or supernatural appearances'. John, however, had 'no doubt but that it is of supernatural origin'. David, too, confessed 'I cannot account for this noise as being produced by any human agency'.[378]

At the same time, Lucretia Pulver, who had been a maid to the last family occupying the house, also gave her testimony. She claimed to have lived and worked there for about three months one winter, during which time she, too, had heard the mysterious rapping sounds and footsteps from downstairs. The dog, she said, would lie under the bed and howl all night long. She claimed that before the sounds were heard a 'foot-pedlar' had called at the house and then strangely was never seen again. She said that she saw her mistress altering coats

---

[376] Todd, pp. 41–2.
[377] Underhill, p. 19.
[378] Underhill, pp. 9–10, 19.

that were too large for her husband. She said she found evidence of strange diggings in the cellar that were explained away as rat-holes.[379]

Anna Pulver also remembered the former mistress of the house complaining of hearing strange footsteps in the night. Former residents Mr and Mrs Weekman came forward to add their testimony, throwing fuel on the fire with more stories of terrified children and unusual noises. Jane C. Lape even claimed to have seen the ghost of the pedlar. The well near the house, when the water smelt so foul in the summer of 1844, was mentioned as something suspicious. A lot of question marks were now beginning to form an accusing finger.[380]

The Foxes abandoned the house, going to live with their son David. People still visited and still claimed to hear rapping noises. The phenomena also transferred themselves to David's house, some two miles distant. At night they would hear the ghastly re-enactment of the murder: 'gurgling, strangling, sawing, planing, and boring'. By the end of July, David and a group of friends returned to resume the digging. The ground had dried out and there was the chance that they might now make some progress. His wife, Elizabeth, laid on a feast of puddings, pies, cakes and sweet-meats, and work began.[381]

On the first day they dug down to a depth of between 4 and 5 feet (1.2 to 1.5 m), finding charcoal and lime, then some hair, then some teeth. Darkness brought a halt to the digging and they returned the next day, but so did the crowds. Cartloads of rowdies with 'shouts of ribaldry and roars of laughter' arrived for the entertainment. The women formed a picket-line round the house, whilst the men rolled up their sleeves and continued digging. This time they unearthed some bones 'which doctors pronounced to be human bones' from the ankle, hands and skull. Meanwhile the crowd outside broke through, crowding

---

[379] Testimony of Lucretia Pulver, dated 11 April 1848, in Underhill, pp. 13–15.
[380] Testimony of Anna Pulver, dated 11 April 1848, in Underhill, p. 16; Underhill, pp. 16–18.
[381] Underhill, pp. 20–2, 32.

into the cellar, spitting and throwing sticks and stones. But the digging went on.[382]

Shovelling out layers of sand and gravel, they hit what appeared to be a board and tried to bore through it. Over their heads the floorboards were creaking with the weight of people trampling through the house. The cellar was mobbed. There were shouts of 'Drag the women out!' and 'Drag the men out!' They were called crazy. Overflowing excitement and barely repressed violence jostled shoulder-to-shoulder. Luckily, perhaps, daylight was fading fast and brought work to a halt once more.[383]

Leah, another of the Foxes' daughters, arrived on the scene. Following the death of her husband, Mr Fish, she had built up a successful business as a music teacher in Rochester. The family decided that Katie should return with Leah. Interestingly, Leah later wrote, 'we hoped, by separating the two children (Maggie and Katie), that we could put a stop to the disturbance'. Mrs Fox had noticed that the noises seemed to occur round Katie in particular.[384]

The mysterious rapping followed them on the canal boat back to Rochester and settled in to its new home on Mechanics' Square, showing every intention of playing merry havoc with their lives. That first night, Leah's daughter Lizzie was reduced to a screaming fit after she felt a cold hand on her face in the darkness. Leah struck a light and read out from a bible, but the girls continued to feel hands upon them. Eventually they were able to put out the light and try sleeping once more. Leah tucked the bible under her pillow, but before she could even put her head down, it shot out from underneath. The box of matches shook in front of her face and 'such a variety of performances ensued that we gave up in despair to our fate, whatever it may be'.[385]

The next night at about midnight, they were rudely awoken

---

[382] Underhill, pp. 22–5.
[383] Underhill, p. 25.
[384] Underhill, p. 32.
[385] Underhill, pp. 33–4.

by the sound of all the tables and chairs being moved about downstairs. Footsteps then clattered on the stairs up to the room next to their bedroom. It sounded as though someone wearing clogs danced a jig to the applause of a sizeable audience. They then all trooped back downstairs, slamming the doors noisily behind them. Similar disturbances followed over the next weeks, until Leah resolved to move – thinking it was the house that was haunted – and took another property on Prospect Street backing onto an old cemetery called 'the Buffalo Burying-ground'. Finally, they spent an uneventful night. The mother, Margaret Fox, arrived with Maggie the next day and Leah excitedly told them that they had escaped the noises.[386]

At midnight the spirits were back. Footsteps were heard creeping up the stairs. 'We could hear them,' Leah wrote, 'shuffling, giggling, and whispering'. Repeatedly, they came into the bedroom to 'give our bed a tremendous shaking, lifting it (and us) entirely from the floor, almost to the ceiling, and let us down with a bang; then pat us with hands'. The whole panoply of poltergeist phenomena manifested itself: objects were lifted, objects were thrown, furniture was moved about, people were slapped and touched, they were pricked with pins, a ghostly figure was seen, the piano played by itself, and a varied range of noises were heard. Katie fell into a trance, describing 'the terrible occurrence at the Hydesville house', sobbing uncontrollably and repeating many verses of poetry.[387]

They had tried to ignore the disturbances, believing them to be caused by evil spirits, but the disturbances would not be ignored. Finally, in the late summer of 1848, they turned to the method first employed by David in Hydesville of calling out the letters of the alphabet and noting which one received a rap in response and in this way were able to receive communications from the source of the noises, whatever it was. The first message read:

---

[386] Underhill, pp. 35–6.
[387] Underhill, pp. 37–41, 45, 48.

Dear friends, you must proclaim these truths to the world. This is the dawning of a new era; and you must not try to conceal it any longer. When you do your duty, God will protect you; and good spirits will watch over you.[388]

They dubbed the system 'God's Telegraph'. As Leah put it, 'We were truly converted [. . .] we had something to live for'. They arranged a signal with the spirits, that they should rap five times when they wanted to communicate. But still they resisted taking the next step until their dead grandfather used the 'telegraph':[389]

My Dear Children:– The time will come when you will understand and appreciate this great dispensation. You must permit your good friends to meet with you and hold commun- ion with their friends in heaven.[390]

They shared the message with their friends and from there it spread. A committee was formed to deal with the wave of enquiries and the 'rushing crowd of curiosity seekers' who wished to hear the 'Rochester Rappings'. People did not just wish to chat with deceased relatives, but wanted to know how to make a fortune, what the secrets of their rivals were, how to resolve their domestic problems, what the winning lottery numbers would be, and what stocks and shares to invest in. Leah recorded that answers were given, but that none ever led to success. She thought that the spirits seemed to delight in deceiving those who asked such questions. It did not stop the crowds. They called at all hours of the day and night. The family scarcely had time to keep the house in order, and Leah lost all of her music pupils.[391]

As Leah told the story, the spirits compelled them to hold a

---

[388] Underhill, pp. 48–9.
[389] Underhill, pp. 49, 51.
[390] Underhill, p. 51.
[391] Underhill, pp. 52–3, 55, 59; Britten, p. 43.

public performance. The Corinthian Hall was hired for the evening of 14 November 1848, and Leah and Maggie displayed 'the manifestations' before a large audience. They also announced that a Committee of Investigation would be formed to search for fraud in their activities. A local paper, the *Rochester Democrat*, scented blood and published a long editorial, denouncing 'the rapping humbug'.[392]

The curtain was up, but it was not humbug. The committee found nothing to suggest deception and as they delivered their report before an audience at a second night at the Corinthian many greeted it with surprise. A second committee was formed and reported on the next evening before an even larger audience: 'there was no kind of probability or possibility of [the sounds] being made by ventriloquism, as some had supposed; and they could not have been made by machinery'. The outcry was even greater than before. A third committee was formed – the 'Infidel Committee' – including, in particular, all of those most vocal in their belief that it was an unmitigated fraud. One would 'forfeit a new hat', another would 'throw myself over Genesee Falls', if they could not prove it to be humbug.[393]

They met in the rooms of Dr Gates in the Rochester House. In a private room beforehand, Leah and Maggie were undressed by three specially appointed women and given clothes provided by the committee. They were brought into the main room and seated at a large table. Leah and Maggie waited. The committee waited. No sounds were heard. They waited all morning, but without any of the usual manifestations. Lunch was served and the committee thought it good sport to tease Leah and Maggie as they ate. Tears streaked Maggie's cheeks. Leah pushed her food around, unable to taste it. The sceptics were in good cheer.[394]

---

[392] Underhill, pp. 63–4.
[393] Underhill, pp. 65–8.
[394] Underhill, pp. 68–9.

As they all sat around the table it suddenly began to shake. One end slowly lifted into the air, then the other. With much creaking in protest, the table rose above their heads. Everyone, except Leah and Maggie, looked on in horror. The waiters ran from the room. The three women comforted the two sisters and the Infidel Committee declared their defeat: 'Girls, you have gained a victory. We will stand by you to the last'.[395]

They still had to make their report public at the Corinthian Hall, however. Warning was sent to the committee that if they gave a favourable report, they would be attacked. The friends of Leah and Maggie thought there would be a riot and urged them not to go. Everyone feared for their own safety. Maggie thought they would surely be lynched. After all, it was 1848.[396]

All the same, they went: Leah and Maggie, and the Infidel Committee. Each member of the committee took centre stage and made his report in turn, explaining the experiment, the precautions taken and the observations made. But the 'rowdy element' would have none of it and worked themselves up into a 'howling mob'. They had warmed a barrel of tar and hidden it near the door to use on Leah, Maggie and the Committee as they left. The police were called. Squibs were set off, violence threatened. But the Chief of Police had cordoned off the stage with policemen and another had brought 'fifty good men' of his own. The rabble dissipated. 'We had,' said Leah, 'passed the fiery ordeal.'[397]

Spiritualism did not begin with the Fox sisters – Leah called what they did 'modern Spiritualism' – but it did now find itself propelled to the centre of the public imagination. Poltergeist phenomena had been recorded long before, of course, and a seventeenth-century Jewish sect had even used 'table-turning' as a centrepiece magico-religious rite. Spirit communication also had an ancient pedigree – attempts to talk to the dead were

---

[395] Underhill, pp. 69–70.
[396] Underhill, p. 71.
[397] Underhill, pp. 71–3, 100.

considered necromancy. Sometimes the dead were believed to try and communicate with the living, as we saw with regard to purposeful ghosts.[398]

Spirit-rapping, said Sir Arthur Conan Doyle, had been heard before. Best known as the creator of Sherlock Holmes, Doyle was also an ardent Spiritualist and had written a two-volume study of the subject, identifying several prior cases of spirit-rapping – in 1520 at Oppenheim in Germany; in 1661 at the house of Mr Mompesson in Tedworth: the famous Drummer of Tedworth; and in 1716 at the vicarage of Epworth.[399]

There were even earlier cases to be found. *The Spiritual Magazine* for March 1861 quoted from the Roman Catholic missionary Évariste Régis Huc's (1813–60) recent account of Christianity in the Orient involving the travels of William of Rubruck (Willem van Ruysbroek), the French ambassador to the Khan of Tartary in the thirteenth century:

> When they (the soothsayers to the Tartar Emperor) were interrogated, they evoked their demons (spirits) by the sound of the tambourine, shaking it furiously; then falling into an ecstasy, they feigned to receive answers from their familiar spirits, and proclaimed them as oracles. It is rather curious, too, that table-rapping and table-turning were in use in the thirteenth century among these Mongols in the wilds of Tartary. Rubru[c]k himself witnessed an instance of the kind. On the eve of the Ascension, when the mother of Mangou [was] feeling very ill, the first soothsayer was summoned for consultation, he 'performed some magic by rapping on a table'.[400]

---

[398] Brian Inglis, *Natural and Supernatural: A History of the Paranormal*, Prism/Unity, 1992, p. 206.

[399] Sir Arthur Conan Doyle, *The History of Spiritualism*, 2 vols, Cassell, 1926, vol. 1, p. 58.

[400] 'Glimpses of Spiritualism in the East', *The Spiritual Magazine*, 1 March 1861, p. 118, quoting Évariste Régis Huc, *Christianity in China, Tartary and Thibet*, 2 vols, Sadlier & Co., 1857, vol. I, p. 199. The same account is

This account reveals its biases, but those aside, it is an interesting case. *The Spiritual Magazine* had delved deep into the past to find this precedent for Spiritualism. In the process it had established a connection with shamanism, which was as yet to receive serious anthropological study.

Nearer the Foxes' own time, Emmanuel Swedenborg's discourses with the disincarnate had given rise to a thriving sect after his death in 1772. Franz Anton Mesmer's spectacular results with 'animal magnetism' led some to suggest that the spirits were involved. The term séance, for example, was used in the context of Mesmerism before it became applied to Spiritualism.[401] Spectacular cases of spontaneous mediumship had been reported in the early years of the nineteenth century: Friederike Hauffe, 'The Seeress of Prevorst', who would talk to the spirits every evening; the maid Mary Jane who could talk to the fairies after being mesmerized by her employer in Massachusetts; Andrew Jackson Davis, 'The Poughkeepsie Seer', uneducated, but able to transcribe learned discourses on philosophy and science, as well as see through walls, whilst in trance.[402]

By 1850 the Fox sisters were holding séances in New York. The business-minded Leah managed Katie and Maggie, steering them to success. They became household names, but they were no longer alone. By 1851 every town and city in New York State had its medium giving public trance lectures or private sittings. Competition was growing on every side and not just from the developing professional and semi-professional medium class. Practical handbooks were being published, telling readers how to hold their own séances. According to Uriah Clarke in his

---

strangely absent from William of Rubruck, *The Journey of William of Rubruck to the Eastern Parts of the World 1253–55*, trans. William W. Rockhill, Hakluyt Society, 1900.

[401] *The Athenæum*, 1845, pp. 268, 334, reference to a 'mesmeric séance'.

[402] Lehman, p. 82; Inglis, pp. 199–203. See Justinus Kerner, *Die Seherin von Prevorst*, 1829; Justinus Kerner, *The Seeress of Prevorst*, trans. Catherine Crowe, Partridge & Brittan, 1855; and Andrew Jackson Davis, *The Principle of Nature, Her Divine Revelation, and a Voice to Mankind*, 1847.

1863 book *Plain Guide to Spiritualism*, for example, the ideal number of sitters ranged from three to twenty with a balanced number of men and women. The participants were instructed to 'put yourselves in sympathy' with whatever it was they believed they were trying to communicate with and 'become an instrument for the manifestations of the spirits'.[403]

SPIRITUAL MISSION.—Three mediums on a spiritual mission to this city for a few days, now stopping at Hungerford's Hotel, in Duane-street, near Hudson-street. They will examine diseases, and prescribe for the same. Price $2; for spiritual investigations $1. – *Tribune*, 8 February 1853

SPIRITUAL MANIFESTATIONS.—Mrs A. L. Coan, declared to be the best medium, for rapping and writing by the influence of departed spirits, in Boston, will receive company for sittings every day in the week, from nine o'clock A.M. till ten P.M. Rooms No. 8 Howard-street, opposite the Athenaeum. Sittings fifty cents each. – *Boston Herald*, 15 February 1853

It was, as Milton said, that 'Millions of spiritual creatures walk the earth / Unseen, both when we wake and when we sleep', but, now, not unheard. Spiritualism was all the rage. It had its own periodicals, such as *The Spirit Messenger, The Shekinah,* and *The Spiritual Magazine*. Sir David Brewster, the inventor of the kaleidoscope, wrote that 'there are *thousands* of tables turning every night in London, so general is the excitement'. Even Queen Victoria and Prince Albert sat down to a séance. By the end of the century there were an estimated three million people in the USA who believed in the powers of the 10,000 or so trance mediums who were then practising.

---

[403] Inglis, pp. 206, 209; Uriah Clarke, *Plain Guide to Spiritualism*, W. White & Co., 1863, p. 172.

Amongst them were many remarkable characters. Marietta Davis went into a trance for nine days. When she came round again she said that she had been in heaven, talking to old friends and meeting Jesus. The teenage Cora Scott was drawing huge crowds with her elevated trance communication and stunning good looks. Perhaps the most startling was Daniel Dunglas Home (1833–86) who flew in and out of windows for an encore.[404]

Born in Currie near Edinburgh, Home claimed to be the illegitimate son of Alexander, tenth Earl of Home. He claimed that his cradle had been rocked by invisible hands and that the supernatural disturbances that attended him led to his eventually being turned out of his home. Active in America from 1851, by 1852 he was holding up to seven sittings a day. From 1855 to 1862 he was touring Europe. But where others hired halls and performed for the masses, Home only appeared before select private audiences. Initially he enjoyed great success amongst the upper classes, was lavished with expensive gifts and made a socially advantageous marriage to the daughter of a Russian general. However, when his wife died in 1862 her relatives seized her assets and Home was cheated out of any inheritance. Travelling to Rome he found himself expelled in 1864 by order of the Vatican for being a 'sorcerer'. Back in London he was cruelly satirized as Robert Browning's 'Mr Sludge the Medium' (1864): 'I cheated when I could, / Rapped with my toe-joints, set sham hands to work [. . .]' He became involved with the wealthy widow Jane Lyon and, initially, his fortunes dramatically improved, especially when the late Mr Lyon told his wife

---

[404] The first edition of *The Spirit Messenger* was published in Springfield, USA, 10 August 1850, edited by Apollos Munn and R. P. Ambler. *The Spiritual Magazine* was first published in London, January 1860; another *Spiritual Magazine*, also known as *The American Spiritual Magazine*, was edited by Samuel Watson, first published in 1875; John Milton, *Paradise Lost*, Bk IV, ll 677–8; Cora Linn Victoria Scott [Richmond/Tappan], *The Discourses Through the Mediumship of Mrs Cora L.V. Tappan*, J. Burns, 1875; Brewster quoted in Inglis, p. 214; Gordon Stein (ed.), *The Encyclopedia of the Paranormal*, Prometheus Books, 1996, p. 154.

to treat Home like a son and present him with several large cash gifts. But when Lyon later changed heart in 1868, she took him to court to recover the money. The court found in her favour: Home had exercised 'improper influence'. He was ordered to return £60,000 – remarkably he was able to do so, but the case brought much adverse publicity. Association with Viscount Adare, who privately published *Experiences in Spiritualism with Mr D. D. Home* in 1869, revived his reputation. He married a second time in 1871 to Julie de Goumeline and her wealth allowed him to retire from Spiritualism.[405]

Home's repertoire included levitation, bodily elongation, immunity to fire, manifestation of spirit-hands ('pseudopods'), spirit music and table-tipping. He had enjoyed the admiration of the great names of his day: Edward Bulwer-Lytton, John Ruskin, William Makepeace Thackeray and Henry Wadsworth Longfellow. Ralph Waldo Emerson thought him a 'prodigious genius'. Investigated by the scientist Sir William Crookes in 1871, he was pronounced genuine. Society for Psychical Research members William Fletcher Barrett and Frederic W. H. Myers came to the same conclusion in 1889, discounting some of the claims of fraud as hearsay. It is frequently said of him that he was never publicly proven to be a charlatan, but research by the noted sceptic the late Dr Gordon Stein has since uncovered several instances in which he was privately caught in the act of deceiving his audience, although this too has been contested.[406]

---

[405] Joseph McCabe, *Spiritualism: A Popular History from 1847*, Unwin, 1920, pp. 94–5; *Enc. Para.*, pp. 325–9.

[406] William Fletcher Barrett and Frederic W. H. Myers, *Journal of the Society of Psychical Research*, July 1889, pp. 104–5; *Enc. Para.*, pp. 325–9; Stuart Gordon, *The Paranormal: An Illustrated Encyclopedia*, Headline, 1992, p. 313. See Gordon Stein, *The Sorcerer of Kings: The Case of Daniel Dunglas Home and William Crookes*, Prometheus Books, 1993, and the review in *Journal of the Society of Psychical Research*, 60, July 1994, pp. 45ff. Peter Lamont was equivocal in *The First Psychic*, Abacus, 2006, p. 267.

Influential Mediums

Name	Lived	Notability
Andrew Jackson Davis, 'The Poughkeepsie Seer'	1826–1910	voluminous trance-writer
Helene Petrovna Blavatsky	1831– 91	founded the Theosophical Society in 1875
Daniel Dunglas Home	1833–86	supposedly never caught cheating
Fox Sisters		started the 'table-rapping' phenomenon leading to the development of Spiritualism
Margaretta	1833–93	
Catherine	1837–92	
William Stainton Moses	1839– 92	one of the founders of the Society for Psychical Research
Davenport Brothers		
Ira Erastus	1839–1911	world-touring spirit cabinet séances
William Henry	1841–77	
Eusapia Palladino	1854–1918	the most famous physical medium
Leonora Piper, 'Mrs Piper'	1859–1950	the most famous direct voice medium
Edgar Cayce, 'The Sleeping Prophet'	1877–1945	psychic diagnoses of illness
Marthe Beraud, aka Eva Carrière	1886 – ?	first produced what was called 'ectoplasm'
Helen Duncan	1897–1956	convicted in 1944 under the Witchcraft Act of 1735
Doris Stokes	1920–87	first medium to play the London Palladium
Jane Roberts	1929–84	channelled the 'Seth Material'
J[udy] Z[ebra] Knight	1946 –	channel of the Lemurian 'Ramtha'

The Davenport Brothers, Ira Erastus Davenport (1839–1911) and William Henry Davenport (1841–77), claimed an earlier pedigree than the Fox sisters. Apparently the spirits had made their presence known in 1846 with a midnight cacophony of 'raps, thumps, loud noises, snaps, crackling noises'. Together with their younger sister Elizabeth they experimented in table-rapping, getting immediate results. Ira developed the gift of automatic writing. Soon all three were levitating and 'hundreds of respectable citizens of Buffalo are reported to have seen these occurrences'. At breakfast the cutlery and dishes would dance a jig. A lead pencil appeared to write with no human hand guiding it. Musical instruments floated in the air, playing themselves.[407]

Their professional career began in 1854, specializing in a 'spirit cabinet' style of séance. Securely tied up, they would be placed in a closed cabinet and spiritual wonders would ensue. One witness said 'hands were seen appearing at a small aperture [. . .] not only seen, but were felt'. When the cabinet was re-opened they would be seen to still be bound as securely as before. Several Harvard professors tested them in 1857, truss-ing the boys up in 500 feet of rope, sealing the knots with linen thread and seating a certain Professor Pierce between them before closing them all in the cabinet. Materializations were observed outside the cabinet. When it was re-opened some of the rope had wrapped itself around the hapless professor's neck. Dumbfounded, the professors decided not to publish their intended report.[408]

The brothers toured Europe in the mid-1860s, visiting first England then France with their 'Spiritualistic Manifestations'. After their first private performance at the Regent Street, London, residence of the then famous actor and playwright Dion Boucicault, a journalist for the *Morning Post* reported that

---

[407] Conan Doyle, vol. 1, pp. 218–19.
[408] Edward Dicey, 'The Davenport Brothers', *Macmillan's Magazine*, XI, November 1864 – April 1864, pp. 35–40; T. L. Nichols, *A Biography of the Brothers Davenport*, Saunder, Otley and Co., 1864, pp. 87–8; Inglis, p. 241.

there could be no 'presumption of fraud'. They were met with great fanfare in France. For their opening night they filled every seat at the Salle Herz in Paris at 25 francs a head for a two-part show of the 'Cabinet' and the 'Dark Séance'. But there was such a great hue and cry that after only forty-five minutes the police were called to clear the hall. The French magician Jean-Eugène Robert-Houdin thought them 'mere performers of juggling tricks', although he did not travel up to the capital to witness the debacle in person. They continued a zig-zag itinerary to Ireland, Germany, Belgium, Russia, Poland and Sweden before coming back to London and finally returning to America. William later died in Melbourne during their Australian tour in the 1870s. Sir Arthur Conan Doyle thought them 'the greatest mediums of their kind that the world has ever seen'. However, in his final years, Ira wrote cryptically to the escapologist Harry Houdini, saying 'We never *in public* affirmed our belief in Spiritualism'.[409]

---

[409] Conan Doyle, vol. 1, pp. 224, 230–2, 234; Jean-Eugène Robert-Houdin, *The Secrets of Stage Conjuring*, trans. Professor Hoffmann, Routledge, 1881, pp. 160–2, 168–70. Conan Doyle, vol. 1, pp. 234–5, questions the veracity of the statements Houdini reproduces as being from Ira Davenport.

Key Terms in Spiritualism

Apports	'Objects are brought from many miles distant, and tossed on the table. These are technically termed *apports*.' (Andrew Lang, 1894)
Control	'Used of the intelligence which purports to communicate messages which are written or uttered by the [. . .] medium.' (F. W. H. Myers, 1896)
Ectoplasm	'A supposedly psychic substance or materialisation which exudes from the medium's body.' (*Pears Cyclopaedia*, 1897)
Involuntary Utterance (later 'xenoglossy')	'Of which the speaker is himself incapable, is not the least noteworthy of the modes and evidences of spirit-intercourse.' (*The Spiritual Magazine*, 1860)
Luminous Phenomena	'Usually described as very brilliant, sometimes they appear as stars, or as balls of fire, at other times they shoot meteor-like through the apartment, or gleam over the walls; or appear as luminous currents circling round a particular centre.' (*The Spiritual Magazine*, 1860)
Medium	'A person through whom communication is deemed to be carried on between living men and spirits of the departed.' (F. W. H. Myers, 1896)
Pseudopods	'Psychic projections from the medium's body.' (E. E. Fournier D'Albe in Schrenck-Notzing, 1920)
Rapping	'A rap, clear, distinct, and free, as if made on, or within the table, by a piece of watch-spring.' (*Blackwood's Edinburgh Magazine*, 1853)
	'Sounds, like raps or detonations, are heard on the table, the chairs, the walls, or the floor, often varying in power and tone.' (*The Spiritual Magazine*, 1860)

Without apparent theology or dogma, only the séance or trance as its central rite, Spiritualism could take myriad forms as its followers chose. A religion to some, scientific inquiry to others, a vehicle for social justice or home entertainment for the rest.[410] Most, if not all, of its adherents couched what they did in Christian terms, even if they had 'Red Indian' spirit guides. The Spiritualists often described that what they did as a spiritual revolution, but it was simply a novel way to express the sentiments of Christianity. After all, Christianity taught that there was an afterlife, and the Bible made famous the necromancy of the Witch of Endor, demonstrating to the believer that our spirits lived on and could be called back to earth and communicated with. It did, however, take Protestantism one step further. If every man should be his own priest, then he could also be his own prophet, speaking to God without intermediaries and bringing back pearls of wisdom.

This was where the revolution lay. This was where the barricades went up, but it was not, ultimately, where the battle was fought – that would be between the mediums and the investigators, many of them distinguished men of science.

Making his report before the Congregational Association of New York and Brooklyn in 1853, Revd Charles Beecher saw two explanations for the phenomena of Spiritualism: the 'Pneumatic Theory' that the human spirit survived death, maintained its identity and could 'continue to act through some imponderable element'; and the 'Apneumatic Hypothesis' that the observed effects were psychological in nature, mediums being '*automatons*, moved by some power inherent in their own brains'. Author Samuel Byron Brittan commended Beecher for not taking the easy route of dismissing Spiritualism out of hand, which he characterized as typical of the clergy. Indeed, Beecher was forced to the conclusion that spirits of the deceased must be involved, but his early consideration of the psychological is notable and shows the sophistication of some of the researchers,

---

[410] Lehman, pp. 81–4, 88.

at least, at that time. In over 150 years, the debate has not advanced much beyond this impasse.[411]

A certain Monsieur Mannet, a French Bachelor of Letters, proposed to the *Scientific Review* that the marvellous phenomena of the séance were produced by the serving of tea spiked with a 'decoction of hemp-resin or haschish [*sic*]'. The editor of the *Scientific Review* said that he had tried it, in the interests of science of course, and could confirm its properties. *The Gentleman's Magazine*, however, pointed out that beverages were not always served at séances.[412]

The mystery of 'spirit-rapping' was claimed to have been solved almost as soon as it appeared. In 1854 a young German girl was holding a séance in Frankfurt am Main. Spirit-rappings were produced, a '*tap, tap*, by which questions were answered'. Dr Schiff sat forward in his seat: how did she make these noises? She sat apart, 'perfectly isolated', and made no perceptible movements. It seemed the usual mystery. Going home afterwards, an idea hit the doctor 'that the noise might be occasioned by straining the tendons and muscles'. We are all familiar with the sound of cracking knuckles, but this usually involves overt manipulation of the joint. Schiff experimented with several methods to find one that could produce the right sound whilst still being virtually undetectable. And he did:

By simply displacing the *peronæus longus* which passes behind the ankle up the leg; such displacing being effected by a scarcely perceptible change in the position of the foot, and being accompanied by a loudish snap.[413]

---

[411] Samuel Byron Brittan, A Review of Revd Charles Beecher's *Report Concerning the Spiritual*, Partridge and Brittan,1853, pp. 9–10; Charles Beecher, *A Review of the Spiritual Manifestations*, G. P. Putnam & Co., 1853.

[412] 'Notes and Incidents', *The Gentleman's Magazine*, June–November, 1868, p. 259.

[413] *Notes and Queries*, 10.244, 1 July 1854, p. 5, footnote.

Schiff practised the technique 'until he got to be a first-rate "medium"'. He presented a paper on his findings to the Académie des Sciences in Paris, 12 June 1854, to their 'gratification and amusement', and it was widely reported in medical journals at the time. Some years later Jobert de Lamballe made similar observations in the diagnosis of a patient with spontaneously occurring 'rapping' sounds. The parents of the patient, a fourteen-year-old girl, were convinced that the origin was supernatural, but Lamballe demonstrated that the sounds were made by involuntary spasms of the peronæus brevis. From this he applied his findings to 'spirit-rapping', declaring it to be a naturally produced phenomenon. Oddly, it had passed almost unnoticed that three medical doctors from the University of Buffalo had reached the same conclusions even earlier, in 1851, and after examining the Fox sisters themselves.[414]

Professor Austin Flint and his colleagues Drs C. B. Coventry and Charles A. Lee visited the sisters, apparently paying a dollar each. At first they were 'surprised and puzzled by the loudness of the sounds, the apparent evidences of non-instrumentality [. . .] and the different directions from which they seemed to emanate'. But as they watched the performance – with Leah 'conducting' and Maggie apparently the source – they became convinced that Maggie was making the sounds herself. They just could not figure out how. They knew, as we all do, that joints could make snapping noises. One of the doctors had once been consulted by a patient with loud popping sounds coming from a joint as he walked. Another accidentally met a man who said his wife could produce such mysterious sounds. She had kept him ignorant of the cause, 'in jest', but on the doctors' asking she revealed that it was her knee-joint. The possibility that something similar was the cause of the 'spirit-rapping' was therefore evident.[415]

---

[414] *Notes and Queries*, 10.244, 1 July 1854, p. 5, footnote; *The Dublin Hospital Gazette*, 15 August 1854, p. 224; 'Audible Knockings of the Muscles', *American Medical Gazette*, 10.10, October 1859, pp. 747–9.

[415] Austin Flint, 'On the Discovery of the Source of the "Rochester Knockings" and

They wrote to the *Commercial Advertiser* on 17 February 1851, exposing the sisters as charlatans. Their evidence: that noisy knee-joint. The sisters saw the letter and wrote back, somewhat indignantly. They were not 'willing to rest under the imputation of being imposters' and offered themselves to a 'proper and decent examination'. A challenge had been made. It was accepted.[416]

It was not a duel to be fought on the heath at dawn. The two parties met in the evening in a comfortably furnished room in Buffalo; the doctors and the sisters with some selected supporters. The sisters sat on a sofa together and, after a pause, the rappings were heard, loud and rapid. The doctors asked the 'spirits' if they would consent to the examination. They rapped in the affirmative. The sisters were removed from the sofa and arranged on chairs, legs extended, feet separated, heels resting on cushions and their toes 'elevated'. The doctors had predetermined that this posture should prevent any knee-joint clicking. They sat back in a semicircle round the sisters and waited. They waited for more than thirty minutes: 'but the "spirits", generally so noisy, were now dumb'. They re-arranged the sisters, putting them back on the sofa, Leah sitting normally at one end, Maggie with her legs stretched out. The doctors asked the 'spirits' to make their presence known. Still nothing was heard. They let Maggie sit normally on the sofa. Rapping was heard. When the doctors held the sisters' knees, no sounds were heard. They concluded that the sounds were coming from the knee-joint of Maggie. And they told the sisters as much, at which point

on Sounds Produced by the Movements of Joints and Tendons', *The Quarterly Journal of Psychological Medicine and Medical Jurisprudence*, 3.3, July 1869, pp. 417–46, which also reprints the original articles by Flint et al.: 'Discovery of the Source of the Rochester Knockings', *Buffalo Medical Journal*, 6, March 1851; 'Rochester Knockings', *Buffalo Medical Journal*, 6 April 1851; and 'Spirit-Rappings in the French Academy of Sciences', *Buffalo Medical Journal*, 10, September 1854. The fact that so many women were 'spirit-rappers' they attributed to the wearing of skirts, which inadvertently concealed the slight movements made.

[416] Flint, pp. 423–6.

Maggie began to 'weep hysterically' and the investigation was brought to a close.[417]

These revelations, however, had little immediate impact on the careers of the Fox sisters, or on anybody else, it seems. Indeed, Flint had recourse to write to the Académie des Sciences in 1854 after reading about Dr Schiff's discoveries, asserting his claim to have got there first, and then to the *Quarterly Journal of Psychology* in 1869, reminding its readers that he had already investigated and resolved the matter.

The keen-eyed Revd Hiram Mattison had seen a report of the investigation and published it in his 1853 book *Spirit Rapping Unveiled!* He could add more to the list: the Revd H. O. Sheldon had discovered the trick and could rap with the best of them on his toe-joint; and the testimony of witnesses at the trial of the teenage medium Almira Bezely for the murder of her brother stated that she had made the rapping with her foot. In 1854 John Netten Radcliffe published the confession of a Mrs Norman Culvers who claimed to have been taught how to crack her toe-joints by Maggie Fox herself. But again these disclosures barely had an effect on the movement's popularity.[418]

Readers of the *New York Herald* opened their papers on 24 September 1888 to read in bold letters: 'God has not ordered it. A celebrated medium says the spirits never return.' It was an announcement by Maggie Fox. 'I am going to expose the very root of corruption in this spiritualist ulcer,' she declared. It was not just simple fraud, but in some cases a cover for 'shameless goings on that vie with the secret Saturnalia of the Romans'.[419]

A few weeks later Rueben Davenport, correspondent for the *New York Herald*, published a complete account in his *The Death-Blow to Spiritualism* with the full blessing and signed statement to that effect of the Fox sisters themselves. Maggie

---

[417] Flint, pp. 426–8, 431.

[418] John Netten Radcliffe, *Fiends, Ghosts and Sprites: Including an Account of the Origin and Nature of Belief in the Supernatural*, R. Bentley, 1854, p. 139.

[419] Quoted in Rueben Briggs Davenport, *The Death-Blow to Spiritualism*, G. W. Dillingham Co., 1888, p. 51.

had already written to the *Herald* on 14 May 1888 denouncing Spiritualism: 'I call it a curse, for it is made use of as a covering for heartless persons like the Diss De Barrs, and the vilest miscreants make use of it to cloak their evil doings [. . .] and a snare to all who meddle with it'. She sailed from Britain to America, intending to reveal all about Spiritualism. A *Herald* journalist was granted an interview ahead of her planned lecture. He described her as 'a small magnetic woman of middle age, whose face bears the traces of much sorrow and of a world-wide experience', adding that she 'was the most famous of the celebrated trio of witches'.[420]

Maggie blamed her older sister Leah. It was she, she said, who had 'made me take up with it'. She blamed her drinking on Spiritualism, saying 'I would drown my remorse in wine'. And she blamed the decline of her career on herself: 'I was too honest to remain a "medium"'.[421]

Before Maggie made her exposure, the *Herald* sought out the opinions of other Spiritualists. From one anonymous medium, the paper printed her opinion that 'I don't believe she [Maggie] can expose any fraud'. She added that 'I have heard that the Fox sisters are dreadfully addicted to drink. I don't know how far it is true, but I wouldn't believe anything she might say in way of exposure.' She finished by hinting at some sort of blackmail: 'May be [*sic*] she's out of money and thinks the spiritualists ought to do something for her.' Henry J. Newton, President of the First Spiritualist Society in New York, called them 'silly pretended revelations'. He had been present at séances given by the Fox sisters themselves and was thoroughly convinced that they were genuine, in spite of what the sisters themselves might say.[422]

Katie, now Mrs Catherine Fox Jencken, arrived on 9 October from London on the steamship SS *Persian Monarch*, apparently

---

[420] Published 27 May 1888, reproduced in Davenport, pp. 30–1, and 32–3.
[421] Davenport, p. 35–6.
[422] Davenport, pp. 45–7.

unexpectedly and immediately declared her intention to stand beside her sister. She, too, blamed Leah.[423]

The Academy of Music in New York was booked for 21 October 1888. It was an ugly Neo-Classical blockhouse that had declined from the grand opera produced in its heyday to a venue for vaudeville. But its 4,000 seats were packed to hear 'The Curse of Spiritualism'. Katie sat in a box near the stage. Spiritualists in the audience heckled. Maggie stood in the glow of the footlights 'trembling with intense feeling'. The audience waited with bated breath as she began: [424]

> That I have been chiefly instrumental in perpetrating the fraud of Spiritualism upon a too confiding public, most of you doubtless know. The greatest sorrow of my life has been that this is true, and though it has come late in my day, I am now prepared to tell the truth, the whole truth and nothing but the truth – so help me God![425]

It sounded like she was on trial. She was. But the real court was her conscience. A four-legged wooden stool was placed in front of her. She removed her shoe and placed her right foot upon it. 'The entire house became breathlessly still,' reported the *New York World*. Several 'little short, sharp raps' rang out. Mr Splitfoot had arrived. Three medical doctors were called up to the stage from the audience. Maggie still had her foot on the stool. More rappings were heard. The doctors bent over her foot and examined it. They 'unhesitatingly agreed that the sounds were made by the action of the first joint of her large toe'.[426]

The *Herald* asked Katie about the earlier manifestations and the finding of bones in the cellar of their old house in Hydesville. 'All humbuggery;' she said, 'every bit of it.' And she denounced

---

[423] Davenport, pp. 54–5.
[424] Davenport, pp. 55, 75.
[425] Davenport, p. 75.
[426] Davenport, p. 77.

her sister Leah's published retelling of the story as 'nothing but falsehood'.[427]

Hydesville was named after Dr Hyde, not Mr, but here there was still something like a split personality at work: two 'innocent' girls and their Mr Splitfoot. Back in that humble cottage in Hydesville in 1848, right at the beginning, before any great fuss had been made about the 'rappings', little Katie had already explained the whole phenomenon: an April Fool's joke. But no one had paid much attention to her words. Forty years later Maggie confessed that it had all been a fraud with Katie looking on, silent. Flint et al., Schiff and Lamballe were all vindicated. The great procession of spirits had indeed been a mere popping of tendons and joints, or had it?

The confession should have been the end of Spiritualism, but it was not. The Fox sisters could only speak for themselves and a year after making it, Maggie retracted her confession and returned to the séance room. Dr Isaac Funk, co-founder of the publishing house Funk & Wagnalls, said of her at the time that 'for five dollars she would have denied her mother'. Within the next four years all three sisters – Leah, Maggie and Katie – would be dead.[428]

In 1904 it was reported in the *Boston Journal* that the skeleton of a man had been found in the 'Spook House' as the Foxes' former home had come to be known. Now in the possession of William H. Hyde, the house had already been thoroughly searched, but 'an almost entire human skeleton' was said to have been found by schoolchildren 'between the earth and crumbling cellar walls'. In 1905 Dr Mellen told her story to the Medico Legal Society of New York. She had treated Maggie in her last bedridden days in a tenement on Ninth Street. Mellen was clear that Maggie could not move hand nor foot at the time, there was neither a hiding place for an accomplice, and yet she had heard

---

[427] Davenport, pp. 57–8.

[428] Isaac K. Funk, *The Widow's Mite and Other Psychic Phenomena*, Funk & Wagnalls, 1904, p. 241; Lewis Spence, *Encyclopedia of Occultism and Parapsychology*, 2 vols, Kessinger, 2003, vol. 1, p. 349.

the knockings – on the wall, on the ceiling, on the floor. Not only were they heard, but they answered in response to questions, just as they had all those years ago in Hydesville. Dr Mellen told the society 'she was as incapable of cracking her toe-joints at this time as I was'. These proofs, if they were proofs, came too late for the Fox sisters.[429]

What was the truth: the confession or the retraction? The psychology of the mediums is complicated, as Derren Brown's famous television experiment 'Séance' showed. With a group of students he recreated all of the classic phenomena of Spiritualism without the participants' conscious knowledge of what they were doing. The fraud, if it is one, seems in some cases to be perpetrated on us by our unconscious. The so-called evidence has only raised many more questions, and the possible answers seem a long way from the more comforting thought that the human personality can survive death.[430]

With the religious manifestation of Spiritualism in steep decline after the 1920s – although the Spiritualist paper *Psychic News* lingered on until 2010 – it found itself reinvented. For the New Age it became 'channelling'. There was nothing new about it. Helene Petrovna Blavatsky had 'channelled' the Mahatmas and written about it at length in the two volumes of *The Secret Doctrine* published in 1888. John Ballou Newbrough (1828–91) had 'channelled' the angels for his automatic typing marathon called *Oahspe*.

With the manifestation of phenomena so closely studied, tested and often exposed as fraudulent, the mediums reduced their repertoire, falling back on the less evidential and therefore less testable form of indirect communication. Derek Acorah (1950–), amongst others, has taken this new stripped down mediumship onto television, most notably with Yvette Fielding's *Most Haunted* series, introducing a new generation to supposed spirit communication.

---

[429] *Boston Journal*, 23 November 1904, reproduced in Todd, pp. 59–60 from 'Truth Crushed to Earth will Rise Again', *Banner of Light*, 3 December 1904; Spence, p. 349.

[430] 'Derren Brown: Séance', first broadcast on Channel 4, 31 May 2004.

Unlike revealed religion, such as Christianity, the claims of Spiritualism could be directly tested. Given that its claims were so tremendous in their implications – proof of the afterlife would overturn the developing materialistic worldview of science – the tests it would be put under would be strenuous. The *ad hoc* committees that had investigated the Fox sisters became more organized. Psychical research, as it was called, developed as a new scientific discipline, even if science did not want to acknowledge it until it wore the more respectable academic robes of parapsychology.

It would not be the last time that it would be claimed that the spirits were knocking on the door to the world of the living. When she was in her early teens, Sophie Harris claimed to have communicated with the dead just like the Fox sisters, only more than 150 years later. Around the year 2007 whilst staying overnight at her grandmother's house – reputedly over a hundred years old – she had the feeling of being watched when she went upstairs to bed. The door would swing open and whoever, or whatever, it was would stand there watching her, or so she thought. An aunt and great-aunt began to feel the presence, too. About a year later, once more in the house, she heard a series of knocking sounds. When she spoke, the rhythm changed. She asked it to knock once for 'yes', twice for 'no'. Her first question was 'Is there someone there?' One knock – yes. 'Can you talk to me without knocking?' Two knocks. 'Do you mean me any harm?' One knock.[431]

---

[431] 'Experiences', *Paranormal*, 56, February 2011, p. 70.

8. Science

The messenger burst into the palace. The empire of Astyages, last king of Media, had fallen. Cyrus the Persian was on the warpath. In his marble hall, Croesus, King of Lydia (modern Turkey) pondered his next move. Astyages had been the husband of his sister in a marriage to cement their alliance. Now he had been deposed and there was no one standing between Cyrus and Lydia. He saw that he must act now, before Cyrus' power grew greater, but should he offer treaty or war? The oracles would know, but which among them could really see beyond the sight of man?[432]

He sent messengers to all the great centres of divination in the sixth century BCE: the oracles of Apollo at Delphi, of Abae in Phocia, of Dodona, of Amphiaraus, of Trophonius, of Branchidae in Milesia, and of Ammon in Libya. His messengers were instructed to keep an accurate reckoning of the time and to consult the oracles on the hundredth day, asking them to describe what Croesus, back in his capital of Sardis, was doing at that moment. The messengers returned, having carefully written down the answers they had received. In order to test them, Croesus had devised an unlikely activity. He had cut up a lamb and a tortoise and cooked them in a bronze pot covered by a bronze lid. Croesus examined the bundle of reports. At Delphi the Pythian priestess had replied:

---

[432] Herodotus, *The Histories*, Bk 1, Ch. 46–53, trans. A. D. Godley, Harvard University Press, 1920.

I know the number of the grains of sand and the extent of the sea,
And understand the mute and hear the voiceless.
The smell has come to my senses of a strong-shelled tortoise
Boiling in a cauldron together with a lamb's flesh,
Under which is bronze and over which is bronze[433]

He had found his oracle. He offered up sacrifices of animals, gold and other riches 'to win the favour of the Delphian god'. When asked what he should do about Cyrus, the oracle answered that 'if he should send an army against the Persians he would destroy a great empire'. Cyrus led his soldiers into battle. In a typically Greek twist, it was Croesus' own empire that he destroyed. Being captured, Cyrus burnt him to death and conquered Lydia.[434]

Croesus, known now for his legendary wealth, might also be regarded as the first to have tested the abilities of self-professed psychics. Like the oracles of the ancient world, the claims being made by the mediums of the industrial age were so extraordinary, so potentially revolutionary, that they demanded investigation. That the initial investigations of the Fox sisters – as recounted by the less than detached Leah – were positive was a major factor in their success. What seems inexplicable is that when they were exposed as frauds, and even after they had confessed as much, people still believed that they, and the other mediums using the same techniques, were genuine. This desire, this demand, to believe, even in the face of the evidence, was and still is cruelly abused. But the chance that there could be a germ of truth in all this chaff has strained the abilities of many extremely able individuals. Mesmerism and Spiritualism created psychical research. Psychical research, in turn, led to the

---

[433] Herodotus, Bk 1, Ch. 47.
[434] Herodotus, Bk 1, Ch. 86. In Ch. 87–8 Herodotus said that Apollo was believed to have extinguished the flames and that Cyrus afterwards made him an adviser, but historically it seems more likely that he was executed. See Stephanie West, 'Croesus' Second Reprieve and Other Tales of the Persian Court', *Classical Quarterly*, 53, 2003, pp. 416–37.

development of parapsychology as a scientific discipline. It was, as Nietzsche said, the magicians who created this hunger for forbidden powers.

Mesmerism

His patients had already arrived and were waiting. He could hear the pianist playing quietly in a side room. He liked the effect. The gentle background music made a nice counterpoint to the sometimes dramatic demonstrations. He pushed open the door into a dimly lit room; a few trimmed wicks flickered and reflected in the mirrors arranged round the walls. Exotic perfumes hung in the air like invisible genies. His patients were standing around the apparatus, a large covered wooden tub with long articulated rods hanging down from the top like spiders' legs. He had more patients than he could treat individually, hence the 'Magnetic Basin', Baquet or Paropothus, as he variously called it. They turned as one as he came in. His purple robe swirled about him as he flourished his magnetic wand; brown eyes, black and glittering in the lamplight. There were gasps of anticipation. 'Magnetized' water loaded with iron filings and ground glass swished against the sides of the oak tub, hidden in the darkness.[435]

'There is only one illness,' he told them, 'and only one cure.'[436] To many, Franz Anton Mesmer was not a scientist. He was a magician. To others he was their saviour.

Mesmer undoubtedly thought of himself as a scientist – after all, he had had scientific training. Born in the village of Iznang on the shores of Lake Constance, Swabia, in 1734, he went on to study medicine at the University of Vienna. In 1766 he argued

---

[435] Mesmer's theatrical style of treatment is well attested. See for example, *Enc. Para.*, p. 337. Other details from the Paris police 'Aufenthalts Karte' reproduced in 'Some Researches of Dr Justinus Kerner', *The Spiritual Magazine*, vol. VI, no. 10, 1 October 1865, p. 434, and p. 449; Lehman, p. 32. Description of the tub based on the sole surviving example now in the Musée d'Histoire de la Médecine et de la Pharmacie, Lyon, France, other varieties of construction can be found in illustrations and descriptions from the period.

[436] Quotation in Waterfield, p. 71, from Mesmer, *Memoir*, 1779, p. 79.

in his doctoral thesis 'On the Influence of the Planets on the Human Body' that a 'subtle fluid [. . .] pervades the universe, and associates all things together in mutual intercourse and harmony'. It was by no means a radical proposition for the times, nor original, much of it being lifted from the work of Richard Mead, but it sufficed to see him through his *viva*. With a doctorate under his belt, he began practising medicine in Vienna from about 1768. Shortly afterwards he married a wealthy widow, Maria Anna von Posch, in St Stephen's Cathedral with the Archbishop of Vienna, no less, presiding. He set up practice at 261 Landstrasse in the most fashionable quarter of town and became a patron of the arts – Wolfgang Amadeus Mozart premiered his first opera, *Bastien und Bastienne*, at Mesmer's home.[437]

Mesmer could have continued in such style, doling out the inefficacious treatments of his time to the wealthy of Vienna, but the ideas fired in his doctoral work drove him to search the subject deeper. His meeting with the Hungarian Jesuit Maximilian Hell in the early to mid 1770s was to prove the turning point. Hell was famous for curing the sick by placing magnetized steel plates on their bodies. Mesmer abandoned the bleeding, blistering and opiates of regular medicine. Using and further developing Hell's technique Mesmer effected many cures, theorizing on the existence of 'animal magnetism', that is, a magnetic force of biological, as opposed to non-organic, origin. When Mesmer said 'There is only one illness', he was referring to the disruption of the flow of the magnetic fluid; 'and only one cure' was, of course, what would later be called Mesmerism.[438]

---

[437] 'Fridericus Antonius Mesmer', 'De planetarum influxu in corpus humanum', Vindibonae, 1766; quoted in Inglis, p. 141; 'Some Researches . . .', *The Spiritual Magazine*, p. 438; Robin Waterfield, *Hidden Depths: The Story of Hypnosis*, Routledge, 2003, pp. 66–7; Judith Pintar and Steven J. Lynn, *Hypnosis: A Brief History*, Wiley-Blackwell, 2008, p. 13.

[438] *Enc. Para.*, pp. 336–7, gives 1774 for the meeting with Hell; 'Some Researches . . .', *The Spiritual Magazine*, p. 438, gives 1772; Waterfield, pp. 66–7; Pintar and Lynn, p. 14.

He made a tour of Hungary, Switzerland and southern Germany to promote his new ideas. In Bavaria in 1775 he was asked to investigate Father Johann Joseph Gassner (1727–79), a country priest and exorcist extraordinaire. Like Mesmer, Gassner was producing near miraculous cures of the sick, but his theoretical underpinning was theology rather than medicine, possession rather than magnetism. The sick in their thousands, and not a few who were simply curious, were flocking to Gassner and asking him to cast out their demons. Gassner's technique was deceptively simple. He had dispensed with the rigmarole of the official rite of exorcism and laid hands on patients as any faith healer might today. He would begin by identifying the nature of the disease by asking, in Latin: 'If there be anything preternatural about this disease, I order in the name of Jesus that it manifest itself immediately'. If convulsions or other symptoms followed, then Gassner took this as a sign that demons were behind the illness. He would then command the demon to demonstrate the illness in various parts of the sufferer's body. He could also produce emotions as diverse as grief, anger and even silliness. Now having the demon perform at his command, he would drive the spirit out through a toe or finger.[439]

Not surprisingly, Mesmer's conclusion was that Gassner was unconsciously using animal magnetism to produce his cures. But for Mesmer, who had taken over Hell's magnetized plates, here was a demonstration that the same cures could be produced without the plates at all. Mesmer's report to the Bavarian Prince-Elector Maximilian III upheld the Enlightenment in the face of this outbreak of the supernatural, supplanting the old spirits with new forms of energy. It was a triumph for Mesmer: he was elected a member of the Bavarian Academy of Sciences. For Gassner it was defeat. Both the Bavarian government and the

---

[439] Pintar and Lynn, p. 15; Waterfield, p. 73; Podmore, p. 27. For a detailed study see H. C. Erik Midelfort, *Exorcism and Enlightenment: Johann Joseph Gassner and the Demons of Eighteenth Century Germany*, Yale University Press, 2005.

Church banned his activities and his books. He died in obscurity four years later.[440]

Despite these early successes, controversy would hound Mesmer out of Vienna. The Royal Academy in Berlin rejected his therapy as 'destitute of foundation and unworthy [of] the slightest attention'.[441] A setback, but that was not the reason he had to leave. The young musician Maria Theresia von Paradis – the protégé of the Empress Maria Theresa, after whom she was named – sought out Mesmer to treat her illness in the mid to late 1770s. Blind from infancy, she believed that the Swabian wonder-worker would be able to cure her. She was then about eighteen years old and her swollen and disfigured eye-sockets already bore witness to more brutal and less successful treatments. With her parents' blessing, she even moved in to Mesmer's house. It is reported that Mesmer was able to alleviate her condition. However, in consequence her musical abilities suffered and the pension from the empress (settled on her because of her blindness) was under threat. When her father came to remove her, she refused. There was a scene. Her father drew his sword. Her mother knocked the girl's head against a wall. She was, at last, dragged off. Rumour-mongers whispered that she had been receiving more than medical treatment. She suffered a relapse and Mesmer's enemies condemned his treatment as a fraud. Mesmer fell into a deep depression. Deciding to abandon his medical practice, his grand estate and his wife, he packed his equipment and left for Paris.[442]

It was as if Paris had been waiting for him. Alchemy, phrenology, and other occult sciences, were all the rage. As Henriette Louise von Waldner, Baroness d'Oberkirch, observed: 'It is

---

[440] Pintar and Lynn, p. 16; Waterfield, p. 74; Alan Gauld, *A History of Hypnotism*, Cambridge University Press, 1995, p. 3.

[441] Benjamin Franklin, *Animal Magnetism: Report of Dr Franklin and Other Commissioners, Charged by the King of France with the Examination of the Animal Magnetism as Practised at Paris*, H. Perkins, 1837, p. 47.

[442] Lehman, p. 33; Pintar and Lynn, pp. 17–18. Variations of Paradis' name include Marie-Thérèse, Paradies and Paradise.

certain that Rosicrucians, adepts, prophets and all that goes with them, were never so numerous or so much listened to'. This had been the Paris of the Comte de Saint-Germain and would yet be the Paris of Cagliostro, as much as it was of the Encyclopedists. Mesmer expected a ready audience. He moved into the Hôtel Bouret on the Place Louis-le-grand, today the Place Vendôme where one will find the Ritz Paris. The Baroness d'Oberkirch visited him there, reporting that 'his apartments were crowded from morning to night'. He had a letter of intro-duction to the Austrian ambassador, Count Florimund Merci-Argenteau. He made overtures to the Académie Royale des Sciences and the Société Royale de Médecine. Both of them snubbed him. Not everyone in Paris was ready to embrace his new ideas. Perhaps they did not like his German accent or Viennese connections.[443]

Mesmer retreated to the outlying village of Créteil and concentrated on building up a practice. His treatments became more theatrical. His patient list grew. As many as 200 people a day were seeking his help. He invented the 'baquet' in order to cope with them all. He moved back to Paris, taking a large prop-erty on the rue Coq Héron. Something like mass hysteria seemed to be sweeping the French capital. The Baroness d'Oberkirch noted that 'Magnetism became quite the fashion'. The novelist Stefan Zweig later called it Mesmeromania. A rumour that a tree in the Bois de Boulogne had been 'magnet-ized' caused Parisians in their hundreds to crowd round it, trying to get close enough to hug it and be cured. He found eager and in many cases influential students, such as Charles d'Eslon, a Doctor Regent of the Faculty of Paris and physician to the King's brother, the Comte d'Artois, and the wealthy

---

[443] Henrietta Louisa von Waldner, Baronne d'Oberkirch, *Memoirs of the Baron-ess d'Oberkirch*, 3 vols, Colburn and Co., 1852, vol. 2, p. 280; *Enc. Para.*, p. 337; Pintar and Lynn, pp. 18, 20; Waterfield, pp. 78–80; Frank Podmore, *Mesmerism and Christian Science: A Short History of Mental Healing*, George W. Jacobs & Co., 1909, pp. 4–5, 7; Gauld, p. 4. See also Mesmer, *Mémoire sur la Découverte du Magnétisme Animal*, 1779.

landowner the Marquis de Puységur. He won the sympathy of Queen Marie Antoinette and through her would even be offered a generous pension, which he ungraciously rebuffed. He formed a semi-Masonic secret society called the 'Society of Universal Harmony' to regulate the teaching and dissemination of his therapeutic method. By the mid 1780s there were an estimated 6,000 unsanctioned mesmerists operating in the Paris area. Between them Mesmer and d'Eslon were thought to have already treated some 8,000 patients. The Académie Royale des Sciences began to take notice.[444]

In 1784 a royal commission was established to investigate Mesmerism. It included the leading lights of the Académie Royale des Sciences and the University of Paris' Faculty of Medicine, such as the famous chemist Antoine-Laurent Lavoisier, Joseph Ignace Guillotin, eponymous inventor of the guillotine, and the American ambassador Benjamin Franklin. However, instead of Mesmer himself, they chose to observe his student d'Elson at work. They were not concerned whether or not Mesmerism worked, but specifically set out to determine whether or not the practice proved that there was a universal fluid as Mesmer claimed.

Franklin and the others watched d'Eslon arrange his patients round the baquet so that the articulated rods could be applied to the affected parts of their bodies. They could also be roped together; sometimes holding hands was sufficient. As well as the physician, a number of assistants brandished iron rods, about 10 to 12 inches in length, supposedly conductors of the magnetic force. The commission observed that some patients remained calm, others coughed or spat, complaining of mild pain, whilst a third group underwent violent and prolonged convulsions. 'Nothing can be more astonishing than these convulsions': they appeared to be contagious, could last up to three hours and put the victim entirely under the power of the mesmerist. It was

[444] D'Oberkirch, ibid.; Christopher Turner, 'Mesmeromania, or, the Tale of the Tub', *Cabinet*, 21, Spring 2006, n.p.; Waterfield, pp. 84, 86.

Mesmer's practice to make a separate, padded *Salle des Crises* available to receive the more violent convulsives. The commission described several cases in the report:[445]

Dame P—

'[. . .] the patient began to feel a nervous shuddering; she had then successively a pain in the back of her head, in her arms, a creeping in her hands, that was her expression, she grew stiff, struck her hands violently together, rose from the seat, stamped with her feet [. . .]'[446]

Mademoiselle B—

'[. . .] she felt a sensation of dejection and suffocation; to these succeeded an interrupted hiccup, a chattering of the teeth, a contraction of the throat, she complained of a pain in the loins; now and then she struck her foot with extreme quickness on the floor; afterwards she stretched her arms behind her, twisting them extremely [. . .]'[447]

The commission had brought an 'electrometer' and a 'needle of iron'. They found that the baquet had neither an electrical current nor a magnetic field. They could not see it, smell it nor feel it as d'Eslon said they would be able. None of the commission who underwent the treatment felt any better after it; if anything, some reported feeling worse. They decided 'to make experiments upon persons really diseased' and chose seven 'out of the lower class'. Again most felt nothing, but three experienced something, although what exactly the committee failed to discover. There was no 'physical agent', they said, capable of producing the supposed effects of Mesmerism. Furthermore, magnetism was least noted in those 'who have submitted to it with any degree of incredulity' and apparent only in those with 'an imagination more easily excited'.[448]

---

[445] Franklin, pp. 10–24.
[446] Franklin, p. 29.
[447] Franklin, p. 34.
[448] Franklin, pp. 10–24.

They concluded that universal magnetic fluid was 'absolutely destitute of proof' and 'that the imagination is the true cause of the effects attributed to the magnetism'. They were right. Mesmer himself had almost reached the same conclusion. 'It cannot be demonstrated,' he told the commission, 'that either the physician or the medicine causes the recovery of the patient.' D'Eslon had come closer: animal magnetism, he told the commission as it gathered in Franklin's house, 'might be no other than the imagination itself, whose power is as extensive as it is little known'.[449]

Despite the credentials of the commission, it was not very scientific. They went about their investigation in an *ad hoc* manner. They readily explained away observed effects and relied for a great part of their evidence upon the experiments of Dr Jumelin, a practising doctor but an untrained mesmerist with a connection to the university. They went so far as to declare Mesmerism dangerous, although they had no proof to that effect. It would not pass muster today, but the commission's report destroyed Mesmer. Within weeks of publication, 20,000 copies had been sold. The Public Ministry were a hair's breadth from outlawing magnetism. The Académie had every practitioner struck off the register, the well-connected d'Eslon included. Criticism and ridicule came from every corner: from the popular stage as much as from academia. He was savagely satirized in the plays of Pierre-Yves Barré and Jean-Baptiste Radet. To compound matters, von Paradis was in town and Mesmer unwisely attended the concert. It was clear to everyone that she was as blind as ever. A French cartoon, *Le Magnétisme dévoilé* of 1784, showed a scene like a Witches' Sabbath: Franklin brandishing his report as Mesmer escapes on a broomstick, leaving a young woman – von Paradis? – blindfold and *déshabillé*, in a state of partial undress.[450]

---

[449] Franklin, pp. 33, 41, 43 – Franklin notes that d'Eslon had made a similar remark as early as 1780; Pintar and Lynn, p. 21; Inglis, p. 143.

[450] Franklin, p. 42; Waterfield, pp. 92–3; Turner, n.p.

Mesmer disappeared. He left Paris without telling even his closest disciples his plans. For the next twenty years some few hints of his existence are scattered across Europe. He died of a stroke in 1815 in a village not far from Iznang.[451]

Away from the scandal and intrigue of the capital, sequestered at his large estate in Buzancy, near Soissons, Armand-Marie-Jacques de Chastenet, Marquis de Puységur, was on leave from the army and finding himself at a loose end he decided to try out Mesmerism on his tenants. It was early 1784 and Mesmer had yet to fall. His brothers had talked him into joining the Society of Universal Harmony and for his 100 louis d'or subscription he had been given some lessons in the new therapy.[452]

Victor Race, a twenty-three-year-old shepherd confined to bed with fever and inflammation of the lungs (*fluxion de poitrine*), was one of his first subjects. Puységur made the mesmeric passes, but instead of becoming violently convulsed, Race appeared to fall asleep. Strangely, even asleep he could still answer his master's questions. He could get up and walk about. He even appeared to have a different personality. Gone was the dull shepherd; in his place was someone of intelligence who spoke about the other self in the third person. Puységur thought it was the 'perfect crisis', but adjusting his terminology he called the state 'mesmeric somnabulism' or 'magnetic sleep'. He was later able to get the mesmerized Race to do things simply by silently willing them. Even more surprisingly, Race could diagnose his own illness and prescribe treatments for it, and not just for his own illness. Others performed similarly. They even developed more paranormal powers of clairvoyance (in both its original French sense of seeing clearly and its later supernatural sense) and prophecy.[453]

---

[451] Pintar and Lynn, p. 22; Waterfield, p. 100.

[452] Pintar and Lynn, p. 23, give 1784; Waterfield, p. 105, gives 1783; Podmore, p. 71, gives 1784. See A. M. J. Chastenet de Puységur, *Mémoires pour Servir a l'Histoire et a l'Etablissement du Magnétisme Animal*, n.p., 1784, and *Du Magnétisme Animal, Consideré dans ces Rapports avec Diverses Branches de la Physique Générale*, Desenne, 1807.

[453] Pintar and Lynn, pp. 23–4; Waterfield, pp. 105–8, 112; Podmore, pp. 72–4;

The Revolution put an end to further experiments. The mesmeric societies that had spread throughout France were disbanded. Puységur had set up his own society to teach his technique and by 1789 had over 200 members. This, too, was dissolved. Puységur spent some years in prison, but escaped the upheaval with his life and, in time, would return to Mesmerism. Many of those who had sat on the commission would not be so lucky.[454]

Ultimately, what was the difference between Gassner and Mesmer, except one of terminology? Exorcism and magnetism, spirits and 'subtle fluids' were simply names for unknown quantities. Mesmer had vanquished exorcism with his 'science', but science had ultimately claimed him, too. Competing interpretations of the paranormal had been trounced by the sceptics. His therapy had brought relief to hundreds of sufferers of diverse disorders, but the grey eminences had swept all that aside in defence of their ivory towers. Mesmer had laid the foundation for his disciple Puységur's discovery of 'magnetic somnambulism' and what Scotsman James Braid would later call 'hypnotism', a technique so powerful that patients might go under the knife with no more than words for an anaesthetic. He had opened a door on inexplicable extra-sensory perceptions, but, like the poet Shelley's Ozymandias, whose shattered statue lies half-buried in the desert sands, only a fragment of Mesmer's reputation remains: one sole surviving 'baquet' in the Musée d'Histoire de la Médecine et de la Pharmacie, Lyon, France.[455]

Sean O'Donnell, 'Science and Psi: A Largely Temporal Phenomenon?', *Paranormal Review*, 33, January 2005, p. 29.

[454] Pintar and Lynn, p. 27; Waterfield, p. 119; Podmore, p. 85.

[455] For further reading see Adam Crabtree, *Animal Magnetism, Early Hypnotism, and Psychical Research, 1766 to 1926: An Annotated Bibliography*, Kraus International Publications, 1988. 'Mesmerism' was also used successfully in place of anaesthetic, for example, by the Scottish surgeon James Esdaile from 1845, see Pintar and Lynn, p. 41, or Gauld, p. 221.

Psychical Research

> A human Skull! I bought it passing cheap,
> No doubt 'twas dearer to its first employer!
> I thought mortality did well to keep
> Some mute memento of the Old Destroyer.
> – Frederick Locker, *London Lyrics*, 1881

It was a London winter, wet and mild under leaden skies. Jaundiced and grey winter fogs crawled along the Thames. In Finchley, far from the polluted miasma, a balding professor with a neatly clipped beard was walking down Hendon Lane to the Villa Rosa, home of a well-known journalist. The professor, William Fletcher Barrett (1844–1925), lectured on physics at the new Royal College of Science for Ireland in Dublin and would later be knighted. The journalist, Edmund Dawson Rogers (1823–1910), had the look of a country parson about him: thin hair brushed back and left to grow over the collar; a long, straggling beard, square-cut, hung down like a napkin across his neck, a bright light shone in his eyes behind the polished glass of small oval spectacles. He had founded the National Press Agency and was then still managing it. He had a reputation for 'blunt frankness' but offset it with an engaging good humour. The professor would later be characterized as 'vain and querulous'; he was undoubtedly ambitious. But the two did not meet to discuss physics, the end of the First Boer War, or the rise of the Muslim extremist known as the Mahdi in Sudan. They met to talk about Death and his imminent redundancy.[456]

In flickering candlelight, Rogers had seen Daniel Dunglas Home give a séance in London with raps, table levitations and

---

[456] Edmund Dawson Rogers, *The Life and Experiences of Edmund Dawson Rogers, Spiritualist and Journalist*, Office of 'Light', 1911, pp. 5, 43; Fraser Nicol, 'The Founders of the SPR', *Proceedings of the Society of Psychical Research*, 55, March 1972, pp. 341–2. On the fog: Max Schlesinger, *Saunterings In and About London*, N. Cooke, 1853, p. 84. See Alan Gauld, *The Founders of Psychical Research*, Schocken, 1968.

disembodied accordion playing. Across the country people were falling into mesmeric trances and exhibiting clairvoyance, talking to the dead in séances, or hunting real ghosts down to their lairs for fun. Mesmerism had reached Britain by the 1830s. It was widely spread when Spiritualism joined the scene in the 1850s. The publication of Catherine Crowe's *Night-Side of Nature* in 1848 had kindled a popular interest in apparitions and related subjects. Cambridge University had its 'Ghost Society' (1851) and Oxford its 'Phasmatological Society' (1879); and The Ghost Club was founded in London in 1862, tracing its beginnings to Trinity College, Cambridge, in the 1850s. Although Sir William Crookes had abandoned psychical research in the face of scandal and the hostility of his peers, there was still a desire to investigate these phenomena more exactly.[457]

Barrett and Rogers sat up late into the night as the professor recounted his paranormal experiences. Since reading a paper on thought-transference to the British Association at Glasgow in 1876, Barrett had been pushing for the establishment of a committee to examine the field in more depth. It was, claimed Rogers, he who suggested that a society be set up 'to attract some of the best minds' to the subject.[458]

Scientists and Spiritualists came together on 6 January 1882 to discuss what could be done. Rogers had invited them to the headquarters of the British National Association of Spiritualists at 38 Great Russell Street, opposite the British Museum, and Barrett presided. The scene of ghost-haunted séances since 1875, it is now a fish and chip shop. Joining them were Frederic W. H. Myers

---

[457] Gordon Stein (ed.), *The Encyclopedia of the Paranormal*, Prometheus Books, 1996, p. 707, incorrectly gives 'Phantasmological'; Rogers, pp. 35–6; Sir Charles Oman, 'The Old Oxford Phasmatological Society', *Journal of the Society of Psychical Research*, 33, March–April 1946, pp. 208–12; Alan Murdie, 'A Very Brief History of the Ghost Club', www.ghostclub.org.uk, 2009, accessed 16 December 2010. The Cambridge group is also sometimes referred to as the Cambridge Ghost Club, as by Nandor Fodor, *Encyclopedia of Psychic Science*, Arthurs Press, 1934.

[458] Rogers, p. 46.

(1843–1901), MA, a former Fellow of Trinity College, Cambridge, Edmund Gurney (1847–88), MA, another former Fellow of Trinity, and the sceptical but vigorous researcher Frank Podmore (1856–1910), a civil servant. They decided to form the Society for Psychical Research (SPR) and persuaded Henry Sidgwick (1838–1900) to be their first president. Sidgwick was another Trinity man, a former member of the Cambridge Ghost Society and shortly to become professor of moral philosophy at Cambridge University. The SPR was formally constituted on 20 February 1882. The society's stated goal was 'to investigate that large body of debatable phenomena designated by such terms as mesmeric, psychical and spiritualistic', expressly 'without prejudice or prepossession of any kind'. By the end of the year they had 150 members who shared these aims.[459]

They took rooms at 14 Dean's Yard, around the corner from Westminster Abbey in London, then the home of SPR member Dr William H. Stone, Fellow of the Royal College of Surgeons and physician to the Clergy Mutual Assurance Society. Sidgwick donated 150 books on psychical research to begin their library, with the other founding members adding more. A special dark room and powerful electro-magnet were installed for experiments. Their accounts to the year end showed a then handsome figure of £216 and 15 shillings.[460]

Its membership never exceeding a 1,000 in the Victorian period, it nonetheless became something of a national institution. Serving Prime Minister William Gladstone, Alfred, Lord Tennyson, John Ruskin, the future Prime Minister (1902–5) Arthur Balfour, Lord Rayleigh and others, all lent their support; the Revd Charles Lutwidge Dodgson, better known by his

---

[459] *Enc. Para.*, p. 708; 'Objects of the Society', *Proceedings of the Society for Psychical Research*, 1, 1882, pp. 3–6; Janet Oppenheim, *The Other World: Spiritualism and Psychical Research in England, 1850–1914*, Cambridge University Press, 1988, p. 57; Roger Luckhurst, *The Invention of Telepathy, 1870–1901*, Oxford University Press, 2002, p. 51; Peter Hallson, 'The Birth of the SPR', *Paranormal Review*, July 2002, pp. 3–5; Nicol, p. 344.

[460] 'Anniversary Meeting', *Proceedings of the Society for Psychical Research*, 1, 1883, pp. 158–60; *Debrett's Peerage*, Dean & Son, 1876, p. 16.

pen-name Lewis Carroll was a member, as was Robert Louis Stevenson. Barrett travelled to the USA and instituted an American Society for Psychical Research, founded in Boston in January 1885, with the astronomer Simon Newcomb as its first president and the famous psychologist William James (1842–1910) as its most notable member. Even with such august members and supporters, the SPR still met with as much sceptical hostility from other scientists, medical doctors and academicians as anyone studying the field today.[461]

The formation of the SPR would, nevertheless, herald a 'golden age' of psychical research. There was a Committee on Thought-Reading, a Committee on Haunted Houses, a Committee on Mesmerism, a Committee on Spontaneous Experiences, a Committee on Physical Phenomena, a Literary Committee, and the Reichenbach Committee on the perception of 'self-luminous' substances as described by the Baron Karl von Reichenbach.[462] Despite the professors on the council and the great and the good among its supporters, most of the spade work would be done by amateurs, albeit Victorian amateurs in the best tradition deserving of that name. From its beginning up until the turn of the century, the society's efforts took three main directions: telepathy, then called thought-reading or 'thought-transference' until Myers coined the new term; what they termed 'hallucinations'; and mediums. The sea-faring nation that had become the world-straddling British Empire was now also a soul-faring one, taking that empire further than anyone had before, beyond the prison of the body, beyond the veil of death.[463]

The first committee to make its report was that on thought-reading. An article published in *Nature* the year before had already dismissed the whole subject as 'so puerile a hypothesis'. On 17 July the society gathered in Willis's Rooms, otherwise

---

[461] *Enc. Para.*, pp. 582, 708; 'First Report on Thought-Reading', *Proceedings of the Society for Psychical Research*, 1, 1882, p. 13, and 1883, pp. 322, 326; Nicol, p. 350.

[462] See *Proceedings of the Society for Psychical Research*, 1, 1882–3.

[463] *Enc. Para.*, pp. 708–9; Nicol, p. 350.

known as Almack's – a suite of assembly rooms on King Street, St James's, that had been famous for its grand balls and concerts – to hear the case for the opposition.[464]

A Revd A. M. Creery of Buxton, Derbyshire, described as 'clergyman of unblemished character', had discovered that four of his five children, all girls, had the apparent ability to read thoughts. Barrett, Gurney and Myers duly arrived on the scene. Over six days in April 1882 they made 382 trials of guessing objects, cards, numbers and fictitious names with three of the children: Alice, Maud and Mary. They took precautions against such things as 'involuntary actions', unconscious lip movement and so on, by having the child wait outside the room when the item was chosen and having her look to the floor when she came in. They ruled out deception and collusion, since they were obviously not cheating themselves. Only chance remained. They calculated that the average number of successes by an 'ordinary guesser' would be 7.33. The children got 127 right on the first guess. Sometimes they were allowed subsequent guesses, bringing the number of 'hits' to 202. Calculating the odds on making eight consecutive successful guesses with the cards, they reckoned they were over 142 million to one. The odds for eight consecutive successful guesses with names they thought were 'something incalculably greater'. They felt they were safe to rule out coincidence.[465]

It seemed like real proof, but the girls' ability began to decline and Gurney, in later tests, caught them cheating by signalling to each other. The reverend, then a Corresponding Member of the SPR, wrote to the society expressing his 'intense pain' at the

[464] William Fletcher Barrett, Edmund Gurney and Frederic W. H. Myers, 'First Report of the Committee on Thought-Reading', *Proceedings of the Society for Psychical Research*, 1, 1882, p. 34; George Romanes, 'Thought-Reading', *Nature*, 23 June 1881; Peter Cunningham, *Hand-Book of London*, 2nd ed., John Murray, 1850, p. 10.

[465] Barrett, Gurney and Myers, pp. 20–7. An earlier series of trials had been made, see Balfour Stewart, 'Note on Thought-Reading', *Proceedings of the Society for Psychical Research*, 1, 1882, pp. 35–42, and A. M. Creery, 'Note on Thought-Reading', in the same issue, pp. 43–6.

revelations and assured them that he did not believe that such subterfuges had been used in the earlier experiments. It made no difference: the evidence was tainted; the proof had vanished like morning mist.[466]

The work on hallucinations began by collecting first-hand accounts from those who had experienced, whilst awake, sober, sane and not suffering from fever, a hallucination – a 'phantasm' as they also called it – of a living thing (human or animal), sounds produced by it, or an emotional awareness of it. Naturally, some of these experiences were simply hallucinations, but they found a number of cases that appeared to be something more. These they called 'veridical'. Such cases included 'crisis apparitions' when someone experiences something uniquely related to a person (appearance, voice) they know at a time when that person undergoes a crisis, very often death; 'collective percipience' (mass hallucination) when more than one person experiences the same phenomenon; and accounts of what we would generally term hauntings, the experience repeated amongst different people at different times of encountering the same thing at the same place.

In 1886 Gurney, Myers and Podmore published the results of their labours in the two-volume, 1,400-page *Phantasms of the Living*. It made *The Times* on the day it was published, 30 October. In all, 701 cases were discussed, of which 352 'phantasmal' experiences were classified as high-quality evidence. Building on their work on 'thought-transference', Gurney theorized that crisis apparitions were mental projections produced by the percipient after becoming telepathically aware of the crisis being experienced by the other. Work continued after

---

[466] The cheating was first brought to notice in an editorial note, *Journal of the Society of Psychical Research*, 3, October 1887, p. 164. A. M. Creery, letter to the Editor, *Journal of the Society of Psychical Research*, 3, November 1887, pp. 175–6. Edmund Gurney, 'Note Relating to Some of the Published Experiments in Thought-Transference', *Proceedings of the Society for Psychical Research*, 5, 1888, pp. 269–70. See the discussion of this case in Matthew Colborn, 'The Decline Effect in Spontaneous and Experimental Psychical Research', *Journal of the Society of Psychical Research*, 71, 2007, p. 2.

Gurney's untimely death two years later, culminating in the monumental 'Census of Hallucinations'. Completed in 1894, the census had surveyed 17,000 people on their experiences of hallucinations, including 'phantasms of the dead'. With all this evidence to work with, Sidgwick and the others determined that crisis apparitions could not be explained away: 'Between deaths and apparitions of the dying-person a connexion exists which is not due to chance alone. This we hold as a proved fact'.[467]

With most of the mediums it was the, by now, old familiar story: lies, deceit and disappointment. The 'physical mediums' – those claiming to be able to produce materializations from the spirit world – were the worst. The 'mental' mediums – those claiming to be in contact with the spirits – were less often detected in fraud. Among them, Leonora Piper is thought to have presented the best evidence for the spirit world; Helena Petrovna Blavatsky and William Eglington, the worst.[468]

Discovered by William James in America in 1885, Leonora Evelina Piper, née Simonds (1859–1950), was investigated on and off for the better part of thirty years. She was born in Nashua, New Hampshire, in 1859. At 22 she married a Boston clerk, William J. Piper. Some time in her mid-twenties, whilst visiting the blind medium J. E. Cocke, she spontaneously went into a trance and a supposed spirit, an Indian girl with the bizarre name of Chlorine, began speaking through her. In time Martin Luther, Commodore Cornelius Vanderbilt, Longfellow, George Washington, Abraham Lincoln, Johann Sebastian Bach, Julius Caesar, even Richard Hodgson and Myers after their deaths, and others, would all be claimed to have spoken through her.[469]

She became a professional medium performing as 'Mrs Piper'. Consequently, the American Society was obliged to

---

[467] *Enc. Para.*, p. 709; Henry Sidgwick, et al., 'Report on the Census of Hallucinations', *Proceedings of the Society for Psychical Research*, 10, 1894, p. 394; Nicol, pp. 353–5.

[468] *Enc. Para.*, p. 709.

[469] *Enc. Para.*, p. 535; Nicol, p. 362.

hand over $10 a sitting: she appears as the very thinly veiled 'Mrs P' in their records. William James learnt of her through the glowing recommendation of his mother-in-law. He and his wife Alice began attending séances in 1885. Alice immediately fell under her spell. James, too, would later pronounce:[470]

> Taking everything that I know of Mrs P into account, the result is to make me feel as absolutely certain as I am of any personal fact in the world that she knows things in her trances which she cannot possibly have heard in her waking state.

For all his reputation, William James' approach was lackadaisical, as he was compelled to concede. He took no notes. He made no tests. He just sat there. His opinion is just that: unverifiable hearsay. Piper was, however, keenly scrutinized by the British. Whilst still in America, Hodgson had her followed by private investigators. When she arrived in Britain in 1889, Oliver Lodge 'overhauled the whole of her luggage' and, with Myers, inspected her letters, but only with her permission did they read them. She was also lodged in members' houses or other chosen locations during her stay in order to provide better opportunities for surveillance and control. The first séance took place on 30 November 1889 at Myers' house in Cambridge. Myers sat behind a curtain to take notes whilst Lodge watched Piper's performance:[471]

> Mrs Piper sat still, leaning forward in her chair, and holding my hands. For some time she could not go off, but at last she said, 'Oh, I am going,' the clock happened to strike one (for a half hour) and she twitched convulsively, ejaculated 'don't,'

---

[470] William James, 'Certain Phenomena of Trance: (5) Part III', *Proceedings of the Society for Psychical Research*, 6, 1890, p. 651.

[471] Nicol, p. 351; James, p. 651; Frederic W. H. Myers, Introduction to 'A Record of Observations of Certain Phenomena of Trance', *Proceedings of the Society for Psychical Research*, 6, 1890, pp. 438–9; Oliver Lodge, 'Account of Sittings with Mrs. Piper. Formal Report', *Proceedings of the Society for Psychical Research*, 6, 1890, pp. 446–7.

and went into apparent epilepsy [. . .] Gradually she became
quiet, and still holding my right hand, cleared her throat in a
male voice, and with distinctly altered and hardened features,
eyes closed and unused the whole time.[472]

After his detectives failed to find evidence of fraud, Hodgson
allowed himself to believe in the sincerity of her mediumship.
Lodge made the cautious assessment that 'much of the information she possesses in the trance state is not acquired by
ordinary commonplace methods', but was certain that she was
'utterly beyond and above suspicion'. Nonetheless, he attributed the source, not to spirits, but to secondary consciousnesses
and trance personalities receiving information telepathically. He
glibly disposed of muscle-reading and 'unconscious-indication'.
Myers did not like 'trance-utterances' and for a good reason,
'since real and pretended trance-utterances have notoriously
been the vehicle of much conscious and unconscious fraud'.
But even Myers had to admit that Piper's 'utterances show that
knowledge has been acquired by some intelligence in some
supernormal fashion'. Even so, he was aware that Piper's trance
personality 'Dr Phinuit' frequently fished for information and,
for a spirit who claimed to be a French doctor, knew precious
little of French or medicine.[473]

On 20 October 1901 Piper shocked her followers with a two-
and-a-half page article in the *New York Herald* disavowing her
spiritual powers. Under the headline 'I Am No Telephone to the
Spirit World', Piper announced that she was retiring from mediumship with the bombshell that 'I must truthfully say that I do
not believe that spirits of the dead have spoken through me'.
She did not, in fact, retire. There would be other séances and
other investigations. She lived out her last years in Boston, dying
in 1950 at the age of 91.[474]

[472] Lodge, p. 444.
[473] Lodge, pp. 443, 447–9, 451; Myers, pp. 430, 440; James, p. 655.
[474] *Enc. Para.*, pp. 537–8.

Helene Petrovna Blavatsky (1831–91) – 'Madame Blavatsky' – is still a name to conjure with in occult circles. Her organization, the Theosophical Society, is still going strong. In the nineteenth century her reputation was enormous and she was making bold paranormal claims. The SPR felt duty bound to investigate. In 1884 the council appointed a committee and the committee sent Hodgson off to India after the evidence. It would result in what Fraser Nicol has called 'the most sensational report on physical phenomena ever published by the SPR'. Often called the Hodgson Report, the committee concluded that Blavatsky was not, as she claimed, 'the mouthpiece of hidden seers', but 'one of the most accomplished, ingenious, and interesting imposters in history'. Even before the investigation, she had already confessed earlier indiscretions to Alexander Aksakof (1832–1903). Much of what she later passed off as messages from Koot Hoomi and other discarnate 'Mahatmas' was plagiarized from other works – something that was noticed by at least one author himself – and the rest was what Dr Theodore Besterman (1904–76), investigating officer for the SPR from 1927 to 1935, would memorably call 'muddled rubbish'.[475]

In 1886 the most famous medium in the world was William Eglington (1857–1933). He had produced apports out of thin air, manifested physically solid spirits, even levitated himself to the ceiling, but he was particularly famed for his slate-writing in broad daylight. He was investigated by Sidgwick's wife Eleanor Mildred, an able researcher in her own right and Principal of Newnham College. In her report for the SPR she concluded that she had 'no hesitation in attributing the performances to clever conjuring'. Eglington countered by publishing forty-four pages of favourable testimony in *Light* and called on Spiritualist supporters in the SPR to resign. Only Stainton Moses and five others saw fit to obey the call. Worse, one of Eglington's previously most impressed clients, S. John Davey, agreed to take part

---

[475] Nicol, pp. 358–9.

in a series of experiments with Hodgson. Playing the role of medium in a fake slate-writing séance, it became painfully clear to Davey how unreliable the sitters' observations were. They saw things that did not take place, generally misinterpreted what did happen and forgot much more besides. Disappointing for the Spiritualists, it was nonetheless a landmark study in the deficiencies of eye-witness testimony that is still relevant today.[476]

Rogers himself resigned soon after the SPR's founding. Like Stainton Moses and the others, he objected to the direction the society was taking. In the hands of Sidgwick, Gurney and Myers it was holding true to science and they felt that Spiritualism, in consequence, was suffering. About two-thirds of the original council had been Spiritualists, but by 1887 that had fallen to a quarter. The SPR's decision to hold no prejudices or prepossessions suited unbiased research but not the faith of the believers. Rogers would instead put his energies into the London Spiritualist Alliance, which he founded with Moses, and into editing its periodical *Light*.[477]

For Rogers, in the oft-quoted words of Philip James Bailey, 'Death is another life [. . .] Larger than this we leave and lovelier'. These were sentiments the scientists would not have disagreed with. For Myers, death as an absolute finality made life pointless. Although he had discredited the Creery children and unmasked a score of cheating mediums, Gurney later remarked that he 'felt the world *without* survival [of the spirit] hopelessly meaningless and largely positively evil'. The sceptics wanted to believe, but, unlike the Spiritualists, that belief had to have a firm basis in fact, for a world based on toe-joints and trickery was worse than meaningless.[478]

---

[476] Nicol, pp. 356–8; Eleanor Mildred Sidgwick, Mr. Eglington, *Journal of the Society of Psychical Research*, June 1886, pp. 282–7.
[477] Nicol, p. 344.
[478] Nicol, p. 347; Rogers, p. 65; Philip James Bailey, *Festus: A Poem*, W. Pickering, 2nd ed., 1845, p. 259.

Parapsychology

On 7 May 1915 the heavy fog that had shrouded the Irish Sea was starting to lift. Kapitänleutnant Walther Schweiger ordered Kaiserliche Marine submarine U-20 to surface. They had been patrolling off the southern coast of Ireland as part of the German U-boat blockade of Britain since 30 April. Oil was running low and there were only two torpedoes left, and not their best ones. Standing in the conning tower, Schweiger swept his binoculars across the sea. At 14:20 (13:20 GMT) Schweiger spotted smoke stacks on the horizon. 'I saw it was a great steamer,' he said afterwards. He ordered diving stations to periscope depth and closed at high speed to 2,296 feet. He launched a single torpedo.[479]

On lookout Able Seaman Leslie Morton saw the telltale wake of the onrushing danger: 'Torpedo coming on starboard side!' It struck 9½ feet below the waterline, punching through to the boiler room before exploding. Almost immediately there was another, much larger explosion. The ship was going down rapidly. Passengers surged on deck.[480]

Among them was Ramon. Around him, people were panicking, frightened, trying to struggle into life-jackets, shouting and screaming in English, a language foreign to him. Ramon had fled Havana under an assumed name for political reasons. That may or may not have been how he got the scar over his left eyebrow. He tore a sheet from his pocket book and scrawled a hurried message. There was the sound of another explosion. He put the message in a bottle, corked it and threw it into the waves. Perhaps the wife and children he had left behind would someday read it. RMS *Lusitania* sank in eighteen minutes, taking with it 1,198 souls. But the story of Ramon would not be known until several years later.[481]

Extra-Sensory Perception (ESP) began in Mexico with a German doctor and a patient with insomnia. Dr Gustav

---

[479] Lowell Thomas, *Raiders of the Deep*, Periscope Publishing, 2002 [1928], pp. 94–5.
[480] Thomas, pp. 94–5; 'Lusitania', *Boy's Life*, May 1964, pp. 22–3.
[481] Thomas, pp. 94–7, 102.

Pagenstecher (1855–1942) was practising medicine in Mexico City in 1919 when an educated and well-to-do lady, Senora Maria Reyes de Z. – later identified as Zierold – came to see him about her sleeping problem. He proceeded to hypnotize her and assessing the depth of her trance state found that she had lost the use of all five senses, although, as she said, 'I can hear nothing except the voice of my hypnotist'. He must have been rather alarmed to have produced such a catatonic condition, but he discovered that if an object were placed in her hand she would automatically grasp it and give information about it – the technique known as psychometry. He tried various things out: a shoe, a tropical plant seed, stone fragments from ancient monuments and so on. When he gave her a piece of marble, Zierold described an open space where 'it seems they are building a town' with something like a church in the background. Pagenstecher did not know anything about the marble, but afterwards found out that it had come from the Forum Romanum. At second and third sittings, Zierold was able to supply more details and made a post-hypnotic sketch: 'it is clear that she had visualized the Forum, as it exists today, with great clearness'.[482]

Despite the apparent loss of her senses, Pagenstecher discovered that she would react as if a light had been shone into her eyes, not when one was actually shone into her eyes, but when Pagenstecher shone it into his own. All of her senses seemed to have been transferred to Pagenstecher. 'I can taste

[482] 'Dr Pagenstecher's Experiments in Psychometry', *Journal of the Society of Psychical Research*, 21, February 1924, pp. 216–19. See also Walter Franklin Prince, 'Psychometrical Experiments with Senora Maria Reyes de Z.', *Proceedings of the Society for Psychical Research*, 15, 1921, pp. 189–312, Journal of the American Society of Psychical Research, 16, 1922, 5–40, and Gustav Pagenstecher, 'Past Events Seership: A Study in Psychometry', *Proceedings of the American Society of Psychical Research*, 16, 1922, 1–136. Z. quoted in W. H. C Tenhaeff, *Aussergewöhnliche Heilkrafte*, Walter-Verlag, 1957, translation in *Journal of the Society of Psychical Research*, 39, March 1958, p. 200. Identification of Z. made incidentally in Alejandro Parra and Juan Carlos Argibay, 'Comparing a Free-Response Psychometry Test with a Free-Response Visual Imagery Test for a Non-Psychic Sample', *Journal of the Society of Psychical Research*, 71, April 2001, p. 92.

[. . .] sugar or salt when these substances are placed on Dr P.'s tongue. I can hear the ticking of a clock held to his ear'. For some reason Pagenstecher also weighed himself and his patient before and after the experiments. Bizarrely, he found that both of them lost weight, although this returned to normal within about half an hour.[483]

A friend of Pagenstecher's, then living in Japan, sent an envelope to a lawyer in Mexico City. Inside the envelope was a letter to Pagenstecher and two sealed envelopes. The letter explained that one of the envelopes contained a note written under conditions of great distress; the other a description of the note's writer. The letter asked Pagenstecher to give the envelope with the note to Zierold to 'read' in her particular way; neither envelope should be opened until the close of the experiment. Dr Walter Franklin Prince, research officer of the ASPR, made a journey in 1921 to see Zierold for himself and was present when Pagenstecher put one of the sealed envelopes into her hand.

Zierold described a ship, frightened people on deck; they were speaking English and trying to put on life belts. A man with a scar over his left eyebrow tore a page out of a notebook and wrote on it. There was an explosion and he threw the note, now sealed in a bottle, into the sea.

Pagenstecher and Prince broke the seals on the envelopes and took out a slip of paper from one. It was torn down one edge. In hastily written Spanish it read:

> The ship is sinking. Farewell my Luisa; see that my children do not forget me. Your Ramon. Havana. May God care for you and me also. Farewell.[484]

From the second envelope they took a short explanation of the circumstances of the note. It had been taken from a bottle that had been found off the coast of the Azores. Enquiries had been

---

[483] 'Dr Pagenstecher's . . .', pp. 216–19.
[484] 'Dr Pagenstecher's . . .', p. 218.

made at Havana. Someone using the name of Ramon P., physically remarkable for the scar over his left eyebrow, had disappeared in the 1910s. A wife, Luisa, and children were tracked down. His handwriting resembled that in the note. Luisa said that he had left for Europe and feared that he had perished with the *Lusitania*.[485]

Pagenstecher made his case to the Mexican Medical Society, which appointed an investigatory commission. They reported favourably, as did Prince for the ASPR. In 1922 Pagenstecher joined the SPR. In writing up his records of Zierold in 1924, he coined the term 'extra-sensory perception'.[486]

Parapsychology (*Parapsychologie*) began in Germany. The psychologist Dr Max Dessoir coined the term in 1889, but it did not gain wider currency until the 1920s. It first appeared in English in 1923, yet it was Baron Albert von Schrenck-Notzing's renaming of Alexander Aksakof's periodical *Psychische Studien* as the *Zeitschrift für Parapsychologie* ('Journal for Parapsychology') in 1926 that established the word and its connotations. In 1928 an Institut für Parapsychologie was established in Berlin. Finally, the publication of Hans Driesch's influential book *Parapsychologie* in 1932 brought the term into common usage.[487]

---

[485] There are a number of discrepancies in the account given: when describing the events around the note, Zierold said that it was night-time; Ramon P. was said to have disappeared in 1916 – it was an afternoon in 1915 when the *Lusitania* sank. For a critical interpretation see Wilhelm Gubisch, *Hellseher, Scharlatane, Demagogen? Kritik an der Parapsychologie*, E. Reinhard, 1961.

[486] Gustav Pagenstecher, *Aussersinnliche Wahrnehmung*, C. Marhold, 1924. For some later experiments see Gustav Pagenstecher, 'Experimentalberichte', *Zeitschrift für Parapsychologie*, in three parts from issue 4–6, April–June 1928.

[487] Max Dessoir, 'Die Parapsychologie', *Sphinx*, 7, 1889, pp. 341–4; still in its German form in T. Konstantin Oesterreich, *Occultism and Modern Science*, 2nd ed., English translation, Methuen, 1923, reviewed by Eric J. Dingwall, *Journal of the Society of Psychical Research*, 21, April 1923, pp. 78–80; Eberhard W. Bauer, 'Periods of Historical Development of Parapsychology in Germany', in D. Delanoy (ed.), *Proceedings of Presented Papers, The Parapsychological Association 34th Annual Convention*, 1991, pp. 18–34 – my thanks to Mr Bauer for sending this and other materials. The *Zeitschrift für Parapsychologie* was established in 1874 by Alexander Aksakof as *Psychische Studien* and was published under the new name from 1926, see the 1st ed., 1926, p. 1, online at http://www.

Up until then people had called what they were doing 'psychical research'. However, this was more than a change of name; it was also a change of emphasis. It put the research next to psychology, implying that the phenomena were a product of the mind, and it brought the research into the laboratory. Whilst the SPR could convert one of their offices into a dark room or séance room as required, it was done on an *ad hoc* basis, and much research was still being conducted under less than satisfactory conditions. With the advent of parapsychology came properly controlled experimental facilities. The era of the gifted amateur was giving way to the era of the professional scientist. Joseph Banks Rhine and William MacDougall, head of the Psychology Department at Duke University, specifically used 'parapsychology' to make the distinction between the old psychical research approach and the new experimental one.[488]

There had been earlier work in Germany, but as in the UK, it had concentrated on mediumship and was organizationally informal. The astrophysicist Friedrich Zöllner (1834–82), for example, had held a series of experimental séances in Leipzig from 1877–8 on the basis of which he argued – controversially – that space was four-dimensional. Max Dessoir had established the Berliner Gesellschaft für Experimental-Psychologie and investigated the medium Henry Slade in 1886. He had followed up on Dr W. Preyer's work on muscle reading and found that he, too, could produce apparently telepathic effects using Preyer's explanation of the method. In 1887 he was voted a corresponding member of the SPR. Schrenck-Notzing already had a well-equipped laboratory in Munich and from 1926 until his sudden death in 1929 he took a leading role in the recently renamed *Zeitschrift für Parapsychologie*.[489]

---

ub.uni-freiburg.de/index.php?id=zs_parapsychologie. Heather Wolffram, *The Stepchildren of Science*, Rodopi, 2009, p. 26.

[488] *Enc. Para.*, p. 496.

[489] Bauer, pp. 18–34; Max Dessoir, 'Experiments in Muscle-Reading and Thought-Transference', *Proceedings of the Society for Psychical Research*, 4, 1886, p. 111; *Journal of the Society of Psychical Research*, 3, October 1887, p. 1.

'Psychical research' continued in the UK, but, as in Germany, it was becoming more scientifically organized. A major step was Harry Price's National Laboratory of Psychical Research in London. Before the ghosts of Borley Rectory, Price had spent his time with the mediums. Elected a member of the SPR in 1920, he was in some ways carrying on the work of its founders in the séance room, but his relationship with the SPR would never be an easy one. He investigated the mediums William Hope and Willi Schneider in 1922, and Stella Cranshaw and Jean Guzik in 1923. He would also hold séances with Helen Duncan in 1931. In March 1925 he held the inaugural meeting of the National Laboratory of Psychical Research (NLPR) at the Royal Societies Club in London. In January 1926 it opened its doors at 16 Queensbury Place in South Kensington – premises shared with the London Spiritualist Alliance. It was a suite of six rooms on the top floor laid out as a laboratory, séance room, 'baffle chamber', dark room, office and a fully equipped workshop, all with enamelled name plates on the doors. Price boasted that the NLPR had 'the finest installation in the world for experimental research work in the field of psychic science'. Whether it was or not, it was certainly well-equipped. Price had stereoscopic cameras, an 'Optiscope', a dictaphone system, a flawless quartz crystal sphere, a specially designed 'transmitting thermograph', radioactive sulphide of zinc for making luminous paint, an electroscope, a galvanometer, and much more besides, all valued at £3,000. Price claimed that it was the first laboratory of its kind in Britain, a country, furthermore, without a 'permanent body of psychical research workers'. Eric Dingwall, the SPR's research officer, called these 'somewhat surprising remarks'. One of the first subjects to be studied there was Eleonore Zugun, the so-called 'poltergeist girl'.[490]

---

[490] Paul G. Adams, 'Harry Price Timeline – 1925–1929', http://www.harrypricewebsite.co.uk/Timeline/1925–1929.htm, 2004–2005, accessed 2 December 2010; Harry Price, 'A Model Psychic Laboratory', *British Journal of Psychical Research*, 1.1, May–June 1926, pp. 11–19; Eric J. Dingwall, 'Notes on Periodicals', *Journal of the Society of Psychical Research*, 23, June 1926,

Price approached both the French Institut Métapsychique International (in 1929) and the SPR (in 1930) with proposals of a merger, only to be rebuffed by both. However, his overtures to the University of London in 1933 to equip a Department of Psychical Research met with more success. A London University Council for Psychical Research was established, although, ultimately, the department was never realized. It would be Bonn University that would seize the opportunity, offering Price his wished-for department in 1937. But war was on the horizon. The failure of Price's plans and the suppression of research in Nazi Germany allowed the torch of parapsychology to pass across the Atlantic.[491]

Telepathy

The odds against it were a hundred billion to one. He shuffled a pack of Zenner Cards – circle, cross (or plus sign), square, star, wavy lines – and took one out, holding it face down. A twenty-six-year-old theology student called Hubert Pearce, a plumber's son from Clarendon, an insignificant dot in the backwoods of Arkansas, was about to become the shining star of parapsychological research. He made his first guess. Dr Joseph Banks Rhine turned over the card: 'Right'. He had turned up one day at one of Rhine's lectures because he was scared that he might be telepathic. Rhine asked him to guess again. 'Right.' He got ten right in a straight run. Rhine paused. Could Pearce do it again? Rhine pulled another ten cards. Pearce called another ten right answers. This was parapsychology's royal flush, twice in a row. Pearce's worst fears were confirmed.[492]

p. 96; Eric. J. Dingwall, 'Notes on Periodicals', *Journal of the Society of Psychical Research*, 24, June 1928, p. 299. Dr Hans Rosenbusch would claim in 1927 to have exposed Zugun not soon after, see 'The Poltergeist Girl – Unmasked in Munich', *Daily News*, 21 February 1927.

[491] Adams; Sofie Lachapelle, 'Attempting Science: The Creation and Early Development of the Institut Métapsychique International in Paris, 1919–1931', *Journal of the History of the Behavioral Sciences*, 41.1, Winter 2005, pp. 1–24.

[492] Odds given by Peter Hallson, 'Some Thoughts on the Decline Effect', *Paranormal Review*, January 1999, p. 15.

The astonishing odds would be chalked up during the first series of ESP tests conducted at Duke University in 1933. Over the next two years Pearce would be repeatedly tested, but he was not the only subject. When Rhine published the results in 1934 in his landmark book *Extra-Sensory Perception*, he and his colleagues had conducted 90,000 trials in the prior three-year period.[493]

Rhine was a botanist by training and had once intended on a career as a minister, but he and his wife, Dr Louisa Rhine, also a botanist, had listened to Sir Arthur Conan Doyle lecturing persuasively on the survival of the spirit and joined the ASPR. They began looking for answers. On 1 July 1926 their quest found them mounting the stairs of 10 Lime Street in Boston, Massachusetts, the home of the then famous medium Mina Crandon (1888–1941), known as 'Margery'. During her exhibitionist séances, at which sitters were served champagne, her thin dressing gown would invariably fall open, revealing that the silk stockings on her legs were the only things she was wearing underneath. Margery was a sensation. Harry Houdini had already imprisoned her in a wooden box to test her powers – inconclusively – and the ASPR were championing her mediumship as solid proof of survival after death. Despite the diversions, the Rhines could see that fraud was involved. The publication of their exposé in 1927 ended their relationship with the ASPR and 'Margery' would ultimately split the ASPR.[494]

In 1928, disappointed with 'Margery', the Rhines moved on

---

[493] J. B. Rhine, *Extra-Sensory Perception*, Boston Society for Psychic Research, 1934, excerpted in Robert Schoch and Logan Yonavjak, *The Parapsychological Revolution*, Tarcher/Penguin, 2008, p. 132.

[494] J. B. Rhine and Louisa E. Rhine, 'One Evening's Observation on the Margery Mediumship', *Journal of Abnormal and Social Psychology*, 24.2, January 1927; Brian Mackenzie, 'The Place of J. B. Rhine in the History of Parapsychology', *Journal of Parapsychology*, 45, March 1981, pp. 75–6; Stacy Horn, *Unbelievable*, HarperCollins, 2009, pp. 17–24; *Enc. Para.*, pp. 393–9. Not everyone at the ASPR had fallen for her charms: with extraordinary dedication E. E. Dudley had discovered that the thumbprint supposedly left by a spirit, Mina's dead brother Walter, was in fact that of her dentist, see *Enc. Para.*, p. 397.

to Lady, 'the telepathic horse', seeking to rule out the problem of human deviousness. Lady would touch her nose to blocks with numbers or letters of the alphabet on them in response to questions put both verbally and mentally. She apparently scored well above chance. The Rhines were aware of Oskar Pfunst's earlier work with a similar beast called 'Clever Hans', and so tried to control for 'unconscious guidance' from the humans around her, although unsuccessfully. By not fully grasping that the cues were entirely involuntary they concluded, incorrectly, that Lady was indeed telepathic. Rhine scouted around for other 'infra-human telepathic subjects', as he put it, but finding none, decided to turn to humans once again.[495]

In 1930 he was having 'guessing contests' with groups of children. Then he moved on to college students. For a time he also tried hypnosis as a means of accessing ESP, but found the process slow and the results insignificant. Trying experiments using ordinary playing cards, Rhine discovered that people had particular preferences for a suit or card. His colleague, the psychologist Dr Karl Zenner (1903–64), devised the famous set of cards around 1930–1 to overcome this problem. A set of five distinctive symbols were used in a deck of twenty-five cards, giving a chance expectation of 5 right in every run. The more trials they conducted the more they found that their modest results began to mount up. His first notable success was with Adam J. Linzmayer. Rhine believed that he was on the brink of proving the possibility of 'the transfer of thought from one mind to another without the intermediation of the sense' – telepathy.[496]

The SPR had early concluded that telepathy was a reality after the Creery case – a finding they would later be forced to reject. After a series of experiments in 1890, Baron Albert von

---

[495] J. B. Rhine and Louisa E. Rhine, 'An Investigation of a "Mind-Reading" Horse', *Journal of Abnormal and Social Psychology*, 23, 1929, pp. 287–92; Rhine, *Extra-Sensory*, p. 132; Mackenzie, pp. 77–8; Oskar Pfungst, *Clever Hans (The Horse of Mr von Osten):A Contribution to Experimental Animal and Human Psychology*, trans. C. L. Rahn, Henry Holt, 1911 [1907].

[496] Rhine, *Extra-Sensory*, pp. 7–10, 132; Mackenzie, p. 80; Horn, p. 31.

Schrenck-Notzing had already argued that there was 'evidence in favour of the reality of true psychical transference'. Some of the pictures he used in his tests were even reminiscent of Zenner's symbols. But the sheer weight of Rhine's evidence, collated through thousands of man-hours of dedicated work, and reduced to clean, compelling statistics would prove more decisive than a series of informal sessions with cheating teenagers or aristocrats. The most important development was the move away from the study of professional 'psychics' and apparently gifted amateurs to the study of (almost) randomly selected 'ordinary' subjects. Some of the psychics could fool some of the scientists some of the time – as Margery did – but with randomized selection the inevitable base temptation of gulling the credulous for money (or anything else) was removed. As Charles Fort (1874–1932) – the man who gave us the word Fortean – once said, 'There is not a physicist in the world who can perceive when a parlor magician palms off playing-cards', but now the parapsychologists were no longer studying 'parlour magicians'.[497]

Clairvoyance

In the late summer of 1933 Pearce called on Rhine's assistant Gaither Pratt, in his research room on the top floor of the Social Science Building, Duke West Campus, as arranged. They synchronized watches and Pearce left. Pratt watched from his window and after a few moments he saw Pearce cross the quadrangle to the library. He waited a few moments more until he was sure Pearce was at his appointed seat at the back of the library. They were ready to begin. Pratt shuffled the Zenner cards and placed the deck on the table in front of him. He checked the time, then took the first card off the top of the deck and put it face down in the centre of the table without looking at it. He waited for one minute, then, putting the card to one side, repeated the action

---

[497] Albert von Schrenck-Notzing, 'Experimental Studies in Thought-Transference', *Proceedings of the Society for Psychical Research*, 7, 1891–1892, p. 6; Charles Hoy Fort, *New Lands: More Unexplained Occurrences*, Forgotten Books, 2008 [1925], p. 56.

with the next card and so on until he had gone through the whole deck. Sitting in the library a hundred yards away, Pearce wrote down his predictions, one every minute. When Pratt finished he turned over the cards and noted their order. Five minutes later he would shuffle the cards again and they would repeat the test. At the end of the experiment they put their records into envelopes and sealed them. They then personally delivered them to Rhine. They discovered that Hubert Pearce was not just telepathic, he was also clairvoyant.[498]

Rhine had decided to test to see if distance had any effect on Hubert's abilities. He also wanted to devise an experiment where collusion (even involuntary) between subject and scientist could be automatically ruled out without having to rely on the participants' good character. With the distance tests, he thought that nobody could ever accuse them of cheating. In a final group of tests, Rhine observed Pratt during the procedure, just to make sure. Also this was not just mind-reading any more. Clairvoyance was, as Rhine defined it, 'the extrasensory perception of objects or objective events, as distinguished from the mental states or thoughts of another person'. Pratt had not looked at the cards. He did not know what they were. Pearce would have to be able to read the cards for himself, despite the fact they were face down on a table a hundred yards away.[499]

At first Pearce's results were not impressive. He was even scoring below chance, but as they continued, he got better. From August 1933 to March 1934 they would conduct 1,850 distance trials in total with distances ranging from 100 to 250 yards. After statistical analysis the results were staggering. As the British mathematician and psychical researcher S. G. Soal

---

[498] J. B. Rhine, 'Some Selected Experiments in Extra-Sensory Perception', *Journal of Abnormal and Social Psychology*, 31, 1936, pp. 216–28; J. B. Rhine and J. G. Pratt, 'A Review of the Pearce–Pratt Distance Series of ESP Tests', *Journal of Parapsychology*, 18, 1954, pp. 165–78; Horn, pp. 38–9.
[499] See C. E. M. Hansel, 'A Critical Analysis of the Pearce–Pratt Experiment', *Journal of Parapsychology*, 25, 1961, pp. 87ff, for his views on the inability of this methodology to automatically exclude fraud; Rhine, *Extra-Sensory*, pp. 7–10.

once said, 'a million persons might go on guessing for years without producing such a series'. Rhine himself gave the odds of this happening due to chance as 10^{-22}. Rhine was convinced that these results 'allow no other interpretation except that they were due to extrasensory perception'.[500]

Then after two years of incredible results, Pearce lost his apparent abilities. The reason, it seems, was a broken heart. Pearce's girlfriend left him shortly after the distance experiments and he never reached the level of his earlier performances. He graduated the next year and went back to Arkansas. His involvement in parapsychology almost cost him the career as a minister he had been striving for. As it was, he was given a rundown country church in the mountains. He would find love again, but those astonishing powers were gone for good.[501]

Despite the setback, it was enough to justify Duke University's decision to create a Parapsychology Laboratory in September 1933 and make Rhine its director. Even with this new recognition, not to mention such apparently black and white experimental results, the scientific establishment was not ready to accept that ESP could be possible. The science writer and sceptic Martin Gardner wrote to Pearce bluntly asking him to confess to having cheated. Mark Hansel spent considerable time thinking of ways, however improbable, that Pearce might have cheated, even suggesting that Pearce had crawled through the ceiling space in order to be able to spy upon Pratt as he turned over the cards. Gardner himself would later come to recognize that 'there is obviously an enormous, irrational prejudice on the part of most American psychologists [. . .] against even the possibility of extra-sensory mental powers'.[502]

---

[500] S. G. Soal, Reviews, *Proceedings of the Society for Psychical Research*, 45, 1938, p. 93; Rhine and Pratt, pp. 171, 174; Horn, p. 39.
[501] Horn, pp. 39–40, 232.
[502] Horn, pp. 51, 78, 155, 228.

Psychokinesis

The idea had come from a young amateur gambler who had visited the lab to tell them he could influence dice rolls with his force of will. Rhine and the gambler got down on the floor of his office and started rolling dice. Rhine was not impressed. 'The gambler went on his way,' wrote Gaither Pratt, 'but he left this beautifully simple idea behind.' They now had what they thought was the perfect way to test for psychokinesis (PK), the power of the mind over matter.[503]

Rhine and Pratt began rolling dice. They got students at the university to roll dice. They even got Rhine's children and their friends to roll dice. They began throwing the dice from cupped hands, then against a wall, next down a chute, and finally they built a machine to do it for them. They gave prizes to the children, making it a party game. They tried drinking coffee and alcohol, and taking the narcotic sodium amytal to see if that made a difference. And they rolled the dice again and again over nine years.[504]

The Rhines' first report excitedly declared that 'the experiments on PK show first that the mind has a force, real kinetic force, and that it can also operate outside of the body'. But were the results due to PK or precognition? Rhine thought he could rule out precognition by agreeing on a 'rigid order of target face' or allowing the subject to choose it for themselves during a trial. But it was the same problem in his ESP experiments, only reversed. What was needed some direct physical effect that could not involve precognition.[505]

---

[503] Louisa E. Rhine and J. B. Rhine, 'The Psychokinetic Effect, I: The First Experiment', *Journal of Parapsychology*, 20, 1943, 20–43; Harvey J. Irwin, *An Introduction to Parapsychology*, 4th ed., McFarland & Company, 2004, p. 107; Pratt quoted in Horn, p. 74.

[504] Horn, pp. 74–5.

[505] Quoted in Horn, p. 74; Rhine and Rhine, 'Psychokinetic', pp. 20–43. For other confirmatory experiments see L. A. Dale, 'The Psychokinetic Effect: The First A.S.P.R. Experiment', *Journal of the American Society of Psychical Research*, 40, 1946, pp. 123–51; Robert A. McConnell, et al., 'Wishing with Dice', *Journal of Experimental Psychology*, 50, 1955, pp. 269–75; J. G. Pratt and H. Forwald, 'Confirmation of the PK Placement Effect', *Journal of Parapsychology*,

The answer, if it was an answer, lay halfway across the world. A six-year-old boy in Tel Aviv, Israel, in the 1950s, stared fascinated as the hands of his watch bent before his eyes. He next tried cutlery, then nails, all bent by the power of his mind. Being abducted by aliens had given him new and amazing powers. At least that is the story that Uri Geller has given of himself. He later retracted the aliens. What is indisputable is that, after being discharged from the Israeli Army in the 1960s, Geller developed a magic routine with Shimson 'Shipi' Shtrang and together they worked nightclubs and private parties performing an act they billed as ESP. They were discovered by American parapsychologist Dr Andrija Puharich and Geller was promoted in the US as the genuine article. To some it looked like the physical evidence was finally available.[506]

After a radio broadcast in Texas in the early 1970s, a number of people claimed that after listening to Geller, metal objects in their homes had bent spontaneously. He used this when appearing on BBC Radio 2's 'The Jimmy Young Show' in the UK on 3 November 1973, asking listeners who believed that they might be able to bend metal to bring some object close to their radio sets so that he could 'trigger' their latent psychokinetic powers. This distance macro-PK experiment apparently worked and for a while was known as 'The Geller Effect'. He was not just proficient in PK, but ESP as well. A study by two scientists at the Stanford Research Institute, California, concluded that 'we can safely say that it is evident that Geller does have paranormal perceptual abilities'. Rhine himself was 'impressed by the number of serious competent people who have seen his demonstrations of physical effects under circumstances which, as reported, would not allow any kind of known sleight of hand or trickery'. He then went on to say that Geller's

22, 1958, pp. 1–19.
[506] Uri Geller, *Uri Geller: My Story*, Holt and Co., 1975, p. 102; Andrija Puharich, *Uri: A Journal of the Mystery of Uri Geller*, Anchor Press/Doubleday, 1974; *Enc. Para.*, pp. 613–14.

effects were 'genuinely parapsychic', although he reserved final judgement.[507]

A number of other spoon-benders soon appeared on the scene: Jean-Pierre Girard in France; Stephen North in the UK; Steve Shaw and Mike Edwards in the USA; Masuaki Kiyota and Merac in Japan. It seemed like a wave of psychic powers had been released, although no one else mentioned aliens. Parapsychology had a new category: PKMB – psychokinetic metal bending.[508]

Rhine was right to remain cautious. According to the then president of the Israel Parapsychology Society, Dr Heinz Berendt, a former girlfriend claimed to have acted as a stooge in Geller's early stage show routine and a former impresario, Dany Pelz, also said that Geller covertly observed his audience before coming onstage and displaying apparent ESP in identifying someone's favourite brand of cigarettes and so on. Berendt reasoned that there was nothing paranormal about Geller's feats because of 'Geller's own admission that he uses tricks' and noted that Geller had ignored their repeated requests to study him. James Randi, former magician turned debunker, would later publish a still taken from Geller's appearance on an American TV programme, Barbara Walter's 'Not for Women Only', that seemed to show that one of the spoons used had been pre-fatigued. Journalist C. Eugene Emery, Jr, claimed to have personally caught Geller cheating in *ad hoc* ESP and PK tests.[509]

---

[507] Russell Targ and Harold Puthoff, 'ESP Experiments with Uri Geller', in J. D. Morris, et al. (eds), *Research In Parapsychology*, Scarecrow Press, 1973, p. 60; and Russel Targ and Harold Puthoff, 'PK Experiments with Uri Geller and Ingo Swann', in Morris, *Parapsychology*, pp. 125–8; Rhine quoted in Heinz C. Berendt, 'Uri Geller – Pro and Con', *Journal of the Society of Psychical Research*, 47, December 1974, pp. 481, 483; *Enc. Para.*, p. 614. Targ and Puthoff also published their findings on Geller in 'Information Transmission Under Conditions of Sensory Shielding', *Nature*, 251, 18 October, pp. 602–7.

[508] *Enc. Para.*, p. 614.

[509] Berendt, p. 477; James Randi, *The Truth About Uri Geller*, Prometheus Books, 1982, p. 179; C. Eugene Emery, 'Psychic or Charlatan: Uri Geller Reverses his Disappearing Act', *Providence Sunday Journal*, 12 April 1987, pp. A21ff, and C. Eugene Emery, 'Catching Geller in the Act', *Skeptical Inquirer*, 12.1, 1987,

At the height of his fame, a 1974 poll by the *Daily Mail* revealed that 95 per cent of its readers believed Geller could produce paranormal phenomena. Now, as SPR member John Randall observed, there is no research into metal-bending being conducted, as far as he is aware, and the subject has been largely (perhaps conveniently) forgotten by parapsychology.[510]

Spoon-bending might be the most well-known example of supposed psychokinesis, but it is surely also the most banal and least convincing. We have already seen how the physical mediums were displaying dramatic phenomena from sound to spirit manifestations and materializations. Parapsychologists now refer to this class of phenomena as macro-PK. Poltergeists, too, are seen by some as an example of macro-PK, or more particularly following Professor William Roll's coinage as 'recurrent spontaneous psychokinesis' (RSPK). Macro-PK applies to any form of PK that is immediately apparent, but there is also a range of weaker effects – micro-PK – that are often only observable through statistical analysis of experimental results. Rhine's dice-rolling experiments were classic studies of micro-PK. Of course, there are also areas, such as psychic healing, that can seemingly involve both macro- and micro-PK effects.[511]

Precognition

In 1952 Rhine called back one of the students he had been testing for ESP, not because Lois Duncan was the next Hubert Pearce, but because, as she put it, 'I had broken a record for incorrect responses'. She would drop out of Duke University, but become a best-selling novelist. The 1997 film adaptation of one of her earlier books, *I Know What You Did Last Summer*

---

pp. 75–80; *Enc. Para.*, p. 614. Stated using 'tricks' in Calev Ben-David, 'A Life of the Mind', *The Jerusalem Report*, 8 September 1994, p. 46.

[510] John Randall, 'The Near-Death Experience: A Reliable Paranormal Phenomenon?', *Journal of the Society of Psychical Research*, 74, October 2010, p. 254.

[511] *Enc. Para.*, pp. 604–5; J. G. Pratt and W. G. Roll, 'The Seaford Disturbances', *Journal of Parapsychology*, 22.2, June 1958, p. 79.

(1973), would take over $125 million at the box office. In 1989, when our story begins, she had completed her thirty-eighth book, but the celebrations would be cut short when the plot of *Don't Look Behind You* became real life. Afterwards, Duncan would come to believe that she had just written a 289-page premonition.[512]

Don't Look Behind You told the story of an FBI agent's daughter called April. April is caught up in her father's violent world when the family is forced into hiding under the US Federal Witness Security Program. Missing her friends, April runs away and returns to the former family home. A hitman discovers her whereabouts and pursues her across Florida.

April was based on Duncan's own daughter Kaitlyn (also Kait) Arquette. Duncan presented her with the bound galleys, inscribed 'For my own special April', adding 'Always be sure to look behind you, Honey!' One month later Kaitlyn was shot twice in the head. She died twenty hours later.[513]

In the novel, April is chased by a hitman driving a Chevrolet Camaro. Kaitlyn was also chased by a Camaro. In the novel the hitman is called Mike Vamp. After Kaitlyn's murder, police indicted a man called Mike who was known by the nickname 'Vamp'. Just as April's family went into hiding under the Federal Witness Security Program, so Duncan and her husband were forced into hiding in 1990 after receiving death threats from the relatives of two suspects in Kaitlyn's murder case.

The police thought Kaitlyn's murder was a random drive-by shooting. Her sister Robin had concerns about Kaitlyn's Vietnamese boyfriend, Dung Nguyen. They were apparently about to break up and Kaitlyn was scared of his friends. There

---

[512] Lois Duncan, *Who Killed My Daughter? The True Story of a Mother's Search for Her Daughter's Murderer* Delacorte Press, 1992; reviewed by William Roll in *Journal of Parapsychology*, 57, 1993, pp. 305–7. See also Lois Duncan and William Roll, *Psychic Connections: A Journey into the Mysterious World of Psi*, Delacorte Press, 1995.

[513] Reported in *The Albuquerque Journal*, 18 July 1989; and *The Albuquerque Tribune*, 18 July 1989.

were rumours of what Duncan called 'a car-wreck scam' – staging rental car crashes to make fraudulent insurance claims. Trying to find out more, Robin went to psychic Betty Muench (1933–2010). Using automatic writing Muench made claims of drug-dealing politicians and gang involvement. Desperate for some progress in a case the police seemed to have abandoned, Duncan would later consult another three psychics – Noreen Renier, Nancy Czetli and Greta Alexander.[514]

These three already had reputations as 'psychic detectives'. Greta Alexander (1932–98) claimed being hit by lightning in 1961 had given her psychic powers. She was a 'cult figure' with a waiting list of seven months to a year. Her clients included the MGM contract actress Debbie Reynolds, who starred in the 1952 film *Singin' in the Rain*, and actress Ruth Warrick, who appeared in Orson Welles' 1941 film *Citizen Kane*. She claimed to have two guardian angels called Raoul and Isaiah – 'her boys', as she called them. Alexander had most famously been involved in the Mary Cousett murder case in 1983 and according to newspaper reports had found missing person Rex Carpenter in 1991.[515]

Nancy Czetli (also known by the surnames Anderson, Myer-Czetli and Myer, her maiden name) took an MA in 'Writing Popular Fiction' before turning to psychic detection. According to her website she has 'assisted in the investigations of over 765 homicides' and claims to have given 'new, accurate information about the case that helps in the search for a resolution' 90 per cent of the time. One of her more famous successes was supposedly finding the body of Sylvester Tonet in 1988, although police detective Will Greenaway, who had worked on the case, had been 'unimpressed' with the information she provided. At the time of writing, she charges $200 an hour.[516]

---

[514] Duncan, ch. 3.
[515] Ward Lucas, 'A Product of the Media: Greta Alexander', in Joe Nickell (ed.), *Psychic Sleuths: ESP and Sensational Cases*, Prometheus Books, 1994, pp. 130–55; 'Psychic Greta Alexander', *Chicago Sun-Times*, 19 July 1998.
[516] http://www.nancymyer-psychicdetective.com/aboutuspagehtml.html,

Noreen Renier (c. 1937–) was said to have predicted the assassination attempt on Ronald Reagan and the successful assassination of Egypt's President Anwar Sadat. At one time or another, she has been billed as 'the only psychic to ever work with the FBI'. Renier had volunteered for a parapsychological study undertaken at Duke University, although details are sketchy. Anthropologist David E. Jones at the University of Central Florida also investigated her supposed psychic abilities and those of three others in the 1970s. He argued that 'a positive conclusion is unavoidable. There are individuals who have abilities which we now refer to as paranormal or psychic'. However, fellow anthropologist Kenneth L. Feder would be less than complimentary about how he came to that conclusion. Renier's fee in the 1990s was around $400 a case.[517]

'My speciality is homicide work,' Renier told Duncan after she contacted her. She went on to explain that 'I've worked with police from all over the United States and as far away as Japan'. Her technique was psychometry: 'If I'm sent an object that was on the body of the victim, I can usually describe the victim and recreate the murder scene'. She said that she would go into a trance and 'get impressions', which she could not remember afterwards. She talked of 'channelling' the spirit of the dead victim.[518]

Duncan sent Renier some of Kaitlyn's personal belongings and arranged a telephone conference to take part in the psychic investigation. 'I feel a knife so strongly,' said Renier. 'Why do I feel a knife?' 'She wasn't killed with a knife,' replied Duncan.

---

accessed 6 December 2010; Joe Nickell, 'Psychic Sleuthing: The Myth-Making Process', *Skeptical Inquirer*, 26 September 2005.

[517] Gary P. Posner, 'The Media's Rising Star Psychic Sleuth: Noreen Renier', in Nickell, pp. 60–85; David E. Jones, *Visions of Time: Experiments in Psychic Archaeology*, Theosophical Publishing House, 1979, p. 16; Kenneth L. Feder, 'Psychic Archaeology: The Anatomy of Irrationalist Prehistoric Studies', *Skeptical Inquirer*, Summer 1980, pp. 32–43; William G. Roll, Review of Noreen Renier, *A Mind for Murder*, Berkley Books, 2005, *Journal of Scientific Exploration*, 20, 2006, p. 140; Duncan, p. 290.

[518] Duncan, pp. 248, 290.

'She was shot.' A moment later Renier stated, 'I wasn't shot. I don't *think* I was shot . . .' 'She was shot while she was driving,' said Duncan. 'Oh, then she was driving?' said Renier. 'Good! I felt so sure of that.'[519]

Like Muench, Czetli also talked about someone involved in politics, and like Muench, Renier also said there was a gang connection. All three would say that Kaitlyn had witnessed a drug transaction. An investigation by an Albuquerque newspaper would later find evidence of a connection between Kaitlyn's murder and a Vietnamese gang, and an anonymous call to Duncan would claim that drugs had been involved. However, it was Renier who would make what is presented as one of the most astonishing revelations.[520]

The police artist Mike Deal sketched from Renier's description of the killer: tight wiry hair, close-set eyes, big ears, long nose, possibly broken at some point, square chin – a boxer's face, or any mobster extra from *The Godfather*. When Duncan saw it she telephoned Renier immediately. 'Something crazy happened with one of the pictures,' she said. 'Your artist drew a character from one of my books. [. . .] Your artist drew my hitman.' The picture had only been used on the cover of the British edition of *Don't Look Behind You* and not the US edition. Few people in the USA were thought to have seen it. Kaitlyn was one of those. She had seen the picture before she died and Renier interpreted it as a message that 'a hitman was hired to kill her because she was going to expose illegal activities'.[521]

It was not the first time that one of her books had seemingly predicted the future. In *Ransom*, her first suspense novel written in 1966 when Duncan was living in Livermore, California, a group of teenagers are kidnapped by the driver of their school bus. Not long after the book was published, school children in Livermore, California, were kidnapped and held to ransom by

---

[519] Duncan, p. 254.
[520] Ken Dornstein, *Accidentally, on Purpose: The Making of a Personal Injury Underworld in America*, Palgrave Macmillan, 1998, p. 328; Duncan, p. 293.
[521] Duncan, p. 258.

their bus driver. One of the children's parents demanded that Duncan be arrested as an accessory because she seemed to know too much about the case.

This was not the first time that an author had apparently predicted the future, either. 'Precognition is quite well established,' William Roll, then Director of the Psychical Research Foundation, told Duncan, 'and creative individuals seem to have more of this ability than others.' He used the *Titanic* as an example. W. T. Stead's 'How the Mail Steamer Went Down in Mid-Atlantic' (1886) and 'From the Old World to the New' (1892), and Morgan Robertson's *Futility, or The Wreck of the Titan* (1898) all seemed to predict the sinking of RMS *Titanic* in 1912. In all three stories an ocean liner goes down after colliding with an iceberg, but there were more parallels than that.[522]

In 'From the Old World to the New' the name of the captain was E. J. Smith, also the name of the captain of the *Titanic*. The fate of Stead himself was curiously linked to that of the ship. In 1892 the chiromancer Teresina told him he would die aged sixty-three. Another palmist, W. de Kerlor, had dreams and visions of a large, dark ship and a watery grave. Stead lost his life on the *Titanic*, aged sixty-three. Robertson also produced other remarkable parallels: the names of the ships were almost identical, both left port in April, both struck icebergs around midnight, both were travelling at a similar speed, both had sixteen watertight compartments and both could carry around 3,000 passengers.[523]

In 1915 Boston businessman Edward Bowen had an important meeting in London and booked passage on the next

---

[522] Duncan, p. 241; W. T. Stead, 'How the Mail Steamer Went Down in Mid-Atlantic', *Pall Mall Gazette*, 22 March 1886, and 'From the Old World to the New', *The Review of Reviews*, Christmas edition, December 1892. See Martin Gardner (ed.), *The Wreck of the Titanic Foretold*, Prometheus Books, 1985, for these and other examples.

[523] Guy Lyon Playfair, Review of Bertrand Méheust, *Histoires Paranormales du Titanic*, J'ai lu, 2006, *Journal of the Society of Psychical Research*, 70, 2006, pp. 241–2; Bob Brier, Review of Martin Gardner (ed.), *The Wreck of the Titanic Foretold?*, Prometheus Books, 1986, *Journal of Parapsychology*, 50, 1986, p. 288.

available transatlantic steamer from New York to Liverpool, despite the German U-boat blockade. It was a luxury liner, the pride of the Cunard Line and the fastest on the seas, more than able to outrun any German submarine. 'It's the best joke I've heard in many days, this talk of torpedoing', said Captain W. T. Turner as the ship prepared to cast off. Nevertheless, 'A feeling grew upon me that something was going to happen,' said Bowen. He talked it over with his wife and cancelled his tickets. The meeting could wait. The theatrical manager, Arthur 'Al' Woods, had taken a stateroom next to the famous playwright Charles Klein – in 1912 they had both cancelled their passage on the *Titanic*. On the morning of sailing, fear overcame him and he gave it up; but not Klein. On the evening before sailing, the ship's mascot, a black cat called Dowie, made an escape down one of the large hawsers. The firemen and stokers saw in it a terrible omen. The ship was the RMS *Lusitania*. As we saw earlier, the *Lusitania* was sunk by a U-boat, going down with huge loss of life.[524]

From the 1880s to the 1950s, Eleanor Sidgwick, Herbert Saltmarsh and Louisa Rhine between them collected a massive number of case reports of precognition. They found that most of them occurred during dreaming as realistic representations of the event. In 1933 J. B. Rhine had tried precognition experiments with Pearce attempting to guess the order of cards before they were dealt. The American parapsychologist W. E. Cox found that days with train crashes had a relatively lower level of passenger traffic. He theorized that people were subconsciously precognisant of the accidents and so avoided travelling on those days. But this only scratches the surface of the amount of work that has been done, and continues to be done, on this subject.[525]

---

[524] Adolph A. Hoehling and Mary Hoehling, *The Last Voyage of the Lusitania*, Holt, 1956, pp. 31–2; Frederick Ellis, *The Tragedy of the Lusitania*, National Publishing Co., 1915, pp. 168, 172, 174–5.
[525] E. M. Sidgwick, 'On the Evidence for Premonitions', *Proceedings of the Society for Psychical Research*, 5, 1888, pp. 288–354; H. F. Saltmarsh, 'Report on Cases of Apparent Precognition', *Proceedings of the Society for Psychical*

After the Aberfan disaster in 1966 in which a colliery slagheap landslide caused considerable loss of life, Dr J. C. Barker, then a consultant psychiatrist at Sheldon Hospital in Shrewsbury, appealed through the media for anyone who had had a presentiment of what had happened. He received numerous replies, thirty-five of which were sufficiently detailed to warrant attention. Barker set up the British Premonitions Bureau (BPB) in 1967 to collect people's experiences. It was his hope that the BPB, based at Grove House in London, might act as a psychic early-warning system to prevent similar disasters in the future. By the early 1970s the BPB had received over 3,000 reports. Sadly, it is no longer operational. A number of other such bureaux were set up around the world. In 1968 a Central Premonitions Registry was established in New York under Robert Nelson and there have been similar efforts in Canada. John L. Peterson's Arlington Institute in Arlington, Virginia, continues to try and predict the future with a specially selected group of 'precognisant dreamers'.[526]

One of the many problems for precognition research has always been 'retro-fitting' or postdiction. Given enough time, the cryptic pronouncements of Nostradamus, for example, can be made to fit actual events from the rise of Hitler to the terrorist attack on the World Trade Center, New York. Likewise, a prolific writer such as Duncan is likely to describe things that eventually happen. The supposed novelistic predictions of the sinking of the *Titanic* were published fourteen to twenty-six years before the event. Some of the information provided by Renier seemed hopelessly off-target – a knife instead of a gun.

Research, 42, 1934, pp. 49–103; Louisa E. Rhine, 'Frequency of Types of Experience in Spontaneous Precognition', *Journal of Parapsychology*, 18, 1954, pp. 93–123; Irwin, pp. 95–7; J. B. Rhine, 'Experiments Bearing on the Precognition Hypothesis: I. Pre-Shuffling Card Calling', *Journal of Parapsychology*, 2, 1938, pp. 38–54; W. E. Cox, 'Precognition: An analysis II', *Journal of the American Society for Psychical Research*, 30, 1956, pp. 99–109.
[526] John C. Barker, 'Premonitions of the Aberfan Disaster', *Journal of the Society of Psychical Research* 44, 1967, pp. 169–81; Andrew MacKenzie, *Riddle of the Future: A Modern Study of Precognition*, Arthur Baker, 1974; Dossey, n.p.

Even Renier's best hit – the supposed match between her mugshot and the cover illustration showing the killer – stretches the imagination. Renier's sketch looked like an Italian, the face on the cover like a cousin of Roger Moore. Despite some of the flawed evidence, precognition cannot be explained away. For example, controlled experiments in the laboratory have uncovered strange effects such as changes in skin conductivity occurring prior to emotional stimuli in randomized tests that seem suspiciously similar to precognition. After analyzing almost two million precognition trials involving more than 50,000 subjects in 309 separate studies conducted between 1935 and 1987, researchers Charles Honorton, then director of Princeton's Psychophysical Research Laboratories, and Diane Ferrari found that 30 per cent had produced significant results in favour.[527]

Rhine had wanted to establish a centre for research that would outlive him. It looked as though he had. The Parapsychology Laboratory had produced excellent work. His long-time research assistant and valued colleague Gaither Pratt was expected to succeed him as director. The university had other plans. They wanted to subsume the lab into a new Center for the Study of the Nature of Man that would include anthropology, psychology, physics, even electronics, and much else besides. Rhine feared that the lab would disappear in this untidy heap. But after confidential discussions with Karl Zener and other senior figures at Duke, the university dropped the whole idea and with it any sort of future for the laboratory. Pratt was left dangling. Rhine would retire with full benefits. Pratt, then in his fifties, had sacrificed his career and had nothing in return.

---

[527] Dean Radin, 'Experiments Testing Models of Mind-Matter Interaction', *Journal of Scientific Exploration*, 20.3, 2006, pp. 375–401. For a critical perspective see Richard Wiseman, 'Dreaming the Future?', *Fortean Times*, 273, April 2011, pp. 36–9. For a fuller analysis see Charles Honorton and Diane C. Ferrari, '"Future Telling": A Meta-Analysis of Forced-Choice Precognition Experiments, 1935–1987', *Journal of Parapsychology*, 53, 1989, pp. 281–308.

The two men parted acrimoniously, although they would be reconciled some years later.[528]

When Rhine officially retired in 1962, the Parapsychology Laboratory at Duke University was no more. Rhine established the independent Foundation for Research on the Nature of Man (FRNM) – renamed the Rhine Research Center in 1995 – and the Institute for Parapsychology to continue his work. Rhine had earlier proposed that a Parapsychological Association be created as a professional organization for scientists working in parapsychology. It was formally established on 19 June 1957 in Durham, North Carolina, with the physicist Dr Robert A. McConnell (1914–2006) as its first president. In 1969 the Parapsychological Association was voted a member of the prestigious American Association for the Advancement of Science – it was a landmark development. Today it has a total membership of 271.[529]

There had been many stumbling blocks along the way, but parapsychology is now an established discipline, albeit still an embattled one. The SPR is still going strong, more than a hundred years later, and across the world many similar endeavours have emerged – more than can be mentioned here. France's Institut Métapsychique International, founded in 1919, also continues to this day. Hans Bender established the Institut für Grenzgebiete der Psychologie und Psychohygiene (Institute for Border Areas of Psychology and Psychohygiene) in Freiburg, Germany, in 1950, and a chair of border psychology was established at Freiburg University in 1954. In 1985 the Koestler Chair of Parapsychology was established at Edinburgh University, funded by a bequest made by the writer Arthur Koestler and his wife Cynthia. Under the first incumbent, Robert L. Morris, a Koestler Parapsychology Unit was also set

---

[528] Horn, pp. 229–30.
[529] Horn, pp. 229–30, 233; J. Gordon Melton (ed.), *Encyclopedia of Occultism and Parapsychology*, 2 vols, 5th ed., Gale, 2001, vol. 2, p. 1185; 'History of the Parapsychological Association', Parapsychological Association, http://www.parapsych.org/history_of_pa.html, accessed 28 December 2010.

up. An indirect outcome of this was the formation of the
Parapsychology Research Group at Liverpool Hope University
in the early 2000s. The Princeton Engineering Anomalies
Research (PEAR) programme lasted from 1979 to 2007,
coming to an end when, after twenty-eight years of research, it
was felt that it had proven that the human mind could exert a
non-physical influence on 'engineering devices and informa-
tion-processing systems'.[530]

Within the English-speaking world, parapsychology as an
academic discipline has followed the lead of the SPR. It tends
not to investigate the whole range of what is popularly known as
'paranormal', but instead concentrates on telepathy, clairvoyance, precognition (premonition) and psychokinesis – the
category of things covered by the term 'psi'. Rhine reduced
everything to ESP and PK, although he still had to admit the
other aspects as sub-categories. Research has broadened today
with investigations into reincarnation, and out-of-body and
near-death experiences, encompassing magnetic field and ultrasound effects, as well as theorizing based on the models of
quantum physics, but still baulks at the full range of phenomena
considered supernatural or paranormal.[531]

Unlike Croesus, what the original members of the SPR,
Rhine and many others were really concerned about was not
whether one would defeat the Persian army, or succeed in any
other future endeavour for that matter, but whether the mind
could operate independently of the body, which is to say,

---

[530] GEEPP website, http://geepp.free.fr/index1024.htm, accessed 31 December 2010; IGPP, http://www.igpp.de/english/welcome.htm, accessed 31
December 2010; Koestler Research Unit, http://www.koestler-parapsychol-
ogy.psy.ed.ac.uk/index.html, accessed 31 December 2010; Parapsychology
Research Unit, http://hopelive.hope.ac.uk/psychology/para/Index.html, accessed 31 December 2010; 'Princeton's PEAR Laboratory to Close', PEAR
Press Release, 10 February 2007; Dr Carl Williams, personal communication,
4 January 2011.
[531] Rhine, p. 7–10; Horn, p. 240; 'Parapsychology FAQ', Parapsychological Association, http://www.parapsych.org/faq_file1.html#4, accessed 28 December
2010.

whether consciousness could survive death. This survival hypothesis ultimately lies behind all the guessing games and spoon-bending. If the answer is yes, then many of these researchers will already know it, but for the rest of us the doubt, and with it the dread, remains. Death, not space, has always been the final frontier.

9. Conclusion:
Explaining the Inexplicable

The American hypnotherapist Dr Steven Heller (1939–97) once told the story of a professor of psychology, his patient, and the rather cruel trick he played on her in the interests of science. The professor had found the perfect hypnotic subject and wanted to test whether she would re-enter the hypnotic state when carrying out a post-hypnotic suggestion. The ideal place to test this, thought the professor, was not under carefully controlled laboratory conditions, but at the faculty party that evening. While hypnotized he planted the suggestion that when the clock struck 10 p.m. she should take off one of her shoes, set it on the dining room table and place some roses in it. As a further twist he told her that she would have no memory of this suggestion, but would instead believe it to be her own idea and would feel a strong compulsion to finish the task.[532]

As the clock struck 10 that evening the woman duly slipped off one of her shoes, put it on the table and started arranging roses in it. One can see the smirk on the professor's face as he asked, in all feigned innocence, what she was doing. She explained that her husband had given her a crystal vase in the shape of a shoe. She had not known what to do with it until the idea had suddenly come to her now of how to arrange flowers in the vase. Not wanting to forget, she had taken off her own shoe, which looked very much like the vase, and was trying out the idea she had had.

---

[532] Steven Heller, *Monsters and Magical Sticks*, Falcon, 1987, pp. 39–40.

Testing the suggestion further, the professor told her how absurd her story was and tried to talk her out of it. She was convinced that what she was saying was true and as the professor pushed further she became more and more defensive, and finally almost hysterical. The professor, at last, terminated the experiment.

The point is, we do not always know what we think we know. People are suggesting things to us all of the time. We are even suggesting things to ourselves all of the time. We invent personally convincing explanations for why anything we believe in is the gospel truth. As William James once said on the subject of survival after death, the evidence is sufficient to convince the believers but is never enough for the sceptics. It is the case with much of what we have examined in this book. It seems, then, that the explanation may not lie with the evidence, but with the human being who interprets it. History is always psychology and that, I would argue, is the point of sociology. So why do some people believe whilst others are sceptical?

A huge amount of research has been conducted on this subject. Most of it tends to find that the reason people develop or adopt 'paranormal beliefs' (variously defined) is due to some sort of mental or social abnormality, such as deficiencies in reality-testing, or a background of childhood abuse. In their book *Paranormal America*, Christopher Bader, F. Carson Mencken and Joseph Baker argued that rather than being deviant, it is actually relatively mainstream to believe in at least one area they defined as paranormal – astrology, the prophecies of Nostradamus, ghosts, monsters (cryptozoology), UFOs, and the New Age. Just over two-thirds (68 per cent) of people in the USA believe in at least one of these areas. The major difference lay in 'conventionality', with more conventional people holding fewer paranormal beliefs or claiming fewer experiences than the less conventional.[533]

---

[533] See, for example, Erich Goode, *Paranormal Beliefs: A Sociological Introduction*, Waveland Press, 2000; Harvey J. Irwin, 'Reality Testing and the Formation of Paranormal Beliefs', *Journal of the Society for Psychical Research*, 68, July 2004, pp. 143–52; S. L. Perkins and R. Allen, 'Childhood Physical Abuse and Differential Development of Paranormal Belief Systems', *Journal of Nervous*

There are certainly some problems in the way the research data are interpreted. For example, Bader, Mencken and Baker stated that 'belief in paranormal topics is at its lowest among people who believe the Bible is the literal word of God'.[534] This is certainly the case according to their definition of 'paranormal topics', which excludes religious belief. However, historical research has shown that the Bible is the work of multiple authors over a considerable span of time. How would we view such claims today, that a certain individual was the son of God, performed various miracles and returned from the dead? What is viewed as relatively normal within society – Christianity, for example – is excluded from what is seen as relatively *ab*normal, or paranormal – such as UFOs.

Contrary to what actually seems to be the case, we do not directly experience reality, we experience an interpretation of reality. Now for most of us, fortunately, our interpretations are fairly similar, but under certain situations that interpretation can be subject to gross distortion. People can speak to teapots and hear their answers as clearly as you are reading this now. We call them psychotics and give them drugs. People can speak to ghosts and hear their answers. We call them psychics and give them money. People can speak to gods and receive their message. We call them prophets and give them our souls. The social definition of who is speaking is more important than the message and until we know what 'normal' is how can we even grasp what is 'paranormal'? As Ralph Noyes, former Honorary Secretary of the Society for Psychical Research, once pertinently remarked, 'it is the "magical imagination" far more than fraud which clutters our field', which is another way of saying TRONDANT. But then how do we know that we are not all arranging roses in a shoe?[535]

---

and Mental Disease, May 2006, 194.5, pp. 349–55. Christopher Bader, et al., *Paranormal America: Ghost Encounters, UFO Sightings, Bigfoot Hunts, and Other Curiosities in Religion and Culture*, New York University, 2010, pp. 197–200, for the breakdown of 'paranormal beliefs' see Table A.6, p. 212.

[534] Bader, et al., p. 196.

[535] 'Backchat', *Paranormal Review*, 1997, p. 70.

If paranormal beliefs are only held by those with a history of childhood abuse or by those who are considered unconventional, then it pushes the paranormal to the fringes where it is little threat to the mainstream. However, Bader, Mencken and Baker, and all of the other surveys we have drawn on in this book, have repeatedly shown that a large proportion, often the majority, of people hold views that could be termed paranormal beliefs. Does this mean that the 68 per cent who believe in the paranormal in the USA are all unconventional? If so, this surely requires a new definition of conventional.[536]

I have never seen the Seychelles sheath-tailed bat, one of the world's rarest animals, in the wild. I have never seen an apparition, either. Both have been seen by other people. Both are well documented and described. So what is the difference? Is it the reliability of the witnesses? Is it a question of their psychology? Is it a question of their scientific training? Is it a question of the repeatability of the experiments? In 1997 the then president of the SPR, Professor David Fontana, said that fifteen laboratories across the world had conducted a total of 2,549 psychical experiments 'producing results in favour of paranormal abilities with combined odds against chance (in layman's terms) of a million billion to one'. In 2010 Professor Emeritus Daryl J. Bem of Cornell University, New York State, announced the results of his own experiments involving over 1,000 volunteers that showed the existence of psi with odds against chance of 74 billion to one. Out of them all – believer, sceptic, scientist – who is arranging flowers in a shoe?[537]

---

[536] See Jeremy Northcote, *The Paranormal and the Politics of Truth: A Sociological Account*, Imprint Academic, 2007.

[537] Fontana was referring specifically to autoganzfeld experiments, see *Paranormal Review*, 4, November 1997, p. 17; Daryl J. Bem, 'Feeling the Future: Experimental Evidence for Anomalous Retroactive Influences on Cognition and Affect', *Journal of Personality and Social Psychology*, forthcoming, discussed in David Sutton, 'Precognition and Porn: New Evidence for Psi', *Fortean Times*, 270, November 2010.

The Results

At the beginning of this book I asked you to take part in some experiments to show the problems associated with research into the supernatural/paranormal.

In the first experiment I asked you to think of a simple shape and draw it on a piece of paper. It is an experiment that has been tried before. In 1885 Max Dessoir was at the home of Baron Dr Goeler von Ravensburg, testing the psychic powers of his wife Elizabeth. Dessoir would draw a simple shape and he and the baron would concentrate on it, whilst Elizabeth, sitting at another table would try and reproduce it. After a while she said, 'It is a circle outside, and there is something else inside it'. She paused. 'A triangle.' She then drew a perfect reproduction of Dessoir's sketch. Using my psychic powers, I can now tell you that you also drew these shapes: a triangle inside a circle.[538]

In the second experiment I asked you to try and find out what number I was thinking of. I was, of course, mentally projecting this for you from a secret location in central Europe, which I find invariably helps. The number was between 1 and 50, and to make it easier both digits were odd, but not the same. If you thought of 35 or 39, then you were close, but if you thought of 37, then you were 100 per cent right.

---

[538] Max Dessoir, 'Experiments in Muscle-Reading and Thought-Transference', *Proceedings of the Society for Psychical Research*, 4, 1886, p. 126; see also Edmund Gurney, et al., 'Second Report on Thought-Transference', *Proceedings of the Society for Psychical Research*, 1, 1882, p. 81.

In the third experiment I asked you to find an old wind-up watch that no longer works, to then hold it in your hands for some minutes, concentrating on making it work, as I broadcast my psychic powers to operate on the machinery. You should have held it for at least ten minutes, repeating 'work, mend, work'. It apparently worked for many people after Uri Geller transmitted his 'psychic energy' from the observation deck of New York's World Trade Center in 1982. It worked for my mother-in-law after watching Geller on television in 2008 and following his instructions. I believe that it may also have worked for you.[539]

Did I read your mind or transmit my thoughts? Did I release your latent psychic powers? In some cases, it may not have worked. The picture-sending experiment did not work for Uri Geller when he tried it out with Helen Kruger of *The Village Voice* in 1973, but then he still managed to interest the US Department of Defense in his apparent abilities and convinced the scientists at the Stanford Research Institute in California. According to the research, however, in at least one in three cases I should have been right. According to that same research the answer lies in simple psychology and mechanics.

There are not many simple geometric shapes to think of and between them the circle, triangle and square just about cover the range. Results show that more people think of a triangle in a circle than a square in a circle, for example. Guessing a number from 1 to 50 sounds impressive, but due to the parameters I set, this actually only leaves seven numbers to choose from: 13, 17, 19, 31, 35, 37 and 39. Professor David Marks and Dr Richard Kammann once took a group of 202 people and posed these same questions. They found that over a third chose a triangle in circle and the number 37.[540]

The reason why broken watches may start working again is

---

[539] Geller's 1982 performance described in John Fairley and Simon Welfare, *Arthur C. Clarke's World of Strange Powers*, William Collins Sons & Co., 1984, ch. 4.

[540] David Marks and Richard Kammann, *The Psychology of the Psychic*, Prometheus, 1980, pp. 59–61.

due to the fact that, as watchmakers will confirm, more than half of all watches sent in for repair do not have a broken mechanism, but have stopped due to dust, dirt, or oil. The simple act of picking it up again, moving it and warming it in one's hand, may be sufficient to clear the blockage. The president of the Israel Parapsychology Society, Dr Heinz Berendt, reported being impressed by this demonstration until his watchmaker told him it was quite common.[541]

As these experiments show, one of the major difficulties in investigating the supernatural – beyond the elusiveness of the subject matter itself – lies in designing tests that reliably show that something paranormal has actually happened. What do you think happened? To post your results and interpretations – and to find out how the other readers did – log on to my website at www.ruickbie.com.[542]

---

[541] Marks and Kammann, *Psychology*, pp. 91–2, 108; David Marks and Richard Kammann, 'The Nonpsychic Powers of Uri Geller', *Zetetic*, 1.2, 1977, pp. 9–17; *Journal of the Society of Psychical Research*, 47, December 1974, p. 479.
[542] Kruger, 'Psychic Uri Geller – The Man Who Bends Forks With His Eyes', *The Village Voice*, 19 April 1973; Susan Blackmore, *The Adventures of a Parapsychologist*, Prometheus Books, 1986, p. 220.

Further Reading

Ghosts

Cornell, Tony, *Investigating the Paranormal*, Helix Press, 2002

Davies, Owen, *The Haunted: A Social History of Ghosts*, Palgrave Macmillan, 2009

Guiley, Rosemary Ellen, *The Encyclopedia of Ghosts and Spirits*, 2nd ed., Facts on File, 2000

Houran, James, and Rense Lange, (eds), *Hauntings and Poltergeists: Multidisciplinary Perspectives*, illus. 2nd ed., McFarland & Co., 2008

Karl, Jason, *Twenty-First Century Ghosts*, New Holland, 2007

Roll, William George, *The Poltergeist*, Cosimo, 2004

The Undead

Barber, Paul, *Vampires, Burial and Death: Folklore and Reality*, Yale University Press, 2010 [1990]

Beresford, Matthew, *From Demons to Dracula: The Creation of the Modern Vampire Myth*, Reaktion Books, 2008

Davis, Wade, *The Serpent and the Rainbow: A Harvard Scientist's Astonishing Journey into the Secret Societies of Haitian Voodoo, Zombis, and Magic*, Simon & Schuster, 1985; Pocket Books, 1997

Day, Jasmine, *The Mummy's Curse: Mummymania in the English-Speaking World*, Routledge, 2006

Seabrook, William, *The Magic Island*, George C. Harrap & Co., 1929; Marlowe & Co., 1994

Angels

Clarke, David, *The Angel of Mons: Phantom Soldiers and Ghostly Guardians*, John Wiley & Sons, 2005

Davidson, Gustav, *A Dictionary of Angels, Including the Fallen Angels*, Simon & Schuster, 1994

Heathcote-James, Emma, *Seeing Angels: True Contemporary Accounts of Hundreds of Angelic Experiences*, John Blake Publishing, 2001

Lumpkin, Joseph B., *The Books of Enoch: A Complete Volume*, Fifth Estate, 2009

Demons

Ashley, Leonard R.N., *The Complete Book of Devils and Demons*, Barricade Books, 1996; Skyhorse Publishing, 2011

Kelly, Henry Angsar, *Satan: A Biography*, Cambridge University Press, 2006

Toorn, Karel van der, Bob Becking and Pieter Willem van der Horst (eds), *Dictionary of Deities and Demons in the Bible*, 2nd ed., Brill/Eerdmans, 1999

Zaffis, John, and Rosemary Ellen Guiley, *The Encyclopedia of Demons and Demonology*, Facts on File, 2009

Extraterrestrials and UFOs

Clancy, Susan, *Abducted: How People Come to Believe They were Kidnapped by Aliens*, Harvard University Press, 2005

Clark, Jerome, *The UFO Book: Encyclopedia of the Extraterrestrial*, Visible Ink, 1997

Hynek, J. Allen, *The UFO Experience: A Scientific Inquiry*, Henry Regnery Co., 1972; De Capo Press, 1998

Kean, Leslie, (ed.), *UFOs: Generals, Pilots and Government Officials Go on the Record*, Harmony Books, 2010

Randle, Kevin D., *The Roswell Encyclopedia*, HarperCollins, 2000

Redfern, Nick, *Contactees: A History of Alien-Human Interaction*, Career Press, 2009

Ruppelt, Edward J., *The Report on Unidentified Flying Objects*, Doubleday & Company, 1956; Cosimo Classics, 2011

Magic

Crowley, Aleister, *Magick in Theory and Practice*, privately published, 1929; reprinted by Prober Publishing, 2011

Davies, Owen, *Grimoires: A History of Magic Books*, Oxford University Press, 2009

Frazer, Sir James George, *The Golden Bough: A Study in Magic and Religion*, 2 vols, Macmillan & Co., 1890; reprinted in one vol. by Oxford Paperbacks, 2009

Kieckhefer, Richard, *Magic in the Middle Ages*, Canto, 2000 [1989]

Ruickbie, Leo, *Faustus: The Life and Times of a Renaissance Magician*, The History Press, 2009

Spiritualism

Lamont, Peter, *The First Psychic*, Abacus, 2006

Melechi, Antonio, *Servants of the Supernatural: The Night Side of the Victorian Mind*, Arrow, 2009

Pearsall, Ronald, *Table-Rappers: The Victorians and the Occult*, The History Press, 2004

Weisberg, Barbara, *Talking to the Dead: Kate and Maggie Fox and the Rise of Spiritualism*, HarperOne, 2004

Psychical Research and Parapsychology

Horn, Stacey, *Unbelievable: Investigations into Ghosts, Poltergeists, Telepathy, and Other Unseen Phenomena from the Duke Parapsychological Laboratory*, Ecco, 2009

Irwin, Harvey J., and Caroline A. Watt, *An Introduction to Parapsychology*, McFarland & Co., 2007

Oppenheim, Janet, *The Other World: Spiritualism and Psychical Research in England, 1850-1914*, Cambridge University Press, 1988

Schoch, Robert, and Logan Yonavjak (eds), *The Parapsychological Revolution: A Concise Anthology of Paranormal and Psychical Research*, Tarcher/Penguin, 2008

General

Bader, Christopher, et al., *Paranormal America: Ghost Encounters, UFO Sightings, Bigfoot Hunts, and Other Curiosities in Religion and Culture*, New York University, 2010

Stein, Gordon (ed.), *The Encyclopedia of the Paranormal*, Prometheus Books, 1996

Gordon, Stuart, *The Paranormal: An Illustrated Encyclopedia*, Headline, 1992

Rosney, Mark, Rob Bethell and Jebby Robinson, *A Beginner's Guide to Paranormal Investigation*, Amberley, 2009

Index